THE NEW
OXFORD BOOK OF
ROMANTIC PERIOD
VERSE

Jerome J. McGann is John Stewart Bryan Professor of English at the University of Virginia. He has written widely on the Romantic Period and is the editor of Byron's *Complete Poetical Works* in seven volumes and of the one-volume Oxford Authors *Byron*. Other publications include *The Romantic Ideology. A Critical Investigation* (1983), *Social Values and Poetic Acts* (1987), and *Towards a Literature of Knowledge* (1989).

THE NEW
OXFORD BOOK OF
ROMANTIC
PERIOD
VERSE

Edited by

JEROME J. McGANN

Oxford   New York
OXFORD UNIVERSITY PRESS
1994

Oxford University Press, Walton Street, Oxford OX2 6DP

Oxford New York Toronto
Delhi Bombay Calcutta Madras Karachi
Kuala Lumpur Singapore Hong Kong Tokyo
Nairobi Dar es Salaam Cape Town
Melbourne Auckland Madrid
and associated companies in
Berlin Ibadan

Oxford is a trade mark of Oxford University Press

Introduction, notes, and selection © Jerome J. McGann 1993

First published 1993
First issued as an Oxford University Press Paperback 1994

British Library Cataloguing in Publication Data
Data available

Library of Congress Cataloging in Publication Data
The New Oxford Book of Romantic period verse / edited by
Jerome J. McGann.
p. cm.
1. English poetry—19th century. 2. English poetry—18th century.
3. Romanticism—Great Britain. I. McGann, Jerome J.
821'.709145—dc20 [PR1222.N48 1994] 93–32333
ISBN 0–19–282329–9

1 3 5 7 9 10 8 6 4 2

Printed in Great Britain by
Clays Ltd
Bungay, Suffolk

CONTENTS

CONTENTS

1789

1790

1791

CONTENTS

1792

CONTENTS

1796

CONTENTS

1799

CONTENTS

CONTENTS

CONTENTS

CONTENTS

CONTENTS

CONTENTS

1821

1822

1823

CONTENTS

1824

1825

1826

1827

CONTENTS

1828

1829

1830

CONTENTS

1831

INTRODUCTION

DECEPTIVE apparitions haunt romantic writing: *ignes fatui*, 'the viewless snow-mist' noticed by Coleridge in 'Constancy to an Ideal Object', and other dangerous shape-changers, like the *fata morgana*. The reader trying to understand romanticism often seems in pursuit of similar phenomena —things longed for but never really seen.

Partly the problem lies in the understanding mind itself. Concepts and ideas—those mental constructions Wordsworth deplored because they are the tools by which we 'murder to dissect'—will never seize the romantic experience. Though famous as theorists of things romantic, Kant and Hegel possess enlightened consciousnesses and—as such—have been among our worst guides to the *Ding an sich*. Far better, if one turns to prose and to Germany, are the less disciplined thoughts of Goethe and Schiller, or Schelling and Schlegel, or the poetical minds of Novalis, Kleist, Hoffmann, and Heine. In face of the romantic experience, the brain works best when it is supple (as are Coleridge and Keats), or when it is passionate and unguarded (as are Blake, Shelley, and Byron).

Romanticism's changing forms are figures of imaginative desire; for to be romantic is to exist under the sign of longing:

> What mad pursuit? What struggle to escape?
> What pipes and timbrels? What wild ecstasy?

At its epipsychic core, as in this famous passage, romanticism is doubled and involuted—not so much passion and desire, which one gets in the generous excesses of Burns and Blake, as a second-order quest for desire itself. Indeed, the romantic experience finally suffocates and implodes when it discovers that very bourne from which no romantic traveller ever returned. Some of the most interesting forms of romanticism—I am thinking of Byron's work after 1816, of Keats, and of certain poets of the 1820s like Felicia Dorothea Hemans and Laetitia Elizabeth Landon—are most successful when the writers choose to remain in those airless regions, when they choose—it involves a kind of artistic suicide—to reveal and explore the fatal gifts of romantic beauty.

Under such (elusive and transformational) conditions, an anthology of writing from the romantic period may be a better resource for study (and even for understanding) than a more theoretical work. The anthology format opens the doors of one's perception to changes of many kinds. In the case of the romantic period, moreover, such flexibility may be especially helpful because of the philosophic and ideological pretensions of so many romantic writers.

As everyone knows, romanticism involved broad-ranging revisionist moves against many traditional cultural ideas and artistic practices. In negotiating those difficult currents and cross-currents, one discovers this crucial historical fact: that the romantic period and its correspondent breeze, the romantic movement, are not the same thing. They differ, for instance, because the movement continued to mutate—mostly via indominant forms—well after the period as such was over. Tennyson, for example, began as a romantic poet and his work never entirely abandoned its romantic inheritance. None the less, Tennyson deliberately sought to place his writing outside the psychic, social, and stylistic boundaries of his romantic forebears. His effort was successful. This collection ends with 'The Palace of Art' because that poem, and the volume from which it is taken, represent Tennyson's hail and farewell to romanticism.

The period also falls out of correspondence with the movement because much of the writing during the period—including some of the best work —is not properly speaking 'romantic'. This fact, including perhaps its importance, comes immediately home to us if we think of the novelists Scott and Austen, or of the poets Coleridge and Crabbe. Scott and Coleridge are dominated by their romanticisms, Austen and Crabbe are not.

When we speak of romantic writing, even within its periodic context, we refer to a body of extremely diverse materials. The historic impossibility of defining the term 'romantic' reflects this diversity. Byron's romanticism —a form that loomed over the practice of nineteenth-century poetry throughout Europe—differs sharply from Wordsworth's and Coleridge's romanticism, which later came to control the way the twentieth-century tended to think about romantic work. Blake's romanticism is yet another thing. Indeed, Blake's special position is fairly well measured by the fact that its proper cultural installation had to await the coming of Pre-Raphaelitism, that unique mixture of late romantic attitudes and early modern gestures.

The romantic movement thus keeps splitting into numerous variant forms. One critical point of departure is the so-called Della Cruscan poetry of sentiment. Launched with *The Florence Miscellany* (Florence, 1785, privately printed), Della Cruscan writing soon found its way back to England, became a great force in the 1790s, and had a signal influence on later writing as well, especially the work of Keats, Shelley, Byron, and the poets of the 1820s. A distinctly urban project, it was committed to extreme displays of stylistic artifice. (In an important sense, Keats is the greatest representative of the Della Cruscan movement, as the attacks and criticisms of John Wilson Croker, Wordsworth, Byron, and later Matthew Arnold show very well.) The contrast of this work with Burns, and ultimately with the programme of Lake School poetry, is striking—even though, in all these cases, 'sensibility' is an important shared element. And the name of Burns reminds us not merely of the differential which he represents in himself, but of the variety of ways his legacy was taken up.

Important as *The Florence Miscellany* was, Burns's volume of the following year—*Poems, Chiefly in the Scottish Dialect*—proved an even more crucial literary resource. Signalling the arrival of a major poet, the book displayed features of style and sensibility that would be central to many subsequent romantic practitioners: the power of natural and even primitive cultural formations, a regional orientation, and what Wordsworth would later call a 'language really used by men'. Wordsworth's entire mythology of the 'common life' is already present, in what Schiller would have called a 'naïve' form, in Burns's great book. (Needless to say, there is nothing truly 'naïve'—in either Schiller's or any other sense—about Burns's volume.)

The satiric and conversational elements in Burns's poems fed other romantic streams, most notably Byron's, just as his investment in the traditions of Scottish song would exert a widespread influence throughout and well beyond the romantic period. In his later work, in fact, Burns was to plunge himself so deeply into those song traditions that his writing seemed at least as much an expression of those traditions as of his own individual identity. In this respect his work appears and is read as a kind of ethnographic expression of Scottish culture.

This view of Burns helps to explain the importance of the work of Sir William Jones to romanticism and the romantic period. Unlike Burns's (dialect, as opposed to his English) poetry, Jones's pseudo-translations of Vedic hymns are not written in a romantic style. None the less, these productions—along with Jones's philological writings on Persian and Arabic materials—were a major source of the romantic orientalism that flooded across the period.

Like *The Florence Miscellany* and Burns's 1786 volume, Jones's poetic translations were first printed outside England—in Calcutta. This apparently odd fact of printing history is not incidental for it signals a distinctive feature of the writing of the period in general: its tendency to break with or to seek places beyond centralized and traditional cultural authorities. Blake's antinomianism, the interest in Scottish, Welsh, and Irish cultural traditions, the cultivation of 'unlearned' writers and popular poetry and song, and the expatriate urgencies of so many of the period's writers: these phenomena exemplify the age's tendency to seek its unity in its diversities, its sameness in its differences.

Jones's translations also locate romanticism's roots in the late eighteenth century's many philological and anthropological projects, and they help to explain the radical connections that hold together such otherwise disparate texts as Blake's *The [First] Book of Urizen*, Coleridge's 'The Rime of the Ancyent Marinere', Byron's *The Giaour*, and Keats's 'Hyperion'. All are 'philological' constructions, and they connect closely with the various lines of ethnographic translation and imitation which can be traced through the writing of the period. Blake, for example, was as fascinated (and influenced) by Jones's reconstructions of Hindu culture as he was by Iolo Morgannwg's of Welsh bardic and Druid culture. Like Burns's songs and dialect poems, Jones's translations are part of an effort to recover or fabricate some alternative or lost world. Such worlds—we encounter similar ones through Wordsworth's *Lyrical Ballads* and Byron's Eastern tales —were invested with cultural values that could be imagined free of contemporary England's preoccupation with getting and spending. (That these otherworlds were equally *reflections* of England's bourgeois values cannot be forgotten; as a discourse grounded in metonymy and metaphor, poetry —certainly romantic poetry—generates itself from just those kinds of contradictions.)

Jones's prefatory note to 'A Hymn to Na′ra′yena', which is this collection's opening text, foreshadows a number of important romantic thoughts. We note, among other things, Jones's critique of 'the *vulgar notion* of *material substances*', and his related idea that 'the whole Creation [is] rather an *energy* than a *work* . . . like a wonderful picture or piece of musick, always varied, yet always uniform; so that all bodies and their qualities exist . . . only as far as they are *perceived*'. That passage, indeed, might be used as an epigraph for a collection of romantic writing. It defines, as well as any of comparable brevity, salient features of many different romantic styles.

It does not, however, define the features of all or even most of the poetry written and read during the romantic period. In this sense, the non-romantic style of Jones's verse translations is the very feature that makes them so important. For Jones's work is radically self-divided, and similar contradictions will play about all the writing of the period. Hazlitt's *The Spirit of the Age* is a far truer and more comprehensive account of the romantic period than (say) Coleridge's *Biographia Literaria* precisely because it allows the period's many counter-spirits to appear on something like their own terms. We call the period 'romantic' because the ideological movement of romanticism came to dominance in that epoch. If we do not remember, however, that romanticism achieved its success only through an intense struggle on various fronts—some of them home fronts—we will understand neither romanticism nor the age in which it was born.

The contradictions of the period help to explain why some of its most impressive writing is not romantic writing. So far as poetry is concerned, Crabbe is the central instance. *The Borough* is a work of such scope and imaginative clarity as to be fitly compared with only the greatest achievements of the age. Literary historians sometimes appear reluctant to acknowledge the importance of Crabbe's work, perhaps because they have been embarrassed to account for it. Most of the (hi)stories we read of the romantic period are romantic (hi)stories, and Crabbe does not easily fit into those romantic narratives. Blake's work has itself been forced to fit only by invoking that familiar trope of romantic ideology, the neglected genius. Though our literary histories do not like to say so, there is an important sense in which Blake is the stranger in the strange land of the romantic period, whereas Crabbe is of that earth, earthy. Once again, Hazlitt's clear-eyed *Spirit of the Age*—which has nothing to say of Blake, but a great deal (mostly negative) of Crabbe—supplies us with an important historical index to the literature of the period.

Crabbe's work recalls another weakness of our literary memory, which is I think a failure of taste as well. Though the romantic period produced a great many women writers and 'bluestockings', they have almost all been forgotten. Even an explicitly feminist anthology like the recent *Norton Anthology of Literature by Women* (1985) could find only one poem of the period, from Dorothy Wordsworth's *Journal*, to illustrate what women were writing at that time. In fact, the age saw a mob of women (mostly gentlewomen) who wrote, and it was only through a great failure of sensibility that we unlearned how to read their work. Felicia Dorothea Hemans was one of the most widely published and widely read poets of the nineteenth century, and numbers of other women from Ann Yearsley and Laetitia Barbauld to Mary Tighe, Lady Morgan, and Laetitia Elizabeth Landon were regarded as writers of real importance, as they are.

The issue involved here strikes to the heart of the period and its dominant cultural movement, romanticism. Richard Polwhele's *The Unsex'd Females* (1798, excerpted below) is important partly as an index of a factual historical emergence of great scope: writing by women would become, in the nineteenth century for the first time, a great and distinctive force. This writing often traces itself back to the Della Cruscan movement, the chief object of Polwhele's attack (as it was of the similar attacks by his friends William Gifford [*The Baviad*, 1791, excerpted below] and Thomas James Mathias [*The Pursuits of Literature*, 1794]).

These reactionary works are perhaps even more important, however, for the ideology of Woman which they represent in such unmistakable ways. A set of contradictions like all ideologies, this one developed alongside some of the central attitudes of romanticism. Most important here is the commitment to what has been called 'the true voice of feeling', a voice located by all the European romanticisms in a certain concept of The Woman (often displaced into that equivalent romantic form, Nature). Lucy, Sara, Astarte, Asia, Moneta: the figure underwent many transformations, but She repeatedly appears as the inspirational source and end of creative activity. It was this (imaginary) Woman who was equally seen as the ideal locus of children's education, a fact most dramatically (if also most equivocally) represented in Blake's early *Songs of Innocence and of Experience*.

The actual writing of women, in this context, proves an indispensable resource. To write out of such an imaginary space—and there is no question that most women writers did so—yields a body of work which is radically self-conflicted, far more so than the work (in this frame of reference) of any writing by men. A limited anthology like this one cannot give back the glory in their flower, but I have attempted (at any rate) to include a good selection of the women poets of the period, partly as an inducement to further and deeper reading.

I have also tried, through the device of a chronological arrangement of the texts, to break down the extreme domination of an author-centred perception of the poetry. Anthologies of this kind typically organize the poems in groups by author, with a consequent loss, it seems to me, of the general scene and context in which the writers and their work interact.

The chronicle-ordering I have followed here will, I hope, throw many of the old familiar poems into new and interesting relationships. (The strength and genuine originality of Felicia Dorothea Hemans' elegy for Byron, 'The Lost Pleiad', are much more evident when the poem is read—as it was in historical fact—right after the appearance of Byron's 'Messalonghi. January 22, 1824. On this day I Complete my Thirty-Sixth Year'.) Such an arrangement should also give a better sense of the ebb and flow of poetry in the period, and of types of poetry. Perhaps most of all, the arrangement makes it easier for a reader to see the work as writing that occupied a certain specific context and space of time. As it still does, as it always does.

THE WORKS AND THE TEXTS

My general purpose is to make a fair representation of the work (as well as the kind of work) being read in the period, of the poetry that was in more or less general circulation. This aim brought me to adopt the following rule: to include only those works that had been printed and distributed at the time. The rule of course yields some startling absences: *The Prelude* most notably, but also Keats's 'On Sitting Down to Read *King Lear* Once Again', Blake's *The Four Zoas*, and (a problematic case, because of its printing history) Shelley's 'Epipsychidion'. It has also kept out the splendid early manuscript poems and uncompleted dramatic work of Thomas Lovell Beddoes.

One could as easily imagine—especially for this period—a collection with a completely different emphasis: one, for example, that collected only those works which did *not* find their way into print, or which were held back from publication by their authors. Such a book would include *The Prelude* and *The Four Zoas* and of course many other works which are now so familiar to us. It would also lead one to sift the manuscript archives for writing that kept its privacy, whether by choice or by chance.

Such a collection would doubtless prove, in one sense, a far more 'romantic' body of work than the present volume—even as it would necessarily convey a less reliable experience of the actual scene of reading and writing in the period. In another sense, however, it would supply a diminished experience of the work of the period, and even of romanticism and romantic writing. To the extent that romanticism was a literary and artistic movement, it polemicized a certain kind of art and sensibility for art. The polemic was executed in public and it was widespread. The occasion of Wordsworth's and Coleridge's *Lyrical Ballads* project (1798–1805) has long stood at the heart of the chronology of English romanticism because of the project's openly revisionist ideas about the nature of poetry and its public functions.

The Preface to *Lyrical Ballads* is not poetry, but it is a central text for the poetry of the period. Besides the importance of its ideas, the work is an index of the polemical character of the writing scene in general. The period is notable for the intensity of its cultural and aesthetic debates, and similar 'manifestos' were produced by many of the writers whose poems appear in this collection. I deeply regret that space limits have prevented me from including a number of the most interesting of these works. From Yearsley and Burns to Peacock and Macauley and Arthur Henry Hallam, writers addressed the question of poetry and argued fiercely about its cultural role. These disputations are a distinct feature of the writing of the period.

Given such an original context, then, I have tried to avoid making this a prescriptive collection. It has been designed, rather, partly as invitation and partly as argument. Its mild apostasies from the conventional academic rules of earlier collections will, I hope, encourage us to adopt some new perspectives on the work of the period. In this respect the collection will be most successful if it stimulates the reader's impulses to imagine other inclusions and exclusions—different collections that would run, perhaps, at strange diagonals to the present one.

As for the other absences that every reader will notice and deplore, they reflect the pressure of space restrictions, and the consequent necessity of making choices. Excluding *The Cenci* was a hard decision which reflects the larger problem of romantic drama in general. The length of these works is a serious problem, and they are difficult to excerpt. For that matter, the many poems printed here in abbreviated forms will inevitably seem more impoverished than the editor or the reader would like them to be.

As for the texts of the works in this collection, the general rule has been to choose the first printed version (purged of printer's errors). This editorial posture has meant that one will read here Coleridge's 'The Rime of the Ancyent Marinere' (1798) rather than the more familiar 'The Rime of the Ancient Mariner' (1816, with the important marginal glosses). On the other hand, the full (seventh edition) text of *The Giaour* is printed here, rather than the shorter first edition. The two cases, in fact, illustrate what has guided my choice when I have included a text other than the first printing. That is to say, if the work displays some process of close and continuous evolution, I have chosen the later version in that evolution. (Twenty years separate Coleridge's two texts, but only a few months separate Byron's.)

One final note on the texts. I have not, in general, corrected the texts against earlier manuscript versions. That is to say, original authorized printed versions are only modified against manuscripts when the printed texts are unambiguously in error. Shelley's 'Mont Blanc', for example, appears here as it was first printed, with all its problems of punctuation. On the other hand, corrections from manuscript have been brought into the text of another famous Shelley work, 'The Triumph of Life', because the first printed text derived from the single manuscript Shelley wrote.

The aim, in short, is to print the texts that had been made available to the poets' original audiences. I have therefore normalized only the long (or 'old face') s. In this I am departing from the series' tradition (as I do in a number of other ways, already discussed) because of my desire to preserve some signs of the poems' original context and circumstances. Conventions of punctuation have not changed so drastically during the past two hundred years as to present any serious difficulties of reading. Besides, the modern historical sense of 'period' began to develop strongly in the romantic age, and many romantic poems positively solicit the slight sense of historical distancing that an 'old-fashioned' textual appearance can give. Coleridge's 'The Rime of the Ancyent Marinere' and Darley's 'It is not beautie I demande' are two well-known instances. So I have stayed close to the original typographical forms. Changes are introduced only when we know that accident, blind contact, or strong necessity interfered with the texts' transmissions.

INDEXES

Besides the chronological table of contents, I have included an index of authors alphabetically arranged, along with the poems by each to be found in this book. There is as well, of course, a separate index of first lines.

THE NEW
OXFORD BOOK OF
ROMANTIC PERIOD
VERSE

[1785]

SIR WILLIAM JONES
1746–1794

I   *A Hymn to Na'ra'yena*

THE ARGUMENT

A COMPLETE introduction to the following Ode would be no less than
a full comment on the VAYDS and PURA'NS of the HINDUS, the
remains of *Egyptian* and *Persian* Theology, and the tenets of the *Ionick* and
Italick Schools; but this is not the place for so vast a disquisition. It will
be sufficient here to premise, that the inextricable difficulties attending
the *vulgar notion* of *material substances*, concerning which

'We know this only, that we nothing know,'

induced many of the wisest among the Ancients, and some of the most
enlightened among the Moderns, to believe, that the whole Creation was
rather an *energy* than a *work*, by which the Infinite Being, who is present
at all times in all places, exhibits to the minds of his creatures a set of
perceptions, like a wonderful picture or piece of musick, always varied,
yet always uniform; so that all bodies and their qualities exist, indeed, to
every wise and useful purpose, but exist only as far they are *perceived*; a
theory no less pious than sublime, and as different from any principle of
Atheism, as the brightest sunshine differs from the blackest midnight.
This *illusive operation* of the Deity the *Hindu* philosophers call, MA'YA',
or *Deception*; and the word occurs in this sense more than once in the
commentary on the *Rig Vayd*, by the great VASISHTHA, of which Mr
HALHED has given us an admirable specimen.

The *first* stanza of the Hymn represents the sublimest attributes of the
Supreme Being, and the three forms, in which they most clearly appear
to us, *Power*, *Wisdom*, and *Goodness*, or, in the language of ORPHEUS and
his disciples, *Love*: the *second* comprises the *Indian* and *Egyptian* doctrine
of the Divine Essence and Archetypal *Ideas*; for a distinct account of which
the reader must be referred to a noble description in the sixth book of
PLATO'S *Republick*; and the fine explanation of that passage in an elegant
discourse by the author of CYRUS, from whose learned work a hint has
been borrowed for the conclusion of this piece. The *third* and *fourth*
are taken from the Institutes of MENU, and the eighteenth *Puran* of
VYA'SA', entitled *Srey Bhagawat*, part of which has been translated into
Persian, not without elegance, but rather too paraphrastically. From
BREHME, or the *Great Being*, in the *neuter* gender, is formed BREHMA',

I

in the *masculine*; and the second word is appropriated to the *creative power* of the Divinity.

The spirit of GOD, call'd NA'RA'YENA, or *moving on the water*, has a multiplicity of other epithets in *Sanscrit*, the principal of which are introduced, expressly or by allusion, in the *fifth* stanza; and two of them contain the names of the *evil beings*, who are feigned to have sprung from the ears of VISHNU; for thus the divine spirit is entitled, when considered as the *preserving power*: the *sixth* ascribes the perception of *secondary* qualities by our *senses* to the immediate influence of MA'YA'; and the *seventh* imputes to her operation the *primary* qualities of *extension* and *solidity*.

> SPIRIT of Spirits, who, through ev'ry part
>   Of space expanded and of endless time,
>   Beyond the stretch of lab'ring thought sublime,
>   Badst uproar into beauteous order start.
>   Before Heav'n was, Thou art;
> Ere spheres beneath us roll'd or spheres above,
>   Ere earth in firmamental ether hung,
>   Thou satst alone; till, through thy mystick Love,
>   Things unexisting to existence sprung,
>   And grateful descant sung.   10
> What first impell'd thee to exert thy might?
>   Goodness unlimited. What glorious light
>   Thy pow'r directed? Wisdom without bound.
> What prov'd it first? Oh! guide my fancy right,
>   Oh! raise from cumbrous ground
>   My soul in rapture drown'd,
>   That fearless it may soar on wings of fire;
> For Thou, who only knowst, Thou only canst inspire.
>
> Wrapt in eternal solitary shade,
>   Th' impenetrable gloom of light intense,   20
>   Impervious, inaccessible, immense,
>   Ere spirits were infus'd or forms display'd,
>   BREHM his own Mind survey'd,
> As mortal eyes (thus finite we compare
>   With infinite) in smoothest mirrors gaze:
>   Swift, at his look, a shape supremely fair
>   Leap'd into being with a boundless blaze,
>   That fifty suns might daze.
> Primeval MAYA was the Goddess nam'd,
>   Who to her sire, with Love divine inflam'd,   30
>   A casket gave with rich *Ideas* fill'd,
> From which this gorgeous Universe he fram'd;
>   For, when th' Almighty will'd,
>   Unnumber'd worlds to build,

From Unity diversified he sprang,
While gay Creation laugh'd, and procreant Nature rang.

First an all-potent all-pervading sound
   Bade flow the waters—and the waters flow'd,
   Exulting in their measureless abode,
   Diffusive, multitudinous, profound,   40
     Above, beneath, around;
Then o'er the vast expanse primordial wind
   Breath'd gently, till a lucid bubble rose,
   Which grew in perfect shape an Egg refin'd:
   Created substance no such lustre shows,
     Earth no such beauty knows.
Above the warring waves it danc'd elate,
   Till from its bursting shell with lovely state
   A form cerulean flutter'd o'er the deep,
   Brightest of beings, greatest of the great: 50
     Who, not as mortals steep,
     Their eyes in dewy sleep,
   But heav'nly-pensive on the Lotos lay,
That blossom'd at his touch and shed a golden ray.

Hail, primal blossom! hail empyreal gem!
   KEMEL, or PEDMA, or whate'er high name
   Delight thee, say, what four-form'd Godhead came,
   With graceful stole and beamy diadem,
     Forth from thy verdant stem?
Full-gifted BREHMA! Rapt in solemn thought   60
   He stood, and round his eyes fire-darting threw;
   But, whilst his viewless origin he sought,
   One plain he saw of living waters blue,
     Their spring nor saw nor knew.
Then, in his parent stalk again retir'd,
   With restless pain for ages he inquir'd
   What were his pow'rs, by whom, and why conferr'd:
   With doubts perplex'd, with keen impatience fir'd
     He rose, and rising heard
     Th' unknown all-knowing Word,   70
   'BREHMA! no more in vain research persist:
My veil thou canst not move—Go; bid all worlds exist.'

Hail, self-existent, in celestial speech
   NARAYEN, from thy watry cradle, nam'd;
   Or VENAMALY may I sing unblam'd,
   With flow'ry braids, that to thy sandals reach,
     Whose beauties, who can teach?

Or high PEITAMBER clad in yellow robes
   Than sunbeams brighter in meridian glow,
   That weave their heav'n-spun light o'er circling globes?   80
Unwearied, lotos-eyed, with dreadful bow,
      Dire Evil's constant foe!
Great PEDMANABHA, o'er thy cherish'd world
   The pointed *Checra*, by thy fingers whirl'd,
   Fierce KYTABH shall destroy and MEDHU grim
To black despair and deep destruction hurl'd.
      Such views my senses dim,
      My eyes in darkness swim:
What eye can bear thy blaze, what utt'rance tell
Thy deeds with silver trump or many-wreathed shell?   90

Omniscient Spirit, whose all-ruling pow'r
   Bids from each sense bright emanations beam;
   Glows in the rainbow, sparkles in the stream,
   Smiles in the bud, and glistens in the flow'r
      That crowns each vernal bow'r;
Sighs in the gale, and warbles in the throat
   Of ev'ry bird, that hails the bloomy spring,
   Or tells his love in many a liquid note,
   Whilst envious artists touch the rival string,
         Till rocks and forests ring;   100
Breathes in rich fragrance from the sandal grove,
   Or where the precious musk-deer playful rove;
   In dulcet juice from clust'ring fruit distills,
   And burns salubrious in the tasteful clove:
      Soft banks and verd'rous hills
      Thy present influence fills;
In air, in floods, in caverns, woods, and plains;
Thy will inspirits all, thy sov'reign MAYA reigns.

Blue crystal vault, and elemental fires,
   That in th' ethereal fluid blaze and breathe;   110
   Thou, tossing main, whose snaky branches wreathe
   This pensile orb with intertwisted gyres;
      Mountains, whose radiant spires
Presumptuous rear their summits to the skies,
   And blend their em'rald hue with sapphire light;
   Smooth meads and lawns, that glow with varying dyes
   Of dew-bespangled leaves and blossoms bright,
      Hence! vanish from my sight:
Delusive Pictures! unsubstantial shows!
   My soul absorb'd One only Being knows,   120
   Of all perceptions One abundant source,

4

Whence ev'ry object ev'ry moment flows:
Suns hence derive their force,
Hence planets learn their course;
But suns and fading worlds I view no more:
GOD only I perceive; GOD only I adore.

ROBERT MERRY ('DELLA CRUSCA')
1755–1798

2 *Madness*

I'VE lost my Love, I know not where,
I ask'd her of the fiend Despair,
He look'd aghast, and bade me go
To the dark abode of woe.
I'll seek her in the glare of day,
I'll seek her in the milky-way,
I'll seek her o'er the raging deep;
Yon wave shall rock her soul to sleep:
Ye wanton Sea-Gods! O beware!
And do not violate my fair.   10
On some far mountain lone, and drear,
With arms across she sits to hear,
How the torrents rage in vain,
Emblems of her Lover's pain.
Or where Moon-light shuns the shade,
Throws her down, my pensive maid.
Tis the Roe-buck bounding by,
Tis the Zephyr seems to sigh
As his careless pinions rove,
Tis perhaps the voice of Love.   20
Do not start, nor haste away,
I have sought thee all the day,
Yes, I sought thee in the cave
Where the frantic furies rave,
Dreadful was the brand they bore,
One, her breast was stained with gore,
One, her snaky locks, display'd,
And told me of my beauteous maid,
Told me she was sunk to rest
On my Rival's burning breast;   30
And the other smiled to hear:
Curse on her malignant sneer!

Now I steal the Eagle's wing,
Like the Bird of Sorrow sing,
I will hover o'er my fair,
And my song shall pierce the air,
Song of fury, mix'd with woe,
Deep, pathetic, wild, and slow;
Echo, if she chance to hear,
Shall only answer with a tear.   40
Once around my fair I twin'd,
Where the rose embraced the wind,
And the plaintive Shepherd's lay
Soothed the parting ear of day.
Was it rapture, was it pain,
Was it hope that fired my vein,
As I pressed my ravish'd fair?
She I loved was never there.
Some are mad for love they say,
Others fight, and others pray,   50
Others lay them down and weep,
Hush, my tyrant sinks to sleep.
Not a leaf shall trembling move
To disturb the maid I love,
Near her bed of many a flower
I will guard her slumb'ring hour,
With the mighty sword, of yore
That the ruthless Giant bore.
Not the Genius of the storm
Shall approach her lovely form,   60
Ruffian! wouldst thou dare possess
Her I love with rude caress?
There's my love, I see her there,
I know her by her streaming hair,
I know her by her bosom's snow,
By her frozen heart below;
I know her by her flaming eye,
Tis she, have mercy, for I die.

WILLIAM PARSONS
fl. 1785–1807

3   *Medoro's Inscription Book* XXIII

[*Translation from Ariosto*]

Liete piante, verdi erbe, limpid' acque
Spelouca opaca, e di fredde ombre grata

DARK cave, that ever dost cool shades retain,
    Gay blooming flow'rs, soft herbs, and limpid spring,
Where my kind fair, by others lov'd in vain,
    Would oft to me her yielding beauties bring.
For all the transports which I here have known,
    All the dear aids that to your scenes belong,
I can repay ye but with verse alone,
    Take then the grateful tribute of my song.

And much all gentle lovers I intreat,
    Whether of mean or of illustrious line,   10
Trav'lers of every kind, whose wand'ring feet
    May enter here, to join their vows with mine;
That on this cave, and flow'rs, and herbs, and tide,
    The Sun, and Moon, and rural Pow'rs may shed
Their influence kind, from hence conducting wide
    All flocks impure, and each unhallow'd tread!

ANN YEARSLEY
1752–1806

4   *Soliloquy*

       —WHAT folly to complain,
Or throw my woes against the face of Heaven?
Ills self-created prey upon my soul,
And rob each coming hour of soften'd Peace.
What then? Is Fate to blame? I chose distress;
Free will was mine; I might have still been happy
From a fore-knowledge of the dire effect,
And the sad bondage of resistless love.
I knew the struggles of a wounded mind,
Not self-indulging, and not prone to vice,   10

Knew all the terrors of conflicting passion,
Too stubborn foe, and ever unsubdued;
Yet rashly parley'd with the mighty victor.
Infectious mists upon my senses hang,
More deadly than LETHÈAN dews which fall
From SOMNUS' bough, on the poor wearied wretch,
Whose woes are fully told!—
The dire contagion creeps thro' all my frame,
Seizes my heart, and drinks my spirit up.
Ah! fatal poison, whither dost thou tend?   20
Tear not my soul with agonizing pains;
There needs no more; the world to me is lost,
And all the whirl of life-unneeded thrift.
I sicken at the Sun, and fly his beams,
Like some sad ghost which loves the moonless night,
And pensive shuns the morn. The deep recess
Where dim-ey'd Melancholy silent sits,
Beckoning the poor desponding, slighted wretch,
Suits well. 'Tis here I find a gloomy rest;
'Tis here the fool's loud clatter leaves me still,   30
Nor force unwilling answers to their tale:
But, ah! this gloom, this lethargy of thought,
Yields not repose; I sigh the hour away;
The next rolls on, and leaves me still opprest.
But, oh! swift-footed Time, thou ceaseless racer,
Thou who hast chac'd five thousand years before thee,
With all their great events, and minute trifles,
Haste, with redoubled speed, bring on the hour,
When dark Oblivion's dusky veil shall shroud
Too painful Memory.—   40

[1786]

ROBERT BURNS
1759–1796

5–9   from *Poems, Chiefly in the Scottish Dialect*

5   *Address to the Deil*

> *O Prince, O chief of many throned pow'rs,*
> *That led th' embattl'd Seraphim to war—*
> MILTON

O THOU, whatever title suit thee!
Auld Hornie, Satan, Nick, or Clootie,
Wha in yon cavern grim an' sooty
   Clos'd under hatches,
Spairges about the brunstane cootie,
   To scaud poor wretches!

Hear me, *auld Hangie*, for a wee,
An' let poor, *damned bodies* bee;
I'm sure sma' pleasure it can gie,
   Ev'n to a *deil*,   10
To skelp an' scaud poor dogs like me,
   An' hear us squeel!

Great is thy pow'r, an' great thy fame;
Far ken'd, an' noted is thy name;
An' tho' yon *lowan heugh*'s thy hame,
   Thou travels far;
An' faith! thou 's neither lag nor lame,
   Nor blate nor scaur.

Whyles, ranging like a roaring lion,
For prey, a' holes an' corners tryin;   20
Whyles, on the strong-wing'd Tempest flyin,
   Tirlan the *kirks*;

5: 2 Clootie] Cloven-hoof 5 Spairges] bespatters brunstane cootie] brimstone tub 6 scaud] scald 7 *Hangie*] Hangman 10 *deil*] devil 11 skelp] smack 15 *lowan heugh*] blazing pit 17 lag] backward 18 blate] bashful scaur] afraid 22 Tirlan] uncovering *kirks*] churches

9

Whyles, in the human bosom pryin,
  Unseen thou lurks.

I've heard my rev'rend *Graunie* say,
In lanely glens ye like to stray;
Or where auld, ruin'd castles, gray,
  Nod to the moon,
Ye fright the nightly wand'rer's way,
  Wi' eldritch croon.   30

When twilight did my *Graunie* summon,
To say her pray'rs, douse, honest woman,
Aft 'yont the dyke she 's heard you bumman,
  Wi' eerie drone;
Or, rustling, thro' the boortries coman,
  Wi' heavy groan.

Ae dreary, windy, winter night,
The stars shot down wi' sklentan light,
Wi' you, *mysel*, I gat a fright
  Ayont the lough;   40
Ye, like a *rash-buss*, stood in sight,
  Wi' waving sugh:

The cudgel in my nieve did shake,
Each bristl'd hair stood like a stake,
When wi' an eldritch, stoor, *quaick, quaick,*
  Amang the springs,
Awa ye squatter'd like a *drake*,
  On whistling wings.

Let *Warlocks* grim, an' wither'd *Hags*,
Tell, how wi' you, on ragweed nags,   50
They skim the muirs an' dizzy crags,
  Wi' wicked speed;
And in kirk-yards renew their leagues,
  Owre howcket dead.

---

25 *Graunie*] grandmother   26 lanely] lonely   30 eldritch croon] un-
earthly moan   32 douse] sober   33 'yont] behind   dyke] wall   bumman]
humming   35 boortries] elder trees   38 sklentan] slanting   40 Ayont]
beyond   lough] loch   41 *rash-buss*] clump of rushes   42 sugh] sound of
wind   43 nieve] fist   45 stoor] harsh   47 squatter'd] fluttered in water
[RB]   50 ragweed] ragwort   51 muirs] moors   54 howcket]
exhumed

Thence, countra wives, wi' toil an' pain,
May plunge an' plunge the *kirn* in vain;
For Och! the yellow treasure 's taen,
          By witching skill;
An' dawtit, twal-pint *Hawkie* 's gane
          As yell 's the Bill.   60

Thence, mystic knots mak great abuse,
On *Young-Guidmen*, fond, keen an' croose;
When the best *warklum* i' the house,
          By cantraip wit,
Is instant made no worth a louse,
          Just at the bit.

When thowes dissolve the snawy hoord,
An' float the jinglan icy boord,
Then, *Water-kelpies* haunt the foord,
          By your direction,   70
An' nighted Trav'llers are allur'd
          To their destruction.

An' aft your moss-traversing *Spunkies*
Decoy the wight that late an' drunk is;
The bleezan, curst, mischievous monkies
          Delude his eyes,
Till in some miry slough he sunk is,
          Ne'er mair to rise.

When MASONS' mystic *word* an' *grip*,
In storms an' tempests raise you up,   80
Some cock, or cat, your rage maun stop,
          Or, strange to tell!
The *youngest Brother* ye wad whip
          Aff straught to *H–ll*.

Lang syne in *Eden*'s bonie yard,
When youthfu' lovers first were pair'd,
An' all the Soul of Love they shar'd,
          The raptur'd hour,

56 *kirn*] churn   59 dawtit] spoiled   twal] twelve   *Hawkie*] cow   60 yell 's]
milkless as   Bill] bull   62 *Guidmen*] husbands   croose] confident   63 *mark-*
lum] work-loom   64 cantraip] magic   66 bit] critical moment   67 thowes]
thaws   snawy hoord] snowy drift   68 jinglan] cracking   boord] surface
69 *Water-kelpies*] waterhorse demons   foord] ford   73 *Spunkies*] will-o'-
the-wisps   75 bleezan] blazing   84 straught] straight   85 Lang
syne] long ago   yard] garden

Sweet on the fragrant, flow'ry swaird,
      In shady bow'r: 90

Then you, ye auld, snick-drawing dog!
Ye cam to Paradise incog,
An' play'd on a man a cursed brogue,
      (Black be your fa'!)
An' gied the infant warld a shog,
      'Maist ruin'd a'.

D'ye mind that day, when in a bizz,
Wi' reeket duds, an' reestet gizz,
Ye did present your smoutie phiz
      'Mang better folk,   100
An' sklented on the *man of Uz*
      Your spitefu' joke?

An' how ye gat him i' your thrall,
An' brak him out o' house an' hal',
While scabs an' botches did him gall,
      Wi' bitter claw,
An' lows'd his ill-tongu'd, wicked *Scawl*
      Was warst ava?

But a' your doings to rehearse,
Your wily snares an' fechtin fierce,
Sin' that day MICHAEL did you pierce,   110
      Down to this time,
Wad ding a' *Lallan* tongue, or *Erse*,
      In Prose or Rhyme.

An' now, auld *Cloots*, I ken ye're thinkan,
A certain *Bardie*'s rantin, drinkin,
Some luckless hour will send him linkan,
      To your black pit;
But faith! he'll turn a corner jinkan,
      An' cheat you yet.   120

89 swaird] sward   91 snick] latch   92 incog] unknown   93 brogue]
trick   95 warld] world   shog] shock   97 mind] remember   bizz]
stir   98 reeket duds] smoky clothes   reestet gizz] 'cured' wig
99 smoutie phiz] ugly face   101 sklented] directed aslant   105 botches]
angry tumours [RB]   106 claw] scratching   107 lows'd] loosed
ill-tongu'd] abusive   *Scawl*] woman   108 warst ava] worst of all
110 fechtin] fighting   113 ding] weary   *Lallan*] Lowland   *Erse*] Gaelic
116 *Bardie*] poet   117 linkan] going briskly   119 jinkan] side-stepping

> But fare you weel, auld *Nickie-ben*!
> O wad ye tak a thought an' men'!
> Ye aiblins might—I dinna ken—
>   Still hae a *stake*—
> I'm wae to think upo' yon den,
>   Ev'n for your sake.

6   *Halloween*

> *Yes! let the Rich deride, the Proud disdain,*
> *The simple pleasures of the lowly train;*
> *To me more dear, congenial to my heart,*
> *One native charm, than all the gloss of art.*
>   GOLDSMITH

I

> UPON that *night*, when Fairies light,
>   On *Cassilis Downans* dance,
> Or owre the lays, in splendid blaze,
>   On sprightly coursers prance;
> Or for *Colean*, the rout is taen,
>   Beneath the moon's pale beams;
> There, up the *Cove*, to stray an' rove,
>   Amang the rocks an' streams
>   To sport that night.

II

> Amang the bonie, winding banks,   10
>   Where *Doon* rins, wimplin, clear,
> Where BRUCE ance rul'd the martial ranks,
>   An' shook his *Carrick* spear,
> Some merry, friendly, countra folks,
>   Together did convene,
> To *burn* their nits, an' *pou* their stocks,
>   An' haud their *Halloween*
>   Fu' blythe that night.

122 an' men'] and mend   123 aiblins] perhaps   124 *stake*] chance   125 wae] unhappy

6:   3 lays] leas   11 rins] runs   wimplin] winding   16 nits] nuts   *pou*] pull   17 haud] hold, keep   18 Fu'] very

III

The lasses feat, an' cleanly neat,
  Mair braw than when they're fine;   20
Their faces blythe, fu' sweetly kythe,
  Hearts leal, an' warm, an' kin':
The lads sae trig, wi' wooer-babs,
  Weel knotted on their garten,
Some unco blate, an' some wi' gabs,
  Gar lasses hearts gang startin
             Whyles fast at night.

IV

Then, first an' foremost, thro' the kail,
  Their *stocks* maun a' be sought ance;
They steek their een, an' grape an' wale,   30
  For muckle anes, an' straught anes.
Poor hav'rel *Will* fell aff the drift,
  An' wander'd thro' the *Bow-kail*,
An' pow't, for want o' better shift,
  A *runt* was like a sow-tail
             Sae bow't that night.

V

Then, straught or crooked, yird or nane,
  They roar an' cry a' throw'ther;
The vera *wee-things*, toddlan, rin,
  Wi' stocks out owre their shouther: 40
An' gif the *custock*'s sweet or sour,
  Wi' joctelegs they taste them;
Syne coziely, aboon the door,
  Wi' cannie care, they've plac'd them
             To lye that night.

19 feat] spruce   20 fine] in their finery   21 kythe] show   22 leal] loyal
kin'] kindly   23 trig] trim   wooer-babs] love-knots   24 garten] garters
25 blate] shy   gabs] chatter   26 Gar] make   28 kail] greens   30 steek]
shut   een] eyes   grape] grope   wale] choose   31 muckle] big   straught]
straight   32 hav'rel] foolish   fell aff the drift] lost the way   33 *Bow-kail*]
cabbage   34 pow't] pulled   shift] choice   35 *runt*] cabbage stalk [which]
36 bow't] bent   37 yird] earth   38 a' throw'ther] in confusion
40 shouther] shoulder   41 gif] if   *custock*] pith   42 joctelegs]
pocket-knives   43 Syne coziely] then snugly   aboon] above   44 cannie]
knowing

VI

The lasses staw frae 'mang them a',
　　To pou their *stalks o' corn*;
But *Rab* slips out, an' jinks about,
　　Behint the muckle thorn:
He grippet *Nelly* hard an' fast;   50
　　Loud skirl'd a' the lasses;
But her *tap-pickle* maist was lost,
　　When kiutlan in the *Fause-house*
　　　　Wi' him that night.

VII

The auld Guidwife's weel-hoordet *nits*
　　Are round an' round divided,
An' monie lads an' lasses fates
　　Are there that night decided:
Some kindle, couthie, side by side,
　　An' *burn* thegither trimly;   60
Some start awa, wi' saucy pride,
　　An' jump out owre the chimlie
　　　　Fu' high that night.

VIII

Jean slips in twa, wi' tentie e'e;
　　Wha 'twas, she wadna tell;
But this is *Jock*, an' this is *me*,
　　She says in to hersel:
He bleez'd owre her, an' she owre him,
　　As they wad never mair part,
Till fuff! he started up the lum,   70
　　An' *Jean* had e'en a sair heart
　　　　To see 't that night.

IX

Poor *Willie*, wi' his *bow-kail runt*,
　　Was *brunt* wi' primsie *Mallie*;

46 staw] stole   48 jinks] dodges   51 skirl'd] screamed   52 *tap-pickle*] top-
most grain   53 kiutlan] cuddling   55 Guidwife] mistress   hoordet]
hoarded   59 couthie] sociably   62 chimlie] fire-place   64 tentie]
watchful   e'e] eye   67 says in] whispers   68 bleez'd] blazed   70 lum]
chimney   71 sair] sore   74 *brunt*] burnt   primsie] prim

An' *Mary*, nae doubt, took the drunt,
  To be compar'd to *Willie*:
Mall's nit lap out, wi' pridefu' fling,
  An' her ain fit, it brunt it;
While *Willie* lap, an' swoor by *jing*,
  'Twas just the way he wanted   80
            To be that night.

                    X

Nell had the *Fause-house* in her min',
  She pits hersel an' *Rob* in;
In loving bleeze they sweetly join,
  Till white in ase they're sobbin:
Nell's heart was dancin at the view;
  She whisper'd *Rob* to leuk for't;
Rob, stownlins, prie'd her bonie mou,
  Fu' cozie in the neuk for't,
            Unseen that night.   90

                    XI

But *Merran* sat behint their backs,
  Her thoughts on *Andrew Bell*;
She lea'es them gashan at their cracks,
  An' slips out by hersel:
She thro' the yard the nearest taks,
  An' for the *kiln* she goes then,
An' darklins grapet for the *bauks*,
  And in the *blue-clue* throws then,
            Right fear't that night.

                    XII

An' ay she *win't*, an' ay she swat,   100
  I wat she made nae jaukin;
Till something *held* within the *pat*,
  Guid L—d! but she was quaukin!

75 drunt] huff   77 lap] leapt   78 ain fit] own foot   79 swoor] swore
83 pits] puts   85 ase] ashes   87 leuk] look   88 stownlins] by stealth
prie'd] kissed   mou] mouth   89 neuk] corner   93 lea'es] leaves   gashan]
gossiping   cracks] talk   97 darklins] in the dark   grapet] groped   *bauks*]
beams   99 Right fear't] thoroughly afraid   100 *win't*] wound   swat]
sweated   101 wat] know   jaukin] trifling   102 *pat*] pot   103 quaukin]
quaking

But whether 'twas the *Deil* himsel,
 Or whether 'twas a *bauk-en'*,
Or whether it was *Andrew Bell*,
 She did na wait on talkin
   To spier that night.

XIII

Wee Jenny to her Graunie says,
 'Will ye go wi' me Graunie?   110
'I'll *eat the apple* at the *glass*,
 'I gat frae uncle Johnie:'
She fuff't her pipe wi' sic a lunt,
 In wrath she was sae vap'rin,
She notic't na, an aizle brunt
 Her braw, new, worset apron
   Out thro' that night.

XIV

'Ye little Skelpie-limmer's-face!
 I daur you try sic sportin,
As seek the *foul Thief* onie place,   120
 For him to spae your fortune:
Nae doubt but ye may get a *sight*!
 Great cause ye hae to fear it;
For monie a ane has gotten a fright,
 An' liv'd an' di'd deleeret,
   'On sic a night.

XV

'Ae Hairst afore the *Sherra-moor*,
 I mind 't as weel 's yestreen,
I was a gilpey then, I'm sure,
 I was na past fyfteen: 130
The Simmer had been cauld an' wat,
 An' *Stuff* was unco green;

104 *Deil*] Devil 105 *bauk-en'*] beam-end 108 spier] ask 113 fuff't]
puffed lunt] smoke 114 vap'rin] vapouring 115 aizle] red ember
116 worset] worsted 118 Skelpie-limmer] naughty hussy 119 daur] dare
121 spae] tell 125 deleeret] delirious 127 Hairst] harvest *Sherra-*
moor] Sheriffmuir 128 yestreen] last night 129 gilpey] girl 131 wat] wet
132 *Stuff*] grain

An' ay a rantan *Kirn* we gat,
    An' just on *Halloween*
        'It fell that night.

XVI

'Our *Stibble-rig* was *Rab M'Graen*,
    A clever, sturdy fallow;
His Sin gat *Eppie Sim* wi' wean,
    That liv'd in Achmacalla:
He gat *hemp-seed*, I mind it weel,   140
    An' he made unco light o't;
But monie a day was *by himsel*,
    He was sae sairly frighted
        'That vera night.'

XVII

Then up gat fechtan *Jamie Fleck*,
    An' he swoor by his conscience,
That he could *saw hemp-seed* a peck;
    For it was a' but nonsense:
The auld guidman raught down the pock,
    An' out a handfu' gied him;   150
Syne bad him slip frae 'mang the folk,
    Sometime when nae ane see'd him,
        An' try't that night.

XVIII

He marches thro' amang the stacks,
    Tho' he was something sturtan;
The *graip* he for a *harrow* taks,
    An' haurls at his curpan:
And ev'ry now an' then, he says,
    'Hemp-seed I saw thee,
'An' her that is to be my lass,   160
    Come after me an' draw thee
        'As fast this night.'

---

133 rantan *Kirn*] jovial harvest-home   136 *Stibble-rig*] chief harvester   138 wean]
child   142 *by*] beside   145 fechtan] fighting   147 *saw*] sow   149 raught]
reached   pock] bag   151 Syne] then   155 sturtan] afraid   156 *harrow*]
dung-fork   157 haurls] drags   curpan] rump

XIX

He whistl'd up *lord Lenox' march*,
   To keep his courage cheary;
Altho' his hair began to arch,
   He was sae fley'd an' eerie:
Till presently he hears a squeak,
   An' then a grane an' gruntle;
He by his showther gae a keek,
   An' tumbl'd wi' a wintle   170
            Out owre that night.

XX

He roar'd a horrid murder-shout,
   In dreadfu' desperation!
An' young an' auld come rinnan out,
   An' hear the sad narration:
He swoor 'twas hilchan *Jean M'Craw*,
   Or crouchie *Merran Humphie*,
Till stop! she trotted thro' them a';
   An' wha was it but *Grumphie*
            Asteer that night?   180

XXI

Meg fain wad to the *Barn* gaen,
   To *winn three wechts o' naething*;
But for to meet the Deil her lane,
   She pat but little faith in:
She gies the Herd a pickle nits,
   An' twa red cheeket apples,
To watch, while for the *Barn* she sets,
   In hopes to see *Tam Kipples*
            That vera night.

XXII

She turns the key, wi' cannie thraw,   190
   An' owre the threshold ventures;
But first on *Sawnie* gies a ca',
   Syne bauldly in she enters:

---

166 sae fley'd] badly scared   168 grane] groan   gruntle] grunt   169 showther]
shoulder   keek] look   170 wintle] roll   176 hilchan] limping   177 crouchie]
hump-backed   179 *Grumphie*] the pig   180 Asteer] astir   181 gaen] have
gone   182 *winn*] winnow   *wechts*] sievesful   183 her lane] alone   184 pat]
put   185 Herd] shepherd   pickle] few   190 cannie thraw] cautious twist
192 *Sawnie*] Sandy

A *ratton* rattl'd up the wa',
   An' she cry'd, L—d preserve her!
An' ran thro' midden-hole an' a',
   An' pray'd wi' zeal and fervour,
      Fu' fast that night.

XXIII

They hoy't out Will, wi' sair advice;
   They hecht him some fine braw ane;   200
It chanc'd the *Stack* he *faddom't thrice*,
   Was timmer-propt for thrawin:
He taks a swirlie, auld *moss-oak*,
   For some black, grousome *Carlin*;
An' loot a winze, an' drew a stroke,
   Till skin in blypes cam haurlin
      Aff's nieves that night.

XXIV

A wanton widow *Leezie* was,
   As cantie as a kittlen;
But Och! that night, amang the shaws,   210
   She gat a fearfu' settlin!
She thro' the whins, an' by the cairn,
   An' owre the hill gaed scrievin,
Whare *three Lairds' lan's met at a burn*,
   To dip her *left sark-sleeve* in,
      Was bent that night.

XXV

Whyles owre a linn the burnie plays,
   As thro' the glen it wimpl't;
Whyles round a rocky scar it strays;
   Whyles in a wiel it dimpl't;   220
Whyles glitter'd to the nightly rays,
   Wi' bickerin, dancin dazzle;

---

194 *ratton*] rat   196 midden-hole] dung gutter   199 hoy't] urged   202 timmer-propt for thrawin] timber-propped against bending   203 swirlie] gnarled   204 *Carlin*] old woman   205 loot a winze] let out an oath   206 blypes] shreds   haurlin] peeling   207 nieves] fists   209 cantie] lively   kittlen] kitten   210 shaws] woods   212 whins] gorse   213 scrievin] careering   214 *lan's*] lands   215 *sark*] shirt   217 linn] waterfall   burnie] stream   220 wiel] eddy

Whyles cooket underneath the braes,
  Below the spreading hazle
              Unseen that night.

XXVI

Amang the brachens, on the brae,
  Between her an' the moon,
The Deil, or else an outler Quey,
  Gat up an' gae a croon:
Poor *Leezie*'s heart maist lap the hool;   230
  Near lav'rock-height she jumpet,
But mist a fit, an' in the *pool*,
  Out owre the lugs she plumpet,
              Wi' a plunge that night.

XXVII

In order, on the clean hearth-stane,
  The *Luggies* three are ranged;
And ev'ry time great care is taen,
  To see them duely changed:
Auld, uncle *John*, wha *wedlock's joys*,
  Sin' *Mar's-year* did desire,   240
Because he gat the toom dish thrice,
  He heav'd them on the fire,
              In wrath that night.

XXVIII

Wi' merry sangs, an' friendly cracks,
  I wat they did na weary;
And unco tales, an' funnie jokes,
  Their sports were cheap an' cheary:
Till *buttr'd So'ns*, wi' fragrant lunt,
  Set a' their gabs a steerin;
Syne, wi' a social glass o' strunt,   250
  They parted aff careerin
              Fu' blythe that night.

223 cooket] hid   braes] hillsides   226 brachens] bracken   228 oulter Quey]
young cow in the open   230 lap the hool] leapt out of her skin   231 lav'rock] lark
232 fit] foot   233 lugs] ears   236 *Luggies*] wooden dishes   240 *Mar's-year*]
1715   241 toom] empty   245 wat] know   248 *buttr'd So'ns*] porridge
lunt] steam   249 gabs] tongues   steerin] wagging   250 strunt] liquor

21

7   *The Cotter's Saturday Night*

Inscribed to R. A****, Esq.

> *Let not Ambition mock their useful toil,*
> *Their homely joys, and destiny obscure;*
> *Nor Grandeur hear, with a disdainful smile,*
> *The short and simple annals of the Poor.*
>   GRAY

I

My lov'd, my honor'd, much respected friend,
  No mercenary Bard his homage pays;
With honest pride, I scorn each selfish end,
  My dearest meed, a friend's esteem and praise:
To you I sing, in simple Scottish lays,
  The *lowly train* in life's sequester'd scene;
The native feelings strong, the guileless ways,
  What A**** in a *Cottage* would have been;
Ah! tho' his worth unknown, far happier there I ween!

II

November chill blaws loud wi' angry sugh;   10
  The short'ning winter-day is near a close;
The miry beasts retreating frae the pleugh;
  The black'ning trains o' craws to their repose:
The toil-worn COTTER frae his labor goes,
  This night his weekly moil is at an end,
Collects his *spades*, his *mattocks* and his *hoes*,
  Hoping the *morn* in ease and rest to spend,
And weary, o'er the muir, his course does hameward bend.

III

At length his lonely *Cot* appears in view,
  Beneath the shelter of an aged tree;   20
Th' expectant wee-things, toddlan, stacher thro'
  To meet their *Dad*, wi' flichterin noise and glee.
His wee-bit ingle, blinkan bonilie,
  His clean hearth-stane, his thrifty *Wifie*'s smile,

7: 4 meed] reward   9 ween] believe   10 blaws] blows   sugh] rushing
sound   12 pleugh] plough   13 craws] crows   14 COTTER] farm-tenant,
cottager   16 moil] drudgery   19 *Cot*] cottage   21 stacher] stagger
22 flichterin] fluttering   23 wee-bit ingle] little bit of fire   24 stane] stone

The *lisping infant*, prattling on his knee,
Does a' his weary kiaugh and care beguile,
And makes him quite forget his labor and his toil.

IV

Belyve, the *elder bairns* come drapping in,
At *Service* out, amang the Farmers roun';
Some ca' the pleugh, some herd, some tentie rin   30
A cannie errand to a neebor toun:
Their eldest hope, their *Jenny*, woman-grown,
In youthfu' bloom, Love sparkling in her e'e,
Comes hame, perhaps to show a braw new gown,
Or deposite her sair-won penny-fee,
To help her *Parents* dear, if they in hardship be.

V

With joy unfeign'd, *brothers* and *sisters* meet,
And each for other's weelfare kindly spiers:
The social hours, swift-wing'd, unnotic'd, fleet;
Each tells the uncos that he sees or hears.   40
The *Parents partial* eye their hopeful years;
Anticipation forward points the view;
The *Mother* wi' her needle and her sheers
Gars auld claes look amaist as weel 's the new;
The *Father* mixes a', wi' admonition due.

VI

Their Master's and their Mistress's command,
The *youngkers* a' are warned to obey;
And mind their labors wi' an eydent hand,
And ne'er, tho' out o' sight, to jauk or play:
'And O! be sure to fear the LORD alway!   50
And mind your *duty*, duely, morn and night!
Lest in temptation's path ye gang astray,
Implore His counsel and assisting might:
They never sought in vain, that sought the LORD aright.'

26 kiaugh] carking anxiety [RB]   28 Belyve] soon   drapping] dropping   30 ca']
drive   tentie] careful   rin] run   31 cannie] quiet   neebor] neighbour-
ing   33 e'e] eye   34 braw] good-looking   35 sair-won] hard-won
38 spiers] asks   40 uncos] news, uncommon things   44 Gars] makes   claes]
clothes   48 eydent] diligent   49 jauk] dally, trifle [RB]

VII

But hark! a rap comes gently to the door;
 Jenny, wha kens the meaning o' the same,
Tells how a neebor lad came o'er the muir,
 To do some errands, and convoy her hame.
The wily Mother sees the *conscious flame*
 Sparkle in *Jenny*'s e'e, and flush her cheek,   60
With heart-struck, anxious care enquires his name,
 While *Jenny* hafflins is afraid to speak;
Weel-pleas'd the Mother hears, it's nae wild, worthless
              Rake.

VIII

With kindly welcome, *Jenny* brings him ben;
 A *strappan youth*, he takes the Mother's eye;
Blythe *Jenny* sees the *visit*'s no ill-taen;
 The Father cracks of horses, pleughs and kye.
The *youngster*'s artless heart o'erflows wi' joy,
 But blate and laithfu', scarce can weel behave;
The mother, wi' a woman's wiles, can spy   70
 What makes the *youth* sae bashfu' and sae grave;
Weel-pleas'd to think her *bairn*'s respected like the lave.

IX

O happy love! where love like this is found!
 O heart-felt raptures! bliss beyond compare!
I've paced much this weary, *mortal round*,
 And sage EXPERIENCE bids me this declare—
'If Heaven a draught of heavenly pleasure spare,
 One *cordial* in this melancholly *Vale*,
'Tis when a youthful, loving, *modest* Pair,
 In other's arms, breathe out the tender tale,   80
Beneath the milk-white thorn that scents the ev'ning gale.'

X

Is there, in human-form, that bears a heart—
 A wretch! a villain! lost to love and truth!
That can, with studied, sly, ensnaring art,
 Betray sweet *Jenny*'s unsuspecting youth?

58 convoy] escort   62 hafflins] half   67 cracks] talks kye] cattle
69 blate] shy laithfu'] bashful   72 lave] rest

Curse on his perjur'd arts! dissembling smoothe!
   Are *Honor, Virtue, Conscience*, all exil'd?
Is there no Pity, no relenting Ruth,
   Points to the Parents fondling o'er their Child?
Then paints the *ruin'd Maid*, and *their* distraction wild!   90

XI

But now the Supper crowns their simple board,
   The healsome *Porritch*, chief of SCOTIA's food:
The soupe their *only Hawkie* does afford,
   That 'yont the hallan snugly chows her cood:
The *Dame* brings forth, in complimental mood,
   To grace the lad, her weel-hain'd kebbuck, fell;
And aft he 's prest, and aft he ca's it guid;
   The frugal *Wifie*, garrulous, will tell,
How 'twas a towmond auld, sin' Lint was i' the bell.

XII

The chearfu' Supper done, wi' serious face,   100
   They, round the ingle, form a circle wide;
The Sire turns o'er, with patriarchal grace,
   The big *ha'-Bible*, ance his *Father*'s pride:
His bonnet rev'rently is laid aside,
   His *lyart haffets* wearing thin and bare;
Those strains that once did sweet in ZION glide,
   He wales a portion with judicious care;
'*And let us worship* GOD!' he says with solemn air.

XIII

They chant their artless notes in simple guise;
   They tune their hearts, by far the noblest aim: 110
Perhaps *Dundee*'s wild-warbling measures rise,
   Or plaintive *Martyrs*, worthy of the name;
Or noble *Elgin* beets the heaven-ward flame,
   The sweetest far of SCOTIA's holy lays:
Compar'd with these, *Italian trills* are tame;
   The tickl'd ears no heart-felt raptures raise;
Nae unison hae they, with our CREATOR's praise.

---

92 healsome] wholesome   *Porritch*] porridge   93 soupe] drink   *Hawkie*]
cow   94 'yont] beyond   hallan] partition   chows] chews   cood] cud
96 hain'd] kept   kebbuck] cheese   fell] pungent   99 towmond] twelvemonth
Lint] flax   bell] flower   103 ha'] hall   105 *lyart*] grey   *haffets*] temples
107 wales] chooses   113 beets] adds fuel to [RB]

XIV

The priest-like Father reads the sacred page,
 How *Abram* was the Friend of GOD on high;
Or, *Moses* bade eternal warfare wage,   120
 With *Amalek*'s ungracious progeny;
Or how the *royal Bard* did groaning lye,
 Beneath the stroke of Heaven's avenging ire;
Or *Job*'s pathetic plaint, and wailing cry;
 Or rapt *Isiah*'s wild, seraphic fire;
Or other *Holy Seers* that tune the *sacred lyre*.

XV

Perhaps the *Christian Volume* is the theme;
 How *guiltless blood* for *guilty man* was shed;
How HE, who bore in Heaven the second name,
 Had not on Earth whereon to lay His head: 130
How His first *followers* and *servants* sped;
 The *Precepts sage* they wrote to many a land:
How *he*, who lone in *Patmos*, banished,
 Saw in the sun a mighty angel stand;
And heard great *Bab'lon*'s doom pronounc'd by
      Heaven's command.

XVI

Then kneeling down to HEAVEN'S ETERNAL KING,
 The *Saint*, the *Father*, and the *Husband* prays:
Hope 'springs exulting on triumphant wing,'
 That *thus* they all shall meet in future days:
There, ever bask in *uncreated rays*,   140
 No more to sigh, or shed the bitter tear,
Together hymning their CREATOR's praise
 In *such society*, yet still more dear;
While circling Time moves round in an eternal sphere.

XVII

Compar'd with this, how poor Religion's pride,
 In all the pomp of *method*, and of *art*,
When men display to congregations wide,
 Devotion's ev'ry grace, except the *heart*!
The POWER, incens'd, the Pageant will desert,
 The pompous strain, the sacredotal stole;   150
But haply, in some *Cottage* far apart,
 May hear, well pleas'd, the language of the *Soul*;
And in His *Book of Life* the Inmates poor enroll.

XVIII

Then homeward all take off their sev'ral way;
 The youngling *Cottagers* retire to rest:
The Parent-pair their *secret homage* pay,
 And proffer up to Heaven the warm request,
That 'HE who stills the *raven*'s clam'rous nest,
 'And decks the *lily* fair in flow'ry pride,
'Would, in the way His *Wisdom* sees the best,   160
 'For *them* and for their *little ones* provide;
'But chiefly, in their hearts with *Grace divine* preside.'

XIX

From Scenes like these, old SCOTIA's grandeur springs,
 That makes her lov'd at home, rever'd abroad:
Princes and lords are but the breath of kings,
 'An honest man 's the noble work of GOD:'
And *certes*, in fair Virtue's heavenly road,
 The *Cottage* leaves the *Palace* far behind:
What is a lordling's pomp? a cumbrous load,
 Disguising oft the *wretch* of human kind,   170
Studied in arts of Hell, in wickedness refin'd!

XX

O SCOTIA! my dear, my native soil!
 For whom my warmest wish to Heaven is sent!
Long may thy hardy sons of *rustic toil*
 Be blest with health and peace and sweet content!
And O may Heaven their simple lives prevent
 From *Luxury*'s contagion, weak and vile!
Then howe'er *crowns* and *coronets* be rent,
 A *virtuous Populace* may rise the while,
And stand a wall of fire, around their much-lov'd ISLE. 180

XXI

O THOU! who pour'd the *patriotic tide*,
 That stream'd thro' great, unhappy WALLACE' heart;
Who dar'd to, nobly, stem tyrannic pride,
 Or *nobly die*, the second glorious part:
(The Patriot's GOD, peculiarly thou art,
 His *friend, inspirer, guardian* and *reward*!)
O never, never SCOTIA's realm desert,
 But still the *Patriot*, and the *Patriot-bard*,
In bright succession raise, her *Ornament* and *Guard*!

8   *To a Louse*

On Seeing one on a Lady's Bonnet at Church

HA! whare ye gaun, ye crowlan ferlie!
Your impudence protects you sairly:
I canna say but ye strunt rarely,
        Owre *gawze* and *lace*;
Tho' faith, I fear ye dine but sparely,
        On sic a place.

Ye ugly, creepan, blastet wonner,
Detested, shunn'd, by saunt an' sinner,
How daur ye set your fit upon her,
        Sae fine a *Lady*!   10
Gae somewhere else and seek your dinner,
        On some poor body.

Swith, in some beggar's haffet squattle;
There ye may creep, and sprawl, and sprattle,
Wi'ther kindred, jumping cattle,
        In shoals and nations;
Whare *horn* nor *bane* ne'er daur unsettle,
        Your thick plantations.

Now haud you there, ye're out of sight,
Below the fatt'rels, snug and tight,   20
Na faith ye yet! ye'll no be right,
        Till ye've got on it,
The vera tapmost, towrin height
        O' *Miss's bonnet*.

My sooth! right bauld ye set your nose out,
As plump an' gray as onie grozet:
O for some rank, mercurial rozet,
        Or fell, red smeddum,

8: 1 crowlan ferlie] crawling wonder   2 sairly] indeed   3 strunt] strut
7 wonner] wonder   8 saunt] saint   9 daur] dare   fit] foot   13 Swith]
off!   haffet] temple   squattle] squat   14 sprattle] scramble   15 cattle]
beasts   16 shoals] families   nations] tribes   17 *horn*] horn   *bane*] bone
19 haud] keep   20 fatt'rels] falderals   23 vera tapmost] very
topmost   25 bauld] bold   26 grozet] gooseberry   27 rozet] resin
28 fell] deadly   smeddum] powder

I'd gie you sic a hearty dose o't,
    Wad dress your droddum!   30

I wad na been surpriz'd to spy
You on an auld wife's *flainen toy*;
Or aiblins some bit duddie boy,
    On's *wylecoat*;
But Miss's fine *Lunardi*, fye!
    How daur ye do't?

O *Jenny* dinna toss your head,
An' set your beauties a' abroad!
Ye little ken what cursed speed
    The blastie's makin!   40
Thae *winks* and *finger-ends*, I dread,
    Are notice takin!

O wad some Pow'r the giftie gie us
To see oursels as others see us!
It wad frae monie a blunder free us
    An' foolish notion:
What airs in dress an' gait wad lea'e us
    And ev'n Devotion!

9   *Song*

Tune: 'Corn Rigs are Bonie'

I

IT was upon a Lammas night,
    When corn rigs are bonie,
Beneath the moon's unclouded light,
    I held awa to Annie:
The time flew by, wi' tentless heed,
    Till 'tween the late and early;
Wi' sma' persuasion she agreed,
    To see me thro' the barley.

30 dress] trash   droddum] backside   32 *flainen toy*] flannel cap   33 aiblins]
perhaps   bit duddie] small ragged   34 *wylecoat*] flannel vest   35 *Lunardi*]
balloon bonnet   37 dinna] do not   38 abread] abroad   40 blastie] ill-
disposed creature   41 Thae] those   43 giftie] little gift

9: 2 rigs] ridges   4 held awa] took my way   5 tentless] careless

29

II

The sky was blue, the wind was still,
　　The moon was shining clearly;   10
I set her down, wi' right good will,
　　Amang the rigs o' barley:
I ken't her heart was a' my ain;
　　I lov'd her most sincerely;
I kiss'd her owre and owre again,
　　Amang the rigs o' Barley.

III

I lock'd her in my fond embrace;
　　Her heart was beating rarely:
My blessings on that happy place,
　　Amang the rigs o' barley!   20
But by the moon and stars so bright,
　　That shone that hour so clearly!
She ay shall bless that happy night,
　　Amang the rigs o' barley.

IV

I hae been blythe wi' Comrades dear;
　　I hae been merry drinking;
I hae been joyfu' gath'rin gear;
　　I hae been happy thinking:
But a' the pleasures e'er I saw,
　　Tho' three times doubl'd fairly,   30
That happy night was worth them a',
　　Amang the rigs o' barley.

CHORUS

Corn rigs, an' barley rigs,
　　An' corn rigs are bonie:
I'll ne'er forget that happy night,
　　Amang the rigs wi' Annie.

13 ain] own   27 gear] money, property

SIR WILLIAM JONES

10

A Hymn to Indra

THE ARGUMENT

So many allusions to *Hindu* Mythology occur in the following Ode, that it would be scarce intelligible without an explanatory introduction, which, on every account and on all occasions, appears preferable to notes in the margin.

A distinct idea of the God, whom the poem celebrates, may be collected from a passage in the ninth section of the *Gítà*, where the sudden change of measure has an effect similar to that of the finest modulation:

> *tè punyamásádya suréndra lócam*
> *asnanti divyán dividévabhógán,*
> *tè tam bhuctwà swergalócam visálam*
> *eshínè punyè mertyalócam visant*

'These, having through virtue reached the mansion of the king of *Sura's*, feast on the exquisite heavenly food of the Gods: they, who have enjoyed this lofty region of SWERGA, *but* whose virtue is exhausted, revisit the habitation of mortals.'

INDRA, therefore, or the *King* of Immortals, corresponds with one of the ancient *Jupiters* (for several of that name were worshipped in *Europe*), and particularly with *Jupiter* the *Conductor*, whose attributes are so nobly described by the *Platonick* Philosophers: one of his numerous titles is *Dyupeti*, or, in the nominative case before certain letters, *Dyupetir*, which means the *Lord of Heaven*, and seems a more probable origin of the *Hetruscan* word than *Juvans Pater*; as *Diespiter* was, probably, not the *Father*, but the *Lord*, of *Day*. He may be considered as the JOVE of ENNIUS in his memorable line:

> Aspice hoc sublime candens, quem invocant omnes *Jovem*,

where the poet clearly means the firmament, of which INDRA is the personification. He is the God of thunder and the five elements, with inferior Genii under his command; and is conceived to govern the Eastern quarter of the world, but to preside, like the *Genius* or *Agathodæmon* of the Ancients, over the celestial bands, which are stationed on the summit of ME'RU, or the North-pole, where he solaces the Gods with nectar and heavenly musick: hence, perhaps, the *Hindus*, who give evidence, and the magistrates, who hear it, are directed to stand fronting the East or the North.

This imaginary mount is here feigned to have been seen in a vision at *Váránasì*, very improperly called *Banáris*, which takes its name from two rivulets, that embrace the city; and the bard, who was favoured with the sight, is supposed to have been VYA'SA, surnamed *Dwaipáyana*, or *Dwelling in an Island*; who, if he really composed the *Gítá*, makes very flattering mention of himself in the tenth chapter. The plant *Latà*, which he describes weaving a net round the mountain *Mandara*, is transported by a poetical liberty to *Suméru*, which the great author of the *Mahabhárat* has richly painted in four beautiful couplets: it is the generick name for a *creeper*, though represented here as a species, of which many elegant varieties are found in *Asia*.

The Genii named *Cinnara's* are the male dancers in *Swerga*, or the Heaven of INDRA; and the *Apsarà's* are his dancing-girls, answering to the *fairies* of the PERSIANS, and to the damsels called in the KORAN *hhúru'lûyùn*, or *with antelopes' eyes*. For the story of *Chitrarat'ha*, the chief musician of the *Indian* paradise, whose *painted car* was burned by ARJUN, and for that of *Chaturdesaretna*, or *fourteen gems*, as they are called, which were produced by churning the ocean, the reader must be referred to Mr. WILKINS'S learned annotations on his accurate version of the *Bhagavadgítà*. The fable of the pomegranate-flower is borrowed from the popular mythology of *Népàl* and *Tibet*.

In this poem the same form of stanza is repeated with *variations*, on a principle entirely new in modern lyrick poetry, which on some future occasion may be fully explained.

> BUT ah! what glories yon blue vault emblaze?
> What living meteors from the zenith stream?
> Or hath a rapt'rous dream
> Perplex'd the isle-born bard in fiction's maze?
> He wakes; he hears; he views no fancied rays.
> 'Tis INDRA mounted on the sun's bright beam;
> And round him revels his empyreal train:
> How rich their tints! how sweet their strain!
>
>   Like shooting stars around his regal seat
> A veil of many-colour'd light they weave,   10
> That eyes unholy would of sense bereave:
> Their sparkling hands and lightly-tripping feet
> Tir'd gales and panting clouds behind them leave.
> With love of song and sacred beauty smit
> The mystick dance they knit;
> Pursuing, circling, whirling, twining, leading,
> Now chasing, now receding;
> Till the gay pageant from the sky descends
> On charm'd *Suméru*, who with homage bends.
>
>   Hail, mountain of delight,   20
> Palace of glory, bless'd by glory's king!

With prosp'ring shade embow'r me, whilst I sing
Thy wonders yet unreach'd by mortal flight.

   Sky-piercing mountain! In thy bow'rs of love
No tears are seen, save where medicinal stalks
Weep drops balsamick o'er the silver'd walks;
No plaints are heard, save where the restless dove
Of coy repulse and mild reluctance talks;
Mantled in woven gold, with gems enchas'd,
With em'rald hillocks grac'd,   30
From whose fresh laps in young fantastick mazes
Soft crystal bounds and blazes
Bathing the lithe convolvulus, that winds
Obsequious, and each flaunting arbour binds.

   When sapient BRAHMA' this new world approv'd,
On woody wings eight primal mountains mov'd;
But INDRA mark'd *Suméru* for his own,
And motionless was ev'ry stone.

   Dazzling the moon he rears his golden head:
Nor bards inspir'd, nor heav'n's all-perfect speech   40
Less may unhallow'd rhyme his beauties teach,
Or paint the pavement which th' immortals tread;
Nor thought of man his awful height can reach:
Who sees it, maddens; who approaches, dies;
For, with flame-darting eyes,
Around it roll a thousand sleepless dragons;
While from their diamond flagons
The feasting Gods exhaustless nectar sip,
Which glows and sparkles on each fragrant lip.

   This feast, in mem'ry of the churned wave   50
Great INDRA gave, when *Amrit* first was won
From impious demons, who to *Máyà*'s eyes
Resign'd the prize, and rued the fight begun.

   Now, while each ardent *Cinnara* persuades
The soft-ey'd *Apsarà* to break the dance,
And leads her loth, yet with love-beaming glance,
To banks of marjoram and *Champac* shades,
Celestial *Genii* tow'rd their king advance
(So call'd by men, in heav'n *Gandharva's* nam'd)
For matchless musick fam'd.   60
Soon, where the bands in lucid rows assemble,
Flutes breathe, and citherns tremble;

Till CHITRARATHA sings—His painted car,
Yet unconsum'd, gleams like an orient star.

Hush'd was ev'ry breezy pinion,
Ev'ry stream his fall suspended:
Silence reign'd; whose sole dominion
Soon was rais'd, but soon was ended.

He sings, how 'whilom from the troubled main
The sov'reign elephant *Airávan* sprang;   70
The breathing shell, that peals of conquest rang;
The parent cow, whom none implores in vain;
The milkwhite steed, the bow with deaf'ning clang;
The Goddesses of beauty, wealth, and wine;
Flow'rs, that unfading shine,
NA'RA'YAN's gem, the moonlight's tender languish;
Blue venom, source of anguish;
The solemn leech, slow-moving o'er the strand,
A vase of long-sought *Amrit* in his hand.

'To soften human ills dread SIVA drank   80
The pois'nous flood, that stain'd his azure neck;
The rest thy mansions deck,
High *Swerga*, stor'd in many a blazing rank,

'Thou, God of thunder, satst on *Méru* thron'd,
Cloud-riding, mountain-piercing, thousand-ey'd,
With young PULO'MAJA', thy blooming bride,
Whilst air and skies thy boundless empire own'd;
Hail, DYUPETIR, dismay to BALA's pride!
Or speaks PURANDER best thy martial fame,
Or SACRA, mystick name?   90
With various praise in odes and hallow'd story
Sweet bards shall hymn thy glory.
Thou, VA'SAVA, from this unmeasur'd height
Shedst pearl, shedst odours o'er the sons of light!'

The Genius rested; for his pow'rful art
Had swell'd the monarch's heart with ardour vain,
That threaten'd rash disdain, and seem'd to low'r
On Gods of loftier pow'r and ampler reign.

He smil'd; and, warbling in a softer mode,
Sang, 'the red light'ning, hail, and whelming rain   100
O'er *Gócul* green and *Vraja*'s nymph-lov'd plain
By INDRA hurl'd, whose altars ne'er had glow'd,

Since infant CRISHNA rul'd the rustick train
Now thrill'd with terrour—Them the heav'nly child
Call'd, and with looks ambrosial smil'd,
Then with one finger rear'd the vast *Govérdhen*,
Beneath whose rocky burden
On pastures dry the maids and herdsmen trod:
The Lord of thunder felt a mightier God!'

    What furies potent modulation soothes!   110
E'en the dilated heart of INDRA shrinks:
His ruffled brow he smoothes,
His lance half-rais'd with listless languor sinks.

    A sweeter strain the sage musician chose:
He told, how 'SACHI, soft as morning light,
Blythe SACHI, from her Lord INDRA'NI' hight,
When through clear skies their car ethereal rose,
Fix'd on a garden trim her wand'ring sight,
Where gay pomegranates, fresh with early dew,
Vaunted their blossoms new: 120
"Oh! pluck, she said, yon gems, which nature dresses
To grace my darker tresses."
In form a shepherd's boy, a God in soul,
He hasten'd, and the bloomy treasure stole.

    'The reckless peasant, who those glowing flow'rs,
Hopeful of rubied fruit, had foster'd long,
Seiz'd and with cordage strong
Shackled the God, who gave him show'rs.'

    Such was the vision, which, on *Varan*'s breast
Or *Asì* pure with offer'd blossoms fill'd,   130
DWAIPA'YAN slumb'ring saw; (thus NA'RED will'd)
For waking eye such glory never bless'd,
Nor waking ear such musick ever thrill'd.
It vanish'd with light sleep: he, rising, prais'd
The guarded mount high-raised,
And pray'd the thund'ring pow'r, that sheafy treasures,
Mild show'rs and vernal pleasures,
The lab'ring youth in mead and vale might cheer,
And cherish'd herdsmen bless th' abundant year.

    Thee, darter of the swift blue bolt, he sang;   140
Sprinkler of genial dews and fruitful rains
O'er hills and thirsty plains!
'When through the waves of war thy charger sprang,

Each rock rebellow'd and each forest rang,
Till vanquish'd *Asurs* felt avenging pains.
Send o'er their seats the snake, that never dies,
But waft the virtuous to thy skies!

'Straight from sev'n winds immortal Genii flew,
Green *Varuna*, whom foamy waves obey,
Bright *Vahni* flaming like the lamp of day,   150
Cuvéra sought by all, enjoyed by few,
Marut, who bids the winged breezes play,
Stern *Yama*, ruthless judge, and *Isa* cold
With *Nairrit* mildly bold:
They with the ruddy flash, that points his thunder,
Rend his vain bands asunder.
Th' exulting God resumes his thousand eyes,
Four arms divine, and robes of changing dyes.'

Soft memory retrac'd the youthful scene:
The thund'rer yielded to resistless charms,   160
Then smil'd enamour'd on his blushing queen,
And melted in her arms.

[1787]

ROBERT MERRY ('DELLA CRUSCA')

I I   *The Adieu and Recall to Love*

Go, idle Boy! I quit thy pow'r;
Thy couch of many a thorn, and flow'r;
Thy twanging bow, thine arrow keen,
Deceitful Beauty's timid mien;
The feign'd surprize, the roguish leer,
The tender smile, the thrilling tear,
Have now no pangs, no joys for me,
So fare thee well, for I am free!
Then flutter hence on wanton wing,
Or lave thee in yon lucid spring,   10
Or take thy bev'rage from the rose,
Or on *Louisa*'s breast repose:
I wish thee well for pleasures past,
Yet bless the hour, I'm free at last.

But sure, methinks, the alter'd day
Scatters around a mournful ray;
And chilling ev'ry zephyr blows,
And ev'ry stream untuneful flows;
No rapture swells the linnet's voice,
No more the vocal groves rejoice;   20
And e'en thy song, *sweet Bird of Eve!*
With whom I lov'd so oft to grieve,
Now scarce regarded meets my ear,
Unanswer'd by a sigh or tear.
No more with devious step I choose
To brush the mountain's morning dews;
To drink the spirit of the breeze,
Or wander midst o'er-arching trees;
Or woo with undisturb'd delight,
The pale-cheek'd Virgin of the Night,   30
That piercing thro' the leafy bow'r,
Throws on the ground a silv'ry show'r.
Alas! is all this boasted ease,
To lose each warm desire to please,
No sweet solicitude to know
For others bliss, for others woe,
A frozen apathy to find,
A sad vacuity of mind?
O hasten back, then, idle Boy,
And with thine anguish bring thy joy!   40
Return with all thy torments here,
And let me hope, and doubt, and fear.
O rend my heart with ev'ry pain!
But let me, let me love again.

MRS HANNAH COWLEY
('ANNA MATILDA')
1743–1809

12   *Invocation. To Horror*

FAR be remov'd each painted scene!
What is to *me* the sapphire sky?
What is to *me* the earth's soft dye?
    Or fragrant vales which sink between
Those velvet hills? yes, there I see—

(Why do those beauties burst on me?)
Pearl-dropping groves bow to the sun;
Seizing his beams, bright rivers run
        That dart redoubled day:
Hope ye vain scenes, to catch the mind   10
To torpid sorrow all resign'd,
        Or bid my heart be gay?
False are those hopes!—I turn—I fly,
Where no enchantment meets the eye,
        Or soft ideas stray.

HORROR! I call thee from the *mould'ring tower*,
The *murky church-yard*, and *forsaken bower*,
        Where 'midst unwholesome damps
        The vap'ry gleamy lamps
Of *ignes fatui*, shew the thick-wove night,   20
        Where morbid MELANCHOLY sits,
        And weeps, and sings, and raves by fits,
And to her bosom strains the fancied sprite.

Or, if amidst the arctic gloom
        Thou toilest at thy sable loom,
Forming the hideous phantoms of Despair—
        Instant thy grisly labours leave,
        With raven wing the concave cleave,
Where floats, self-borne, the dense nocturnal air.

Oh! bear me to th' impending cliffs,   30
        Under whose brow the dashing skiffs
Beholds *Thee* seated on thy rocky throne;
        There, 'midst the shrieking wild wind's roar,
        Thy influence, HORROR, I'll adore,
And at thy magic touch, congeal to stone.

Oh! hide the Moon's obtrusive orb,
        The gleams of ev'ry star absorb,
And let CREATION be a moment thine!
        Bid billows dash; let whirlwinds roar,
        And the stern, rocky-pointed shore,   40
The stranded bark, back to the waves resign!
        Then, whilst from yonder turbid cloud,
        Thou roll'st thy thunders long, and loud,
And light'nings flash upon the deep below,
        Let the *expiring Seaman*'s cry,
        The *Pilot*'s agonizing sigh
Mingle, and in the dreadful chorus flow!

38

HORROR! far back thou dat'st thy reign;
Ere KINGS th' *historic page* could stain
With records black, or deeds of lawless power;   50
Ere empires *Alexanders* curst,
Or Faction, mad'ning *Cæsars* nurst,
The frighted World receiv'd thy awful dower!

Whose pen JEHOVAH's self inspir'd;
He, who in eloquence attir'd,
Led *Israel's squadrons* o'er the earth,
Grandly terrific, paints thy birth.
Th' ALMIGHTY, 'midst his fulgent seat on high,
Where glowing *Seraphs* round his footstool fly,
Beheld the wanton cities of the plain,   60
With acts of deadly name his laws disdain;
He gave th' irrevocable sign,
Which mark'd to man the hate divine;
And sudden from the starting sky
The Angels of his wrath bid fly!
Then HORROR! thou presidest o'er the whole,
And fill'd, and rapt, each self-accusing soul!
Thou did'st ascend to guide the burning shower—
On THEE th' Omnipotent bestow'd the hour!

'Twas thine to scourge the sinful land,   70
'Twas thine to toss the fiery brand;
Beneath thy glance the temples fell,
And mountains crumbled at thy yell.
ONCE MORE thou'lt triumph in a fiery storm;
ONCE MORE the Earth behold thy direful form;
Then shalt thou seek, as holy prophets tell,
Thy *native throne*, amidst th' *eternal shades of* HELL!

13   *To Della Crusca. The Pen*

O! SEIZE again thy golden quill,
And with its point my bosom thrill;
With magic touch explore my heart,
And bid the tear of passion start.
Thy golden quill APOLLO gave—
Drench'd first in bright Aonia's wave:
He snatch'd it flutt'ring thro' the sky,
Borne on the vapour of a sigh;

It fell from *Cupid*'s burnish'd wing
As forcefully he drew the string;   10
    Which sent his keenest, surest dart
Thro' a rebellious frozen heart;
That had till then defy'd his pow'r,
And vacant beat thro' each dull hour.

    Be worthy then the sacred loan!
Seated on Fancy's air-built throne;
Immerse it in her rainbow hues,
Nor, what the Godheads bid, refuse.
APOLLO, CUPID shall inspire,
And aid thee with their blended fire.   20
The *one*, poetic language give,
The *other* bid thy passion live;
With soft ideas fill thy lays,
And crown with LOVE thy wintry days!

[1788]

14   *Ode to Della Crusca*

    O THOU!
Who from '*a wilderness of Suns*'
Canst stoop to where the low brook runs!
Thro' space with rapid comets glow;—
Or mark where, soft, the snow-drops grow!
O THOU!
Whose burning Pen now rapture paints!
Then moralizes, cold, with Saints!
Now trembling ardors can infuse—
Then, seems as dipp'd in cloister'd dews—   10
O say! thy BEING quick declare,
Art thou a Son of Earth, or Air?
Celestial Bard! though thy sweet song
Might to a Seraph's strains belong,
Its wondrous beauty, and its art
Can only *touch*, not *change*, my heart.
So Heaven-sent light'ning *powerless* plays,
And wanton, throws its purple rays;
It leaps through Night's scarce pervious gloom
Attracted by the Rose's bloom,   20

Th' illumin'd shrub then quiv'ring round,
It seems each scented bud to wound;
Morn shakes her locks, and see the Rose
In renovated beauty blows!
Smiles at the dart which past away,
And flings her perfume on the day.

Thy light'ning Pen 'tis thus I greet,
Fearless its subtile point I meet;
Ne'er shall its spells my sad heart move,
From the calm state it vows to love.   30
All other bliss I've proved is vain—
All other bliss is dash'd with pain.
My waist with myrtles has been bound,
MY BROW WITH LAURELS HAS BEEN CROWN'D;
LOVE, has sigh'd hopeless at my feet,
LOVE, on my couch, has pour'd each sweet;
All these I've known, and now I fly
With thee, INDIFFERENCE, to die!

Nor is thy gift '*dull torpid ease,*'
The Mind's quick powers that dost not freeze: 40
No! blest by *Thee*, the soul expands,
And darts o'er new-created lands;
Springs from the confines of the earth
To where new systems struggle into birth;
The germ of future Worlds beholds,
The secrets of dark space unfolds;
Can watch how far th' ERRATIC runs,
And gaze on DELLA CRUSCA'S Suns;
In some new Orb can meet, '*his starry mail,*'
And him, on earth unknown, in Heaven with transport   50
    hail.

15   *To Anna Matilda*

> *Age, jam meorum,*
> *Finis amorum.*

AND have I strove in vain to move
Thy Heart, *fair Phantom* of my Love?
And cou'dst thou think 'twas my design,
Calmly to list thy Notes Divine,
That I responsive Lays might send,
To gain a cold *Platonic Friend?*
Far other hopes thy Verse inspir'd,
And all my Breast with Passion fir'd.
For Fancy to my mind had given
Thy form, as of the forms of Heaven—   10
Had bathed thy lips with vermil dew;
Had touch'd thy cheek with Morning's hue!
And down thy neck had sweetly roll'd
Luxuriant locks of mazy gold.

Yes, I had hopes, at least to press,
And lure thee to the chaste caress;
Catch from thy breath the quiv'ring sigh,
And meet the *murder of thine eye.*
Ah! when I deem'd such joys at hand,
Remorseless comes the stern command,   20
Nor calls my wand'ring footsteps home,
But far, and farther bids me roam;
And then thy Vestal Notes dispense
The meed of COLD INDIFFERENCE!
Curs'd Pow'r! that to myself unknown,
Still turns the heart I love, to stone!
Dwells with the Fair whom most I prize,
And scorns my tears, and mocks my sighs.

Yes, ANNA! I will hasten forth
To the bleak regions of the North,   30
Where *Erickson,* immortal Lord!
Pour'd on the Dane his vengeful sword;
Or where wide o'er the barb'rous plain,
Fierce Rurick held his ancient reign.
Then once more will I trace the Rhine,
And mark the Rhone's swift billows shine;

Once more on VIRGIL's tomb I'll muse,
And *Laura*'s, gemm'd with evening dews;
Once more ROME's *Via Sacra* tread,
And ponder on the mighty dead.   40
    More Eastward then direct my way,
    To thirsty *Egypt*'s desarts stray,
    Fix in wonder, to behold
    The Pyramids renown'd of old;
    Fallen near one of which, I ween,
    The *Hieroglyphic Sphinx* is seen!
    The Lion Virgin Sphinx, that shows
    What time the rich Nile overflows.
    Then will I sail th' Egean tide,
    Or seek *Scamander*'s tuneful side;   50
    Wander the secret groves among,
    Where HOMER wak'd th' immortal Song;
    Traverse the Nemæan Wood,
    Mark the spot where *Sparta* stood;
    Or at humbled *Athens* see
    Its still remaining Majesty!—
    Yet to *Indiff'rence* e'er a foe,
    May Beauty other joys bestow;
    Her rapt'rous Science I'll pursue,
    The Science NEWTON *never knew.*   60

Now blows the wind with melancholy force,
And o'er the *Baltic* points my weary course;
Loud shout the Mariners, the white sails swell—
ANNA MATILDA! fare thee, fare thee well!
Farewell, whoe'er thou art, and may'st thou find
Health and repose, and lasting peace of mind;
Still pour the various Verse with fancy clear,
To thrill the pulse, and charm th' attentive ear;
Nor may relentless Care thy days destroy,
But ev'ry hope be ripen'd into joy!   70

   And O! farewell to distant Britain's shore,
Which I perhaps am doom'd to see no more;
Where Valour, Wisdom, Taste, and Virtue dwell,
Dear Land of Liberty, alas! farewell!—
Yet oft, *e'en there*, by wild Ambition tost,
The Soul's best season settles in a frost.
Yet even *there*, desponding, late I knew,
That Friendship, *foreign-form'd*, is rarely true.
For they, whom most I lov'd, whose kindness sav'd
My shatter'd Bark, when erst the tempest rav'd: 80

43

At Home, e'en with the common herd could fly,
Gaze on the wounded Deer, and *pass him by!*
Nor yet can Pride subdue my pangs severe,
But Scorn itself evap'rates in a Tear.

   Thou too, delusive Maid! whose winning charms
Seduc'd me first from slow Wealth's beck'ning arms;
Sweet POETRY! my earliest, falsest Friend,
Here shall my frantic adoration end.
Take back the simple Flute thy treach'ry gave,
Take back, and plunge it in Oblivion's wave,   90
So shall its sad Notes hence no malice raise—
The Bard unknown—forgotten be the Lays.—
But should, with ANNA's Verse, his hapless Rhime,
In future meet th' impartial eye of Time,
Say, that thy wretched victim long endur'd,
Pains which are seldom felt, and never cur'd!
Say 'midst the lassitude of hopes o'erthrown,
MATILDA's *strain* could comfort him alone.
Yet was the veil mysterious ne'er remov'd,
From *him th' admiring*, and from *her the lov'd*,   100
And no kind intercourse the Song repaid,
But each to each remain'd—*a Shadow and a Shade.*

MILES PETER ANDREWS ('ARLEY')
d. 1814

16   *Elegy on the Death of Mr Sterne*

Which happened at the time of the general election, 1768.

    WHILE venal crowds for worthless men engage,
   Who basely promise what they won't perform;
While Freedom's purchas'd, and while Faction's rage
   Rends England's peace with her septennial storm;

Unaw'd by pow'r, unsway'd by partial views,
   Deaf to the clam'rous roar of public strife,
Calmly contemplative, the private muse
   Marks the calamities of private life:

Sees worth and wisdom daily sink away,
   Sees, and laments them, with a kind concern,   10
E'en now to sorrow yields the pensive lay,
   And drops a tear for genius and for *Sterne.*

O! form'd to please, to urge the social sigh,
    The gloomy hours of anguish to beguile,
To temper humour with humanity,
    And melt the bosom, while you force the smile!

Soon shall thy works, the darts of slander stemm'd,
    By Wisdom cherish'd, and by Virtue priz'd,
Be by Hypocrisy alone condemn'd,
    By prudish ignorance alone despis'd.   20

For what is wisdom, what is virtue worth?
    Hard-hearted spleen, and rigor to destroy,
To raise compassion, call our feelings forth,
    And sooth life's cares with inoffensive joy?

Let Folly's sons, to malice ever prone,
    Deem all thy labors vain, caprice and whim,
Benignity and Truth, will ever own
    The generous *Toby* and the faithful *Trim*.

Grant, decency may sometimes discommend,
    And plead its outward barriers you assault;   30
Maria's woes, and poor *Le Fevre*'s end
    Make ample recompense for every fault:

Long Gratitude thy memory shall revere,
    Long, as benevolence and virtue reign;
Pity, thy monumental stone shall rear,
    And daily dew it, with a tear humane.

There honor, love, and friendship, shall attend,
    Wait round thy silent ashes as they sleep;
There, wit and genius mourn their common friend,
    And mirth, unpatroniz'd, shall learn to weep.   40

ANONYMOUS

17

Lady T–rc———l's Ring

YOUR husband gave to you a Ring,
Set round with Jewels rare:
    You gave to him a better thing—
—A Ring set round with Hair.

ERASMUS DARWIN
1731–1802

18   from *The Loves of the Plants*

WEAK with nice sense, the chaste MIMOSA* stands,
From each rude touch withdraws her timid hands;
Oft as light clouds o'erpass the Summer-glade,
Alarm'd she trembles at the moving shade;
And feels, alive through all her tender form,
The whisper'd murmurs of the gathering storm;
Shuts her sweet eye-lids to approaching night;
And hails with freshen'd charms the rising light.

Veil'd, with gay decency and modest pride,
Slow to the mosque she moves, an eastern bride;   10
There her soft vows unceasing love record,
Queen of the bright seraglio of her Lord.—
So sinks or rises with the changeful hour
The liquid silver in its glassy tower.
So turns the needle to the pole it loves,
With fine librations quivering, as it moves.

(I. 247–62)

* *Mimosa.* The sensitive plant. Of the class Polygamy, one house. Naturalists have not explained the immediate cause of the collapsing of the sensitive plant; the leaves meet and close in the night during the sleep of the plant, or when exposed to much cold in the day time, in the same manner as when they are affected by external violence, folding their upper surfaces together, and in part over each other like scales or tiles; so as to expose as little of the upper surface as may be to the air; but do not indeed collapse quite so far, since I have found, when touched in the night during their sleep, they fall still further; especially when touched on the foot-stalks between the stems and the leaflets, which seems to be their most sensitive or irritable part. Now as their situation after being exposed to external violence resembles their sleep, but with a greater degree of collapse, may it not be owing to a numbness or paralysis consequent to too violent irritation, like the faintings of animals from pain or fatigue? I kept a sensitive plant in a dark room till some hours after day break, its leaves and leaf-stalks were collapsed as in its most profound sleep, and on exposing it to the light, above twenty minutes passed before the plant was thoroughly awake and had quite expanded itself. During the night the upper or smoother surfaces of the leaves are appressed together, this would seem to shew that the office of this surface of the leaf was to expose the fluids of the plant to the light as well as to the air. Many flowers close up their petals during the night.

On DOVE's green brink the fair TREMELLA* stood,
And view'd her playful image in the flood;
To each rude rock, lone dell, and echoing grove
Sung the sweet sorrows of her *secret* love.
'Oh, stay!—return!'—along the sounding shore
Cry'd the sad Naiads,—she return'd no more!—
Now girt with clouds the sullen Evening frown'd,
And withering Eurus swept along the ground;
The misty moon withdrew her horned light,
And sunk with Hesper in the skirt of night;   10
No dim electric streams, (the northern dawn,)
With meek effulgence quiver'd o'er the lawn;
No star benignant shot one transient ray
To guide or light the wanderer on her way.
Round the dark craggs the murmuring whirlwinds blow,
Woods groan above, and waters roar below;
As o'er the steeps with pausing foot she moves,
The pitying Dryads shriek amid their groves;
She flys,—she stops,—she pants—she looks behind,
And hears a demon howl in every wind.   20
—As the bleak blast unfurls her fluttering vest,
Cold beats the snow upon her shuddering breast;
Through her numb'd limbs the chill sensations dart,
And the keen ice-bolt trembles at her heart.
'I sink, I fall! oh, help me, help!' she cries,

---

* *Tremella.* Clandestine marriage. I have frequently observed funguses of this Genus on old rails and on the ground to become a transparent jelly, after they had been frozen in autumnal mornings; which is a curious property, and distinguishes them from some other vegetable mucilage; for I have observed that the paste, made by boiling wheat-flour in water, ceases to be adhesive after having been frozen. I suspected that the Tremella Nostoc, or star-jelly, also had been thus produced; but have since been well informed, that the Tremella Nostoc is a mucilage voided by Herons after they have eaten frogs; hence it has the appearance of having been pressed through a hole; and limbs of frogs are said sometimes to be found amongst it; it is always seen upon plains or by the sides of water, places which Herons generally frequent.

Some of the Funguses are so acrid, that a drop of their juice blisters the tongue; others intoxicate those who eat them. The Ostrahs in Siberia use them for the latter purpose; one Fungus of the species, Agaricus muscarum, eaten raw; or the decoction of three of them, produces intoxication for 12 or 16 hours. History of Russia. V. 1. Nichols. 1780. As all acrid plants become less so, if exposed to a boiling heat, it is probable the common mushroom may sometimes disagree from being not sufficiently stewed. The Ostiacks blister their skin by a fungus found on Birch-trees; and use the Agaricus officin. for Soap. (ib.)

There was a dispute whether the funguses should be classed in the animal or vegetable department. Their animal taste in cookery, and their animal smell when burnt, together with their tendency to putrefaction, insomuch that the Phallus impudicus has gained the name of stink-horn, and lastly their growing and continuing healthy without light, as the fungus vinosus in dark cellars, and the esculent mushrooms on beds covered thick with straw, would seem to shew, that they approach towards the animals, or make a kind of isthmus connecting the two mighty kingdoms of animal and of vegetable nature.

Her stiffening tongue the unfinish'd sound denies;
Tear after tear adown her cheek succeeds,
And pearls of ice bestrew the glistering meads;
Congealing snows her lingering feet surround,
Arrest her flight, and root her to the ground;   30
With suppliant arms she pours the silent prayer,
Her suppliant arms hang crystal in the air;
Pellucid films her shivering neck o'erspread,
Seal her mute lips, and silver o'er her head,
Veil her pale bosom, glaze her lifted hands,
And shrined in ice the beauteous statue stands.
—DOVE's azure nymphs on each revolving year
For fair TREMELLA shed the tender tear;
With rush-wove crowns in sad procession move,
And sound the sorrowing shell to hapless love.   40

(I. 373–412)

CARYO's sweet smile DIANTHUS* proud admires,
And gazing burns with unallow'd desires;
With sighs and sorrows her compassion moves,
And wins the damsel to illicit loves.
The Monster-offspring heirs the father's pride,
Mask'd in the damask beauties of the bride.
So, when the Nightingale in eastern bowers
On quivering pinion woos the Queen of flowers;

* *Dianthus*. Superbus. Proud Pink. There is a kind of pink called Fairchild's mule, which is here supposed to be produced between a Dianthus superbus, and the Caryophyllus, Clove. The Dianthus superbus emits a most fragrant odour, particularly at night. Vegetable mules supply an irrefragable argument in favour of the sexual system of botany. They are said to be numerous, and like the mules of the animal kingdom not always to continue their species by seed. There is an account of a curious mule from the Antirrhinum linaria, Toad-flax, in the Amænit. academ. V. 1. No. 3. and many hybrid plants described in No. 32. The Urtica alienata is an evergreen plant, which appears to be a nettle from the male flowers, and a Pellitory (Parietaria) from the female ones and the fruit; and is hence between both. Murray. Syst. Veg. Amongst the English indigenous plants the veronica hybrida mule Speedwel is supposed to have originated from the officinal one, and the spiked one, and the Sibthorpia europæa to have for its parents the golden saxifrage, and marsh pennywort. Pulteney's view of Linneus, p. 250. Mr. Graberg, Mr. Schreber, and Mr. Ramstrom seem of opinion, that the internal structure or parts of fructification in mule plants resemble the female parent, but that the habit or external structure resembles the male parent. See treatises under the above names in V. 6. Amænit. academic. The mule produced from a horse and the ass resembles the horse externally with his ears, main, and tail; but with the nature or manners of an ass: but the Hinnus, or creature produced from a male ass, and a mare, resembles the father externally, in stature, ash-colour, and the black cross, but with the nature or manners of a horse. The breed from Spanish rams and Swedish ewes resembled the Spanish sheep in wool, stature and external form; but was as hardy as the Swedish sheep; and the contrary of those, which were produced from Swedish rams and Spanish ewes. The offspring from the male goat of Angora and the Swedish female goat had long soft camel's-hair; but that from the male Swedish goat, and the female one of Angora, had no improvement of their wool. An English ram without horns, and a Swedish horned ewe produced sheep without horns, Amæn. academ. V. 6. p. 13.

Inhales her fragrance, as he hangs in air,
And melts with melody the blushing fair;   10
Half-rose, half-bird, a beauteous Monster springs,
Waves his thin leaves, or claps his glossy wings;
Long horrent thorns his mossy legs surround,
And tendril-talons root him to the ground;
Green films of rind his wrinkled neck o'erspread,
And crimson petals crest his curled head;
Soft warbling beaks in each bright blossom move,
And vocal Rosebuds thrill the enchanted grove!—
Admiring Evening stays her beamy star,
And still Night listens from his ebon car;   20
While on white wings descending Houries throng,
And drink the floods of odour and of song.

(IV. 207–26)

—Fair CHUNDA* smiles amid the burning waste,
Her brow unturban'd, and her zone unbrac'd;
Ten brother-youths with light umbrellas shade,
Or fan with busy hands the panting maid;
Loose wave her locks, disclosing, as they break,
The rising bosom and averted cheek;
Clasp'd round her ivory neck with studs of gold
Flows her thin vest in many a silky fold;
O'er her light limbs the dim transparence plays,
And the fair form, it seems to hide, betrays.   10

(IV. 237–46)

Where cool'd by rills, and curtain'd round by woods,
Slopes the green dell to meet the briny floods,
The sparkling noon-beams trembling on the tide,

---

* *Chunda.* Chundali Borrum is the name, which the natives give to this plant; it is the
Hedysarum movens, or moving plant; its class is two brotherhoods ten males. Its leaves are
continually in spontaneous motion, some rising and others falling, and others whirling circu-
larly by twisting their stems; this spontaneous movement of the leaves, when the air is quite
still, and very warm, seems to be necessary to the plant, as perpetual respiration is to animal
life.

There are many other instances of spontaneous movements of the parts of vegetables. In
the Marchantia polymorpha some yellow wool proceeds from the flower-bearing anthers,
which moves spontaneously in the anther, while it drops its dust like atoms. Murray. Syst.
Veg. See note on Collinsonia for other instances of vegetable spontaneity. Add to this, that
as the sleep of animals consists in a suspension of voluntary motion, and as vegetables are
likewise subject to sleep; there is reason to conclude, that the various actions of opening and
closing their petals and foliage may be justly ascribed to a voluntary power: for without the
faculty of volition, sleep would not have been necessary to them.

The PROTEUS-LOVER* woos his playful bride.
To win the fair he tries a thousand forms,
Basks on the sands, or gambols in the storms.—
A Dolphin now, his scaly sides he laves,
And bears the sportive damsel on the waves;
She strikes the cymbal, as he moves along,
And wondering Ocean listens to the song.   10
—And now a spotted pard the Lover stalks,
Plays round her steps, and guards her favour'd walks;
As with white teeth he prints her hand, caress'd,
And lays his velvet paw upon her breast,
O'er his round face her snowy fingers strain
The silken knots, and fit the ribbon-rein.
—And now a Swan, he spreads his plumy sails,
And proudly glides before the fanning gales;
Pleas'd on the flowery brink with graceful hand
She waves her floating lover to the land;   20
Bright shines his sinuous neck, with crimson beak
He prints fond kisses on her glowing cheek,
Spreads his broad wings, elates his ebon crest,
And clasps the beauty to his downy breast.

(IV. 363–86)

---

* *The Proteus-lover.* Conserva-polymorpha. This vegetable is put amongst the cryptogamia, or clandestine marriages, by Linneus; but according to Mr. Ellis the males and females are on different plants. Philos. Trans. V. 57. It twice changes its colour, from red to brown, and then to black; and changes its form by losing its lower leaves, and elongating some of the upper ones, so as to be mistaken by the unskilful for different plants, it grows on the shores of this country.

  There is another plant, Medicago polymorpha, which may be said to assume a great variety of shapes; as the seed-vessels resemble sometimes snail-horns, at other times caterpillars with or without long hair upon them, by which means it is probable they sometimes elude the depredations of those insects. Salicornia also assumes an animal similitude. Phil. Bot. p. 87. See note on Rubia.

THOMAS RUSSELL
1762–1788

19   *Sonnet to Valclusa*

WHAT tho', VALCLUSA, the fond Bard be fled
   That woo'd his Fair in thy sequester'd bowers,
Long lov'd her living, long bemoan'd her dead,
   And hung her visionary shrine with flowers!
What tho' no more he teach thy shades to mourn
   The hapless chances that to Love belong,
As erst, when drooping o'er her turf forlorn
   He charm'd wild ECHO with his plaintive song!
Yet still, enamour'd of the tender tale,
   Pale Passion haunts thy grove's romantic gloom,   10
Yet still soft Music breathes in every gale,
   Still undecay'd the Fairy-garlands bloom,
Still heavenly incense fills each fragrant vale,
Still PETRARCH's GENIUS weeps o'er LAURA's tomb.

20   *Sonnet Suppos'd to be Written at Lemnos*

ON THIS lone Isle, whose rugged rocks affright
   The cautious pilot, ten revolving years
   Great Pæan's Son, unwonted erst to tears,
   Wept o'er his wound: alike each rolling light
Of heaven he watch'd, and blam'd it's lingering flight,
   By day the sea-mew screaming round his cave
   Drove slumber from his eyes, the chiding wave,
   And savage howlings chas'd his dreams by night.
HOPE still was his: in each low breeze, that sigh'd
   Thro' his rude grot, he heard a coming oar,   10
   In each white cloud a coming sail he spied;
Nor seldom listen'd to the fancied roar
   Of Oeta's torrents, or the hoarser tide
   That parts fam'd Trachis from th' Euboic shore.

SIR WILLIAM JONES

　　　　　A Hymn to Su'rya

THE ARGUMENT

A PLAUSIBLE opinion has been entertained by learned men, that the principal source of idolatry among the ancients was their enthusiastick admiration of the Sun; and that, when the primitive religion of mankind was lost amid the distractions of establishing regal government, or neglected amid the allurements of vice, they ascribed to the great visible luminary, or to the wonderful fluid, of which it is the general reservoir, those powers of pervading all space and animating all nature, which their wiser ancestors had attributed to one eternal MIND, by whom the substance of fire had been created as an inanimate and secondary cause of natural phenomena. The Mythology of the East confirms this opinion; and it is probable, that the *triple Divinity* of the *Hindus* was originally no more than a personification of the Sun, whom they call *Treyitenu,* or *Three-bodied,* in his triple capacity of producing forms by his genial *heat,* preserving them by his *light,* or destroying them by the concentrated force of his *igneous* matter: this, with the wilder conceit of a *female power* united with the Godhead, and ruling nature by his authority, will account for nearly the whole system of *Egyptian, Indian,* and *Grecian* polytheism, distinguished from the sublime Theology of the Philosophers, whose understandings were too strong to admit the popular belief, but whose influence was too weak to reform it.

SU'RYA, the PHOEBUS of *European* heathens, has near fifty names or epithets in the *Sanscrit* language; most of which, or at least the meanings of them, are introduced in the following Ode; and every image, that seemed capable of poetical ornament, has been selected from books of the highest authority among the *Hindus:* the title *Arca* is very singular; and it is remarkable, that the *Tibetians* represent the Sun's car in the form of a *boat.*

It will be necessary to explain a few other particulars of the *Hindu* Mythology, to which allusions are made in the poem. SOMA, or the Moon, is a *male* Deity in the *Indian* system, as *Mona* was, I believe, among the *Saxons,* and *Lunus* among some of the nations, who settled in *Italy:* his titles also, with one or two of the ancient fables, to which they refer, are exhibited in the second stanza. Most of the *Lunar mansions* are believed to be the daughters of *Casyapa,* the first production of *Brahmà's* head, and from their names are derived those of the twelve months, who are here feigned to have married as many constellations: this primeval *Bráhman* and *Vinatà* are also supposed to have been the parents of *Arun,* the charioteer of the Sun, and of the bird *Garuda,* the eagle of the great *Indian* JOVE, one of whose epithets is *Mádhava.*

After this explanation the Hymn will have few or no difficulties, especially if the reader has perused and studied the *Bhagavadgítà*, with which our literature has been lately enriched, and the fine episode from the *Mahábhárat*, on the production of the *Amrita*, which seems to be almost wholly astronomical, but abounds with poetical beauties. Let the following description of the demon *Ráhu*, decapitated by *Náráyan*, be compared with similar passages in *Hesiod* and *Milton*:

> *tach ch'hailasringapratiman dánavasya sirò mahat*
> *chacrach'hinnam c'hamutpatya nenádíti bhayancaram,*
> *tat cabandham pepátásya visp'hurad dharanítalè*
> *sapervatavanadwípán daityasyácampayanmahím.*

FOUNTAIN of living light,
That o'er all nature streams,
Of this vast microcosm both nerve and soul;
Whose swift and subtil beams,
Eluding mortal sight,
Pervade, attract, sustain th' effulgent whole,
Unite, impel, dilate, calcine,
Give to gold its weight and blaze,
Dart from the diamond many-tinted rays,
Condense, protrude, transform, concoct, refine   10
The sparkling daughters of the mine;
Lord of the lotos, father, friend, and king,
O Sun, thy pow'rs I sing:
Thy substance *Indra* with his heav'nly bands
Nor sings nor understands;
Nor e'en the *Védas* three to man explain
Thy mystick orb triform, though *Brahmà* tun'd the strain.

Thou, nectar-beaming Moon,
Regent of dewy night,
From yon black roe, that in thy bosom sleeps,   20
Fawn-spotted *Sasin* hight;
Wilt thou desert so soon
Thy night-flow'rs pale, whom liquid odour steeps,
And *Oshadhi*'s transcendent beam
Burning in the darkest glade?
Will no lov'd name thy gentle mind persuade
Yet one short hour to shed thy cooling stream?
But ah! we court a passing dream:
Our pray'r nor *Indu* nor *Himánsu* hears;
He fades; he disappears—   30
E'en *Casyapa*'s gay daughters twinkling die,
And silence lulls the sky,

Till *Chátacs* twitter from the moving brake,
And sandal-breathing gales on beds of ether wake.

   Burst into song, ye spheres;
A greater light proclaim,
And hymn, concentrick orbs, with sev'nfold chime
The God with many a name;
Nor let unhallow'd ears
Drink life and rapture from your charm sublime: 40
'Our bosoms, *Aryama*, inspire,
Gem of heav'n, and flow'r of day,
Vivaswat, lancer of the golden ray,
Divácara, pure source of holy fire,
Victorious *Ráma*'s fervid sire,
Dread child of *Aditi*, *Martunda* bless'd,
Or *Súra* be address'd,
Ravi, or *Mihira*, or *Bhánu* bold,
Or *Arca*, title old,
Or *Heridaswa* drawn by green-hair'd steeds,   50
Or *Carmasacshi* keen, attesting secret deeds.

   'What fiend, what monster fierce
E'er durst thy throne invade?
Malignant *Ráhu*. Him thy wakeful sight,
That could the deepest shade
Of snaky *Narac* pierce,
Mark'd quaffing nectar; when by magick sleight
A *Sura*'s lovely form he wore,
Rob'd in light, with lotos crown'd,
What time th' immortals peerless treasures found   60
On the churn'd Ocean's gem-bespangled shore,
And *Mandar*'s load the tortoise bore:
Thy voice reveal'd the daring sacrilege;
Then, by the deathful edge
Of bright *Sudersan* cleft, his dragon head
Dismay and horror spread
Kicking the skies, and struggling to impair
The radiance of thy robes, and stain thy golden hair.

   'With smiles of stern disdain
Thou, sov'reign victor, seest   70
His impious rage: soon from the mad assault
Thy coursers fly releas'd;
Then toss each verdant mane,
And gallop o'er the smooth aerial vault;
Whilst in charm'd *Gócul*'s od'rous vale

Blue-ey'd *Yamunà* descends
Exulting, and her tripping tide suspends,
The triumph of her mighty sire to hail:
So must they fall, who Gods assail!
For now the demon rues his rash emprise,   80
Yet, bellowing blasphemies
With pois'nous throat, for horrid vengeance thirsts,
And oft with tempest bursts,
As oft repell'd he groans in fiery chains,
And o'er the realms of day unvanquish'd *Súrya* reigns.'

    Ye clouds, in wavy wreathes
Your dusky van unfold;
O'er dimpled sands, ye surges, gently flow,
With sapphires edg'd and gold!
Loose-tressed morning breathes,   90
And spreads her blushes with expansive glow;
But chiefly where heav'n's op'ning eye
Sparkles at her saffron gate,
How rich, how regal in his orient state!
Erelong he shall emblaze th' unbounded sky:
The fiends of darkness yelling fly;
While birds of liveliest note and lightest wing
The rising daystar sing,
Who skirts th' horizon with a blazing line
Of topazes divine;   100
E'en, in their prelude, brighter and more bright,
Flames the red east, and pours insufferable light.

    First o'er blue hills appear,
With many an agate hoof
And pasterns fring'd with pearl, sev'n coursers green;
Nor boasts yon arched woof,
That girds the show'ry sphere,
Such heav'n-spun threads of colour'd light serene,
As tinge the reins, which *Arun* guides,
Glowing with immortal grace,   110
Young *Arun*, loveliest of *Vinatian* race,
Though younger He, whom *Mádhava* bestrides,
When high on eagle-plumes he rides:
But oh! what pencil of a living star
Could paint that gorgeous car,
In which, as in an ark supremely bright,
The lord of boundless light
Ascending calm o'er th' empyrean sails,
And with ten thousand beams his awful beauty veils.

Behind the glowing wheels   120
Six jocund seasons dance,
A radiant month in each quick-shifting hand;
Alternate they advance,
While buxom nature feels
The grateful changes of the frolick band:
Each month a constellation fair
Knit in youthful wedlock holds,
And o'er each bed a varied sun unfolds,
Lest one vast blaze our visual force impair,
A canopy of woven air.   130
Vasanta blythe with many a laughing flow'r
Decks his *Candarpa*'s bow'r;
The drooping pastures thirsty *Gríshma* dries,
Till *Vershà* bids them rise;
Then *Sarat* with full sheaves the champaign fills,
Which *Sisira* bedews, and stern *Hémanta* chills.

Mark, how the all-kindling orb
Meridian glory gains!
Round *Méru*'s breathing zone he winds oblique
O'er pure cerulean plains: 140
His jealous flames absorb
All meaner lights, and unresisted strike
The world with rapt'rous joy and dread.
Ocean, smit with melting pain,
Shrinks, and the fiercest monster of the main
Mantles in caves profound his tusky head
With sea-weeds dank and coral spread:
Less can mild earth and her green daughters bear
The noon's wide-wasting glare;
To rocks the panther creeps; to woody night   150
The vulture steals his flight;
E'en cold cameleons pant in thickets dun,
And o'er the burning grit th' unwinged locusts run!

But when thy foaming steeds
Descend with rapid pace
Thy fervent axle hast'ning to allay,
What majesty, what grace
Dart o'er the western meads
From thy relenting eye their blended ray!
Soon may th' undazzled sense behold   160
Rich as *Vishnu*'s diadem,
Or *Amrit* sparkling in an azure gem,
Thy horizontal globe of molten gold,

Which pearl'd and rubied clouds infold.
It sinks; and myriads of diffusive dyes
Stream o'er the tissued skies,
Till *Sóma* smiles, attracted by the song
Of many a plumed throng
In groves, meads, vales; and, whilst he glides above,
Each bush and dancing bough quaffs harmony and love.   170

   Then roves thy poet free,
Who with no borrow'd art
Dares hymn thy pow'r, and durst provoke thy blaze,
But felt thy thrilling dart;
And now, on lowly knee,
From him, who gave the wound, the balsam prays.
Herbs, that assuage the fever's pain,
Scatter from thy rolling car,
Cull'd by sage *Aswin* and divine *Cumàr*;
And, if they ask, 'What mortal pours the strain?'   180
Say (for thou seest earth, air, and main)
Say: 'From the bosom of yon silver isle,
Where skies more softly smile,
He came; and, lisping our celestial tongue
Though not from *Brahmà* sprung,
Draws orient knowledge from its fountains pure,
Through caves obstructed long, and paths too long obscure.'

   Yes; though the *Sanscrit* song
Be strown with fancy's wreathes,
And emblems rich, beyond low thoughts refin'd,   190
Yet heav'nly truth it breathes
With attestation strong,
That, loftier than thy sphere, th' Eternal Mind,
Unmov'd, unrival'd, undefil'd,
Reigns with providence benign:
He still'd the rude abyss, and bade it shine
(Whilst Sapience with approving aspect mild
Saw the stupendous work, and smil'd);
Next thee, his flaming minister, bade rise
O'er young and wondering skies.   200
Since thou, great orb, with all-enlight'ning ray
Rulest the golden day,
How far more glorious He, who said serene,
BE, and *thou wast*—Himself unform'd, unchang'd, unseen!

WILLIAM LISLE BOWLES
1762–1850

22   *Sonnet V*

EVENING, as slow thy placid shades descend,
   Veiling with gentlest hush the landscape still,
   The lonely battlement, and farthest hill
And wood, I think of those that have no friend,
Who now, perhaps, by melancholy led,
   From the broad blaze of day, where pleasure flaunts,
   Retiring, wander 'mid thy lonely haunts
Unseen; and watch the tints that o'er thy bed
Hang lovely, to their pensive fancy's eye
   Presenting fairy vales, where the tir'd mind   10
   Might rest, beyond the murmurs of mankind,
Nor hear the hourly moans of misery!
Ah! beauteous views, that Hope's fair gleams the while
Should smile like you, and perish as they smile!

WILLIAM BLAKE
1757–1827

23–30   from *Songs of Innocence*

23   *Introduction*

PIPING down the valleys wild
Piping songs of pleasant glee
On a cloud I saw a child.
And he laughing said to me.

Pipe a song about a Lamb;
So I piped with merry chear,
Piper pipe that song again—
So I piped, he wept to hear.

Drop thy pipe thy happy pipe
Sing thy songs of happy chear,   10
So I sung the same again
While he wept with joy to hear

Piper sit thee down and write
In a book that all may read—
So he vanish'd from my sight.
And I pluck'd a hollow reed.

And I made a rural pen,
And I stain'd the water clear,
And I wrote my happy songs
Every child may joy to hear   20

24   *The Lamb*

Little Lamb who made thee
Dost thou know who made thee
Gave thee life & bid thee feed.
By the stream & o'er the mead;
Gave thee clothing of delight,
Softest clothing wooly bright;
Gave thee such a tender voice,
Making all the vales rejoice!
Little Lamb who made thee
Dost thou know who made thee   10

Little Lamb I'll tell thee,
Little Lamb I'll tell thee!
He is called by thy name.
For he calls himself a Lamb:
He is meek & he is mild,
He became a little child:
I a child & thou a lamb,
We are called by his name.
Little Lamb God bless thee.
Little Lamb God bless thee.   20

25   *The Little Black Boy*

My mother bore me in the southern wild,
And I am black, but O! my soul is white;
White as an angel is the English child:
But I am black as if bereav'd of light.

My mother taught me underneath a tree
And sitting down before the heat of day,
She took me on her lap and kissed me,
And pointing to the east began to say.

Look on the rising sun: there God does live
And gives his light, and gives his heat away.   10
And flowers and trees and beasts and men recieve
Comfort in morning joy in the noon day.

And we are put on earth a little space,
That we may learn to bear the beams of love,
And these black bodies and this sun-burnt face
Is but a cloud, and like a shady grove.

For when our souls have learn'd the heat to bear
The cloud will vanish we shall hear his voice.
Saying: come out from the grove my love & care,
And round my golden tent like lambs rejoice.   20

Thus did my mother say and kissed me,
And thus I say to little English boy.
When I from black and he from white cloud free,
And round the tent of God like lambs we joy:

I'll shade him from the heat till he can bear,
To lean in joy upon our fathers knee.
And then I'll stand and stroke his silver hair,
And be like him and he will then love me.

26   *The Divine Image*

To Mercy Pity Peace and Love,
All pray in their distress:
And to these virtues of delight
Return their thankfulness.

For Mercy Pity Peace and Love,
Is God our father dear:
And Mercy Pity Peace and Love,
Is Man his child and care.

For Mercy has a human heart
Pity, a human face: 10
And Love, the human form divine,
And Peace, the human dress.

Then every man of every clime,
That prays in his distress,
Prays to the human form divine
Love Mercy Pity Peace.

And all must love the human form,
In heathen, turk or jew.
Where Mercy, Love & Pity dwell,
There God is dwelling too.   20

27   *Holy Thursday*

Twas on a Holy Thursday their innocent faces clean
The children walking two & two in red & blue & green
Grey headed beadles walkd before with wands as white as snow
Till into the high dome of Pauls they like Thames waters flow

O what a multitude they seemd these flowers of London town
Seated in companies they sit with radiance all their own
The hum of multitudes was there but multitudes of lambs
Thousands of little boys & girls raising their innocent hands

Now like a mighty wind they raise to heaven the voice of song
Or like harmonious thunderings the seats of heaven among   10
Beneath them sit the aged men wise guardians of the poor
Then cherish pity, lest you drive an angel from your door

28   *A Dream*

Once a dream did weave a shade,
O'er my Angel-guarded bed,
That an Emmet lost its way
Where on grass methought I lay.

Troubled wilderd and forlorn
Dark benighted travel-worn,
Over many a tangled spray
All heart-broke I heard her say.

O my children! do they cry
Do they hear their father sigh.   10
Now they look abroad to see,
Now return and weep for me.

Pitying I drop'd a tear:
But I saw a glow-worm near:
Who replied. What wailing wight
Calls the watchman of the night.

I am set to light the ground,
While the beetle goes his round:
Follow now the beetles hum,
Little wanderer hie thee home.   20

29   *The Little Girl Lost*

In futurity
I prophetic see,
That the earth from sleep,
(Grave the sentence deep)

Shall arise and seek
For her maker meek:
And the desart wild
Become a garden mild.

In the southern clime,
Where the summers prime,   10
Never fades away;
Lovely Lyca lay.

Seven summers old
Lovely Lyca told,
She had wanderd long,
Hearing wild birds song.

Sweet sleep come to me
Underneath this tree;
Do father, mother weep.—
Where can Lyca sleep.   20

Lost in desart wild
Is your little child.
How can Lyca sleep,
If her mother weep.

If her heart does ake,
Then let Lyca wake;
If my mother sleep,
Lyca shall not weep.

Frowning frowning night,
O'er this desart bright,   30
Let thy moon arise,
While I close my eyes.

Sleeping Lyca lay;
While the beasts of prey,
Come from caverns deep,
View'd the maid asleep

The kingly lion stood
And the virgin view'd,
Then he gambold round
O'er the hallowd ground;   40

Leopards, tygers play,
Round her as she lay;
While the lion old,
Bow'd his mane of gold.

And her bosom lick,
And upon her neck,
From his eyes of flame,
Ruby tears there came;

While the lioness,
Loos'd her slender dress,   50
And naked they convey'd
To caves the sleeping maid.

30   *The Little Girl Found*

All the night in woe,
Lyca's parents go:
Over vallies deep,
While the desarts weep.

Tired and woe-begone,
Hoarse with making moan:
Arm in arm seven days,
They trac'd the desart ways.

Seven nights they sleep,
Among shadows deep: 10
And dream they see their child
Starv'd in desert wild.

Pale thro' pathless ways
The fancied image strays,
Famish'd, weeping, weak
With hollow piteous shriek

Rising from unrest,
The trembling woman prest,
With feet of weary woe;
She could no further go.   20

In his arms he bore,
Her arm'd with sorrow sore;
Till before their way,
A couching lion lay.

Turning back was vain,
Soon his heavy mane,
Bore them to the ground;
Then he stalk'd around,

Smelling to his prey.
But their fears allay,   30
When he licks their hands;
And silent by them stands.

They look upon his eyes
Fill'd with deep surprise:
And wondering behold,
A spirit arm'd in gold.

On his head a crown
On his shoulders down,
Flow'd his golden hair.
Gone was all their care.   40

Follow me he said,
Weep not for the maid;
In my palace deep,
Lyca lies asleep.

Then they followed,
Where the vision led:
And saw their sleeping child,
Among tygers wild.

To this day they dwell
In a lonely dell   50
Nor fear the wolvish howl,
Nor the lions growl.

ROBERT BURNS

31 *John Anderson my Jo*

JOHN Anderson my jo, John,
　　When we were first acquent;
Your locks were like the raven,
　　Your bony brow was brent;
But now your brow is beld, John,
　　Your locks are like the snaw;
But blessings on your frosty pow,
　　John Anderson my Jo.

John Anderson my jo, John,
　　We clamb the hill the gither;　　　　　　10
And mony a canty day, John,
　　We've had wi' ane anither:
Now we maun totter down, John,
　　And hand in hand we'll go;
And sleep the gither at the foot,
　　John Anderson my Jo.

HELEN MARIA WILLIAMS
1762–1827

32 from *An Address to Poetry*

BLEST Poesy! Oh sent to calm
The human pains which all must feel;
　　Still shed on life thy precious balm,
And every wound of nature heal!
　　Is there a heart of human frame
Along the burning track of torrid light,
　　Or 'mid the fearful waste of polar night,
That never glow'd at thy inspiring name?

　　Ye southern isles, emerg'd so late
Where the pacific billow rolls,　　　　　　10
　　Witness, tho' rude your simple state,

65

How heav'n-taught verse can melt your souls:
  Say, when you hear the wand'ring bard,
How thrill'd ye listen to his lay,
  By what kind arts ye court his stay,
All savage life affords, his sure reward.

  So, when great Homer's chiefs prepare,
A while from war's rude toils releas'd,
  The pious hecatomb, and share
The flowing bowl, and genial feast;   20
  Some heav'nly minstrel sweeps the lyre,
While all applaud the poet's native art,
  For him they heap the viands choicest part,
And copious goblets crown the muses fire.

  Ev'n *here*, in scenes of pride and gain,
Where faint each genuine feeling glows;
  Here, Nature asks, in want and pain,
The dear illusions verse bestows;
  The poor, from hunger, and from cold,
Spare one small coin, the ballad's price;   30
  Admire their poet's quaint device,
And marvel much at all his rhymes unfold.

  Ye children, lost in forests drear,
Still o'er your wrongs each bosom grieves,
  And long the red-breast shall be dear
Who strew'd each little corpse with leaves;
  For you, my earliest tears were shed,
For you, the gaudy doll I pleas'd forsook,
  And heard with hands up-rais'd, and eager look,
The cruel tale, and wish'd ye were not dead!   40

  And still on Scotia's northern shore,
'At times, between the rushing blast,'
  Recording mem'ry loves to pour
The mournful song of ages past;
  Come, lonely bard 'of other years!'
While dim the half-seen moon of varying skies,
  While sad the wind along the grey-moss sighs,
And give my pensive heart 'the joy of tears!'

  The various tropes that splendour dart
Around the modern poet's line,   50
  Where, borrow'd from the sphere of art,

66

Unnumber'd gay allusions shine,
  Have not a charm my breast to please
Like the blue mist, the meteor's beam,
  The dark-brow'd rock, the mountain stream,
And the light thistle waving in the breeze.

  Wild Poesy, in haunts sublime,
Delights her lofty note to pour;
  She loves the hanging rock to climb,
And hear the sweeping torrent roar: 60
  The little scene of cultur'd grace
But faintly her expanded bosom warms;
  She seeks the daring stroke, the aweful charms,
Which Nature's pencil throws on Nature's face.

(lines 89–152)

ROBERT MERRY ('DELLA CRUSCA')

33   from *The Laurel of Liberty. A Poem*

GENIUS, or Muse, whate'er thou art! whose thrill
Exalts the fancy, and inflames the will,
Bids o'er the heart sublime sensation roll,
And wakes extatic fervour in the soul;
Who lov'st to throw thy wild ungovern'd gaze
Where starry Night weaves thick her tissued rays,
And chasing envious shadow from the globe,
Leads the meek moon array'd in virgin robe,
To glance soft lustre from her chrystal eye,
And deck the heav'ns with pearly panoply: 10
Or, whether, random-cast, beside some stream,
Whose rippling current laves the falling beam,
Thou ponder'st, philosophical, alone,
Entranc'd by Sorrow's desultory groan,
While from dark dell the plumed minstrel's throat
Swells the long anguish of disast'rous note:
Or dost thou hasten to the lawny vale,
When yellow morning breathes her sweetest gale,
And drops on ev'ry flow'r luxuriant hues,
And bathes the landscape with celestial dews: 20
Whate'er thy pleasures are, or O! thy pains,
Attend thy suppliant and assist his strains;
With smiles benign thy ardent vot'ry hear,
Hang o'er his eye thy gossamery tear,

Wake the true throb, the living flame impart,
Usurp his mind, and seize upon his heart!
Not *now* he strays where other times are brought
By mem'ry's pow'rful magic to the thought,
With all that Folly plann'd, or Pride essay'd,
The earliest efforts men or monarchs made;   30
Nor calls the shad'wy trains again to birth,
Who trod, a moment trod, the realms of earth;
Valour's rough sons, and Beauty's daughters fair,
And those that bled, and those that triumph'd there,
Ambition's Robbers, Poets with their lay,
Alike th' important nothings of a day.
Not *now*, he fondly courts thee to renew
The lovesick song, some trem'lous maid to woo;
As when his youthful hand was wont to fling
A grateful incense to the op'ning Spring,   40
Who sweetly pacing from her blossom'd bow'r,
Unbound the streams, and shed the perfum'd show'r;
Who taught faint Echo in her cave serene,
With Passion's tend'rest tones to charm the green,
Wreathe round her airy harp the tim'rous joy,
And with delight her hundred tongues employ.
Nor yet, as *once*, for graceful COWLEY's brow,
He blends the laurel and the myrtle bough,
Drinks her rich strain with extacy divine,
Dares the bold flight, and maddens on the line;   50
But a still nobler, grander theme inspires,
And Love is lost in Reason's purer fires.

                                          (lines 1–52)

68

ROBERT BURNS

34   *Tam o' Shanter. A Tale*

WHEN chapman billies leave the street,
And drouthy neebors, neebors meet,
As market-days are wearing late,
And folk begin to tak the gate;
While we sit bowsing at the nappy,
And gettin fou and unco happy,
We think na on the lang Scots miles,
The waters, mosses, slaps, and styles,
That lie between us and our hame,
Whare sits our sulky sullen dame,   10
Gathering her brows like gathering storm,
Nursing her wrath to keep it warm.

This truth fand honest *Tam o' Shanter*,
As he frae Ayr ae night did canter,
(Auld Ayr, whom ne'er a town surpasses,
For honest men and bonny lasses.)

O *Tam*! hadst thou but been sae wise,
As ta'en thy ain wife *Kate*'s advice!
She tauld thee weel thou was a skellum,
A bletherin, blusterin, drunken blellum;   20
That frae November till October,
Ae market-day thou was na sober;
That ilka melder wi' the miller,
Thou sat as long as thou had siller;
That every naig was ca'd a shoe on,
The smith and thee gat roaring fou on;
That at the L—d's house, even on Sunday,
Thou drank wi' Kirkton Jean till Monday.
She prophesied that late or soon,
Thou wad be found deep-drown'd in Doon;   30

34: 1 chapman billies] pedlars   2 drouthy] thirsty   4 gate] road
5 nappy] ale   6 fou and unco] full and mighty   8 slaps] bogs   styles]
breaches   19 skellum] good-for-nothing   20 blellum] babbler   23 melder]
meal-grinding   24 siller] money

Or catch'd wi' warlocks in the mirk,
By *Alloway*'s auld haunted kirk.

Ah, gentle dames! it gars me greet,
To think how mony counsels sweet,
How mony lengthen'd sage advices,
The husband frae the wife despises!

But to our tale:—Ae market-night,
Tam had got planted unco right;
Fast by an ingle bleezing finely,
Wi' reamin swats that drank divinely;   40
And at his elbow, Souter Johnie,
His ancient, trusty, drouthy cronie;
Tam lo'ed him like a vera brither;
They had been fou for weeks thegither.—
The night drave on wi' sangs and clatter,
And ay the ale was growing better:
The landlady and *Tam* grew gracious,
Wi' favours, secret, sweet, and precious:
The Souter tauld his queerest stories;
The landlord's laugh was ready chorus: 50
The storm without might rair and rustle,
Tam did na mind the storm a whistle.—
Care, mad to see a man sae happy,
E'en drown'd himsel amang the nappy:
As bees flee hame wi' lades o' treasure,
The minutes wing'd their way wi' pleasure:
Kings may be blest, but *Tam* was glorious,
O'er a' the ills o' life victorious!

But pleasures are like poppies spread,
You seize the flower, its bloom is shed;   60
Or like the snow falls in the river,
A moment white—then melts for ever;
Or like the borealis race,
That flit ere you can point their place;
Or like the rainbow's lovely form
Evanishing amid the storm.—
Nae man can tether time or tide,
The hour approaches *Tam* maun ride;
That hour, o' night's black arch the key-stane,

---

33 gars] makes   greet] weep   40 reamin swats] foaming new ale   41 Souter]
Cobbler

That dreary hour he mounts his beast in;   70
And sic a night he taks the road in,
As ne'er poor sinner was abroad in.

   The wind blew as 'twad blawn its last;
The rattling showers rose on the blast;
The speedy gleams the darkness swallow'd;
Loud, deep, and lang, the thunder bellow'd:
That night, a child might understand,
The Deil had business on his hand.

   Weel mounted on his gray mare, *Meg*,
A better never lifted leg,   80
Tam skelpit on thro' dub and mire,
Despising wind, and rain, and fire;
Whiles holding fast his gude blue bonnet;
Whiles crooning o'er an auld Scots sonnet;
Whiles glowring round wi' prudent cares,
Lest bogles catch him unawares:
Kirk-Aloway was drawing nigh,
Whare ghaists and houlets nightly cry.

   By this time he was cross the ford,
Whare in the snaw the chapman smoor'd;   90
And past the birks and meikle stane,
Whare drunken *Charlie* brak 's neck-bane;
And thro' the whins, and by the cairn,
Whare hunters fand the murder'd bairn;
And near the tree, aboon the well,
Whare *Mungo*'s mither hang'd hersel.—
Before him, *Doon* pours all his floods;
The doubling storm roars thro' the woods;
The lightnings flash from pole to pole;
Near, and more near, the thunders roll: 100
When, glimmering thro' groaning trees,
Kirk-Aloway seem'd in a bleeze;
Thro' ilka bore the beams were glancing;
And loud resounded mirth and dancing.—

   Inspiring, bold *John Barleycorn*!
What dangers thou canst make us scorn!
Wi' tippeny, we fear nae evil;

81 dub] puddle   86 bogles] bogies   88 houlets] owls   90 smoor'd] smoth-
ered   91 birks] birches   meikle] big   93 whins] furze   95 aboon]
above   103 ilka bore] every chink   107 tippeny] ale

Wi' usquabae, we'll face the devil!
The swats sae ream'd in *Tammie*'s noddle,
Fair play, he car'd na deils a boddle.   110
But *Maggie* stood, right sair astonish'd,
Till, by the heel and hand admonish'd,
She ventured forward on the light;
And, wow! *Tam* saw an unco sight!

Warlocks and witches in a dance;
Nae cotillion brent new frae *France*,
But hornpipes, jigs, strathspeys, and reels,
Put life and mettle in their heels.—
A winnock-bunker in the east,
There sat auld Nick in shape o' beast;   120
A towzie tyke, black, grim, and large,
To gie them music was his charge:
He screw'd the pipes and gart them skirl,
Till roof and rafters a' did dirl.—
Coffins stood round, like open presses,
That shaw'd the dead in their last dresses;
And (by some devilish cantraip slight)
Each in its cauld hand held a light.—
By which heroic *Tam* was able
To note upon the haly table,   130
A murderer's banes, in gibbet airns;
Twa span-lang, wee, unchristen'd bairns;
A thief, new-cutted frae a rape,
Wi' his last gasp his gab did gape;
Five tomahawks, wi' blude red-rusted;
Five scymitars, wi' murder crusted;
A garter which a babe had strangled;
A knife a father's throat had mangled,
Whom his ain son o' life bereft,
The grey hairs yet stack to the heft;   140
Wi' mair o' horrible and awefu',
Which even to name wad be unlawfu'.
Three lawyers tongues, turn'd inside out,
Wi' lies seam'd like a beggar's clout;
Three priests' hearts, rotten, black as muck,
Lay stinking, vile, in every neuk.—

110 boddle] farthing   116 brent] brand   119 winnock-bunker] window-
seat   121 towzie tyke] shaggy dog   123 skirl] squeal   124 dirl]
ring   125 presses] cupboards   127 cantraip] magic device   131 airns]
irns   134 gab] mouth

As *Tammie* glow'rd, amaz'd, and curious,
The mirth and fun grew fast and furious:
The piper loud and louder blew;
The dancers quick and quicker flew;   150
They reel'd, they set, they cross'd, they cleekit,
Till ilka carlin swat and reekit,
And coost her duddies on the wark,
And linket at it in her sark!

Now, *Tam*, O *Tam*! had thae been queans,
A' plump and strapping in their teens,
Their sarks, instead o' creeshie flannen,
Been snaw-white seventeen-hunder linnen!
Thir breeks o' mine, my only pair,
That ance were plush, o' gude blue hair,   160
I wad hae gi'en them off my hurdies,
For ae blink o' the bonie burdies!
But wither'd beldams, auld and droll,
Rigwoodie hags wad spean a foal,
Lowpin and flingin on a crummock,
I wonder didna turn thy stomach.

But *Tam* kend what was what fu' brawlie,
There was ae winsome wench and walie,
That night enlisted in the core,
(Lang after kend on *Carrick* shore;   170
For mony a beast to dead she shot,
And perish'd mony a bony boat,
And shook baith meikle corn and bear,
And kept the country-side in fear)—
Her cutty-sark, o' Paisley harn,
That while a lassie she had worn,
In longitude tho' sorely scanty,
It was her best, and she was vauntie.—
Ah! little thought thy reverend grannie,
That sark she coft for her wee Nannie,   180
Wi' twa pund Scots ('twas a' her riches)
Should ever grac'd a dance of witches!

151 cleekit] took hold   152 carlin] beldam   swat and reekit] sweated and steamed   153 duddies] rags   154 linket] tripped   sark] shirt   157 creeshie] greasy   161 hurdies] buttocks   162 burdies] maidens   164 Rigwoodie] ancient   spean] wean   165 Lowpin] leaping   flingin] kicking   crummock] cudgel   167 fu'] well   168 winsome] choice   173 bear] barley   175 cutty-sark] short shrift   harn] coarse cloth   178 vauntie] proud   180 coft] bought

But here my Muse her wing maun cour,
Sic flights are far beyond her power;
To sing how Nannie lap and flang,
(A souple jad she was, and strang),
And how *Tam* stood, like ane bewitch'd,
And thought his very een enrich'd;
Even Satan glowr'd, and fidg'd fu' fain,
And hotch'd, and blew wi' might and main: 190
Till first ae caper—syne anither—
Tam lost his reason a' thegither,
And roars out—'Weel done, Cutty-sark!'
And in an instant all was dark:
And scarcely had he Maggie rallied,
When out the hellish legion sallied.

As bees bizz out wi' angry fyke,
When plundering herds assail their byke;
As open pussie's mortal foes,
When, pop! she stars before their nose;   200
As eager runs the market-croud,
When 'Catch the thief!' resounds aloud;
So Maggie rins, the witches follow,
Wi' mony an eldritch shout and hollo.

Ah, *Tam*! Ah, *Tam*! thou'll get thy fairin!
In hell they'll roast thee like a herrin!
In vain thy *Kate* awaits thy comin!
Kate soon will be a woefu' woman!
Now, do thy speedy utmost, Meg,
And win the key-stane of the brig;   210
There at them thou thy tail may toss,
A running stream they dare na cross.
But ere the key-stane she could make,
The fient a tail she had to shake!
For Nannie, far before the rest,
Hard upon noble Maggie prest,
And flew at *Tam* wi' furious ettle;
But little kend she Maggie's mettle!
Ae spring brought off her master hale,
But left behind her ain gray tail: 220

183 cour]stoop   185 lap] leaped   flang] kicked   189 fidg'd] fidgeted
fain] fond   190 hotch'd] jerked   191 syne] then   197 fyke] fret
198 byke] hive   199 pussie] the hare   205 fairin] beating   214 fient] devil
217 ettle] aim   219 hale] whole

74

The carlin claught her by the rump,
And left poor Maggie scarce a stump.

Now, wha this tale o' truth shall read,
Ilk man and mother's son, take heed:
Whene'er to drink you are inclin'd,
Or cutty-sarks rin in your mind,
Think, ye may buy the joys o'er dear,
Remember Tam o' Shanter's mere.

MARY ROBINSON ('LAURA MARIA')
1758–1800

35   *Canzonet*

SLOW the limpid currents twining,
    Brawl along the lonely dell,
'Till in one wild stream combining,
    Nought its rapid course can quell;
So at first LOVE's poisons stealing,
    Round the heart unheeded play,
While we hope our pangs concealing,
    Vainly hope to check his sway.

If amidst the glassy river
    Aught impedes its placid course,   10
Ah! it glides more swift than ever,
    While opposing gives it force;
So when HOPE and PASSION blending,
    Warm the feeble trembling frame;
REASON sickens by contending,
    Fanning only feeds the flame.

34: 221 claught] seized

ANN RADCLIFFE
1764–1823

36   *Night*

Now Ev'ning fades! her pensive step retires,
   And Night leads on the dews, and shadowy hours;
Her awful pomp of planetary fires,
   And all her train of visionary powers.

These paint with fleeting shapes the dream of sleep,
   These swell the waking soul with pleasing dread;
These through the glooms in forms terrific sweep,
   And rouse the thrilling horrors of the dead!

Queen of the solemn thought—mysterious Night!
   Whose step is darkness, and whose voice is fear!   10
Thy shades I welcome with severe delight,
   And hail thy hollow gales, that sigh so drear!

When, wrapt in clouds, and riding in the blast,
   Thou roll'st the storm along the sounding shore,
I love to watch the whelming billows cast
   On rocks below, and listen to the roar.

Thy milder terrors, Night, I frequent woo,
   Thy silent lightnings, and thy meteor's glare,
Thy northern fires, bright with ensanguine hue,
   That light in heaven's high vault the fervid air.   20

But chief I love thee, when thy lucid car
   Sheds through the fleecy clouds a trembling gleam,
And shews the misty mountain from afar,
   The nearer forest, and the valley's stream:

And nameless objects in the vale below,
   That floating dimly to the musing eye,
Assume, at Fancy's touch, fantastic shew,
   And raise her sweet romantic visions high.

Then let me stand amidst thy glooms profound
   On some wild woody steep, and hear the breeze   30
That swells in mournful melody around,
   And faintly dies upon the distant trees.

76

What melancholy charm steals o'er the mind!
   What hallow'd tears the rising rapture greet!
While many a viewless spirit in the wind
   Sighs to the lonely hour in accents sweet!

Ah! who the dear illusions pleas'd would yield,
   Which Fancy wakes from silence and from shades,
For all the sober forms of Truth reveal'd,
   For all the scenes that Day's bright eye pervades!   40

WILLIAM GIFFORD
1756–1826

37   from *The Baviad*

LO, DELLA CRUSCA! In his closet pent,
He toils to give the crude conception vent.
Abortive thoughts that right and wrong confound,
Truth sacrific'd to letters, sense to sound,
False glare, incongruous images, combine;
And noise, and nonsense, clatter through the line.
'Tis done. Her house the generous Piozzi lends,
And thither summons her blue-stocking friends;
The summons her blue-stocking friends obey,
Lur'd by the love of Poetry—and Tea.   10
The BARD steps forth in birth-day splendour drest,
His right hand graceful waving o'er his breast;
His left extending, so that all may see,
A roll inscrib'd 'THE WREATH OF LIBERTY.'
So forth he steps, and with complacent air,
Bows round the circle, and assumes the chair:
With lemonade he gargles first his throat,
Then sweetly preludes to the liquid note:
And now 'tis silence all. 'GENIUS OR MUSE'—
Thus while the flow'ry subject he pursues,   20
A wild delirium round th' assembly flies;
Unusual lustre shoots from Emma's eyes;
Luxurious Arno drivels as he stands;
And Anna frisks, and Laura claps her hands.
O wretched man! And dost thou toil to please,
At this late hour, such prurient ears as these?
Is thy poor pride contented to receive
Such transitory fame as fools can give?
Fools, who unconscious of the critics' laws,

Rain in such show'rs their indistinct applause.   30
That THOU, even THOU, who liv'st upon renown,
And with eternal puffs insult'st the town,
Art forc'd at length to check the idiot roar,
And cry, 'For heaven's sweet sake, no more, no more!'

ANONYMOUS

38   *The Trumpet of Liberty*

THE Trumpet of Liberty sounds through the World,
    And the universe starts at the sound,
Her Standard Philosophy's hand has unfurl'd,
    And the Nations are thronging around.

CHORUS

    Fall Tyrants! fall! fall! fall!
    These are the Days of Liberty!
    Fall Tyrants! fall!

How noble the Ardor that seizes the Soul!
    How it bursts from the Yoke and the Chain!
What Powers can the Fervor of Freedom controul,   10
    Or its terrible Vengeance refrain,
                            Fall Tyrants! fall! etc.

Proud Castles of Despotism, Dungeons, and Cells,
    The Tempest shall sweep you away;
From the East to the West the dread Hurricane swells,
    And the Tyrants are chill'd with Dismay.
                            Fall Tyrants! fall! etc.

The Slave on whose Neck the proud Despot has trod,
    Now feels that Himself is a Man,
While the Lordly Usurper, who rul'd with a Nod,   20
    Hides his Head 'midst his Servile Divan.
                            Fall Tyrants! fall! &c.

Poor Vassals, who crawl by the Vistula's stream,
    Hear, Hear the glad Call and obey!
Rise, Nations, who worship the Sun's sacred Beam,
    And drive your Pizaroes away.
                            Fall Tyrants! fall! &c.

The cruel Dominion of Priestcraft is o'er,
  Its Thunders, its Faggots, and Chains;
Mankind will endure the vile Bondage no more,   30
  While Religion its freedom maintains.
                              Fall Tyrants! fall! &c.

Shall Britons the Chorus of Liberty hear,
  With a cold and insensible mind?
No—the Triumph of Freedom each Briton shall share,
  And contend for the Rights of Mankind.
                              Fall Tyrants! fall! &c.

[1792]

ROBERT BURNS

39   *Song*

Tune: 'Rory Dall's Port'

AE fond kiss, and then we sever;
Ae fareweel, and then for ever!
Deep in heart-wrung tears I'll pledge thee,
Warring sighs and groans I'll wage thee.—

Who shall say that Fortune grieves him,
While the star of hope she leaves him:
Me, nae chearful twinkle lights me;
Dark despair around benights me.—

I'll ne'er blame my partial fancy,
Naething could resist my Nancy: 10
But to see her, was to love her;
Love but her, and love for ever.—

Had we never lov'd sae kindly,
Had we never lov'd sae blindly!
Never met—or never parted,
We had ne'er been broken-hearted.—

Fare-thee-weel, thou first and fairest!
Fare-thee-weel, thou best and dearest!

Thine be ilka joy and treasure,
Peace, Enjoyment, Love and Pleasure!—   20

Ae fond kiss, and then we sever!
Ae fareweel, Alas, for ever!
Deep in heart-wrung tears I'll pledge thee,
Warring sighs and groans I'll wage thee.—

[1793]

WILLIAM BLAKE

40   *The Marriage of Heaven and Hell*

[PLATE 2]

THE ARGUMENT

RINTRAH roars & shakes his fires in the burdend air;
Hungry clouds swag on the deep

Once meek, and in a perilous path,
The just man kept his course along
The vale of death.
Roses are planted where thorns grow.
And on the barren heath
Sing the honey bees.

Then the perilous path was planted:
And a river, and a spring   10
On every cliff and tomb;
And on the bleached bones
Red clay brought forth.

Till the villain left the paths of ease,
To walk in perilous paths, and drive
The just man into barren climes.

Now the sneaking serpent walks
In mild humility.
And the just man rages in the wilds
Where lions roam.   20

Rintrah roars & shakes his fires in the burdend air;
Hungry clouds swag on the deep.

[PLATE 3]

As a new heaven is begun, and it is now thirty-three years since its advent: the Eternal Hell revives. And lo! Swedenborg is the Angel sitting at the tomb; his writings are the linen clothes folded up. Now is the dominion of Edom, & the return of Adam into Paradise; see Isaiah XXXIV & XXXV Chap.

Without Contraries is no progression. Attraction and Repulsion, Reason and Energy, Love and Hate, are necessary to Human existence.

From these contraries spring what the religious call Good & Evil. Good is the passive that obeys Reason. Evil is the active springing from Energy.

Good is Heaven. Evil is Hell.

[PLATE 4]

THE VOICE OF THE DEVIL

All Bibles or sacred codes. have been the causes of the following Errors:

1. That Man has two real existing principles Viz: a Body & a Soul.
2. That Energy. calld Evil. is alone from the Body. & that Reason. calld Good. is alone from the Soul.
3. That God will torment Man in Eternity for following his Energies.

But the following Contraries to these are True:

1. Man has no Body distinct from his Soul for that calld Body is a portion of Soul discernd by the five Senses. the chief inlets of Soul in this age.
2. Energy is the only life and is from the Body and Reason is the bound or outward circumference of Energy.
3. Energy is Eternal Delight.

[PLATE 5]

Those who restrain desire, do so because theirs is weak enough to be restrained; and the restrainer or reason usurps its place & governs the unwilling.

And being restraind it by degrees becomes passive till it is only the shadow of desire.

The history of this is written in Paradise Lost. & the Governor or Reason is call'd Messiah.

And the original Archangel or possessor of the command of the heavenly host, is calld the Devil or Satan and his children are call'd Sin & Death.

But in the Book of Job Miltons Messiah is call'd Satan.

For this history has been adopted by both parties.

It indeed appear'd to Reason as if Desire was cast out. but the Devils account is, that the Messi[PL 6]ah fell. & formed a heaven of what he stole from the Abyss

This is shewn in the Gospel, where he prays to the Father to send the comforter or Desire that Reason may have Ideas to build on, the Jehovah of the Bible being no other than he, who dwells in flaming fire.

Know that after Christs death, he became Jehovah.

But in Milton; the Father is Destiny, the Son, a Ratio of the five senses. & the Holy-ghost, Vacuum!

Note. The reason Milton wrote in fetters when he wrote of Angels & God, and at liberty when of Devils & Hell, is because he was a true Poet and of the Devils party without knowing it

A MEMORABLE FANCY

As I was walking among the fires of hell, delighted with the enjoyments of Genius; which to Angels look like torment and insanity. I collected some of their Proverbs: thinking that as the sayings used in a nation, mark its character, so the Proverbs of Hell, shew the nature of Infernal wisdom better than any description of buildings or garments.

When I came home; on the abyss of the five senses, where a flat sided steep frowns over the present world. I saw a mighty Devil folded in black clouds, hovering on the sides of the rock, with cor[PL 7]roding fires he wrote the following sentence now percieved by the minds of men, & read by them on earth.

How do you know but ev'ry Bird that cuts the airy way,
Is an immense world of delight, clos'd by your senses five?

PROVERBS OF HELL

In seed time learn, in harvest teach, in winter enjoy.
Drive your cart and your plow over the bones of the dead.
The road of excess leads to the palace of wisdom.
Prudence is a rich ugly old maid courted by Incapacity.
He who desires but acts not, breeds pestilence.
The cut worm forgives the plow.
Dip him in the river who loves water.
A fool sees not the same tree that a wise man sees.
He whose face gives no light, shall never become a star.
Eternity is in love with the productions of time.   10
The busy bee has no time for sorrow.
The hours of folly are measur'd by the clock, but of wisdom: no clock can measure.
All wholsom food is caught without a net or a trap.
Bring out number weight & measure in a year of dearth.
No bird soars too high. if he soars with his own wings.
A dead body revenges not injuries.
The most sublime act is to set another before you.

If the fool would persist in his folly he would become wise.
Folly is the cloke of knavery.
Shame is Prides cloke. 20

[PLATE 8]

Prisons are built with stones of Law, Brothels with bricks of Religion.
The pride of the peacock is the glory of God.
The lust of the goat is the bounty of God.
The wrath of the lion is the wisdom of God.
The nakedness of woman is the work of God.
Excess of sorrow laughs. Excess of joy weeps.
The roaring of lions, the howling of wolves, the raging of the stormy
sea, and the destructive sword. are portions of eternity too great for the
eye of man.
The fox condemns the trap, not himself.
Joys impregnate. Sorrows bring forth.
Let man wear the fell of the lion. woman the fleece of the sheep. 30
The bird a nest, the spider a web, man friendship.
The selfish smiling fool. & the sullen frowning fool. shall be both
thought wise. that they may be a rod.
What is now proved was once, only imagin'd.
The rat, the mouse, the fox, the rabbet; watch the roots, the lion, the
tyger, the horse, the elephant, watch the fruits.
The cistern contains: the fountain overflows.
One thought. fills immensity.
Always be ready to speak your mind, and a base man will avoid
you.
Every thing possible to be believ'd is an image of truth.
The eagle never lost so much time. as when he submitted to learn of
the crow.

[PLATE 9]

The fox provides for himself. but God provides for the lion. 40
Think in the morning, Act in the noon, Eat in the evening, Sleep in
the night.
He who has sufferd you to impose on him knows you.
As the plow follows words, so God rewards prayers.
The tygers of wrath are wiser than the horses of instruction
Expect poison from the standing water.
You never know what is enough unless you know what is more than
enough.
Listen to the fools reproach! it is a kingly title!
The eyes of fire, the nostrils of air, the mouth of water, the beard of
earth.
The weak in courage is strong in cunning.

The apple tree never asks the beech how he shall grow, nor the lion.
the horse; how he shall take his prey.   50
The thankful reciever bears a plentiful harvest.
If others had not been foolish. we should be so.
The soul of sweet delight. can never be defil'd.
When thou seest an Eagle, thou seest a portion of Genius. lift up thy
head!
As the catterpiller chooses the fairest leaves to lay her eggs on, so the
priest lays his curse on the fairest joys.
To create a little flower is the labour of ages.
Damn. braces: Bless relaxes.
The best wine is the oldest. the best water the newest.
Prayers plow not! Praises reap not!
Joys laugh not! Sorrows weep not!   60

[PLATE 10]

The head Sublime, the heart Pathos, the genitals Beauty, the hands &
feet Proportion.
As the air to a bird or the sea to a fish, so is contempt to the con-
temptible.
The crow wish'd every thing was black, the owl, that every thing was
white.
Exuberance is Beauty.
If the lion was advised by the fox. he would be cunning.
Improvement makes strait roads, but the crooked roads without
Improvement, are roads of Genius.
Sooner murder an infant in its cradle than nurse unacted desires.
Where man is not nature is barren.
Truth can never be told so as to be understood, and not be believ'd.

Enough! or Too much.   70

[PLATE 11]

The ancient Poets animated all sensible objects with Gods or Geniuses,
calling them by the names and adorning them with the properties of woods,
rivers, mountains, lakes, cities, nations, and whatever their enlarged &
numerous senses could percieve.
And particularly they studied the genius of each city & country. placing
it under its mental deity.
Till a system was formed, which some took advantage of & enslav'd the
vulgar by attempting to realize or abstract the mental dieties from their
objects: thus began Priesthood.
Choosing forms of worship from poetic tales.
And at length they pronounced that the Gods had orderd such things.
Thus men forgot that All deities reside in the human breast.

[PLATE 12]

A MEMORABLE FANCY

The Prophets Isaiah and Ezekiel dined with me, and I asked them how they dared so roundly to assert. that God spake to them; and whether they did not think at the time, that they would be misunderstood, & so be the cause of imposition.

Isaiah answer'd. I saw no God. nor heard any, in a finite organical perception; but my senses discover'd the infinite in every thing, and as I was then perswaded. & remain confirm'd; that the voice of honest indignation is the voice of God, I cared not for consequences but wrote.

Then I asked: does a firm perswasion that a thing is so, make it so?

He replied. All poets believe that it does, & in ages of imagination this firm perswasion removed mountains; but many are not capable of a firm perswasion of any thing.

Then Ezekiel said. The philosophy of the east taught the first principles of human perception   some nations held one principle for the origin & some another, we of Israel taught that the Poetic Genius (as you now call it) was the first principle and all the others merely derivative, which was the cause of our despising the Priests & Philosophers of other countries, and prophecying that all Gods [PL 13] would at last be proved. to originate in ours & to be the tributaries of the Poetic Genius, it was this. that our great poet King David desired so fervently & invokes so patheticly, saying by this he conquers enemies & governs kingdoms; and we so loved our God. that we cursed in his name all the deities of surrounding nations, and asserted that they had rebelled; from these opinions the vulgar came to think that all nations would at last be subject to the jews.

This said he, like all firm perswasions, is come to pass, for all nations believe the jews code and worship the jews god, and what greater subjection can be

I heard this with some wonder, & must confess my own conviction. After dinner I ask'd Isaiah to favour the world with his lost works, he said none of equal value was lost. Ezekiel said the same of his.

I also asked Isaiah what made him go naked and barefoot three years? he answerd, the same that made our friend Diogenes the Grecian.

I then asked Ezekiel. why he eat dung, & lay so long on his right & left side? he answerd. the desire of raising other men into a perception of the infinite   this the North American tribes practise. & is he honest who resists his genius or conscience. only for the sake of present ease or gratification?

[PLATE 14]

The ancient tradition that the world will be consumed in fire at the end of six thousand years is true. as I have heard from Hell.

For the cherub with his flaming sword is hereby commanded to leave his guard at the tree of life, and when he does, the whole creation will be consumed, and appear infinite. and holy whereas it now appears finite & corrupt.

This will come to pass by an improvement of sensual enjoyment.

But first the notion that man has a body distinct from his soul, is to be expunged; this I shall do, by printing in the infernal method, by corrosives, which in Hell are salutary and medicinal, melting apparent surfaces away, and displaying the infinite which was hid.

If the doors of perception were cleansed every thing would appear to man as it is: infinite.

For man has closed himself up, till he sees all things thro' narrow chinks of his cavern.

[PLATE 15]

A MEMORABLE FANCY

I was in a Printing house in Hell & saw the method in which knowledge is transmitted from generation to generation.

In the first chamber was a Dragon-Man, clearing away the rubbish from a caves mouth; within, a number of Dragons were hollowing the cave,

In the second chamber was a Viper folding round the rock & the cave, and others adorning it with gold silver and precious stones.

In the third chamber was an Eagle with wings and feathers of air, he caused the inside of the cave to be infinite, around were numbers of Eagle like men, who built palaces in the immense cliffs.

In the fourth chamber were Lions of flaming fire raging around & melting the metals into living fluids.

In the fifth chamber were Unnam'd forms, which cast the metals into the expanse.

There they were reciev'd by Men who occupied the sixth chamber, and took the forms of books & were arranged in libraries.

[PLATE 16]

The Giants who formed this world into its sensual existence and now seem to live in it in chains; are in truth. the causes of its life & the sources of all activity, but the chains are, the cunning of weak and tame minds. which have power to resist energy. according to the proverb, the weak in courage is strong in cunning.

Thus one portion of being, is the Prolific. the other, the Devouring: to the devourer it seems as if the producer was in his chains, but it is not so, he only takes portions of existence and fancies that the whole.

But the Prolific would cease to be Prolific unless the Devourer as a sea reciev'd the excess of his delights.

Some will say, Is not God alone the Prolific? I answer, God only Acts & Is, in existing beings or Men.

These two classes of men are always upon earth, & they should be enemies; whoever tries [PL 17] to reconcile them seeks to destroy existence.

Religion is an endeavour to reconcile the two.

Note. Jesus Christ did not wish to unite but to separate them, as in the Parable of sheep and goats! & he says I came not to send Peace but a Sword.

Messiah or Satan or Tempter was formerly thought to be one of the Antediluvians who are our Energies.

A MEMORABLE FANCY

An Angel came to me and said. O pitiable foolish young man! O horrible! O dreadful state! consider the hot burning dungeon thou art preparing for thyself to all eternity, to which thou art going in such career.

I said. perhaps you will be willing to shew me my eternal lot & we will contemplate together upon it and see whether your lot or mine is most desirable

So he took me thro' a stable & thro' a church & down into the church vault at the end of which was a mill: thro' the mill we went, and came to a cave. down the winding cavern we groped our tedious way till a void boundless as a nether sky appeard beneath us & we held by the roots of trees and hung over this immensity; but I said, if you please we will commit ourselves to this void, and see whether providence is here also, if you will not I will? but he answerd. do not presume O young-man but as we here remain behold thy lot which will soon appear when the darkness passes away

So I remaind with him sitting in the twisted [PL 18] root of an oak. he was suspended in a fungus which hung with the head downward into the deep:

By degrees we beheld the infinite Abyss, fiery as the smoke of a burning city; beneath us at an immense distance was the sun, black but shining[;] round it were fiery tracks on which revolv'd vast spiders, crawling after their prey; which flew or rather swum in the infinite deep, in the most terrific shapes of animals sprung from corruption. & the air was full of them, & seemd composed of them; these are Devils. and are called Powers of the air, I now asked my companion which was my eternal lot? he said, between the black & white spiders

But now, from between the black & white spiders a cloud and fire burst and rolled thro the deep blackning all beneath, so that the nether deep grew black as a sea & rolled with a terrible noise: beneath us was nothing now to be seen but a black tempest, till looking east between the clouds & the waves, we saw a cataract of blood mixed with fire and not many stones throw from us appeard and sunk again the scaly fold of a monstrous serpent. at last to the east, distant about three degrees appeard a fiery

crest above the waves slowly it reared like a ridge of golden rocks till we
discoverd two globes of crimson fire. from which the sea fled away in
clouds of smoke, and now we saw, it was the head of Leviathan. his
forehead was divided into streaks of green & purple like those on a tygers
forehead: soon we saw his mouth & red gills hang just above the raging
foam tinging the black deep with beams of blood, advancing toward
[PL 19] us with all the fury of a spiritual existence.

My friend the Angel climb'd up from his station into the mill; I remain'd
alone, & then this appearance was no more, but I found myself sitting on
a pleasant bank beside a river by moon light hearing a harper who sung
to the harp. & his theme was, The man who never alters his opinion is
like standing water, & breeds reptiles of the mind.

But I arose, and sought for the mill, & there I found my Angel, who
surprised asked me, how I escaped?

I answerd. All that we saw was owing to your metaphysics: for when
you ran away, I found myself on a bank by moonlight hearing a harper,
But now we have seen my eternal lot, shall I shew you yours? he laughd
at my proposal: but I by force suddenly caught him in my arms, & flew
westerly thro' the night, till we were elevated above the earths shadow:
then I flung myself with him directly into the body of the sun, here I
clothed myself in white, & taking in my hand Swedenborgs volumes sunk
from the glorious clime, and passed all the planets till we came to saturn,
here I staid to rest & then leap'd into the void, between saturn & the fixed
stars.

Here said I! is your lot, in this space, if space it may be calld, Soon we
saw the stable and the church, & I took him to the altar and open'd the
Bible, and lo! it was a deep pit, into which I descended driving the Angel
before me, soon we saw seven houses of brick, one we enterd; in it were
a [PL 20] number of monkeys, baboons, & all of that species chaind by
the middle, grinning and snatching at one another, but witheld by the
shortness of their chains: however I saw that they sometimes grew numer-
ous, and then the weak were caught by the strong and with a grinning
aspect, first coupled with & then devourd, by plucking off first one limb
and then another till the body was left a helpless trunk. this after grinning
& kissing it with seeming fondness they devourd too; and here & there I
saw one savourily picking the flesh off of his own tail; as the stench terribly
annoyd us both we went into the mill, & I in my hand brought the skeleton
of a body, which in the mill was Aristotles Analytics.

So the Angel said: thy phantasy has imposed upon me & thou oughtest
to be ashamed.

I answerd: we impose on one another, & it is but lost time to converse
with you whose works are only Analytics.

Opposition is true Friendship.

[PLATE 21]

I have always found that Angels have the vanity to speak of themselves as the only wise; this they do with a confident insolence sprouting from systematic reasoning:

Thus Swedenborg boasts that what he writes is new; tho' it is only the Contents or Index of already publish'd books.

A man carried a monkey about for a shew, & because he was a little wiser than the monkey, grew vain, and conciev'd himself as much wiser than seven men. It is so with Swedenborg; he shews the folly of churches & exposes hypocrites, till he imagines that all are religious. & himself the single [PL 22] one on earth that ever broke a net.

Now hear a plain fact: Swedenborg has not written one new truth: Now hear another: he has written all the old falshoods.

And now hear the reason. He conversed with Angels who are all religious, & conversed not with Devils who all hate religion, for he was incapable thro' his conceited notions.

Thus Swedenborgs writings are a recapitulation of all superficial opinions, and an analysis of the more sublime, but no further.

Have now another plain fact: Any man of mechanical talents may from the writings of Paracelsus or Jacob Behmen, produce ten thousand volumes of equal value with Swedenborg's. and from those of Dante or Shakespear, an infinite number.

But when he has done this, let him not say that he knows better than his master, for he only holds a candle in sunshine.

A MEMORABLE FANCY

Once I saw a Devil in a flame of fire. who arose before an Angel that sat on a cloud. and the Devil utterd these words.

The worship of God is. Honouring his gifts in other men each according to his genius. and loving the [PL 23] greatest men best, those who envy or calumniate great men hate God, for there is no other God.

The Angel hearing this became almost blue but mastering himself he grew yellow, & at last white pink & smiling, and then replied,

Thou Idolater, is not God One? & is not he visible in Jesus Christ? and has not Jesus Christ given his sanction to the law of ten commandments and are not all other men fools, sinners, & nothings?

The Devil answer'd; bray a fool in a morter with wheat. yet shall not his folly be beaten out of him: if Jesus Christ is the greatest man, you ought to love him in the greatest degree; now hear how he has given his sanction to the law of ten commandments: did he not mock at the sabbath, and so mock the sabbaths God? murder those who were murderd because of him? turn away the law from the woman taken in adultery? steal the labor of others to support him? bear false witness when he omitted making a defence before Pilate? covet when he pray'd for his disciples, and when he bid them shake off the dust of their feet against such as refused to lodge them? I tell you, no virtue can exist without breaking these ten commandments: Jesus was all virtue, and acted from im[PL 24]pulse: not from rules.

When he had so spoken: I beheld the Angel who stretched out his arms embracing the flame of fire & he was consumed and arose as Elijah.

Note. This Angel, who is now become a Devil, is my particular friend: we often read the Bible together in its infernal or diabolical sense which the world shall have if they behave well

I have also: The Bible of Hell: which the world shall have whether they will or no.

One Law for the Lion & Ox is Oppression.

[PLATE 25]

A SONG OF LIBERTY

1. The Eternal Female groand! it was heard over all the Earth:
2. Albions coast is sick silent; the American meadows faint!
3. Shadows of Prophecy shiver along by the lakes and the rivers and mutter across the ocean! France rend down thy dungeon;
4. Golden Spain burst the barriers of old Rome;
5. Cast thy keys O Rome into the deep down falling, even to eternity down falling,
6. And weep!
7. In her trembling hands she took the new born terror howling;
8. On those infinite mountains of light now barr'd out by the atlantic sea, the new born fire stood before the starry king!
9. Flag'd with grey brow'd snows and thunderous visages the jealous wings wav'd over the deep.
10. The speary hand burned aloft, unbuckled was the shield, forth went the hand of jealousy among the flaming hair, and [PL 26] hurl'd the new born wonder thro' the starry night.
11. The fire, the fire, is falling!
12. Look up! look up! O citizen of London. enlarge thy countenance; O Jew, leave counting gold! return to thy oil and wine; O African! black African! (go, winged thought widen his forehead.)
13. The fiery limbs, the flaming hair, shot like the sinking sun into the western sea.
14. Wak'd from his eternal sleep, the hoary element roaring fled away:
15. Down rushd beating his wings in vain the jealous king: his grey brow'd councellors, thunderous warriors, curl'd veterans, among helms, and shields, and chariots horses, elephants: banners, castles, slings and rocks,

16. Falling, rushing, ruining! buried in the ruins, on Urthona's dens.

17. All night beneath the ruins, then their sullen flames faded emerge round the gloomy king,

18. With thunder and fire: leading his starry hosts thro' the waste wilderness [PL 27] he promulgates his ten commands, glancing his beamy eyelids over the deep in dark dismay,

19. Where the son of fire in his eastern cloud, while the morning plumes her golden breast,

20. Spurning the clouds written with curses, stamps the stony law to dust, loosing the eternal horses from the dens of night, crying

Empire is no more! and now the lion & wolf shall cease.

CHORUS

Let the Priests of the Raven of dawn, no longer in deadly black, with hoarse note curse the sons of joy. Nor his accepted brethren whom, tyrant, he calls free; lay the bound or build the roof. Nor pale religious letchery call that virginity, that wishes but acts not!

For every thing that lives is Holy.

ANONYMOUS

41   *The Humble Petition of the British Jacobins*
            to their Brethren of France

WHILE to you we true children of Liberty pray,
     Great Tag, Rag, and Bobtail, attend;
Who with heads on your pikes so facetiously play,
     Mirth and murder so merrily blend!

O ye boasts of proud France, ye bright lights of the earth,
     Who, in fine philosophical speeches,
Prove the only criterion of virtue and worth
     Consists in the bareness of breeches!

Brother Jacobins, listen; and, if you can cease
     To gaze on your glorious Convention,   10
Where the point of the dagger best propagates peace,
     Where concord grows out of contention;

Cast a glance of compassion on Britons, who lie
     By old superstitions opprest;
For, ah! still like the night-mare, an incubus fly,
     Sits Monarchy squat on our breast!

Come, come, at our call; nor thus let us beneath
  Such hateful incumbency groan.
In the hearts of our rulers your poignards, oh, sheathe,
  And hoist a red cap on our throne!   20

Ah! consider how many long months are past over,
  And how many ling'ring long days,
Since you promised to hasten from Calais to Dover,
  Wretched Britons from slavery to raise;

To reclaim us at length from political vice,
  To write reformation in blood;
To bestow on us liberty not without lice,
  All, all, for our ultimate good.

For, Britons, alas! are a nation of slaves,
  More full of plumb-pudding than wit,   30
Warm with rapture, while Burke against anarchy raves,
  Ever licking the spittle of Pitt!

Ah! think, gallant Frenchmen, while thus you delay,
  What misfortunes your friends here betide:
Ah! think how the tyrants their leaders dismay,
  Forc'd in holes, like true adders, to hide!

ANONYMOUS

42   *Translation of 'Pax Bello Potior',*

A Latin Poem, in the European Magazine *for July 1793.*
Peace More Desirable Than War

GRANT us, O God! great Ruler of the Skies!
  That which our love to thee will much increase,
The source from which life's choicest treasures rise,
  The first of human blessings,—heav'n-born *Peace.*

Beneath her shade Science her views extends,
  Cities and people with their laws improve;
Justice, her sister Virtue's rights defends,
  And reigns with them in dignity and love.

But where mad War is, thence no good can spring,
  The Laws grow dumb, Religion dormant lies;   10
Probity feels, alas! a venom'd sting,
  Droops her fair form, and disregarded dies.

May Heaven favour this our native land,
  Each social blessing may her sons enjoy;
May *George* with golden Peace reign hand in hand,
  His power of doing good with zeal employ.

                                               W.R.N.

Ipswich

[1794]

WILLIAM BLAKE

43–54   from *Songs of Experience*

43   *Introduction*

HEAR the voice of the Bard!
Who Present, Past, & Future sees
Whose ears have heard,
The Holy Word,
That walk'd among the ancient trees.

Calling the lapsed Soul
And weeping in the evening dew:
That might controll,
The starry pole;
And fallen fallen light renew!   10

O Earth O Earth return!
Arise from out the dewy grass;
Night is worn,
And the morn
Rises from the slumberous mass.

Turn away no more:
Why wilt thou turn away
The starry floor
The watry shore
Is giv'n thee till the break of day.   20

44   *Earth's Answer*

    EARTH rais'd up her head,
    From the darkness dread & drear.
    Her light fled:
    Stony dread!
    And her locks cover'd with grey despair.

    Prison'd on watry shore
    Starry Jealousy does keep my den
    Cold and hoar
    Weeping o'er
    I hear the Father of the ancient men   10

    Selfish father of men
    Cruel jealous selfish fear
    Can delight

    Chain'd in night
    The virgins of youth and morning bear.

    Does spring hide its joy
    When buds and blossoms grow?
    Does the sower?
    Sow by night?
    Or the plowman in darkness plow?   20

    Break this heavy chain,
    That does freeze my bones around
    Selfish! vain!
    Eternal bane!
    That free Love with bondage bound.

45   *Holy Thursday*

    Is this a holy thing to see,
    In a rich and fruitful land,
    Babes reduced to misery,
    Fed with cold and usurous hand?

    Is that trembling cry a song?
    Can it be a song of joy?
    And so many children poor?
    It is a land of poverty!

And their sun does never shine.
And their fields are bleak & bare.   10
And their ways are fill'd with thorns.
It is eternal winter there.

For where-e'er the sun does shine,
And where-e'er the rain does fall:
Babe can never hunger there,
Nor poverty the mind appall.

46   *The Sick Rose*

O ROSE thou art sick.
The invisible worm,
That flies in the night
In the howling storm:

Has found out thy bed
Of crimson joy:
And his dark secret love
Does thy life destroy.

47   *The Fly*

LITTLE Fly
Thy summers play,
My thoughtless hand
Has brush'd away.

Am not I
A fly like thee?
Or art not thou
A man like me?

For I dance
And drink & sing: 10
Till some blind hand
Shall brush my wing.

If thought is life
And strength & breath:
And the want
Of thought is death;

Then am I
A happy fly,
If I live,
Or if I die.   20

48   *The Tyger*

    TYGER Tyger, burning bright,
    In the forests of the night;
    What immortal hand or eye,
    Could frame thy fearful symmetry?

    In what distant deeps or skies,
    Burnt the fire of thine eyes?
    On what wings dare he aspire?
    What the hand, dare sieze the fire?

    And what shoulder, & what art,
    Could twist the sinews of thy heart?   10
    And when thy heart began to beat,
    What dread hand? & what dread feet?

    What the hammer? what the chain,
    In what furnace was thy brain?
    What the anvil? what dread grasp,
    Dare its deadly terrors clasp!

    When the stars threw down their spears
    And water'd heaven with their tears:
    Did he smile his work to see?
    Did he who made the Lamb make thee?   20

    Tyger Tyger burning bright,
    In the forests of the night:
    What immortal hand or eye,
    Dare frame thy fearful symmetry?

49   *My Pretty Rose Tree*

    A FLOWER was offerd to me;
    Such a flower as May never bore.
    But I said I've a Pretty Rose-tree:
    And I passed the sweet flower o'er.

    Then I went to my Pretty Rose-tree;
    To tend her by day and by night.
    But my Rose turnd away with jealousy:
    And her thorns were my only delight.

50   ## Ah! Sun-Flower

AH Sun-flower! weary of time,
Who countest the steps of the Sun:
Seeking after that sweet golden clime
Where the travellers journey is done.

Where the Youth pined away with desire,
And the pale Virgin shrouded in snow:
Arise from their graves and aspire,
Where my Sun-flower wishes to go.

51   ## The Lilly

THE modest Rose puts forth a thorn:
The humble Sheep, a threatning horn:
While the Lilly white, shall in Love delight,
Nor a thorn nor a threat stain her beauty bright.

52   ## London

I WANDER thro' each charter'd street,
Near where the charter'd Thames does flow.
And mark in every face I meet
Marks of weakness, marks of woe.

In every cry of every Man,
In every Infants cry of fear,
In every voice: in every ban,
The mind-forg'd manacles I hear

How the Chimney-sweepers cry
Every blackning Church appalls,   10
And the hapless Soldiers sigh
Runs in blood down Palace walls

But most thro' midnight streets I hear
How the youthful Harlots curse
Blasts the new-born Infants tear
And blights with plagues the Marriage hearse

53   *The Human Abstract*

PITY would be no more,
If we did not make somebody Poor:
And Mercy no more could be,
If all were as happy as we;

And mutual fear brings peace;
Till the selfish loves increase.
Then Cruelty knits a snare,
And spreads his baits with care.

He sits down with holy fears,
And waters the ground with tears: 10
Then Humility takes its root
Underneath his foot.

Soon spreads the dismal shade
Of Mystery over his head;
And the Catterpiller and Fly,
Feed on the Mystery.

And it bears the fruit of Deceit,
Ruddy and sweet to eat;
And the Raven his nest has made
In its thickest shade.   20

The Gods of the earth and sea,
Sought thro' Nature to find this Tree
But their search was all in vain:
There grows one in the Human Brain.

54   *A Poison Tree*

I WAS angry with my friend;
I told my wrath, my wrath did end.
I was angry with my foe:
I told it not, my wrath did grow.

And I waterd it in fears,
Night & morning with my tears:
And I sunned it with smiles,
And with soft deceitful wiles.

And it grew both day and night,
Till it bore an apple bright;   10
And my foe beheld it shine,
And he knew that it was mine,

And into my garden stole,
When the night had veild the pole;
In the morning glad I see;
My foe outstretchd beneath the tree.

55   *The* [First] *Book of Urizen*

[PLATE 2]

PRELUDIUM TO THE [*FIRST*] BOOK OF URIZEN

OF the primeval Priests assum'd power,
When Eternals spurn'd back his religion;
And gave him a place in the north,
Obscure, shadowy, void, solitary.

Eternals I hear your call gladly,
Dictate swift winged words, & fear not
To unfold your dark visions of torment.

[PLATE 3]

CHAP: I

1. Lo, a shadow of horror is risen
In Eternity! Unknown, unprolific!
Self-closd, all-repelling: what Demon
Hath form'd this abominable void
This soul-shudd'ring vacuum?—Some said
'It is Urizen', But unknown, abstracted
Brooding secret, the dark power hid.

2. Times on times he divided, & measur'd
Space by space in his ninefold darkness
Unseen, unknown! changes appeard   10
In his desolate mountains rifted furious
By the black winds of perturbation

3. For he strove in battles dire
In unseen conflictions with shapes

Bred from his forsaken wilderness,
Of beast, bird, fish, serpent & element
Combustion, blast, vapour and cloud.

4. Dark revolving in silent activity:
Unseen in tormenting passions;
An activity unknown and horrible;   20
A self-contemplating shadow,
In enormous labours occupied

5. But Eternals beheld his vast forests
Age on ages he lay, clos'd, unknown,
Brooding shut in the deep; all avoid
The petrific abominable chaos

6. His cold horrors silent, dark Urizen
Prepar'd: his ten thousands of thunders
Rang'd in gloom'd array stretch out across
The dread world, & the rolling of wheels   30
As of swelling seas, sound in his clouds
In his hills of stor'd snows, in his mountains
Of hail & ice; voices of terror,
Are heard, like thunders of autumn,
When the cloud blazes over the harvests

CHAP: II

1. Earth was not: nor globes of attraction
The will of the Immortal expanded
Or contracted his all flexible senses.
Death was not, but eternal life sprung

2. The sound of a trumpet the heavens   40
Awoke & vast clouds of blood roll'd
Round the dim rocks of Urizen, so nam'd
That solitary one in Immensity

3. Shrill the trumpet: & myriads of Eternity,

[PLATE 4]

Muster around the bleak desarts
Now fill'd with clouds, darkness & waters
That roll'd perplex'd labring & utter'd
Words articulate, bursting in thunders
That roll'd on the tops of his mountains

4. From the depths of dark solitude. From
The eternal abode in my holiness,
Hidden set apart in my stern counsels
Reserv'd for the days of futurity,
I have sought for a joy without pain,   10
For a solid without fluctuation
Why will you die O Eternals?
Why live in unquenchable burnings?

5. First I fought with the fire; consum'd
Inwards, into a deep world within:
A void immense, wild dark & deep,
Where nothing was: Natures wide womb

And self balanc'd stretch'd o'er the void
I alone, even I! the winds merciless
Bound; but condensing, in torrents   20
They fall & fall; strong I repell'd
The vast waves, & arose on the waters
A wide world of solid obstruction

6. Here alone I in books formd of metals
Have written the secrets of wisdom
The secrets of dark contemplation
By fightings and conflicts dire,
With terrible monsters Sin-bred:
Which the bosoms of all inhabit;
Seven deadly Sins of the soul.   30

7. Lo! I unfold my darkness: and on
This rock, place with strong hand the Book
Of eternal brass, written in my solitude.

8. Laws of peace, of love, of unity:
Of pity, compassion, forgiveness.
Let each chuse one habitation:
His ancient infinite mansion:
One command, one joy, one desire,
One curse, one weight, one measure
One King, one God, one Law.   40

CHAP: III

1. The voice ended, they saw his pale visage
Emerge from the darkness; his hand
On the rock of eternity unclasping
The Book of brass. Rage siez'd the strong

2. Rage, fury, intense indignation
In cataracts of fire blood & gall
In whirlwinds of sulphurous smoke:
And enormous forms of energy;
All the seven deadly sins of the soul

[PLATE 5]

In living creations appear'd
In the flames of eternal fury.

3. Sund'ring, dark'ning, thund'ring!
Rent away with a terrible crash
Eternity roll'd wide apart
Wide asunder rolling
Mountainous all around
Departing; departing; departing:
Leaving ruinous fragments of life
Hanging frowning cliffs & all between   10
An ocean of voidness unfathomable.

4. The roaring fires ran o'er the heav'ns
In whirlwinds & cataracts of blood
And o'er the dark desarts of Urizen
Fires pour thro' the void on all sides
On Urizens self-begotten armies.

5. But no light from the fires. all was darkness
In the flames of Eternal fury

6. In fierce anguish & quenchless flames
To the desarts and rocks He ran raging   20
To hide, but He could not: combining
He dug mountains & hills in vast strength,
He piled them in incessant labour,
In howlings & pangs & fierce madness
Long periods in burning fires labouring
Till hoary, and age-broke, and aged,
In despair and the shadows of death.

7. And a roof, vast petrific around,
On all sides He fram'd: like a womb;
Where thousands of rivers in veins   30
Of blood pour down the mountains to cool
The eternal fires beating without

From Eternals; & like a black globe
View'd by sons of Eternity, standing
On the shore of the infinite ocean
Like a human heart strugling & beating
The vast world of Urizen appear'd.

8. And Los round the dark globe of Urizen,
Kept watch for Eternals to confine,
The obscure separation alone;
For Eternity stood wide apart,   40

[PLATE 6]

As the stars are apart from the earth

9. Los wept howling around the dark Demon:
And cursing his lot; for in anguish,
Urizen was rent from his side;
And a fathomless void for his feet;
And intense fires for his dwelling.

10. But Urizen laid in a stony sleep
Unorganiz'd, rent from Eternity

11. The Eternals said: What is this? Death
Urizen is a clod of clay.   10

[PLATE 7]

12: Los howld in a dismal stupor,
Groaning! gnashing! groaning!
Till the wrenching apart was healed

13: But the wrenching of Urizen heal'd not
Cold, featureless, flesh or clay,
Rifted with direful changes
He lay in a dreamless night

14: Till Los rouz'd his fires, affrighted
At the formless unmeasurable death.

[PLATE 8]

CHAP: IV [a]

1: Los smitten with astonishment
Frightend at the hurtling bones

2: And at the surging sulphureous
Perturbed Immortal mad raging

3: In whirlwinds & pitch & nitre
Round the furious limbs of Los

4: And Los formed nets & gins
And threw the nets round about

5: He watch'd in shuddring fear
The dark changes & bound every change   10
With rivets of iron & brass;

6. And these were the changes of Urizen.

[PLATE 10]

CHAP: IV [b]

1. Ages on ages roll'd over him!
In stony sleep ages roll'd over him!
Like a dark waste stretching chang'able
By earthquakes riv'n, belching sullen fires
On ages roll'd ages in ghastly
Sick torment; around him in whirlwinds
Of darkness the eternal Prophet howl'd
Beating still on his rivets of iron
Pouring sodor of iron; dividing
The horrible night into watches.   10

2. And Urizen (so his eternal name)
His prolific delight obscurd more & more
In dark secresy hiding in surgeing
Sulphureous fluid his phantasies.
The Eternal Prophet heavd the dark bellows,
And turn'd restless the tongs; and the hammer
Incessant beat; forging chains new & new
Numb'ring with links. hours, days & years

3. The eternal mind bounded began to roll
Eddies of wrath ceaseless round & round,   20
And the sulphureous foam surgeing thick
Settled, a lake, bright, & shining clear:
White as the snow on the mountains cold.

4. Forgetfulness, dumbness, necessity!
In chains of the mind locked up,

Like fetters of ice shrinking together
Disorganiz'd, rent from Eternity,
Los beat on his fetters of iron;
And heated his furnaces & pour'd
Iron sodor and sodor of brass   30

5. Restless turnd the immortal inchain'd
Heaving dolorous! anguish'd! unbearable
Till a roof shaggy wild inclos'd
In an orb, his fountain of thought.

6. In a horrible dreamful slumber;
Like the linked infernal chain;
A vast Spine writh'd in torment
Upon the winds; shooting pain'd
Ribs, like a bending cavern
And bones of solidness, froze   40
Over all his nerves of joy.
And a first Age passed over,
And a state of dismal woe.

[PLATE 11]

7. From the caverns of his jointed Spine,
Down sunk with fright a red
Round globe hot burning deep
Deep down into the Abyss:
Panting: Conglobing, Trembling
Shooting out ten thousand branches
Around his solid bones.
And a second Age passed over,
And a state of dismal woe.

8. In harrowing fear rolling round;   10
His nervous brain shot branches
Round the branches of his heart.
On high into two little orbs
And fixed in two little caves
Hiding carefully from the wind,
His Eyes beheld the deep,
And a third Age passed over:
And a state of dismal woe.

9. The pangs of hope began,
In heavy pain striving, struggling.   20
Two Ears in close volutions.

From beneath his orbs of vision
Shot spiring out and petrified
As they grew. And a fourth Age passed
And a state of dismal woe.

10. In ghastly torment sick;
Hanging upon the wind;

[PLATE 13]

Two Nostrils bent down to the deep.
And a fifth Age passed over;
And a state of dismal woe.

11. In ghastly torment sick;
Within his ribs bloated round,
A craving Hungry Cavern;
Thence arose his channeld Throat,
And like a red flame a Tongue
Of thirst & of hunger appeard.
And a sixth Age passed over: 10
And a state of dismal woe.

12. Enraged & stifled with torment
He threw his right Arm to the north
His left Arm to the south
Shooting out in anguish deep,
And his Feet stampd the nether Abyss
In trembling & howling & dismay.
And a seventh Age passed over:
And a state of dismal woe.

CHAP: V

1. In terrors Los shrunk from his task: 20
His great hammer fell from his hand:
His fires beheld, and sickening,
Hid their strong limbs in smoke.
For with noises ruinous loud;
With hurtlings & clashings & groans
The Immortal endur'd his chains,
Tho' bound in a deadly sleep.

2. All the myriads of Eternity:
All the wisdom & joy of life:
Roll like a sea around him,   30

Except what his little orbs
Of sight by degrees unfold.

3. And now his eternal life
Like a dream was obliterated

4. Shudd'ring, the Eternal Prophet smote
With a stroke, from his north to south region
The bellows & hammer are silent now
A nerveless silence, his prophetic voice
Siez'd; a cold solitude & dark void
The Eternal Prophet & Urizen clos'd   40

5. Ages on ages rolld over them
Cut off from life & light frozen
Into horrible forms of deformity
Los suffer'd his fires to decay
Then he look'd back with anxious desire
But the space undivided by existence
Struck horror into his soul.

6. Los wept obscur'd with mourning:
His bosom earthquak'd with sighs;
He saw Urizen deadly black,   50
In his chains bound, & Pity began,

7. In anguish dividing & dividing
For pity divides the soul
In pangs eternity on eternity
Life in cataracts pourd down his cliffs
The void shrunk the lymph into Nerves
Wand'ring wide on the bosom of night
And left a round globe of blood
Trembling upon the Void

[PLATE 15]

Thus the Eternal Prophet was divided
Before the death-image of Urizen
For in changeable clouds and darkness
In a winterly night beneath,
The Abyss of Los stretch'd immense:
And now seen, now obscur'd, to the eyes
Of Eternals, the visions remote
Of the dark seperation appear'd.
As glasses discover Worlds

In the endless Abyss of space,   10
So the expanding eyes of Immortals
Beheld the dark visions of Los,
And the globe of life blood trembling.

[PLATE 18]

8. The globe of life blood trembled
Branching out into roots;
Fib'rous, writhing upon the winds;
Fibres of blood, milk and tears;
In pangs, eternity on eternity.
At length in tears & cries imbodied
A female form trembling and pale
Waves before his deathy face

9. All Eternity shudderd at sight
Of the first female now separate   10
Pale as a cloud of snow
Waving before the face of Los

10. Wonder, awe, fear, astonishment,
Petrify the eternal myriads;
At the first female form now separate

[PLATE 19]

They call'd her Pity, and fled

11. 'Spread a Tent, with strong curtains around them
Let cords & stakes bind in the Void
That Eternals may no more behold them'

12. They began to weave curtains of darkness
They erected large pillars round the Void
With golden hooks fastend in the pillars
With infinite labour the Eternals
A woof wove, and called it Science

CHAP: VI

1. But Los saw the Female & pitied   10
He embrac'd her, she wept, she refus'd
In perverse and cruel delight
She fled from his arms, yet he followd

2. Eternity shudder'd when they saw,
Man begetting his likeness,
On his own divided image.

3. A time passed over, the Eternals
Began to erect the tent;
When Enitharmon sick,
Felt a Worm within her womb.   20

4. Yet helpless it lay like a Worm
In the trembling womb
To be moulded into existence

5. All day the worm lay on her bosom
All night within her womb
The worm lay till it grew to a serpent
With dolorous hissings & poisons
Round Enitharmons loins folding,

6. Coild within Enitharmons womb
The serpent grew casting its scales,   30
With sharp pangs the hissings began
To change to a grating cry,
Many sorrows and dismal throes,
Many forms of fish, bird & beast,
Brought forth an Infant form
Where was a worm before.

7. The Eternals their tent finished
Alarm'd with these gloomy visions
When Enitharmon groaning
Produc'd a man Child to the light.   40

8. A shriek ran thro' Eternity:
And a paralytic stroke;
At the birth of the Human shadow.

9. Delving earth in his resistless way;
Howling, the Child with fierce flames
Issu'd from Enitharmon.

10. The Eternals, closed the tent
They beat down the stakes the cords

[PLATE 20]

Stretch'd for a work of eternity;
No more Los beheld Eternity.

11. In his hands he siez'd the infant
He bathed him in springs of sorrow
He gave him to Enitharmon.

CHAP: VII

1. They named the child Orc, he grew
Fed with milk of Enitharmon

2. Los awoke her; O sorrow & pain!
A tight'ning girdle grew,
Around his bosom. In sobbings   10
He burst the girdle in twain,
But still another girdle
Opressd his bosom, In sobbings
Again he burst it. Again
Another girdle succeeds
The girdle was form'd by day;
By night was burst in twain.

3. These falling down on the rock
Into an iron Chain
In each other link by link lock'd   20

4. They took Orc to the top of a mountain.
O how Enitharmon wept!
They chain'd his young limbs to the rock
With the Chain of Jealousy
Beneath Urizens deathful shadow

5. The dead heard the voice of the child
And began to awake from sleep
All things. heard the voice of the child
And began to awake to life.

6. And Urizen craving with hunger   30
Stung with the odours of Nature
Explor'd his dens around

7. He form'd a line & a plummet
To divide the Abyss beneath.
He form'd a dividing rule:

8. He formed scales to weigh;
He formed massy weights;
He formed a brazen quadrant;
He formed golden compasses
And began to explore the Abyss   40
And he planted a garden of fruits

9. But Los encircled Enitharmon
With fires of Prophecy
From the sight of Urizen & Orc.

10. And she bore an enormous race

CHAP: VIII

1. Urizen explor'd his dens
Mountain, moor, & wilderness,
With a globe of fire lighting his journey
A fearful journey, annoy'd
By cruel enormities: forms   50

[PLATE 23]

Of life on his forsaken mountains

2. And his world teemd vast enormities
Frightning; faithless; fawning
Portions of life; similitudes
Of a foot, or a hand, or a head
Or a heart, or an eye, they swam mischevous
Dread terrors! delighting in blood

3. Most Urizen sicken'd to see
His eternal creations appear
Sons & daughters of sorrow on mountains   10
Weeping! wailing! first Thiriel appear'd
Astonish'd at his own existence
Like a man from a cloud born, & Utha
From the waters emerging, laments!
Grodna rent the deep earth howling
Amaz'd! his heavens immense cracks
Like the ground parch'd with heat; then Fuzon
Flam'd out! first begotten, last born.
All his eternal sons in like manner
His daughters from green herbs & cattle   20
From monsters, & worms of the pit.

111

4. He in darkness clos'd, view'd all his race
And his soul sicken'd! he curs'd
Both sons & daughters; for he saw
That no flesh nor spirit could keep
His iron laws one moment.

5. For he saw that life liv'd upon death

[PLATE 25]

The Ox in the slaughter house moans
The Dog at the wintry door
And he wept, & he called it Pity
And his tears flowed down on the winds

6. Cold he wander'd on high, over their cities
In weeping & pain & woe!
And where-ever he wanderd in sorrows
Upon the aged heavens
A cold shadow follow'd behind him
Like a spiders web, moist, cold, & dim   10
Drawing out from his sorrowing soul
The dungeon-like heaven dividing.
Where ever the footsteps of Urizen
Walk'd over the cities in sorrow.

7. Till a Web dark & cold, throughout all
The tormented element stretch'd
From the sorrows of Urizens soul
And the Web is a Female in embrio
None could break the Web, no wings of fire.

8. So twisted the cords, & so knotted   20
The meshes: twisted like to the human brain

9. And all calld it, The Net of Religion

CHAP: IX

1. Then the Inhabitants of those Cities:
Felt their Nerves change into Marrow
And hardening Bones began
In swift diseases and torments,
In throbbings & shootings & grindings
Thro' all the coasts; till weaken'd
The Senses inward rush'd shrinking,
Beneath the dark net of infection.   30

2. Till the shrunken eyes clouded over
Discernd not the woven hipocrisy
But the streaky slime in their heavens
Brought together by narrowing perceptions
Appeard transparent air; for their eyes
Grew small like the eyes of a man
And in reptile forms shrinking together
Of seven feet stature they remain

3. Six days they shrunk up from existence
And on the seventh day they rested   40
And they bless'd the seventh day, in sick hope:
And forgot their eternal life

4. And their thirty cities divided
In form of a human heart
No more could they rise at will
In the infinite void, but bound down
To earth by their narrowing perceptions

[PLATE 28]

They lived a period of years
Then left a noisom body
To the jaws of devouring darkness

5. And their children wept, & built
Tombs in the desolate places,
And form'd laws of prudence, and call'd them
The eternal laws of God

6. And the thirty cities remaind
Surrounded by salt floods, now call'd
Africa: its name was then Egypt.   10

7. The remaining sons of Urizen
Beheld their brethren shrink together
Beneath the Net of Urizen;
Perswasion was in vain;
For the ears of the inhabitants,
Were wither'd, & deafen'd, & cold:
And their eyes could not discern,
Their brethren of other cities.

8. So Fuzon call'd all together
The remaining children of Urizen: 20
And they left the pendulous earth:
They called it Egypt, & left it.

9. And the salt ocean rolled englob'd

The End of the [*first*] book of Urizen

ANONYMOUS

56   *Hymn*

*Sung at a meeting of the Friends of Peace and Reform in
Sheffield, held on the late Fast Day*

O GOD of Hosts, thine Ear incline,
Regard our Prayers, our Cause be thine;
When Orphans cry, when Babes complain,
When Widows weep—can'st thou refrain?

Now red and terrible thine Hand,
Scourges with WAR our guilty Land:
Europe thy flaming Vengeance feels,
And from her deep Foundation reels.

Her Rivers bleed like mighty Veins;
Her Towers are Ashes, Graves her plains;   10
Slaughter her groaning Vallies fills,
And reeking Carnage melts her Hills.

O THOU! whose awful Word can bind,
The raging Waves, the raving Wind,
Mad TYRANTS tame; break down the High
Whose haughty Foreheads beat the Sky;

Make bare thine Arm, great King of Kings!
That Arm alone Salvation brings,
That Wonder-working Arm which broke,
From Israel's Neck th' Egyptian Yoke.   20

ANONYMOUS

57   *Epigram*

*On hearing that the French had melted down their Saints to
purchase Artillery*

SAYS a Reverend Priest to a less Rev'rend friend,
Where at length will the crimes of these French villains end,
Who their Saints and their Martyrs thus impiously sell,
And convert into damnable engines of hell!
Prithee why, quoth his friend, are you so much surpriz'd,
That Saints have their desert and are all—CANONIZ'D?

JOHN THELWALL
1764–1834

58   *Anacreontic*

1

'TIS not how long we have to live,
   But how much Pleasure is to come,
That real Wisdom would enquire;
   Could Oracles proclaim our doom.

2

Could we, like those before the Flood,
   Instead of years, by centuries count,
If fetter'd by monastic rules,
   Say, what would be the vast amount?

3

Days, months, and years—the driveller's tale—
   Are cyphers—and for nothing tell: 10
Enjoyments are the numeral signs
   That Life's intrinsic value swell.

4

Then let us seize the present hour,
   The bliss within our grasp enjoy;

For Jove himself the Bliss possess'd,
    Nor all his thunders can destroy.

                    5

Who will, Oppression's power may aid,
    (Crouching beneath the iron rod!)
And yield his cheerful powers of mind
    Obsequious to the haughty nod.   20

                    6

For me—what force would grasp in vain
    I scorn, from timid awe, to give:—
My Life the Tyrant may destroy;—
    But not my Pleasures while I live.

18 October 1794

JOHN WOLCOT ('PETER PINDAR')
1738–1819

59   *Hymn to the Guillotine*

                By Peter Pindar, Esq.

DAUGHTER of Liberty! whose knife
So busy chops the threads of life,
And frees from cumbrous clay the spirit;
    Ah! why alone shall Gallia feel
    The beauties of thy pond'rous steel?
Why must not Britain mark thy merit?

Hark! 'tis the dungeon's groan I hear;
And lo, a squalid band appear,
With sallow cheek, and hollow eye!
    Unwilling, lo, the neck they bend;   10
    Yet, through thy pow'r, their terrors end,
And with their *heads* the sorrows fly.

O let us view thy lofty grace;
To Britons shew thy blushing face,
And bless Rebellion's life—tir'd train!
    Joy to my soul! she's on her way,
    Led by her *dearest* friends, Dismay,
Death, and the Devil, and Tom Paine!

WILLIAM CROWE
1745–1829

60   *'In evil hour, and with unhallow'd voice'*

IN evil hour, and with unhallow'd voice
Profaning the pure gift of poesy
Did he begin to sing, he first who sung
Of arms and combats, and the proud array
Of warriors on the embattled plain and raised
The aspiring spirit to hopes of fair renown
By deeds of violence. For since that time
The imperious victor, oft unsatisfied
With bloody spoil and tyrannous conquest, dares
To challenge fame and honour; and too oft   10
The poet, bending low to lawless power,
Hath paid unseemly reverence, yea, and brought
Streams clearest of the Aonian fount, to wash
Blood-stain'd ambition. If the stroke of war
Fell certain on the guilty head none else;
If they who make the cause might taste the effect,
And drink themselves the bitter cut they mix,
Then might the bard (though child of peace) delight
To twine fresh wreaths around the conqueror's brow,
Or haply strike his high toned harp to swell   20
The trumpet's martial sound, and bid them on,
Whom justice arms for vengeance: but alas!
That undistinguishing and deathful storm
Beats heaviest on the exposed Innocent;
And they that stir its fury, while it raves
Stand at safe distance; send their mandate forth
Unto the mortal Ministers that wait
To do their bidding—Ah! who then regards
The Widow's tears, the friendless Orphan's cry,
And Famine, and the ghastly train of woes   30
That follow at the dogged heels of war?
They in the pomp and pride of victory,
Rejoicing o'er the desolated Earth,
As at an altar wet with human blood,
And flaming with the fire of cities burnt,
Sing their mad hymns of triumph, hymns to God

O'er the destruction of his gracious works!—
Hymns to the Father o'er his slaughter'd Sons!
Detested by their sword, abhorred their name,
And scorn'd the tongues that praise them.   40

[1796]

ROBERT BURNS

61   'O my Luve's like a red, red rose'

O MY Luve's like a red, red rose,
    That's newly sprung in June;
O my Luve's like the melodie
    That 's sweetly play'd in tune.—

As fair art thou, my bonie lass,
    So deep in luve am I;
And I will love thee still, my Dear,
    Till a' the seas gang dry.—

Till a' the seas gang dry, my Dear,
    And the rocks melt wi' the sun:
I will love thee still, my Dear,
    While the sands o' life shall run.—   10

And fare thee weel, my only Luve!
    And fare thee weel, a while!
And I will come again, my Luve,
    Tho' it were ten thousand mile!

SAMUEL TAYLOR COLERIDGE
1772–1834

62   *The Eolian Harp*

Composed at Clevedon, Somersetshire

MY pensive Sara! thy soft cheek reclined
Thus on mine arm, most soothing sweet it is
To sit beside our Cot, our Cot o'ergrown
With white-flower'd Jasmin, and the broad-leav'd Myrtle,
(Meet emblems they of Innocence and Love!)
And watch the clouds, that late were rich with light,
Slow saddening round, and mark the star of eve
Serenely brilliant (such should Wisdom be)
Shine opposite! How exquisite the scents
Snatch'd from yon bean-field! and the world *so* hush'd!   10
The stilly murmur of the distant Sea
Tells us of silence.
                    And that simplest Lute,
Placed length-ways in the clasping casement, hark!
How by the desultory breeze caress'd,
Like some coy maid half yielding to her lover,
It pours such sweet upbraidings, as must needs
Tempt to repeat the wrong! And now, its strings
Boldlier swept, the long sequacious notes
Over delicious surges sink and rise,
Such a soft floating witchery of sound—   20
Methinks, it should have been impossible
Not to love all things in a World like this,
Where e'en the Breezes of the simple Air
Possess the power and Spirit of Melody!

And thus, my Love! as on the midway slope
Of yonder hill I stretch my limbs at noon,
Whilst through my half-clos'd eye-lids I behold
The sunbeams dance, like diamonds, on the main,
And tranquil muse upon tranquillity;
Full many a thought uncall'd and undetain'd,   30
And many idle flitting phantasies,
Traverse my indolent and passive brain,
As wild and various as the random gales
That swell and flutter on this subject Lute!

    Or what if all of animated nature
Be but organic Harps diversely fram'd,
That tremble into thought, as o'er them sweeps
Plastic and vast, one intellectual breeze,
At once the Soul of each, and God of all?

    But thy more serious eye a mild reproof   40
Darts, O belovéd Woman! nor such thoughts
Dim and unhallow'd dost thou not reject,
And biddest me walk humbly with my God.
Meek Daughter in the family of Christ!
Well hast thou said and holily disprais'd
These shapings of the unregenerate mind;
Bubbles that glitter as they rise and break
On vain Philosophy's aye-babbling spring.
For never guiltless may I speak of him,
The Incomprehensible! save when with awe   50
I praise him, and with Faith that inly *feels*;
Who with his saving mercies healéd me,
A sinful and most miserable man,
Wilder'd and dark, and gave me to possess
Peace, and this Cot, and thee, heart-honour'd Maid!

WILLIAM TAYLOR
1765–1836

63 *Ellenore*

AT break of day from frightful dreams
  Upstarted Ellenore:
My William, art thou slayn, she sayde,
  Or dost thou love no more?

He went abroade with Richard's host
  The paynim foes to quell;
But he no word to her had writt,
  An he were sick or well.

With blore of trump and thump of drum
  His fellow-soldyers come,   10
Their helms bedeckt with oaken boughs,
  They seeke their long'd-for home.

And evry road and evry lane
  Was full of old and young
To gaze at the rejoycing band,
  To haile with gladsom toung.

'Thank God!' their wives and children sayde,
  'Welcome!' the brides did saye;
But grief or kiss gave Ellenore
  To none upon that daye.   20

And when the soldyers all were bye,
  She tore her raven hair,
And cast herself upon the growne,
  In furious despair.

Her mother ran and lyfte her up,
  And clasped her in her arm,
'My child, my child, what dost thou ail?
  God shield thy life from harm!'

'O mother, mother! William's gone
  What's all besyde to me?   30
There is no mercie, sure, above!
  All, all were spar'd but he!'

'Kneele downe, thy paternoster saye,
  'T will calm thy troubled spright:
The Lord is wise, the Lord is good;
  What He hath done is right.'

'O mother, mother! saye not so;
  Most cruel is my fate:
I prayde, and prayde; but watte avaylde?
  'T is now, alas! too late.'   40

'Our Heavenly Father, if we praye,
  Will help a suffring child:
Go take the holy sacrament;
  So shall thy grief grow mild.'

'O mother, what I feele within,
  No sacrament can staye;
No sacrament can teche the dead
  To bear the sight of daye.'

'May-be, among the heathen folk
  Thy William false doth prove,   50
And put away his faith and troth,
  And take another love.

'Then wherefor sorrowe for his loss?
  Thy moans are all in vain:
But when his soul and body parte,
  His falsehode brings him pain.'

'O mother, mother! gone is gone:
  My hope is all forlorn;
The grave my only safeguard is—
  O had I ne'er been born!   60

'Go out, go out, my lamp of life;
  In grizely darkness die:
There is no mercie, sure, above.
  Forever let me lie.'

'Almighty God! O do not judge
  My poor unhappy child;
She knows not what her lips pronounce,
  Her anguish makes her wild.

'My girl, forget thine earthly woe,
  And think on God and bliss;   70
For so, at least shall not thy soul
  Its heavenly bridegroom miss.'

'O mother, mother! what is bliss,
  And what the fiendis cell?
With him 'tis heaven any where,
  Without my William, hell.

'Go out, go out, my lamp of life,
  In endless darkness die:
Without him I must loathe the earth,
  Without him scorn the skie.'   80

And so despair did rave and rage
  Athwarte her boiling veins;
Against the Providence of God
  She hurlde her impious strains.

She bet her breast, and wrung her hands,
  And rollde her tearless eye,
From rise of morn, til the pale stars
  Again orespread the skye.

When harke! abroade she herde the tramp
  Of nimble-hoofed steed;   90
She herde a knight with clank alighte,
  And climbe the stair in speed.

And soon she herde a tinkling hand,
  That twirled at the pin;
And thro her door, that opened not,
  These words were breathed in.

'What ho! what ho! thy door undo;
  Art watching or asleepe?

My love, dost yet remember me,
　And dost thou laugh or weepe?'　　　　　　100

'Ah! William here so late at night!
　Oh! I have wachte and wak'd:
Whense art thou come? For thy return
　My heart has sorely ak'd.'

'At midnight only we may ride;
　I come ore land and see:
I mounted late, but soone I go;
　Aryse, and come with mee.'

'O William, enter first my bowre,
　And give me one embrace:　　　　　　110
The blasts athwarte the hawthorn hiss;
　Awayte a little space.'

'Tho blasts athwarte the hawthorn hiss,
　I may not harbour here;
My spurs are sett, my courser pawes,
　My hour of flight is nere.

'All as thou lyest upon thy couch,
　Aryse, and mount behinde;
To-night we'le ride a thousand miles,
　The bridal bed to finde.'　　　　　　120

'How, ride to-night a thousand miles?
　Thy love thou dost bemock:
Eleven is the stroke that still
　Rings on within the clock.'

'Looke up; the moon is bright, and we
　Outstride the earthly men:
I'le take thee to the bridal bed,
　And night shall end but then.'

'And where is then thy house, and home,
　And bridal bed so meet?'　　　　　　130
' 'Tis narrow, silent, chilly, low,
　Six planks, one shrouding sheet.'

'And is there any room for me,
　Wherein that I may creepe?'

'There's room enough for thee and me,
    Wherein that we may sleepe.

'All as thou lyest upon thy couch,
    Aryse, no longer stop;
The wedding-guests thy coming wayte,
    The chamber-door is ope.'   140

All in her sarke, as there she lay,
    Upon his horse she sprung;
And with her lily hands so pale
    About her William clung.

And hurry-skurry off they go,
    Unheeding wet or dry;
And horse and rider snort and blow,
    And sparkling pebbles fly.

How swift the flood, the mead, the wood,
    Aright, aleft, are gone!   150
The bridges thunder as they pass,
    But earthly sowne is none.

Tramp, tramp, across the land they speede;
    Splash, splash, across the see:
'Hurrah! the dead can ride apace;
    Dost fear to ride with me?

'The moon is bright, and blue the night;
    Dost quake the blast to stem?
Dost shudder, mayd, to seeke the dead?'
    'No, no, but what of them?'   160

How glumly sownes yon dirgy song!
    Night-ravens flappe the wing.
What knell doth slowly tolle ding dong?
    The psalms of death who sing?

Forth creeps a swarthy funeral train,
    A corse is on the biere;
Like croke of todes from lonely moores,
    The chauntings meete the eere.

'Go, beare her corse when midnight's past,
  With song, and tear, and wail;   170
I've gott my wife, I take her home,
  My hour of wedlock hail!

'Leade forth, O clark, the chaunting quire,
  To swell our spousal-song:
Come, preest, and reade the blessing soone;
  For our dark bed we long.'

The bier is gon, the dirges hush;
  His bidding all obaye,
And headlong rush thro briar and bush,
  Beside his speedy waye.   180

Halloo! halloo! how swift they go,
  Unheeding wet or dry;
And horse and rider snort and blow,
  And sparkling pebbles fly.

How swift the hill, how swift the dale,
  Aright, aleft, are gon!
By hedge and tree, by thorp and town,
  They gallop, gallop on.

Tramp, tramp, across the land they speede;
  Splash, splash, across the see: 190
'Hurrah! the dead can ride apace;
  Dost feare to ride with mee?

'Look up, look up, an airy crew
  In roundel dances reele:
The moon is bright, and blue the night,
  Mayst dimly see them wheele.

'Come to, come to, ye ghostly crew,
  Come to, and follow me,
And daunce for us the wedding daunce,
  When we in bed shall be.'   200

And brush, brush, brush, the ghostly crew,
  Came wheeling ore their heads,
All rustling like the witherd leaves
  That wide the whirlwind spreads.

Halloo! halloo! away they go,
  Unheeding wet or dry;
And horse and rider snort and blow,
  And sparkling pebbles fly.

And all that in the moonshyne lay,
  Behind them fled afar;   210
And backward scudded overhead
  The skie and every star.

Tramp, tramp, across the land they speede;
  Splash, splash, across the see:
'Hurrah! the dead can ride apace;
  Dost fear to ride with mee?

'I weene the cock prepares to crowe;
  The sand will soone be run:
I snuffe the early morning air;
  Downe, downe! our work is done.   220

'The dead, the dead can ride apace:
  Our wed-bed here is fit:
Our race is ridde, our journey ore,
  Our endless union knit.'

And lo! an yron-grated gate
  Soon biggens to their view:
He crackde his whyppe; the locks, the bolts,
  Cling, clang! asunder flew.

They passe, and 'twas on graves they trodde;
  ' 'Tis hither we are bound:'   230
And many a tombstone ghastly white
  Lay in the moonshyne round.

And when he from his steed alytte,
  His armure, black as cinder,
Did moulder, moulder all awaye,
  As were it made of tinder.

His head became a naked skull;
  Nor hair nor eyne had he:

His body grew a skeleton,
  Whilome so blithe of ble.   240

And at his dry and boney heel
  No spur was left to bee;
And in his witherd hand you might
  The scythe and hour-glass see.

And lo! his steed did thin to smoke,
  And charnel-fires outbreathe;
And pal'd, and bleachde, then vanishde quite
  The mayd from underneathe.

And hollow howlings hung in air,
  And shrekes from vaults arose: 250
Then knewe the mayd she might no more
  Her living eyes unclose.

But onward to the judgment-seat,
  Thro' mist and moonlight dreare,
The ghostly crew their flight persewe,
  And hollowe in her eare:

'Be patient; tho thyne heart should breke,
  Arrayne not Heaven's decree;
Thou nowe art of thy bodie reft,
  Thy soul forgiven bee!'   260

MATTHEW GREGORY LEWIS
1775–1818

64   *The Erl-King*

WHO is it that rides through the forest so fast,
While night frowns around him, while shrill roars the blast?
The father, who holds his young son in his arm,
And close in his mantle has wrapp'd him up warm.

—'Why trembles my darling? why shrinks he with fear?'—
—'Oh, father! my father! the Erl-King is near!
The Erl-King, with his crown and his beard long and white!'
—'Oh! your eyes are deceived by the vapours of night.'—

—'Come, baby, sweet baby, with me go away!
Fine clothes you shall wear, we will play a fine play;   10
Fine flowers are growing, white, scarlet, and blue,
On the banks of yon river, and all are for you.'—

—'Oh! father! my father! and dost thou not hear,
What words the Erl-King whispers low in mine ear?'—
—'Now hush thee, my darling, thy terrors appease;
Thou hear'st, 'mid the branches, where murmurs the breeze.'

—'Oh! baby, sweet baby, with me go away!
My daughter shall nurse you, so fair and so gay;
My daughter, in purple and gold who is dress'd,
Shall tend you, and kiss you, and sing you to rest!'   20

—'Oh! father! my father! and dost thou not see
The Erl-King and his daughter are waiting for me?'—
—'Oh! shame thee, my darling, 'tis fear makes thee blind:
Thou see'st the dark willows which wave in the wind.'—

—'I love thee! I doat on thy face so divine!
I must and will have thee, and force makes thee mine!'—
—'My father! my father! oh! hold me now fast!
He pulls me! he hurts, and will have me at last!'—

The father he trembled, he doubled his speed;
O'er hills and through forests he spurr'd his black steed;   30
But when he arrived at his own castle door,
Life throbb'd in the sweet baby's bosom no more.

65   *Alonzo the Brave and the Fair Imogine*

A WARRIOR so bold and a virgin so bright
    Conversed, as they sat on the green;
They gazed on each other with tender delight:
Alonzo the Brave was the name of the knight,
    The maid's was the Fair Imogine.

—'And, oh!' said the youth, 'since to-morrow I go
    To fight in a far-distant land,
Your tears for my absence soon leaving to flow,
Some other will court you, and you will bestow
    On a wealthier suitor your hand.'—   10

—'Oh! hush these suspicions,' Fair Imogine said,
    'Offensive to love and to me!
For, if you be living, or if you be dead,
I swear by the Virgin, that none in your stead
    Shall husband of Imogine be.

'If e'er I, by lust or by wealth led aside,
    Forget my Alonzo the Brave,
God grant that, to punish my falsehood and pride,
Your ghost at the marriage may sit by my side,
May tax me with perjury, claim me as bride,   20
    And bear me away to the grave!'—

To Palestine hasten'd the hero so bold;
    His love she lamented him sore:
But scarce had a twelvemonth elapsed, when behold,
A Baron all cover'd with jewels and gold
    Arrived at Fair Imogine's door.

His treasure, his presents, his spacious domain,
    Soon made her untrue to her vows:
He dazzled her eyes; he bewilder'd her brain;
He caught her affections so light and so vain,   30
    And carried her home as his spouse.

And now had the marriage been blest by the priest;
    The revelry now was begun:
The tables they groan'd with the weight of the feast;
Nor yet had the laughter and merriment ceased,
    When the bell of the castle told—'one!'

Then first with amazement Fair Imogine found
  That a stranger was placed by her side:
His air was terrific; he utter'd no sound;
He spoke not, he moved not, he look'd not around,   40
  But earnestly gazed on the bride.

His vizor was closed, and gigantic his height;
  His armour was sable to view:
All pleasure and laughter were hush'd at his sight;
The dogs as they eyed him drew back in affright;
  The lights in the chamber burned blue!

His presence all bosoms appeared to dismay;
  The guests sat in silence and fear:
At length spoke the bride, while she trembled:—'I pray,
Sir Knight, that your helmet aside you would lay,   50
  And deign to partake of our chear.'—

The lady is silent: the stranger complies,
  His vizor he slowly unclosed:
Oh! God! what a sight met Fair Imogine's eyes!
What words can express her dismay and surprise,
  When a skeleton's head was exposed!

All present then uttered a terrified shout;
  All turned with disgust from the scene.
The worms they crept in, and the worms they crept out,
And sported his eyes and his temples about,   60
  While the spectre addressed Imogine:

'Behold me, thou false one! behold me!' he cried;
  'Remember Alonzo the Brave!
God grants, that to punish thy falsehood and pride,
My ghost at thy marriage should sit by thy side,
Should tax thee with perjury, claim thee as bride,
  And bear thee away to the grave!'

Thus saying, his arms round the lady he wound,
  While loudly she shriek'd in dismay;
Then sank with his prey through the wide-yawning ground: 70
Nor ever again was Fair Imogine found,
  Or the spectre who bore her away.

Not long lived the Baron: and none since that time
  To inhabit the castle presume;
For chronicles tell, that, by order sublime,

There Imogine suffers the pain of her crime,
  And mourns her deplorable doom.

At midnight four times in each year does her sprite,
  When mortals in slumber are bound,
Arrayed in her bridal apparel of white,   80
Appear in the hall with the Skeleton-Knight,
  And shriek as he whirls her around.

While they drink out of skulls newly torn from the grave,
  Dancing round them the spectres are seen:
Their liquor is blood, and this horrible stave
They howl:—'To the health of Alonzo the Brave,
  And his consort, the False Imogine!'

[1797]

ROBERT SOUTHEY
1774–1843

66   *The Widow*

Sapphics

COLD was the night wind, drifting fast the snow fell,
Wide were the downs and shelterless and naked,
When a poor Wanderer struggled on her journey,
  Weary and way-sore.

Drear were the downs, more dreary her reflections.
Cold was the night-wind, colder was her bosom:
She had no home, the world was all before her,
  She had no shelter.

Fast o'er the heath a chariot rattled by her,
'Pity me!' feebly cried the lonely wanderer;   10
'Pity me, strangers! lest with cold and hunger
  Here I should perish.

'Once I had friends,—though now by all forsaken!
Once I had parents,—they are now in Heaven!
I had a home once—I had once a husband—
  Pity me, strangers!

'I had a home once—I had once a husband—
I am a widow, poor and broken-hearted!'
Loud blew the wind, unheard was her complaining,
    On drove the chariot.   20

Then on the snow she laid her down to rest her;
She heard a horseman, 'Pity me!' she groan'd out;
Loud was the wind, unheard was her complaining,
    On went the horseman.

Worn out with anguish, toil and cold and hunger,
Down sunk the Wanderer, sleep had seized her senses;
There did the traveller find her in the morning;
    God had released her.

Bristol, 1795

GEORGE CANNING and
JOHN HOOKHAM FRERE
1770–1827 and 1769–1846

67   *Sapphics*

The Friend of Humanity and the Knife-Grinder

FRIEND OF HUMANITY.

'NEEDY Knife-grinder! whither are you going?
Rough is the road, your wheel is out of order—
Bleak blows the blast;—your hat has got a hole in't,
    So have your breeches!

'Weary Knife-grinder! little think the proud ones,
Who in their coaches roll along the turnpike-
-road, what hard work 'tis crying all day, "Knives and
    Scissars to grind O!"

'Tell me, Knife-grinder, how came you to grind knives?
Did some rich man tyrannically use you?   10
Was it the squire? or parson of the parish?
    Or the attorney?

'Was it the squire, for killing of his game? or
Covetous parson, for his tithes distraining?
Or roguish lawyer made you lose your little
          All in a lawsuit?

'(Have you not read the Rights of Man, by Tom Paine?)
Drops of compassion tremble on my eyelids,
Ready to fall as soon as you have told your
          Pitiful story.'   20

KNIFE-GRINDER.

'Story! God bless you! I have none to tell, sir,
Only last night a-drinking at the Chequers,
This poor old hat and breeches, as you see, were
          Torn in a scuffle.

'Constables came up for to take me into
Custody; they took me before the justice;
Justice Oldmixon put me in the parish-
          -Stocks for a vagrant.

'I should be glad to drink your Honour's health in
A pot of beer, if you will give me sixpence;   30
But for my part, I never love to meddle
          With politics, sir.'

FRIEND OF HUMANITY.

'*I* give thee sixpence! I will see thee damn'd first—
Wretch! whom no sense of wrongs can rouse to vengeance—
Sordid, unfeeling, reprobate, degraded,
          Spiritless outcast?'

[*Kicks the Knife-grinder, overturns his wheel, and exit in a transport
of Republican enthusiasm and universal philanthropy.*]

[1798]

GEORGE CANNING and
WILLIAM GIFFORD

68   *The Progress of Man*

*A Didactic Poem in Forty Cantos, with Notes Critical and
Explanatory: Chiefly of a Philosophical Tendency*

Dedicated to R. P. Knight, Esq.

CANTO FIRST

CONTENTS

*The Subject proposed.—Doubts and Waverings.—Queries not to be answered.
—Formation of the stupendous Whole.—Cosmogony; or the Creation of the
World: the Devil—Man—Various Classes of Being:*—ANIMATED BEINGS
*—Birds—Fish—Beasts—the Influence of the Sexual Appetite—on Tigers—
on Whales—on Crimpt Cod—on Perch—on Shrimps—on Oysters.—Various
Stations assigned to different Animals:—Birds—Bears—Mackarel.—Bears
remarkable for their fur—Mackarel cried on a Sunday—Birds do not graze—
nor Fishes fly—nor Beasts live in the Water.—Plants equally contented with
their lot:—Potatoe—Cabbage—Lettuce—Leeks—Cucumbers.—*MAN *only
discontented—born a Savage; not choosing to continue so, becomes polished—
resigns his Liberty—Priestcraft—Kingcraft—Tyranny of Laws and Institutions.
—Savage Life—description thereof:—The Savage free—roaming Woods—
feeds on Hips and Haws—Animal Food—first notion of it from seeing a Tiger
tearing his Prey—wonders if it is good—resolves to try—makes a Bow and
Arrow—kills a Pig—resolves to roast a part of it—lights a Fire—*APOS-
TROPHE *to Fires—Spits and Jacks not yet invented.—Digression.—*COR-
INTH—SHEFFIELD.—*Love the most natural desire after Food.—Savage
Courtship.—Concubinage recommended.—Satirical Reflections on Parents and
Children—Husbands and Wives—against collateral Consanguinity.—*FREE-
DOM *the only Morality, &c. &c. &c.*

> WHETHER some great, supreme, o'er-ruling Power
> Stretch'd forth its arm at nature's natal hour,
> Composed this mighty whole with plastic skill,
> Wielding the jarring elements at will?
> Or whether sprung from Chaos' mingling storm,
> The mass of matter started into form?
> Or Chance o'er earth's green lap spontaneous fling

The fruits of autumn and the flowers of spring?
Whether material substance unrefined,
Owns the strong impulse of instinctive mind,   10
Which to one centre points diverging lines,
Confounds, refracts, invig'rates, and combines?
Whether the joys of earth, the hopes of heaven,
By Man to God, or God to Man, were given?
If virtue leads to bliss, or vice to woe?
Who rules above? or who resides below?
Vain questions all—shall Man presume to know?
On all these points, and points obscure as these,
Think they who will,—and think whate'er they please!

    Let us a plainer, steadier theme pursue—   20
Mark the grim savage scoop his light canoe;
Mark the dark rook, on pendant branches hung,
With anxious fondness feed her cawing young.—
Mark the fell leopard through the desert prowl,
Fish prey on fish, and fowl regale on fowl;
How Lybian tigers' chawdrons love assails,
And warms, midst seas of ice, the melting whales;—
Cools the crimpt cod, fierce pangs to perch imparts,
Shrinks shrivell'd shrimps, but opens oysters' hearts;—
Then say, how all these things together tend   30
To one great truth, prime object, and good end?
    First—to each living thing, whate'er its kind,
Some lot, some part, some station is assign'd.
The feather'd race with pinions skim the *air*—
Not so the mackarel, and still less the bear:
This roams the *wood*, carniv'rous, for his prey;
That with soft roe, pursues his *watery* way:—
This slain by hunters yields his shaggy hide;
That, caught by fishers, is on *Sundays* cried.—

but each contented with his humble sphere,   40
Moves unambitious through the circling year;
Nor e'er forgets the fortune of his race,
Nor pines to quit, or strives to change his place.
Ah! who has seen the mailed lobster rise,
Clap her broad wings, and soaring claim the skies?
When did the owl, descending from her bow'r,
Crop, 'midst the fleecy flocks, the tender flower;
Or the young heifer plunge, with pliant limb,
In the salt wave, and fish-like strive to swim?

The same with plants—potatoes 'tatoes breed—   50
Uncostly cabbage springs from cabbage seed;
Lettuce to lettuce, leeks to leeks succeed;
Nor e'er did cooling cucumbers presume
To flow'r like myrtle, or like violets bloom.
—Man, only—rash, refined, presumptuous Man,
Starts from his rank, and mars creation's plan.
Born the free heir of Nature's wide domain,
To art's strict limits bound his narrow reign;
Resigns his native rights for meaner things,
For Faith and Fetters—Laws, and Priests, and Kings.   60

(*To be continued.*)

We are sorry to be obliged to break off here.—The
remainder of this admirable and instructive poem is in
the press, and will be continued the first opportunity.

THE EDITOR

RICHARD POLWHELE
1760–1838

69   from *The Unsex'd Females*

THOU, who with all the poet's genuine rage,
Thy 'fine eye rolling' o'er 'this aweful age,'
Where polish'd life unfolds its various views,
Hast mark'd the magic influence of the muse;
Sever'd, with nice precision, from her beam
Of genial power, her false or feeble gleam;
Expos'd the Sciolist's vain-glorious claim,
And boldly thwarted Innovation's aim,
Where witlings wildly think, or madly dare,
With Honor, Virtue, Truth, announcing war;   10
Survey with me, what ne'er our fathers saw,
A female band despising NATURE's law,
As 'proud defiance' flashes from their arms,
And vengeance smothers all their softer charms.
    I shudder at the new unpictur'd scene,
Where unsex'd woman vaunts the imperious mien;
Where girls, affecting to dismiss the heart,
Invoke the Proteus of petrific art;
With equal ease, in body or in mind,
To Gallic freaks or Gallic faith resign'd.   20

.   .   .   .

  Alas! in every aspiration bold,
I saw the creature of a mortal mould:
Yes! not untrembling (tho' I half ador'd
A mind by Genius fraught, by Science stor'd)
I saw the Heroine mount the dazzling dome
Where Shakspeare's spirit kindled, to illume
His favourite FUSELI, and with magic might
To earthly sense unlock'd a world of light!
  Full soon, amid the high pictorial blaze,
I saw a Sibyl-transport in her gaze: 30
To the great Artist, from his wondrous Art,
I saw transferr'd the whole enraptur'd Heart;
Till, mingling soul with soul, in airy trance,
Enlighten'd and inspir'd at every glance,
And from the dross of appetite refin'd,
And, grasping at angelic food, all mind,
Down from the empyreal heights she sunk, betray'd
To poor Philosophy—a love-sick maid!
—But hark! lascivious murmurs melt around;
And pleasure trembles in each dying sound.   40
A myrtle bower, in fairest bloom array'd,
To laughing Venus streams the silver shade:
Thrill'd with fine ardors *Collinsonias* glow,
And, bending, breathe their loose desires below.
Each gentle air a swelling anther heaves,
Wafts its full sweets, and shivers thro' the leaves.
  Bath'd in new bliss, the Fair-one greets the bower,
And ravishes a flame from every flower;
Low at her feet inhales the master's sighs,
And darts voluptuous poison from her eyes.   50
Yet, while each heart-pulse, in the Paphian grove,
Beats quick to IMLAY and licentious love,
A sudden gloom the gathering tempest spreads;
The floral arch-work withers o'er their heads;
Whirlwinds the paramours asunder tear;
And wisdom falls, the victim of despair.

        (lines 1–20, 124–59)

ANONYMOUS

70   *The Age of War*

HENCE, stupid Peace! thy pride and song
    No more shall childish joy impart,
A nobler zeal inspires the throng,
    They pant to learn the killing art.
This is THE AGE OF WAR the age
When ev'ry bosom swells with rage,
    And burns with military fame,
When Mamlucks, Pr[ie]sts, and foplings arm,
Whilst Europe sounds the loud alarm,
    And pride her children's breasts inflame.   10

O! what a vast resistless train
    The Minister can now command!
The threats of enemies are vain,
    They'll find their graves if they should land.
See heroes now of ev'ry trade,
In military garb array'd,
    Pimps, Pr[e]l[a]t[e]s, Taylors, Lawyers shine,
Embodied to support the laws,
In their good King and Country's cause,
    The gen'rous Yeomanry combine.   20

Long may they wield the shining sword,
    While *watchful* fleets the *heroes guard*,
And, seated round the social board,
    Eat beef and pudding *undeterr'd*.
Long may the Church and State protect,
And heav'n-born R[oyalty] respect;
    Tho' business should neglected lie,
Enroll'd to guard the rights of P[i]tt,
Whenev'er their MASTER shall think fit,
    Those Warriors in his cause will die.   30

WALTER SAVAGE LANDOR
1775–1864

71   from *Gebir*

Now to Aurora, borne by dappled steeds,
The sacred gate of orient pearl and gold,
Smitten with Lucifer's light silver wand,
Expanded slow in strains of harmony;
The waves beneath, in purpling rows, like doves
Glancing with wanton coyness tow'rd their queen,
Heav'd softly: thus the damsel's bosom heaves
When, from her sleeping lover's downy cheek,
To which so warily her own she brings
Each moment nearer, she perceives the warmth   10
(Blithe warmth!) of kisses fann'd by playful Dreams
Ocean, and earth, and heaven, was jubilee.
For 'twas the morning, pointed out by Fate,
When an immortal maid and mortal man
Should share each other's nature, knit in bliss.

The brave Iberians far the beach o'erspread
Ere dawn, with distant awe: none hear the mew,
None mark the curlew, flapping o'er the field:
Silence held all, and fond expectancy.
Now suddenly the conch above the sea   20
Sounds, and goes sounding thro' the woods profound.
They, where they hear the echo, turn their eyes;
But nothing see they, save a purple mist
Roll from the distant mountain down the shore.
It rolls, it sails, it settles, it dissolves.
Now shines the Nymph to human eye reveal'd,
And leads her Tamar timorous o'er the waves.
Immortals, crowding round, congratulate
The shepherd; he shrinks back, of breath bereft.
His vesture clinging closely round his limbs   30
Unfelt, while they the whole fair form admire,
He fears that he has lost it; then he fears
The wave has mov'd it; most to look he fears.
Scarce the sweet-flowing music he imbibes,
Or sees the peopled ocean: scarce he sees
Spio, with sparkling eyes, and Beröe
Demure, and young Ione, less renown'd,
Not less divine, mildnatured, Beauty form'd
Her face, her heart Fidelity; for Gods

Design'd, a mortal, too, Ione loved.   40
These were the Nymphs elected for the hour
Of Hesperus and Hymen; these had strewn
The bridal bed: these tuned afresh the shells,
Wiping the green that hoarsen'd them within:
These wove the chaplets; and at night resolved
To drive the dolphins from the wreathed door.

(Book VI, lines 1–46)

Sleepless, with pleasure and expiring fears,
Had Gebir risen ere the break of dawn,
And o'er the plains appointed for the feast
Hurried with ardent step: the swains admired
What could so transversely sweep off the dew,
For never long one path had Gebir trod,
Nor long, unheeding man, one pace preserved.
Not thus Charoba. She despair'd the day.
The day was present: true: yet she despair'd.
In the too tender and once tortured heart   10
Doubts gather strength from habit, like disease;
Fears, like the needle verging to the pole,
Tremble and tremble into certainty.
How often, when her maids with merry voice
Call'd her, and told the sleepless queen 'twas morn,
How often would she feign some fresh delay,
And tell them (tho' they saw) that she arose.
Next to her chamber, closed by cedar doors,
A bath, of purest marble, purest wave,
On its fair surface bore its pavement high.   20
Arabian gold inclosed the crystal roof,
With fluttering boys adorn'd and girls unrobed,
These, when you touch the quiet water, start
From their aërial sunny arch, and pant
Entangled midst each other's flowery wreaths,
And each pursuing is in turn pursued.
   Here came at last, as ever wont at morn,
Charoba: long she linger'd at the brink,
Often she sighed, and, naked as she was,
Sat down, and leaning on the couch's edge,   30
On the soft inward pillow of her arm
Rested her burning cheek: she moved her eyes;
She blush'd; and blushing plung'd into the wave.
   Now brazen chariots thunder thro' each street,
And neighing steeds paw proudly from delay.
While o'er the palace breathes the dulcimer,
Lute, and aspiring harp, and lisping reed;

Loud rush the trumpets, bursting thro' the throng,
And urge the high-shoulder'd vulgar; now are heard
Curses and quarrels and constricted blows,   40
Threats and defiance and suburban war.
Hark! the reiterated clangor sounds!
Now murmurs, like the sea, or like the storm,
Or like the flames on forests, move and mount
From rank to rank, and loud and louder roll,
Till all the people is one vast applause.

(Book VII, lines 63–108)

CHARLES LAMB
1775–1834

72   *The Old Familiar Faces*

WHERE are they gone, the old familiar faces?

I had a mother, but she died, and left me,
Died prematurely in a day of horrors—
All, all are gone, the old familiar faces.

I have had playmates, I have had companions,
In my days of childhood, in my joyful school-days,
All, all are gone, the old familiar faces.

I have been laughing, I have been carousing,
Drinking late, sitting late, with my bosom cronies,
All, all are gone, the old familiar faces.   10

I loved a love once, fairest among women;
Closed are her doors on me, I must not see her—
All, all are gone, the old familiar faces.

I have a friend, a kinder friend has no man;
Like an ingrate, I left my friend abruptly;
Left him, to muse on the old familiar faces.

Ghost-like, I paced round the haunts of my childhood.
Earth seemed a desart I was bound to traverse,
Seeking to find the old familiar faces.

Friend of my bosom, thou more than a brother,   20
Why wert not thou born in my father's dwelling?
So might we talk of the old familiar faces—

How some they have died, and some they have left me,
And some are taken from me; all are departed;
All, all are gone, the old familiar faces.

WILLIAM WORDSWORTH
1770–1850
and SAMUEL TAYLOR COLERIDGE

73–79   from *Lyrical Ballads* (vol. i)

73   *The Rime of the Ancyent Marinere,*
          In Seven Parts

ARGUMENT

How a Ship having passed the Line was driven by Storms to the cold Country
towards the South Pole; and how from thence she made her course to the Tropical
Latitude of the Great Pacific Ocean; and of the strange things that befell; and in
what manner the Ancyent Marinere came back to his own Country.

I

IT is an ancyent Marinere,
    And he stoppeth one of three:
'By thy long grey beard and thy glittering eye
    Now wherefore stoppest me?

'The Bridegroom's doors are open'd wide,
    And I am next of kin;
The Guests are met, the Feast is set,—
    May'st hear the merry din.'

But still he holds the wedding-guest—
    There was a Ship, quoth he—   10
'Nay, if thou'st got a laughsome tale,
    Marinere! come with me.'

He holds him with his skinny hand,
    Quoth he, there was a Ship—
'Now get thee hence, thou grey-beard Loon!
    Or my Staff shall make thee skip.'

He holds him with his glittering eye—
 The wedding guest stood still
And listens like a three year's child;
 The Marinere hath his will.   20

The wedding-guest sate on a stone,
 He cannot chuse but hear:
And thus spake on that ancyent man,
 The bright-eyed Marinere.

The Ship was cheer'd, the Harbour clear'd—
 Merrily did we drop
Below the Kirk, below the Hill,
 Below the Light-house top.

The Sun came up upon the left,
 Out of the Sea came he: 30
And he shone bright, and on the right
 Went down into the Sea.

Higher and higher every day,
 Till over the mast at noon—
The wedding-guest here beat his breast,
 For he heard the loud bassoon.

The Bride hath pac'd into the Hall,
 Red as a rose is she;
Nodding their heads before her goes
 The merry Minstralsy.   40

The wedding-guest he beat his breast,
 Yet he cannot chuse but hear:
And thus spake on that ancyent Man,
 The bright-eyed Marinere.

Listen, Stranger! Storm and Wind,
 A Wind and Tempest strong!
For days and weeks it play'd us freaks—
 Like Chaff we drove along.

Listen, Stranger! Mist and Snow,
 And it grew wond'rous cauld: 50
And Ice mast-high came floating by
 As green as Emerauld.

And thro' the drifts the snowy clifts
  Did send a dismal sheen;
Ne shapes of men ne beasts we ken—
  The Ice was all between.

The Ice was here, the Ice was there,
  The Ice was all around:
It crack'd and growl'd, and roar'd and howl'd—
  Like noises of a swound.   60

At length did cross an Albatross,
  Thorough the Fog it came;
And an it were a Christian Soul,
  We hail'd it in God's name.

The Marineres gave it biscuit-worms,
  And round and round it flew:
The Ice did split with a Thunder-fit,
  The Helmsman steer'd us thro'.

And a good south wind sprung up behind,
  The Albatross did follow;   70
And every day for food or play
  Came to the Marinere's hollo!

In mist or cloud on mast or shroud,
  It perch'd for vespers nine,
Whiles all the night thro' fog-smoke white,
  Glimmer'd the white moon-shine.

'God save thee, ancyent Marinere!
  From the fiends that plague thee thus—
Why look'st thou so?'—with my cross bow
  I shot the Albatross.   80

II

The Sun came up upon the right,
  Out of the Sea came he;
And broad as a weft upon the left
  Went down into the Sea.

And the good south wind still blew behind,
  But no sweet Bird did follow
Ne any day for food or play
  Came to the Marinere's hollo!

And I had done an hellish thing
  And it would work 'em woe: 90
For all averr'd, I had kill'd the Bird
  That made the Breeze to blow.

Ne dim ne red, like God's own head,
  The glorious Sun uprist:
Then all averr'd, I had kill'd the Bird
  That brought the fog and mist.
'Twas right, said they, such birds to slay
  That bring the fog and mist.

The breezes blew, the white foam flew,
  The furrow follow'd free: 100
We were the first that ever burst
  Into that silent Sea.

Down dropt the breeze, the Sails dropt down,
  'Twas sad as sad could be
And we did speak only to break
  The silence of the Sea.

All in a hot and copper sky
  The bloody sun at noon,
Right up above the mast did stand,
  No bigger than the moon.   110

Day after day, day after day,
  We stuck, ne breath ne motion,
As idle as a painted Ship
  Upon a painted Ocean.

Water, water, every where,
  And all the boards did shrink;
Water, water, everywhere,
  Ne any drop to drink.

The very deeps did rot: O Christ!
  That ever this should be!   120
Yea, slimy things did crawl with legs
  Upon the slimy Sea.

About, about, in reel and rout,
  The Death-fires danc'd at night;
The water, like a witch's oils,
  Burnt green and blue and white.

And some in dreams assured were
   Of the Spirit that plagued us so:
Nine fathom deep he had follow'd us
   From the Land of Mist and Snow.   130

And every tongue thro' utter drouth
   Was wither'd at the root;
We could not speak no more than if
   We had been choked with soot.

Ah wel-a-day! what evil looks
   Had I from old and young;
Instead of the Cross the Albatross
   About my neck was hung.

III

I saw a something in the Sky
   No bigger than my fist;   140
At first it seem'd a little speck
   And then it seem'd a mist:
It mov'd and mov'd, and took at last
   A certain shape, I wist.

A speck, a mist, a shape, I wist!
   And still it ner'd and ner'd;
And, an it dodg'd a water-sprite,
   It plung'd and tack'd and veer'd.

With throat unslack'd, with black lips bak'd
   Ne could we laugh, ne wail: 150
Then while thro' drouth all dumb they stood
I bit my arm and suck'd the blood
   And cry'd, A sail! a sail!

With throat unslack'd, with black lips bak'd
   Agape they hear'd me call:
Gramercy! they for joy did grin
And all at once their breath drew in
   As they were drinking all.

She doth not tack from side to side—
   Hither to work us weal   160
Withouten wind, withouten tide
   She steddies with upright keel.

The western wave was all a flame,
  The day was well nigh done!
Almost upon the western wave
  Rested the broad bright Sun;
When that strange shape drove suddenly
  Betwixt us and the Sun.

And strait the Sun was fleck'd with bars
  (Heaven's mother send us grace)   170
As if thro' a dungeon grate he peer'd
  With broad and burning face.

Alas! (thought I, and my heart beat loud)
  How fast she neres and neres!
Are those *her* Sails that glance in the Sun
  Like restless gossameres?

Are those *her* naked ribs, which fleck'd
  The sun that did behind them peer?
And are these two all, all the crew,
  That woman and her fleshless Pheere?   180

His bones were black with many a crack,
  All black and bare, I ween;
Jet-black and bare, save where with rust
Of mouldy damps and charnel crust
  They're patch'd with purple and green.

Her lips are red, *her* looks are free,
  Her locks are yellow as gold:
Her skin is as white as leprosy,
And she is far liker Death than he;
  Her flesh makes the still air cold.   190

The naked Hulk alongside came
  And the Twain were playing dice;
'The Game is done! I've won, I've won!'
  Quoth she, and whistled thrice.

A gust of wind sterte up behind
  And whistled thro' his bones;
Thro' the holes of his eyes and the hole of his mouth
  Half-whistles and half-groans.

With never a whisper in the Sea
  Off darts the Spectre-ship;   200

While clombe above the Eastern bar
The horned Moon, with one bright Star
  Almost atween the tips.

One after one by the horned Moon
  (Listen, O Stranger! to me)
Each turn'd his face with a ghastly pang
  And curs'd me with his ee.

Four times fifty living men,
  With never a sigh or groan,
With heavy thump, a lifeless lump   210
  They dropp'd down one by one.

Their souls did from their bodies fly,—
  They fled to bliss or woe;
And every soul it pass'd me by,
  Like the whiz of my Cross-bow.

IV

'I fear thee, ancyent Marinere!
  I fear thy skinny hand;
And thou art long, and lank, and brown,
  As is the ribb'd Sea-sand.

'I fear thee and thy glittering eye   220
  And thy skinny hand so brown—'
Fear not, fear not, thou wedding guest!
  This body dropt not down.

Alone, alone, all all alone
  Alone on the wide wide Sea;
And Christ would take no pity on
  My soul in agony.

The many men so beautiful,
  And they all dead did lie!
And a million million slimy things   230
  Liv'd on—and so did I.

I look'd upon the rotting Sea,
  And drew my eyes away;
I look'd upon the eldritch deck,
  And there the dead men lay.

I look'd to Heav'n, and try'd to pray;
   But or ever a prayer had gusht,
A wicked whisper came and made
   My heart as dry as dust.

I clos'd my lids and kept them close,   240
   Till the balls like pulses beat;
For the sky and the sea, and the sea and the sky
Lay like a load on my weary eye,
   And the dead were at my feet.

The cold sweat melted from their limbs,
   Ne rot, ne reek did they;
The look with which they look'd on me,
   Had never pass'd away.

An orphan's curse would drag to Hell
   A spirit from on high: 250
But O! more horrible than that
   Is the curse in a dead man's eye!
Seven days, seven nights I saw that curse,
   And yet I could not die.

The moving Moon went up the sky,
   And no where did abide:
Softly she was going up
   And a star or two beside—

Her beams bemock'd the sultry main
   Like morning frosts yspread;   260
But where the ship's huge shadow lay,
The charmed water burnt alway
   A still and awful red.

Beyond the shadow of the ship
   I watch'd the water-snakes:
They mov'd in tracks of shining white;
And when they rear'd, the elfish light
   Fell off in hoary flakes.

Within the shadow of the ship
   I watch'd their rich attire: 270
Blue, glossy green, and velvet black
They coil'd and swam; and every track
   Was a flash of golden fire.

O happy living things! no tongue
  Their beauty might declare:
A spring of love gusht from my heart,
  And I bless'd them unaware!
Sure my kind saint took pity on me,
  And I bless'd them unaware.

The self-same moment I could pray;   280
  And from my neck so free
The Albatross fell off, and sank
  Like lead into the sea.

V

O sleep, it is a gentle thing,
  Belov'd from pole to pole!
To Mary-queen the praise be yeven
She sent the gentle sleep from heaven
  That slid into my soul.

The silly buckets on the deck
  That had so long remain'd,   290
I dreamt that they were fill'd with dew
  And when I awoke it rain'd.

My lips were wet, my throat was cold,
  My garments all were dank;
Sure I had drunken in my dreams
  And still my body drank.

I mov'd and could not feel my limbs,
  I was so light, almost
I thought that I had died in sleep,
  And was a blessed Ghost.   300

The roaring wind! it roar'd far off,
  It did not come anear;
But with its sound it shook the sails
  That were so thin and sere.

The upper air bursts into life,
  And a hundred fire-flags sheen
To and fro they are hurried about;
And to and fro, and in and out
  The stars dance on between.

The coming wind doth roar more loud;   310
  The sails do sigh, like sedge:
The rain pours down from one black cloud
  And the Moon is at its edge.

Hark! hark! the thick black cloud is cleft,
  And the Moon is at its side:
Like waters shot from some high crag,
The lightning falls with never a jag
  A river steep and wide.

The strong wind reach'd the ship: it roar'd
  And dropp'd down, like a stone!   320
Beneath the lightning and the moon
  The dead men gave a groan.

They groan'd, they stirr'd, they all uprose,
  Ne spake, ne mov'd their eyes:
It had been strange, even in a dream
  To have seen those dead men rise.

The helmsman steer'd, the ship mov'd on;
  Yet never a breeze up-blew;
The Marineres all 'gan work the ropes,
  Where they were wont to do: 330
They rais'd their limbs like lifeless tools—
  We were a ghastly crew.

The body of my brother's son
  Stood by me knee to knee:
The body and I pull'd at one rope,
  But he said nought to me—
And I quak'd to think of my own voice
  How frightful it would be!
          .   .   .   .   .   .

The day-light dawn'd—they dropp'd their arms,
  And cluster'd round the mast: 340
Sweet sounds rose slowly thro' their mouths
  And from their bodies pass'd.

Around, around, flew each sweet sound,
  Then darted to the sun:
Slowly the sounds came back again
  Now mix'd, now one by one.

Sometimes a dropping from the sky
   I heard the Lavrock sing;
Sometimes all little birds that are
How they seem'd to fill the sea and air   350
   With their sweet jargoning.

And now 'twas like all instruments,
   Now like a lonely flute;
And now it is an angel's song
   That makes the heavens be mute.

It ceas'd: yet still the sails made on
   A pleasant noise till noon,
A noise like of a hidden brook
   In the leafy month of June,
That to the sleeping woods all night   360
   Singeth a quiet tune.

Listen, O listen, thou Wedding-guest!
   'Marinere! thou hast thy will:
For that, which comes out of thine eye, doth make
   My body and soul to be still.'

Never sadder tale was told
   To a man of woman born:
Sadder and wiser thou wedding-guest!
   Thou'lt rise to-morrow morn.

Never sadder tale was heard   370
   By a man of woman born:
The Marineres all return'd to work
   As silent as beforne.

The Marineres all 'gan pull the ropes,
   But look at me they n'old:
Thought I, I am as thin as air—
   They cannot me behold.

Till noon we silently sail'd on
   Yet never a breeze did breathe:
Slowly and smoothly went the ship   380
   Mov'd onward from beneath.

Under the keel nine fathom deep
   From the land of mist and snow
The spirit slid: and it was He

That made the Ship to go.
The sails at noon left off their tune
And the Ship stood still also.

The sun right up above the mast
    Had fix'd her to the ocean:
But in a minute she 'gan stir   390
    With a short uneasy motion—
Backwards and forwards half her length
    With a short uneasy motion.

Then, like a pawing horse let go,
    She made a sudden bound:
It flung the blood into my head,
    And I fell into a swound.

How long in that same fit I lay,
    I have not to declare;
But ere my living life return'd,   400
I heard and in my soul discern'd
    Two voices in the air,

'Is it he?' quoth one, 'Is this the man?
    By him who died on cross,
With his cruel bow he lay'd full low
    The harmless Albatross.

'The spirit who 'bideth by himself
    In the land of mist and snow,
He lov'd the bird that lov'd the man
    Who shot him with his bow.'   410

The other was a softer voice,
    As soft as honey-dew:
Quoth he the man hath penance done,
    And penance more will do.

VI

FIRST VOICE.

'But tell me, tell me! speak again,
    Thy soft response renewing—
What makes that ship drive on so fast?
    What is the Ocean doing?'

SECOND VOICE.

'Still as a Slave before his Lord,
    The Ocean hath no blast: 420
His great bright eye most silently
    Up to the moon is cast—

'If he may know which way to go,
    For she guides him smooth or grim.
See, brother, see! how graciously
    She looketh down on him.'

FIRST VOICE.

'But why drives on that ship so fast
    Withouten wave or wind?'

SECOND VOICE.

'The air is cut away before,
    And closes from behind.   430

'Fly, brother, fly! more high, more high,
    Or we shall be belated:
For slow and slow that ship will go,
    When the Marinere's trance is abated.'

I woke, and we were sailing on
    As in a gentle weather:
'Twas night, calm night, the moon was high;
    The dead men stood together.

All stood together on the deck,
    For a charnel-dungeon fitter: 440
All fix'd on me their stony eyes
    That in the moon did glitter.

The pang, the curse, with which they died,
    Had never pass'd away:
I could not draw my een from theirs
    Ne turn them up to pray.

And in its time the spell was snapt,
    And I could move my een:
I look'd far-forth, but little saw
    Of what might else be seen.   450

155

Like one, that on a lonely road
  Doth walk in fear and dread,
And having once turn'd round, walks on
  And turns no more his head:
Because he knows, a frightful fiend
  Doth close behind him tread.

But soon there breath'd a wind on me,
  Ne sound ne motion made:
Its path was not upon the sea
  In ripple or in shade.   460

It rais'd my hair, it fann'd my cheek,
  Like a meadow-gale of spring—
It mingled strangely with my fears,
  Yet it felt like a welcoming.

Swiftly, swiftly flew the ship,
  Yet she sail'd softly too:
Sweetly, sweetly blew the breeze—
  On me alone it blew.

O dream of joy! is this indeed
  The light-house top I see?   470
Is this the Hill? Is this the Kirk?
  Is this mine own countrée?

We drifted o'er the Harbour-bar,
  And I with sobs did pray—
'O let me be awake, my God!
  Or let me sleep alway!'

The harbour-bay was clear as glass,
  So smoothly it was strewn!
And on the bay the moon light lay,
  And the shadow of the moon.   480

The moonlight bay was white all o'er,
  Till rising from the same,
Full many shapes, that shadows were,
  Like as of torches came.

A little distance from the prow
  Those dark-red shadows were;
But soon I saw that my own flesh
  Was red as in a glare.

I turn'd my head in fear and dread,
    And by the holy rood,   490
The bodies had advanc'd, and now
    Before the mast they stood.

They lifted up their stiff right arms,
    They held them strait and tight;
And each right-arm burnt like a torch,
    A torch that's borne upright.
Their stony eye-balls glitter'd on
    In the red and smoky light.

I pray'd and turn'd my head away,
    Forth looking as before.   500
There was no breeze upon the bay,
    No wave against the shore.

The rock shone bright, the kirk no less
    That stands above the rock:
The moonlight steep'd in silentness
    The steady weathercock.

And the bay was white with silent light,
    Till rising from the same
Full many shapes, that shadows were,
    In crimson colours came.   510

A little distance from the prow
    Those crimson shadows were:
I turn'd my eyes upon the deck—
    O Christ! what saw I there?

Each corse lay flat, lifeless and flat;
    And by the Holy rood
A man all light, a seraph-man,
    On every corse there stood.

This seraph-band, each wav'd his hand:
    It was a heavenly sight: 520
They stood as signals to the land,
    Each one a lovely light:

This seraph-band, each wav'd his hand,
    No voice did they impart—
No voice; but O! the silence sank,
    Like music on my heart.

Eftsones I heard the dash of oars,
　　I heard the pilot's cheer:
My head was turn'd perforce away
　　And I saw a boat appear.　　　　　　　　　　530

Then vanish'd all the lovely lights;
　　The bodies rose anew:
With silent pace, each to his place,
　　Came back the ghastly crew.
The wind, that shade nor motion made,
　　On me alone it blew.

The pilot, and the pilot's boy
　　I heard them coming fast:
Dear Lord in Heaven! it was a joy,
　　The dead men could not blast.　　　　　　　540

I saw a third—I heard his voice:
　　It is the Hermit good!
He singeth loud his godly hymns
　　That he makes in the wood.
He'll shrieve my soul, he'll wash away
　　The Albatross's blood.

VII

This Hermit good lives in that wood
　　Which slopes down to the Sea.
How loudly his sweet voice he rears!
He loves to talk with Marineres　　　　　　　550
　　That come from a far Contrée.

He kneels at morn and noon and eve—
　　He hath a cushion plump:
It is the moss, that wholly hides
　　The rotted old Oak-stump.

The Skiff-boat ne'rd: I heard them talk,
　　'Why, this is strange, I trow!
Where are those lights so many and fair
　　That signal made but now?

'Strange, by my faith! the Hermit said—　　560
　　And they answer'd not our cheer.
The planks look warp'd, and see those sails
　　How thin they are and sere!

I never saw aught like to them
  Unless perchance it were

'The skeletons of leaves that lag
  My forest-brook along:
When the Ivy-tod is heavy with snow,
And the Owlet whoops to the wolf below
  That eats the she-wolf's young.   570

'Dear Lord! it has a fiendish look—'
  (The Pilot made reply)
'I am afear'd'—'Push on, push on!'
  Said the Hermit cheerily.

The Boat came closer to the Ship,
  But I ne spake ne stirr'd!
The Boat came close beneath the Ship,
  And strait a sound was heard!

Under the water it rumbled on,
  Still louder and more dread: 580
It reach'd the Ship, it split the bay;
  The Ship went down like lead.

Stunn'd by that loud and dreadful sound,
  Which sky and ocean smote:
Like one that had been seven days drown'd
  My body lay afloat:
But, swift as dreams, myself I found
  Within the Pilot's boat.

Upon the whirl, where sank the Ship,
  The boat spun round and round: 590
And all was still, save that the hill
  Was telling of the sound.

I mov'd my lips: the Pilot shriek'd
  And fell down in a fit.
The Holy Hermit rais'd his eyes
  And pray'd where he did sit.

I took the oars: the Pilot's boy,
  Who now doth crazy go,
Laugh'd loud and long, and all the while
  His eyes went to and fro,   600
'Ha! ha!' quoth he—'full plain I see,
  The devil knows how to row.'

And now all in mine own Countrée
  I stood on the firm land!
The Hermit stepp'd forth from the boat,
  And scarcely he could stand.

'O shrieve me, shrieve me, holy Man!'
  The Hermit cross'd his brow—
'Say quick,' quoth he, 'I bid thee say
  What manner man art thou?'   610

Forthwith this frame of mine was wrench'd
  With a woeful agony,
Which forc'd me to begin my tale
  And then it left me free.

Since then at an uncertain hour,
  Now oftimes and now fewer,
That anguish comes and makes me tell
  My ghastly aventure.

I pass, like night, from land to land;
  I have strange power of speech;   620
The moment that his face I see
I know the man that must hear me;
  To him my tale I teach.

What loud uproar bursts from that door!
  The Wedding-guests are there;
But in the Garden-bower the Bride
  And Bride-maids singing are:
And hark the little Vesper-bell
  Which biddeth me to prayer.

O Wedding-guest! this soul hath been   630
  Alone on a wide wide sea:
So lonely 'twas, that God himself
  Scarce seemed there to be.

O sweeter than the Marriage-feast,
  'Tis sweeter far to me
To walk together to the Kirk
  With a goodly company.

To walk together to the Kirk
  And all together pray,
While each to his great Father bends,   640

Old men, and babes, and loving friends,
  And Youths, and Maidens gay.

Farewell, farewell! but this I tell
  To thee, thou wedding-guest!
He prayeth well who loveth well,
  Both man and bird and beast.

He prayeth best who loveth best,
  All things both great and small:
For the dear God, who loveth us,
  He made and loveth all.   650

The Marinere, whose eye is bright,
  Whose beard with age is hoar,
Is gone; and now the wedding-guest
  Turn'd from the bridegroom's door.

He went, like one that hath been stunn'd
  And is of sense forlorn:
A sadder and a wiser man
  He rose the morrow morn.

74   *We Are Seven*

A SIMPLE child, dear brother Jim,
  That lightly draws its breath,
And feels its life in every limb,
  What should it know of death?

I met a little cottage girl,
  She was eight years old, she said;
Her hair was thick with many a curl
  That cluster'd round her head.

She had a rustic, woodland air,
  And she was wildly clad;   10
Her eyes were fair, and very fair,
  —Her beauty made me glad.

'Sisters and brothers, little maid,
  How many may you be?'
'How many? seven in all,' she said,
  And wondering looked at me.

'And where are they, I pray you tell?'
She answered, 'Seven are we,
And two of us at Conway dwell,
And two are gone to sea.   20

'Two of us in the church-yard lie,
My sister and my brother,
And in the church-yard cottage, I
Dwell near them with my mother.'

'You say that two at Conway dwell,
And two are gone to sea,
Yet you are seven; I pray you tell
Sweet Maid, how this may be?'

Then did the little Maid reply,
'Seven boys and girls are we;   30
Two of us in the church-yard lie,
Beneath the church-yard tree.'

'You run about, my little maid,
Your limbs they are alive;
If two are in the church-yard laid,
Then ye are only five.'

'Their graves are green, they may be seen,'
The little Maid replied,
'Twelve steps or more from my mother's door,
And they are side by side.   40

'My stockings there I often knit,
My 'kerchief there I hem;
And there upon the ground I sit—
I sit and sing to them.

'And often after sunset, Sir,
When it is light and fair,
I take my little porringer,
And eat my supper there.

'The first that died was little Jane;
In bed she moaning lay,   50
Till God released her of her pain,
And then she went away.

'So in the church-yard she was laid,
And all the summer dry,

Together round her grave we played,
My brother John and I.

'And when the ground was white with snow,
And I could run and slide,
My brother John was forced to go,
And he lies by her side.'   60

'How many are you then,' said I,
'If they two are in Heaven?'
The little Maiden did reply,
'O Master! we are seven.'

'But they are dead; those two are dead!
Their spirits are in heaven!'
'Twas throwing words away; for still
The little Maid would have her will,
And said, 'Nay, we are seven!'

75   *Lines Written in Early Spring*

I HEARD a thousand blended notes,
While in a grove I sate reclined,
In that sweet mood when pleasant thoughts
Bring sad thoughts to the mind.

To her fair works did nature link
The human soul that through me ran;
And much it griev'd my heart to think
What man has made of man.

Through primrose-tufts, in that sweet bower,
The periwinkle trail'd its wreathes;   10
And 'tis my faith that every flower
Enjoys the air it breathes.

The birds around me hopp'd and play'd:
Their thoughts I cannot measure,
But the least motion which they made,
It seem'd a thrill of pleasure.

The budding twigs spread out their fan,
To catch the breezy air;
And I must think, do all I can,
That there was pleasure there.   20

If I these thoughts may not prevent,
If such be of my creed the plan,
Have I not reason to lament
What man has made of man?

76   *The Idiot Boy*

'TIS eight o'clock,—a clear March night,
The moon is up—the sky is blue,
The owlet in the moonlight air,
He shouts from nobody knows where;
He lengthens out his lonely shout,
Halloo! halloo! a long halloo!

—Why bustle thus about your door,
What means this bustle, Betty Foy?
Why are you in this mighty fret?
And why on horseback have you set   10
Him whom you love, your idiot boy?

Beneath the moon that shines so bright,
Till she is tired, let Betty Foy
With girt and stirrup fiddle-faddle;
But wherefore set upon a saddle
Him whom she loves, her idiot boy?

There's scarce a soul that's out of bed;
Good Betty! put him down again;
His lips with joy they burr at you,
But, Betty! what has he to do   20
With stirrup, saddle, or with rein?

The world will say 'tis very idle,
Bethink you of the time of night;
There's not a mother, no not one,
But when she hears what you have done,
Oh! Betty she'll be in a fright.

But Betty's bent on her intent,
For her good neighbour, Susan Gale,
Old Susan, she who dwells alone,
Is sick, and makes a piteous moan,   30
As if her very life would fail.

There's not a house within a mile,
No hand to help them in distress:

Old Susan lies a bed in pain,
And sorely puzzled are the twain,
For what she ails they cannot guess.
And Betty's husband's at the wood,
Where by the week he doth abide,
A woodman in the distant vale;
There's none to help poor Susan Gale,   40
What must be done? what will betide?

And Betty from the lane has fetched
Her pony, that is mild and good,
Whether he be in joy or pain,
Feeding at will along the lane,
Or bringing faggots from the wood.

And he is all in travelling trim,
And by the moonlight, Betty Foy
Has up upon the saddle set,
The like was never heard of yet,   50
Him whom she loves, her idiot boy.

And he must post without delay
Across the bridge that's in the dale,
And by the church, and o'er the down,
To bring a doctor from the town,
Or she will die, old Susan Gale.

There is no need of boot or spur,
There is no need of whip or wand,
For Johnny has his holly-bough,
And with a hurly-burly now   60
He shakes the green bough in his hand.

And Betty o'er and o'er has told
The boy who is her best delight,
Both what to follow, what to shun,
What do, and what to leave undone,
How turn to left, and how to right.

And Betty's most especial charge,
Was, 'Johnny! Johnny! mind that you
Come home again, nor stop at all,
Come home again, whate'er befal,   70
My Johnny do, I pray you do.'

To this did Johnny answer make,
Both with his head, and with his hand,
And proudly shook the bridle too,
And then! his words were not a few,
Which Betty well could understand.

And now that Johnny is just going,
Though Betty's in a mighty flurry,
She gently pats the pony's side,
On which her idiot boy must ride,   80
And seems no longer in a hurry.

But when the pony moved his legs,
Oh! then for the poor idiot boy!
For joy he cannot hold the bridle,
For joy his head and heels are idle,
He's idle all for very joy.

And while the pony moves his legs,
In Johnny's left-hand you may see,
The green bough's motionless and dead;
The moon that shines above his head   90
Is not more still and mute than he.

His heart it was so full of glee,
That till full fifty yards were gone,
He quite forgot his holly whip,
And all his skill in horsemanship,
Oh! happy, happy, happy John.

And Betty's standing at the door,
And Betty's face with joy o'erflows,
Proud of herself, and proud of him,
She sees him in his travelling trim;   100
How quietly her Johnny goes.

The silence of her idiot boy,
What hopes it sends to Betty's heart!
He's at the guide-post—he turns right,
She watches till he's out of sight,
And Betty will not then depart.

Burr, burr—now Johnny's lips they burr,
As loud as any mill, or near it,
Meek as a lamb the pony moves,
And Johnny makes the noise he loves,   110
And Betty listens, glad to hear it.

Away she hies to Susan Gale:
And Johnny's in a merry tune,
The owlets hoot, the owlets curr,
And Johnny's lips they burr, burr, burr,
And on he goes beneath the moon.

His steed and he right well agree,
For of this pony there's a rumour,
That should he lose his eyes and ears,
And should he live a thousand years,   120
He never will be out of humour.

But then he is a horse that thinks!
And when he thinks his pace is slack;
Now, though he knows poor Johnny well,
Yet for his life he cannot tell
What he has got upon his back.

So through the moonlight lanes they go,
And far into the moonlight dale,
And by the church, and o'er the down,
To bring a doctor from the town,   130
To comfort poor old Susan Gale.

And Betty, now at Susan's side,
Is in the middle of her story,
What comfort Johnny soon will bring,
With many a most diverting thing,
Of Johnny's wit and Johnny's glory.

And Betty's still at Susan's side:
By this time she's not quite so flurried;
Demure with porringer and plate
She sits, as if in Susan's fate   140
Her life and soul were buried.

But Betty, poor good woman! she,
You plainly in her face may read it,
Could lend out of that moment's store
Five years of happiness or more,
To any that might need it.

But yet I guess that now and then
With Betty all was not so well,
And to the road she turns her ears,
And thence full many a sound she hears,   150
Which she to Susan will not tell.

Poor Susan moans, poor Susan groans,
'As sure as there's a moon in heaven,'
Cries Betty, 'he'll be back again;
They'll both be here, 'tis almost ten,
They'll both be here before eleven.'

Poor Susan moans, poor Susan groans,
The clock gives warning for eleven;
'Tis on the stroke—'If Johnny's near,'
Quoth Betty 'he will soon be here,   160
As sure as there's a moon in heaven.'

The clock is on the stroke of twelve,
And Johnny is not yet in sight,
The moon's in heaven, as Betty sees,
But Betty is not quite at ease;
And Susan has a dreadful night.

And Betty, half an hour ago,
On Johnny vile reflections cast;
'A little idle sauntering thing!'
With other names, an endless string,   170
But now that time is gone and past.

And Betty's drooping at the heart,
That happy time all past and gone,
'How can it be he is so late?
The doctor he has made him wait,
Susan! they'll both be here anon.'

And Susan's growing worse and worse,
And Betty's in a sad quandary;
And then there's nobody to say
If she must go or she must stay: 180
—She's in a sad quandary.

The clock is on the stroke of one;
But neither Doctor nor his guide
Appear along the moonlight road,
There's neither horse nor man abroad,
And Betty's still at Susan's side.

And Susan she begins to fear
Of sad mischances not a few,
That Johnny may perhaps be drown'd,
Or lost perhaps, and never found;   190
Which they must both for ever rue.

She prefaced half a hint of this
With, 'God forbid it should be true!'
At the first word that Susan said
Cried Betty, rising from the bed,
'Susan, I'd gladly stay with you.

'I must be gone, I must away,
Consider, Johnny's but half-wise;
Susan, we must take care of him,
If he is hurt in life or limb'—   200
'Oh God forbid!' poor Susan cries.

'What can I do?' says Betty, going,
'What can I do to ease your pain?
Good Susan tell me, and I'll stay;
I fear you're in a dreadful way,
But I shall soon be back again.'

'Good Betty go, good Betty go,
There's nothing that can ease my pain.'
Then off she hies, but with a prayer
That God poor Susan's life would spare,   210
Till she comes back again.

So, through the moonlight lane she goes,
And far into the moonlight dale;
And how she ran, and how she walked,
And all that to herself she talked,
Would surely be a tedious tale.

In high and low, above, below,
In great and small, in round and square,
In tree and tower was Johnny seen,
In bush and brake, in black and green,   220
'Twas Johnny, Johnny, every where.

She's past the bridge that's in the dale,
And now the thought torments her sore,
Johnny perhaps his horse forsook,
To hunt the moon that's in the brook,
And never will be heard of more.

And now she's high upon the down,
Alone amid a prospect wide;
There's neither Johnny nor his horse,
Among the fern or in the gorse;   230
There's neither doctor nor his guide.

'Oh saints! what is become of him?
Perhaps he's climbed into an oak,
Where he will stay till he is dead;
Or sadly he has been misled,
And joined the wandering gypsey-folk.

'Or him that wicked pony's carried
To the dark cave, the goblins' hall,
Or in the castle he's pursuing,
Among the ghosts, his own undoing;   240
Or playing with the waterfall.'

At poor old Susan then she railed,
While to the town she posts away;
'If Susan had not been so ill,
Alas! I should have had him still,
My Johnny, till my dying day.'

Poor Betty! in this sad distemper,
The doctor's self would hardly spare,
Unworthy things she talked and wild,
Even he, of cattle the most mild,   250
The pony had his share.

And now she's got into the town,
And to the doctor's door she hies;
'Tis silence all on every side;
The town so long, the town so wide,
Is silent as the skies.

And now she's at the doctor's door,
She lifts the knocker, rap, rap, rap,
The doctor at the casement shews,
His glimmering eyes that peep and doze;   260
And one hand rubs his old night-cap.

'Oh Doctor! Doctor! where's my Johnny?'
'I'm here, what is't you want with me?'
'Oh Sir! you know I'm Betty Foy,
And I have lost my poor dear boy,
You know him—him you often see;

'He's not so wise as some folks be.'
'The devil take his wisdom!' said
The Doctor, looking somewhat grim,
'What, woman! should I know of him?'   270
And, grumbling, he went back to bed.

'O woe is me! O woe is me!
Here will I die; here will I die;
I thought to find my Johnny here,
But he is neither far nor near,
Oh! what a wretched mother I!'

She stops, she stands, she looks about,
Which way to turn she cannot tell.
Poor Betty! it would ease her pain
If she had heart to knock again;   280
—The clock strikes three—a dismal knell!

Then up along the town she hies,
No wonder if her senses fail,
This piteous news so much it shock'd her,
She quite forgot to send the Doctor,
To comfort poor old Susan Gale.

And now she's high upon the down,
And she can see a mile of road,
'Oh cruel! I'm almost three-score;
Such night as this was ne'er before,   290
There's not a single soul abroad.'

She listens, but she cannot hear
The foot of horse, the voice of man;
The streams with softest sound are flowing,
The grass you almost hear it growing,
You hear it now if e'er you can.

The owlets through the long blue night
Are shouting to each other still:
Fond lovers, yet not quite hob nob,
They lengthen out the tremulous sob,   300
That echoes far from hill to hill.

Poor Betty now has lost all hope,
Her thoughts are bent on deadly sin;
A green-grown pond she just has pass'd,
And from the brink she hurries fast,
Lest she should drown herself therein.

And now she sits her down and weeps;
Such tears she never shed before;
'Oh dear, dear pony! my sweet joy!
Oh carry back my idiot boy!   310
And we will ne'er o'erload thee more.'

A thought is come into her head;
'The pony he is mild and good,
And we have always used him well;
Perhaps he's gone along the dell,
And carried Johnny to the wood.'

Then up she springs as if on wings;
She thinks no more of deadly sin;
If Betty fifty ponds should see,
The last of all her thoughts would be,   320
To drown herself therein.

Oh reader! now that I might tell
What Johnny and his horse are doing
What they've been doing all this time,
Oh could I put it into rhyme,
A most delightful tale pursuing!

Perhaps, and no unlikely thought!
He with his pony now doth roam
The cliffs and peaks so high that are,
To lay his hands upon a star,   330
And in his pocket bring it home.

Perhaps he's turned himself about,
His face unto his horse's tail,
And still and mute, in wonder lost,
All like a silent horseman-ghost,
He travels on along the vale.

And now, perhaps, he's hunting sheep,
A fierce and dreadful hunter he!
Yon valley, that's so trim and green,
In five months' time, should he be seen,   340
A desart wilderness will be.

Perhaps, with head and heels on fire,
And like the very soul of evil,
He's galloping away, away,
And so he'll gallop on for aye,
The bane of all that dread the devil.

I to the muses have been bound,
These fourteen years, by strong indentures;
Oh gentle muses! let me tell
But half of what to him befel,   350
For sure he met with strange adventures.

Oh gentle muses! is this kind?
Why will ye thus my suit repel?
Why of your further aid bereave me?
And can ye thus unfriended leave me?
Ye muses! whom I love so well.

Who's yon, that, near the waterfall,
Which thunders down with headlong force,
Beneath the moon, yet shining fair,
As careless as if nothing were,   360
Sits upright on a feeding horse?

Unto his horse, that's feeding free,
He seems, I think, the rein to give;
Of moon or stars he takes no heed;
Of such we in romances read,
—'Tis Johnny! Johnny! as I live.

And that's the very pony too.
Where is she, where is Betty Foy?
She hardly can sustain her fears;
The roaring water-fall she hears,   370
And cannot find her idiot boy.

Your pony's worth his weight in gold,
Then calm your terrors, Betty Foy!
She's coming from among the trees,
And now, all full in view, she sees
Him whom she loves, her idiot boy.

And Betty sees the pony too:
Why stand you thus Good Betty Foy?
It is no goblin, 'tis no ghost,
'Tis he whom you so long have lost,   380
He whom you love, your idiot boy.

She looks again—her arms are up—
She screams—she cannot move for joy;
She darts as with a torrent's force,
She almost has o'erturned the horse,
And fast she holds her idiot boy.

And Johnny burrs and laughs aloud,
Whether in cunning or in joy,
I cannot tell; but while he laughs,
Betty a drunken pleasure quaffs,   390
To hear again her idiot boy.

And now she's at the pony's tail,
And now she's at the pony's head,
On that side now, and now on this,
And almost stifled with her bliss,
A few sad tears does Betty shed.

She kisses o'er and o'er again,
Him whom she loves, her idiot boy,
She's happy here, she's happy there,
She is uneasy every where;   400
Her limbs are all alive with joy.

She pats the pony, where or when
She knows not, happy Betty Foy!
The little pony glad may be,
But he is milder far than she,
You hardly can perceive his joy.

'Oh! Johnny, never mind the Doctor;
You've done your best, and that is all.'
She took the reins, when this was said,
And gently turned the pony's head   410
From the loud water-fall.

By this the stars were almost gone,
The moon was setting on the hill,
So pale you scarcely looked at her:
The little birds began to stir,
Though yet their tongues were still.

The pony, Betty, and her boy,
Wind slowly through the woody dale:
And who is she, be-times abroad,
That hobbles up the steep rough road?   420
Who is it, but old Susan Gale?

Long Susan lay deep lost in thought,
And many dreadful fears beset her,
Both for her messenger and nurse;
And as her mind grew worse and worse,
Her body it grew better.

She turned, she toss'd herself in bed,
On all sides doubts and terrors met her;
Point after point did she discuss;
And while her mind was fighting thus,   430
Her body still grew better.

'Alas! what is become of them?
These fears can never be endured,
I'll to the wood.'—The word scarce said,
Did Susan rise up from her bed,
As if by magic cured.

Away she posts up hill and down,
And to the wood at length is come,
She spies her friends, she shouts a greeting;
Oh me! it is a merry meeting,   440
As ever was in Christendom.

The owls have hardly sung their last,
While our four travellers homeward wend;
The owls have hooted all night long,
And with the owls began my song,
And with the owls must end.

For while they all were travelling home,
Cried Betty, 'Tell us Johnny, do,
Where all this long night you have been,
What you have heard, what you have seen,   450
And Johnny, mind you tell us true.'

Now Johnny all night long had heard
The owls in tuneful concert strive;
No doubt too he the moon had seen;
For in the moonlight he had been
From eight o'clock till five.

And thus to Betty's question, he
Made answer, like a traveller bold,
(His very words I give to you,)
'The cocks did crow to-whoo, to-whoo,   460
And the sun did shine so cold.'
—Thus answered Johnny in his glory,
And that was all his travel's story.

77   *Expostulation and Reply*

'Why William, on that old grey stone,
Thus for the length of half a day,
Why William, sit you thus alone,
And dream your time away?

'Where are your books? that light bequeath'd
To beings else forlorn and blind!
Up! Up! and drink the spirit breath'd
From dead men to their kind.

'You look round on your mother earth,
As if she for no purpose bore you;   10
As if you were her first-born birth,
And none had lived before you!'

One morning thus, by Esthwaite lake,
When life was sweet I knew not why,
To me my good friend Matthew spake,
And thus I made reply.

'The eye it cannot chuse but see,
We cannot bid the ear be still;
Our bodies feel, where'er they be,
Against, or with our will.   20

'Nor less I deem that there are powers,
Which of themselves our minds impress,
That we can feed this mind of ours,
In a wise passiveness.

'Think you, mid all this mighty sum
Of things for ever speaking,
That nothing of itself will come,
But we must still be seeking?

'—Then ask not wherefore, here, alone,
Conversing as I may,   30
I sit upon this old grey stone,
And dream my time away.'

78   *The Tables Turned*

An Evening Scene, on the Same Subject

UP! up! my friend, and clear your looks,
Why all this toil and trouble?
Up! up! my friend, and quit your books,
Or surely you'll grow double.

The sun above the mountain's head,
A freshening lustre mellow,
Through all the long green fields has spread,
His first sweet evening yellow.

Books! 'tis a dull and endless strife,
Come, hear the woodland linnet,   10
How sweet his music; on my life
There's more of wisdom in it.

And hark! how blithe the throstle sings!
And he is no mean preacher;
Come forth into the light of things,
Let Nature be your teacher.

She has a world of ready wealth,
Our minds and hearts to bless—
Spontaneous wisdom breathed by health,
Truth breathed by chearfulness.   20

One impulse from a vernal wood
May teach you more of man;
Of moral evil and of good,
Than all the sages can.

Sweet is the lore which nature brings;
Our meddling intellect
Misshapes the beauteous forms of things;
—We murder to dissect.

Enough of science and of art;
Close up these barren leaves;   30
Come forth, and bring with you a heart
That watches and receives.

79   *Lines Written a Few Miles above Tintern Abbey*

On Revisiting the Banks of the Wye during a Tour,
July 13, 1798

FIVE years have passed; five summers, with the length
Of five long winters! and again I hear
These waters, rolling from their mountain-springs
With a sweet inland murmur.—Once again
Do I behold these steep and lofty cliffs,
Which on a wild secluded scene impress
Thoughts of more deep seclusion; and connect
The landscape with the quiet of the sky.
The day is come when I again repose
Here, under this dark sycamore, and view   10
These plots of cottage-ground, these orchard-tufts,
Which, at this season, with their unripe fruits,
Among the woods and copses lose themselves,
Nor, with their green and simple hue, disturb
The wild green landscape. Once again I see
These hedge-rows, hardly hedge-rows, little lines
Of sportive wood run wild; these pastoral farms
Green to the very door; and wreathes of smoke
Sent up, in silence, from among the trees,
With some uncertain notice, as might seem,   20
Of vagrant dwellers in the houseless woods,
Or of some hermit's cave, where by his fire
The hermit sits alone.

      Though absent long,
These forms of beauty have not been to me,
As is a landscape to a blind man's eye:
But oft, in lonely rooms, and mid the din
Of towns and cities, I have owed to them,
In hours of weariness, sensations sweet,
Felt in the blood, and felt along the heart,
And passing even into my purer mind   30
With tranquil restoration:—feelings too
Of unremembered pleasure; such, perhaps,
As may have had no trivial influence
On that best portion of a good man's life;
His little, nameless, unremembered acts
Of kindness and of love. Nor less, I trust,
To them I may have owed another gift,
Of aspect more sublime; that blessed mood,

In which the burthen of the mystery,
In which the heavy and the weary weight   40
Of all this unintelligible world
Is lighten'd:—that serene and blessed mood,
In which the affections gently lead us on,
Until, the breath of this corporeal frame,
And even the motion of our human blood
Almost suspended, we are laid asleep
In body, and become a living soul:
While with an eye made quiet by the power
Of harmony, and the deep power of joy,
We see into the life of things.

                    If this   50
Be but a vain belief, yet, oh! how oft,
In darkness, and amid the many shapes
Of joyless day-light; when the fretful stir
Unprofitable, and the fever of the world,
Have hung upon the beatings of my heart,
How oft, in spirit, have I turned to thee
O sylvan Wye! Thou wanderer through the woods,
How often has my spirit turned to thee!
And now, with gleams of half-extinguish'd thought,
With many recognitions dim and faint,   60
And somewhat of a sad perplexity,
The picture of the mind revives again:
While here I stand, not only with the sense
Of present pleasure, but with pleasing thoughts
That in this moment there is life and food
For future years. And so I dare to hope
Though changed, no doubt, from what I was, when first
I came among these hills; when like a roe
I bounded o'er the mountains, by the sides
Of the deep rivers, and the lonely streams,   70
Wherever nature led; more like a man
Flying from something that he dreads, than one
Who sought the thing he loved. For nature then
(The coarser pleasures of my boyish days,
And their glad animal movements all gone by,)
To me was all in all.—I cannot paint
What then I was. The sounding cataract
Haunted me like a passion: the tall rock,
The mountain, and the deep and gloomy wood,
Their colours and their forms, were then to me   80
An appetite: a feeling and a love,
That had no need of a remoter charm,

By thought supplied, or any interest
Unborrowed from the eye.—That time is past,
And all its aching joys are now no more,
And all its dizzy raptures. Not for this
Faint I, nor mourn nor murmur: other gifts
Have followed, for such loss, I would believe,
Abundant recompence. For I have learned
To look on nature, not as in the hour   90
Of thoughtless youth, but hearing oftentimes
The still, sad music of humanity,
Not harsh nor grating, though of ample power
To chasten and subdue. And I have felt
A presence that disturbs me with the joy
Of elevated thoughts; a sense sublime
Of something far more deeply interfused,
Whose dwelling is the light of setting suns,
And the round ocean, and the living air,
And the blue sky, and in the mind of man,   100
A motion and a spirit, that impels
All thinking things, all objects of all thought,
And rolls through all things. Therefore am I still
A lover of the meadows and the woods,
And mountains; and of all that we behold
From this green earth; of all the mighty world
Of eye and ear, both what they half-create,
And what perceive; well pleased to recognize
In nature and the language of the sense,
The anchor of my purest thoughts, the nurse,   110
The guide, the guardian of my heart, and soul
Of all my moral being.

               Nor, perchance,
If I were not thus taught, should I the more
Suffer my genial spirits to decay:
For thou art with me, here, upon the banks
Of this fair river; thou, my dearest Friend,
My dear, dear Friend, and in thy voice I catch
The language of my former heart, and read
My former pleasures in the shooting lights
Of thy wild eyes. Oh! yet a little while   120
May I behold in thee what I was once,
My dear, dear Sister! And this prayer I make,
Knowing that Nature never did betray
The heart that loved her; 'tis her privilege,
Through all the years of this our life, to lead
From joy to joy: for she can so inform

The mind that is within us, so impress
With quietness and beauty, and so feed
With lofty thoughts, that neither evil tongues,
Rash judgments, nor the sneers of selfish men,   130
Nor greetings where no kindness is, nor all
The dreary intercourse of daily life,
Shall e'er prevail against us, or disturb
Our chearful faith that all which we behold
Is full of blessings. Therefore let the moon
Shine on thee in thy solitary walk;
And let the misty mountain winds be free
To blow against thee: and in after years,
When these wild ecstasies shall be matured
Into a sober pleasure, when thy mind   140
Shall be a mansion for all lovely forms,
Thy memory be as a dwelling-place
For all sweet sounds and harmonies; Oh! then,
If solitude, or fear, or pain, or grief,
Should be thy portion, with what healing thoughts
Of tender joy wilt thou remember me,
And these my exhortations! Nor, perchance,
If I should be, where I no more can hear
Thy voice, nor catch from thy wild eyes these gleams
Of past existence, wilt thou then forget   150
That on the banks of this delightful stream
We stood together; and that I, so long
A worshipper of Nature, hither came,
Unwearied in that service: rather say
With warmer love, oh! with far deeper zeal
Of holier love. Nor wilt thou then forget,
That after many wanderings, many years
Of absence, these steep woods and lofty cliffs,
And this green pastoral landscape, were to me
More dear, both for themselves, and for thy sake.   160

SAMUEL TAYLOR COLERIDGE

80   *Frost at Midnight*

THE Frost performs its secret ministry,
Unhelp'd by any wind. The owlet's cry
Came loud—and hark, again! loud as before.
The inmates of my cottage, all at rest,
Have left me to that solitude, which suits

Abstruser musings: save that at my side
My cradled infant slumbers peacefully.
'Tis calm indeed! so calm, that it disturbs
And vexes meditation with its strange
And extreme silentness. Sea, hill, and wood,   10
This populous village! Sea, and hill, and wood,
With all the numberless goings on of life,
Inaudible as dreams! The thin blue flame
Lies on my low-burnt fire, and quivers not:
Only that film, which flutter'd on the grate,
Still flutters there, the sole unquiet thing,
Methinks, its motion in this hush of nature
Gives it dim sympathies with me, who live,
Making it a companionable form,
With which I can hold commune. Idle thought!   20
But still the living spirit in our frame,
That loves not to behold a lifeless thing,
Transfuses into all its own delights
Its own volition, sometimes with deep faith,
And sometimes with fantastic playfulness.
Ah me! amus'd by no such curious toys
Of the self-watching subtilizing mind,
How often in my early school-boy days,
With most believing superstitious wish
Presageful have I gaz'd upon the bars,   30
To watch the *stranger* there! and oft belike,
With unclos'd lids, already had I dreamt
Of my sweet birthplace, and the old church-tower,
Whose bells, the poor man's only music, rang
From morn to evening, all the hot fair-day,
So sweetly, that they stirr'd and haunted me
With a wild pleasure, falling on mine ear
Most like articulate sounds of things to come!
So gaz'd I, till the soothing things, I dreamt,
Lull'd me to sleep, and sleep prolong'd my dreams!   40
And so I brooded all the following morn,
Aw'd by the stern preceptor's face, mine eye
Fix'd with mock study on my swimming book:
Save if the door half-open'd, and I snatch'd
A hasty glance, and still my heart leapt up,
For still I hop'd to see the *stranger's* face,
Townsman, or aunt, or sister more belov'd,
My play-mate when we both were cloth'd alike!

    Dear babe, that sleepest cradled by my side,
Whose gentle breathings, heard in this dead calm,   50

Fill up the interspersed vacancies
And momentary pauses of the thought!
My babe so beautiful! it fills my heart
With tender gladness, thus to look at thee,
And think, that thou shalt learn far other lore,
And in far other scenes! For I was rear'd
In the great city, pent mid cloisters dim,
And saw nought lovely but the sky and stars.
But *thou*, my babe! shalt wander, like a breeze,
By lakes and sandy shores, beneath the crags   60
Of ancient mountain, and beneath the clouds,
Which image in their bulk both lakes and shores
And mountain crags: so shalt thou see and hear
The lovely shapes and sounds intelligible
Of that eternal language, which thy God
Utters, who from eternity doth teach
Himself in all, and all things in himself.
Great universal Teacher! he shall mould
Thy spirit, and by giving make it ask.

Therefore all seasons shall be sweet to thee,   70
Whether the summer clothe the general earth
With greenness, or the redbreasts sit and sing
Betwixt the tufts of snow on the bare branch
Of mossy apple-tree, while all the thatch
Smokes in the sun-thaw: whether the eave-drops fall
Heard only in the trances of the blast,
Or whether the secret ministery of cold
Shall hang them up in silent icicles,
Quietly shining to the quiet moon,
Like those, my babe! which, ere to-morrow's warmth   80
Have capp'd their sharp keen points with pendulous drops,
Will catch thine eye, and with their novelty
Suspend thy little soul; then make thee shout,
And stretch and flutter from thy mother's arms
As thou would'st fly for very eagerness.

February 1798

SIR WILLIAM JONES

81   from *The Yarjurveda*

1. As a tree, the lord of the forest, even so, without fiction, is man: his hairs are as leaves; his skin, as exterior bark.

2. Through the skin flows blood; through the rind, sap: from a wounded man, therefore, blood gushes, as the vegetable fluid from a tree *that is* cut.

3. His muscles are as interwoven fibres; the membrane round his bones as interior bark, which is closely fixed: his bones are as the hard pieces of wood within: their marrow is composed of pith.

4. Since the tree, when felled, springs again, still fresher, from the root, from what root springs mortal man when felled by the hand of death?

5. Say not, he springs from seed: seed surely comes from the living. A tree, no doubt, rises from seed, and after death has a visible renewal.

6. But a tree which they have plucked up by the root, flourishes individually no more. From what root then springs mortal man when felled by the hand of death?

7. Say not he was born before; he is born: who can make him spring again to birth?

8. GOD, who is perfect wisdom, perfect happiness, He is the final refuge of the man, who has liberally bestowed his wealth, who has been firm in virtue, who knows and adores that Great One.

82   *A Hymn to the Night*

NIGHT approaches illumined with stars and planets, and looking on all sides with numberless eyes, overpowers all meaner lights. The immortal goddess pervades the firmament covering the low valleys and shrubs and the lofty mountains and trees, but soon she disturbs the gloom with celestial effulgence. Advancing with brightness, at length she recalls her sister Morning; and the nightly shade gradually melts away.

May she, at this time, be propitious! She, in whose early watch, we may calmly recline in our mansion, as birds repose on the tree.

Mankind now sleep in their towns; now herds and flocks peacefully slumber, and winged creatures, even swift falcons and vultures.

O Night, avert from us the she-wolf and the wolf; and oh! suffer us to pass thee in soothing rest!

O Morn, remove, in due time, this black, yet visible, overwhelming darkness which at present infolds me, as thou enablest me to remove the cloud of their debts.

Daughter of heaven, I approach thee with praise, as the cow approaches her milker; accept, O Night, not the hymn only, but the oblation of thy suppliant, who prays that his foes may be subdued.

ROBERT BURNS

83   *Love and Liberty. A Cantata*

RECITATIVO

WHEN lyart leaves bestrow the yird,
Or wavering like the Bauckie-bird,
   Bedim cauld Boreas' blast;
When hailstanes drive wi' bitter skyte,
And infant Frosts begin to bite,
   In hoary cranreuch drest;
Ae night at e'en a merry core
   O' randie, gangrel bodies,
In Poosie-Nansie's held the splore,
   To drink their orra dudies: 10
     Wi' quaffing, and laughing,
      They ranted an' they sang;
     Wi' jumping, an' thumping,
      The vera girdle rang.

First, niest the fire, in auld, red rags,
Ane sat; weel brac'd wi' mealy bags,
   And knapsack a' in order;
His doxy lay within his arm;
Wi' USQEBAE an' blankets warm,
   She blinket on her Sodger: 20
An' ay he gies the tozie drab
   The tither skelpan kiss,

83: 1 lyart] streaked   4 skyte] blow   6 cranreuch] frost   8 gangrel]
vagrant   9 splore] carousal   10 orra dudies] old clothes   14 girdle]
griddle   21 tozie] tipsy   22 skelpan] smacking

While she held up her greedy gab,
  Just like an aumous dish:
    Ilk smack still, did crack still,
    Just like a cadger's whip;
  Then staggering, an' swaggering,
    He roar'd this ditty up—

Air. *Tune, Soldier's joy*

I AM a Son of Mars who have been in many wars,
  And show my cuts and scars wherever I come;   30
This here was for a wench, and that other in a trench,
  When welcoming the French at the sound of the drum.
                              Lal de daudle &c.

My Prenticeship I past where my LEADER breath'd his last,
  When the bloody die was cast on the heights of ABRAM;
And I served out my TRADE when the gallant *game* was play'd,
  And the MORO low was laid at the sound of the drum.

I lastly was with Curtis among the *floating batt'ries*,
  And there I left for witness, an arm and a limb;
Yet let my Country need me, with ELLIOT to head me,
  I'd clatter on my stumps at the sound of a drum.   40

And now tho' I must beg, with a wooden arm and leg,
  And many a tatter'd rag hanging over my bum,
I'm as happy with my wallet, my bottle and my Callet,
  As when I us'd in scarlet to follow a drum.

What tho', with hoary locks, I must stand the winter shocks,
  Beneath the woods and rocks oftentimes for a home,
When the tother bag I sell and the tother bottle tell,
  I could meet a troop of HELL at the sound of a drum.

RECITATIVO

He ended; and the kebars sheuk,
  Aboon the chorus roar;   50
While frighted rattons backward leuk,
  An' seek the benmost bore:

23 gab] mouth   24 aumous dish] alms-dish   26 cadger] hawker   43 Callet]
wench   49 kebars] rafters   51 rattons] rats   52 benmost bore] inmost
crevice

A fairy FIDDLER frae the neuk,
　He skirl'd out, ENCORE.
But up arose the martial CHUCK,
　An' laid the loud uproar—

Air. *Tune, Sodger laddie*

I ONCE was a Maid, tho' I cannot tell when,
And still my delight is in proper young men:
Some one of a troop of DRAGOONS was my dadie,
No wonder I'm fond of a SODGER LADDIE.　　　　　　60
　　　　Sing lal de dal &c.

The first of my LOVES was a swaggering blade,
To rattle the thundering drum was his trade;
His leg was so tight and his cheek was so ruddy,
Transported I was with my SODGER LADDIE.

But the godly old Chaplain left him in the lurch,
The sword I forsook for the sake of the church;
He ventur'd the SOUL, and I risked the BODY,
'Twas then I prov'd false to my SODGER LADDIE.

Full soon I grew sick of my sanctified *Sot*,
The Regiment AT LARGE for a HUSBAND I got;　　　　70
From the gilded SPONTOON to the FIFE I was ready;
I asked no more but a SODGER LADDIE.

But the PEACE it reduc'd me to beg in despair,
Till I met my old boy in a CUNNINGHAM fair;
His RAGS REGIMENTAL they flutter'd so gaudy,
My heart it rejoic'd at a SODGER LADDIE.

And now I have lived—I know not how long,
And still I can join in a cup and a song;
But whilst with both hands I can hold the glass steady,
Here 's to thee, MY HERO, MY SODGER LADDIE.　　　　80

RECITATIVO

Then niest outspak a raucle Carlin,
Wha ken't fu' weel to cleek the Sterlin;
For mony a pursie she had hooked,
An' had in mony a well been douked:

54 skirl'd]yelled　　　55 CHUCK]Maid　　　71 SPONTOON]half-pike　　　81 raucle]
sturdy　　　82 cleek the Sterlin] pinch the ready

Her LOVE had been a HIGHLAND LADDIE,
But weary fa' the waefu' woodie!
Wi' sighs an' sobs she thus began
To wail her braw JOHN HIGHLANDMAN—

Air. *Tune, O an' ye were dead Gudeman*

A HIGHLAND lad my Love was born,
The lalland laws he held in scorn;   90
But he still was faithfu' to his clan,
My gallant, braw JOHN HIGHLANDMAN.

CHORUS

   Sing hey my braw John Highlandman!
   Sing ho my braw John Highlandman!
   There 's not a lad in a' the lan'
   Was match for my John Highlandman.

With his Philibeg, an' tartan Plaid,
An' guid Claymore down by his side,
The ladies' hearts he did trepan,
My gallant, braw John Highlandman.   100
      Sing hey &c.

We ranged a' from Tweed to Spey,
An' liv'd like lords an' ladies gay:
For a lalland face he feared none,
My gallant, braw John Highlandman.
      Sing hey &c.

They banish'd him beyond the sea,
But ere the bud was on the tree,
Adown my cheeks the pearls ran,
Embracing my John Highlandman.
      Sing hey &c.

But Och! they catch'd him at the last,
And bound him in a dungeon fast,   110
My curse upon them every one,
They've hang'd my braw John Highlandman.
      Sing hey &c.

86 weary fa'] plague upon   woodie] gallows   88 braw] gaily dressed   90 lalland]
lowland   97 Philibeg] kilt

And now a Widow I must mourn
The Pleasures that will ne'er return;
No comfort but a hearty can,
When I think on John Highlandman.
          Sing hey &c.

RECITATIVO

A pigmy Scraper wi' his Fiddle,
Wha us'd to trystes an' fairs to driddle,
Her strappan limb an' gausy middle,
          (He reach'd nae higher)   120
Had hol'd his HEARTIE like a riddle,
          An' blawn 't on fire.

Wi' hand on hainch, and upward e'e,
He croon'd his gamut, ONE, TWO, THREE,
Then in an ARIOSO key,
          The wee Apollo
Set off wi' ALLEGRETTO glee
          His GIGA SOLO—

          Air. *Tune, Whistle owre the lave o't*

LET me ryke up to dight that tear,
An' go wi' me an' be my DEAR;   130
An' then your every CARE an' FEAR
          May whistle owre the lave o't.

CHORUS

I am a Fiddler to my trade,
An' a' the tunes that e'er I play'd,
The sweetest still to WIFE or MAID,
          Was whistle owre the lave o't.

At KIRNS an' WEDDINS we'se be there,
An' O sae nicely 's we will fare!
We'll bowse about till Dadie CARE
          Sing whistle owre the lave o't.   140
          I am &c.

118 driddle] toddle   119 gausy] buxom   123 hainch] hip   129 ryke]
reach   dight] wipe   132 lave] rest   137 Kirns] harvest-homes

Sae merrily 's the banes we'll pyke,
An' sun oursells about the dyke;
An' at our leisure when ye like
    We'll whistle owre the lave o't.
        I am &c.

But bless me wi' your heav'n o' charms,
An' while I kittle hair on thairms
HUNGER, CAULD, an' a' sic harms
    May whistle owre the lave o't.
        I am &c.

RECITATIVO

Her charms had struck a sturdy CAIRD,
    As weel as poor GUTSCRAPER;   150
He taks the Fiddler by the beard,
    An' draws a roosty rapier—
He swoor by a' was swearing worth
    To speet him like a Pliver,
Unless he would from that time forth
    Relinquish her for ever:

Wi' ghastly e'e poor TWEEDLEDEE
    Upon his hunkers bended,
An' pray'd for grace wi' ruefu' face,
    An' so the quarrel ended;   160
But tho' his little heart did grieve,
    When round the TINKLER prest her,
He feign'd to snirtle in his sleeve
    When thus the CAIRD address'd her—

Air. *Tune, Clout the Caudron*

MY bonie lass I work in brass,
    A TINKLER is my station;
I've travell'd round all Christian ground
    In this my occupation;
I've ta'en the gold an' been enroll'd
    In many a noble squadron;   170
But vain they search'd when off I march'd
    To go an' clout the CAUDRON.
        I've ta'en the gold &c.

141 banes] bones   pyke] pick   146 kittle] tickle   thairms] catgut   149 CAIRD]
tinker   158 hunkers] hams   163 snirtle] snicker   172 clout] patch

Despise that SHRIMP, that withered IMP,
   With a' his noise an' cap'rin;
An' take a share, with those that bear
   The *budget* and the *apron*!
And *by* that STOWP! my faith an' houpe,
   And *by* that dear KILBAIGIE,
If e'er ye want, or meet with scant,
   May I ne'er weet my CRAIGIE!   180
        And by that Stowp, &c.

RECITATIVO

The Caird prevail'd—th' unblushing fair
   In his embraces sunk;
Partly wi' LOVE o'ercome sae sair,
   An' partly she was drunk:
SIR VIOLINO with an air,
   That show'd a man o' spunk,
Wish'd UNISON between the PAIR,
   An' made the bottle clunk
        To their health that night.

But hurchin Cupid shot a shaft,   190
   That play'd a DAME a shavie—
The Fiddler RAK'D her, FORE AND AFT,
   Behint the Chicken cavie:
Her lord, a wight of HOMER's craft,
   Tho' limpan wi' the Spavie,
He hirpl'd up an' lap like daft,
   An' shor'd them DAINTY DAVIE
        O' *boot* that night.

He was a care-defying blade,
   As ever BACCHUS listed!   200
Tho' Fortune sair upon him laid,
   His heart she ever miss'd it.
He had no WISH but—to be glad,
   Nor WANT but—when he thristed;
He hated nought but—to be sad,
   An' thus the Muse suggested
        His sang that night.

176 *budget*] tinker's bag of tools   177 STOWP] pot   180 CRAIGIE] throat
190 hurchin] urchin   191 shavie] trick   193 cavie] coop   195 Spavie]
spavin   196 hirpl'd] limped   lap] leapt   197 shor'd] offered   DAINTY
DAVIE] penis   198 *boot*] gratis

Air. *Tune, For a' that an' a' that*

I AM a BARD of no regard,
   Wi' gentle folks an' a' that;
But HOMER LIKE the glowran byke,   210
   Frae town to town I draw that.

CHORUS

For a' that an' a' that,
   An' twice as muckle 's a' that,
I've lost but ANE, I've TWA behin',
   I've WIFE ENEUGH for a' that.

I never drank the Muses' STANK,
   Castalia's burn an a' that,
But there it streams an' richly reams,
   My HELICON I ca' that.
           For a' that &c.

Great love I bear to all the FAIR,   220
   Their humble slave an' a' that;
But lordly WILL, I hold it still
   A mortal sin to thraw that.
           For a' that &c.

In raptures sweet this hour we meet,
   Wi' mutual love an' a' that;
But for how lang the FLIE MAY STANG,
   Let INCLINATION law that.
           For a' that &c.

Their tricks an' craft hae put me daft,
   They've ta'en me in, an' a' that,
But clear your decks an' here 's the SEX!   230
   I like the jads for a' that.
     For a' that an' a' that.
       An' twice as muckle 's a' that,
       My DEAREST BLUID to do them guid,
       They're welcome till 't for a' that.

210 glowran byke] staring crowd   216 STANK] pond   217 burn] brook
218 reams] foams   223 thraw] thwart   226 FLIE] fly   STANG] sting

RECITATIVO

So sung the BARD—and Nansie's waws
Shook with a thunder of applause
   Re-echo'd from each mouth!
They toom'd their pocks, they pawn'd their duds,
They scarcely left to coor their fuds   240
   To quench their lowan drouth:
Then owre again the jovial thrang
   The Poet did request
To lowse his PACK an' wale a sang,
   A BALLAD o' the best.
     He, rising, rejoicing,
       Between his TWA DEBORAHS,
     Looks round him an' found them
       Impatient for the Chorus.

   Air. *Tune, Jolly Mortals fill your glasses*

SEE the smoking bowl before us,   250
   Mark our jovial, ragged ring!
Round and round take up the Chorus,
   And in raptures let us sing—

CHORUS

A fig for those by law protected!
   LIBERTY's a glorious feast!
Courts for Cowards were erected,
   Churches built to please the PRIEST.

What is TITLE, what is TREASURE,
   What is REPUTATION's care?
If we lead a life of pleasure,   260
   'Tis no matter HOW or WHERE.
     A fig, &c.

With the ready trick and fable
   Round we wander all the day;
And at night, in barn or stable,
   Hug our doxies on the hay.
     A fig for &c.

236 waws] walls   239 toom'd] emptied   240 coor] cover   fuds] tails
241 lowan] flaming   244 lowse] untie

Does the train-attended CARRIAGE
  Thro' the country lighter rove?
Does the sober bed of MARRIAGE
  Witness brighter scenes of love?
      A fig for &c.

Life is all a VARIORUM,   270
  We regard not how it goes;
Let them cant about DECORUM,
  Who have character to lose.
      A fig for &c.

Here's to BUDGETS, BAGS and WALLETS!
  Here's to all the wandering train!
Here's our ragged BRATS and CALLETS!
  One and all cry out, AMEN!
    A fig for those by LAW protected,
      LIBERTY's a glorious feast!
    COURTS for cowards were erected,   280
      CHURCHES built to please the Priest.

ANNA LAETITIA BARBAULD

1743–1825

84   *To Mr [S. T.] C[olerid]ge*

MIDWAY the hill of science, after steep
And rugged paths that tire the unpractised feet,
A grove extends; in tangled mazes wrought,
And filled with strange enchantment:—dubious shapes
Flit through dim glades, and lure the eager foot
Of youthful ardour to eternal chase.
Dreams hang on every leaf: unearthly forms
Glide through the gloom; and mystic visions swim
Before the cheated sense. Athwart the mists,
Far into vacant space, huge shadows stretch   10
And seem realities; while things of life,
Obvious to sight and touch, all glowing round,
Fade to the hue of shadows.—Scruples here,
With filmy net, most like the autumnal webs
Of floating gossamer, arrest the foot
Of generous enterprise; and palsy hope

And fair ambition with the chilling touch
Of sickly hesitation and blank fear.
Nor seldom Indolence these lawns among
Fixes her turf-built seat; and wears the garb   20
Of deep philosophy, and museful sits
In dreamy twilight of the vacant mind,
Soothed by the whispering shade; for soothing soft
The shades; and vistas lengthening into air,
With moonbeam rainbows tinted.—Here each mind
Of finer mould, acute and delicate,
In its high progress to eternal truth
Rests for a space, in fairy bowers entranced;
And loves the softened light and tender gloom;
And, pampered with most unsubstantial food,   30
Looks down indignant on the grosser world,
And matter's cumbrous shapings. Youth beloved
Of Science—of the Muse beloved,—not here,
Not in the maze of metaphysic lore,
Build thou thy place of resting! lightly tread
The dangerous ground, on noble aims intent;
And be this Circe of the studious cell
Enjoyed, but still subservient. Active scenes
Shall soon with healthful spirit brace thy mind;
And fair exertion, for bright fame sustained,   40
For friends, for country, chase each spleen-fed fog
That blots the wide creation.—
Now heaven conduct thee with a parent's love!

MARY ROBINSON

85   *Modern Female Fashions*

A FORM, as any taper, fine;
    A head like half-pint bason;
Where golden cords, and bands entwine,
    As rich as fleece of JASON.

A pair of shoulders strong and wide,
    Like *country clown* enlisting;
Bare arms long dangling by the side,
    And shoes of ragged listing!

Cravats like towels, thick and broad,
   Long tippets made of bear-skin,   10
Muffs that a RUSSIAN might applaud,
   And *rouge* to spoil a fair skin.

Long petticoats to *hide* the feet,
   Silk hose with clocks of scarlet;
A load of perfume, sick'ning sweet,
   Bought of PARISIAN VARLET.

A bush of hair, the brow to shade,
   Sometimes the eyes to cover;
A necklace that might be display'd
   By OTAHEITEAN lover!   20

A bowl of straw to deck the head,
   Like porringer unmeaning;
A bunch of POPPIES flaming red,
   With motly ribands streaming.

Bare ears on either side the head,
   Like wood-wild savage SATYR;
Tinted with deep vermilion red,
   To shame the blush of nature.

Red elbows, gauzy gloves, that add
   An icy cov'ring merely;   30
A wadded coat, the shape to pad,
   Like Dutch-women—or nearly.

Such is CAPRICE! but, lovely kind!
   Oh! let each mental feature
Proclaim the labour of the *mind*,
   And leave your charms to NATURE.

86　　　　　*Modern Male Fashions*

CROPS like hedgehogs, high-crown'd hats,
　Whiskers like Jew MOSES;
Padded collars, thick cravats,
　And cheeks as red as roses.

Faces *painted pink* and *brown*;
　Waistcoats strip'd and gaudy;
Sleeves thrice doubled thick with down,
　And straps to brace the body.

Short great-coats that reach the knees,
　Boots like French postillion;　　　　　　　10
Worn the G—— race to please,
　But laugh'd at by the million.

Square-toed shoes, with silken strings,
　Pantaloons *not* fitting;
Finger deck'd with *wedding* rings,
　And small-clothes made of knitting.

Curricles so low, that they
　Along the ground seem dragging;
Hacks that weary half the day
　In Rotten-row are fagging.　　　　　　　20

Bull-dogs grim, and boxers bold,
　In noble trains attending;
Science which is bought with gold,
　And flatt'rers vice commending.

Hair-cords, and *plain* rings, to shew
　Many a LADY's favour,
BOUGHT by ev'ry vaunting *beau*,
　With mischievous endeavour.

Such is giddy FASHION's son!
　Such a MODERN LOVER!　　　　　　　30
Oh! wou'd their reign had ne'er begun!
　And may it soon BE OVER!

WILLIAM WORDSWORTH

from *Lyrical Ballads* (vol. ii)

87   ['There was a Boy']

There was a Boy, ye knew him well, ye Cliffs
And Islands of Winander! many a time,
At evening, when the stars had just begun
To move along the edges of the hills,
Rising or setting, would he stand alone,
Beneath the trees, or by the glimmering lake,
And there, with fingers interwoven, both hands
Press'd closely palm to palm and to his mouth
Uplifted, he, as through an instrument,
Blew mimic hootings to the silent owls   10
That they might answer him. And they would shout
Across the wat'ry vale and shout again
Responsive to his call, with quivering peals,
And long halloos, and screams, and echoes loud
Redoubled and redoubled, a wild scene
Of mirth and jocund din. And, when it chanced
That pauses of deep silence mock'd his skill,
Then, sometimes, in that silence, while he hung
Listening, a gentle shock of mild surprize
Has carried far into his heart the voice   20
Of mountain torrents, or the visible scene
Would enter unawares into his mind
With all its solemn imagery, its rocks,
Its woods, and that uncertain heaven, receiv'd
Into the bosom of the steady lake.
     Fair are the woods, and beauteous is the spot,
The vale where he was born: the Church-yard hangs
Upon a slope above the village school,
And there along that bank when I have pass'd
At evening, I believe, that near his grave   30
A full half-hour together I have stood,
Mute—for he died when he was ten years old.

88   ['Strange fits of passion I have known']

Strange fits of passion I have known,
And I will dare to tell,
But in the lover's ear alone,
What once to me befel.

When she I lov'd, was strong and gay
And like a rose in June,
I to her cottage bent my way,
Beneath the evening moon.

Upon the moon I fix'd my eye,
All over the wide lea;   10
My horse trudg'd on, and we drew nigh
Those paths so dear to me.

And now we reach'd the orchard plot,
And, as we climb'd the hill,
Towards the roof of Lucy's cot
The moon descended still.

In one of those sweet dreams I slept,
Kind Nature's gentlest boon!
And, all the while, my eyes I kept
On the descending moon.   20

My horse mov'd on; hoof after hoof
He rais'd and never stopp'd:
When down behind the cottage roof
At once the planet dropp'd.

What fond and wayward thoughts will slide
Into a Lover's head—
'O mercy!' to myself I cried,
'If Lucy should be dead!'

89 *Song*

She dwelt among th' untrodden ways
    Beside the springs of Dove,
A Maid whom there were none to praise
    And very few to love.

A Violet by a mossy stone
    Half-hidden from the Eye!
—Fair, as a star when only one
    Is shining in the sky!

She *liv'd* unknown, and few could know
    When Lucy ceas'd to be;   10
But she is in her Grave, and Oh!
    The difference to me.

90 ['A slumber did my spirit seal']

A slumber did my spirit seal,
    I had no human fears:
She seem'd a thing that could not feel
    The touch of earthly years.

No motion has she now, no force
    She neither hears nor sees
Roll'd round in earth's diurnal course
    With rocks and stones and trees!

91 *Lucy Gray*

Oft I had heard of Lucy Gray,
And when I cross'd the Wild,
I chanc'd to see at break of day
The solitary Child.

No Mate, no comrade Lucy knew;
She dwelt on a wild Moor,
The sweetest Thing that ever grew
Beside a human door!

You yet may spy the Fawn at play,
The Hare upon the Green; 10
But the sweet face of Lucy Gray
Will never more be seen.

'To-night will be a stormy night,
You to the Town must go,
And take a lantern, Child, to light
Your Mother thro' the snow.'

'That, Father! will I gladly do;
'Tis scarcely afternoon—
The Minster-clock has just struck two,
And yonder is the Moon.' 20

At this the Father rais'd his hook
And snapp'd a faggot-band;
He plied his work, and Lucy took
The lantern in her hand.

Not blither is the mountain roe,
With many a wanton stroke
Her feet disperse the powd'ry snow
That rises up like smoke.

The storm came on before its time,
She wander'd up and down, 30
And many a hill did Lucy climb
But never reach'd the Town.

The wretched Parents all that night
Went shouting far and wide;
But there was neither sound nor sight
To serve them for a guide.

At day-break on a hill they stood
That overlook'd the Moor;
And thence they saw the Bridge of Wood
A furlong from their door. 40

And now they homeward turn'd, and cry'd
'In Heaven we all shall meet!'
When in the snow the Mother spied
The print of Lucy's feet.

Then downward from the steep hill's edge
They track'd the footmarks small;

And through the broken hawthorn-hedge,
And by the long stone-wall;

And then an open field they cross'd,
The marks were still the same;   50
They track'd them on, nor ever lost,
And to the Bridge they came.

They follow'd from the snowy bank
The footmarks, one by one,
Into the middle of the plank,
And further there were none.

Yet some maintain that to this day
She is a living Child,
That you may see sweet Lucy Gray
Upon the lonesome Wild.   60

O'er rough and smooth she trips along,
And never looks behind;
And sings a solitary song
That whistles in the wind.

92   *Nutting*

                                    It seems a day,
(I speak of one from many singled out)
One of those heavenly days which cannot die,
When forth I sallied from our cottage-door,
And with a wallet o'er my shoulder slung,
A nutting crook in hand, I turn'd my steps
Towards the distant woods, a Figure quaint,
Trick'd out in proud disguise of Beggar's weeds
Put on for the occasion, by advice
And exhortation of my frugal Dame.   10
Motley accoutrement! of power to smile
At thorns, and brakes, and brambles, and, in truth,
More ragged than need was. Among the woods,
And o'er the pathless rocks, I forc'd my way
Until, at length, I came to one dear nook
Unvisited, where not a broken bough
Droop'd with its wither'd leaves, ungracious sign
Of devastation, but the hazels rose
Tall and erect, with milk-white clusters hung,
A virgin scene!—A little while I stood,   20
Breathing with such suppression of the heart

As joy delights in; and with wise restraint
Voluptuous, fearless of a rival, eyed
The banquet, or beneath the trees I sate
Among the flowers, and with the flowers I play'd;
A temper known to those, who, after long
And weary expectation, have been bless'd
With sudden happiness beyond all hope.—
—Perhaps it was a bower beneath whose leaves
The violets of five seasons re-appear   30
And fade, unseen by any human eye,
Where fairy water-breaks do murmur on
For ever, and I saw the sparkling foam,
And with my cheek on one of those green stones
That, fleec'd with moss, beneath the shady trees,
Lay round me scatter'd like a flock of sheep,
I heard the murmur and the murmuring sound,
In that sweet mood when pleasure loves to pay
Tribute to ease, and, of its joy secure
The heart luxuriates with indifferent things,   40
Wasting its kindliness on stocks and stones,
And on the vacant air. Then up I rose,
And dragg'd to earth both branch and bough, with crash
And merciless ravage; and the shady nook
Of hazels, and the green and mossy bower
Deform'd and sullied, patiently gave up
Their quiet being: and unless I now
Confound my present feelings with the past,
Even then, when from the bower I turn'd away,
Exulting, rich beyond the wealth of kings   50
I felt a sense of pain when I beheld
The silent trees and the intruding sky.—

Then, dearest Maiden! move along these shades
In gentleness of heart, with gentle hand
Touch,—for there is a Spirit in the woods.

93   *A Fragment*

Between two sister moorland rills
There is a spot that seems to lie
Sacred to flowrets of the hills,
And sacred to the sky.
And in this smooth and open dell
There is a tempest-stricken tree;
A corner-stone by lightning cut,

The last stone of a cottage hut;
And in this dell you see
A thing no storm can e'er destroy,   10
The shadow of a Danish Boy.

In clouds above, the lark is heard,
He sings his blithest and his best;
But in this lonesome nook the bird
Did never build his nest.
No beast, no bird hath here his home;
The bees borne on the breezy air
Pass high above those fragrant bells
To other flowers, to other dells,
Nor ever linger there.   20
The Danish Boy walks here alone:
The lovely dell is all his own.

A spirit of noon day is he,
He seems a Form of flesh and blood;
A piping Shepherd he might be,
A Herd-boy of the wood.
A regal vest of fur he wears,
In colour like a raven's wing;
It fears nor rain, nor wind, nor dew,
But in the storm 'tis fresh and blue   30
As budding pines in Spring;
His helmet has a vernal grace,
Fresh as the bloom upon his face.

A harp is from his shoulder slung;
He rests the harp upon his knee,
And there in a forgotten tongue
He warbles melody.
Of flocks and herds both far and near
He is the darling and the joy,
And often, when no cause appears,   40
The mountain ponies prick their ears,
They hear the Danish Boy,
While in the dell he sits alone
Beside the tree and corner-stone.

When near this blasted tree you pass,
Two sods are plainly to be seen
Close at its root, and each with grass
Is cover'd fresh and green.
Like turf upon a new-made grave

These two green sods together lie,   50
Nor heat, nor cold, nor rain, nor wind
Can these two sods together bind,
Nor sun, nor earth, nor sky,
But side by side the two are laid,
As if just sever'd by the spade.

There sits he: in his face you spy
No trace of a ferocious air,
Nor ever was a cloudless sky
So steady or so fair.
The lovely Danish Boy is blest   60
And happy in his flowery cove;
From bloody deeds his thoughts are far;
And yet he warbles songs of war;
They seem like songs of love,
For calm and gentle is his mien;
Like a dead Boy he is serene.

94   *Michael*

A Pastoral Poem

IF from the public way you turn your steps
Up the tumultuous brook of Green-head Gill,
You will suppose that with an upright path
Your feet must struggle; in such bold ascent
The pastoral Mountains front you, face to face.
But, courage! for beside that boisterous Brook
The mountains have all open'd out themselves,
And made a hidden valley of their own.
No habitation there is seen; but such
As journey thither find themselves alone   10
With a few sheep, with rocks and stones, and kites
That overhead are sailing in the sky.

It is in truth an utter solitude,
Nor should I have made mention of this Dell
But for one object which you might pass by,
Might see and notice not. Beside the brook
There is a straggling heap of unhewn stones!
And to that place a story appertains,
Which, though it be ungarnish'd with events,
Is not unfit, I deem, for the fire-side,   20

Or for the summer shade. It was the first,
The earliest of those tales that spake to me
Of Shepherds, dwellers in the vallies, men
Whom I already lov'd, not verily
For their own sakes, but for the fields and hills
Where was their occupation and abode.
And hence this Tale, while I was yet a boy
Careless of books, yet having felt the power
Of Nature, by the gentle agency
Of natural objects led me on to feel   30
For passions that were not my own, and think
At random and imperfectly indeed
On man; the heart of man and human life.
Therefore, although it be a history
Homely and rude, I will relate the same
For the delight of a few natural hearts,
And with yet fonder feeling, for the sake
Of youthful Poets, who among these Hills
Will be my second self when I am gone.

Upon the Forest-side in Grasmere Vale   40
There dwelt a Shepherd, Michael was his name,
An old man, stout of heart, and strong of limb.
His bodily frame had been from youth to age
Of an unusual strength; his mind was keen
Intense and frugal, apt for all affairs,
And in his Shepherd's calling he was prompt
And watchful more than ordinary men.
Hence he had learn'd the meaning of all winds,
Of blasts of every tone, and often-times
When others heeded not, He heard the South   50
Make subterraneous music, like the noise
Of Bagpipers on distant Highland hills;
The Shepherd, at such warning, of his flock
Bethought him, and he to himself would say
The winds are now devising work for me!
And truly at all times the storm, that drives
The Traveller to a shelter, summon'd him
Up to the mountains: he had been alone
Amid the heart of many thousand mists
That came to him and left him on the heights.   60
So liv'd he till his eightieth year was pass'd.

And grossly that man errs, who should suppose
That the green Valleys, and the Streams and Rocks
Were things indifferent to the Shepherd's thoughts.

Fields, where with chearful spirits he had breath'd
The common air; the hills, which he so oft
Had climb'd with vigorous steps; which had impress'd
So many incidents upon his mind
Of hardship, skill or courage, joy or fear;
Which like a book preserv'd the memory   70
Of the dumb animals, whom he had sav'd,
Had fed or shelter'd, linking to such acts,
So grateful in themselves, the certainty
Of honorable gains; these fields, these hills
Which were his living Being, even more
Than his own Blood—what could they less? had laid
Strong hold on his affections, were to him
A pleasurable feeling of blind love,
The pleasure which there is in life itself.

He had not passed his days in singleness.   80
He had a Wife, a comely Matron, old
Though younger than himself full twenty years.
She was a woman of a stirring life
Whose heart was in her house: two wheels she had
Of antique form, this large for spinning wool,
That small for flax, and if one wheel had rest,
It was because the other was at work.
The Pair had but one Inmate in their house,
An only Child, who had been born to them
When Michael telling o'er his years began   90
To deem that he was old, in Shepherd's phrase,
With one foot in the grave. This only son,
With two brave sheep dogs tried in many a storm,
The one of an inestimable worth,
Made all their Household. I may truly say,
That they were as a proverb in the vale
For endless industry. When day was gone,
And from their occupations out of doors
The Son and Father were come home, even then
Their labour did not cease, unless when all   100
Turn'd to their cleanly supper-board, and there
Each with a mess of pottage and skimm'd milk,
Sate round their basket pil'd with oaten cakes,
And their plain home-made cheese. Yet when their meal
Was ended, LUKE (for so the Son was nam'd)
And his old Father, both betook themselves
To such convenient work, as might employ
Their hands by the fire-side; perhaps to card
Wool for the House-wife's spindle, or repair

Some injury done to sickle, flail, or scythe,   110
Or other implement of house or field.
Down from the ceiling by the chimney's edge,
Which in our ancient uncouth country style
Did with a huge projection overbrow
Large space beneath, as duly as the light
Of day grew dim, the House-wife hung a lamp;
An aged utensil, which had perform'd
Service beyond all others of its kind.
Early at evening did it burn and late,
Surviving Comrade of uncounted Hours   120
Which going by from year to year had found
And left the Couple neither gay perhaps
Nor chearful, yet with objects and with hopes
Living a life of eager industry.
And now, when LUKE was in his eighteenth year,
There by the light of this old lamp they sate,
Father and Son, while late into the night
The House-wife plied her own peculiar work,
Making the cottage thro' the silent hours
Murmur as with the sound of summer flies.   130
Not with a waste of words, but for the sake
Of pleasure, which I know that I shall give
To many living now, I of this Lamp
Speak thus minutely: for there are no few
Whose memories will bear witness to my tale.
The Light was famous in its neighbourhood,
And was a public Symbol of the life,
The thrifty Pair had liv'd. For, as it chanc'd,
Their Cottage on a plot of rising ground
Stood single, with large prospect North and South,   140
High into Easedale, up to Dunmal-Raise,
And Westward to the village near the Lake.
And from this constant light so regular
And so far seen, the House itself by all
Who dwelt within the limits of the vale,
Both old and young, was nam'd The Evening Star.

Thus living on through such a length of years,
The Shepherd, if he lov'd himself, must needs
Have lov'd his Help-mate; but to Michael's heart
This Son of his old age was yet more dear—   150
Effect which might perhaps have been produc'd
By that instinctive tenderness, the same
Blind Spirit, which is in the blood of all,
Or that a child, more than all other gifts,

Brings hope with it, and forward-looking thoughts,
And stirrings of inquietude, when they
By tendency of nature needs must fail.
From such, and other causes, to the thoughts
Of the old Man his only Son was now
The dearest object that he knew on earth.   160
Exceeding was the love he bare to him,
His Heart and his Heart's joy! For oftentimes
Old Michael, while he was a babe in arms,
Had done him female service, not alone
For dalliance and delight, as is the use
Of Fathers, but with patient mind enforc'd
To acts of tenderness; and he had rock'd
His cradle with a woman's gentle hand.

And in a later time, ere yet the Boy
Had put on Boy's attire, did Michael love,   170
Albeit of a stern unbending mind,
To have the young one in his sight, when he
Had work by his own door, or when he sate
With sheep before him on his Shepherd's stool,
Beneath that large old Oak, which near their door
Stood, and from its enormous breadth of shade
Chosen for the Shearer's covert from the sun,
Thence in our rustic dialect was call'd
The CLIPPING TREE, a name which yet it bears.
There, while they two were sitting in the shade,   180
With others round them, earnest all and blithe,
Would Michael exercise his heart with looks
Of fond correction and reproof bestow'd
Upon the child, if he disturb'd the sheep
By catching at their legs, or with his shouts
Scar'd them, while they lay still beneath the shears.
And when by Heaven's good grace the Boy grew up
A healthy Lad, and carried in his cheek
Two steady roses that were five years old,
Then Michael from a winter coppice cut   190
With his own hand a sapling, which he hoop'd
With iron, making it throughout in all
Due requisites a perfect Shepherd's Staff,
And gave it to the Boy; wherewith equipp'd
He as a Watchman oftentimes was plac'd
At gate or gap, to stem or turn the flock,
And to his office prematurely call'd
There stood the urchin, as you will divine,
Something between a hindrance and a help,

And for this cause not always, I believe,　　　　　200
Receiving from his Father hire of praise.
Though nought was left undone which staff or voice,
Or looks, or threatening gestures could perform.
But soon as Luke, full ten years old, could stand
Against the mountain blasts, and to the heights,
Not fearing toil, nor length of weary ways,
He with his Father daily went, and they
Were as companions, why should I relate
That objects which the Shepherd loved before
Were dearer now? that from the Boy there came　　210
Feelings and emanations, things which were
Light to the sun and music to the wind;
And that the Old Man's heart seemed born again.
Thus in his Father's sight the Boy grew up:
And now when he had reached his eighteenth year,
He was his comfort and his daily hope.

While this good household thus were living on
From day to day, to Michael's ear there came
Distressful tidings. Long before the time
Of which I speak, the Shepherd had been bound　　220
In surety for his Brother's Son, a man
Of an industrious life, and ample means,
But unforeseen misfortunes suddenly
Had press'd upon him, and old Michael now
Was summon'd to discharge the forfeiture,
A grievous penalty, but little less
Than half his substance. This un-look'd for claim
At the first hearing, for a moment took
More hope out of his life than he supposed
That any old man ever could have lost.　　　　230
As soon as he had gather'd so much strength
That he could look his trouble in the face,
It seem'd that his sole refuge was to sell
A portion of his patrimonial fields.
Such was his first resolve; he thought again,
And his heart fail'd him. 'Isabel,' said he,
Two evenings after he had heard the news,
'I have been toiling more than seventy years,
And in the open sun-shine of God's love
Have we all liv'd, yet if these fields of ours　　240
Should pass into a Stranger's hand, I think
That I could not lie quiet in my grave.
Our lot is a hard lot; the Sun itself
Has scarcely been more diligent than I,

And I have liv'd to be a fool at last
To my own family. An evil Man
That was, and made an evil choice, if he
Were false to us; and if he were not false,
There are ten thousand to whom loss like this
Had been no sorrow. I forgive him—but   250
'Twere better to be dumb than to talk thus.

When I began, my purpose was to speak
Of remedies and of a chearful hope.
Our Luke shall leave us, Isabel; the land
Shall not go from us, and it shall be free,
He shall possess it, free as is the wind
That passes over it. We have, thou knowest,
Another Kinsman, he will be our friend
In this distress. He is a prosperous man,
Thriving in trade, and Luke to him shall go,   260
And with his Kinsman's help and his own thrift,
He quickly will repair this loss, and then
May come again to us. If here he stay,
What can be done? Where every one is poor
What can be gain'd?' At this, the old man paus'd,
And Isabel sate silent, for her mind
Was busy, looking back into past times.
There's Richard Bateman, thought she to herself,
He was a parish-boy—at the church-door
They made a gathering for him, shillings, pence,   270
And halfpennies, wherewith the Neighbours bought
A Basket, which they fill'd with Pedlar's wares,
And with this Basket on his arm, the Lad
Went up to London, found a Master there,
Who out of many chose the trusty Boy
To go and overlook his merchandise
Beyond the seas, where he grew wond'rous rich,
And left estates and monies to the poor,
And at his birth-place built a Chapel, floor'd
With Marble, which he sent from foreign lands.   280
These thoughts, and many others of like sort,
Pass'd quickly thro' the mind of Isabel,
And her face brighten'd. The Old Man was glad,
And thus resum'd. 'Well! Isabel, this scheme
These two days has been meat and drink to me.
Far more than we have lost is left us yet.
—We have enough—I wish indeed that I
Were younger, but this hope is a good hope.
—Make ready Luke's best garments, of the best
Buy for him more, and let us send him forth   290

To-morrow, or the next day, or to-night:
—If he could go, the Boy should go to-night.'

Here Michael ceas'd, and to the fields went forth
With a light heart. The House-wife for five days
Was restless morn and night, and all day long
Wrought on with her best fingers to prepare
Things needful for the journey of her Son.
But Isabel was glad when Sunday came
To stop her in her work; for, when she lay
By Michael's side, she for the two last nights   300
Heard him, how he was troubled in his sleep:
And when they rose at morning she could see
That all his hopes were gone. That day at noon
She said to Luke, while they two by themselves
Were sitting at the door, 'Thou must not go,
We have no other Child but thee to lose,
None to remember—do not go away,
For if thou leave thy Father he will die.'
The Lad made answer with a jocund voice,
And Isabel, when she had told her fears,   310
Recover'd heart. That evening her best fare
Did she bring forth, and all together sate
Like happy people round a Christmas fire.
Next morning Isabel resum'd her work,
And all the ensuing week the house appear'd
As cheerful as a grove in Spring: at length
The expected letter from their Kinsman came,
With kind assurances that he would do
His utmost for the welfare of the Boy,
To which requests were added that forthwith   320
He might be sent to him. Ten times or more
The letter was read over; Isabel
Went forth to shew it to the neighbours round:
Nor was there at that time on English Land
A prouder heart than Luke's. When Isabel
Had to her house return'd, the Old Man said,
'He shall depart to-morrow.' To this word
The House-wife answered, talking much of things
Which, if at such short notice he should go,
Would surely be forgotten. But at length   330
She gave consent, and Michael was at ease.

Near the tumultous brook of Green-head Gill,
In that deep Valley, Michael had design'd
To build a Sheep-fold, and, before he heard

The tidings of his melancholy loss,
For this same purpose he had gathered up
A heap of stones, which close to the brook side
Lay thrown together, ready for the work.
With Luke that evening thitherward he walk'd;
And soon as they had reach'd the place he stopp'd,   340
And thus the Old Man spake to him. 'My Son,
To-morrow thou wilt leave me; with full heart
I look upon thee, for thou art the same
That wert a promise to me ere thy birth,
And all thy life hast been my daily joy.
I will relate to thee some little part
Of our two histories; 'twill do thee good
When thou art from me, even if I should speak
Of things thou canst not know of.—After thou
First cam'st into the world, as it befalls   350
To new-born infants, thou didst sleep away
Two days, and blessings from thy Father's tongue
Then fell upon thee. Day by day pass'd on,
And still I lov'd thee with encreasing love.
Never to living ear came sweeter sounds
Than when I heard thee by our own fire-side
First uttering without words a natural tune,
When thou, a feeding babe, didst in thy joy
Sing at thy Mother's breast. Month follow'd month,
And in the open fields my life was pass'd   360
And in the mountains, else I think that thou
Hadst been brought up upon thy father's knees.
—But we were playmates, Luke; among these hills,
As well thou know'st, in us the old and young
Have play'd together, nor with me didst thou
Lack any pleasure which a boy can know.'

Luke had a manly heart; but at these words
He sobb'd aloud; the Old Man grasp'd his hand,
And said, 'Nay do not take it so—I see
That these are things of which I need not speak.   370
—Even to the utmost I have been to thee
A kind and a good Father: and herein
I but repay a gift which I myself
Receiv'd at others hands, for, though now old
Beyond the common life of man, I still
Remember them who lov'd me in my youth.
Both of them sleep together: here they liv'd
As all their Forefathers had done, and when
At length their time was come, they were not loth

To give their bodies to the family mold.　　　　　　380
I wish'd that thou should'st live the life they liv'd.
But 'tis a long time to look back, my Son,
And see so little gain from sixty years.
These fields were burthen'd when they came to me;
'Till I was forty years of age, not more
Than half of my inheritance was mine.
I toil'd and toil'd; God bless'd me in my work,
And 'till these three weeks past the land was free.
—It looks as if it never could endure
Another Master. Heaven forgive me, Luke,　　　　390
If I judge ill for thee, but it seems good
That thou should'st go.' At this the Old Man paus'd,
Then, pointing to the Stones near which they stood,
Thus, after a short silence, he resum'd:
'This was a work for us, and now, my Son,
It is a work for me. But, lay one Stone—
Here, lay it for me, Luke, with thine own hands.
I for the purpose brought thee to this place.
Nay, Boy, be of good hope:—we both may live
To see a better day. At eighty-four　　　　　　　400
I still am strong and stout;—do thou thy part,
I will do mine.—I will begin again
With many tasks that were resign'd to thee;
Up to the heights, and in among the storms,
Will I without thee go again, and do
All works which I was wont to do alone,
Before I knew thy face.—Heaven bless thee, Boy!
Thy heart these two weeks has been beating fast
With many hopes—it should be so—yes—yes—
I knew that thou could'st never have a wish　　　410
To leave me, Luke, thou hast been bound to me
Only by links of love, when thou art gone
What will be left to us!—But, I forget
My purposes. Lay now the corner-stone,
As I requested, and hereafter, Luke,
When thou art gone away, should evil men
Be thy companions, let this Sheep-fold be
Thy anchor and thy shield; amid all fear
And all temptation, let it be to thee
An emblem of the life thy Fathers liv'd,　　　　　420
Who, being innocent, did for that cause
Bestir them in good deeds. Now, fare thee well—
When thou return'st, thou in this place wilt see
A work which is not here, a covenant
'Twill be between us—but whatever fate

Befall thee, I shall love thee to the last,
And bear thy memory with me to the grave.'

The Shepherd ended here; and Luke stoop'd down,
And as his Father had requested, laid
The first stone of the Sheep-fold; at the sight   430
The Old Man's grief broke from him, to his heart
He press'd his Son, he kissed him and wept;
And to the House together they return'd.

Next morning, as had been resolv'd, the Boy
Began his journey, and when he had reach'd
The public Way, he put on a bold face;
And all the Neighbours as he pass'd their doors
Came forth, with wishes and with farewell pray'rs,
That follow'd him 'till he was out of sight.
A good report did from their Kinsman come,   440
Of Luke and his well-doing; and the Boy
Wrote loving letters, full of wond'rous news,
Which, as the House-wife phrased it, were throughout
The prettiest letters that were ever seen.
Both parents read them with rejoicing hearts.
So, many months pass'd on: and once again
The Shepherd went about his daily work
With confident and cheerful thoughts; and now
Sometimes when he could find a leisure hour
He to that valley took his way, and there   450
Wrought at the Sheep-fold. Meantime Luke began
To slacken in his duty, and at length
He in the dissolute city gave himself
To evil courses: ignominy and shame
Fell on him, so that he was driven at last
To seek a hiding-place beyond the seas.

There is a comfort in the strength of love;
'Twill make a thing endurable, which else
Would break the heart:—Old Michael found it so.
I have convers'd with more than one who well   460
Remember the Old Man, and what he was
Years after he had heard this heavy news.
His bodily frame had been from youth to age
Of an unusual strength. Among the rocks
He went, and still look'd up upon the sun,
And listen'd to the wind; and as before
Perform'd all kinds of labour for his Sheep,
And for the land his small inheritance.

And to that hollow Dell from time to time
Did he repair, to build the Fold of which   470
His flock had need. 'Tis not forgotten yet
The pity which was then in every heart
For the Old Man—and 'tis believ'd by all
That many and many a day he thither went,
And never lifted up a single stone.

There, by the Sheep-fold, sometimes was he seen
Sitting alone, with that his faithful Dog,
Then old, beside him, lying at his feet.
The length of full seven years from time to time
He at the building of this Sheep-fold wrought,   480
And left the work unfinished when he died.

Three years, or little more, did Isabel,
Survive her Husband: at her death the estate
Was sold, and went into a Stranger's hand.
The Cottage which was nam'd The Evening Star
Is gone, the ploughshare has been through the ground
On which it stood; great changes have been wrought
In all the neighbourhood, yet the Oak is left
That grew beside their Door; and the remains
Of the unfinished Sheep-fold may be seen   490
Beside the boisterous brook of Green-head Gill.

[1801]

ROBERT BURNS

95   *Holy Willie's Prayer*

And send the Godly in a pet to pray—
                    POPE

ARGUMENT

Holy Willie was a rather oldish batchelor Elder in the parish of Mauchline,
and much and justly famed for that polemical chattering which ends in
tippling Orthodoxy, and for that Spiritualized Bawdry which refines to
Liquorish Devotion.—In a Sessional process with a gentleman in Mauch-
line, a Mr Gavin Hamilton, Holy Willie, and his priest, father Auld, after

full hearing in the Presbytry of Ayr, came off but second best; owing partly
to the oratorical powers of Mr Robt Aiken, Mr Hamilton's Counsel; but
chiefly to Mr Hamilton's being one of the most irreproachable and truly
respectable characters in the country.—On losing his Process, the Muse
overheard him at his devotions as follows—

> O THOU that in the heavens does dwell!
> Wha, as it pleases best thysel,
> Sends ane to heaven and ten to h—ll,
> > A' for thy glory!
> And no for ony gude or ill
> > They've done before thee.—
>
> I bless and praise thy matchless might,
> When thousands thou has left in night,
> That I am here before thy sight,
> > For gifts and grace,   10
> A burning and a shining light
> > To a' this place.—
>
> What was I, or my generation,
> That I should get such exaltation?
> I, wha deserv'd most just damnation,
> > For broken laws
> Sax thousand years ere my creation,
> > Thro' Adam's cause!
>
> When from my mother's womb I fell,
> Thou might hae plunged me deep in hell,   20
> To gnash my gooms, and weep, and wail,
> > In burning lakes,
> Where damned devils roar and yell
> > Chain'd to their stakes.—
>
> Yet I am here, a chosen sample,
> To shew thy grace is great and ample:
> I'm here, a pillar o' thy temple
> > Strong as a rock,
> A guide, a ruler and example
> > To a' thy flock.—   30
>
> But yet—O L—d—confess I must—
> At times I'm fash'd wi' fleshly lust;

95:   21 gooms] gums   32 fash'd] irked

And sometimes too, in warldly trust
　　　　Vile Self gets in;
But thou remembers we are dust,
　　　　Defil'd wi' sin.—

O L—d—yestreen—thou kens—wi' Meg—
Thy pardon I sincerely beg!
O may 't ne'er be a living plague,
　　　　To my dishonor!　　　　　　　　　　40
And I'll ne'er lift a lawless leg
　　　　Again upon her.—

Besides, I farther maun avow,
Wi' Leezie's lass, three times—I trow—
But L—d, that friday I was fou
　　　　When I cam near her;
Or else, thou kens, thy servant true
　　　　Wad never steer her.—

Maybe thou lets this fleshy thorn
Buffet thy servant e'en and morn,　　　　　50
Lest he o'er proud and high should turn,
　　　　That he 's sae gifted;
If sae, thy hand maun e'en be borne
　　　　Untill thou lift it.—

L—d bless thy Chosen in this place,
For here thou has a chosen race:
But G—d, confound their stubborn face,
　　　　And blast their name,
Wha bring thy rulers to disgrace
　　　　And open shame.—　　　　　　　　60

L—d mind Gaun Hamilton's deserts!
He drinks, and swears, and plays at cartes,
Yet has sae mony taking arts
　　　　Wi' Great and Sma',
Frae G—d's ain priest the people's hearts
　　　　He steals awa.—

And when we chasten'd him therefore,
Thou kens how he bred sic a splore,

45　fou] drunk　　　48　steer] meddle with　　　68　splore] row

And set the warld in a roar
        O' laughin at us: 70
Curse thou his basket and his store,
        Kail and potatoes.—

L—d hear my earnest cry and prayer
Against that Presbytry of Ayr!
Thy strong right hand, L—d, make it bare
        Upon their heads!
L—d visit them, and dinna spare,
        For their misdeeds!

O L—d my G–d, that glib-tongu'd Aiken!
My very heart and flesh are quaking   80
To think how I sat, sweating, shaking,
        And p–ss'd wi' dread,
While Auld wi' hingin lip gaed sneaking
        And hid his head!

L—d, in thy day o' vengeance try him!
L—d visit him that did employ him!
And pass not in thy mercy by them,
        Nor hear their prayer;
But for thy people's sake destroy them,
        And dinna spare!   90

But L—d, remember me and mine
Wi' mercies temporal and divine!
That I for grace and gear may shine,
        Excell'd by nane!
And a' the glory shall be thine!
        AMEN! AMEN!

ANONYMOUS

96   *The Bleeding Nun*

WHERE yon proud turrets crown the rock,
    Seest thou a warrior stand?
He sighs to hear the castle clock
    Say midnight is at hand.

83 hingin] sneering   93 gear] wealth

It strikes, and now his lady fair
　　Comes tripping from her hall,
Her heart is rent by deep despair,
　　And tears in torrents fall.

—'Ah! woe is me, my love,' she cried,
　　'What anguish wrings my heart:　　　　　　10
Ah! woe is me,' she said, and sigh'd,
　　'We must for ever part.

'Know, ere three days are past and flown,
　　(Tears choak the piteous tale!)
A parents vow, till now unknown,
　　Devotes me to the veil.'—

—'Not so, my Agnes!' Raymond cried,
　　'For leave thee will I never;
Thou art mine, and I am thine,
　　Body and soul for ever!　　　　　　　　20

'Then quit thy cruel father's bower,
　　And fly, my love, with me.'—
'Ah! how can I escape his power,
　　Or who can set me free.

'I cannot leap yon wall so high,
　　Nor swim the fosse with thee;
I can but wring my hands, and sigh
　　That none can set me free.'—

—'Now list, my lady, list, my love,
　　I pray thee list to me,　　　　　　　　　30
For I can all your fears remove,
　　And I can set you free.

'Oft have you heard old Ellinore,
　　Your nurse, with horror tell,
How, robed in white, and stain'd with gore,
　　Appears a spectre fell,

'And each fifth year, at dead of night,
　　Stalks through the castle gate,
Which, by an ancient solemn rite,
　　For her must open wait.　　　　　　　　40

'Soon as to some far distant land,
　　Retires to-morrow's sun,

With torch and dagger in her hand,
  Appears the Bleeding Nun.

'Now you shall play the bleeding Nun,
  Array'd in robes so white,
And at the solemn hour of one,
  Stalk forth to meet your knight.

'Our steeds shall bear us far away,
  Beyond your father's power,   50
And Agnes, long ere break of day,
  Shall rest in Raymond's bower.'—

—'My heart consents, it must be done,
  —Father, 'tis your decree,—
And I will play the Bleeding Nun,
  And fly, my love, with thee.

'For I am thine,' fair Agnes cried,
  'And leave thee will I never;
I am thine, and thou art mine,
  Body and soul for ever!'—   60

Fair Agnes sat within her bower,
  Array'd in robes so white,
And waited the long wish'd-for hour,
  When she should meet her knight.

And Raymond, as the clock struck one,
  Before the castle stood;
And soon came forth his lovely Nun,
  Her white robes stain'd in blood.

He bore her in his arms away,
  And placed her on her steed;   70
And to the maid he thus did say,
  As on they rode with speed:

—'Oh Agnes! Agnes! thou art mine,
  And leave thee will I never;
Thou art mine, and I am thine,
  Body and soul for ever!'—

—'Oh Raymond! Raymond, I am thine,
  And leave thee will I never;
I am thine, and thou art mine,
  Body and soul for ever!'—   80

At length,—'We're safe!'—the warrior cried;
  'Sweet love abate thy speed;'—
But madly still she onwards hied
  Nor seem'd his call to heed.

Through wood and wild, they speed their way,
  Then sweep along the plain,
And almost at the break of day,
  The Danube's banks they gain.

—'Now stop ye, Raymond, stop ye here,
  And view the farther side;   90
Dismount, and say Sir Knight, do'st fear,
  With me to stem the tide.'—

Now on the utmost brink they stand,
  And gaze upon the flood,
She seized Don Raymond by the hand,
  Her grasp it froze his blood.

A whirling blast from off the stream
  Threw back the maiden's veil;
Don Raymond gave a hideous scream,
  And felt his spirits fail.   100

Then down his limbs, in strange affright,
  Cold dews to pour begun;
No Agnes met his shudd'ring sight,
  —'God! 'Tis the Bleeding Nun!'—

A form of more than mortal size,
  All ghastly, pale, and dead,
Fix'd on the Knight her livid eyes,
  And thus the Spectre said.

—'Oh Raymond! Raymond! I am thine,
  And leave thee will I never;   110
I am thine, and thou art mine,
  Body and soul for ever!'—

Don Raymond shrieks, he faints; the blood
  Ran cold in every vein,
He sank into the roaring flood,
  And never rose again!

97

Sonnet VI.
To the Torrid Zone

PATHWAY of light! o'er thy empurpled zone,
With lavish charms perennial summer strays;
Soft 'midst thy spicy groves the zephyr plays,
While far around the rich perfumes are thrown:
The amadavid-bird for thee alone,
Spreads his gay plumes that catch thy vivid rays;
For thee the gems with liquid lustre blaze,
And nature's various wealth is all thy own.
But, ah! not thine is twilight's doubtful gloom,
Those mild gradations, mingling day with night;   10
Here, instant darkness shrouds thy genial bloom,
Nor leaves my pensive soul that ling'ring light,
When musing mem'ry would each trace resume
Of fading pleasures in successive flight.

ROBERT SOUTHEY

98   from *Thalaba the Destroyer*

[Thalaba finds the Sorceress Maimuna spinning]

COLD! cold! 'tis a chilly clime
That the youth in his journey hath reach'd,
And he is aweary now,
And faint for lack of food.
Cold! cold! there is no Sun in heaven,
A heavy and uniform cloud
Overspreads the face of the sky,
And the snows are beginning to fall.
Dost thou wish for thy deserts, O Son of Hodeirah?
Dost thou long for the gales of Arabia?   10
Cold! cold! his blood flows languidly,
His hands are red, his lips are blue,
His feet are sore with the frost.
Cheer thee! cheer thee! Thalaba!
A little yet bear up!

All waste! no sign of life
But the track of the wolf and the bear!
No sound but the wild, wild wind,
And the snow crunching under his feet!
Night is come; neither moon, nor stars,   20
Only the light of the snow!
But behold a fire in a cave of the hill,
A heart-reviving fire;
And thither with strength renew'd
Thalaba presses on.

He found a Woman in the cave,
A solitary Woman,
Who by the fire was spinning,
And singing as she spun.
The pine boughs were cheerfully blazing,   30
And her face was bright with the flame;
Her face was as a Damsel's face,
And yet her hair was grey.
She bade him welcome with a smile,
And still continued spinning,
And singing as she spun.
The thread the woman drew
Was finer than the silkworm's,
Was finer than the gossamer;
The song she sung was low and sweet,   40
But Thalaba knew not the words.

He laid his bow before the hearth,
For the string was frozen stiff;
He took the quiver from his neck,
For the arrow-plumes were iced.
Then as the cheerful fire
Revived his languid limbs,
The adventurer ask'd for food.
The Woman answer'd him,
And still her speech was song: 50
'The She Bear she dwells near to me,
And she hath cubs, one, two, and three;
She hunts the deer, and brings him here,
And then with her I make good cheer;
And now to the chase the She Bear is gone,
And she with her prey will be here anon.'

She ceased her spinning while she spake;
And when she had answer'd him,

Again her fingers twirl'd the thread,
And again the Woman began,   60
In low, sweet tones to sing
The unintelligible song.

The thread she spun it gleam'd like gold
In the light of the odorous fire,
Yet was it so wondrously thin,
That, save when it shone in the light,
You might look for it closely in vain.
The youth sate watching it,
And she observed his wonder,
And then again she spake,   70
And still her speech was song:
'Now twine it round thy hands I say,
Now twine it round thy hands I pray!
My thread is small, my thread is fine,
But he must be
A stronger than thee,
Who can break this thread of mine!'

And up she raised her bright blue eyes,
And sweetly she smiled on him,
And he conceived no ill;   80
And round and round his right hand,
And round and round his left,
He wound the thread so fine.
And then again the Woman spake,
And still her speech was song,
'Now thy strength, O Stranger, strain!
Now then break the slender chain.'

Thalaba strove, but the thread
By magic hands was spun,
And in his cheek the flush of shame   90
Arose, commixt with fear.
She beheld and laugh'd at him,
And then again she sung,
'My thread is small, my thread is fine,
But he must be
A stronger than thee,
Who can break this thread of mine!'

And up she raised her bright blue eyes,
And fiercely she smiled on him:
'I thank thee, I thank thee, Hodeirah's son!   100

I thank thee for doing what can't be undone
For binding thyself in the chain I have spun!'
Then from his head she wrench'd
A lock of his raven hair,
And cast it in the fire,
And cried aloud as it burnt,
'Sister! Sister! hear my voice!
Sister! Sister! come and rejoice!

The thread is spun,
The prize is won,   110
The work is done,
For I have made captive Hodeirah's Son.'

(from Book VIII)

THOMAS MOORE
1779–1852

99   *The Kiss*

GROW to my lip, thou sacred kiss,
On which my soul's beloved swore
That there should come a time of bliss,
When she would mock my hopes no more;
And fancy shall thy glow renew,
In sighs at morn, and dreams at night,
And none shall steal thy holy dew
Till thou 'rt absolv'd by rapture's rite.
Sweet hours that are to make me blest,
Oh! fly, like breezes, to the goal,   10
And let my love, my more than soul,
Come panting to this fever'd breast;
And while in every glance I drink
The rich o'erflowings of her mind,
Oh! let her all impassion'd sink,
In sweet abandonment resign'd,
Blushing for all our struggles past,
And murmuring 'I am thine at last!'

MARY LAMB
1764–1847

100　　　　*Helen*

HIGH-BORN Helen, round your dwelling
　These twenty years I've paced in vain:
Haughty beauty, thy lover's duty
　Hath been to glory in his pain.

High-born Helen, proudly telling
　Stories of thy cold disdain;
I starve, I die, now you comply,
　And I no longer can complain.

These twenty years I've lived on tears,
　Dwelling for ever on a frown;　　　　　　10
On sighs I've fed, your scorn my bread;
　I perish now you kind are grown.

Can I, who loved my beloved
　But for the scorn 'was in her eye',
Can I be moved for my beloved,
　When she 'returns me sigh for sigh'?

In stately pride, by my bed-side,
　High-born Helen's portrait's hung;
Deaf to my praise, my mournful lays
　Are nightly to the portrait sung.　　　　20

To that I weep, nor ever sleep,
　Complaining all night long to her—
Helen, grown old, no longer cold,
　Said, 'you to all men I prefer.'

The Camp

TENTS, *marquees*, and baggage-waggons;
Suttling-houses, beer in flagons;
Drums and trumpets, singing, firing;
Girls seducing, beaux admiring;
Country lasses gay and smiling,
City lads their hearts beguiling;
Dusty roads, and horses frisky,
Many an *Eton Boy* in whisky;
Tax'd carts full of farmers' daughters;
Brutes condemn'd, and man who slaughters!   10
Public-houses, booths, and castles,
Belles of fashion, serving vassals;
Lordly gen'rals fiercely staring,
Weary soldiers, sighing, swearing!
Petit-maitres always dressing,
In the glass themselves caressing;
Perfum'd, painted, patch'd, and blooming
Ladies—manly airs assuming!
Dowagers of fifty, simp'ring,
Misses for their lovers whimp'ring;   20
Husbands drill'd to household tameness;
Dames heart sick of wedded sameness.
Princes setting girls a-madding,
Wives for ever fond of gadding;
Princesses with lovely faces,
Beauteous children of the Graces!
Britain's pride and virtue's treasure,
Fair and gracious beyond measure!
Aid-de-camps and youthful pages,
Prudes and vestals of all ages!   30
Old coquets and matrons surly,
Sounds of distant hurly-burly!
Mingled voices, uncouth singing,
Carts full laden, forage bringing;
Sociables and horses weary,
Houses warm, and dresses airy;
Loads of fatten'd poultry; pleasure
Serv'd (to nobles) without measure;
Doxies, who the waggons follow;
Beer, for thirsty hinds to swallow;   40
Washerwomen, fruit-girls cheerful,

Ancient ladies—*chaste* and *fearful!!*
Tradesmen, leaving shops, and seeming
More of *war* than profit dreaming;
Martial sounds and braying asses,
Noise, that ev'ry noise surpasses!
All confusion, din, and riot,
Nothing clean—and nothing quiet.

SAMUEL TAYLOR COLERIDGE

102

Dejection.

An Ode, Written April 4, 1802

'LATE, late yestreen I saw the New Moon,
    With the Old Moon in her arms;
And I fear, I fear, my master dear,
    We shall have a deadly storm.'

Ballad of Sir Patrick Spence

WELL! if the Bard was weather-wise, who made
    The grand Old Ballad of Sir PATRICK SPENCE,
    This night, so tranquil now, will not go hence
Unrous'd by winds, that ply a busier trade
Than those, which mould yon clouds in lazy flakes,
Or this dull sobbing draft, that drones and rakes
Upon the strings of this Œolian lute,
Which better far were mute.
For lo! the New Moon, winter-bright!
And overspread with phantom light,   10
(With swimming phantom light o'erspread,
But rimm'd and circled by a silver thread)
I see the Old Moon in her lap, foretelling
    The coming on of rain and squally blast:
And O! that even now the gust were swelling,
    And the slant night-show'r driving loud and fast!
Those sounds which oft have rais'd me, while they aw'd,
And sent my soul abroad,
Might now perhaps their wonted impulse give,
Might startle this dull pain, and make it move and live!   20

II

A grief without a pang, void, dark, and drear,
    A stifled, drowsy, unimpassion'd grief,

Which finds no nat'ral outlet, no relief
In word, or sigh, or tear—
O EDMUND! in this wan and heartless mood,
To other thoughts by yonder throstle woo'd,
All this long eve, so balmy and serene,
   Have I been gazing on the Western sky,
And its peculiar tint of yellow-green:
   And still I gaze—and with how blank an eye!   30
And those thin clouds above, in flakes and bars,
That give away their motion to the stars;
Those stars, that glide behind them, or between,
Now sparkling, now bedimm'd, but always seen;
Yon crescent moon, as fix'd as if it grew,
In its own cloudless, starless lake of blue,
A boat becalm'd! a lovely sky-canoe!
I see them all, so excellently fair—
I *see*, not *feel*, how beautiful they are!

III

   My genial spirits fail,   40
     And what can these avail,
To lift the smoth'ring weight from off my breast!
     It were a vain endeavour,
     Tho' I should gaze for ever
On that green light that lingers in the west:
I may not hope from outward forms to win
The passion and the life, whose fountains are within!

IV

O EDMUND! we receive but what we give,
And in *our* life alone does Nature live:
Ours is her wedding-garment, ours her shroud!   50
And would we aught behold, of higher worth,
Than that inanimate cold world, *allow'd*
To the poor loveless ever-anxious crowd,
Ah from the soul itself must issue forth,
A light, a glory, a fair luminous cloud
Enveloping the earth—
And from the soul itself must there be sent
A sweet and potent voice, of its own birth,
Of all sweet sounds the life and element!
O pure of heart! Thou need'st not ask of me   60
What this strong music in the soul may be?
What, and wherein it doth exist,

This light, this glory, this fair luminous mist,
This beautiful and beauty-making pow'r?
JOY, virtuous EDMUND! joy, that ne'er was given,
Save to the pure, and in their purest hour,
Joy, EDMUND! is the spirit and the pow'r,
Which wedding Nature to us gives in dow'r
    A new earth and new Heaven,
Undream'd of by the sensual and the proud— 70
JOY is the sweet voice, JOY the luminous cloud—
    We, we ourselves rejoice!
And thence flows all that charms or ear or sight,
All melodies the echoes of that voice
All colours a suffusion from that light.

V

Yes, dearest EDMUND, yes!
  There was a time when, tho' my path was rough,
    This joy within me dallied with distress,
  And all misfortunes were but as the stuff
    Whence fancy made me dreams of happiness: 80
For hope grew round me, like the twining vine,
And fruits and foliage, not my own, seem'd mine.
But now afflictions bow me down to earth:
Nor care I, that they rob me of my mirth,
  But O! each visitation
Suspends what nature gave me at my birth,
  My shaping spirit of imagination.

[The sixth and seventh Stanzas omitted.]

*   *   *   *   *
*   *   *   *   *
*   *   *   *   *

VIII

O wherefore did I let it haunt my mind,
  This dark distressful dream?
I turn from it and listen to the wind 90
  Which long has rav'd unnotic'd. What a scream
Of agony, by torture, lengthen'd out,
That lute sent forth! O wind, that rav'st without,
  Bare crag, or mountain tairn, or blasted tree,
Or pine-grove, whither woodman never clomb,
Or lonely house, long held the witches' home,
  Methinks were fitter instruments for thee,
Mad Lutanist! who, in this month of show'rs,

Of dark-brown gardens, and of peeping flow'rs,
Mak'st devil's yule, with worse than wintry song,   100
The blossoms, buds, and tim'rous leaves among.
    Thou Actor, perfect in all tragic sounds!
        Thou mighty Poet, ev'n to frenzy bold!
What tell'st thou now about?
'Tis of the rushing of an host in rout,
    With many groans of men with smarting wounds—
        At once they groan with pain, and shudder with the cold!
But hush! there is a pause of deepest silence!
    And all that noise, as of a rushing crowd,
        With groans and tremulous shudderings—all is over!   110
    It tells another tale, with sounds less deep and loud—
        A tale of less affright,
      And temper'd with delight,
As EDMUND's self had fram'd the tender lay—
      'Tis of a little child,
      Upon a lonesome wild,
Not far from home; but she has lost her way—
And now moans low, in utter grief and fear;
And now screams loud, and hopes to make her mother *hear!*

IX

'Tis midnight, and small thoughts have I of sleep;   120
Full seldom may my friend such vigils keep!
Visit him, gentle Sleep, with wings of healing,
    And may this storm be but a mountain birth,
May all the stars hang bright above his dwelling,
    Silent, as tho' they *watch'd* the sleeping earth!
      With light heart may he rise,
      Gay fancy, cheerful eyes,
And sing his lofty song, and teach me to rejoice!
O EDMUND, friend of my devoutest choice,
O rais'd from anxious dread and busy care,   130
By the immenseness of the good and fair
Which thou see'st ev'ry where
Joy lifts thy spirit, joy attunes thy voice,
To thee do all things live from pole to pole,
Their life the eddying of thy living soul!
O simple spirit, guided from above,
O lofty Poet, full of light and love,
Brother and friend of my devoutest choice,
Thus may'st thou ever evermore rejoice!

ΕΣΤΗΣΕ

WILLIAM COWPER
1731–1800

103   *The Castaway*

OBSCUREST night involved the sky,
   Th' Atlantic billows roar'd,
When such a destined wretch as I
   Wash'd headlong from on board
Of friends, of hope, of all bereft,
His floating home for ever left.

No braver chief could Albion boast
   Than he with whom he went,
Nor ever ship left Albion's coast
   With warmer wishes sent.   10
He loved them both, but both in vain,
Nor him beheld nor her again.

Not long beneath the whelming brine,
   Expert to swim, he lay;
Nor soon he felt his strength decline,
   Or courage die away,
But waged with death a lasting strife,
Supported by despair of life.

He shouted: nor his friends had fail'd
   To check the vessel's course,   20
But so the furious blast prevail'd,
   That, pitiless perforce,
They left their outcast mate behind,
And scudded still before the wind.

Some succour yet they could afford;
   And, such as storms allow,
The cask, the coop, the floated cord,
   Delay'd not to bestow.
But he (they knew) nor ship nor shore,
Whate'er they gave, should visit more.   30

Nor, cruel as it seem'd, could he
    Their haste himself condemn,
Aware that flight, in such a sea,
    Alone could rescue them;
Yet bitter felt it still to die
Deserted, and his friends so nigh.

He long survives, who lives an hour
    In ocean, self-upheld;
And so long he, with unspent pow'r,
    His destiny repell'd;   40
And ever, as the minutes flew,
Entreated help, or cried—'Adieu!'

At length, his transient respite past,
    His comrades, who before
Had heard his voice in ev'ry blast,
    Could catch the sound no more.
For then, by toil subdued, he drank
The stifling wave, and then he sank.

No poet wept him: but the page
    Of narrative sincere,   50
That tells his name, his worth, his age,
    Is wet with Anson's tear.
And tears by bards or heroes shed
Alike immortalize the dead.

I therefore purpose not or dream,
    Descanting on his fate,
To give the melancholy theme
    A more enduring date:
But mis'ry still delights to trace
Its semblance in another's case.   60

No voice divine the storm allay'd,
    No light propitious shone,
When, snatched from all effectual aid,
    We perish'd, each, alone:
But I beneath a rougher sea,
And whelm'd in deeper gulphs than he.

THOMAS CAMPBELL
1777–1844

Hohenlinden

ON Linden, when the sun was low,
All bloodless lay the untrodden snow,
And dark as winter was the flow
    Of Iser, rolling rapidly.

But Linden saw another sight
When the drum beat at dead of night,
Commanding fires of death to light
    The darkness of her scenery.

By torch and trumpet fast arrayed,
Each horseman drew his battle blade,   10
And furious every charger neighed
    To join the dreadful revelry.

Then shook the hills with thunder riven,
Then rushed the steed to battle driven,
And louder than the bolts of heaven
    Far flashed the red artillery.

But redder yet that light shall glow
On Linden's hills of stainèd snow,
And bloodier yet the torrent flow
    Of Iser, rolling rapidly.   20

'Tis morn, but scarce yon level sun
Can pierce the war-clouds, rolling dun,
Where furious Frank and fiery Hun
    Shout in their sulphurous canopy.

The combat deepens. On, ye brave,
Who rush to glory, or the grave!
Wave, Munich! all thy banners wave,
    And charge with all thy chivalry!

Few, few shall part where many meet!
The snow shall be their winding-sheet,   30
And every turf beneath their feet
    Shall be a soldier's sepulchre.

[1804]

ANONYMOUS

105 *To Buonaparte*

The English are nothing but a Nation of Shopkeepers, &c.

Vide MONITEUR

WHEN the Corsican Chief, with a view to degrade,
Says, we're nothing but shopmen, and sneers at our trade:
Let none to the obvious assertion object,
Nor a charge contradict so extremely correct;
'Tis true, Buonaparte—and we wish you to know,
That the firm of our partnership's, *One King and Co.*
Tho' our *first rate* productions so oft you decline,
And always seem hurt when we send you *a line*,
Yet try us for once, we're quite ready to deal
With a capital stock of lead, iron, and steel,   10
And a warehouse long open'd, and constantly fill'd
With the *choicest* of *Spirits*, most ably distill'd,
Not smuggled from France, but, according to my sense,
Of full *British proof*, which *we sell with a licence.*
Should none of these articles prove to your liking,
We can shew you some others, tho' nothing so striking.
Perhaps you've a wish for our virgins and wives,
But these if we sell we must sell with our lives;
And as for our lives, Buonaparte, I much fear,
The price that we ask is a little too dear   20
Ten French for one English—we cannot abate,
So *high* are the *duties* they owe to the state.
These terms if you like, you are welcome to come,
Assur'd that you always will find us at *home.*
For the sale we're prepar'd—when you please we'll begin it;
Upon honour we serve, you shall not wait a minute.

G.C.

WILLIAM BLAKE

106   from *Milton*

[PLATE 2]

 AND did those feet in ancient time,
Walk upon Englands mountains green:
And was the holy Lamb of God,
On Englands pleasant pastures seen!

And did the Countenance Divine,
Shine forth upon our clouded hills?
And was Jerusalem builded here,
Among these dark Satanic Mills?

Bring me my Bow of burning gold:
Bring me my Arrows of desire: 10
Bring me my Spear: O clouds unfold!
Bring me my Chariot of fire!

I will not cease from Mental Fight,
Nor shall my Sword sleep in my hand:
Till we have built Jerusalem,
In Englands green & pleasant Land.

[PLATE 24]

But the Wine-press of Los is eastward of Golgonooza, before the
    Seat
Of Satan. Luvah laid the foundation & Urizen finish'd it in howling
    woe.
How red the sons & daughters of Luvah! here they tread the grapes.
Laughing & shouting drunk with odours many fall oerwearied
Drownd in the wine is many a youth & maiden: those around
Lay them on skins of Tygers & of the spotted Leopard & the Wild
    Ass
Till they revive, or bury them in cool grots, making lamentation.

This Wine-press is call'd War on Earth, it is the Printing-Press
Of Los; and here he lays his words in order above the mortal brain
As cogs are formd in a wheel to turn the cogs of the adverse wheel.   10

Timbrels & violins sport round the Wine-presses; the little Seed;
The sportive Root, the Earth-worm, the gold Beetle; the wise Emmet;

237

Dance round the Wine-presses of Luvah: the Centipede is there:
The ground Spider with many eyes: the Mole clothed in velvet
The ambitious Spider in his sullen web; the lucky golden Spinner;
The Earwig armd: the tender Maggot emblem of immortality:
The Flea: Louse: Bug: the Tape-Worm: all the Armies of Disease:
Visible or invisible to the slothful vegetating Man.
The slow Slug: the Grasshopper that sings & laughs & drinks:
Winter comes, he folds his slender bones without a murmur.   20
The cruel Scorpion is there: the Gnat: Wasp: Hornet & the Honey
    Bee:
The Toad & venomous Newt; the Serpent clothd in gems & gold:
They throw off their gorgeous raiment: they rejoice with loud jubilee
Around the Wine-presses of Luvah, naked & drunk with wine.

There is the Nettle that stings with soft down; and there
The indignant Thistle: whose bitterness is bred in his milk:
Who feeds on contempt of his neighbour: there all the idle Weeds
That creep around the obscure places, shew their various limbs.
Naked in all their beauty dancing round the Wine-presses.

But in the Wine-presses the Human grapes sing not, nor dance   30
They howl & writhe in shoals of torment; in fierce flames consuming,
In chains of iron & in dungeons circled with ceaseless fires.
In pits & dens & shades of death: in shapes of torment & woe.
The plates & screws & wracks & saws & cords & fires & cisterns
The cruel joys of Luvahs Daughters lacerating with knives
And whips their Victims & the deadly sport of Luvahs Sons.

They dance around the dying, & they drink the howl & groan
They catch the shrieks in cups of gold, they hand them to one another:
These are the sports of love, & these the sweet delights of amorous
    play
Tears of the grape, the death sweat of the cluster the last sigh   40
Of the mild youth who listens to the lureing songs of Luvah

[PLATE 30]

There is a place where Contrarieties are equally True
This place is called Beulah, It is a pleasant lovely Shadow
Where no dispute can come. Because of those who Sleep.
Into this place the Sons & Daughters of Ololon descended
With solemn mourning into Beulahs moony shades & hills
Weeping for Milton: mute wonder held the Daughters of Beulah
Enrapturd with affection sweet and mild benevolence

Beulah is evermore Created around Eternity; appearing
To the Inhabitants of Eden, around them on all sides.

But Beulah to its Inhabitants appears within each district   10
As the beloved infant in his mothers bosom round incircled
With arms of love & pity & sweet compassion. But to
The Sons of Eden the moony habitations of Beulah,
Are from Great Eternity a mild & pleasant Rest.

And it is thus Created. Lo the Eternal Great Humanity
To whom be Glory & Dominion Evermore Amen
Walks among all his awful Family seen in every face
As the breath of the Almighty. such are the words of man to man
In the great Wars of Eternity, in fury of Poetic Inspiration,
To build the Universe stupendous: Mental forms Creating   20

But the Emanations trembled exceedingly, nor could they
Live, because the life of Man was too exceeding unbounded
His joy became terrible to them they trembled & wept
Crying with one voice. Give us a habitation & a place
In which we may be hidden under the shadow of wings
For if we who are but for a time, & who pass away in winter
Behold these wonders of Eternity we shall consume
But you O our Fathers & Brothers, remain in Eternity
But grant us a Temporal Habitation. do you speak
To us; we will obey your words as you obey Jesus   30
The Eternal who is blessed for ever & ever. Amen

So spake the lovely Emanations; & there appeard a pleasant
Mild Shadow above: beneath: & on all sides round,

[PLATE 31]

Into this pleasant Shadow all the weak & weary
Like Women & Children were taken away as on wings
Of dovelike softness, & shadowy habitations prepared for them
But every Man returnd & went still going forward thro'
The Bosom of the Father in Eternity on Eternity
Neither did any lack or fall into Error without
A Shadow to repose in all the Days of happy Eternity.

Into this pleasant Shadow Beulah, all Ololon descended
And when the Daughters of Beulah heard the lamentation
All Beulah wept, for they saw the Lord coming in the Clouds   10
And the Shadows of Beulah terminate in rocky Albion.

And all Nations wept in affliction Family by Family
Germany wept towards France & Italy: England wept & trembled
Towards America: India rose up from his golden bed:

As one awakend in the night: they saw the Lord coming
In the Clouds of Ololon with Power & Great Glory!

And all the Living Creatures of the Four Elements, wail'd
With bitter wailing: these in the aggregate are named Satan
And Rahab: they know not of Regeneration, but only of Generation
The Fairies, Nymphs, Gnomes & Genii of the Four Elements   20
Unforgiving & unalterable: these cannot be Regenerated
But must be Created, for they know only of Generation
These are the Gods of the Kingdoms of the Earth: in contrarious
And cruel opposition: Element against Element, opposed in War
Not Mental, as the Wars of Eternity, but a Corporeal Strife
In Los's Halls continual labouring in the Furnaces of Golgonooza
Orc howls on the Atlantic: Enitharmon trembles: All Beulah weeps

Thou hearest the Nightingale begin the Song of Spring;
The Lark sitting upon his earthy bed: just as the morn
Appears; listens silent; then springing from the waving Corn-field!
    loud
                                                            30
He leads the Choir of Day! trill, trill, trill, trill,
Mounting upon the wings of light into the Great Expanse:
Reecchoing against the lovely blue & shining heavenly Shell:
His little throat labours with inspiration; every feather
On throat & breast & wings vibrates with the effluence Divine
All Nature listens silent to him & the awful Sun
Stands still upon the Mountain looking on this little Bird
With eyes of soft humility, & wonder love & awe.
Then loud from their green covert all the Birds begin their Song
The Thrush, the Linnet & the Goldfinch, Robin & the Wren   40
Awake the Sun from his sweet reverie upon the Mountain:
The Nightingale again assays his song, & thro the day,
And thro the night warbles luxuriant; every Bird of Song
Attending his loud harmony with admiration & love.
This is a Vision of the lamentation of Beulah over Ololon!

Thou percievest the Flowers put forth their precious Odours!
And none can tell how from so small a center comes such sweets
Forgetting that within that Center Eternity expands
Its ever during doors, that Og & Anak fiercely guard[.]
First eer the morning breaks joy opens in the flowery bosoms   50
Joy even to tears, which the Sun rising dries; first the Wild Thyme
And Meadow-sweet downy & soft waving among the reeds.
Light springing on the air lead the sweet Dance: they wake
The Honeysuckle sleeping on the Oak: the flaunting beauty
Revels along upon the wind; the White-thorn lovely May
Opens her many lovely eyes: listening the Rose still sleeps

None dare to wake her. soon she bursts her crimson curtaind bed
And comes forth in the majesty of beauty; every Flower:
The Pink, the Jessamine, the Wall-flower, the Carnation
The Jonquil, the mild Lilly opes her heavens! every Tree,   60
And Flower & Herb soon fill the air with an innumerable Dance
Yet all in order sweet & lovely, Men are sick with Love!
Such is a Vision of the lamentation of Beulah over Ololon.

107   *from Jerusalem*

[PLATE 15]

I SEE the Four-fold Man. The Humanity in deadly sleep
And its fallen Emanation. The Spectre & its cruel Shadow.
I see the Past, Present & Future, existing all at once
Before me; O Divine Spirit sustain me on thy wings!
That I may awake Albion from his long & cold repose.
For Bacon & Newton sheathd in dismal steel, their terrors hang
Like iron scourges over Albion, Reasonings like vast Serpents
Infold around my limbs, bruising my minute articulations

I turn my eyes to the Schools & Universities of Europe
And there behold the Loom of Locke whose Woof rages dire   10
Washd by the Water-wheels of Newton. black the cloth
In heavy wreathes folds over every Nation; cruel Works
Of many Wheels I view, wheel without wheel, with cogs tyrannic
Moving by compulsion each other: not as those in Eden: which
Wheel within Wheel in freedom revolve in harmony & peace.

I see in deadly fear in London Los raging round his Anvil
Of death: forming an Ax of gold: the Four Sons of Los
Stand round him cutting the Fibres from Albions hills
That Albions Sons may roll apart over the Nations
While Reuben enroots his brethren in the narrow Canaanite   20
From the Limit Noah to the Limit Abram in whose Loins
Reuben in his Twelve-fold majesty & beauty shall take refuge
As Abraham flees from Chaldea shaking his goary locks
But first Albion must sleep, divided from the Nations

I see Albion sitting upon his Rock in the first Winter
And thence I see the Chaos of Satan & the World of Adam
When the Divine Hand went forth on Albion in the mid Winter
And at the place of Death when Albion sat in Eternal Death
Among the Furnaces of Los in the Valley of the Son of Hinnom

[PLATE 16]

Hampstead Highgate Finchley Hendon Muswell hill: rage loud
Before Bromions iron Tongs & glowing Poker reddening fierce
Hertfordshire glows with fierce Vegetation! in the Forests
The Oak frowns terrible, the Beech & Ash & Elm enroot
Among the Spiritual fires; loud the Corn fields thunder along
The Soldiers fife; the Harlots shriek; the Virgins dismal groan
The Parents fear: the Brothers jealousy: the Sisters curse
Beneath the Storms of Theotormon & the thundring Bellows
Heaves in the hand of Palamabron who in Londons darkness
Before the Anvil, watches the bellowing flames: thundering   10
The Hammer loud rages in Rintrahs strong grasp swinging loud
Round from heaven to earth down falling with heavy blow
Dead on the Anvil, where the red hot wedge groans in pain
He quenches it in the black trough of his Forge; Londons River
Feeds the dread Forge, trembling & shuddering along the Valleys

Humber & Trent roll dreadful before the Seventh Furnace
And Tweed & Tyne anxious give up their Souls for Albions sake
Lincolnshire Derbyshire Nottinghamshire Leicestershire
From Oxfordshire to Norfolk on the Lake of Udan Adan
Labour within the Furnaces, walking among the Fires   20
With Ladles huge & iron Pokers over the Island white.

JOSEPH LEES
1748–1824

108   *Jone o' Grinfilt*

SAYS Jone to his woife on a whot summer's day,
'Aw'm resolvt i' Grinfilt no lunger to stay;
For aw'll goo to Owdham os fast os aw can,
So fare thee weel, Grinfilt, an' fare thee weel, Nan;
For a sodger aw'll be, an' brave Owdham aw'll see,
An' aw'll ha'e a battle wi' th' French.'

'Dear Jone,' said eawr Nan, un' hoo bitterly cried,
'Wilt be one o' th' foote, or theaw meons for t' ride?'
'Ods eawns! wench, aw'll ride oather ass or a mule,
Ere aw'll keawer i' Grinfilt os black os th' dule,   10
Both clemmin', un' starvin', un' never a fardin',
It'ud welly drive ony mon mad.'

'Ay, Jone, sin' we coom i' Grinfilt for t' dwell,
Wey'n had mony a bare meal, aw con vara weel tell.'
'Bare meal, ecod! ay, that aw vara weel know,
There's bin two days this wick 'ot wey'n had nowt at o';
Aw'm vara near sided, afore aw'll abide it,
Aw'll feight oather Spanish or French.'

Then says my Noant Marget, 'Ah! Jone, theaw'rt so whot,
Aw'd ne'er go to Owdham, boh i' England aw'd stop.'   20
'It matters nowt, Madge, for to Owdham aw'll goo,
Aw'st ne'er clem to deeoth, boh sumbry shall know:
Furst Frenchmon aw find, aw'll tell him meh mind,
Un' if he'll naw feight, he shall run.'

Then deawn th' broo aw coom, for weh livent at top,
Aw thowt aw'd raich Owdham ere ever aw stop;
Ecod! heaw they staret when aw getten to th' Mumps,
Meh owd hat i' my hont, un' meh clogs full o' stumps;

108: 10 keawer] hide away   dule] devil   11 clemmin', un' starvin'] cold and
hungry   12 welly] almost   17 sided] decided   22 sumbry] some-
body   25 broo] hill

Boh aw soon towd 'um, aw're gooin' to Owdham,
Un' aw'd ha'e a battle wi' th' French.   30

Aw kept eendway thro' th' lone, un' to Owdham aw went,
Aw ax'd a recruit if they'd made up their keawnt?
'Nowe, Nowe, honest lad' (for he tawked like a king),
'Goo wi' meh thro' th' street, un' thee aw will bring
Wheere, if theaw'rt willin', theaw may ha'e a shillin'.'
Ecod! aw thowt this wur rare news.

He browt meh to th' pleck, where they measurn their height,
Un' if they bin height, there's nowt said abeawt weight;
Aw ratched meh un' stretch'd meh, un' never did flinch:
Says th' mon, 'Aw believe theaw'rt meh lad to an inch.'   40
Aw thowt, this'll do; aw'st ha'e guineas enoo'.
Ecod! Owdham, brave Owdham for me.

So fare thee weel, Grinfilt, a soger aw'm made:
Aw getten new shoon, un' a rare cockade;
Aw'll feight for Owd England os hard os aw con,
Oather French, Dutch, or Spanish, to me it's o' one;
Aw'll mak 'em to stare, like a new-started hare,
Un' aw'll tell 'em fro' Owdham aw coom.

CHARLOTTE DACRE
('ROSA MATILDA')
1782–*c*.1841

109   *The Female Philosopher*

YOU tell me, fair one, that you ne'er can love,
    And seem with scorn to mock the dangerous fire;
But why, then, trait'ress, do you seek to move
    In others what *your* breast can ne'er inspire?

You tell me, you my *friend* alone will be,
    Yet speak of friendship in a voice so sweet,
That, while I struggle to be coldly free,
    I feel my heart with wildest throbbings beat.

31 eendway] straight on   37 pleck] spot

Vainly indiff'rence would you bid us feel,
  While so much languor in those eyes appear;   10
Vainly the stoic's happiness reveal,
  While soft emotion all your features wear.

O, form'd for love! O, wherefore should you fly
  From the seducing charm it spreads around?
O why enshrine your soul with apathy?
  Or wish in frozen fetters to be bound?

Life is a darksome and a dreary day,
  The solitary wretch no pleasure knows;
Love is the star that lights him on his way,
  And guides him on to pleasure and repose.   20

But oft, forgetful of thy plan severe,
  I've seen thee fondly gaze—I've heard thee sigh;
I've mark'd thy strain of converse, sadly dear,
  While softest rapture lighten'd from thine eye.

Then have I thought some wayward youth employ'd
  Thy secret soul, but left thee to despair,
And oft with pleasing sorrow have enjoy'd
  The task of chasing thy corrosive care.

Yet pride must save me from a dastard love,
  A grov'ling love, that cannot hope return: 30
A soul like mine was never form'd to prove
  Those viler passions with which some can burn.

Then fear not me; for since it is thy will,
  Adhere with stubborn coolness to thy vow;
Grant me thy philosophic friendship still—
  I'll grant thee *mine* with all the powers I know.

110   *The Kiss*

              THE greatest bliss
                Is in a kiss—
          A kiss of love refin'd,
              When springs the soul
                Without controul,
          And blends the bliss with mind.

For if desire
Alone inspire,
The kiss not *me* can charm;
The eye must beam   10
With *chasten'd* gleam
That would *my* soul disarm.

What fond delight
Does love excite
When sentiment takes part!
The falt'ring sigh,
Voluptuous eye,
And palpitating heart.

Ye fleet too fast—
Sweet moments, last   20
A little longer mine!
Like Heaven's bow
Ye fade—ye go;
Too tremulously fine!

III   *The Power of Love*

THE sweet enthusiast, on a rock reclin'd,
  With transport listen'd to the dashing waves;
Her snowy garments swam upon the wind,
  And Silence spread her wing amid the caves.

Now sportive Fancy did her eye-lids close,
  And Memory brought the happy past to view;
A group of visionary friends arose,
  And in a dance confus'd around her drew.

Borne on Imagination's ardent wing,
  Again a child, she skimm'd the yellow mead,   10
Again threw pebbles in the cloud-pav'd spring—
  Again in baby gambols took the lead.

And now, her childhood past, a busier scene
  Floats on the bosom of the silent night;
Her lover's form, all deck'd in sea-weeds green,
  Swam wet and shiv'ring in her startled sight.

Light on the trembling surge he seem'd to stand;
  Pale was his face, loose hung his dripping hair,

246

His shroud he held within his clay-cold hand,
   And, sighing deeply, threw his bosom bare.   20

Then pointed Melancholy to the wave;
   'Say, wilt thou come, sweet love? behold my fate!
This element hath been thy lover's grave;
   Say, dost thou love me still—or dost thou hate?'

In haste the beauteous dreamer op'd her eyes,
   To lose the vision from her rocky pillow;
In vain, alas! whatever side she tries,
   The sprite remains, still pointing to the billow!

And now a sterner look assum'd his face;
   'Thou dost not love me, or thou wouldst not stay,   30
Come plunge, my love!—soon, soon shall we embrace!
   Midnight has past:—haste, haste, I must away!'

The sweet enthusiast heard her lover groan;
   And sighing from the promontory's steep,
'See, dear-lov'd spirit!—I am thine alone!'
   She said; and plunging sought him 'midst the deep.

112

Sappho;
or, The Resolve

YES, I have lov'd: yet often have I said,
   Love in this breast shall never revel more;
   But I will listen to wild ocean's roar,
Or, like some out-cast solitary shade,
   Will cling upon the howlings of the wind,
   Till I grow deaf and lifeless, cold and blind.
But, ah! enchantress, cease the tender lay,
   Nor tune thy lyre to notes, thus softly slow;
Those eyes—oh take those melting eyes away!
   Nor let those lips with honey'd sweets o'erflow;—   10
Nor let meek Pity pale that lovely cheek,
   Nor weep, as wretches their long-sufferings speak.
With forms so fair endued, oh! Venus, why
   Are Lesbian maids, or with such weakness I?
Do Lesbian damsels touch the melting lyre?
   My lyre is mute; and I in silence gaze;
As tho' the muse did not this breast inspire,
   I lose in tenderer loves the love of praise.

Oh! Sappho, how art thou imprisoned round,
Beauty's weak captive, fast-enchain'd with sound!   20
  Frail, frail resolve! vain promise of a day!
  I see, I hear, I feel, and die away.

113   *Simile*

  The little moth round candle turning,
  Stops not till its wings are burning:
  So woman, dazzled by man's wooing,
  Rushes to her own undoing.

MARY TIGHE
1772–1810

114   from *Psyche*

[*Psyche Introduced*]

'MID the thick covert of that woodland shade,
A flowery bank there lay undressed by art,
But of the mossy turf spontaneous made;
Here the young branches shot their arms athwart,
And wove the bower so thick in every part,
That the fierce beams of Phœbus glancing strong
Could never through the leaves their fury dart;
But the sweet creeping shrubs that round it throng,
Their loving fragrance mix, and trail their flowers along.

And close beside a little fountain played,   10
Which through the trembling leaves all joyous shone,
And with the cheerful birds sweet music made,
Kissing the surface of each polished stone
As it flowed past: sure as her favourite throne
Tranquillity might well esteem the bower,
The fresh and cool retreat have called her own,
A pleasant shelter in the sultry hour,
A refuge from the blast, and angry tempest's power.

Wooed by the soothing silence of the scene
Here Psyche stood, and looking round, lest aught   20
Which threatened danger near her might have been,
Awhile to rest her in that quiet spot

She laid her down, and piteously bethought
Herself on the sad changes of her fate,
Which in so short a space so much had wrought,
And now had raised her to such high estate,
And now had plunged her low in sorrow desolate.

Oh! how refreshing seemed the breathing wind
To her faint limbs! and while her snowy hands
From her fair brow her golden hair unbind,   30
And of her zone unloose the silken bands,
More passing bright unveiled her beauty stands;
For faultless was her form as beauty's queen,
And every winning grace that Love demands,
With mild attempered dignity was seen
Play o'er each lovely limb, and deck her angel mien.

(Canto I, lines 46–81)

[Psyche's Return to the Palace of Love]

Illumined bright now shines the splendid dome,
Melodious accents her arrival hail:
But not the torches' blaze can chase the gloom,
And all the soothing powers of music fail;
Trembling she seeks her couch with horror pale,
But first a lamp conceals in secret shade,
While unknown terrors all her soul assail.
Thus half their treacherous counsel is obeyed,
For still her gentle soul abhors the murderous blade.

And now, with softest whispers of delight,   10
Love welcomes Psyche still more fondly dear;
Not unobserved, though hid in deepest night,
The silent anguish of her secret fear.
He thinks that tenderness excites the tear
By the late image of her parents' grief,
And half offended seeks in vain to cheer,
Yet, while he speaks, her sorrows feel relief,
Too soon more keen to sting from this suspension brief.

Allowed to settle on celestial eyes
Soft Sleep exulting now exerts his sway,   20
From Psyche's anxious pillow gladly flies
To veil those orbs, whose pure and lambent ray
The powers of heaven submissively obey.
Trembling and breathless then she softly rose
And seized the lamp, where it obscurely lay,

With hand too rashly daring to disclose
The sacred veil which hung mysterious o'er her woes.

Twice, as with agitated step she went,
The lamp expiring shone with doubtful gleam,
As though it warned her from her rash intent: 30
And twice she paused, and on its trembling beam
Gazed with suspended breath, while voices seem
With murmuring sound along the roof to sigh;
As one just waking from a troublous dream,
With palpitating heart and straining eye,
Still fixed with fear remains, still thinks the danger nigh.

Oh, daring Muse! wilt thou indeed essay
To paint the wonders which that lamp could shew?
And canst thou hope in living words to say
The dazzling glories of that heavenly view?   40
Ah! well I ween, that if with pencil true
That splendid vision could be well exprest,
The fearful awe imprudent Psyche knew
Would seize with rapture every wondering breast,
When Love's all potent charms divinely stood confest.

All imperceptible to human touch,
His wings display celestial essence light,
The clear effulgence of the blaze is such,
The brilliant plumage shines so heavenly bright
That mortal eyes turn dazzled from the sight;   50
A youth he seems in manhood's freshest years;
Round his fair neck, as clinging with delight,
Each golden curl resplendently appears,
Or shades his darker brow, which grace majestic wears.

Or o'er his guileless front the ringlets bright
Their rays of sunny lustre seem to throw,
That front than polished ivory more white!
His blooming cheeks with deeper blushes glow
Than roses scattered o'er a bed of snow:
While on his lips, distilled in balmy dews,   60
(Those lips divine that even in silence know
The heart to touch) persuasion to infuse
Still hangs a rosy charm that never vainly sues.

The friendly curtain of indulgent sleep
Disclosed not yet his eyes' resistless sway,
But from their silky veil there seemed to peep
Some brilliant glances with a softened ray,

Which o'er his features exquisitely play,
And all his polished limbs suffuse with light.
Thus through some narrow space the azure day   70
Sudden its cheerful rays diffusing bright,
Wide darts its lucid beams, to gild the brow of night.

His fatal arrows and celestial bow
Beside the couch were negligently thrown,
Nor needs the god his dazzling arms, to show
His glorious birth, such beauty round him shone
As sure could spring from Beauty's self alone;
The gloom which glowed o'er all of soft desire,
Could well proclaim him Beauty's cherished son;
And Beauty's self will oft these charms admire,   80
And steal his witching smile, his glance's living fire.

Speechless with awe, in transport strangely lost
Long Psyche stood with fixed adoring eye;
Her limbs immoveable, her senses tost
Between amazement, fear, and ecstasy,
She hangs enamoured o'er the Deity.
Till from her trembling hand extinguished falls
The fatal lamp—He starts—and suddenly
Tremendous thunders echo through the halls,
While ruin's hideous crash bursts o'er the affrighted walls.   90

Dread horror seizes on her sinking heart,
A mortal chillness shudders at her breast,
Her soul shrinks fainting from death's icy dart,
The groan scarce uttered dies but half exprest,
And down she sinks in deadly swoon opprest:
But when at length, awaking from her trance,
The terrors of her fate stand all confest,
In vain she casts around her timid glance,
The rudely frowning scenes her former joys enhance.

No traces of those joys, alas, remain!   100
A desert solitude alone appears.
No verdant shade relieves the sandy plain,
The wide spread waste no gentle fountain cheers,
One barren face the dreary prospect wears;
Nought through the vast horizon meets her eye
To calm the dismal tumult of her fears,
No trace of human habitation nigh,
A sandy wild beneath, above a threatening sky.

(Canto II, lines 155–262)

WALTER SAVAGE LANDOR

115   *[Rose Aylmer]*

AH what avails the sceptred race,
    Ah what the form divine!
What, every virtue, every grace!
    For, Aylmer, all were thine.

Sweet Aylmer, whom these wakeful eyes
    May weep, but never see,
A night of sorrows and of sighs
    I consecrate to thee.

JANE TAYLOR
1783–1824

116   *The Star*

TWINKLE, twinkle, little star,
How I wonder what you are!
Up above the world so high,
Like a diamond in the sky.

When the blazing sun is gone,
When he nothing shines upon,
Then you show your little light,
Twinkle, twinkle, all the night.

Then the traveller in the dark,
Thanks you for your tiny spark!   10
He could not see which way to go,
If you did not twinkle so.

In the dark blue sky you keep,
And often through my curtains peep,
For you never shut your eye
Till the sun is in the sky.

As your bright and tiny spark
Lights the traveller in the dark,
Though I know not what you are,
Twinkle, twinkle, little star.   20

WILLIAM ROSCOE
1753–1831

117   *The Butterfly's Ball and the*
              Grasshopper's Feast

COME take up your Hats, and away let us haste
To the *Butterfly's* Ball, and the *Grasshopper's* Feast.
The Trumpeter, *Gad-fly*, has summon'd the Crew,
And the Revels are now only waiting for you.

So said little Robert, and pacing along,
His merry Companions came forth in a Throng.
And on the smooth Grass, by the side of a Wood,
Beneath a broad Oak that for Ages had stood,

Saw the Children of Earth, and the Tenants of Air,
For an Evening's Amusement together repair.   10
And there came the *Beetle*, so blind and so black,
Who carried the *Emmet*, his Friend, on his Back.

And there was the *Gnat* and the *Dragon-fly* too,
With all their Relations, Green, Orange, and Blue.
And there came the *Moth*, with his Plumage of Down,
And the *Hornet* in Jacket of Yellow and Brown;

Who with him the *Wasp*, his Companion, did bring,
But they promis'd, that Evening, to lay by their Sting.
And the sly little *Dormouse* crept out of his Hole,
And brought to the Feast his blind Brother, the *Mole*.   20

And the *Snail*, with his Horns peeping out of his Shell,
Came from a great Distance, the Length of an Ell.
A Mushroom their Table, and on it was laid
A Water-dock Leaf, which a Table-cloth made.

The Viands were various, to each of their Taste,
And the *Bee* brought her Honey to crown the Repast.

Then close on his Haunches, so solemn and wise,
The *Frog* from a Corner, look'd up to the Skies.

And the *Squirrel* well pleas'd such Diversions to see,
Mounted high over Head, and look'd down from a Tree.   30
Then out came the *Spider*, with Finger so fine,
To shew his Dexterity on the tight Line.

From one Branch to another, his Cobwebs he slung,
Then quick as an Arrow he darted along,
But just in the Middle,—Oh! shocking to tell,
From his Rope, in an Instant, poor Harlequin fell.

Yet he touch'd not the Ground, but with Talons outspread,
Hung suspended in Air, at the End of a Thread.
Then the *Grasshopper* came with a Jerk and a Spring,
Very long was his Leg, though but short was his Wing;   40

He took but three Leaps, and was soon out of Sight,
Then chirp'd his own Praises the rest of the Night.
With Step so majestic the *Snail* did advance,
And promis'd the Gazers a Minuet to dance.

But they all laugh'd so loud that he pull'd in his Head,
And went in his own little Chamber to Bed.
Then, as Evening gave Way to the Shadows of Night,
Their Watchman, the *Glow-worm*, came out with a Light.

Then Home let us hasten, while yet we can see,
For no Watchman is waiting for you and for me.   50
So said little Robert, and pacing along,
His merry Companions returned in a Throng.

END OF THE BUTTERFLY'S BALL.

CHARLOTTE SMITH
1749–1806

118   from *Beachy Head*

ON thy stupendous summit, rock sublime!
That o'er the channel rear'd, half way at sea
The mariner at early morning hails,
I would recline; while Fancy should go forth,
And represent the strange and awful hour
Of vast concussion; when the Omnipotent
Stretch'd forth his arm, and rent the solid hills,
Bidding the impetuous main flood rush between
The rifted shores, and from the continent
Eternally divided this green isle.   10
Imperial lord of the high southern coast!
From thy projecting head-land I would mark
Far in the east the shades of night disperse,
Melting and thinned, as from the dark blue wave
Emerging, brilliant rays of arrowy light
Dart from the horizon; when the glorious sun
Just lifts above it his resplendent orb.
Advances now, with feathery silver touched,
The rippling tide of flood; glisten the sands,
While, inmates of the chalky clefts that scar   20
Thy sides precipitous, with shrill harsh cry,
Their white wings glancing in the level beam,
The terns, and gulls, and tarrocks, seek their food,
And thy rough hollows echo to the voice
Of the gray choughs, and ever restless daws,
With clamour, not unlike the chiding hounds,
While the lone shepherd, and his baying dog,
Drive to thy turfy crest his bleating flock.

The high meridian of the day is past,
And Ocean now, reflecting the calm Heaven,   30
Is of cerulean hue; and murmurs low
The tide of ebb, upon the level sands.
The sloop, her angular canvas shifting still,
Catches the light and variable airs
That but a little crisp the summer sea,
Dimpling its tranquil surface.

SYDNEY OWENSON
(later LADY MORGAN)
1776–1859

119

Joy

Fragment XXXVII

Joy's a fix'd state—a tenure, not a start.

YOUNG

I

'JOY a fix'd state—a tenure, not a start!'
Whence came that thought, sublime and pensive sage?
Did Joy e'er play upon thy grief-chill'd heart,
Or flash its warm beam o'er the life's sad page?

II

And felt'st thou not 'twas but a *start* indeed,
A *rainbow* lustre o'er the clouds of care;
Of many an anxious hope the golden meed,
The bright, tho' transient *heaven* of despair?

III

Oh Joy, *I* know thee well! and in that hour
Which gave me to the dearest father's arms,   10
(Arms long unfill'd by me) have felt thy pow'r
Sweetly dispelling absence' fond alarms.

IV

And I have felt thy evanescent gleam
Illume the vision youthful *fancy* brought;
Have known thee in my slumbers' rosy dream
Give many a bliss *I (waking)* vainly sought.

V

From thee what sweet truths would cold REASON borrow,
Whilst thou (tumultuous in thy reign) would chase
Each gloomy phantom of my bosom's sorrow,
And send thy sunny spirits in their place.   20

VI

Wild, warm, and tender, was thy witching hour,
Delight's wild throb, and rapture's tear was thine,
And every *feeling* own'd thy melting pow'r;
Oh! such *at least* thou wert, when thou wert mine.

VII

Transient indeed, as young spring's *iris sky*,
And ever fleetest in thy dearest bliss;
Chas'd by a doubt, a frown, a tear, a sigh;
Lured by a glance, a thought, a smile, a kiss.

VIII

Yet though so fleeting in thy poignant pleasure,
Though thy brief span is scarce a raptured hour,   30
Though still *least* palpable thy *richest* treasure,
Though as we *cull*, still *fades* thy *sweetest* flow'r;

IX

Yet come! delicious Joy! ere yet the chill
Of age repels thy influence o'er my heart,
While yet each sense responsive meets thy thrill,
Oh come! delicious Joy! *all transient* as thou art!

WILLIAM WORDSWORTH

120–131   from *Poems, in Two Volumes*

120   *Ode to Duty*

STERN Daughter of the Voice of God!
O Duty! if that name thou love
Who art a Light to guide, a Rod
To check the erring, and reprove;
Thou who art victory and law
When empty terrors overawe;
From vain temptations dost set free;
From strife and from despair; a glorious ministry.

There are who ask not if thine eye
Be on them; who, in love and truth,   10

Where no misgiving is, rely
Upon the genial sense of youth:
Glad Hearts! without reproach or blot;
Who do thy work, and know it not:
May joy be theirs while life shall last!
And Thou, if they should totter, teach them to stand fast!

Serene will be our days and bright,
And happy will our nature be,
When love is an unerring light,
And joy its own security.   20
And bless'd are they who in the main
This faith, even now, do entertain:
Live in the spirit of this creed;
Yet find that other strength, according to their need.

I, loving freedom, and untried;
No sport of every random gust,
Yet being to myself a guide,
Too blindly have reposed my trust:
Resolved that nothing e'er should press
Upon my present happiness,   30
I shoved unwelcome tasks away;
But thee I now would serve more strictly, if I may.

Through no disturbance of my soul,
Or strong compunction in me wrought,
I supplicate for thy controul;
But in the quietness of thought:
Me this uncharter'd freedom tires;
I feel the weight of chance desires:
My hopes no more must change their name,
I long for a repose which ever is the same.   40

Yet not the less would I throughout
Still act according to the voice
Of my own wish; and feel past doubt
That my submissiveness was choice:
Not seeking in the school of pride
For 'precepts over dignified,'
Denial and restraint I prize
No farther than they breed a second Will more wise.

Stern Lawgiver! yet thou dost wear
The Godhead's most benignant grace;   50
Nor know we any thing so fair

As is the smile upon thy face:
Flowers laugh before thee on their beds;
And Fragrance in thy footing treads;
Thou dost preserve the Stars from wrong;
And the most ancient Heavens through Thee are fresh
  and strong.

To humbler functions, awful Power!
I call thee: I myself commend
Unto thy guidance from this hour;
Oh! let my weakness have an end!   60
Give unto me, made lowly wise,
The spirit of self-sacrifice;
The confidence of reason give;
And in the light of truth thy Bondman let me live!

121   *Resolution and Independence*

THERE was a roaring in the wind all night;
The rain came heavily and fell in floods;
But now the sun is rising calm and bright;
The birds are singing in the distant woods;
Over his own sweet voice the Stock-dove broods;
The Jay makes answer as the Magpie chatters;
And all the air is fill'd with pleasant noise of waters.

All things that love the sun are out of doors;
The sky rejoices in the morning's birth;
The grass is bright with rain-drops; on the moors   10
The Hare is running races in her mirth;
And with her feet she from the plashy earth
Raises a mist; which, glittering in the sun,
Runs with her all the way, wherever she doth run.

I was a Traveller then upon the moor;
I saw the Hare that rac'd about with joy;
I heard the woods, and distant waters, roar;
Or heard them not, as happy as a Boy:
The pleasant season did my heart employ:
My old remembrances went from me wholly;   20
And all the ways of men, so vain and melancholy.

But, as it sometimes chanceth, from the might
Of joy in minds that can no farther go,

259

As high as we have mounted in delight
In our dejection do we sink as low,
To me that morning did it happen so;
And fears, and fancies, thick upon me came;
Dim sadness, and blind thoughts I knew not nor could name.

I heard the Sky-lark singing in the sky;
And I bethought me of the playful Hare: 30
Even such a happy Child of earth am I;
Even as these blissful Creatures do I fare;
Far from the world I walk, and from all care;
But there may come another day to me,
Solitude, pain of heart, distress, and poverty.

My whole life I have liv'd in pleasant thought,
As if life's business were a summer mood;
As if all needful things would come unsought
To genial faith, still rich in genial good;
But how can He expect that others should   40
Build for him, sow for him, and at his call
Love him, who for himself will take no heed at all?

I thought of Chatterton, the marvellous Boy,
The sleepless Soul that perish'd in its pride;
Of Him who walk'd in glory and in joy
Behind his plough, upon the mountain-side:
By our own spirits are we deified;
We Poets in our youth begin in gladness;
But thereof comes in the end despondency and madness.

Now, whether it were by peculiar grace,   50
A leading from above, a something given,
Yet it befel, that, in this lonely place,
When up and down my fancy thus was driven,
And I with these untoward thoughts had striven,
I saw a Man before me unawares:
The oldest Man he seem'd that ever wore grey hairs.

My course I stopped as soon as I espied
The Old Man in that naked wilderness:
Close by a Pond, upon the further side,
He stood alone: a minute's space I guess   60
I watch'd him, he continuing motionless:
To the Pool's further margin then I drew;
He being all the while before me full in view.

As a huge Stone is sometimes seen to lie
Couch'd on the bald top of an eminence;
Wonder to all who do the same espy
By what means it could thither come, and whence;
So that it seems a thing endued with sense:
Like a Sea-beast crawl'd forth, which on a shelf
Of rock or sand reposeth, there to sun itself.   70

Such seem'd this Man, not all alive nor dead,
Nor all asleep; in his extreme old age:
His body was bent double, feet and head
Coming together in their pilgrimage;
As if some dire constraint of pain, or rage
Of sickness felt by him in times long past,
A more than human weight upon his frame had cast.

Himself he propp'd, his body, limbs, and face,
Upon a long grey Staff of shaven wood:
And, still as I drew near with gentle pace,   80
Beside the little pond or moorish flood
Motionless as a Cloud the Old Man stood;
That heareth not the loud winds when they call;
And moveth altogether, if it move at all.

At length, himself unsettling, he the Pond
Stirred with his Staff, and fixedly did look
Upon the muddy water, which he conn'd,
As if he had been reading in a book:
And now such freedom as I could I took;
And, drawing to his side, to him did say,   90
'This morning gives us promise of a glorious day.'

A gentle answer did the Old Man make,
In courteous speech which forth he slowly drew:
And him with further words I thus bespake,
'What kind of work is that which you pursue?
This is a lonesome place for one like you.'
He answer'd me with pleasure and surprize;
And there was, while he spake, a fire about his eyes.

His words came feebly, from a feeble chest,
Yet each in solemn order follow'd each,   100
With something of a lofty utterance drest;
Choice word, and measured phrase; above the reach

261

Of ordinary men; a stately speech!
Such as grave Livers do in Scotland use,
Religious men, who give to God and Man their dues.

He told me that he to this Pond had come
To gather Leeches, being old and poor:
Employment hazardous and wearisome!
And he had many hardships to endure:
From Pond to Pond he roam'd, from moor to moor,   110
Housing, with God's good help, by choice or chance:
And in this way he gain'd an honest maintenance.

The Old Man still stood talking by my side;
But now his voice to me was like a stream
Scarce heard; nor word from word could I divide;
And the whole Body of the man did seem
Like one whom I had met with in a dream;
Or like a Man from some far region sent,
To give me human strength, and strong admonishment.

My former thoughts return'd: the fear that kills;   120
The hope that is unwilling to be fed;
Cold, pain, and labour, and all fleshly ills;
And mighty Poets in their misery dead.
And now, not knowing what the Old Man had said,
My question eagerly did I renew,
'How is it that you live, and what is it you do?'

He with a smile did then his words repeat;
And said, that, gathering Leeches, far and wide
He travelled; stirring thus about his feet
The waters of the Ponds where they abide.   130
'Once I could meet with them on every side;
But they have dwindled long by slow decay;
Yet still I persevere, and find them where I may.'

While he was talking thus, the lonely place,
The Old Man's shape, and speech, all troubled me:
In my mind's eye I seem'd to see him pace
About the weary moors continually,
Wandering about alone and silently.
While I these thoughts within myself pursued,
He, having made a pause, the same discourse renewed.   140

And soon with this he other matter blended,
Chearfully uttered, with demeanour kind,

But stately in the main; and, when he ended,
I could have laugh'd myself to scorn, to find
In that decrepit Man so firm a mind.
'God,' said I, 'be my help and stay secure;
I'll think of the Leech-gatherer on the lonely moor.'

122 *Composed Upon Westminster Bridge*

Sept. 3, 1803

EARTH has not any thing to shew more fair:
Dull would he be of soul who could pass by
A sight so touching in its majesty:
This City now doth like a garment wear
The beauty of the morning; silent, bare,
Ships, towers, domes, theatres, and temples lie
Open unto the fields, and to the sky;
All bright and glittering in the smokeless air.
Never did sun more beautifully steep
In his first splendor valley, rock, or hill;　　　　10
Ne'er saw I, never felt, a calm so deep!
The river glideth at his own sweet will:
Dear God! the very houses seem asleep;
And all that mighty heart is lying still!

123 ['The world is too much with us']

THE world is too much with us; late and soon,
Getting and spending, we lay waste our powers:
Little we see in nature that is ours;
We have given our hearts away, a sordid boon!
This Sea that bares her bosom to the moon;
The Winds that will be howling at all hours
And are up-gathered now like sleeping flowers;
For this, for every thing, we are out of tune;
It moves us not. Great God! I'd rather be
A Pagan suckled in a creed outworn;　　　　10
So might I, standing on this pleasant lea,
Have glimpses that would make me less forlorn;
Have sight of Proteus coming from the sea;
Or hear old Triton blow his wreathed horn.

124   ['It is a beauteous Evening']

IT is a beauteous Evening, calm and free;
The holy time is quiet as a Nun
Breathless with adoration; the broad sun
Is sinking down in its tranquillity;
The gentleness of heaven is on the Sea:
Listen! the mighty Being is awake
And doth with his eternal motion make
A sound like thunder—everlastingly.
Dear Child! dear Girl! that walkest with me here,
If thou appear'st untouch'd by solemn thought,   10
Thy nature is not therefore less divine:
Thou liest in Abraham's bosom all the year;
And worshipp'st at the Temple's inner shrine,
God being with thee when we know it not.

125   *London*

                1802

MILTON! thou should'st be living at this hour:
England hath need of thee: she is a fen
Of stagnant waters: altar, sword, and pen,
Fireside, the heroic wealth of hall and bower,
Have forfeited their ancient English dower
Of inward happiness. We are selfish men;
Oh! raise us up, return to us again;
And give us manners, virtue, freedom, power.
Thy soul was like a Star and dwelt apart:
Thou hadst a voice whose sound was like the sea;   10
Pure as the naked heavens, majestic, free,
So didst thou travel on life's common way,
In chearful godliness; and yet thy heart
The lowliest duties on itself did lay.

126   *The Solitary Reaper*

BEHOLD her, single in the field,
Yon solitary Highland Lass!
Reaping and singing by herself;
Stop here, or gently pass!
Alone she cuts, and binds the grain,

And sings a melancholy strain;
O listen! for the Vale profound
Is overflowing with the sound.

No Nightingale did ever chaunt
So sweetly to reposing bands   10
Of Travellers in some shady haunt,
Among Arabian Sands:
No sweeter voice was ever heard
In spring-time from the Cuckoo-bird,
Breaking the silence of the seas
Among the farthest Hebrides.

Will no one tell me what she sings?
Perhaps the plaintive numbers flow
For old, unhappy, far-off things,
And battles long ago: 20
Or is it some more humble lay,
Familiar matter of today?
Some natural sorrow, loss, or pain,
That has been, and may be again!

Whate'er the theme, the Maiden sang
As if her song could have no ending;
I saw her singing at her work,
And o'er the sickle bending;
I listen'd till I had my fill:
And, as I mounted up the hill,   30
The music in my heart I bore,
Long after it was heard no more.

127   ['My heart leaps up']

MY heart leaps up when I behold
          A Rainbow in the sky:
So was it when my life began;
So is it now I am a Man;
So be it when I shall grow old,
          Or let me die!
The Child is Father of the Man;
And I could wish my days to be
Bound each to each by natural piety.

128   ['I wandered lonely as a Cloud']

I WANDERED lonely as a Cloud
That floats on high o'er Vales and Hills,
When all at once I saw a crowd
A host of dancing Daffodils;
Along the Lake, beneath the trees,
Ten thousand dancing in the breeze.

The waves beside them danced, but they
Outdid the sparkling waves in glee:—
A Poet could not but be gay
In such a laughing company: 10
I gazed—and gazed—but little thought
What wealth the shew to me had brought:

For oft when on my couch I lie
In vacant or in pensive mood,
They flash upon that inward eye
Which is the bliss of solitude,
And then my heart with pleasure fills,
And dances with the Daffodils.

129   *To the Cuckoo*

O BLITHE New-comer! I have heard,
I hear thee and rejoice:
O Cuckoo! shall I call thee Bird,
Or but a wandering Voice?

While I am lying on the grass,
I hear thy restless shout:
From hill to hill it seems to pass,
About, and all about!

To me, no Babbler with a tale
Of sunshine and of flowers,   10
Thou tellest, Cuckoo! in the vale
Of visionary hours.

Thrice welcome, Darling of the Spring!
Even yet thou art to me
No Bird; but an invisible Thing,
A voice, a mystery.

The same whom in my School-boy days
I listen'd to; that Cry
Which made me look a thousand ways;
In bush, and tree, and sky.   20

To seek thee did I often rove
Through woods and on the green;
And thou wert still a hope, a love;
Still long'd for, never seen!

And I can listen to thee yet;
Can lie upon the plain
And listen, till I do beget
That golden time again.

O blessed Bird! the earth we pace
Again appears to be   30
An unsubstantial, faery place;
That is fit home for Thee!

130   *Elegiac Stanzas*

*Suggested by a Picture of Peele Castle, in a Storm, painted by
Sir George Beaumont*

I WAS thy Neighbour once, thou rugged Pile!
Four summer weeks I dwelt in sight of thee:
I saw thee every day; and all the while
Thy Form was sleeping on a glassy sea.

So pure the sky, so quiet was the air!
So like, so very like, was day to day!
Whene'er I look'd, thy Image still was there;
It trembled, but it never pass'd away.

How perfect was the calm! it seem'd no sleep;
No mood, which season takes away, or brings: 10
I could have fancied that the mighty Deep
Was even the gentlest of all gentle Things.

Ah! THEN, if mine had been the Painter's hand,
To express what then I saw; and add the gleam,
The light that never was, on sea or land,
The consecration, and the Poet's dream;

I would have planted thee, thou hoary Pile!
Amid a world how different from this!
Beside a sea that could not cease to smile;
On tranquil land, beneath a sky of bliss: 20

Thou shouldst have seem'd a treasure-house, a mine
Of peaceful years; a chronicle of heaven:—
Of all the sunbeams that did ever shine
The very sweetest had to thee been given.

A Picture had it been of lasting ease,
Elysian quiet, without toil or strife;
No motion but the moving tide, a breeze,
Or merely silent Nature's breathing life.

Such, in the fond delusion of my heart,
Such Picture would I at that time have made: 30
And seen the soul of truth in every part;
A faith, a trust, that could not be betray'd.

So once it would have been,—'tis so no more;
I have submitted to a new controul:
A power is gone, which nothing can restore;
A deep distress hath humaniz'd my Soul.

Not for a moment could I now behold
A smiling sea and be what I have been:
The feeling of my loss will ne'er be old;
This, which I know, I speak with mind serene.   40

Then, Beaumont, Friend! who would have been the Friend,
If he had lived, of Him whom I deplore,
This Work of thine I blame not, but commend;
This sea in anger, and that dismal shore.

Oh 'tis a passionate Work!—yet wise and well;
Well chosen is the spirit that is here;
That Hulk which labours in the deadly swell,
This rueful sky, this pageantry of fear!

And this huge Castle, standing here sublime,
I love to see the look with which it braves,   50
Cased in the unfeeling armour of old time,
The light'ning, the fierce wind, and trampling waves.

Farewell, farewell the Heart that lives alone,
Hous'd in a dream, at distance from the Kind!
Such happiness, wherever it be known,
Is to be pitied; for 'tis surely blind.

But welcome fortitude, and patient chear,
And frequent sights of what is to be borne!
Such sights, or worse, as are before me here.—
Not without hope we suffer and we mourn.   60

131   *Ode*

[*Intimations of Immortality*]

Paulò majora canamus.

THERE was a time when meadow, grove, and stream,
The earth, and every common sight,
          To me did seem
          Apparelled in celestial light,
The glory and the freshness of a dream.
It is not now as it has been of yore;—
          Turn wheresoe'er I may,
          By night or day,
The things which I have seen I now can see no more.

          The Rainbow comes and goes,   10
          And lovely is the Rose,
          The Moon doth with delight
Look round her when the heavens are bare;
          Waters on a starry night
          Are beautiful and fair;
          The sunshine is a glorious birth;
          But yet I know, where'er I go,
That there hath passed away a glory from the earth.

Now, while the Birds thus sing a joyous song,
          And while the young Lambs bound   20
          As to the tabor's sound,
To me alone there came a thought of grief:
A timely utterance gave that thought relief,
          And I again am strong.
The Cataracts blow their trumpets from the steep,
No more shall grief of mine the season wrong;

I hear the Echoes through the mountains throng,
The Winds come to me from the fields of sleep,
      And all the earth is gay,
         Land and sea
    Give themselves up to jollity,
      And with the heart of May
Doth every Beast keep holiday,
      Thou Child of Joy
Shout round me, let me hear thy shouts, thou happy Shepherd Boy!

Ye blessed Creatures, I have heard the call
    Ye to each other make; I see
The heavens laugh with you in your jubilee;
    My heart is at your festival,
      My head hath its coronal,
The fullness of your bliss, I feel—I feel it all.
      Oh evil day! if I were sullen
      While the Earth herself is adorning,
        This sweet May-morning,
    And the Children are pulling,
        On every side,
    In a thousand vallies far and wide,
    Fresh flowers; while the sun shines warm,
And the Babe leaps up on his mother's arm:—
      I hear, I hear, with joy I hear!
      —But there's a Tree, of many one,
A single Field which I have looked upon,
Both of them speak of something that is gone:
      The Pansy at my feet
      Doth the same tale repeat:
Whither is fled the visionary gleam?
Where is it now, the glory and the dream?

Our birth is but a sleep and a forgetting:
The Soul that rises with us, our life's Star,
      Hath had elsewhere its setting,
        And cometh from afar:
      Not in entire forgetfulness,
      And not in utter nakedness,
But trailing clouds of glory do we come
        From God, who is our home:
Heaven lies about us in our infancy!
Shades of the prison-house begin to close
      Upon the growing Boy,
But He beholds the light, and whence it flows,
      He sees it in his joy;

The Youth, who daily farther from the East
   Must travel, still is Nature's Priest,
     ·   And by the vision splendid
       Is on his way attended;
At length the Man perceives it die away,
And fade into the light of common day.

Earth fills her lap with pleasures of her own;
Yearnings she hath in her own natural kind,
And, even with something of a Mother's mind,
     And no unworthy aim,   80
   The homely Nurse doth all she can
To make her Foster-child, her Inmate Man,
    Forget the glories he hath known,
And that imperial palace whence he came.
Behold the Child among his new-born blisses,
A four year's Darling of a pigmy size!
See, where 'mid work of his own hand he lies,
Fretted by sallies of his Mother's kisses,
With light upon him from his Father's eyes!
See, at his feet, some little plan or chart,   90
Some fragment from his dream of human life,
Shaped by himself with newly-learned art;
      A wedding or a festival,
      A mourning or a funeral;
        And this hath now his heart,
      And unto this he frames his song:
        Then will he fit his tongue
To dialogues of business, love, or strife;
      But it will not be long
      Ere this be thrown aside,   100
      And with new joy and pride
The little Actor cons another part,
Filling from time to time his 'humorous stage'
With all the Persons, down to palsied Age,
That Life brings with her in her Equipage;
      As if his whole vocation
      Were endless imitation.

Thou, whose exterior semblance doth belie
      Thy Soul's immensity;
Thou best Philosopher, who yet dost keep   110
Thy heritage, thou Eye among the blind,
That, deaf and silent, read'st the eternal deep,
Haunted for ever by the eternal mind,—

Mighty Prophet! Seer blest!
On whom those truths do rest,
Which we are toiling all our lives to find;
Thou, over whom thy Immortality
Broods like the Day, a Master o'er a Slave,
A Presence which is not to be put by;
　　　　To whom the grave　　　　　　　　120
Is but a lonely bed without the sense or sight
　　　Of day or the warm light,
A place of thought where we in waiting lie;
Thou little Child, yet glorious in the might
Of untamed pleasures, on thy Being's height,
Why with such earnest pains dost thou provoke
The Years to bring the inevitable yoke,
Thus blindly with thy blessedness at strife?
Full soon thy Soul shall have her earthly freight,
And custom lie upon thee with a weight,　　　　130
Heavy as frost, and deep almost as life!

　　　　O joy! that in our embers
　　　　Is something that doth live,
　　　　That nature yet remembers
　　　　What was so fugitive!
The thought of our past years in me doth breed
Perpetual benedictions: not indeed
For that which is most worthy to be blest;
Delight and liberty, the simple creed
Of Childhood, whether fluttering or at rest,　　　140
With new-born hope for ever in his breast:—
　　　　Not for these I raise
　　　　The song of thanks and praise;
　　　But for those obstinate questionings
　　　Of sense and outward things,
　　　Fallings from us, vanishings;
　　　Blank misgivings of a Creature
Moving about in worlds not realized,
High instincts, before which our mortal Nature
Did tremble like a guilty Thing surprised:　　　150
　　　But for those first affections,
　　　Those shadowy recollections,
　　　　Which, be they what they may,
Are yet the fountain light of all our day,
Are yet a master light of all our seeing;
　　　Uphold us, cherish us, and make
Our noisy years seem moments in the being
Of the eternal Silence: truths that wake,

To perish never;
Which neither listlessness, nor mad endeavour,   160
Nor Man nor Boy,
Nor all that is at enmity with joy,
Can utterly abolish or destroy!
Hence, in a season of calm weather,
Though inland far we be,
Our Souls have sight of that immortal sea
Which brought us hither,
Can in a moment travel thither,
And see the Children sport upon the shore,
And hear the mighty waters rolling evermore.   170

Then, sing ye Birds, sing, sing a joyous song!
And let the young Lambs bound
As to the tabor's sound!
We in thought will join your throng,
Ye that pipe and ye that play,
Ye that through your hearts today
Feel the gladness of the May!
What though the radiance which was once so bright
Be now for ever taken from my sight,
Though nothing can bring back the hour   180
Of splendour in the grass, of glory in the flower;
We will grieve not, rather find
Strength in what remains behind,
In the primal sympathy
Which having been must ever be,
In the soothing thoughts that spring
Out of human suffering,
In the faith that looks through death,
In years that bring the philosophic mind.

And oh ye Fountains, Meadows, Hills, and Groves,   190
Think not of any severing of our loves!
Yet in my heart of hearts I feel your might;
I only have relinquished one delight
To live beneath your more habitual sway.
I love the Brooks which down their channels fret,
Even more than when I tripped lightly as they;
The innocent brightness of a new-born Day
Is lovely yet;
The Clouds that gather round the setting sun
Do take a sober colouring from an eye   200
That hath kept watch o'er man's mortality;

Another race hath been, and other palms are won.
Thanks to the human heart by which we live,
Thanks to its tenderness, its joys, and fears,
To me the meanest flower that blows can give
Thoughts that do often lie too deep for tears.

[1808]

AMELIA OPIE
1769–1853

132 *To a Maniac*

THERE was a time, poor phrensied maid,
When I could o'er thy grief have mourned,
And still with tears the tale repaid
Of sense by sorrow's sway o'erturned.

But now thy state my envy moves:
For thou art woe's unconscious prize;
Thy heart no sense of suffering proves,
No fruitless tears bedew thine eyes.

Excess of sorrow, kind to thee,
At once destroyed thy reason's power;   10
But reason still remains to me,
And only bids me grieve the more.

WALTER SCOTT
1771–1832

from *Marmion*

Song

WHERE shall the lover rest,
  Whom the fates sever
From his true maiden's breast,
  Parted for ever?
Where, through groves deep and high,
  Sounds the far billow,
Where early violets die,
  Under the willow.

CHORUS

Eleu loro, &c. Soft shall be his pillow.

There, through the summer day,   10
  Cool streams are laving;
There, while the tempests sway,
  Scarce are boughs waving;
There, thy rest shalt thou take,
  Parted for ever,
Never again to wake,
  Never, O never!

CHORUS

Eleu loro, &c. Never, O never!

Where shall the traitor rest,
  He, the deceiver,   20
Who could win maiden's breast,
  Ruin, and leave her?
In the lost battle,
  Borne down by the flying,
Where mingles war's rattle
  With groans of the dying.

CHORUS

Eleu loro, &c. There shall he be lying.

Her wing shall the eagle flap
  O'er the false-hearted;
His warm blood the wolf shall lap,   30
  Ere life be parted.
Shame and dishonour sit
  By his grave ever;
Blessing shall hallow it,
  Never, O never!

CHORUS

Eleu loro, &c. Never, O never!

(Canto III. x, xi)

[1809]

REVD THOMAS BECK
fl. 1780–1820

134   *Sonnet to Nothing*

MYSTERIOUS Nothing! how shall I define
  Thy shapeless, baseless, placeless emptiness,
Nor form, nor colour, sound, nor size, are thine,
  Nor words, nor figures, can thy void express:
But though we cannot thee to aught compare,
  To thee a thousand things may liken'd be;
And though thou art with *nobody, nowhere,*
  Yet half mankind devote their lives to thee.
How many books thy history contain!
  How many heads thy mighty plans pursue   10
What lab'ring hands thy portion only gain!
  What busy men thy doings only do!
To thee the great, the proud, the giddy bend,
And, *like my Sonnet, all in nothing end.*

THOMAS CAMPBELL

Lord Ullin's Daughter

A CHIEFTAIN to the Highlands bound
  Cries 'Boatman, do not tarry!
And I'll give thee a silver pound
  To row us o'er the ferry.'

'Now who be ye would cross Lochgyle,
  This dark and stormy water?'
'O, I'm the chief of Ulva's isle,
  And this Lord Ullin's daughter.

'And fast before her father's men
  Three days we've fled together,   10
For, should he find us in the glen,
  My blood would stain the heather.

'His horsemen hard behind us ride;
  Should they our steps discover,
Then who will cheer my bonny bride
  When they have slain her lover?'

Outspoke the hardy Highland wight,
  'I'll go, my chief! I'm ready;
It is not for your silver bright,
  But for your winsome lady.   20

'And, by my word! the bonny bird
  In danger shall not tarry;
So, though the waves are raging white
  I'll row you o'er the ferry.'

By this the storm grew loud apace,
  The water-wraith was shrieking;
And in the scowl of heaven each face
  Grew dark as they were speaking.

But still, as wilder blew the wind,
  And as the night grew drearer,   30
Adown the glen rode armèd men—
  Their trampling sounded nearer.

'O haste thee, haste!' the lady cries,
  'Though tempests round us gather;
I'll meet the raging of the skies
  But not an angry father.'

The boat has left a stormy land,
  A stormy sea before her,—
When, oh! too strong for human hand,
  The tempest gathered o'er her.   40

And still they rowed amidst the roar
  Of waters fast prevailing:
Lord Ullin reached that fatal shore,—
  His wrath was changed to wailing.

For sore dismayed, through storm and shade,
  His child he did discover:
One lovely hand she stretched for aid,
  And one was round her lover.

'Come back! come back!' he cried in grief
  Across the stormy water: 50
'And I'll forgive your Highland chief,
  My daughter! oh my daughter!'

'Twas vain: the loud waves lashed the shore,
  Return or aid preventing;
The waters wild went o'er his child,
  And he was left lamenting.

[1810]

ROBERT SOUTHEY

136   from *The Curse of Kehama*

I CHARM thy life
From the weapons of strife,
From stone and from wood,
From fire and from flood,
From the serpent's tooth,
And the beasts of blood:
From Sickness I charm thee,

And Time shall not harm thee;
But Earth which is mine,
Its fruits shall deny thee;   10
And Water shall hear me,
And know thee and fly thee;
And the Winds shall not touch thee
When they pass by thee,
And the Dews shall not wet thee,
When they fall nigh thee:
And thou shalt seek Death
To release thee, in vain;
Thou shalt live in thy pain
While Kehama shall reign,   20
With a fire in thy heart,
And a fire in thy brain;
And Sleep shall obey me,
And visit thee never,
And the Curse shall be on thee
For ever and ever.

There where the Curse had stricken him,
There stood the miserable man,
There stood Ladurlad, with loose-hanging arms,
And eyes of idiot wandering.   30
Was it a dream? alas,
He heard the river flow,
He heard the crumbling of the pile,
He heard the wind which shower'd
The thin white ashes round.
There motionless he stood,
As if he hoped it were a dream,
And feared to move, lest he should prove
The actual misery;
And still at times he met Kehama's eye,   40
Kehama's eye that fastened on him still.

(II. 14–15)

279

ANNA SEWARD

1742–1809

137   *Speech of the Nymph*

*of that Brook, which, after Heavy Rain, becomes a Deep, Violent,
and Formidable Torrent*

> Lo! down yon steep of vales proud Deva borne,
> Rolls the hoarse treasures of her flashing urn!
> Yet bears my stream, as o'er the rocks it raves,
> Not tribute, but defiance to her waves.

138   *Sonnet*

*Laid in the drawer of the thatched shed by the brook at Plas
Nwydd, the Villa of the Right Hon. Lady Eleanor Butler, and
Miss Ponsonby, in Llangollen Vale*

Written in Autumn 1799

> STRANGER, when o'er yon slant, warm field no cloud
>   Steals,—at its foot, the verge of a wild brook,
>   In tangled dell, where sun-beams never look,
>   Press this screen'd seat, and mark the waters crowd
> Close to the cliff down their steep channel rude;
>   Leaping o'er rugged stones, that aye provoke
>   Foam and hoarse murmur; while the pendant oak
>   Frowns o'er the little, clamorous, lonely flood.—
> Impetuous Deva's honours yield to thine,
>   Dear brook, for O! thy scanty billows lave   10
>   Friendship and Fancy's consecrated shrine;
> And thou may'st tell the stream of mightier wave,
>   Here oft they muse the noontide hours away,
>   Who gild thy vale with intellectual ray.

ANN TAYLOR
1782–1866

The Maniac's Song

BRING me a garland, bring me a wreath;
  Bring me a flower from the dank stream side;
Bring me a herb smelling sweetly of death,
  Wet with the drowsy tide.

Haste to the pool with the green-weed breast,
  Where the dark wave crawls through the sedge;
Where the bittern of the wilderness builds her nest,
  In the flags of its oozy edge;

Where no sun shines through the live-long day,
  Because of the blue-wreathed mist,   10
Where the cockatrice creeps her foul egg to lay,
  And the speckled snake has hissed:

And bring me the flag that is moist with the wave,
  And the rush where the heath-winds sigh,
And the hemlock plant, that flourishes so brave,
  And the poppy, with its coal-black eye;

And weave them tightly, and weave them well,
  The fever of my head to allay;—
And soon shall I faint with the death-weed smell,
  And sleep these throbbings away.   20

And my hot, hot heart, that is fluttering so fast,
  Shall shudder with a strange, cold thrill;
And the damp hand of Death o'er my forehead shall be passed,
  And my lips shall be stiff and still.

And crystals of ice on my bosom shall arise,
  Prest out from the shivering pore;
And oft shall it struggle with pent-up sighs,
  But soon it shall struggle no more.

For the poppy on my head shall her cool breath shed,
  And wind through the blue, blue tide;   30
And the bony wand of Death shall draw my last breath,
  All by the dark stream side.

WALTER SCOTT

Coronach

HE is gone on the mountain,
  He is lost to the forest,
Like a summer-dried fountain,
  When our need was the sorest.
The font, reappearing,
  From the rain-drops shall borrow,
But to us comes no cheering,
  To Duncan no morrow!

The hand of the reaper
  Takes the ears that are hoary,   10
But the voice of the weeper
  Wails manhood in glory.
The autumn winds rushing
  Waft the leaves that are searest,
But our flower was in flushing,
  When blighting was nearest.

Fleet foot on the correi,
  Sage counsel in cumber,
Red hand in the foray,
  How sound is thy slumber!   20
Like the dew on the mountain,
  Like the foam on the river,
Like the bubble on the fountain,
  Thou art gone, and for ever!

(from *The Lady of the Lake*,
Canto III, lines 370–93)

140: 17 correi] lee hillside   18 cumber] trouble

GEORGE CRABBE
1754–1832

Peter Grimes

> Was a sordid soul,
> Such as does murder for a meed;
> Who but for fear knows no controul,
> Because his conscience, sear'd and foul,
>   Feels not the import of the deed;
> One whose brute feeling ne'er aspires
> Beyond his own more brute desires.
>
>   SCOTT, *Marmion* [II. xxii]

Methought the souls of all that I had murder'd came to my tent, and every one did threat—

                         SHAKSPEARE, *Richard III* [V. iii]

> The time hath been,
> That when the brains were out the man would die,
> And there an end; but now they rise again,
> With twenty mortal murders on their crowns,
> And push us from our stools.
>
>   *Macbeth* [III. iv]

The Father of Peter *a Fisherman.—Peter's early Conduct.—His Grief for the old Man.—He takes an Apprentice.—The Boy's Suffering and Fate.—A second Boy: how he died.—*Peter *acquitted.—A third Apprentice.—A Voyage by Sea: the Boy does not return.—Evil Report on* Peter: *he is tried and threatened.— Lives alone.—His Melancholy and incipient Madness.—Is observed and visited. —He escapes and is taken; is lodged in a Parish-House: Women attend and watch him.—He speaks in a Delirium: grows more collected.—His Account of his Feelings and visionary Terrors previous to his Death.*

> OLD *Peter Grimes* made Fishing his employ,
> His Wife he cabin'd with him and his Boy,
> And seem'd that Life laborious to enjoy:
> To Town came quiet *Peter* with his Fish,
> And had of all a civil word and wish.
> He left his Trade upon the Sabbath-Day,
> And took young *Peter* in his hand to pray;
> But soon the stubborn Boy from care broke loose,
> At first refus'd, then added his abuse:
> His Father's Love he scorn'd, his Power defied,   10
> But being drunk, wept sorely when he died.

Yes! then he wept, and to his Mind there came
Much of his Conduct, and he felt the Shame,—
How he had oft the good Old Man revil'd,
And never paid the Duty of a Child:
How, when the Father in his Bible read,
He in contempt and anger left the Shed:
'It is the Word of Life,' the Parent cried;
—'This is the Life itself,' the Boy replied;
And while Old *Peter* in amazement stood,   20
Gave the hot Spirit to his boiling Blood:—
How he, with Oath and furious Speech, began
To prove his Freedom and assert the Man;
And when the Parent check'd his impious Rage,
How he had curs'd the Tyranny of Age,—
Nay, once had dealt the sacrilegious Blow
On his bare Head and laid his Parent low:
The Father groan'd—'If thou art old,' said he,
'And hast a Son—thou wilt remember me:
Thy Mother left me in an happy Time,   30
Thou kill'dst not her—Heav'n spares the double Crime.'

On an Inn-settle, in his maudlin Grief,
This he revolv'd and drank for his Relief.

Now liv'd the Youth in freedom, but debarr'd
From constant Pleasure, and he thought it hard;
Hard that he could not every Wish obey,
But must awhile relinquish Ale and Play;
Hard! that he could not to his Cards attend,
But must acquire the Money he would spend.

With greedy eye he look'd on all he saw,   40
He knew not Justice, and he laugh'd at Law;
On all he mark'd, he stretch'd his ready Hand;
He fish'd by Water and he filch'd by Land:
Oft in the Night has *Peter* dropt his Oar,
Fled from his Boat and sought for Prey on shore;
Oft up the Hedge-row glided, on his Back
Bearing the Orchard's Produce in a Sack,
Or Farm-yard Load, tugg'd fiercely from the Stack;
And as these Wrongs to greater numbers rose,
The more he look'd on all Men as his Foes.   50

He built a mud-wall'd Hovel, where he kept
His various Wealth, and there he oft-times slept;
But no Success could please his cruel Soul,

He wish'd for One to trouble and controul;
He wanted some obedient Boy to stand
And bear the blow of his outrageous hand;
And hop'd to find in some propitious hour
A feeling Creature subject to his Power.

Peter had heard there were in London then,—
Still have they being?—Workhouse-clearing Men,   60
Who, undisturb'd by Feelings just or kind,
Would Parish-Boys to needy Tradesmen bind:
They in their want a trifling Sum would take,
And toiling Slaves of piteous Orphans make.

Such *Peter* sought, and when a Lad was found,
The Sum was dealt him and the Slave was bound.
Some few in Town observ'd in *Peter*'s Trap
A Boy, with Jacket blue and woollen Cap;
But none enquir'd how *Peter* us'd the Rope,
Or what the Bruise, that made the Stripling stoop;   70
None could the Ridges on his Back behold,
None sought him shiv'ring in the Winter's Cold;
None put the question,—'*Peter*, dost thou give
The Boy his Food?—What, Man! the Lad must live:
Consider, *Peter*, let the Child have Bread,
He'll serve thee better if he's strok'd and fed.'
None reason'd thus—and some, on hearing Cries,
Said calmly, '*Grimes* is at his Exercise.'

Pin'd, beaten, cold, pinch'd, threaten'd, and abus'd,—
His Efforts punish'd and his Food refus'd,—   80
Awake tormented,—soon arous'd from sleep,—
Struck if he wept, and yet compell'd to weep,
The trembling Boy dropt down and strove to pray,
Receiv'd a Blow and trembling turn'd away,
Or sobb'd and hid his piteous face;—while he,
The savage Master, grinn'd in horrid glee;
He'd now the power he ever lov'd to show,
A feeling Being subject to his Blow.

Thus liv'd the Lad in Hunger, Peril, Pain,
His Tears despis'd, his Supplications vain: 90
Compell'd by fear to lie, by need to steal,
His Bed uneasy and unblest his Meal,
For three sad Years the Boy his Tortures bore,
And then his Pains and Trials were no more.

'How died he, *Peter?*' when the People said,
He growl'd—'I found him lifeless in his Bed;'
Then try'd for softer tone, and sigh'd, 'Poor *Sam* is dead.'
Yet murmurs were there and some questions ask'd,—
How he was fed, how punish'd, and how task'd?
Much they suspected, but they little prov'd,   100
And *Peter* pass'd untroubled and unmov'd.

Another Boy with equal ease was found,
The Money granted and the Victim bound;
And what his Fate?—One night it chanc'd he fell
From the Boat's Mast and perish'd in her Well,
Where Fish were living kept, and where the Boy
(So reason'd Men) could not himself destroy:—

'Yes! so it was,' said *Peter*, 'in his play,
For he was idle both by night and day;
He climb'd the Main-mast and then fell below;'—   110
Then show'd his Corpse and pointed to the Blow:
'What said the Jury?'—they were long in doubt,
But sturdy *Peter* faced the matter out:
So they dismiss'd him, saying at the time,
'Keep fast your Hatchway when you've Boys who climb.'
This hit the Conscience, and he colour'd more
Than for the closest questions put before.

Thus all his fears the Verdict set aside,
And at the Slave-shop *Peter* still applied.

Then came a Boy, of Manners soft and mild,—   120
Our Seamen's Wives with grief beheld the Child;
All thought (tho' Poor themselves) that he was one
Of gentle Blood, some noble Sinner's Son,
Who had, belike, deceiv'd some humble Maid,
Whom he had first seduc'd and then betray'd:—
However this, he seem'd a gracious Lad,
In Grief submissive and with Patience sad.

Passive he labour'd, till his slender Frame
Bent with his Loads, and he at length was lame:
Strange that a Frame so weak could bear so long   130
The grossest Insult and the foulest Wrong;
But there were causes—in the Town they gave
Fire, Food, and Comfort, to the gentle Slave;
And though stern *Peter*, with a cruel Hand,
And knotted Rope, enforc'd the rude Command,

Yet he consider'd what he'd lately felt,
And his vile Blows with selfish Pity dealt.

One day such Draughts the cruel Fisher made,
He could not vend them in his Borough-Trade,
But sail'd for London-Mart: the Boy was ill,   140
But ever humbled to his Master's will;
And on the River, where they smoothly sail'd,
He strove with terror and awhile prevail'd;
But new to Danger on the angry Sea,
He clung affrighted to his Master's knee:
The Boat grew leaky and the Wind was strong,
Rough was the Passage and the Time was long;
His Liquor fail'd, and *Peter*'s Wrath arose, . . . :
No more is known—the rest we must suppose,
Or learn of *Peter*;—'*Peter*,' says he, 'spied   150
The Stripling's danger and for Harbour tried;
Meantime the Fish and then th'Apprentice died.'

The pitying Women rais'd a Clamour round,
And weeping said, 'Thou hast thy 'Prentice drown'd.'

Now the stern Man was summon'd to the Hall,
To tell his Tale before the Burghers all:
He gave th'Account; profess'd, the Lad he lov'd,
And kept his brazen Features all unmov'd.
The Mayor himself with tone severe replied,
'Henceforth with thee shall never Boy abide;   160
Hire thee a Freeman, whom thou durst not beat,
But who, in thy despite, will sleep and eat:
Free thou art now!—again shouldst thou appear,
Thou'lt find thy Sentence, like thy Soul, severe.'

Alas! for *Peter* not an helping Hand,
So was he hated, could he now command;
Alone he row'd his Boat, alone he cast
His Nets beside, or made his Anchor fast;
To hold a Rope or hear a Curse was none,—
He toil'd and rail'd; he groan'd and swore alone.   170

Thus by himself compell'd to live each day,
To wait for certain hours the Tide's delay;
At the same times the same dull views to see,
The bounding Marsh-bank and the blighted Tree;
The Water only, when the Tides were high,
When low, the Mud half-cover'd and half-dry;

The Sun-burnt Tar that blisters on the Planks,
And Bank-side Stakes in their uneven ranks;
Heaps of entangled Weeds that slowly float,
As the Tide rolls by the impeded Boat.   180

When Tides were neap, and, in the sultry day,
Through the tall bounding Mud-banks made their way,
Which on each side rose swelling, and below
The dark warm Flood ran silently and slow;
There anchoring, *Peter* chose from Man to hide,
There hang his Head, and view the lazy Tide
In its hot slimy Channel slowly glide;
Where the small Eels that left the deeper way
For the warm Shore, within the Shallows play;
Where gaping Muscles, left upon the Mud,   190
Slope their slow passage to the fallen Flood;—
Here dull and hopeless he'll lie down and trace
How sidelong Crabs had scrawl'd their crooked race;
Or sadly listen to the tuneless cry
Of fishing *Gull* or clanging *Golden-eye*;
What time the Sea-birds to the Marsh would come,
And the loud *Bittern*, from the Bull-rush home,
Gave from the Salt-ditch side the bellowing Boom:
He nurst the Feelings these dull Scenes produce,
And lov'd to stop beside the opening Sluice;   200
Where the small Stream, confin'd in narrow bound,
Ran with a dull, unvaried, sad'ning sound;
Where all presented to the Eye or Ear,
Oppress'd the Soul! with Misery, Grief, and Fear.

Besides these objects, there were places three,
Which *Peter* seem'd with certain dread to see;
When he drew near them he would turn from each,
And loudly whistle till he pass'd the *Reach*.

A change of Scene to him brought no relief,
In Town, 'twas plain, Men took him for a Thief: 210
The Sailors' Wives would stop him in the Street,
And say, 'Now, *Peter*, thou'st no Boy to beat:'
Infants at play, when they perceiv'd him, ran,
Warning each other—'That's the wicked Man:'
He growl'd an oath, and in an angry tone
Curs'd the whole Place and wish'd to be alone.

Alone he was, the same dull Scenes in view,
And still more gloomy in his sight they grew:

Though Man he hated, yet employ'd alone
At bootless labour, he would swear and groan,   220
Cursing the Shoals that glided by the spot,
And *Gulls* that caught them when his arts could not.

Cold nervous Tremblings shook his sturdy Frame,
And strange Disease—he couldn't say the name;
Wild were his Dreams, and oft he rose in fright,
Wak'd by his view of Horrors in the Night,—
Horrors that would the sternest Minds amaze,
Horrors that Dæmons might be proud to raise:
And though he felt forsaken, griev'd at heart,
To think he liv'd from all Mankind apart;   230
Yet, if a Man approach'd, in terrors he would start.

A Winter past since *Peter* saw the Town,
And Summer Lodgers were again come down;
These, idly-curious, with their glasses spied
The Ships in Bay as anchor'd for the Tide,—
The River's Craft,—the Bustle of the Quay,—
And Sea-port Views, which Landmen love to see.

One, up the River, had a Man and Boat
Seen day by day, now anchor'd, now afloat;
Fisher he seem'd, yet us'd no Net nor Hook,   240
Of Sea-fowl swimming by, no heed he took,
But on the gliding Waves still fix'd his lazy look:
At certain stations he would view the Stream,
As if he stood bewilder'd in a Dream,
Or that some Power had chain'd him for a time,
To feel a Curse or meditate on Crime.

This known, some curious, some in pity went,
And others question'd—'Wretch, dost thou repent?'
He heard, he trembled, and in fear resign'd
His Boat: new terror fill'd his restless Mind: 250
Furious he grew and up the Country ran,
And there they seiz'd him—a distemper'd Man:—
Him we receiv'd, and to a Parish-bed,
Follow'd and curs'd, the groaning Man was led.

Here when they saw him, whom they us'd to shun,
A lost, lone Man, so harass'd and undone;
Our gentle Females, ever prompt to feel,
Perceiv'd Compassion on their Anger steal;
His Crimes they could not from their Memories blot,
But they were griev'd and trembled at his Lot.   260

A Priest too came, to whom his words are told,
And all the signs they shudder'd to behold.

'Look! look!' they cried; 'his Limbs with horror shake,
And as he grinds his Teeth, what noise they make!
How glare his angry Eyes, and yet he's not awake:
See! what cold drops upon his Forehead stand,
And how he clenches that broad bony Hand.'

The Priest attending, found he spoke at times
As one alluding to his Fears and Crimes:
'It was the fall,' he mutter'd, 'I can show   270
The manner how—I never struck a blow:'—
And then aloud—'Unhand me, free my Chain;
On Oath, he fell—it struck him to the Brain:– – –
Why ask my Father?—that old Man will swear
Against my Life; besides, he wasn't there:– – –
What, all agreed?—Am I to die to-day?—
My Lord, in mercy, give me time to pray.'

Then as they watch'd him, calmer he became,
And grew so weak he couldn't move his Frame,
But murmuring spake,—while they could see and hear   280
The start of Terror and the groan of Fear;
See the large Dew-beads on his Forehead rise,
And the cold Death-drop glaze his sunken Eyes;
Nor yet he died, but with unwonted force,
Seem'd with some fancied Being to discourse:
He knew not us, or with accustom'd art
He hid the knowledge, yet expos'd his Heart;
'Twas part Confession and the rest Defence,
A Madman's Tale, with gleams of waking Sense.

'I'll tell you all,' he said, 'the very day   290
When the old Man first plac'd them in my way:
My Father's Spirit—he who always tried
To give me trouble, when he liv'd and died—
When he was gone, he could not be content
To see my Days in painful Labour spent,
But would appoint his Meetings, and he made
Me watch at these, and so neglect my Trade.

' 'Twas one hot Noon, all silent, still, serene,
No living Being had I lately seen;
I paddled up and down and dipt my Net,   300
But (such his pleasure) I could nothing get,—

A Father's pleasure! when his Toil was done,
To plague and torture thus an only Son;
And so I sat and look'd upon the Stream,
How it ran on; and felt as in a Dream:
But Dream it was not; No!—I fix'd my Eyes
On the mid Stream and saw the Spirits rise;
I saw my Father on the Water stand,
And hold a thin pale Boy in either hand;
And there they glided ghastly on the top   310
Of the salt Flood and never touch'd a drop:
I would have struck them, but they knew th'intent,
And smil'd upon the Oar, and down they went.

'Now, from that day, whenever I began
To dip my Net, there stood the hard Old Man—
He and those Boys: I humbled me and pray'd
They would be gone;—they heeded not, but stay'd:
Nor could I turn, nor would the Boat go by,
But gazing on the Spirits, there was I;
They bade me leap to death, but I was loth to die: 320
And every day, as sure as day arose,
Would these three Spirits meet me ere the close;
To hear and mark them daily was my doom,
And "Come," they said, with weak, sad voices, "come."
To row away with all my strength I try'd,
But there were they, hard by me in the Tide,
The three unbodied Forms—and "Come," still "come,"
        they cried.

'Fathers should pity—but this old Man shook
His hoary Locks and froze me by a Look:
Thrice, when I struck them, through the water came   330
An hollow Groan, that weaken'd all my Frame:
"Father!" said I, "have Mercy:"—He replied,
I know not what—the angry Spirit lied,—
"Didst thou not draw thy Knife?" said he:—'Twas true,
But I had Pity and my Arm withdrew:
He cried for Mercy, which I kindly gave,
But he has no Compassion in his Grave.

'There were three places, where they ever rose,—
The whole long River has not such as those,—
Places accurs'd, where, if a Man remain,   340
He'll see the things which strike him to the Brain;
And there they made me on my Paddle lean,
And look at them for hours;—accursed Scene!

When they would glide to that smooth Eddy-space,
Then bid me leap and join them in the place;
And at my Groans each little villain Sprite
Enjoy'd my Pains and vanish'd in delight.

'In one fierce Summer-day, when my poor Brain
Was burning-hot and cruel was my Pain,
Then came this Father-foe, and there he stood　　　　350
With his two Boys again upon the Flood;
There was more Mischief in their Eyes, more Glee
In their pale Faces when they glar'd at me:
Still did they force me on the Oar to rest,
And when they saw me fainting and opprest,
He, with his Hand, the old Man, scoop'd the Flood,
And there came Flame about him mix'd with Blood;
He bade me stoop and look upon the place,
Then flung the hot-red Liquor in my Face;
Burning it blaz'd, and then I roar'd for Pain,　　　　360
I thought the Dæmons would have turn'd my Brain.

'Still there they stood, and forc'd me to behold
A place of Horrors—they cannot be told—
Where the Flood open'd, there I heard the Shriek
Of tortur'd Guilt—no earthly Tongue can speak:
"All Days alike! for ever!" did they say,
"And unremitted Torments every Day."—
Yes, so they said:'—But here he ceas'd and gaz'd
On all around, affrighten'd and amaz'd;
And still he try'd to speak and look'd in dread　　　　370
Of frighten'd Females gathering round his Bed;
Then dropt exhausted and appear'd at rest,
Till the strong Foe the vital Powers possest;
Then with an inward, broken voice he cried,
'Again they come,' and mutter'd as he died.

MARY RUSSELL MITFORD
1787–1855

142   *Song*

THE fairest things are those which live,
And vanish ere their name we give;
The rosiest clouds in evening's sky,
Are those which soonest fade and fly;
The loveliest hue which decks the rose,
Is when the mossy buds unclose,
Half-opening forth with smiling air,
Like red lips of my lady fair.

The balmiest hour the seasons bring,
Is that which summer joins to spring;   10
The sweetest moment of the day,
Is when the grey dawn slides away;
The brightest rays are those which fly
Through April showers, and dance, and die;
Just quivering through the dewy air,
Like eye-beams of my lady fair.

[1812]

WILLIAM TENNANT
1784–1848

143   from *Anster Fair*

UPON a little dappled nag, whose mane
    Seem'd to have robb'd the steeds of Phaeton,
Whose bit and pad, and fairly-fashion'd rein,
    With silvery adornments richly shone,
Came MAGGIE LAUDER forth, enwheel'd with train
    Of knights and lairds around her trotting on;
At James' right hand she rode, a beauteous bride,
That well deserv'd to go by haughtiest Monarch's side.

Her form was as the Morning's blithesome star
   That, capp'd with lustrous coronet of beams,   10
Rides up the dawning orient in her car
   New-wash'd, and doubly fulgent from the streams;
The Chaldee shepherd eyes her light afar,
   And on his knees adores her as she gleams:
So shone the stately form of MAGGIE LAUDER,
And so th' admiring crowds pay homage and applaud her.

Each little step her trampling palfrey took
   Shak'd her majestic person into grace,
And, as at times, his glossy sides she strook
   Endearingly with whip's green silken lace,   20
(The prancer seem'd to court such kind rebuke
   Loit'ring with wilful tardiness of pace)
By Jove, the very waving of her arm
Had pow'r a brutish lout t' unbrutify and charm!

Her face was as the summer cloud, whereon
   The dawning sun delights to rest his rays;
Compar'd with it, old Sharon's vale, o'ergrown
   With flaunting roses had resign'd its praise;
For why? Her face with Heav'n's own roses shone,
   Mocking the morn, and witching men to gaze,   30
And he that gaz'd with cold unsmitten soul,
That blockhead's heart was ice thrice bak'd beneath the pole.

Her locks, apparent tufts of wiry gold,
   Lay on her lily temples, fairly dangling,
And on each hair, so harmless to behold,
   A lover's soul hung mercilessly strangling;
The piping silly zephyrs vied t' infold
   The tresses in their arms so slim and tangling,
And thrid in sport these lover-noosing snares,
And play'd at hide-and-seek amid the golden hairs.   40

Her eye was as an honour'd palace, where
   A choir of lightsome graces frisk and dance;
What object drew her gaze, how mean so e'er,
   Got dignity and honour from the glance;
Woe to the man on whom she unaware
   Did the dear witch'ry of her eye elance!
'Twas such a thrilling, killing, keen, regard—
May Heav'n from such a look preserve each tender bard.

Beneath its shading tucker heav'd a breast
 Fashion'd to take with ravishment mankind,   50
For never did the flimsy Chian vest
 Hide such a bosom in its gauze of wind;
Ev'n a pure angel, looking had confest
 A sinless transport passing o'er his mind,
For, in the nicest turning-loom of Jove,
Turn'd were these charming hills t' inspire a holy love.

So on she rode in virgin majesty,
 Charming the thin dead air to kiss her lips,
And with the light and grandeur of her eye
 Shaming the proud sun into dim eclipse,   60
While, round her presence clust'ring far and nigh,
 On horseback some, with silver spurs and whips,
And some afoot with shoes of dazzling buckles,
Attended knights, and lairds, and clowns with horny knuckles.

Not with such crowd surrounded nor so fair
 In form, rode forth Semiramis of old,
On chariot where she sat in iv'ry chair,
 Beneath a sky of carbuncle and gold,
When to Euphrates' banks to take the air,
 Or her new rising brickwalls to behold,   70
Abroad she drove, whilst round her wheels were pour'd
Satrap, and turban'd squire, and pursy Chaldee lord.

Soon to the Loan came MAG, and from her pad
 Dismounting with a queen-like dignity,
(So from his buoyant cloud, man's heart to glad,
 Lights a bright angel on a hill-top high,)
On a small mound, with turfy greenness clad
 She lit, and walk'd enchantment on the eye;
Then on two chairs, that on its top stood ready,
Down sat the good King James, and ANSTER's bonny lady. 80

Their chairs were finely carv'd, and overlaid
 With the thin lustre of adorning gold,
And o'er their heads a canopy was spread
 Of arras, flower'd with figures manifold,
Supported by four boys, of silver made,
 Whose glitt'ring hands the vault of cloth uphold;
On each side sat or stood, to view the sport,
Stout lord, and lady fair, the flow'r of Scotland's court.

(Canto III, sts. xii –xxii)

GEORGE GORDON, LORD BYRON
1788–1824

144   from *Childe Harold's Pilgrimage. A Romaunt*

1

COME, blue-eyed maid of heaven!—but thou, alas!
Didst never yet one mortal song inspire—
Goddess of Wisdom! here thy temple was,
And is, despite of war and wasting fire,
And years, that bade thy worship to expire:
But worse than steel, and flame, and ages slow,
Is the dread sceptre and dominion dire
Of men who never felt the sacred glow,
That thoughts of thee and thine on polish'd breasts bestow.

2

Ancient of days! august Athena! where,   10
Where are thy men of might? thy grand in soul?
Gone—glimmering through the dream of things that were:
First in the race that led to Glory's goal,
They won, and pass'd away—is this the whole?
A school-boy's tale, the wonder of an hour!
The warrior's weapon and the sophist's stole
Are sought in vain, and o'er each mouldering tower,
Dim with the mist of years, grey flits the shade of power.

3

Son of the morning, rise! approach you here!
Come—but molest not yon defenceless urn: 20
Look on this spot—a nation's sepulchre!
Abode of gods, whose shrines no longer burn.
Even gods must yield—religions take their turn:
'Twas Jove's—'tis Mahomet's—and other creeds
Will rise with other years, till man shall learn
Vainly his incense soars, his victim bleeds;
Poor child of Doubt and Death, whose hope is built on reeds.

4

Bound to the earth, he lifts his eye to heaven—
Is't not enough, unhappy thing! to know
Thou art? Is this a boon so kindly given,   30

That being, thou wouldst be again, and go,
Thou know'st not, reck'st not to what region, so
On earth no more, but mingled with the skies?
Still wilt thou dream on future joy and woe?
Regard and weigh yon dust before it flies:
That little urn saith more than thousand homilies.

5

Or burst the vanish'd Hero's lofty mound;
Far on the solitary shore he sleeps:
He fell, and falling nations mourn'd around;
But now not one of saddening thousands weeps,   40
Nor warlike worshipper his vigil keeps
Where demi-gods appear'd, as records tell.
Remove yon skull from out the scatter'd heaps:
Is that a temple where a God may dwell?
Why ev'n the worm at last disdains her shatter'd cell!

6

Look on its broken arch, its ruin'd wall,
Its chambers desolate, and portals foul:
Yes, this was once Ambition's airy hall,
The dome of Thought, the palace of the Soul:
Behold through each lack-lustre, eyeless hole,   50
The gay recess of Wisdom and of Wit
And Passion's host, that never brook'd control:
Can all, saint, sage, or sophist ever writ,
People this lonely tower, this tenement refit?

7

Well didst thou speak, Athena's wisest son!
'All that we know is, nothing can be known.'
Why should we shrink from what we cannot shun?
Each has his pang, but feeble sufferers groan
With brain-born dreams of evil all their own.
Pursue what Chance or Fate proclaimeth best;   60
Peace waits us on the shores of Acheron:
There no forc'd banquet claims the sated guest,
But Silence spreads the couch of ever welcome rest.

8

Yet if, as holiest men have deem'd, there be
A land of souls beyond that sable shore,

To shame the doctrine of the Sadducee
And sophists, madly vain of dubious lore;
How sweet it were in concert to adore
With those who made our mortal labours light!
To hear each voice we fear'd to hear no more!   70
Behold each mighty shade reveal'd to sight,
The Bactrian, Samian sage, and all who taught the right!

9

There, thou!—whose love and life together fled,
Have left me here to love and live in vain—
Twin'd with my heart, and can I deem thee dead,
When busy Memory flashes on my brain?
Well—I will dream that we may meet again,
And woo the vision to my vacant breast;
If aught of young Remembrance then remain,
Be as it may Futurity's behest,   80
For me 'twere bliss enough to know thy spirit blest!

(Canto II)

SAMUEL ROGERS
1763–1855

145   *The Boy of Egremond*

'SAY what remains when Hope is fled?'
She answered, 'Endless weeping!'
For in the herdsman's eye she read
Who in his shroud lay sleeping.
   At Embsay rung the matin-bell,
The stag was roused on Barden-fell;
The mingled sounds were swelling, dying,
And down the Wharfe a hern was flying;
When near the cabin in the wood,
In tartan clad and forest-green,   10
With hound in leash and hawk in hood,
The Boy of Egremond was seen.
Blithe was his song, a song, of yore;
But where the rock is rent in two,
And the river rushes through,
His voice was heard no more!
'Twas but a step! the gulf he passed;

But that step—it was his last!
As through the mist he winged his way,
(A cloud that hovers night and day,)   20
The hound hung back, and back he drew
The Master and his merlin too.
That narrow place of noise and strife
Received their little all of Life!
   There now the matin-bell is rung;
The 'Miserere!' duly sung;
And holy men in cowl and hood
Are wandering up and down the wood.
But what avail they? Ruthless Lord,
Thou didst not shudder when the sword   30
Here on the young its fury spent,
The helpless and the innocent.
Sit now and answer, groan for groan.
The child before thee is thy own.
And she who wildly wanders there,
The mother in her long despair,
Shall oft remind thee, waking, sleeping,
Of those who by the Wharfe were weeping;
Of those who would not be consoled
When red with blood the river rolled.   40

146   *Written in a Sick Chamber*

1793

THERE, in that bed so closely curtained round,
Worn to a shade, and wan with slow decay,
A father sleeps! Oh hushed be every sound!
Soft may we breathe the midnight hours away!

   He stirs—yet still he sleeps. May heavenly dreams
Long o'er his smooth and settled pillow rise;
Nor fly, till morning thro' the shutter streams,
And on the hearth the glimmering rush-light dies.

HORACE SMITH and JAMES SMITH
1779–1849 and 1775–1839

Cui Bono?

By Lord B.

I

SATED with home, of wife, of children tired,
The restless soul is driven abroad to roam;
Sated abroad, all seen yet nought admired,
The restless soul is driven to ramble home;
Sated with both, beneath new Drury's dome
The fiend Ennui awhile consents to pine,
There growls, and curses, like a deadly Gnome,
Scorning to view fantastic Columbine,
Viewing with scorn and hate the nonsense of the Nine.

II

Ye reckless dupes, who hither wend your way   10
To gaze on puppets in a painted dome,
Pursuing pastimes glittering to betray,
Like falling stars in life's eternal gloom,
What seek ye here? Joy's evanescent bloom?
Woe 's me! the brightest wreaths she ever gave
Are but as flowers that decorate a tomb.
Man's heart, the mournful urn o'er which they wave,
Is sacred to despair, its pedestal the grave.

III

Has life so little store of real woes,
That here ye wend to taste fictitious grief?   20
Or is it that from truth such anguish flows,
Ye court the lying drama for relief?
Long shall ye find the pang, the respite brief:
Or if one tolerable page appears
In folly's volume, 'tis the actor's leaf,
Who dries his own by drawing others' tears,
And, raising present mirth, makes glad his future years.

IV

Albeit, how like young Betty doth he flee!
Light as the moat that danceth in the beam,

He liveth only in man's present e'e;   30
His life a flash, his memory a dream,
Oblivious down he drops in Lethe's stream.
Yet what are they, the learned and the great?
Awhile of longer wonderment the theme!
Who shall presume to prophesy *their* date,
Where nought is certain, save the uncertainty of fate?

V

This goodly pile, upheaved by Wyatt's toil,
Perchance than Holland's edifice more fleet,
Again red Lemnos' artisan may spoil;
The fire-alarm and midnight drum may beat,   40
And all bestrewed ysmoking at your feet!
Start ye? perchance Death's angel may be sent,
Ere from the flaming temple ye retreat;
And ye who met, on revel idlesse bent,
May find, in pleasure's fane, your grave and monument.

VI

Your debts mount high—ye plunge in deeper waste;
The tradesman duns—no warning voice ye hear;
The plaintiff sues—to public shows ye haste;
The bailiff threats—ye feel no idle fear.
Who can arrest your prodigal career?   50
Who can keep down the levity of youth?
What sound can startle age's stubborn ear?
Who can redeem from wretchedness and ruth
Men true to falsehood's voice, false to the voice of truth?

VII

To thee, blest saint! who doffed thy skin to make
The Smithfield rabble leap from theirs with joy,
We dedicate the pile—arise! awake!—
Knock down the Muses, wit and sense destroy,
Clear our new stage from reason's dull alloy,
Charm hobbling age, and tickle capering youth   60
With cleaver, marrow-bone, and Tunbridge toy;
While, vibrating in unbelieving tooth,
Harps twang in Drury's walls, and make her boards a booth.

VIII

For what is Hamlet, but a hare in March?
And what is Brutus, but a croaking owl?

And what is Rolla? Cupid steeped in starch,
Orlando's helmet in Augustin's cowl.
Shakespeare, how true thine adage, 'fair is foul!'
To him whose soul is with fruition fraught,
The song of Braham is an Irish howl,   70
Thinking is but an idle waste of thought,
And nought is everything, and everything is nought.

IX

Sons of Parnassus! whom I view above,
Not laurel-crown'd, but clad in rusty black;
Not spurring Pegasus through Tempè's grove,
But pacing Grub-street on a jaded hack;
What reams of foolscap, while your brains ye rack,
Ye mar to make again! for sure, ere long,
Condemn'd to tread the bard's time-sanction'd track,
Ye all shall join the bailiff-haunted throng,   80
And reproduce, in rags, the rags ye blot in song.

X

So fares the follower in the Muses' train;
He toils to starve, and only lives in death;
We slight him, till our patronage is vain,
Then round his skeleton a garland wreathe,
And o'er his bones an empty requiem breathe—
Oh! with what tragic horror would he start,
(Could he be conjured from the grave beneath)
To find the stage again a Thespian cart,
And elephants and colts down trampling Shakespeare's art. 90

XI

Hence, pedant Nature! with thy Grecian rules!
Centaurs (not fabulous) those rules efface;
Back, sister Muses, to your native schools;
Here booted grooms usurp Apollo's place,
Hoofs shame the boards that Garrick used to grace,
The play of limbs succeeds the play of wit,
Man yields the drama to the Hou'yn'm race,
His prompter spurs, his licenser the bit,
The stage a stable-yard, a jockey-club the pit.

XII

Is it for these ye rear this proud abode?   100
Is it for these your superstition seeks

To build a temple worthy of a god,
To laud a monkey, or to worship leeks!
Then be the stage, to recompense your freaks,
A motley chaos, jumbling age and ranks,
Where Punch, the lignum-vitæ Roscius, squeaks,
And Wisdom weeps, and Folly plays his pranks,
And moody Madness laughs and hugs the chain he clanks.

ANNA LAETITIA BARBAULD

148   *Eighteen Hundred and Eleven*

STILL the loud death drum, thundering from afar,
O'er the vext nations pours the storm of war:
To the stern call still Britain bends her ear,
Feeds the fierce strife, th' alternate hope and fear;
Bravely, though vainly, dares to strive with Fate,
And seeks by turns to prop each sinking state.
Colossal power with overwhelming force
Bears down each fort of Freedom in its course;
Prostrate she lies beneath the Despot's sway,
While the hushed nations curse him—and obey.   10

Bounteous in vain, with frantic man at strife,
Glad Nature pours the means—the joys of life;
In vain with orange-blossoms scents the gale,
The hills with olives clothes, with corn the vale;
Man calls to Famine, nor invokes in vain,
Disease and Rapine follow in her train;
The tramp of marching hosts disturbs the plough,
The sword, not sickle, reaps the harvest now,
And where the soldier gleans the scant supply,
The helpless peasant but retires to die;   20
No laws his hut from licensed outrage shield,
And war's least horror is th' ensanguined field.

Fruitful in vain, the matron counts with pride
The blooming youths that grace her honoured side;
No son returns to press her widowed hand,
Her fallen blossoms strew a foreign strand.
—Fruitful in vain, she boasts her virgin race,
Whom cultured arts adorn and gentlest grace;
Defrauded of its homage, Beauty mourns,

And the rose withers on its virgin thorns.   30
Frequent, some stream obscure, some uncouth name,
By deeds of blood is lifted into fame;
Oft o'er the daily page some soft one bends
To learn the fate of husband, brothers, friends,
Or the spread map with anxious eye explores,
Its dotted boundaries and penciled shores,
Asks where the spot that wrecked her bliss is found,
And learns its name but to detest the sound.

And think'st thou, Britain, still to sit at ease,
An island queen amidst thy subject seas,   40
While the vext billows, in their distant roar,
But soothe thy slumbers, and but kiss thy shore?
To sport in wars, while danger keeps aloof,
Thy grassy turf unbruised by hostile hoof?
So sing thy flatterers;—but, Britain, know,
Thou who hast shared the guilt must share the woe.
Nor distant is the hour; low murmurs spread,
And whispered fears, creating what they dread;
Ruin, as with an earthquake shock, is here,
There, the heart-witherings of unuttered fear,   50
And that sad death, whence most affection bleeds,
Which sickness, only of the soul, precedes.
Thy baseless wealth dissolves in air away,
Like mists that melt before the morning ray:
No more on crowded mart or busy street
Friends, meeting friends, with cheerful hurry greet;
Sad, on the ground thy princely merchants bend
Their altered looks, and evil days portend,
And fold their arms, and watch with anxious breast
The tempest blackening in the distant West.   60

There walks a Spirit o'er the peopled earth,
Secret his progress is, unknown his birth;
Moody and viewless as the changing wind,
No force arrests his foot, no chains can bind;
Where'er he turns, the human brute awakes,
And, roused to better life, his sordid hut forsakes:
He thinks, he reasons, glows with purer fires,
Feels finer wants, and burns with new desires:
Obedient Nature follows where he leads;
The steaming marsh is changed to fruitful meads;   70
The beasts retire from man's asserted reign,
And prove his kingdom was not given in vain.
Then from its bed is drawn the ponderous ore,

Then Commerce pours her gifts on every shore,
Then Babel's towers and terraced gardens rise,
And pointed obelisks invade the skies;
The prince commands, in Tyrian purple drest,
And Egypt's virgins weave the linen vest.
Then spans the graceful arch the roaring tide,
And stricter bounds the cultured fields divide.   80
Then kindles Fancy, then expands the heart,
Then blow the flowers of Genius and of Art;
Saints, heroes, sages, who the land adorn,
Seem rather to descend than to be born;
Whilst History, midst the rolls consigned to fame,
With pen of adamant inscribes their name.

The Genius now forsakes the favoured shore,
And hates, capricious, what he loved before;
Then empires fall to dust, then arts decay,
And wasted realms enfeebled despots sway;   90
Even Nature's changed; without his fostering smile
Ophir no gold, no plenty yields the Nile;
The thirsty sand absorbs the useless rill,
And spotted plagues from putrid fens distill.
In desert solitudes then Tadmor sleeps,
Stern Marius then o'er fallen Carthage weeps;
Then with enthusiast love the pilgrim roves
To seek his footsteps in forsaken groves,
Explores the fractured arch, the ruined tower,
Those limbs disjointed of gigantic power;   100
Still at each step he dreads the adder's sting,
The Arab's javelin, or the tiger's spring;
With doubtful caution treads the echoing ground,
And asks where Troy or Babylon is found.

And now the vagrant Power no more detains
The vale of Tempe, or Ausonian plains;
Northward he throws the animating ray,
O'er Celtic nations bursts the mental day:
And, as some playful child the mirror turns,
Now here now there the moving lustre burns;   110
Now o'er his changeful fancy more prevail
Batavia's dykes than Arno's purple vale,
And stinted suns, and rivers bound with frost,
Than Enna's plains or Baia's viny coast;
Venice the Adriatic weds in vain,
And Death sits brooding o'er Campania's plain;
O'er Baltic shores and through Hercynian groves,

Stirring the soul, the mighty impulse moves;
Art plies his tools, and Commerce spreads her sail,
And wealth is wafted in each shifting gale.   120
The sons of Odin tread on Persian looms,
And Odin's daughters breathe distilled perfumes.
Loud minstrel bards, in Gothic halls, rehearse
The Runic rhyme, and 'build the lofty verse:'
The Muse, whose liquid notes were wont to swell
To the soft breathings of the' Æolian shell,
Submits, reluctant, to the harsher tone,
And scarce believes the altered voice her own.
And now, where Cæsar saw with proud disdain
The wattled hut and skin of azure stain,   130
Corinthian columns rear their graceful forms,
And light varandas brave the wintry storms,
While British tongues the fading fame prolong
Of Tully's eloquence and Maro's song.
Where once Bonduca whirled the scythed car,
And the fierce matrons raised the shriek of war,
Light forms beneath transparent muslins float,
And tutored voices swell the artful note.
Light-leaved acacias and the shady plane
And spreading cedar grace the woodland reign;   140
While crystal walls the tenderer plants confine,
The fragrant orange and the nectared pine;
The Syrian grape there hangs her rich festoons,
Nor asks for purer air, or brighter noons:
Science and Art urge on the useful toil,
New mould a climate and create the soil,
Subdue the rigour of the northern Bear,
O'er polar climes shed aromatic air,
On yielding Nature urge their new demands,
And ask not gifts but tribute at her hands.   150

London exults:—on London Art bestows
Her summer ices and her winter rose;
Gems of the East her mural crown adorn,
And Plenty at her feet pours forth her horn;
While even the exiles her just laws disclaim,
People a continent, and build a name:
August she sits, and with extended hands
Holds forth the book of life to distant lands.

But fairest flowers expand but to decay;
The worm is in thy core, thy glories pass away;   160
Arts, arms and wealth destroy the fruits they bring;

306

Commerce, like beauty, knows no second spring.
Crime walks thy streets, Fraud earns her unblest bread,
O'er want and woe thy gorgeous robe is spread,
And angel charities in vain oppose:
With grandeur's growth the mass of misery grows.
For see,—to other climes the Genius soars,
He turns from Europe's desolated shores;
And lo, even now, midst mountains wrapt in storm,
On Andes' heights he shrouds his awful form;   170
On Chimborazo's summits treads sublime,
Measuring in lofty thought the march of Time;
Sudden he calls:—' 'Tis now the hour!' he cries,
Spreads his broad hand, and bids the nations rise.
La Plata hears amidst her torrents' roar;
Potosi hears it, as she digs the ore:
Ardent, the Genius fans the noble strife,
And pours through feeble souls a higher life,
Shouts to the mingled tribes from sea to sea,
And swears—Thy world, Columbus, shall be free.   180

GEORGE CRABBE

149   *Procrastination*

Heaven witness
I have been to you ever true and humble.

Henry VIII, II. iv

Gentle lady,
When first I did impart my love to you,
I freely told you all the wealth I had.

Merchant of Venice, III. ii

The fatal time
Cuts off all ceremonies and vows of love,
And ample interchange of sweet discourse,
Which so long sunder'd friends should dwell upon.

Richard III, v. iii

I know thee not, old Man, fall to thy prayers.

2 Henry IV, v. v

Farewell,
Thou pure impiety, thou impious purity,
For thee I'll lock up all the gates of love.

Much Ado about Nothing, IV. ii

LOVE will expire; the gay, the happy dream
Will turn to scorn, indiff'rence, or esteem:
Some favour'd pairs, in this exchange, are blest,
Nor sigh for raptures in a state of rest:
Others, ill match'd, with minds unpair'd, repent
At once the deed, and know no more content;
From joy to anguish they, in haste, decline,
And with their fondness, their esteem resign:
More luckless still their fate, who are the prey
Of long-protracted hope and dull delay;   10
'Mid plans of bliss, the heavy hours pass on,
Till love is wither'd, and till joy is gone.

This gentle flame two youthful hearts possess'd,
The sweet disturber of unenvied rest:
The prudent *Dinah* was the maid belov'd,
And the kind *Rupert* was the swain approv'd:
A wealthy Aunt her gentle Niece sustain'd,
He, with a father, at his desk remain'd;
The youthful couple, to their vows sincere,
Thus lov'd expectant! year succeeding year,   20
With pleasant views and hopes, but not a prospect near.
Rupert some comfort in his station saw,
But the poor Virgin liv'd in dread and awe;
Upon her anxious looks the Widow smil'd,
And bade her wait, 'for she was yet a child.'
She for her neighbour had a due respect,
Nor would his son encourage or reject;
And thus the pair, with expectations vain,
Beheld the seasons change and change again:
Meantime the Nymph her tender tales perus'd,   30
Where cruel aunts impatient girls refus'd;
While hers, though teazing, boasted to be kind,
And she, resenting, to be all resign'd.

The Dame was sick, and when the Youth applied
For her consent, she groan'd, and cough'd, and cried;
Talk'd of departing, and again her breath
Drew hard, and cough'd, and talk'd again of death:
'Here you may live, my *Dinah!* here the boy
And you together my estate enjoy;'
Thus to the lovers was her mind express'd,   40
Till they forbore to urge the fond request.

Servant, and nurse, and comforter, and friend,
Dinah had still some duty to attend;

But yet their walk, when *Rupert*'s evening call
Obtain'd an hour, made sweet amends for all:
So long they now each other's thoughts had known,
That nothing seem'd exclusively their own;
But with the common wish, the mutual fear,
They now had travell'd to their thirtieth year.

At length a prospect open'd,—but, alas!   50
Long time must yet, before the union, pass:
Rupert was call'd in other clime, t'increase
Another's wealth and toil for future peace:
Loth were the Lovers; but the Aunt declar'd
'Twas fortune's call, and they must be prepar'd;
'You now are young, and for this brief delay,
And *Dinah*'s care, what I bequeath will pay;
All will be yours; nay, love, suppress that sigh,
The kind must suffer, and the best must die:'
Then came the cough, and strong the signs it gave   60
Of holding long contention with the grave.

The Lovers parted with a gloomy view,
And little comfort, but that both were true;
He for uncertain duties doom'd to steer,
While hers remain'd too certain and severe.

Letters arriv'd, and *Rupert* fairly told
'His cares were many, and his hopes were cold;
The view more clouded, that was never fair,
And Love alone preserv'd him from despair:'
In other letters brighter hopes he drew,   70
'His friends were kind, and he believ'd them true.'

When the sage Widow *Dinah*'s grief descried,
She wonder'd much why one so happy sigh'd;
Then bade her see how her poor Aunt sustain'd
The ills of life, nor murmur'd nor complain'd.
To vary pleasures, from the Lady's chest
Were drawn the pearly string and tabby-vest;
Beads, jewels, laces,—all their value shown,
With the kind notice—'They will be your own.'

This hope, these comforts cherish'd day by day,   80
To *Dinah*'s bosom made a gradual way;
Till love of treasure had as large a part,
As love of *Rupert*, in the Virgin's heart.
Whether it be that tender passions fail,

From their own nature, while the strong prevail;
Or whether Av'rice, like the poison-tree,
Kills all beside it, and alone will be;
Whatever cause prevail'd, the pleasure grew
In *Dinah*'s soul,—she lov'd the hoards to view;
With lively joy those comforts she survey'd,   90
And Love grew languid in the careful Maid.

Now the grave Niece partook the Widow's cares,
Look'd to the great, and rul'd the small affairs;
Saw clean'd the plate, arrang'd the china-show,
And felt her passion for a shilling grow:
Th'indulgent Aunt increas'd the Maid's delight,
By placing tokens of her wealth in sight;
She lov'd the value of her bonds to tell,
And spake of stocks, and how they rose and fell.

This passion grew, and gain'd at length such sway,   100
That other passions shrank to make it way;
Romantic notions now the heart forsook,
She read but seldom, and she chang'd her book;
And for the verses she was wont to send,
Short was her prose, and 'she was *Rupert*'s Friend.'
Seldom she wrote, and then the Widow's cough,
And constant call, excus'd her breaking off;
Who, now oppress'd, no longer took the air,
But sate and doz'd upon an easy chair.
The cautious Doctor saw the case was clear,   110
But judg'd it best to have companions near;
They came, they reason'd, they prescrib'd—at last,
Like honest men, they said their hopes were past:
Then came a Priest—'tis comfort to reflect,
When all is over, there was no neglect:
And all was over—by her Husband's bones,
The Widow rests beneath the sculptur'd stones;
That yet record their fondness and their fame,
While all they left, the Virgin's care became;
Stocks, bonds, and buildings;—it disturb'd her rest,   120
To think what load of troubles she possess'd:
Yet, if a trouble, she resolv'd to take
Th'important duty, for the donor's sake;
She too was heiress to the Widow's taste,
Her love of hoarding, and her dread of waste.

Sometimes the past would on her mind intrude,
And then a conflict full of care ensued;

The thoughts of *Rupert* on her mind would press,
His worth she knew, but doubted his success:
Of old she saw him heedless; what the boy   130
Forbore to save, the man would not enjoy;
Oft had he lost the chance that care would seize,
Willing to live, but more to live at ease:
Yet could she not a broken vow defend,
And Heav'n, perhaps, might yet enrich her friend.

Month after month was pass'd, and all were spent
In quiet comfort and in rich content:
Miseries there were, and woes, the world around,
But these had not her pleasant dwelling found;
She knew that mothers griev'd, and widows wept,   140
And she was sorry, said her prayers, and slept:
Thus pass'd the seasons, and to *Dinah*'s board
Gave what the seasons to the rich afford;
For she indulg'd, nor was her heart so small,
That one strong passion should engross it all.

A love of splendour now with av'rice strove,
And oft appear'd to be the stronger love:
A secret pleasure fill'd the Widow's breast,
When she reflected on the hoards possess'd;
But livelier joys inspir'd th' ambitious Maid,   150
When she the purchase of those hoards display'd:
In small but splendid room she lov'd to see
That all was plac'd in view and harmony;
There as with eager glance she look'd around,
She much delight in every object found;
While books devout were near her—to destroy,
Should it arise, an overflow of joy.

Within that fair apartment, guests might see
The comforts cull'd for wealth by vanity:
Around the room an Indian paper blaz'd,   160
With lively tint and figures boldly rais'd;
Silky and soft upon the floor below,
Th' elastic carpet rose with crimson glow;
All things around implied both cost and care,
What met the eye, was elegant or rare:
Some curious trifles round the room were laid,
By Hope presented to the wealthy Maid:
Within a costly case of varnish'd wood,
In level rows, her polish'd volumes stood;
Shown as a favour to a chosen few,   170

To prove what beauty for a book could do:
A silver urn with curious work was fraught;
A silver lamp from Grecian pattern wrought:
Above her head, all gorgeous to behold,
A time-piece stood on feet of burnish'd gold;
A stag's-head crest adorn'd the pictur'd case,
Through the pure chrystal shone th' enamell'd face;
And, while on brilliants mov'd the hands of steel,
It click'd from pray'r to pray'r, from meal to meal.

Here as the Lady sate, a friendly pair   180
Stepp'd in t' admire the view, and took their chair:
They then related how the young and gay
Were thoughtless wandering in the broad high-way;
How tender damsels sail'd in tilted boats,
And laugh'd with wicked men in scarlet coats;
And how we live in such degen'rate times,
That men conceal their wants, and show their crimes;
While vicious deeds are screen'd by fashion's name,
And what was once our pride is now our shame.

Dinah was musing, as her friends discours'd,   190
When these last words a sudden entrance forc'd
Upon her mind, and what was once her pride
And now her shame, some painful views supplied;
Thoughts of the past within her bosom press'd,
And there a change was felt, and was confess'd:
While thus the Virgin strove with secret pain,
Her mind was wandering o'er the troubled main;
Still she was silent, nothing seem'd to see,
But sate and sigh'd in pensive reverie.

The friends prepar'd new subjects to begin,   200
When tall *Susannah*, maiden starch, stalk'd in;
Not in her ancient mode, sedate and slow,
As when she came, the mind she knew, to know;
Nor as, when list'ning half an hour before,
She twice or thrice tapp'd gently at the door;
But, all decorum cast in wrath aside,
'I think the devil's in the man!' she cried;
'A huge tall Sailor, with his tawny cheek
And pitted face, will with my Lady speak;
He grinn'd an ugly smile, and said he knew,   210
Please you, my Lady, 'twould be joy to you;
What must I answer?' Trembling and distress'd
Sank the pale *Dinah*, by her fears oppress'd;

When thus alarm'd, and brooking no delay,
Swift to her room the stranger made his way.

    'Revive, my love,' said he, 'I've done thee harm,
Give me thy pardon,' and he look'd alarm:
Meantime the prudent *Dinah* had contriv'd
Her soul to question, and she then reviv'd.

    'See! my good friend,' and then she rais'd her head,   220
'The bloom of life, the strength of youth is fled;
Living we die; to us the world is dead;
We parted blest with health, and I am now
Age-struck and feeble, so I find art thou;
Thine eye is sunken, furrow'd is thy face,
And downward look'st thou—so we run our race:
And happier they, whose race is nearly run,
Their troubles over, and their duties done.'

    'True, Lady, true, we are not girl and boy;
But time has left us something to enjoy.'   230

    'What! thou hast learn'd my fortune?—yes, I live
To feel how poor the comforts wealth can give.
Thou too perhaps art wealthy; but our fate
Still mocks our wishes, wealth is come too late.'

    'To me nor late nor early; I am come
Poor as I left thee to my native home:
Nor yet,' said *Rupert*, 'will I grieve; 'tis mine
To share thy comforts, and the glory thine;
For thou wilt gladly take that generous part
That both exalts and gratifies the heart;   240
While mine rejoices.'—'Heavens!' return'd the Maid,
'This talk to one so wither'd and decay'd?
No! all my care is now to fit my mind
For other spousal, and to die resign'd:
As friend and neighbour, I shall hope to see
These noble views, this pious love in thee;
That we together may the change await,
Guides and spectators in each other's fate;
When, fellow-pilgrims, we shall daily crave
The mutual prayer that arms us for the grave.'   250

    Half angry, half in doubt, the Lover gaz'd
On the meek Maiden, by her speech amaz'd:
'*Dinah*,' said he, 'dost thou respect thy vows?

What spousal mean'st thou?—thou art *Rupert*'s spouse;
The chance is mine to take, and thine to give;
But, trifling this, if we together live:
Can I believe, that, after all the past,
Our vows, our loves, thou wilt be false at last?
Something thou hast—I know not what—in view;
I find thee pious—let me find thee true.'　　　　260

　　'Ah! cruel this; but do, my friend, depart,
And to its feelings leave my wounded heart.'

　　'Nay, speak at once; and *Dinah*, let me know,
Mean'st thou to take me, now I'm wreck'd, in tow:
Be fair, nor longer keep me in the dark;
Am I forsaken for a trimmer spark?
Heav'n's spouse thou art not; nor can I believe
That God accepts her, who will Man deceive:
True I am shatter'd, I have service seen,
And service done, and have in trouble been;　　　270
My cheek—it shames me not—has lost its red,
And the brown buff is o'er my features spread;
Perchance my speech is rude, for I among
Th' untam'd have been, in temper and in tongue;
Have been trepann'd, have liv'd in toil and care,
And wrought for wealth I was not doom'd to share:
It touch'd me deeply, for I felt a pride
In gaining riches for my destin'd bride:
Speak then my fate; for these my sorrows past,
Time lost, youth fled, hope wearied, and at last　　　280
This doubt of thee—a childish thing to tell,
But certain truth—my very throat they swell;
They stop the breath, and but for shame could I
Give way to weakness, and with passion cry;
These are unmanly struggles, but I feel
This hour must end them, and perhaps will heal.'—

　　Here *Dinah* sigh'd as if afraid to speak—
And then repeated,—'They were frail and weak;
His soul she lov'd, and hop'd he had the grace
To fix his thoughts upon a better place.'　　　290

　　She ceas'd;—with steady glance, as if to see
The very root of this hypocrisy,—
He her small fingers moulded in his hard
And bronz'd broad hand; then told her his regard,
His best respect were gone, but Love had still

Hold in his heart, and govern'd yet the will—
Or he would curse her:—saying this, he threw
The hand in scorn away, and bade adieu
To every ling'ring hope, with every care in view.

    Proud and indignant, suffering, sick, and poor,   300
He griev'd unseen, and spoke of Love no more—
Till all he felt in Indignation died,
As hers had sunk in Avarice and Pride.

    In health declining as in mind distress'd,
To some in power his troubles he confess'd,
And shares a parish-gift;—at prayers he sees
The pious *Dinah* dropp'd upon her knees;
Thence as she walks the street with stately air,
As chance directs, oft meet the parted pair:
When he, with thickset coat of Badge-man's blue,   310
Moves near her shaded silk of changeful hue;
When his thin locks of grey approach her braid,
A costly purchase, made in beauty's aid;
When his frank air, and his unstudied pace,
Are seen with her soft manner, air, and grace,
And his plain artless look with her sharp meaning face;
It might some wonder in a stranger move,
How these together could have talk'd of love.

    Behold them now! see there a Tradesman stands,
And humbly hearkens to some fresh commands;   320
He moves to speak—she interrupts him—'Stay!'
Her air expresses,—'Hark! to what I say:'—
Ten paces off, poor *Rupert* on a seat
Has taken refuge from the noon-day heat,
His eyes on her intent, as if to find
What were the movements of that subtle mind:
How still!—how earnest is he!—it appears
His thoughts are wand'ring through his earlier years;
Through years of fruitless labour, to the day
When all his earthly prospects died away;   330
'Had I,' he thinks, 'been wealthier of the two,
Would she have found me so unkind, untrue?
Or knows not man when poor, what man when rich will do?
Yes, yes! I feel that I had faithful prov'd,
And should have sooth'd and rais'd her, blest and lov'd.'

    But *Dinah* moves—she had observ'd before,
The pensive *Rupert* at an humble door:

Some thoughts of pity rais'd by his distress,
Some feeling touch of ancient tenderness;
Religion, duty urg'd the Maid to speak   340
In terms of kindness to a man so weak:
But pride forbad, and to return would prove
She felt the shame of his neglected love;
Nor wrapp'd in silence could she pass, afraid
Each eye should see her, and each heart upbraid;
One way remain'd—the way the Levite took,
Who without mercy could on misery look;
(A way perceiv'd by Craft, approv'd by Pride,)
She cross'd and pass'd him on the other side.

[1813]

GEORGE GORDON, LORD BYRON

150   *The Giaour*

A Fragment of a Turkish Tale

One fatal remembrance—one sorrow that throws
Its bleak shade alike o'er our joys and our woes—
To which Life nothing darker nor brighter can bring,
For which joy hath no balm—and affliction no sting.

MOORE

No breath of air to break the wave
That rolls below the Athenian's grave,
That tomb which, gleaming o'er the cliff,*
First greets the homeward-veering skiff,
High o'er the land he saved in vain—
When shall such hero live again?
   .   .   .   .   .

  Fair clime! where every season smiles
Benignant o'er those blessed isles,
Which seen from far Colonna's height,
Make glad the heart that hails the sight,   10
And lend to loneliness delight.
There mildly dimpling—Ocean's cheek
Reflects the tints of many a peak

line 3. A tomb above the rocks on the promontory, by some supposed the sepulchre of
Themistocles.

Caught by the laughing tides that lave
These Edens of the eastern wave;
And if at times a transient breeze
Break the blue chrystal of the seas,
Or sweep one blossom from the trees,
How welcome is each gentle air,
That wakes and wafts the odours there!   20
For there—the Rose o'er crag or vale,
Sultana of the Nightingale,*
    The maid for whom his melody—
    His thousand songs are heard on high,
Blooms blushing to her lover's tale;
His queen, the garden queen, his Rose,
Unbent by winds, unchill'd by snows,
Far from the winters of the west
By every breeze and season blest,
Returns the sweets by nature given   30
In softest incense back to heaven;
And grateful yields that smiling sky
Her fairest hue and fragrant sigh.
And many a summer flower is there,
And many a shade that love might share,
And many a grotto, meant for rest,
That holds the pirate for a guest;
Whose bark in sheltering cove below
Lurks for the passing peaceful prow,
Till the gay mariner's guitar*   40
Is heard, and seen the evening star;
Then stealing with the muffled oar,
Far shaded by the rocky shore,
Rush the night-prowlers on the prey,
And turn to groans his roundelay.
Strange—that where Nature lov'd to trace,
As if for Gods, a dwelling-place,
And every charm and grace hath mixed
Within the paradise she fixed—
There man, enamour'd of distress,   50
Should mar it into wilderness,
And trample, brute-like, o'er each flower
That tasks not one laborious hour;
Nor claims the culture of his hand
To bloom along the fairy land,

    line 22. The attachment of the nightingale to the rose is a well-known Persian fable. If I mistake not, the 'Bulbul of a thousand tales' is one of his appellations.
    line 40. The guitar is the constant amusement of the Greek sailor by night: with a steady fair wind, and during a calm, it is accompanied always by the voice, and often by dancing.

But springs as to preclude his care,
And sweetly woos him—but to spare!
Strange—that where all is peace beside
There passion riots in her pride,
And lust and rapine wildly reign,   60
To darken o'er the fair domain.
It is as though the fiends prevail'd
Against the seraphs they assail'd,
And fixed, on heavenly thrones, should dwell
The freed inheritors of hell—
So soft the scene, so form'd for joy,
So curst the tyrants that destroy!

He who hath bent him o'er the dead,
Ere the first day of death is fled;
The first dark day of nothingness,   70
The last of danger and distress;
(Before Decay's effacing fingers
Have swept the lines where beauty lingers)
And mark'd the mild angelic air—
The rapture of repose that's there—
The fixed yet tender traits that streak
The languor of the placid cheek,
And—but for that sad shrouded eye,
    That fires not—wins not—weeps not—now—
    And but for that chill changeless brow,   80
Where cold Obstruction's apathy*
Appals the gazing mourner's heart,
As if to him it could impart
The doom he dreads, yet dwells upon—
Yes—but for these and these alone,
Some moments—aye—one treacherous hour,
He still might doubt the tyrant's power,
So fair—so calm—so softly seal'd
The first—last look—by death reveal'd!*
Such is the aspect of this shore—   90
'Tis Greece—but living Greece no more!

line 81.   Ay, but to die and go we know not where,
                      To lie in cold obstruction.
                                    Measure for Measure, III. i. 118–19
    line 89. I trust that few of my readers have ever had an opportunity of witnessing what is
here attempted in description, but those who have will probably retain a painful remembrance
of that singular beauty which pervades, with few exceptions, the features of the dead, a few
hours, and but for a few hours, after 'the spirit is not there'. It is to be remarked in cases of
violent death by gun-shot wounds, the expression is always that of languor, whatever the
natural energy of the sufferer's character; but in death from a stab the countenance preserves
its traits of feeling or ferocity, and the mind its bias, to the last.

So coldly sweet, so deadly fair,
We start—for soul is wanting there.
Hers is the loveliness in death,
That parts not quite with parting breath;
But beauty with that fearful bloom,
That hue which haunts it to the tomb—
Expression's last receding ray,
A gilded halo hovering round decay,
The farewell beam of Feeling past away!   100
Spark of that flame—perchance of heavenly birth—
Which gleams—but warms no more its cherish'd earth!

Clime of the unforgotten brave!—
Whose land from plain to mountain-cave
Was Freedom's home or Glory's grave—
Shrine of the mighty! can it be,
That this is all remains of thee?
Approach thou craven crouching slave—
Say, is not this Thermopylae?
These waters blue that round you lave   110
Oh servile offspring of the free—
Pronounce what sea, what shore is this?
The gulf, the rock of Salamis!
These scenes—their story not unknown—
Arise, and make again your own;
Snatch from the ashes of your sires
The embers of their former fires,
And he who in the strife expires
Will add to theirs a name of fear,
That Tyranny shall quake to hear,   120
And leave his sons a hope, a fame,
They too will rather die than shame;
For Freedom's battle once begun,
Bequeathed by bleeding Sire to Son,
Though baffled oft is ever won.
Bear witness, Greece, thy living page,
Attest it many a deathless age!
While kings in dusty darkness hid,
Have left a nameless pyramid,
Thy heroes—though the general doom   130
Hath swept the column from their tomb,
A mightier monument command,
The mountains of their native land!
There points thy Muse to stranger's eye,
The graves of those that cannot die!
'Twere long to tell, and sad to trace,

Each step from splendour to disgrace,
Enough—no foreign foe could quell
Thy soul, till from itself it fell,
Yes! Self-abasement pav'd the way   140
To villain-bonds and despot-sway.

What can he tell who treads thy shore?
  No legend of thine olden time,
No theme on which the muse might soar,
High as thine own in days of yore,
  When man was worthy of thy clime.
The hearts within thy valleys bred,
The fiery souls that might have led
  Thy sons to deeds sublime;
Now crawl from cradle to the grave,   150
Slaves—nay, the bondsmen of a slave,*
  And callous, save to crime;
Stain'd with each evil that pollutes
Mankind, where least above the brutes;
Without even savage virtue blest,
Without one free or valiant breast.
Still to the neighbouring ports they waft
Proverbial wiles, and ancient craft,
In this the subtle Greek is found,
For this, and this alone, renown'd.   160
In vain might Liberty invoke
The spirit to its bondage broke,
Or raise the neck that courts the yoke:
No more her sorrows I bewail,
Yet this will be a mournful tale,
And they who listen may believe,
Who heard it first had cause to grieve.

              .   .   .   .   .   .

  Far, dark, along the blue sea glancing,
The shadows of the rocks advancing,
Start on the fisher's eye like boat   170
Of island-pirate or Mainote;
And fearful for his light caique
He shuns the near but doubtful creek,
Though worn and weary with his toil,
And cumber'd with his scaly spoil,
Slowly, yet strongly, plies the oar,

---

line 151. Athens is the property of the Kislar Aga (the slave of the seraglio and guardian
of the women), who appoints the Waywode. A pandar and eunuch—these are not polite, yet
true appellations—now *governs* the *governor* of Athens!

Till Port Leone's safer shore
Receives him by the lovely light
That best becomes an Eastern night.
    .   .   .   .

   Who thundering comes on blackest steed?   180
With slacken'd bit and hoof of speed,
Beneath the clattering iron's sound
The cavern'd echoes wake around
In lash for lash, and bound for bound;
The foam that streaks the courser's side,
Seems gather'd from the ocean-tide:
Though weary waves are sunk to rest,
There's none within his rider's breast,
And though to-morrow's tempest lower,
'Tis calmer than thy heart, young Giaour!*   190
I know thee not, I loathe thy race,
But in thy lineaments I trace
What time shall strengthen, not efface;
Though young and pale, that sallow front
Is scath'd by fiery passion's brunt,
Though bent on earth thine evil eye
As meteor-like thou glidest by,
Right well I view, and deem thee one
Whom Othman's sons should slay or shun.

   On—on he hastened—and he drew   200
My gaze of wonder as he flew:
Though like a demon of the night
He passed and vanished from my sight;
His aspect and his air impressed
A troubled memory on my breast;
And long upon my startled ear
Rung his dark courser's hoofs of fear.
He spurs his steed—he nears the steep,
That jutting shadows o'er the deep—
He winds around—he hurries by—   210
The rock relieves him from mine eye—
For well I ween unwelcome he
Whose glance is fixed on those that flee;
And not a star but shines too bright
On him who takes such timeless flight.
He wound along—but ere he passed
One glance he snatched—as if his last—
A moment checked his wheeling steed—

                    line 190. Infidel.

                        321

A moment breathed him from his speed—
A moment on his stirrup stood—   220
Why looks he o'er the olive wood?—
The crescent glimmers on the hill,
The Mosque's high lamps are quivering still;
Though too remote for sound to wake
In echoes of the far tophaike,*
The flashes of each joyous peal
Are seen to prove the Moslem's zeal.
To-night—set Rhamazani's sun—
To-night—the Bairam feast's begun—
To-night—but who and what art thou   230
Of foreign garb and fearful brow?
And what are these to thine or thee,
That thou should'st either pause or flee?
He stood—some dread was on his face—
Soon Hatred settled in its place—
It rose not with the reddening flush
Of transient Anger's hasty blush,
But pale as marble o'er the tomb,
Whose ghastly whiteness aids its gloom.
His brow was bent—his eye was glazed—   240
He raised his arm, and fiercely raised;
And sternly shook his hand on high,
As doubting to return or fly;—
Impatient of his flight delayed
Here loud his raven charger neighed—
Down glanced that hand, and grasped his blade—
That sound had burst his waking dream,
As Slumber starts at owlet's scream.—
The spur hath lanced his courser's sides—
Away—away—for life he rides—   250
Swift as the hurled on high jerreed,*
Springs to the touch his startled steed,
The rock is doubled—and the shore
Shakes with the clattering tramp no more—
The crag is won—no more is seen
His Christian crest and haughty mien.—

line 225. 'Tophaike', musquet.—The Bairam is announced by the cannon at sunset; the illumination of the Mosques, and the firing of all kinds of small arms, loaded with *ball*, proclaim it during the night.

line 251. Jerreed, or Djerrid, a blunted Turkish Javelin, which is darted from horseback with great force and precision. It is a favourite exercise of the Mussulmans; but I know not if it can be called a *manly* one, since the most expert in the art are the Black Eunuchs of Constantinople.—I think, next to these, a Mamlouk at Smyrna was the most skilful that came within my observation.

'Twas but an instant—he restrained
That fiery barb so sternly reined—
'Twas but a moment that he stood,
Then sped as if by death pursued;   260
But in that instant, o'er his soul
Winters of Memory seemed to roll,
And gather in that drop of time
A life of pain, an age of crime.
O'er him who loves, or hates, or fears,
Such moment pours the grief of years—
What felt *he* then—at once opprest
By all that most distracts the breast?
That pause—which pondered o'er his fate,
Oh, who its dreary length shall date!   270
Though in Time's record nearly nought,
It was Eternity to Thought!
For infinite as boundless space
The thought that Conscience must embrace,
Which in itself can comprehend
Woe without name—or hope—or end.—

The hour is past, the Giaour is gone,
And did he fly or fall alone?
Woe to that hour he came or went,
The curse for Hassan's sin was sent   280
To turn a palace to a tomb;
He came, he went, like the Simoom,*
That harbinger of fate and gloom,
Beneath whose widely-wasting breath
The very cypress droops to death—
Dark tree—still sad, when others' grief is fled,
The only constant mourner o'er the dead!

The steed is vanished from the stall,
No serf is seen in Hassan's hall;
The lonely Spider's thin grey pall   290
Waves slowly widening o'er the wall;
The Bat builds in his Haram bower;
And in the fortress of his power
The Owl usurps the beacon-tower;
The wild-dog howls o'er the fountain's brim,
With baffled thirst, and famine, grim,

line 282. The blast of the desert, fatal to every thing living, and alluded to in eastern
poetry.

For the stream has shrunk from its marble bed,
Where the weeds and the desolate dust are spread.
'Twas sweet of yore to see it play
And chase the sultriness of day—   300
As springing high the silver dew
In whirls fantastically flew,
And flung luxurious coolness round
The air, and verdure o'er the ground.—
'Twas sweet, when cloudless stars were bright,
To view the wave of watery light,
And hear its melody by night.—
And oft had Hassan's Childhood played
Around the verge of that cascade;
And oft upon his mother's breast   310
That sound had harmonized his rest;
And oft had Hassan's Youth along
Its bank been sooth'd by Beauty's song;
And softer seemed each melting tone
Of Music mingled with its own.—
But ne'er shall Hassan's Age repose
Along the brink at Twilight's close—
The stream that filled that font is fled—
The blood that warmed his heart is shed!—
And here no more shall human voice   320
Be heard to rage—regret—rejoice—
The last sad note that swelled the gale
Was woman's wildest funeral wail—
That quenched in silence—all is still,
But the lattice that flaps when the wind is shrill—
Though raves the gust, and floods the rain,
No hand shall close its clasp again.
On desart sands 'twere joy to scan
The rudest steps of fellow man,
So here the very voice of Grief   330
Might wake an Echo like relief—
At least 'twould say, 'all are not gone;
There lingers Life, though but in one'—
For many a gilded chamber's there,
Which Solitude might well forbear;
Within that dome as yet Decay
Hath slowly worked her cankering way—
But Gloom is gathered o'er the gate,
Nor there the Fakir's self will wait;
Nor there will wandering Dervise stay,   340
For Bounty cheers not his delay;
Nor there will weary stranger halt

To bless the sacred 'bread and salt'.*
Alike must Wealth and Poverty
Pass heedless and unheeded by,
For Courtesy and Pity died
With Hassan on the mountain side.—
His roof—that refuge unto men—
Is Desolation's hungry den.—
The guest flies the hall, and the vassal from labour,   350
Since his turban was cleft by the infidel's sabre!*

       .   .   .   .   .   .

   I hear the sound of coming feet,
But not a voice mine ear to greet—
More near—each turban I can scan,
And silver-sheathed ataghan;*
The foremost of the band is seen
An Emir by his garb of green:*
   'Ho! who art thou!'—'this low salam*
   Replies of Moslem faith I am.'
'The burthen ye so gently bear,   360
Seems one that claims your utmost care,
And, doubtless, holds some precious freight,
My humble bark would gladly wait.'

   'Thou speakest sooth, thy skiff unmoor,
And waft us from the silent shore;
Nay, leave the sail still furl'd, and ply
The nearest oar that's scatter'd by,
And midway to those rocks where sleep
The channel'd waters dark and deep.—
Rest from your task—so—bravely done,
Our course has been right swiftly run,   370
Yet 'tis the longest voyage, I trow,
That one of'—   .   .   .   .

line 343. To partake of food, to break bread and salt with your host, insures the safety of the guest: even though an enemy, his person from that moment is sacred.

line 351. I need hardly observe, that Charity and Hospitality are the first duties enjoined by Mahomet; and to say truth, very generally practised by his disciples. The first praise that can be bestowed on a chief, is a panegyric on his bounty; the next, on his valour.

line 355. The ataghan, a long dagger worn with pistols in the belt, in a metal scabbard, generally of silver; and, among the wealthier, gilt, or of gold.

line 357. Green is the privileged colour of the prophet's numerous pretended descendants; with them, as here, faith (the family inheritance) is supposed to supersede the necessity of good works; they are the worst of a very indifferent brood.

line 358. Salam aleikoum! aleikoum salam! peace be with you; be with you peace—the salutation reserved for the faithful,—to a Christian, 'Urlarula', a good journey; or saban hiresem, saban serula; good morn, good even; and sometimes, 'may your end be happy'; are the usual salutes.

. . . .

   Sullen it plunged, and slowly sank,
The calm wave rippled to the bank;
I watch'd it as it sank, methought
Some motion from the current caught
Bestirr'd it more,—'twas but the beam
That chequer'd o'er the living stream—
I gaz'd, till vanishing from view,
Like lessening pebble it withdrew;   380
Still less and less, a speck of white
That gemm'd the tide, then mock'd the sight;
And all its hidden secrets sleep,
Known but to Genii of the deep,
Which, trembling in their coral caves,
They dare not whisper to the waves.

. . . . .

   As rising on its purple wing
The insect-queen of eastern spring,*
O'er emerald meadows of Kashmeer
Invites the young pursuer near,   390
And leads him on from flower to flower
A weary chase and wasted hour,
Then leaves him, as it soars on high
With panting heart and tearful eye:
So Beauty lures the full-grown child
With hue as bright, and wing as wild;
A chase of idle hopes and fears,
Begun in folly, closed in tears.
If won, to equal ills betrayed,   400
Woe waits the insect and the maid,
A life of pain, the loss of peace,
From infant's play, or man's caprice:
The lovely toy so fiercely sought
Has lost its charm by being caught,
For every touch that wooed its stay
Has brush'd the brightest hues away
Till charm, and hue, and beauty gone,
'Tis left to fly or fall alone.
With wounded wing, or bleeding breast,   410
Ah! where shall either victim rest?
Can this with faded pinion soar
From rose to tulip as before?
Or Beauty, blighted in an hour,

---

line 389. The blue-winged butterfly of Kashmeer, the most rare and beautiful of the species.

Find joy within her broken bower?
No: gayer insects fluttering by
Ne'er droop the wing o'er those that die,
And lovelier things have mercy shewn
To every failing but their own,
And every woe a tear can claim   420
Except an erring sister's shame.

 . . . . . .

The Mind, that broods o'er guilty woes,
 Is like the Scorpion girt by fire,
In circle narrowing as it glows
The flames around their captive close,
Till inly search'd by thousand throes,
 And maddening in her ire,
One sad and sole relief she knows,
The sting she nourish'd for her foes,
Whose venom never yet was vain,   430
Gives but one pang, and cures all pain,
And darts into her desperate brain.—
So do the dark in soul expire,
Or live like Scorpion girt by fire;*
So writhes the mind Remorse hath riven,
Unfit for earth, undoom'd for heaven,
Darkness above, despair beneath,
Around it flame, within it death!—

 . . . . . .

 Black Hassan from the Haram flies,
Nor bends on woman's form his eyes,   440
The unwonted chase each hour employs,
Yet shares he not the hunter's joys.
Not thus was Hassan wont to fly
When Leila dwelt in his Serai.
Doth Leila there no longer dwell?
That tale can only Hassan tell:
Strange rumours in our city say
Upon that eve she fled away;
When Rhamazan's last sun was set,*
And flashing from each minaret   450
Millions of lamps proclaim'd the feast

line 434. Alluding to the dubious suicide of the scorpion, so placed for experiment by gentle philosophers. Some maintain that the position of the sting, when turned towards the head, is merely a convulsive movement; but others have actually brought in the verdict 'Felo de se'. The scorpions are surely interested in a speedy decision of the question; as, if once fairly established as insect Catos, they will probably be allowed to live as long as they think proper, without being martyred for the sake of an hypothesis.

line 449. The cannon at sunset close the Rhamazan; see note [to l. 225].

Of Bairam through the boundless East.
'Twas then she went as to the bath,
Which Hassan vainly search'd in wrath,
But she was flown her master's rage
In likeness of a Georgian page;
And far beyond the Moslem's power
Had wrong'd him with the faithless Giaour.
Somewhat of this had Hassan deem'd,
But still so fond, so fair she seem'd,   460
Too well he trusted to the slave
Whose treachery deserv'd a grave:
And on that eve had gone to mosque,
And thence to feast in his kiosk.
Such is the tale his Nubians tell,
Who did not watch their charge too well;
But others say, that on that night,
By pale Phingari's trembling light,*
The Giaour upon his jet-black steed
Was seen—but seen alone to speed   470
With bloody spur along the shore,
Nor maid nor page behind him bore.
        .   .   .   .   .   .

    Her eye's dark charm 'twere vain to tell,
But gaze on that of the Gazelle,
It will assist thy fancy well,
As large, as languishingly dark,
But Soul beam'd forth in every spark
That darted from beneath the lid,
Bright as the jewel of Giamschid.*
Yea, *Soul*, and should our prophet say   480
That form was nought but breathing clay,
By Alla! I would answer nay;
Though on Al-Sirat's arch I stood,*
Which totters o'er the fiery flood,
With Paradise within my view,

line 468. Phingari, the moon.
 line 479. The celebrated fabulous ruby of Sultan Giamschid, the embellisher of Istakhar:
from its splendour, named Schebgerag, 'the torch of night'; also, the 'cup of the sun', etc.—
In the first editions 'Giamschid' was written as a word of three syllables, so d'Herbelot has
it; but I am told Richardson reduces it to a dissyllable, and writes 'Jamshid'. I have left in the
text the orthography of the one with the pronunciation of the other.
 line 483. Al-Sirat, the bridge of breadth less than the thread of a famished spider, over
which the Mussulmans must *skate* into Paradise, to which it is the only entrance; but this is
not the worst, the river beneath being hell itself, into which, as may be expected, the unskilful
and tender of foot contrive to tumble with a 'facilis descensus Averni', not very pleasing in
prospect to the next passenger. There is a shorter cut downwards for the Jews and Chris-
tians.

And all his Houris beckoning through.
Oh! who young Leila's glance could read
And keep that portion of his creed*
Which saith, that woman is but dust,
A soulless toy for tyrant's lust?   490
On her might Muftis gaze, and own
That through her eye the Immortal shone—
On her fair cheek's unfading hue,
The young pomegranate's blossoms strew*
Their bloom in blushes ever new—
Her hair in hyacinthine flow*
When left to roll its folds below,
As midst her handmaids in the hall
She stood superior to them all,
Hath swept the marble where her feet   500
Gleamed whiter than the mountain sleet
Ere from the cloud that gave it birth,
It fell, and caught one stain of earth.
The cygnet nobly walks the water—
So moved on earth Circassia's daughter—
The loveliest bird of Franguestan!*
As rears her crest the ruffled Swan,
    And spurns the wave with wings of pride,
When pass the steps of stranger man
    Along the banks that bound her tide;   510
Thus rose fair Leila's whiter neck:—
Thus armed with beauty would she check
Intrusion's glance, till Folly's gaze
Shrunk from the charms it meant to praise.
Thus high and graceful was her gait;
Her heart as tender to her mate—
Her mate—stern Hassan, who was he?
Alas! that name was not for thee!
           .   .   .   .   .

    Stern Hassan hath a journey ta'en
With twenty vassals in his train,   520
Each arm'd as best becomes a man

---

line 488. A vulgar error; the Koran allots at least a third of Paradise to well-behaved women; but by far the greater number of Mussulmans interpret the text their own way, and exclude their moieties from heaven. Being enemies to Platonics, they cannot discern 'any fitness of things' in the souls of the other sex, conceiving them to be superseded by the Houris.

line 494. An Oriental simile, which may, perhaps, though fairly stolen, be deemed 'plus Arabe qu'en Arabie'.

line 496. Hyacinthine, in Arabic, 'Sunbul', as common a thought in the eastern poets as it was among the Greeks.

line 506. 'Franguestan', Circassia.

With arquebuss and ataghan;
The chief before, as deck'd for war,
Bears in his belt the scimitar
Stain'd with the best of Arnaut blood,
When in the pass the rebels stood,
And few return'd to tell the tale
Of what befell in Parne's vale.
The pistols which his girdle bore
Were those that once a pasha wore,   530
Which still, though gemm'd and boss'd with gold,
Even robbers tremble to behold.—
'Tis said he goes to woo a bride
More true than her who left his side;
The faithless slave that broke her bower,
And, worse than faithless, for a Giaour!—

　　·　　·　　·　　·　　·

The sun's last rays are on the hill,
And sparkle in the fountain rill,
Whose welcome waters cool and clear,
Draw blessings from the mountaineer;   540
Here may the loitering merchant Greek
Find that repose 'twere vain to seek
In cities lodg'd too near his lord,
And trembling for his secret hoard—
Here may he rest where none can see,
In crowds a slave, in desarts free;
And with forbidden wine may stain
The bowl a Moslem must not drain.—

　　·　　·　　·　　·　　·

The foremost Tartar's in the gap,
Conspicuous by his yellow cap,   550
The rest in lengthening line the while
Wind slowly through the long defile;
Above, the mountain rears a peak,
Where vultures whet the thirsty beak,
And theirs may be a feast to-night,
Shall tempt them down ere morrow's light.
Beneath, a river's wintry stream
Has shrunk before the summer beam,
And left a channel bleak and bare,
Save shrubs that spring to perish there.   560
Each side the midway path there lay
Small broken crags of granite gray,
By time or mountain lightning riven,
From summits clad in mists of heaven;
For where is he that hath beheld

The peak of Liakura unveil'd?

.   .   .   .   .   .

They reach the grove of pine at last,
'Bismillah! now the peril's past;*
For yonder view the opening plain,
And there we'll prick our steeds amain':   570
The Chiaus spake, and as he said,
A bullet whistled o'er his head;
The foremost Tartar bites the ground!
   Scarce had they time to check the rein
Swift from their steeds the riders bound,
   But three shall never mount again;
Unseen the foes that gave the wound,
   The dying ask revenge in vain.
With steel unsheath'd, and carbine bent,
Some o'er their courser's harness leant,   580
   Half shelter'd by the steed,
Some fly behind the nearest rock,
And there await the coming shock,
   Nor tamely stand to bleed
Beneath the shaft of foes unseen,
Who dare not quit their craggy screen.
Stern Hassan only from his horse
Disdains to light, and keeps his course,
Till fiery flashes in the van
Proclaim too sure the robber-clan   590
Have well secur'd the only way
Could now avail the promis'd prey;
Then curl'd his very beard with ire,*
And glared his eye with fiercer fire.
'Though far and near the bullets hiss,
I've scaped a bloodier hour than this.'
And now the foe their covert quit,
And call his vassals to submit;
But Hassan's frown and furious word
Are dreaded more than hostile sword,   600
Nor of his little band a man
Resign'd carbine or ataghan——
Nor raised the craven cry, Amaun!*

line 568. Bismillah—'In the name of God', the commencement of all the chapters of the
Koran but one, and of prayer and thanksgiving.

line 593. A phenomenon not uncommon with an angry Mussulman. In 1809, the Capitan
Pacha's whiskers at a diplomatic audience were no less lively with indignation than a tiger
cat's, to the horror of all the dragomans; the portentous mustachios twisted, they stood erect
of their own accord, and were expected every moment to change their colour, but at last
condescended to subside, which, probably, saved more heads than they contained hairs.

line 603. 'Amaun', quarter, pardon.

In fuller sight, more near and near,
The lately ambush'd foes appear,
And issuing from the grove advance,
Some who on battle charger prance.—
Who leads them on with foreign brand,
Far flashing in his red right hand?
' 'Tis he—'tis he—I know him now,   610
I know him by his pallid brow;
I know him by the evil eye*
That aids his envious treachery;
I know him by his jet-black barb,
Though now array'd in Arnaut garb,
Apostate from his own vile faith,
It shall not save him from the death;
'Tis he, well met in any hour,
Lost Leila's love—accursed Giaour!'

   As rolls the river into ocean,   620
In sable torrent wildly streaming;
   As the sea-tide's opposing motion
In azure column proudly gleaming,
Beats back the current many a rood,
In curling foam and mingling flood;
While eddying whirl, and breaking wave,
Roused by the blast of winter rave;
Through sparkling spray in thundering clash,
The lightnings of the waters flash
In awful whiteness o'er the shore,   630
That shines and shakes beneath the roar;
Thus—as the stream and ocean greet,
With waves that madden as they meet—
Thus join the bands whom mutual wrong,
And fate and fury drive along.
The bickering sabres' shivering jar;
   And pealing wide—or ringing near,
   Its echoes on the throbbing ear,
The deathshot hissing from afar—
The shock—the shout—the groan of war—   640
   Reverberate along that vale,
   More suited to the shepherd's tale:
Though few the numbers—theirs the strife,
That neither spares nor speaks for life!

line 612. The 'evil eye', a common superstition in the Levant, and of which the imaginary
effects are yet very singular to those who conceive themselves affected.

Ah! fondly youthful hearts can press,
To seize and share the dear caress;
But Love itself could never pant
For all that Beauty sighs to grant,
With half the fervour Hate bestows
Upon the last embrace of foes,   650
When grappling in the fight they fold
Those arms that ne'er shall lose their hold;
Friends meet to part—Love laughs at faith;—
True foes, once met, are joined till death!

    ·   ·   ·   ·   ·

With sabre shiver'd to the hilt,
Yet dripping with the blood he spilt;
Yet strain'd within the sever'd hand
Which quivers round that faithless brand;
His turban far behind him roll'd,
And cleft in twain its firmest fold;   660
His flowing robe by falchion torn,
And crimson as those clouds of morn
That streak'd with dusky red, portend
The day shall have a stormy end;
A stain on every bush that bore
A fragment of his palampore,*
His breast with wounds unnumber'd riven,
His back to earth, his face to heaven,
Fall'n Hassan lies—his unclos'd eye
Yet lowering on his enemy,   670
As if the hour that seal'd his fate,
Surviving left his quenchless hate;
And o'er him bends that foe with brow
As dark as his that bled below.—

    ·   ·   ·   ·   ·

  'Yes, Leila sleeps beneath the wave,
But his shall be a redder grave;
Her spirit pointed well the steel
Which taught that felon heart to feel.
He call'd the Prophet, but his power
Was vain against the vengeful Giaour: 680
He call'd on Alla—but the word
Arose unheeded or unheard.
Thou Paynim fool!—could Leila's prayer
Be pass'd, and thine accorded there?
I watch'd my time, I leagu'd with these,

---

line 666. The flowered shawls generally worn by persons of rank.

The traitor in his turn to seize;
My wrath is wreak'd, the deed is done,
And now I go—but go alone.'

    .   .   .

The browzing camels' bells are tinkling—
His Mother looked from her lattice high,   690
  She saw the dews of eve besprinkling
The pasture green beneath her eye,
  She saw the planets faintly twinkling,
' 'Tis twilight—sure his train is nigh.'—
She could not rest in the garden-bower,
But gazed through the grate of his steepest tower—
'Why comes he not? his steeds are fleet,
Nor shrink they from the summer heat;
Why sends not the Bridegroom his promised gift,
Is his heart more cold, or his barb less swift?   700
Oh, false reproach! yon Tartar now
Has gained our nearest mountain's brow,
And warily the steep descends,
And now within the valley bends;
And he bears the gift at his saddle bow—
How could I deem his courser slow?
Right well my largess shall repay
His welcome speed, and weary way.'—
The Tartar lighted at the gate,
But scarce upheld his fainting weight;   710
His swarthy visage spake distress,
But this might be from weariness;
His garb with sanguine spots was dyed,
But these might be from his courser's side;—
He drew the token from his vest—
Angel of Death! 'tis Hassan's cloven crest!
His calpac rent—his caftan red—*
'Lady, a fearful bride thy Son hath wed—
Me, not from mercy, did they spare,
But this empurpled pledge to bear.   720
Peace to the brave! whose blood is spilt—
Woe to the Giaour! for his the guilt.'

    .   .   .   .

A turban carv'd in coarsest stone,*

line 717. The 'Calpac' is the solid cap or centre part of the headdress; the shawl is wound round it, and forms the turban.

line 723. The turban, pillar, and inscriptive verse, decorate the tombs of the Osmanlies, whether in the cemetery or the wilderness. In the mountains you frequently pass similar mementos; and on enquiry you are informed that they record some victim of rebellion, plunder, or revenge.

A pillar with rank weeds o'ergrown,
Wheron can now be scarcely read
The Koran verse that mourns the dead;
Point out the spot where Hassan fell
A victim in that lonely dell.
There sleeps as true an Osmanlie
As e'er at Mecca bent the knee;   730
As ever scorn'd forbidden wine,
Or pray'd with face towards the shrine,
In orisons resumed anew
At solemn sound of 'Alla Hu!'*
Yet died he by a stranger's hand,
And stranger in his native land—
Yet died he as in arms he stood,
And unaveng'd, at least in blood.
But him the maids of Paradise
    Impatient to their halls invite,   740
And the dark Heaven of Houri's eyes
    On him shall glance for ever bright;
They come—their kerchiefs green they wave,*
And welcome with a kiss the brave!
Who falls in battle 'gainst a Giaour,
Is worthiest an immortal bower.

                .   .   .   .   .

    But thou, false Infidel! shalt writhe
Beneath avenging Monkir's scythe;*
And from its torment 'scape alone
To wander round lost Eblis' throne;*   750
And fire unquench'd, unquenchable—
Around—within—thy heart shall dwell,
Nor ear can hear, nor tongue can tell
The tortures of that inward hell!—

line 734. 'Alla Hu!' the concluding words of the muezzin's call to prayer from the highest gallery on the exterior of the Minaret. On a still evening, when the muezzin has a fine voice, which is frequently the case, the effect is solemn and beautiful beyond all the bells in Christendom.

line 743. The following is part of a battle song of the Turks:—'I see—I see a dark-eyed girl of Paradise, and she waves a handkerchief, a kerchief of green; and cries aloud, Come, kiss me, for I love thee,' etc.

line 748. Monkir and Nekir are the inquisitors of the dead, before whom the corpse undergoes a slight noviciate and preparatory training for damnation. If the answers are none of the clearest, he is hauled up with a scythe and thumped down with a red hot mace till properly seasoned, with a variety of subsidiary probations. The office of these angels is no sinecure; there are but two, and the number of orthodox deceased being in a small proportion to the remainder, their hands are always full.

line 750. Eblis, the Oriental Prince of Darkness.

But first, on earth as Vampire sent,*
Thy corse shall from its tomb be rent;
Then ghastly haunt thy native place,
And suck the blood of all thy race,
There from thy daughter, sister, wife,
At midnight drain the stream of life;   760
Yet loathe the banquet which perforce
Must feed thy livid living corse;
Thy victims ere they yet expire
Shall know the daemon for their sire,
As cursing thee, thou cursing them,
Thy flowers are wither'd on the stem.
But one that for thy crime must fall—
The youngest—most belov'd of all,
Shall bless thee with a *father*'s name—
That word shall wrap thy heart in flame!   770
Yet must thou end thy task, and mark
Her cheek's last tinge, her eye's last spark,
And the last glassy glance must view
Which freezes o'er its lifeless blue;
Then with unhallowed hand shalt tear
The tresses of her yellow hair,
Of which in life a lock when shorn,
Affection's fondest pledge was worn;
But now is borne away by thee,
Memorial of thine agony!   780
Wet with thine own best blood shall drip,*
Thy gnashing tooth and haggard lip;
Then stalking to thy sullen grave—
Go—and with Gouls and Afrits rave;
Till these in horror shrink away
From spectre more accursed than they!

　　　　　·　·　·　·　·

'How name ye yon lone Caloyer?
　　His features I have scann'd before
In mine own land—'tis many a year,

line 755. The Vampire superstition is still general in the Levant. Honest Tournefort tells
a long story, which Mr Southey, in the notes on Thalaba, quotes about these 'Vroucolochas',
as he calls them. The Romaic term is 'Vardoulacha'. I recollect a whole family being terrified
by the scream of a child, which they imagined must proceed from such a visitation. The
Greeks never mention the word without horror. I find that 'Broucolokas' is an old legitimate
Hellenic appellation—at least is so applied to Arsenius, who, according to the Greeks, was
after his death animated by the Devil.—The moderns, however, use the word I men-
tion.
line 781. The freshness of the face, and the wetness of the lip with blood, are the never-
failing signs of a Vampire. The stories told in Hungary and Greece of these foul feeders are
singular, and some of them most *incredibly* attested.

Since, dashing by the lonely shore,   790
I saw him urge as fleet a steed
As ever serv'd a horseman's need.
But once I saw that face—yet then
It was so mark'd with inward pain
I could not pass it by again;
It breathes the same dark spirit now,
As death were stamped upon his brow.'

' 'Tis twice three years at summer tide
    Since first among our freres he came;
And here it soothes him to abide   800
    For some dark deed he will not name.
But never at our vesper prayer,
Nor e'er before confession chair
Kneels he, nor recks he when arise
Incense or anthem to the skies,
But broods within his cell alone,
His faith and race alike unknown.
The sea from Paynim land he crost,
And here ascended from the coast,
Yet seems he not of Othman race,   810
But only Christian in his face:
I'd judge him some stray renegade,
Repentant of the change he made,
Save that he shuns our holy shrine,
Nor tastes the sacred bread and wine.
Great largess to these walls he brought,
And thus our abbot's favour bought;
But were I Prior, not a day
Should brook such stranger's further stay,
Or pent within our penance cell   820
Should doom him there for aye to dwell.
Much in his visions mutters he
Of maiden 'whelmed beneath the sea;
Of sabres clashing—foemen flying,
Wrongs aveng'd—and Moslem dying.
On cliff he hath been known to stand,
And rave as to some bloody hand
Fresh sever'd from its parent limb,
Invisible to all but him,
Which beckons onward to his grave,   830
And lures to leap into the wave.'

.   .   .   .   .   .

Dark and unearthly is the scowl
That glares beneath his dusky cowl—

The flash of that dilating eye
Reveals too much of times gone by—
Though varying—indistinct its hue,
Oft will his glance the gazer rue—
For in it lurks that nameless spell
Which speaks—itself unspeakable—
A spirit yet unquelled and high   840
That claims and keeps ascendancy,
And like the bird whose pinions quake—
But cannot fly the gazing snake—
Will others quail beneath his look,
Nor 'scape the glance they scarce can brook.
From him the half-affrighted Friar
When met alone would fain retire—
As if that eye and bitter smile
Transferred to others fear and guile—
Not oft to smile descendeth he,   850
And when he doth 'tis sad to see
That he but mocks at Misery.
How that pale lip will curl and quiver!
Then fix once more as if for ever—
As if his sorrow or disdain
Forbade him e'er to smile again.—
Well were it so—such ghastly mirth
From joyaunce ne'er deriv'd its birth.—
But sadder still it were to trace
What once were feelings in that face—   860
Time hath not yet the features fixed,
But brighter traits with evil mixed—
And there are hues not always faded,
Which speak a mind not all degraded
Even by the crimes through which it waded—
The common crowd but see the gloom
Of wayward deeds—and fitting doom—
The close observer can espy
A noble soul, and lineage high.—
Alas! though both bestowed in vain,   870
Which Grief could change—and Guilt could stain—
It was no vulgar tenement
To which such lofty gifts were lent,
And still with little less than dread
    On such the sight is riveted.—
The roofless cot decayed and rent,
    Will scarce delay the passer by—
The tower by war or tempest bent,
While yet may frown one battlement,

Demands and daunts the stranger's eye—   880
Each ivied arch—and pillar lone,
Pleads haughtily for glories gone!
'His floating robe around him folding,
   Slow sweeps he through the columned aisle—
With dread beheld—with gloom beholding
   The rites that sanctify the pile.
But when the anthem shakes the choir,
And kneel the monks—his steps retire—
By yonder lone and wavering torch
His aspect glares within the porch;   890
There will he pause till all is done—
And hear the prayer—but utter none.
See—by the half-illumin'd wall
His hood fly back—his dark hair fall—
That pale brow wildly wreathing round,
As if the Gorgon there had bound
The sablest of the serpent-braid
That o'er her fearful forehead strayed.
For he declines the convent oath,
And leaves those locks' unhallowed growth—   900
But wears our garb in all beside;
And—not from piety but pride
Gives wealth to walls that never heard
Of his one holy vow nor word.—
Lo!—mark ye—as the harmony
Peals louder praises to the sky—
That livid cheek—that stoney air
Of mixed defiance and despair!
Saint Francis! keep him from the shrine!
Else may we dread the wrath divine   910
Made manifest by awful sign.—
If ever evil angel bore
The form of mortal, such he wore—
By all my hope of sins forgiven
Such looks are not of earth nor heaven!'

To love the softest hearts are prone,
But such can ne'er be all his own;
Too timid in his woes to share,
Too meek to meet, or brave, despair;
And sterner hearts alone may feel   920
The wound that time can never heal.
The rugged metal of the mine
Must burn before its surface shine,
But plung'd within the furnace-flame,

It bends and melts—though still the same;
Then tempered to thy want, or will,
'Twill serve thee to defend or kill;
A breast-plate for thine hour of need,
Or blade to bid thy foeman bleed;
But if a dagger's form it bear,   930
Let those who shape its edge, beware!
Thus passion's fire, and woman's art,
Can turn and tame the sterner heart;
From these its form and tone are ta'en,
And what they make it, must remain,
But break—before it bend again.

   .   .   .   .   .

If solitude succeed to grief,
Release from pain is slight relief;
The vacant bosom's wilderness
Might thank the pang that made it less.   940
We loathe what none are left to share—
Even bliss—'twere woe alone to bear;
The heart once left thus desolate,
Must fly at last for ease—to hate.
It is as if the dead could feel
The icy worm around them steal,
And shudder, as the reptiles creep
To revel o'er their rotting sleep
Without the power to scare away
The cold consumers of their clay!   950
It is as if the desart-bird,*
  Whose beak unlocks her bosom's stream
  To still her famish'd nestlings' scream,
Nor mourns a life to them transferr'd,
Should rend her rash devoted breast,
And find them flown her empty nest.
The keenest pangs the wretched find
  Are rapture to the dreary void—
The leafless desart of the mind—
  The waste of feelings unemploy'd—   960
Who would be doom'd to gaze upon
A sky without a cloud or sun?
Less hideous far the tempest's roar,
Than ne'er to brave the billows more—
Thrown, when the war of winds is o'er,
A lonely wreck on fortune's shore,

---

line 951. The pelican is, I believe, the bird so libelled, by the imputation of feeding her chickens with her blood.

'Mid sullen calm, and silent bay,
Unseen to drop by dull decay;—
Better to sink beneath the shock
Than moulder piecemeal on the rock!   970
    .   .   .   .   .

'Father! thy days have pass'd in peace,
    'Mid counted beads, and countless prayer;
To bid the sins of others cease,
    Thyself without a crime or care,
Save transient ills that all must bear,
Has been thy lot, from youth to age,
And thou wilt bless thee from the rage
Of passions fierce and uncontroll'd,
Such as thy penitents unfold,
Whose secret sins and sorrows rest   980
Within thy pure and pitying breast.
My days, though few, have pass'd below
In much of joy, but more of woe;
Yet still in hours of love or strife,
I've 'scap'd the weariness of life;
Now leagu'd with friends, now girt by foes,
I loath'd the languor of repose;
Now nothing left to love or hate,
No more with hope or pride elate;
I'd rather be the thing that crawls   990
Most noxious o'er a dungeon's walls,
Than pass my dull, unvarying days,
Condemn'd to meditate and gaze—
Yet, lurks a wish within my breast
For rest—but not to feel 'tis rest—
Soon shall my fate that wish fulfil;
    And I shall sleep without the dream
Of what I was, and would be still;
    Dark as to thee my deeds may seem—
My memory now is but the tomb   1000
Of joys long dead—my hope—their doom—
Though better to have died with those
Than bear a life of lingering woes—
My spirit shrunk not to sustain
The searching throes of ceaseless pain;
Nor sought the self-accorded grave
Of ancient fool, and modern knave:
Yet death I have not fear'd to meet,
And in the field it had been sweet
Had danger wooed me on to move   1010
The slave of glory, not of love.

341

I've brav'd it—not for honour's boast;
I smile at laurels won or lost.—
To such let others carve their way,
For high renown, or hireling pay;
But place again before my eyes
Aught that I deem a worthy prize;—
The maid I love—the man I hate—
And I will hunt the steps of fate,
(To save or slay—as these require)
Through rending steel, and rolling fire;   1020
Nor need'st thou doubt this speech from one
Who would but do—what he *hath* done.
Death is but what the haughty brave—
The weak must bear—the wretch must crave—
Then let Life go to him who gave:
I have not quailed to danger's brow—
When high and happy—need I *now?*

    .   .   .   .   .

'I lov'd her, friar! nay, adored—
   But these are words that all can use—   1030
I prov'd it more in deed than word—
There's blood upon that dinted sword—
   A stain its steel can never lose:
'Twas shed for her, who died for me,
   It warmed the heart of one abhorred:
Nay, start not—no—nor bend thy knee,
   Nor midst my sins such act record,
Thou wilt absolve me from the deed,
For he was hostile to thy creed!
The very name of Nazarene   1040
Was wormwood to his Paynim spleen,
Ungrateful fool! since but for brands,
Well wielded in some hardy hands;
And wounds by Galileans given,
The surest pass to Turkish heav'n;
For him his Houris still might wait
Impatient at the prophet's gate.
I lov'd her—love will find its way
Through paths where wolves would fear to prey,
And if it dares enough, 'twere hard   1050
If passion met not some reward—
No matter how—or where—or why,
I did not vainly seek—nor sigh:
Yet sometimes with remorse in vain
I wish she had not lov'd again.
She died—I dare not tell thee how,

But look—'tis written on my brow!
There read of Cain the curse and crime,
In characters unworn by time:
Still, ere thou dost condemn me—pause—   1060
Not mine the act, though I the cause;
Yet did he but what I had done
Had she been false to more than one;
Faithless to him—he gave the blow,
But true to me—I laid him low;
Howe'er deserv'd her doom might be,
Her treachery was truth to me;
To me she gave her heart, that all
Which tyranny can ne'er enthrall;
And I, alas! too late to save,   1070
Yet all I then could give—I gave—
'Twas some relief—our foe a grave.
His death sits lightly; but her fate
Has made me—what thou well may'st hate.
His doom was seal'd—he knew it well,
Warn'd by the voice of stern Taheer,
Deep in whose darkly boding ear*

Line 1077. This superstition of a second-hearing (for I never met with downright second-sight in the East) fell once under my own observation.—On my third journey to Cape Colonna early in 1811, as we passed through the defile that leads from the hamlet between Keratia and Colonna, I observed Dervish Tahiri riding rather out of the path, and leaning his head upon his hand, as if in pain. I rode up and enquired. 'We are in peril,' he answered. 'What Peril? we are not now in Albania, nor in the passes to Ephesus, Messalunghi, or Lepanto; there are plenty of us, well armed, and the Choriates have not courage to be thieves?'—'True, Affendi, but nevertheless the shot is ringing in my ears.'—'The shot! not a tophaike has been fired this morning.'—'I hear it notwithstanding—Bom—Bom—as plainly as I hear your voice.'—'Psha.'—'As you please, Affendi; if it is written, so will it be.' I left this quick-eared predestinarian, and rode up to Basili, his Christian compatriot, whose ears, though not at all prophetic, by no means relished the intelligence. We all arrived at Colonna, remained some hours, and returned leisurely, saying a variety of brilliant things, in more languages than spoiled the building of Babel, upon the mistaken seer. Romaic, Arnaout, Turkish, Italian, and English were all exercised, in various conceits, upon the unfortunate Mussulman. While we were contemplating the beautiful prospect, Dervish was occupied about the columns. I thought he was deranged into an antiquarian, and asked him if he had become a '*Palao-castro*' man: 'No,' said he, 'but these pillars will be useful in making a stand'; and added other remarks, which at least evinced his own belief in his troublesome faculty of *fore-hearing*. On our return to Athens, we heard from Leoné (a prisoner set ashore some days after) of the intended attack of the Mainotes, mentioned, with the cause of its not taking place, in the notes to *Childe Harold*, Canto [11st. 12]. I was at some pains to question the man, and he described the dresses, arms, and marks of the horses of our party so accurately, that with other circumstances, we could not doubt of *his* having been in 'villainous company', and ourselves in a bad neighbour-hood. Dervish became a soothsayer for life, and I dare say is now hearing more musquetry than ever will be fired, to the great refreshment of the Arnaouts of Berat, and his native mountains.—I shall mention one trait more of this singular race. In March 1811, a remarkably stout and active Arnaout came (I believe the 50th on the same errand), to offer himself as an attendant, which was declined: 'Well, Affendi,' quoth he, 'may you live!—you would have

The deathshot peal'd of murder near—
As filed the troop to where they fell!
He died too in the battle broil—   1080
A time that heeds nor pain nor toil—
One cry to Mahomet for aid,
One prayer to Alla—all he made:
He knew and crossed me in the fray—
I gazed upon him where he lay,
And watched his spirit ebb away;
Though pierced like Pard by hunters' steel,
He felt not half that now I feel.
I search'd, but vainly search'd to find,
The workings of a wounded mind;   1090
Each feature of that sullen corse
Betrayed his rage, but no remorse.
Oh, what had Vengeance given to trace
Despair upon his dying face!
The late repentance of that hour,
When Penitence hath lost her power
To tear one terror from the grave—
And will not soothe, and can not save!
        .   .   .   .   .   .

'The cold in clime are cold in blood,
    Their love can scarce deserve the name;   1100
But mine was like the lava flood
    That boils in Aetna's breast of flame.
I cannot prate in puling strain
Of ladye-love, and beauty's chain;
If changing cheek, and scorching vein—
Lips taught to writhe, but not complain—
If bursting heart, and madd'ning brain—
And daring deed, and vengeful steel—
And all that I have felt—and feel—
Betoken love—that love was mine,   1110
And shewn by many a bitter sign.
'Tis true, I could not whine nor sigh,
I knew but to obtain or die.
I die—but first I have possest,
And come what may, I *have been* blest;
Shall I the doom I sought upbraid?

found me useful. I shall leave the town for the hills to-morrow, in the winter I return, perhaps you will then receive me.'—Dervish, who was present, remarked as a thing of course, and of no consequence, 'in the mean time he will join the Klephtes' (robbers), which was true to the letter.—If not cut off, they come down in the winter, and pass it unmolested in some town, where they are often as well known as their exploits.

No—reft of all—yet undismay'd
But for the thought of Leila slain,
Give me the pleasure with the pain,
So would I live and love again.   1120
I grieve, but not, my holy guide!
For him who dies, but her who died;
She sleeps beneath the wandering wave—
Ah! had she but an earthly grave,
This breaking heart and throbbing head
Should seek and share her narrow bed.
She was a form of life and light—
That seen—became a part of sight,
And rose—where'er I turned mine eye—
The Morning-star of Memory!   1130

'Yes, Love indeed is light from heaven—
    A spark of that immortal fire
With angels shar'd—by Alla given,
    To lift from earth our low desire.
Devotion wafts the mind above,
But Heaven itself descends in love—
A feeling from the Godhead caught,
To wean from self each sordid thought—
A Ray of him who form'd the whole—
A Glory circling round the soul!   1140
I grant *my* love imperfect—all
That mortals by the name miscall—
Then deem it evil—what thou wilt—
But say, oh say, *hers* was not guilt!
She was my life's unerring light—
That quench'd—what beam shall break my night?
Oh! would it shone to lead me still,
Although to death or deadliest ill!—
Why marvel ye? if they who lose
    This present joy, this future hope,   1150
    No more with sorrow meekly cope—
In phrenzy then their fate accuse—
In madness do those fearful deeds
    That seem to add but guilt to woe.
Alas! the breast that inly bleeds
    Hath nought to dread from outward blow—
Who falls from all he knows of bliss,
Cares little into what abyss.—
Fierce as the gloomy vulture's now
    To thee, old man, my deeds appear—   1160
I read abhorrence on thy brow,

345

And this too was I born to bear!
'Tis true, that, like that bird of prey,
With havoc have I mark'd my way—
But this was taught me by the dove—
To die—and know no second love.
This lesson yet hath man to learn,
Taught by the thing he dares to spurn—
The bird that sings within the brake,
The swan that swims upon the lake,   1170
One mate, and one alone, will take.
And let the fool still prone to range,
And sneer on all who cannot change—
Partake his jest with boasting boys,
I envy not his varied joys—
But deem such feeble, heartless man,
Less than yon solitary swan—
Far—far beneath the shallow maid
He left believing and betray'd.
Such shame at least was never mine—   1180
Leila—each thought was only thine!—
My good, my guilt, my weal, my woe,
My hope on high—my all below.
Earth holds no other like to thee,
Or if it doth, in vain for me—
For worlds I dare not view the dame
Resembling thee, yet not the same.
The very crimes that mar my youth,
This bed of death—attest my truth—
'Tis all too late—thou wert—thou art   1190
The cherished madness of my heart!

'And she was lost—and yet I breathed,
    But not the breath of human life—
A serpent round my heart was wreathed,
    And stung my every thought to strife.—
Alike all time—abhorred all place,
Shuddering I shrunk from Nature's face,
Where every hue that charmed before
The blackness of my bosom wore:—
The rest—thou dost already know,   1200
And all my sins and half my woe—
But talk no more of penitence,
Thou see'st I soon shall part from hence—
And if thy holy tale were true—
The deed that's done can'st *thou* undo?
Think me not thankless—but this grief

346

Looks not to priesthood for relief.*
My soul's estate in secret guess—
But would'st thou pity more—say less—
When thou can'st bid my Leila live,   1210
Then will I sue thee to forgive;
Then plead my cause in that high place
Where purchased masses proffer grace—
Go—when the hunter's hand hath wrung
From forest-cave her shrieking young,
And calm the lonely lioness—
But soothe not—mock not *my* distress!

'In early days, and calmer hours,
    When heart with heart delights to blend,
Where bloom my native valley's bowers—   1220
    I had—Ah! have I now?—a friend!—
To him this pledge I charge thee send—
    Memorial of a youthful vow;
I would remind him of my end,—
    Though souls absorbed like mine allow
Brief thought to distant friendship's claim,
Yet dear to him my blighted name.
'Tis strange—he prophesied my doom,
    And I have smil'd—(I then could smile—)
When Prudence would his voice assume,   1230
    And warn—I reck'd not what—the while—
But now remembrance whispers o'er
Those accents scarcely mark'd before.
Say—that his bodings came to pass,
    And he will start to hear their truth,
    And wish his words had not been sooth.
Tell him—unheeding as I was—
    Through many a busy bitter scene
    Of all our golden youth had been—
In pain, my faltering tongue had tried   1240
To bless his memory ere I died;
But heaven in wrath would turn away,
If Guilt should for the guiltless pray.
I do not ask him not to blame—
Too gentle he to wound my name;

---

line 1207. The monk's sermon is omitted. It seems to have had so little effect upon the patient, that it could have no hopes from the reader. It may be sufficient to say, that it was of a customary length (as may be perceived from the interruptions and uneasiness of the penitent), and was delivered in the nasal tone of all orthodox preachers.

And what have I to do with fame?
I do not ask him not to mourn,
Such cold request might sound like scorn;
And what than friendship's manly tear
May better grace a brother's bier?   1250
But bear this ring—his own of old—
And tell him—what thou dost behold!
The wither'd frame, the ruined mind,
The wrack by passion left behind—
A shrivelled scroll, a scatter'd leaf,
Sear'd by the autumn blast of grief!

   .   .   .   .   .   .

'Tell me no more of fancy's gleam,
No, father, no, 'twas not a dream;
Alas! the dreamer first must sleep,
I only watch'd, and wish'd to weep;   1260
But could not, for my burning brow
Throbb'd to the very brain as now.
I wish'd but for a single tear,
As something welcome, new, and dear;
I wish'd it then—I wish it still,
Despair is stronger than my will.
Waste not thine orison—despair
Is mightier than thy pious prayer;
I would not, if I might, be blest,
I want no paradise—but rest.   1270
'Twas then, I tell thee, father! then
I saw her—yes—she liv'd again;
And shining in her white symar,*
As through yon pale grey cloud—the star
Which now I gaze on, as on her
Who look'd and looks far lovelier;
Dimly I view its trembling spark—
To-morrow's night shall be more dark—
And I—before its rays appear,
That lifeless thing the living fear.   1280
I wander, father! for my soul
Is fleeting towards the final goal;
I saw her, friar! and I rose,
Forgetful of our former woes;
And rushing from my couch, I dart,
And clasp her to my desperate heart;
I clasp—what is it that I clasp?

line 1273. 'Symar'—Shroud.

No breathing form within my grasp,
No heart that beats reply to mine,
Yet, Leila! yet the form is thine!   1290
And art thou, dearest, chang'd so much,
As meet my eye, yet mock my touch?
Ah! were thy beauties e'er so cold,
I care not—so my arms enfold
The all they ever wish'd to hold.
Alas! around a shadow prest,
They shrink upon my lonely breast;
Yet still—'tis there—in silence stands,
And beckons with beseeching hands!
With braided hair, and bright-black eye—   1300
I knew 'twas false—she could not die!
But he is dead—within the dell
I saw him buried where he fell;
He comes not—for he cannot break
From earth—why then art thou awake?
They told me, wild waves roll'd above
The face I view, the form I love;
They told me—'twas a hideous tale!
I'd tell it—but my tongue would fail—
If true—and from thine ocean-cave   1310
Thou com'st to claim a calmer grave,
Oh! pass thy dewy fingers o'er
This brow that then will burn no more;
Or place them on my hopeless heart—
But, shape or shade!—whate'er thou art,
In mercy, ne'er again depart—
Or farther with thee bear my soul,
Than winds can waft—or waters roll!—

                .   .   .   .

'Such is my name, and such my tale,
   Confessor—to thy secret ear,   1320
I breathe the sorrows I bewail,
   And thank thee for the generous tear
This glazing eye could never shed.
Then lay me with the humblest dead,
And save the cross above my head,
Be neither name nor emblem spread
By prying stranger to be read,
Or stay the passing pilgrim's tread.'
He pass'd—nor of his name and race
Hath left a token or a trace,   1330
Save what the father must not say
Who shrived him on his dying day;

This broken tale was all we knew
Of her he lov'd, or him he slew.*

ANONYMOUS

151   *War the Source of Riches*

WHAT nonsense they talk who complain of a War
Which makes us all greater and richer by far:
And tho' no War known, ever lasted so long,
Yet this may go on to the end of the song.

I remember the time when we all were at peace,
When rich men and poor men all liv'd at their ease;
When the great could drink claret, the midling sort port,
And ale or grog flow'd for th' inferior sort.
But War levels all, or makes us all rich,
Whether buried in th' Abbey, or dead in a ditch.   10

I remember, that formerly Cits worth a plum
Were call'd very rich—but now such a sum
Is a younger child's portion—since some worth a million
Have fail'd!—or jigg'd off in death's dance of cotillion.
Then what nonsense to talk of the horrors of War,
Which makes the small great, and the poor richer far.

line 1334. The circumstance to which the above story relates was not very uncommon in
Turkey. A few years ago the wife of Muchtar Pacha complained to his father of his son's
supposed infidelity; he asked with whom, and she had the barbarity to give in a list of the
twelve handsomest women in Yanina. They were seized, fastened up in sacks, and drowned
in the lake the same night! One of the guards who was present informed me, that not one of
the victims uttered a cry, or shewed a symptom of terror at so sudden a 'wrench from all we
know, from all we love'. The fate of Phrosine, the fairest of this sacrifice, is the subject of
many a Romaic and Arnaout ditty. The story in the text is one told of a young Venetian many
years ago, and now nearly forgotten. I heard it by accident recited by one of the coffee-house
story-tellers who abound in the Levant, and sing or recite their narratives. The additions and
interpolations by the translator will be easily distinguished from the rest by the want of Eastern
imagery; and I regret that my memory has retained so few fragments of the original.

For the contents of some of the notes I am indebted partly to d'Herbelot, and partly
to that most eastern, and, as Mr Weber justly entitles it, 'sublime tale', the 'Caliph Vathek'.
I do not know from what source the author of that singular volume may have drawn his
materials; some of his incidents are to be found in the *Bibliothèque Orientale*; but for
correctness of costume, beauty of description, and power of imagination, it far surpasses
all European imitations; and bears such marks of originality, that those who have visited
the East will find some difficulty in believing it to be more than a translation. As an
Eastern tale, even Rasselas must bow before it; his 'Happy Valley' will not bear a
comparison with the 'Hall of Eblis'.

Say, how can this happen; has England more acres?
No, the land is the same, but your great fortune makers
Without gold or silver can purchase the land,
And this is the thing that some can't understand;   20
Now the thing is as plain as your A, B, and C,
For those that can't read can get money, we see:

As thus—an army must have cloaths and food,
(With powder and ball for the enemies good,)
Then who must supply them, and who are the factors?
Why Agents, and Brokers, and army Contractors.
Messrs. A. B. and C. and so quite down to Zed,
Men who cypher and sum, tho' they little have read,
And if twenty-four of such letters agree,
They establish a bank—Messrs. A. B. and C.   30

Their notes go for guineas, next year something more,
The next for more still, till at length a full score
Will scarce buy so much as a guinea before;
Yet he who possesses the most of such rags,
Is rich without silver or gold in his bags.

Then what nonsense to talk of the ruin of War,
When such riches are coin'd without bullion from far:
Thus no one *can tell* what by War's won or lost,
But the *Tellers*, who're paid for *not telling* its cost.

H.R.

JAMES MONTGOMERY
1771–1854

152   from *The Bramin*

Extract from Canto 1

ONCE on the mountain's balmy lap reclined,
The Sage unlocked the treasures of his mind;
Pure from his lips, sublime instruction came,
As the blest altar breathes celestial flame:
A band of youths and virgins round him pressed,
Whom thus the prophet and the sage addressed.

'Thro' the wide universe's boundless range,
All that exist decay, revive and change:

No atom torpid or inactive lies;
A being, once created, never dies.   10
The waning moon, when quenched in shades of night,
Renews her youth with all the charms of light;
The flowery beauties of the blooming year
Shrink from the shivering blast, and disappear;
Yet, warmed with quickening showers of genial rain,
Spring from their graves, and purple all the plain.
As day the night, and night succeeds the day,
So death reanimates, so lives decay:
Like billows on the undulating main,
The swelling fall, the falling swell again;   20
Thus on the tide of time, inconstant, roll
The dying body and the living soul.
In every animal, inspired with breath,
The flowers of life produce the seeds of death;—
The seeds of death, though scattered in the tomb,
Spring with new vigour, vegetate and bloom.

   'When wasted down to dust the creature dies,
Quick, from its cell, the enfranchised spirit flies;
Fills, with fresh energy, another form,
And towers an elephant, or glides a worm;   30
The awful lion's royal shape assumes;
The fox's subtlety, or peacock's plumes;
Swims, like an eagle, in the eye of noon,
Or wails, a screech owl, to the deaf, cold moon;
Haunts the dread brakes, where serpents hiss and glare,
Or hums, a glittering insect, in the air.
The illustrious souls of great and virtuous men,
In noble animals revive again:
But base and vicious spirits wind their way,
In scorpions, vultures, sharks and beasts of prey.   40
The fair, the gay, the witty, and the brave,
The fool, the coward, courtier, tyrant, slave;
Each, in congenial animals, shall find
An home and kindred for his wandering mind.

   'Even the cold body, when enshrined in earth,
Rises again in vegetable birth:
From the vile ashes of the bad proceeds
A baneful harvest of pernicious weeds;
The relics of the good, awaked by showers,
Peep from the lap of death, and live in flowers;   50
Sweet modest flowers, that blush along the vale,
Whose fragrant lips embalm the passing gale.'

JANE TAYLOR

153   *The Fairies' Song*

HARK! for the beetle winds his horn,
The dew-drop glitters on the thorn;
Now let us to the daisied lawn,
                 Dancing along.

From acorn cells we spring to view,
In robes of moonshine, ting'd with blue,
And pearly bands of evening dew
                 Bound in our hair.

And now we form the magic ring,
And merrily dance, and merrily sing;   10
A fairy's dance is a pretty thing
                 In the moonshine;

But ere the dawn returns again,
We wind along the wooded lane,
And glow-worm torches light the train
                 All the way home.

GEORGE GORDON, LORD BYRON

154   from *The Corsair*

9

UNLIKE the heroes of each ancient race,
Demons in act, but Gods at least in face,
In Conrad's form seems little to admire,
Though his dark eye-brow shades a glance of fire;
Robust but not Herculean—to the sight
No giant frame sets forth his common height;
Yet, in the whole, who paused to look again,
Saw more than marks the crowd of vulgar men;
They gaze and marvel how—and still confess
That thus it is, but why they cannot guess.   10

Sun-burnt his cheek, his forehead high and pale
The sable curls in wild profusion veil;
And oft perforce his rising lip reveals
The haughtier thought it curbs, but scarce conceals.
Though smooth his voice, and calm his general mien,
Still seems there something he would not have seen:
His features' deepening lines and varying hue
At times attracted, yet perplexed the view,
As if within that murkiness of mind
Worked feelings fearful, and yet undefined;   20
Such might it be—that none could truly tell—
Too close enquiry his stern glance would quell.
There breathe but few whose aspect might defy
The full encounter of his searching eye;
He had the skill, when Cunning's gaze would seek
To probe his heart and watch his changing cheek,
At once the observer's purpose to espy,
And on himself roll back his scrutiny,
Lest he to Conrad rather should betray
Some secret thought, than drag that chief's to day.   30
There was a laughing Devil in his sneer,
That raised emotions both of rage and fear;
And where his frown of hatred darkly fell,
Hope withering fled—and Mercy sighed farewell!

10

Slight are the outward signs of evil thought,
Within—within—'twas there the spirit wrought!
Love shows all changes—Hate, Ambition, Guile,
Betray no further than the bitter smile;
The lip's least curl, the lightest paleness thrown
Along the governed aspect, speak alone   40
Of deeper passions; and to judge their mien,
He, who would see, must be himself unseen.
Then—with the hurried tread, the upward eye,
The clenched hand, the pause of agony,
That listens, starting, lest the step too near
Approach intrusive on that mood of fear:
Then—with each feature working from the heart,
With feelings loosed to strengthen—not depart;
That rise—convulse—contend—that freeze, or glow,
Flush in the cheek, or damp upon the brow;   50
Then—Stranger! if thou canst, and tremblest not,
Behold his soul—the rest that soothes his lot!
Mark—how that lone and blighted bosom sears

The scathing thought of execrated years!
Behold—but who hath seen, or e'er shall see,
Man as himself—the secret spirit free?

11

Yet was not Conrad thus by Nature sent
To lead the guilty—guilt's worst instrument—
His soul was changed, before his deeds had driven
Him forth to war with man and forfeit heaven.   60
Warped by the world in Disappointment's school,
In words too wise, in conduct *there* a fool;
Too firm to yield, and far too proud to stoop,
Doomed by his very virtues for a dupe,
He cursed those virtues as the cause of ill,
And not the traitors who betrayed him still;
Nor deemed that gifts bestowed on better men
Had left him joy, and means to give again.
Feared—shunned—belied—ere youth had lost her force,
He hated man too much to feel remorse,   70
And thought the voice of wrath a sacred call,
To pay the injuries of some on all.
He knew himself a villain—but he deemed
The rest no better than the thing he seemed;
And scorned the best as hypocrites who hid
Those deeds the bolder spirit plainly did.
He knew himself detested, but he knew
The hearts that loathed him, crouched and dreaded too.
Lone, wild, and strange, he stood alike exempt
From all affection and from all contempt: 80
His name could sadden, and his acts surprise;
But they that feared him dared not to despise:
Man spurns the worm, but pauses ere he wake
The slumbering venom of the folded snake:
The first may turn—but not avenge the blow;
The last expires—but leaves no living foe;
Fast to the doomed offender's form it clings,
And he may crush—not conquer—still it stings!

12

None are all evil—quickening round his heart,
One softer feeling would not yet depart;   90
Oft could he sneer at others as beguiled
By passions worthy of a fool or child;
Yet 'gainst that passion vainly still he strove,

And even in him it asks the name of Love!
Yes, it was love—unchangeable—unchanged,
Felt but for one from whom he never ranged;
Though fairest captives daily met his eye,
He shunned, nor sought, but coldly passed them by;
Though many a beauty drooped in prisoned bower,
None ever soothed his most unguarded hour.   100
Yes—it was Love—if thoughts of tenderness,
Tried in temptation, strengthened by distress,
Unmoved by absence, firm in every clime,
And yet—Oh more than all!—untired by time;
Which nor defeated hope, not baffled wile,
Could render sullen were she ne'er to smile,
Nor rage could fire, nor sickness fret to vent
On her one murmur of his discontent;
Which still would meet with joy, with calmness part,
Lest that his look of grief should reach her heart;   110
Which nought removed, nor menaced to remove—
If there be love in mortals—this was love!
He was a villain—ay—reproaches shower
On him—but not the passion, nor its power,
Which only proved, all other virtues gone,
Not guilt itself could quench this loveliest one!

                                                      (Canto 1)

155   from *Lara*

                            17

IN him inexplicably mix'd appeared
Much to be loved and hated, sought and feared;
Opinion varying o'er his hidden lot,
In praise or railing ne'er his name forgot;
His silence formed a theme for others' prate—
They guess'd—they gazed—they fain would know his fate.
What had he been? what was he, thus unknown,
Who walked their world, his lineage only known?
A hater of his kind? yet some would say,
With them he could seem gay amidst the gay;   10
But own'd, that smile if oft observed and near,
Waned in its mirth and withered to a sneer;
That smile might reach his lip, but passed not by,
None e'er could trace its laughter to his eye:
Yet there was softness too in his regard,
At times, a heart as not by nature hard,

                            356

But once perceiv'd, his spirit seem'd to chide
Such weakness, as unworthy of its pride,
And steel'd itself, as scorning to redeem
One doubt from others' half withheld esteem;   20
In self-inflicted penance of a breast
Which tenderness might once have wrung from rest;
In vigilance of grief that would compel
The soul to hate for having lov'd too well.

18

There was in him a vital scorn of all:
As if the worst had fall'n which could befall
He stood a stranger in this breathing world,
An erring spirit from another hurled;
A thing of dark imaginings, that shaped
By choice the perils he by chance escaped;   30
But 'scaped in vain, for in their memory yet
His mind would half exult and half regret:
With more capacity for love than earth
Bestows on most of mortal mould and birth,
His early dreams of good outstripp'd the truth,
And troubled manhood followed baffled youth;
With thought of years in phantom chase misspent,
And wasted powers for better purpose lent;
And fiery passions that had poured their wrath
In hurried desolation o'er his path,   40
And left the better feelings all at strife
In wild reflection o'er his stormy life;
But haughty still, and loth himself to blame,
He called on Nature's self to share the shame,
And charged all faults upon the fleshly form
She gave to clog the soul, and feast the worm;
'Till he at last confounded good and ill,
And half mistook for fate the acts of will:
Too high for common selfishness, he could
At times resign his own for others' good,   50
But not in pity, not because he ought,
But in some strange perversity of thought,
That swayed him onward with a secret pride
To do what few or none would do beside;
And this same impulse would in tempting time
Mislead his spirit equally to crime;
So much he soared beyond, or sunk beneath
The men with whom he felt condemned to breathe,
And longed by good or ill to separate

Himself from all who shared his mortal state;   60
His mind abhorring this had fixed her throne
Far from the world, in regions of her own;
Thus coldly passing all that passed below,
His blood in temperate seeming now would flow:
Ah! happier if it ne'er with guilt had glowed,
But ever in that icy smoothness flowed!
'Tis true, with other men their path he walked,
And like the rest in seeming did and talked,
Nor outraged Reason's rules by flaw nor start,
His madness was not of the head, but heart;   70
And rarely wandered in his speech, or drew
His thoughts so forth as to offend the view.

19

With all that chilling mystery of mien,
And seeming gladness to remain unseen;
He had (if 'twere not nature's boon) an art
Of fixing memory on another's heart:
It was not love perchance—nor hate—nor aught
That words can image to express the thought;
But they who saw him did not see in vain,
And once beheld, would ask of him again: 80
And those to whom he spake remembered well,
And on the words, however light, would dwell:
None knew, nor how, nor why, but he entwined
Himself perforce around the hearer's mind;
There he was stamp'd, in liking, or in hate,
If greeted once; however brief the date
That friendship, pity, or aversion knew,
Still there within the inmost thought he grew.
You could not penetrate his soul, but found,
Despite your wonder, to your own he wound;   90
His presence haunted still; and from the breast
He forced an all unwilling interest;
Vain was the struggle in that mental net,
His spirit seemed to dare you to forget!

(Canto I)

WILLIAM WORDSWORTH

from *The Excursion*

[*The Ruined Cottage*]

                SUPINE the Wanderer lay,
His eyes as if in drowsiness half shut,
The shadows of the breezy elms above
Dappling his face. He had not heard my steps
As I approached; and near him did I stand
Unnotic'd in the shade, some minutes' space.
At length I hailed him, seeing that his hat
Was moist with water-drops, as if the brim
Had newly scooped a running stream. He rose,
And ere the pleasant greeting that ensued   10
Was ended, ' 'Tis,' said I, 'a burning day;
My lips are parched with thirst, but you, I guess,
Have somewhere found relief.' He, at the word,
Pointing towards a sweet-briar, bade me climb
The fence hard by, where that aspiring shrub
Looked out upon the road. It was a plot
Of garden-ground run wild, its matted weeds
Marked with the steps of those, whom, as they pass'd
The gooseberry trees that shot in long lank slips,
Or currants hanging from their leafless stems   20
In scanty strings, had tempted to o'erleap
The broken wall. I looked around, and there,
Where two tall hedge-rows of thick alder boughs
Joined in a cold damp nook, espied a Well
Shrouded with willow-flowers and plumy fern.
My thirst I slaked, and from the chearless spot
Withdrawing, straightway to the shade returned
Where sate the Old Man on the Cottage bench;
And, while, beside him, with uncovered head,
I yet was standing, freely to respire,   30
And cool my temples in the fanning air,
Thus did he speak. 'I see around me here
Things which you cannot see: we die, my Friend,
Nor we alone, but that which each man loved
And prized in his peculiar nook of earth
Dies with him, or is changed; and very soon
Even of the good is no memorial left.
—The Poets, in their elegies and songs
Lamenting the departed, call the groves,

They call upon the hills and streams to mourn,   40
And senseless rocks; nor idly; for they speak,
In these their invocations, with a voice
Obedient to the strong creative power
Of human passion. Sympathies there are
More tranquil, yet perhaps of kindred birth,
That steal upon the meditative mind,
And grow with thought. Beside yon Spring I stood,
And eyed its waters till we seemed to feel
One sadness, they and I. For them a bond
Of brotherhood is broken: time has been   50
When, every day, the touch of human hand
Dislodged the natural sleep that binds them up
In mortal stillness; and they minister'd
To human comfort. As I stooped to drink,
Upon the slimy foot-stone I espied
The useless fragment of a wooden bowl,
Green with the moss of years; a pensive sight
That moved my heart!—recalling former days
When I could never pass that road but She
Who lived within these walls, at my approach,   60
A Daughter's welcome gave me; and I loved her
As my own child. O Sir! the good die first,
And they whose hearts are dry as summer dust
Burn to the socket. Many a Passenger
Hath blessed poor Margaret for her gentle looks,
When she upheld the cool refreshment drawn
From that forsaken Spring; and no one came
But he was welcome; no one went away
But that it seemed she loved him. She is dead,
The light extinguished of her lonely Hut,   70
The Hut itself abandoned to decay,
And She forgotten in the quiet grave!

      'I speak,' continued he, 'of One whose stock
Of virtues bloom'd beneath this lowly roof.
She was a Woman of a steady mind,
Tender and deep in her excess of love,
Not speaking much, pleased rather with the joy
Of her own thoughts: by some especial care
Her temper had been framed, as if to make
A Being—who by adding love to peace   80
Might live on earth a life of happiness.
Her wedded Partner lacked not on his side
The humble worth that satisfied her heart:
Frugal, affectionate, sober, and withal

Keenly industrious. She with pride would tell
That he was often seated at his loom,
In summer, ere the Mower was abroad
Among the dewy grass,—in early spring,
Ere the last Star had vanished.—They who passed
At evening, from behind the garden fence   90
Might hear his busy spade, which he would ply,
After his daily work, until the light
Had failed, and every leaf and flower were lost
In the dark hedges. So their days were spent
In peace and comfort; and a pretty Boy
Was their best hope,—next to the God in Heaven.

  Not twenty years ago, but you I think
Can scarcely bear it now in mind, there came
Two blighting seasons when the fields were left
With half a harvest. It pleased heaven to add   100
A worse affliction in the plague of war;
This happy Land was stricken to the heart!
A Wanderer then among the Cottages
I, with my freight of winter raiment, saw
The hardships of that season; many rich
Sank down, as in a dream, among the poor;
And of the poor did many cease to be
And their place knew them not. Meanwhile abridg'd
Of daily comforts, gladly reconciled
To numerous self-denials, Margaret   110
Went struggling on through those calamitous years
With chearful hope: but ere the second autumn
Her life's true Help-mate on a sick-bed lay,
Smitten with perilous fever. In disease
He lingered long; and when his strength return'd,
He found the little he had stored, to meet
The hour of accident or crippling age,
Was all consumed. Two children had they now,
One newly born. As I have said, it was
A time of trouble; shoals of Artisans   120
Were from their daily labour turn'd adrift
To seek their bread from public charity,
They, and their wives and children—happier far
Could they have lived as do the little birds
That peck along the hedges, or the Kite
That makes his dwelling on the mountain Rocks!

  A sad reverse it was for Him who long
Had filled with plenty, and possess'd in peace,

This lonely Cottage. At the door he stood,
And whistled many a snatch of merry tunes   130
That had no mirth in them; or with his knife
Carved uncouth figures on the heads of sticks—
Then, not less idly, sought, through every nook
In house or garden, any casual work
Of use or ornament; and with a strange,
Amusing, yet uneasy novelty,
He blended, where he might, the various tasks
Of summer, autumn, winter, and of spring.
But this endured not; his good humour soon
Became a weight in which no pleasure was: 140
And poverty brought on a petted mood
And a sore temper: day by day he drooped,
And he would leave his work—and to the Town,
Without an errand, would direct his steps,
Or wander here and there among the fields.
One while he would speak lightly of his Babes,
And with a cruel tongue: at other times
He toss'd them with a false unnatural joy:
And 'twas a rueful thing to see the looks
Of the poor innocent children. "Every smile,"   150
Said Margaret to me, here beneath these trees,
"Made my heart bleed." '
                          At this the Wanderer paused;
And, looking up to those enormous Elms,
He said, ' 'Tis now the hour of deepest noon.—
At this still season of repose and peace,
This hour, when all things which are not at rest
Are chearful; while this multitude of flies
Is filling all the air with melody;
Why should a tear be in an Old Man's eye?
Why should we thus, with an untoward mind,   160
And in the weakness of humanity,
From natural wisdom turn our hearts away,
To natural comfort shut our eyes and ears,
And, feeding on disquiet, thus disturb
The calm of nature with our restless thoughts?'

HE spake with somewhat of a solemn tone:
But, when he ended, there was in his face
Such easy chearfulness, a look so mild,
That for a little time it stole away
All recollection, and that simple Tale   170
Passed from my mind like a forgotten sound.
A while on trivial things we held discourse,

To me soon tasteless. In my own despite
I thought of that poor Woman as of one
Whom I had known and loved. He had rehearsed
Her homely Tale with such familiar power,
With such an active countenance, an eye
So busy, that the things of which he spake
Seemed present; and, attention now relax'd,
There was a heart-felt chillness in my veins.—   180
I rose; and, turning from the breezy shade,
Went forth into the open air, and stood
To drink the comfort of the warmer sun.
Long time I had not staid, ere, looking round
Upon that tranquil Ruin, I return'd,
And begged of the Old Man that, for my sake,
He would resume his story.—
                                        He replied,
'It were a wantonness, and would demand
Severe reproof, if we were Men whose hearts
Could hold vain dalliance with the misery   190
Even of the dead; contented thence to draw
A momentary pleasure, never marked
By reason, barren of all future good.
But we have known that there is often found
In mournful thoughts, and always might be found,
A power to virtue friendly; were't not so,
I am a Dreamer among men, indeed
An idle Dreamer! 'Tis a common Tale,
An ordinary sorrow of Man's life,
A tale of silent suffering, hardly clothed   200
In bodily form.—But, without further bidding,
I will proceed.—
                                        While thus it fared with them,
To whom this Cottage, till those hapless years,
Had been a blessed home, it was my chance
To travel in a Country far remote.
And glad I was, when, halting by yon gate
That leads from the green lane, once more I saw
These lofty elm-trees. Long I did not rest:
With many pleasant thoughts I chear'd my way
O'er the flat Common.—Having reached the door   210
I knock'd,—and, when I entered with the hope
Of usual greeting, Margaret looked at me
A little while; then turn'd her head away
Speechless,—and sitting down upon a chair
Wept bitterly. I wist not what to do,
Or how to speak to her. Poor Wretch! at last

She rose from off her seat, and then,—O Sir!
I cannot *tell* how she pronounced my name.—
With fervent love, and with a face of grief
Unutterably helpless, and a look   220
That seemed to cling upon me, she enquired
If I had seen her Husband. As she spake
A strange surprize and fear came to my heart,
Nor had I power to answer ere she told
That he had disappear'd—not two months gone.
He left his House: two wretched days had pass'd,
And on the third, as wistfully she rais'd
Her head from off her pillow, to look forth,
Like one in trouble, for returning light,
Within her chamber-casement she espied   230
A folded paper, lying as if placed
To meet her waking eyes. This tremblingly
She open'd—found no writing, but therein
Pieces of money carefully enclosed,
Silver and gold.—"I shuddered at the sight,"
Said Margaret, "for I knew it was his hand
Which placed it there; and ere that day was ended,
That long and anxious day! I learned from One
Sent hither by my Husband to impart
The heavy news,—that he had joined a Troop   240
Of Soldiers, going to a distant Land.
—He left me thus—he could not gather heart
To take a farewell of me; for he fear'd
That I should follow with my Babes, and sink
Beneath the misery of that wandering Life."

    This Tale did Margaret tell with many tears:
And when she ended I had little power
To give her comfort, and was glad to take
Such words of hope from her own mouth as served
To chear us both:—but long we had not talked   250
Ere we built up a pile of better thoughts,
And with a brighter eye she look'd around
As if she had been shedding tears of joy.
We parted.—'Twas the time of early spring;
I left her busy with her garden tools;
And well remember, o'er that fence she looked,
And, while I paced along the foot-way path,
Called out, and sent a blessing after me,
With tender chearfulness; and with a voice
That seem'd the very sound of happy thoughts.   260

I roved o'er many a hill and many a dale,
With my accustomed load; in heat and cold,
Through many a wood, and many an open ground,
In sunshine and in shade, in wet and fair,
Drooping, or blithe of heart, as might befal;
My best companions now the driving winds,
And now the "trotting brooks" and whispering trees,
And now the music of my own sad steps,
With many a short-lived thought that pass'd between,
And disappeared.—I journey'd back this way   270
Towards the wane of Summer; when the wheat
Was yellow; and the soft and bladed grass
Springing afresh had o'er the hay-field spread
Its tender verdure. At the door arrived,
I found that she was absent. In the shade,
Where now we sit, I waited her return.
Her Cottage, then a chearful Object, wore
Its customary look,—only, I thought,
The honeysuckle, crowding round the porch,
Hung down in heavier tufts: and that bright weed,   280
The yellow stone-crop, suffered to take root
Along the window's edge, profusely grew,
Blinding the lower panes. I turned aside,
And strolled into her garden. It appeared
To lag behind the season, and had lost
Its pride of neatness. From the border lines
Composed of daisy and resplendent thrift,
Flowers straggling forth had on those paths encroached
Which they were used to deck:—Carnations, once
Prized for surpassing beauty, and no less   290
For the peculiar pains they had required,
Declined their languid heads—without support.
The cumbrous bind-weed, with its wreaths and bells,
Had twined about her two small rows of pease,
And dragged them to the earth.—Ere this an hour
Was wasted.—Back I turned my restless steps,
And, as I walked before the door, it chanced
A Stranger passed; and, guessing whom I sought,
He said that she was used to ramble far.—
The sun was sinking in the west; and now   300
I sate with sad impatience. From within
Her solitary Infant cried aloud;
Then, like a blast that dies away self-stilled,
The voice was silent. From the bench I rose;
But neither could divert nor soothe my thoughts.
The spot, though fair, was very desolate—

The longer I remained more desolate.
And, looking round, I saw the corner stones,
Till then unnotic'd, on either side the door
With dull red stains discolour'd, and stuck o'er   310
With tufts and hairs of wool, as if the Sheep,
That fed upon the Common, thither came
Familiarly; and found a couching-place
Even at her threshold. Deeper shadows fell
From these tall elms;—the Cottage-clock struck eight;—
I turned, and saw her distant a few steps.
Her face was pale and thin, her figure too
Was changed. As she unlocked the door, she said,
"It grieves me you have waited here so long,
But, in good truth, I've wandered much of late,   320
And, sometimes,—to my shame I speak, have need
Of my best prayers to bring me back again."
While on the board she spread our evening meal,
She told me,—interrupting not the work
Which gave employment to her listless hands,
That she had parted with her elder Child;
To a kind Master on a distant farm
Now happily apprenticed—"I perceive
You look at me, and you have cause; to-day
I have been travelling far; and many days   330
About the fields I wander, knowing this
Only, that what I seek I cannot find.
And so I waste my time: for I am changed;
And to myself," said she, "have done much wrong
And to this helpless Infant. I have slept
Weeping, and weeping I have waked; my tears
Have flowed as if my body were not such
As others are; and I could never die.
But I am now in mind and in my heart
More easy; and I hope," said she, "that heaven   340
Will give me patience to endure the things
Which I behold at home." It would have grieved
Your very soul to see her; Sir, I feel
The story linger in my heart: I fear
'Tis long and tedious; but my spirit clings
To that poor Woman:—so familiarly
Do I perceive her manner, and her look,
And presence, and so deeply do I feel
Her goodness, that, not seldom, in my walks
A momentary trance comes over me;   350
And to myself I seem to muse on One
By sorrow laid asleep;—or borne away,

A human being destined to awake
To human life, or something very near
To human life, when he shall come again
For whom she suffered. Yes, it would have grieved
Your very soul to see her: evermore
Her eyelids drooped, her eyes were downward cast;
And, when she at her table gave me food,
She did not look at me. Her voice was low,   360
Her body was subdued. In every act
Pertaining to her house affairs, appeared
The careless stillness of a thinking mind
Self-occupied; to which all outward things
Are like an idle matter. Still she sighed,
But yet no motion of the breast was seen,
No heaving of the heart. While by the fire
We sate together, sighs came on my ear,
I knew not how, and hardly whence they came.

   Ere my departure to her care I gave,   370
For her Son's use, some tokens of regard,
Which with a look of welcome She received;
And I exhorted her to have her trust
In God's good love, and seek his help by prayer.
I took my staff, and, when I kissed her babe
The tears stood in her eyes. I left her then
With the best hope and comfort I could give;
She thanked me for my wish;—but for my hope
Methought she did not thank me.
                    I returned,
And took my rounds along this road again   380
Ere on its sunny bank the primrose flower
Peeped forth, to give an earnest of the Spring.
I found her sad and drooping; she had learned
No tidings of her Husband; if he lived
She knew not that he lived; if he were dead
She knew not he was dead. She seem'd the same
In person and appearance; but her House
Bespake a sleepy hand of negligence.
The floor was neither dry nor neat, the hearth
Was comfortless, and her small lot of books,   390
Which, in the Cottage window, heretofore
Had been piled up against the corner panes
In seemly order, now, with straggling leaves
Lay scattered here and there, open or shut,
As they had chanced to fall. Her Infant Babe
Had from its Mother caught the trick of grief,

And sighed among its playthings. Once again
I turned towards the garden gate, and saw,
More plainly still, that poverty and grief
Were now come nearer to her: weeds defaced   400
The harden'd soil, and knots of wither'd grass;
No ridges there appeared of clear black mold,
No winter greenness; of her herbs and flowers,
It seemed the better part were gnawed away
Or trampled into earth; a chain of straw,
Which had been twined about the slender stem
Of a young apple-tree, lay at its root;
The bark was nibbled round by truant Sheep.
—Margaret stood near, her Infant in her arms,
And, noting that my eye was on the tree,   410
She said, "I fear it will be dead and gone
Ere Robert come again." Towards the House
Together we returned; and she enquired
If I had any hope:—but for her Babe
And for her little orphan Boy, she said,
She had no wish to live, that she must die
Of sorrow. Yet I saw the idle loom
Still in its place; his Sunday garments hung
Upon the self-same nail; his very staff
Stood undisturbed behind the door. And when,   420
In bleak December, I retraced this way,
She told me that her little Babe was dead,
And she was left alone. She now, released
From her maternal cares, had taken up
The employment common through these Wilds, and gain'd
By spinning hemp a pittance for herself;
And for this end had hired a neighbour's Boy
To give her needful help. That very time
Most willingly she put her work aside,
And walked with me along the miry road   430
Heedless how far; and, in such piteous sort
That any heart had ached to hear her, begged
That, wheresoe'er I went, I still would ask
For him whom she had lost. We parted then,
Our final parting; for from that time forth
Did many seasons pass ere I return'd
Into this tract again.
                        Nine tedious years;
From their first separation, nine long years,
She lingered in unquiet widowhood;
A Wife and Widow. Needs must it have been   440
A sore heart-wasting! I have heard, my Friend,

That in yon arbour oftentimes she sate
Alone, through half the vacant Sabbath-day,
And if a dog passed by she still would quit
The shade, and look abroad. On this old Bench
For hours she sate; and evermore her eye
Was busy in the distance, shaping things
That made her heart beat quick. You see that path,
Now faint,—the grass has crept o'er its grey line;
There, to and fro, she paced through many a day   450
Of the warm summer, from a belt of hemp
That girt her waist, spinning the long drawn thread
With backward steps. Yet ever as there pass'd
A man whose garments shewed the Soldier's red,
Or crippled Mendicant in Sailor's garb,
The little Child who sate to turn the wheel
Ceas'd from his task; and she with faultering voice
Made many a fond enquiry; and when they,
Whose presence gave no comfort, were gone by,
Her heart was still more sad. And by yon gate,   460
That bars the Traveller's road, she often stood,
And when a stranger Horseman came, the latch
Would lift, and in his face look wistfully;
Most happy, if, from aught discovered there
Of tender feeling, she might dare repeat
The same sad question. Meanwhile her poor Hut
Sank to decay: for he was gone—whose hand,
At the first nipping of October frost,
Closed up each chink, and with fresh bands of straw
Chequered the green-grown thatch. And so she lived   470
Through the long winter, reckless and alone;
Until her House by frost, and thaw, and rain,
Was sapped; and while she slept the nightly damps
Did chill her breast; and in the stormy day
Her tattered clothes were ruffled by the wind;
Even at the side of her own fire. Yet still
She loved this wretched spot, nor would for worlds
Have parted hence; and still that length of road,
And this rude bench, one torturing hope endeared,
Fast rooted at her heart: and here, my Friend,   480
In sickness she remained; and here she died,
Last human Tenant of these ruined Walls.'

    The Old Man ceased: he saw that I was moved;
From that low Bench, rising instinctively
I turn'd aside in weakness, nor had power
To thank him for the Tale which he had told.

I stood, and leaning o'er the Garden wall,
Reviewed that Woman's sufferings; and it seemed
To comfort me while with a Brother's love
I bless'd her—in the impotence of grief.   490
At length towards the Cottage I returned
Fondly,—and traced with interest more mild,
That secret spirit of humanity
Which, mid the calm oblivious tendencies
Of Nature, mid her plants, and weeds, and flowers,
And silent overgrowings, still survived.
The Old Man, noting this, resumed, and said,
'My Friend! enough to sorrow you have given,
The purposes of wisdom ask no more;
Be wise and chearful; and no longer read   500
The forms of things with an unworthy eye.
She sleeps in the calm earth, and peace is here.
I well remember that those very plumes,
Those weeds, and the high spear-grass on that wall,
By mist and silent rain-drops silver'd o'er,
As once I passed, did to my heart convey
So still an image of tranquillity,
So calm and still, and looked so beautiful
Amid the uneasy thoughts which filled my mind,
That what we feel of sorrow and despair   510
From ruin and from change, and all the grief
The passing shews of Being leave behind,
Appeared an idle dream, that could not live
Where meditation was. I turned away
And walked along my road in happiness.'

   He ceased. Ere long the sun declining shot
A slant and mellow radiance, which began
To fall upon us, while beneath the trees
We sate on that low Bench: and now we felt,
Admonished thus, the sweet hour coming on.   520
A linnet warbled from those lofty elms,
A thrush sang loud, and other melodies,
At distance heard, peopled the milder air.
The Old Man rose, and, with a sprightly mien
Of hopeful preparation, grasped his Staff:
Together casting then a farewell look
Upon those silent walls, we left the Shade;
And, ere the Stars were visible, had reached
A Village Inn,—our Evening resting-place.

                              (Book I, lines 433–961)

GEORGE GORDON, LORD BYRON

157   *She Walks in Beauty*

1

SHE walks in beauty, like the night
　Of cloudless climes and starry skies;
And all that's best of dark and bright
　Meet in her aspect and her eyes:
Thus mellow'd to that tender light
　Which heaven to gaudy day denies.

2

One shade the more, one ray the less,
　Had half impair'd the nameless grace
Which waves in every raven tress,
　Or softly lightens o'er her face;   10
Where thoughts serenely sweet express
　How pure, how dear their dwelling place.

3

And on that cheek, and o'er that brow,
　So soft, so calm, yet eloquent,
The smiles that win, the tints that glow,
　But tell of days in goodness spent,
A mind at peace with all below,
　A heart whose love is innocent!

158　　*Stanzas for Music*

> *O Lachrymarum fons, tenero sacros*
> *Ducentium ortus ex animo: quater*
> *Felix! in imo qui scatentem*
> *Pectore te, pia Nympha, sensit.*
>
> GRAY's *Poemata*

1

THERE'S not a joy the world can give like that it takes away,
When the glow of early thought declines in feeling's dull decay;
'Tis not on youth's smooth cheek the blush alone, which fades so
　　fast,
But the tender bloom of heart is gone, ere youth itself be past.

2

Then the few whose spirits float above the wreck of happiness,
Are driven o'er the shoals of guilt or ocean of excess:
The magnet of their course is gone, or only points in vain
The shore to which their shiver'd sail shall never stretch again.

3

Then the mortal coldness of the soul like death itself comes down;
It cannot feel for others' woes, it dare not dream its own;　　10
That heavy chill has frozen o'er the fountain of our tears,
And tho' the eye may sparkle still, 'tis where the ice appears.

4

Tho' wit may flash from fluent lips, and mirth distract the breast,
Through midnight hours that yield no more their former hope of rest;
'Tis but as ivy-leaves around the ruin'd turret wreath,
All green and wildly fresh without but worn and grey beneath.

5

Oh could I feel as I have felt,—or be what I have been,
Or weep as I could once have wept, o'er many a vanished scene:
As springs in deserts found seem sweet, all brackish though they be,
So midst the wither'd waste of life, those tears would flow to me.　　20

159 *The Time I've Lost in Wooing*

THE time I've lost in wooing,
In watching and pursuing
   The light, that lies
   In woman's eyes,
Has been my heart's undoing.
Tho' Wisdom oft has sought me,
I scorn'd the lore she brought me,
   My only books
   Were woman's looks,
And folly's all they've taught me.   10

Her smile when Beauty granted,
I hung with gaze enchanted,
   Like him the Sprite,
   Whom maids, by night,
Oft meet in glen that's haunted.
Like him, too, Beauty won me,
But while her eyes were on me,
   If once their ray
   Was turn'd away,
O! winds could not outrun me.   20

And are those follies going?
And is my proud heart growing
   Too cold or wise
   For brilliant eyes
Again to set it glowing?
No,—vain, alas! th' endeavour
From bonds so sweet to sever;—
   Poor Wisdom's chance
   Against a glance
Is now as weak as ever.   30

GEORGE GORDON, LORD BYRON

160 *Fare Thee Well!*

Alas! they had been friends in Youth;
But whispering tongues can poison truth;
And constancy lives in realms above:
And Life is thorny; and youth is vain:
And to be wroth with one we love,
Doth work like madness in the brain:
  .   .   .   .   .

But never either found another
To free the hollow heart from paining—
They stood aloof, the scars remaining,
Like cliffs, which had been rent asunder;
A dreary sea now flows between,
But neither heat, nor frost, nor thunder
Shall wholly do away, I ween,
The marks of that which once hath been.

COLERIDGE'S *Christabel* (398–404, 410–17)

FARE thee well! and if for ever—
  Still for ever, fare *thee well*—
Even though unforgiving, never
  'Gainst thee shall my heart rebel.—
Would that breast were bared before thee
  Where thy head so oft hath lain,
While that placid sleep came o'er thee
  Which thou ne'er can'st know again:
Would that breast by thee glanc'd over,
  Every inmost thought could show!   10
Then, thou wouldst at last discover
  'Twas not well to spurn it so—
Though the world for this commend thee—
  Though it smile upon the blow,
Even its praises must offend thee,
  Founded on another's woe—
Though my many faults defaced me,
  Could no other arm be found
Than the one which once embraced me,
  To inflict a cureless wound!   20
Yet—oh, yet—thyself deceive not—
  Love may sink by slow decay,

But by sudden wrench, believe not,
  Hearts can thus be torn away;
Still thine own its life retaineth—
  Still must mine—though bleeding—beat,
And the undying thought which paineth
  Is—that we no more may meet.—
These are words of deeper sorrow
  Than the wail above the dead,   30
Both shall live—but every morrow
  Wake us from a widowed bed.—
And when thou wouldst solace gather—
  When our child's first accents flow—
Wilt thou teach her to say—'Father!'
  Though his care she must forgo?
When her little hands shall press thee—
  When her lip to thine is prest—
Think of him whose prayer shall bless thee—
  Think of him thy love had bless'd.   40
Should her lineaments resemble
  Those thou never more may'st see—
Then thy heart will softly tremble
  With a pulse yet true to me.—
All my faults—perchance thou knowest—
  All my madness—none can know;
All my hopes—where'er thou goest—
  Wither—yet with *thee* they go.—
Every feeling hath been shaken,
  Pride—which not a world could bow—   50
Bows to thee—by thee forsaken
  Even my soul forsakes me now.—
But 'tis done—all words are idle—
  Words from me are vainer still;
But the thoughts we cannot bridle
  Force their way without the will.—
Fare thee well!—thus disunited—
  Torn from every nearer tie—
Seared in heart—and lone—and blighted—
  More than this, I scarce can die.   60

Christabel

PREFACE

THE first part of the following poem was written in the year 1797, at Stowey, in the county of Somerset. The second part, after my return from Germany, in the year 1800, at Keswick, Cumberland. Since the latter date, my poetic powers have been, till very lately, in a state of suspended animation. But as, in my very first conception of the tale, I had the whole present to my mind, with the wholeness, no less than the liveliness of a vision; I trust that I shall be able to embody in verse the three parts yet to come, in the course of the present year. It is probable that if the poem had been finished at either of the former periods, or if even the first and second part had been published in the year 1800, the impression of its originality would have been much greater than I dare at present expect. But for this I have only my own indolence to blame. The dates are mentioned for the exclusive purpose of precluding charges of plagiarism or servile imitation from myself. For there is amongst us a set of critics, who seem to hold, that every possible thought and image is traditional; who have no notion that there are such things as fountains in the world, small as well as great; and who would therefore charitably derive every rill they behold flowing, from a perforation made in some other man's tank. I am confident, however, that as far as the present poem is concerned, the celebrated poets whose writings I might be suspected of having imitated, either in particular passages, or in the tone and the spirit of the whole, would be among the first to vindicate me from the charge, and who, on any striking coincidence, would permit me to address them in this doggerel version of two monkish Latin hexameters.

> 'Tis mine and it is likewise yours;
> But an if this will not do;
> Let it be mine, good friend! for I
> Am the poorer of the two.

I have only to add that the metre of Christabel is not, properly speaking, irregular, though it may seem so from its being founded on a new principle: namely, that of counting in each line the accents, not the syllables. Though the latter may vary from seven to twelve, yet in each line the accents will be found to be only four. Nevertheless, this occasional variation in number of syllables is not introduced wantonly, or for the mere ends of convenience, but in correspondence with some transition in the nature of the imagery or passion.

PART I

'Tis the middle of night by the castle clock,
And the owls have awakened the crowing cock;
Tu—whit!——Tu—whoo!
And hark, again! the crowing cock,
How drowsily it crew.
Sir Leoline, the Baron rich,
Hath a toothless mastiff bitch;
From her kennel beneath the rock
She makes answer to the clock,
Four for the quarters, and twelve for the hour;   10
Ever and aye, by moonshine or shower,
Sixteen short howls, not over loud;
Some say, she sees my lady's shroud.

Is the night chilly and dark?
The night is chilly, but not dark.
The thin gray cloud is spread on high,
It covers but not hides the sky.
The moon is behind, and at the full;
And yet she looks both small and dull.
The night is chill, the cloud is gray: 20
'Tis a month before the month of May,
And the Spring comes slowly up this way.

The lovely lady, Christabel,
Whom her father loves so well,
What makes her in the wood so late,
A furlong from the castle gate?
She had dreams all yesternight
Of her own betrothéd knight;
Dreams that made her moan and leap,
As on her bed she lay in sleep.   30
And she in the midnight wood will pray
For the weal of her lover that's far away.

She stole along, she nothing spoke,
The breezes they were still also,
And naught was green upon the oak
But moss and rarest mistletoe:
She kneels beneath the huge oak tree,
And in silence prayeth she.

The lady leaps up suddenly,
The lovely lady, Christabel!   40

377

It moaned as near, as near can be,
But what it is she cannot tell.—
On the other side it seems to be,
Of the huge, broad-breasted, old oak tree.

The night is chill; the forest bare;
Is it the wind that moaneth bleak?
There is not wind enough in the air
To move away the ringlet curl
From the lovely lady's cheek—
There is not wind enough to twirl   50
The one red leaf, the last of its clan,
That dances as often as dance it can,
Hanging so light, and hanging so high,
On the topmost twig that looks up at the sky.

Hush, beating heart of Christabel!
Jesu, Maria, shield her well!
She folded her arms beneath her cloak,
And stole to the other side of the oak.
        What sees she there?

There she sees a damsel bright,   60
Drest in a silken robe of white,
That shadowy in the moonlight shone:
The neck that made that white robe wan,
Her stately neck, and arms were bare;
Her blue-veined feet unsandal'd were,
And wildly glittered here and there
The gems entangled in her hair.

I guess, 'twas frightful there to see
A lady so richly clad as she—
Beautiful exceedingly!   70

Mary mother, save me now!
(Said Christabel,) And who art thou?

The lady strange made answer meet,
And her voice was faint and sweet:—
Have pity on my sore distress,
I scarce can speak for weariness:
Stretch forth thy hand, and have no fear!
Said Christabel, How camest thou here?
And the lady, whose voice was faint and sweet,
Did thus pursue her answer meet:—   80

378

My sire is of a noble line,
And my name is Geraldine:
Five warriors seized me yestermorn,
Me, even me, a maid forlorn:
They choked my cries with force and fright,
And tied me on a palfrey white.
The palfrey was as fleet as wind,
And they rode furiously behind.
They spurred amain, their steeds were white:
And once we crossed the shade of night.   90
As sure as Heaven shall rescue me,
I have no thought what men they be;
Nor do I know how long it is
(For I have lain in fits, I wis)
Since one, the tallest of the five,
Took me from the palfrey's back,
A weary woman, scarce alive.
Some muttered words his comrades spoke:
He placed me underneath this oak;
He swore they would return with haste;   100
Whither they went I cannot tell—
I thought I heard, some minutes past,
Sounds as of a castle bell.
Stretch forth thy hand (thus ended she),
And help a wretched maid to flee.

Then Christabel stretched forth her hand,
And comforted fair Geraldine:
Saying that she should command
The service of Sir Leoline;
And straight be convoy'd, free from thrall,   110
Back to her noble father's hall.

So up she rose and forth they pass'd
With hurrying steps and nothing fast.
Her lucky stars the lady blest,
And Christabel she sweetly said—
All our household are at rest,
Each one sleeping in his bed;
Sir Leoline is weak in health,
And may not well awakened be,
So to my room we'll creep in stealth,   120
And you to-night must sleep with me.

They crossed the moat, and Christabel
Took the key that fitted well;

A little door she opened straight,
All in the middle of the gate;
The gate that was ironed within and without,
Where an army in battle array had marched out.
The lady sank, belike through pain,
And Christabel with might and main
Lifted her up, a weary weight,   130
Over the threshold of the gate:
Then the lady rose again,
And moved, as she were not in pain.

So free from danger, free from fear,
They crossed the court: right glad they were.
And Christabel devoutly cried
To the lady by her side,
Praise we the Virgin all divine
Who hath rescued thee from thy distress!

Alas, alas! said Geraldine,   140
I cannot speak for weariness.
So free from danger, free from fear,
They crossed the court: right glad they were.

Outside her kennel, the mastiff old
Lay fast asleep, in moonshine cold.
The mastiff old did not awake,
Yet she an angry moan did make!
And what can ail the mastiff bitch?
Never till now she uttered yell
Beneath the eye of Christabel.   150
Perhaps it is the owlet's scritch:
For what can ail the mastiff bitch?

They passed the hall, that echoes still,
Pass as lightly as you will!
The brands were flat, the brands were dying,
Amid their own white ashes lying;
But when the lady passed, there came
A tongue of light, a fit of flame;
And Christabel saw the lady's eye,
And nothing else saw she thereby,   160
Save the boss of the shield of Sir Leoline tall,
Which hung in a murky old nitch in the wall.
O softly tread, said Christabel,
My father seldom sleepeth well.

Sweet Christabel her feet she bares,
And they are creeping up the stairs,
Now in glimmer, and now in gloom.
And now they pass the Baron's room,
As still as death, with stifled breath!
And now have reached her chamber door;   170
And now with eager feet press down
The rushes of her chamber floor.

The moon shines dim in the open air,
And not a moonbeam enters here.
But they without its light can see
The chamber carved so curiously,
Carved with figures strange and sweet,
All made out of the carver's brain,
For a lady's chamber meet:
The lamp with twofold silver chain   180
Is fastened to an angel's feet.

The silver lamp burns dead and dim;
But Christabel the lamp will trim.
She trimmed the lamp, and made it bright,
And left it swinging to and fro,
While Geraldine, in wretched plight,
Sank down upon the floor below.

O weary lady, Geraldine,
I pray you, drink this cordial wine!
It is a wine of virtuous powers;   190
My mother made it of wild flowers.

And will your mother pity me,
Who am a maiden most forlorn?
Christabel answered—Woe is me!
She died the hour that I was born.
I have heard the grey-haired friar tell
How on her death-bed she did say,
That she should hear the castle-bell
Strike twelve upon my wedding-day.
O mother dear! that thou wert here!   200
I would, said Geraldine, she were!

But soon with altered voice, said she—
'Off, wandering mother! Peak and pine!
I have power to bid thee flee.'
Alas! what ails poor Geraldine?

Why stares she with unsettled eye?
Can she the bodiless dead espy?
And why with hollow voice cries she,
'Off, woman, off! this hour is mine—
Though thou her guardian spirit be,   210
Off, woman, off! 'tis given to me.'

Then Christabel knelt by the lady's side,
And raised to heaven her eyes so blue—
Alas! said she, this ghastly ride—
Dear lady! it hath wildered you!
The lady wiped her moist cold brow,
And faintly said, ' 'tis over now!'

Again the wild-flower wine she drank:
Her fair large eyes 'gan glitter bright,
And from the floor whereon she sank,   220
The lofty lady stood upright:
She was most beautiful to see,
Like a lady of a far countrée.

And thus the lofty lady spake—
'All they who live in the upper sky,
Do love you, holy Christabel!
And you love them, and for their sake
And for the good which me befel,
Even I in my degree will try,
Fair maiden, to requite you well.   230
But now unrobe yourself; for I
Must pray, ere yet in bed I lie.'

Quoth Christabel, So let it be!
And as the lady bade, did she.
Her gentle limbs did she undress,
And lay down in her loveliness.

But through her brain of weal and woe
So many thoughts moved to and fro,
That vain it were her lids to close;
So half-way from the bed she rose,   240
And on her elbow did recline
To look at the lady Geraldine.

Beneath the lamp the lady bowed,
And slowly rolled her eyes around;
Then drawing in her breath aloud,

Like one that shuddered, she unbound
The cincture from beneath her breast:
Her silken robe, and inner vest,
Dropt to her feet, and full in view,
Behold! her bosom and half her side——   250
A sight to dream of, not to tell!
And she is to sleep with Christabel.

She took two paces and a stride,
And lay down by the Maiden's side!—
And in her arms the maid she took,
   Ah wel-a-day!
And with low voice and doleful look
These words did say:
'In the touch of this bosom there worketh a spell,
Which is lord of thy utterance, Christabel!
Thou knowest to-night, and wilt know to-morrow,   260
This mark of my shame, this seal of my sorrow;
  But vainly thou warrest,
   For this is alone in
  Thy power to declare,
   That in the dim forest
  Thou heard'st a low moaning,
And found'st a bright lady, surpassingly fair;
And didst bring her home with thee in love and in charity,
To shield her and shelter her from the damp air.'

THE CONCLUSION TO PART I

It was a lovely sight to see   270
The lady Christabel, when she
Was praying at the old oak tree.
  Amid the jaggéd shadows
  Of mossy leafless boughs,
  Kneeling in the moonlight,
  To make her gentle vows;
Her slender palms together prest,
Heaving sometimes on her breast;
Her face resigned to bliss or bale—
Her face, oh call it fair not pale,   280
And both blue eyes more bright than clear,
Each about to have a tear.

With open eyes (ah woe is me!)
Asleep, and dreaming fearfully,
Fearfully dreaming, yet, I wis,

Dreaming that alone, which is—
O sorrow and shame! Can this be she,
The lady, who knelt at the old oak tree?
And lo! the worker of these harms,
That holds the maiden in her arms,   290
Seems to slumber still and mild,
As a mother with her child.

A star hath set, a star hath risen,
O Geraldine! since arms of thine
Have been the lovely lady's prison.
O Geraldine! one hour was thine—
Thou'st had thy will! By tairn and rill,
The night-birds all that hour were still.
But now they are jubilant anew,
From cliff and tower, tu—whoo! tu—whoo!   300
Tu—whoo! tu—whoo! from wood and fell!

And see! the lady Christabel
Gathers herself from out her trance;
Her limbs relax, her countenance
Grows sad and soft; the smooth thin lids
Close o'er her eyes; and tears she sheds—
Large tears that leave the lashes bright!
And oft the while she seems to smile
As infants at a sudden light!

Yea, she doth smile, and she doth weep,   310
Like a youthful hermitess,
Beauteous in a wilderness,
Who, praying always, prays in sleep.
And, if she move unquietly,
Perchance, 'tis but the blood so free
Comes back and tingles in her feet.
No doubt, she hath a vision sweet.
What if her guardian spirit 'twere,
What if she knew her mother near?
But this she knows, in joys and woes,   320
That saints will aid if men will call:
For the blue sky bends over all!

PART II

Each matin bell, the Baron saith,
Knells us back to a world of death.
These words Sir Leoline first said,

When he rose and found his lady dead:
These words Sir Leoline will say
Many a morn to his dying day!

And hence the custom and law began
That still at dawn the sacristan,   330
Who duly pulls the heavy bell,
Five and forty beads must tell
Between each stroke—a warning knell,
Which not a soul can choose but hear
From Bratha Head to Wyn'dermere.

Saith Bracy the bard, So let it knell!
And let the drowsy sacristan
Still count as slowly as he can!
There is no lack of such, I ween,
As well fill up the space between.   340
In Langdale Pike and Witch's Lair,
And Dungeon-ghyll so foully rent,
With ropes of rock and bells of air
Three sinful sextons' ghosts are pent,
Who all give back, one after t'other,
The death-note to their living brother;
And oft too, by the knell offended,
Just as their one! two! three! is ended,
The devil mocks the doleful tale
With a merry peal from Borrowdale.   350

The air is still! through mist and cloud
That merry peal comes ringing loud;
And Geraldine shakes off her dread,
And rises lightly from the bed;
Puts on her silken vestments white,
And tricks her hair in lovely plight,
And nothing doubting of her spell
Awakens the lady Christabel.
'Sleep you, sweet lady Christabel?
I trust that you have rested well.'   360

And Christabel awoke and spied
The same who lay down by her side—
O rather say, the same whom she
Raised up beneath the old oak tree!
Nay, fairer yet! and yet more fair!
For she belike hath drunken deep
Of all the blessedness of sleep!

And while she spake, her looks, her air
Such gentle thankfulness declare,
That (so it seemed) her girded vests   370
Grew tight beneath her heaving breasts.
'Sure I have sinn'd!' said Christabel,
'Now heaven be praised if all be well!'
And in low faltering tones, yet sweet,
Did she the lofty lady greet
With such perplexity of mind
As dreams too lively leave behind.

So quickly she rose, and quickly arrayed
Her maiden limbs, and having prayed
That He, who on the cross did groan,   380
Might wash away her sins unknown,
She forthwith led fair Geraldine
To meet her sire, Sir Leoline.

The lovely maid and the lady tall
Are pacing both into the hall,
And pacing on through page and groom,
Enter the Baron's presence-room.

The Baron rose, and while he prest
His gentle daughter to his breast,
With cheerful wonder in his eyes   390
The lady Geraldine espies,
And gave such welcome to the same,
As might beseem so bright a dame!

But when he heard the lady's tale,
And when she told her father's name,
Why waxed Sir Leoline so pale,
Murmuring o'er the name again,
Lord Roland de Vaux of Tryermaine?

Alas! they had been friends in youth;
But whispering tongues can poison truth;   400
And constancy lives in realms above;
And life is thorny; and youth is vain;
And to be wroth with one we love
Doth work like madness in the brain.
And thus it chanced, as I divine,
With Roland and Sir Leoline.
Each spake words of high disdain
And insult to his heart's best brother:

They parted—ne'er to meet again!
But never either found another   410
To free the hollow heart from paining—
They stood aloof, the scars remaining,
Like cliffs which had been rent asunder;
A dreary sea now flows between;—
But neither heat, nor frost, nor thunder,
Shall wholly do away, I ween,
The marks of that which once hath been.

Sir Leoline, a moment's space,
Stood gazing on the damsel's face:
And the youthful Lord of Tryermaine   420
Came back upon his heart again.

O then the Baron forgot his age,
His noble heart swelled high with rage;
He swore by the wounds in Jesu's side
He would proclaim it far and wide,
With trump and solemn heraldry,
That they, who thus had wronged the dame,
Were base as spotted infamy!
'And if they dare deny the same,
My herald shall appoint a week,   430
And let the recreant traitors seek
My Tournay court—that there and then
I may dislodge their reptile souls
From the bodies and forms of men!'
He spake: his eye in lightning rolls!
For the lady was ruthlessly seized; and he kenned
In the beautiful lady the child of his friend!

And now the tears were on his face,
And fondly in his arms he took
Fair Geraldine, who met the embrace,   440
Prolonging it with joyous look.
Which when she viewed, a vision fell
Upon the soul of Christabel,
The vision of fear, the touch and pain!
She shrunk and shuddered, and saw again—
(Ah, woe is me! Was it for thee,
Thou gentle maid! such sights to see?)

Again she saw that bosom old,
Again she felt that bosom cold,
And drew in her breath with a hissing sound: 450

Whereat the Knight turned wildly round,
And nothing saw, but his own sweet maid
With eyes upraised, as one that prayed.

The touch, the sight, had passed away,
And in its stead that vision blest,
Which comforted her after-rest
While in the lady's arms she lay,
Had put a rapture in her breast,
And on her lips and o'er her eyes
Spread smiles like light!
      With new surprise,   460
'What ails then my belovéd child?'
The Baron said—His daughter mild
Made answer, 'All will yet be well!'
I ween, she had no power to tell
Aught else: so mighty was the spell.

Yet he, who saw this Geraldine,
Had deemed her sure a thing divine:
Such sorrow with such grace she blended,
As if she feared she had offended
Sweet Christabel, that gentle maid!   470
And with such lowly tones she prayed
She might be sent without delay
Home to her father's mansion.
        'Nay!
Nay, by my soul!' said Leoline.
'Ho! Bracy the bard, the charge be thine!
Go thou, with music sweet and loud,
And take two steeds with trappings proud,
And take the youth whom thou lov'st best
To bear thy harp, and learn thy song,
And clothe you both in solemn vest,   480
And over the mountains haste along,
Lest wandering folk, that are abroad,
Detain you on the valley road.

'And when he has crossed the Irthing flood,
My merry bard! he hastes, he hastes
Up Knorren Moor, through Halegarth Wood,
And reaches soon that castle good
Which stands and threatens Scotland's wastes.

'Bard Bracy! bard Bracy! your horses are fleet,
Ye must ride up the hall, your music so sweet,   490

More loud than your horses' echoing feet!
And loud and loud to Lord Roland call,
Thy daughter is safe in Langdale hall!
Thy beautiful daughter is safe and free—
Sir Leoline greets thee thus through me!
He bids thee come without delay
With all thy numerous array
And take thy lovely daughter home:
And he will meet thee on the way
With all his numerous array   500
White with their panting palfreys' foam:
And, by mine honour! I will say,
That I repent me of the day
When I spake words of fierce disdain
To Roland de Vaux of Tryermaine!—
—For since that evil hour hath flown,
Many a summer's sun hath shone;
Yet ne'er found I a friend again
Like Roland de Vaux of Tryermaine.'

The lady fell, and clasped his knees,   510
Her face upraised, her eyes o'erflowing;
And Bracy replied, with faltering voice,
His gracious Hail on all bestowing!—
'Thy words, thou sire of Christabel,
Are sweeter than my harp can tell;
Yet might I gain a boon of thee,
This day my journey should not be,
So strange a dream hath come to me,
That I had vowed with music loud
To clear yon wood from thing unblest,   520
Warned by a vision in my rest!
For in my sleep I saw that dove,
That gentle bird, whom thou dost love,
And call'st by thy own daughter's name—
Sir Leoline! I saw the same
Fluttering, and uttering fearful moan,
Among the green herbs in the forest alone.
Which when I saw and when I heard,
I wonder'd what might ail the bird;
For nothing near it could I see,   530
Save the grass and green herbs underneath the old tree.

'And in my dream methought I went
To search out what might there be found;
And what the sweet bird's trouble meant,

That thus lay fluttering on the ground.
I went and peered, and could descry
No cause for her distressful cry;
But yet for her dear lady's sake
I stooped, methought, the dove to take,
When lo! I saw a bright green snake   540
Coiled around its wings and neck.
Green as the herbs on which it couched,
Close by the dove's its head it crouched;
And with the dove it heaves and stirs,
Swelling its neck as she swelled hers!
I woke; it was the midnight hour,
The clock was echoing in the tower;
But though my slumber was gone by,
This dream it would not pass away—
It seems to live upon my eye!   550
And thence I vowed this self-same day
With music strong and saintly song
To wander through the forest bare,
Lest aught unholy loiter there.'

Thus Bracy said: the Baron, the while,
Half-listening heard him with a smile;
Then turned to Lady Geraldine,
His eyes made up of wonder and love;
And said in courtly accents fine,
'Sweet maid, Lord Roland's beauteous dove,   560
With arms more strong than harp or song,
Thy sire and I will crush the snake!'
He kissed her forehead as he spake,
And Geraldine in maiden wise
Casting down her large bright eyes,
With blushing cheek and courtesy fine
She turned her from Sir Leoline;
Softly gathering up her train,
That o'er her right arm fell again;
And folded her arms across her chest,   570
And couched her head upon her breast,
And looked askance at Christabel——
Jesu, Maria, shield her well!

A snake's small eye blinks dull and shy;
And the lady's eyes they shrunk in her head,
Each shrunk up to a serpent's eye,
And with somewhat of malice, and more of dread,
At Christabel she looked askance!—

One moment—and the sight was fled!
But Christabel in dizzy trance   580
Stumbling on the unsteady ground
Shuddered aloud, with a hissing sound;
And Geraldine again turned round,
And like a thing, that sought relief,
Full of wonder and full of grief,
She rolled her large bright eyes divine
Wildly on Sir Leoline.

The maid, alas! her thoughts are gone,
She nothing sees—no sight but one!
The maid, devoid of guile and sin,   590
I know not how, in fearful wise,
So deeply had she drunken in
That look, those shrunken serpent eyes,
That all her features were resigned
To this sole image in her mind:
And passively did imitate
That look of dull and treacherous hate!
And thus she stood, in dizzy trance,
Still picturing that look askance
With forced unconscious sympathy   600
Full before her father's view——
As far as such a look could be
In eyes so innocent and blue!

But when the trance was o'er, the maid
Paused awhile, and inly prayed:
Then falling at her Father's feet,
'By my mother's soul do I entreat
That thou this woman send away!'
She said: and more she could not say:
For what she knew she could not tell,   610
O'er-mastered by the mighty spell.

Why is thy cheek so wan and wild,
Sir Leoline? Thy only child
Lies at thy feet, thy joy, thy pride,
So fair, so innocent, so mild;
The same, for whom thy lady died!
O by the pangs of her dear mother
Think thou no evil of thy child!
For her, and thee, and for no other,
She prayed the moment ere she died: 620
Prayed that the babe for whom she died,

391

Might prove her dear lord's joy and pride!
  That prayer her deadly pangs beguiled,
    Sir Leoline!
  And would'st thou wrong thy only child,
    Her child and thine?

Within the Baron's heart and brain
If thoughts, like these, had any share,
They only swelled his rage and pain,
And did but work confusion there.   630
His heart was cleft with pain and rage,
His cheeks they quivered, his eyes were wild,
Dishonoured thus in his old age;
Dishonoured by his only child,
And all his hospitality
To the insulted daughter of his friend
By more than woman's jealousy
Brought thus to a disgraceful end—
He rolled his eye with stern regard
Upon the gentle minstrel bard,   640
And said in tones abrupt, austere—
'Why, Bracy! dost thou loiter here?
I bade thee hence!' The bard obeyed;
And turning from his own sweet maid,
The agéd knight, Sir Leoline,
Led forth the lady Geraldine!

THE CONCLUSION TO PART II

A little child, a limber elf,
Singing, dancing to itself,
A fairy thing with red round cheeks,
That always finds, and never seeks,   650
Makes such a vision to the sight
As fills a father's eyes with light;
And pleasures flow in so thick and fast
Upon his heart, that he at last
Must needs express his love's excess
With words of unmeant bitterness.
Perhaps 'tis pretty to force together
Thoughts so all unlike each other;
To mutter and mock a broken charm,
To dally with wrong that does no harm.   660
Perhaps 'tis tender too and pretty
At each wild word to feel within
A sweet recoil of love and pity.

And what, if in a world of sin
(O sorrow and shame should this be true!)
Such giddiness of heart and brain
Comes seldom save from rage and pain,
So talks as it 's most used to do.

162   *Kubla Khan*

Or, A Vision in a Dream. A Fragment.

THE following fragment is here published at the request of a poet of great
and deserved celebrity, and, as far as the Author's own opinions are
concerned, rather as a psychological curiosity, than on the ground of any
supposed *poetic* merits.

In the summer of the year 1797, the Author, then in ill health, had
retired to a lonely farm-house between Porlock and Linton, on the Exmoor
confines of Somerset and Devonshire. In consequence of a slight indispo-
sition, an anodyne had been prescribed, from the effects of which he fell
asleep in his chair at the moment that he was reading the following sen-
tence, or words of the same substance, in 'Purchas's Pilgrimage': 'Here
the Khan Kubla commanded a palace to be built, and a stately garden
thereunto. And thus ten miles of fertile ground were inclosed with a wall.'
The Author continued for about three hours in a profound sleep, at least
of the external senses, during which time he has the most vivid confidence,
that he could not have composed less than from two to three hundred
lines; if that indeed can be called composition in which all the images rose
up before him as *things*, with a parallel production of the correspondent
expressions, without any sensation or consciousness of effort. On awaking
he appeared to himself to have a distinct recollection of the whole, and
taking his pen, ink, and paper, instantly and eagerly wrote down the lines
that are here preserved. At this moment he was unfortunately called out
by a person on business from Porlock, and detained by him above an
hour, and on his return to his room, found, to his no small surprise and
mortification, that though he still retained some vague and dim recollection
of the general purport of the vision, yet, with the exception of some eight
or ten scattered lines and images, all the rest had passed away like the
images on the surface of a stream into which a stone has been cast, but,
alas! without the after restoration of the latter!

Then all the charm
Is broken—all that phantom-world so fair
Vanishes, and a thousand circlets spread,
And each mis-shape[s] the other. Stay awhile,
Poor youth! who scarcely dar'st lift up thine eyes—
The stream will soon renew its smoothness, soon
The visions will return! And lo, he stays,

> And soon the fragments dim of lovely forms
> Come trembling back, unite, and now once more
> The pool becomes a mirror.

Yet from the still surviving recollections in his mind, the Author has frequently purposed to finish for himself what had been originally, as it were, given to him. Αὔριον ἄδιοη ἄσω: but the to-morrow is yet to come.

As a contrast to this vision, I have annexed a fragment of a very different character, describing with equal fidelity the dream of pain and disease.

In Xanadu did Kubla Khan
A stately pleasure-dome decree:
Where Alph, the sacred river, ran
Through caverns measureless to man
  Down to a sunless sea.
So twice five miles of fertile ground
With walls and towers were girdled round:
And there were gardens bright with sinuous rills,
Where blossomed many an incense-bearing tree;
And here were forests ancient as the hills,   10
And folding sunny spots of greenery.

But oh! that deep romantic chasm which slanted
Down the green hill athwart a cedarn cover!
A savage place! as holy and enchanted
As e'er beneath a waning moon was haunted
By woman wailing for her demon-lover!
And from this chasm, with ceaseless turmoil seething,
As if this earth in fast thick pants were breathing,
A mighty fountain momently was forced:
Amid whose swift half-intermitted burst   20
Huge fragments vaulted like rebounding hail,
Or chaffy grain beneath the thresher's flail:
And 'mid these dancing rocks at once and ever
It flung up momently the sacred river.
Five miles meandering with a mazy motion
Through wood and dale the sacred river ran,
Then reached the caverns measureless to man,
And sank in tumult to a lifeless ocean:
And 'mid this tumult Kubla heard from far
Ancestral voices prophesying war!   30
  The shadow of the dome of pleasure
  Floated midway on the waves;
  Where was heard the mingled measure
  From the fountain and the caves.

It was a miracle of rare device,
A sunny pleasure-dome with caves of ice!
   A damsel with a dulcimer
   In a vision once I saw:
   It was an Abyssinian maid,
   And on her dulcimer she played,   40
   Singing of Mount Abora.
   Could I revive within me
   Her symphony and song,
   To such a deep delight 'twould win me,
That with music loud and long,
I would build that dome in air,
That sunny dome! those caves of ice!
And all who heard should see them there,
And all should cry, Beware! Beware!
His flashing eyes, his floating hair!   50
Weave a circle round him thrice,
And close your eyes with holy dread,
For he on honey-dew hath fed,
And drunk the milk of Paradise.

WALTER SCOTT

163   *Jock of Hazeldean*

         'WHY weep ye by the tide, ladie?
            Why weep ye by the tide?
         I'll wed ye to my youngest son,
            And ye sall be his bride:
         And ye sall be his bride, ladie,
            Sae comely to be seen'—
         But aye she loot the tears down fa'
            For Jock of Hazeldean.

         'Now let this wilfu' grief be done,
            And dry that cheek so pale;   10
         Young Frank is chief of Errington,
            And lord of Langley-dale;
         His step is first in peaceful ha',
            His sword in battle keen'—
         But aye she loot the tears down fa'
            For Jock of Hazeldean.

'A chain of gold ye sall not lack,
   Nor braid to bind your hair;
Nor mettled hound, nor managed hawk,
   Nor palfrey fresh and fair;   20
And you, the foremost o' them a',
   Shall ride our forest queen'—
But aye she loot the tears down fa'
   For Jock of Hazeldean.

The kirk was deck'd at morning-tide,
   The tapers glimmer'd fair;
The priest and bridegroom wait the bride,
   And dame and knight are there.
They sought her baith by bower and ha';
   The ladie was not seen!   30
She's o'er the Border, and awa'
   Wi' Jock of Hazeldean.

JOHN HOOKHAM FRERE

164   from *Prospectus and Specimen of an intended
National Work by William and Robert Whistlecraft
. . . relating to King Arthur and his Round Table*

[*Proem*]

I

I'VE often wish'd that I could write a book,
   Such as all English people might peruse;
I never should regret the pains it took,
   That's just the sort of fame that I should choose:
To sail about the world like Captain Cook,
   I'd sling a cot up for my favourite Muse,
And we'd take verses out to Demerara,
To New South Wales, and up to Niagara.

II

Poets consume exciseable commodities,
   They raise the nation's spirit when victorious,   10
They drive an export trade in whims and oddities,

Making our commerce and revenue glorious;
As an industrious and pains-taking body 'tis
    That Poets should be reckon'd meritorious:
And therefore I submissively propose
To erect one Board for Verse and one for Prose.

III

Princes protecting Sciences and Art
    I've often seen, in copper-plate and print;
I never saw them elsewhere, for my part,
    And therefore I conclude there's nothing in't;   20
But everybody knows the Regent's heart;
    I trust he won't reject a well-meant hint;
Each Board to have twelve members, with a seat
To bring them in per ann. five-hundred neat:—

IV

From Princes I descend to the Nobility:
    In former times all persons of high stations,
Lords, Baronets, and Persons of gentility
    Paid twenty guineas for the dedications:
This practice was attended with utility;
    The patrons lived to future generations,   30
The poets lived by their industrious earning,—
So men alive and dead could live by Learning.

V

Then, twenty guineas was a little fortune;
    Now, we must starve unless the times should mend:
Our poets now-a-days are deem'd importune
    If their addresses are diffusely penn'd;
Most fashionable authors make a short one
    To their own wife, or child, or private friend,
To show their independence, I suppose;
And that may do for Gentlemen like those.   40

VI

the common people I beseech—
    Dear People! if you think my verses clever,
Preserve with care your noble Parts of speech,
    And take it as a maxim to endeavour
To talk as your good mothers used to teach,
    And then these lines of mine may last for ever;
And don't confound the language of the nation
With long-tail'd words in *osity* and *ation*.

VII

I think that Poets (whether Whig or Tory)
    (Whether they go to meeting or to church)   50
Should study to promote their country's glory
    With patriotic, diligent research;
That children yet unborn may learn the story,
    With grammars, dictionaries, canes, and birch:
It stands to reason—This was Homer's plan,
And we must do—like him—the best we can.

VIII

Madoc and Marmion, and many more,
    Are out in print, and most of them have sold;
Perhaps together they may make a score;
    Richard the First has had his story told,   60
But there were Lords and Princes long before,
    That had behaved themselves like warriors bold;
Among the rest there was the great KING ARTHUR,
What hero's fame was ever carried farther?

IX

King Arthur, and the Knights of his Round Table,
    Were reckon'd the best King, and bravest Lords,
Of all that flourish'd since the Tower of Babel,
    At least of all that history records;
Therefore I shall endeavour, if I'm able,
    To paint their famous actions by my words: 70
Heroes exert themselves in hopes of Fame,
And having such a strong decisive claim,

X

It grieves me much, that Names that were respected
    In former ages, Persons of such mark,
And Countrymen of ours, should lie neglected,
    Just like old portraits lumbering in the dark:
An error such as this should be corrected,
    And if my Muse can strike a single spark,
Why then (as poets say) I'll string my lyre;
And then I'll light a great poetic Fire;   80

XI

I'll air them all, and rub down the Round Table,
    And wash the Canvas clean, and scour the Frames,

And put a coat of varnish on the Fable,
    And try to puzzle out the Dates and Names;
Then (as I said before) I'll heave my cable,
    And take a pilot, and drop down the Thames—
—These first eleven stanzas make a Proem,
And now I must sit down and write my Poem.

LEIGH HUNT
1784–1859

165   from *The Story of Rimini*

ONE day,—'twas on a gentle, autumn noon,
When the cicale cease to mar the tune
Of birds and brooks—and morning work is done,
And shades have heavy outlines in the sun,—
The Princess came to her accustomed bower
To get her, if she could, a soothing hour;
Trying, as she was used, to leave her cares
Without, and slumberously enjoy the airs,
And the low-talking leaves, and that cool light
The vines let in, and all that hushing sight   10
Of closing wood seen through the opening door,
And distant plash of waters tumbling o'er,
And smell of citron blooms, and fifty luxuries more.

She tried as usual for the trial's sake,
For even that diminish'd her heart-ache;
And never yet, how ill soe'er at ease,
Came she for nothing 'midst the flowers and trees.
Yet how it was she knew not, but that day
She seem'd to feel too lightly borne away,—
Too much reliev'd,—too much inclin'd to draw   20
A careless joy from every thing she saw,
And looking round her with a new-born eye,
As if some tree of knowledge had been nigh,
To taste of nature primitive and free,
And bask at ease in her heart's liberty.

Painfully clear those rising thoughts appear'd,
With something dark at bottom that she fear'd,
And turning from the trees her thoughtful look,
She reach'd o'er head, and took her down a book,

And fell to reading with as fix'd an air,
As though she had been wrapt since morning there.
'Twas 'Launcelot of the Lake,' a bright romance,
That like a trumpet made young pulses dance,
Yet had a softer note that shook still more:—
She had begun it but the day before,
And read with a full heart, half sweet, half sad,
How old King Ban was spoil'd of all he had
But one fair castle: how one summer's day
With his fair queen and child he went away
In hopes King Arthur might resent his wrong;   40
How reaching by himself a hill ere long,
He turn'd to give his castle a last look,
And saw its calm white face; and how a smoke,
As he was looking, burst in volumes forth,
And good King Ban saw all that he was worth,
And his fair castle burning to the ground,
So that his wearied pulse felt overwound,
And he lay down, and said a prayer apart
For those he lov'd, and broke his poor old heart.
Then read she of the queen with her young child,   50
How she came up, and nearly had gone wild,
And how in journeying on in her despair,
She reach'd a lake, and met a lady there,
Who pitied her, and took the baby sweet
Into her arms, when lo! with closing feet
She sprang up all at once, like bird from brake,
And vanish'd with him underneath the lake.
Like stone thereat the mother stood, alas!—

The fairy of the place the lady was,
And Launcelot (so the boy was call'd) became   60
Her pupil, till in search of knightly fame
He went to Arthur's court, and play'd his part
So rarely, and display'd so frank a heart,
That what with all his charms of look and limb,
The Queen Geneura fell in love with him:—
And here, such interest in the tale she took,
Francesca's eyes went deeper in the book.
Ready she sat with one hand to turn o'er
The leaf, to which her thoughts ran on before,
The other on the table, half enwreath'd   70
In the thick tresses over which she breath'd.
So sat she fix'd, and so observ'd was she
Of one, who at the door stood tenderly,—
Paulo,—who from a window seeing her

Go straight across the lawn, and guessing where,
Had thought she was in tears, and found, that day,
His usual efforts vain to keep away.
Twice had he seen her since the Prince was gone,
On some small matter needing unison;
Twice linger'd, and convers'd, and grown long friends;   80
But not till now where no one else attends.—
'May I come in?' said he:—it made her start,—
That smiling voice;—she colour'd, press'd her heart
A moment, as for breath, and then with free
And usual tone said,—'O yes,——certainly.'
There's wont to be, at conscious times like these,
An affectation of a bright-eyed ease,
An air of something quite serene and sure,
As if to seem so, were to be, secure.
With this the lovers met, with this they spoke,   90
With this sat down to read the self-same book.

And Paulo, by degrees, gently embrac'd
With one permitted arm her lovely waist;
And both their cheeks, like peaches on a tree,
Came with a touch together thrillingly,
And o'er the book they hung, and nothing said,
And every lingering page grew longer as they read.

As thus they sat, and felt with leaps of heart
Their colour change, they came upon the part
Where fond Geneura, with her flame long nurst,   100
Smil'd upon Launcelot, when he kiss'd her first:—
That touch, at last, through every fibre slid;
And Paulo turn'd, scarce knowing what he did,
Only he felt he could no more dissemble,
And kiss'd her, mouth to mouth, all in a tremble.—
Oh then she wept,—the poor Francesca wept;
And pardon oft he pray'd; and then she swept
The tears away, and look'd him in the face,
And, well as words might save the truth disgrace,
She told him all, up to that very hour,   110
The father's guile, th' undwelt-in bridal bower,—
And wish'd for wings on which they two might soar
Far, far away, as doves to their own shore,
With claim from none.—That day they read no more.

(Canto III, lines 504–608)

401

JOHN KEATS
1795–1821

166   *On First Looking into Chapman's Homer*

> MUCH have I travell'd in the realms of gold,
>   And many goodly states and kingdoms seen;
>   Round many western islands have I been
> Which bards in fealty to Apollo hold.
> Oft of one wide expanse had I been told
>   That deep-brow'd Homer ruled as his demesne;
>   Yet did I never breathe its pure serene
> Till I heard Chapman speak out loud and bold:
> Then felt I like some watcher of the skies
>   When a new planet swims into his ken;   10
> Or like stout Cortez when with eagle eyes
>   He star'd at the Pacific—and all his men
> Look'd at each other with a wild surmise—
>   Silent, upon a peak in Darien.

GEORGE GORDON, LORD BYRON

167   from *Childe Harold's Pilgrimage*

3

> IN my youth's summer I did sing of One,
> The wandering outlaw of his own dark mind;
> Again I seize the theme then but begun,
> And bear it with me, as the rushing wind
> Bears the cloud onwards: in that Tale I find
> The furrows of long thought, and dried-up tears,
> Which, ebbing, leave a sterile track behind,
> O'er which all heavily the journeying years
> Plod the last sands of life,—where not a flower appears.

4

> Since my young days of passion—joy, or pain,   10
> Perchance my heart and harp have lost a string,
> And both may jar: it may be, that in vain
> I would essay as I have sung to sing.

Yet, though a dreary strain, to this I cling;
So that it wean me from the weary dream
Of selfish grief or gladness—so it fling
Forgetfulness around me—it shall seem
To me, though to none else, a not ungrateful theme.

5

He, who grown aged in this world of woe,
In deeds, not years, piercing the depths of life,   20
So that no wonder waits him; nor below
Can love, or sorrow, fame, ambition, strife,
Cut to his heart again with the keen knife
Of silent, sharp endurance: he can tell
Why thought seeks refuge in lone caves, yet rife
With airy images, and shapes which dwell
Still unimpair'd, though old, in the soul's haunted cell.

6

'Tis to create, and in creating live
A being more intense, that we endow
With form our fancy, gaining as we give   30
The life we image, even as I do now.
What am I? Nothing; but not so art thou,
Soul of my thought! with whom I traverse earth,
Invisible but gazing, as I glow
Mix'd with thy spirit, blended with thy birth,
And feeling still with thee in my crush'd feelings' dearth.

34

There is a very life in our despair,
Vitality of poison,—a quick root
Which feeds these deadly branches; for it were
As nothing did we die; but Life will suit   40
Itself to Sorrow's most detested fruit,
Like to the apples on the Dead Sea's shore,
All ashes to the taste: Did man compute
Existence by enjoyment, and count o'er
Such hours 'gainst years of life,—say, would he name
    threescore?

35

The Psalmist numbered out the years of man:
They are enough; and if thy tale be *true*,

Thou, who didst grudge him even that fleeting span,
More than enough, thou fatal Waterloo!
Millions of tongues record thee, and anew   50
Their children's lips shall echo them, and say—
'Here, where the sword united nations drew,
Our countrymen were warring on that day!'
And this is much, and all which will not pass away.

36

There sunk the greatest, nor the worst of men,
Whose spirit antithetically mixt
One moment of the mightiest, and again
On little objects with like firmness fixt,
Extreme in all things! hadst thou been betwixt,
Thy throne had still been thine, or never been;   60
For daring made thy rise as fall: thou seek'st
Even now to re-assume the imperial mien,
And shake again the world, the Thunderer of the scene!

37

Conqueror and captive of the earth art thou!
She trembles at thee still, and thy wild name
Was ne'er more bruited in men's minds than now
That thou art nothing, save the jest of Fame,
Who wooed thee once, thy vassal, and became
The flatterer of thy fierceness, till thou wert
A god unto thyself; nor less the same   70
To the astounded kingdoms all inert,
Who deem'd thee for a time whate'er thou didst assert.

38

Oh, more or less than man—in high or low,
Battling with nations, flying from the field;
Now making monarchs' necks thy footstool, now
More than thy meanest soldier taught to yield;
An empire thou couldst crush, command, rebuild,
But govern not thy pettiest passion, nor,
However deeply in men's spirits skill'd,
Look through thine own, nor curb the lust of war,   80
Nor learn that tempted Fate will leave the loftiest star.

39

Yet well thy soul hath brook'd the turning tide
With that untaught innate philosophy,

Which, be it wisdom, coldness, or deep pride,
Is gall and wormwood to an enemy.
When the whole host of hatred stood hard by,
To watch and mock thee shrinking, thou hast smiled
With a sedate and all-enduring eye;—
When Fortune fled her spoil'd and favourite child,
He stood unbowed beneath the ills upon him piled.   90

40

Sager than in thy fortunes; for in them
Ambition steel'd thee on too far to show
That just habitual scorn which could contemn
Men and their thoughts; 'twas wise to feel, not so
To wear it ever on thy lip and brow,
And spurn the instruments thou wert to use
Till they were turn'd unto thine overthrow:
'Tis but a worthless world to win or lose;
So hath it proved to thee, and all such lot who choose.

41

If, like a tower upon a headlong rock,   100
Thou hadst been made to stand or fall alone,
Such scorn of man had help'd to brave the shock;
But men's thoughts were the steps which paved thy throne,
Their admiration thy best weapon shone;
The part of Philip's son was thine, not then
(Unless aside thy purple had been thrown)
Like stern Diogenes to mock at men;
For sceptred cynics earth were far too wide a den.

42

But quiet to quick bosoms is a hell,
And *there* hath been thy bane; there is a fire   110
And motion of the soul which will not dwell
In its own narrow being, but aspire
Beyond the fitting medium of desire;
And, but once kindled, quenchless evermore,
Preys upon high adventure, nor can tire
Of aught but rest; a fever at the core,
Fatal to him who bears, to all who ever bore.

43

This makes the madmen who have made men mad
By their contagion; Conquerors and Kings,

Founders of sects and systems, to whom add   120
Sophists, Bards, Statesmen, all unquiet things
Which stir too strongly the soul's secret springs,
And are themselves the fools to those they fool;
Envied, yet how unenviable! what stings
Are theirs! One breast laid open were a school
Which would unteach mankind the lust to shine or rule:

44

Their breath is agitation, and their life
A storm whereon they ride, to sink at last,
And yet so nurs'd and bigotted to strife,
That should their days, surviving perils past,   130
Melt to calm twilight, they feel overcast
With sorrow and supineness, and so die;
Even as a flame unfed, which runs to waste
With its own flickering, or a sword laid by
Which eats into itself, and rusts ingloriously.

45

He who ascends to mountain-tops, shall find
The loftiest peaks most wrapt in clouds and snow;
He who surpasses or subdues mankind,
Must look down on the hate of those below.
Though high *above* the sun of glory glow,   140
And far *beneath* the earth and ocean spread,
Round him are icy rocks, and loudly blow
Contending tempests on his naked head,
And thus reward the toils which to those summits led.

68

Lake Leman woos me with its crystal face,
The mirror where the stars and mountains view
The stillness of their aspect in each trace
Its clear depth yields of their far height and hue:
There is too much of man here, to look through
With a fit mind the might which I behold;   150
But soon in me shall Loneliness renew
Thoughts hid, but not less cherish'd than of old,
Ere mingling with the herd had penn'd me in their fold.

69

To fly from, need not be to hate, mankind;
All are not fit with them to stir and toil,

Nor is it discontent to keep the mind
Deep in its fountain, lest it overboil
In the hot throng, where we become the spoil
Of our infection, till too late and long
We may deplore and struggle with the coil,   160
In wretched interchange of wrong for wrong
'Midst a contentious world, striving where none are strong.

70

There, in a moment, we may plunge our years
In fatal penitence, and in the blight
Of our own soul, turn all our blood to tears,
And colour things to come with hues of Night;
The race of life becomes a hopeless flight
To those that walk in darkness: on the sea,
The boldest steer but where their ports invite,
But there are wanderers o'er Eternity   170
Whose bark drives on and on, and anchored ne'er shall be.

71

Is it not better, then, to be alone,
And love Earth only for its earthly sake?
By the blue rushing of the arrowy Rhone,
Or the pure bosom of its nursing lake,
Which feeds it as a mother who doth make
A fair but froward infant her own care,
Kissing its cries away as these awake;—
Is it not better thus our lives to wear,
Than join the crushing crowd, doom'd to inflict or bear?   180

72

I live not in myself, but I become
Portion of that around me; and to me,
High mountains are a feeling, but the hum
Of human cities torture: I can see
Nothing to loathe in nature, save to be
A link reluctant in a fleshly chain,
Class'd among creatures, when the soul can flee,
And with the sky, the peak, the heaving plain
Of ocean, or the stars, mingle, and not in vain.

73

And thus I am absorb'd, and this is life: 190
I look upon the peopled desert past,

As on a place of agony and strife,
Where, for some sin, to Sorrow I was cast,
To act and suffer, but remount at last
With a fresh pinion; which I feel to spring,
Though young, yet waxing vigorous, as the blast
Which it would cope with, on delighted wing,
Spurning the clay-cold bonds which round our being cling.

74

And when, at length, the mind shall be all free
From what it hates in this degraded form,   200
Reft of its carnal life, save what shall be
Existent happier in the fly and worm,—
When elements to elements conform,
And dust is as it should be, shall I not
Feel all I see, less dazzling, but more warm?
The bodiless thought? the Spirit of each spot?
Of which, even now, I share at times the immortal lot?

75

Are not the mountains, waves, and skies, a part
Of me and of my soul, as I of them?
Is not the love of these deep in my heart   210
With a pure passion? should I not contemn
All objects, if compared with these? and stem
A tide of suffering, rather than forgo
Such feelings for the hard and worldly phlegm
Of those whose eyes are only turn'd below,
Gazing upon the ground, with thoughts which dare not glow?

76

But this is not my theme; and I return
To that which is immediate, and require
Those who find contemplation in the urn,
To look on One, whose dust was once all fire,   220
A native of the land where I respire
The clear air for a while—a passing guest,
Where he became a being,—whose desire
Was to be glorious; 'twas a foolish quest,
The which to gain and keep, he sacrificed all rest.

77

Here the self-torturing sophist, wild Rousseau,
The apostle of affliction, he who threw

Enchantment over passion, and from woe
· Wrung overwhelming eloquence, first drew
The breath which made him wretched; yet he knew   230
How to make madness beautiful, and cast
O'er erring deeds and thoughts, a heavenly hue
Of words, like sunbeams, dazzling as they past
The eyes, which o'er them shed tears feelingly and fast.

78

His love was passion's essence—as a tree
On fire by lightning; with ethereal flame
Kindled he was, and blasted; for to be
Thus, and enamoured, were in him the same.
But his was not the love of living dame,
Nor of the dead who rise upon our dreams,   240
But of ideal beauty, which became
In him existence, and o'erflowing teems
Along his burning page, distempered though it seems.

79

This breathed itself to life in Júlie, *this*
Invested her with all that's wild and sweet;
This hallowed, too, the memorable kiss
Which every morn his fevered lip would greet,
From hers, who but with friendship his would meet;
But to that gentle touch, through brain and breast
Flash'd the thrill'd spirit's love-devouring heat;   250
In that absorbing sigh perchance more blest,
Than vulgar minds may be with all they seek possest.

80

His life was one long war with self-sought foes,
Or friends by him self-banish'd; for his mind
Had grown Suspicion's sanctuary, and chose
For its own cruel sacrifice, the kind,
'Gainst whom he raged with fury strange and blind.
But he was phrenzied,—wherefore, who may know?
Since cause might be which skill could never find;
But he was phrenzied by disease or woe,   260
To that worst pitch of all, which wears a reasoning show.

81

For then he was inspired, and from him came,
As from the Pythian's mystic cave of yore,

Those oracles which set the world in flame,
Nor ceased to burn till kingdoms were no more:
Did he not this for France? which lay before
Bowed to the inborn tyranny of years?
Broken and trembling, to the yoke she bore,
Till by the voice of him and his compeers,
Roused up to too much wrath which follows o'ergrown
    fears?   270

82

They made themselves a fearful monument!
The wreck of old opinions—things which grew
Breathed from the birth of time: the veil they rent,
And what behind it lay, all earth shall view.
But good with ill they also overthrew,
Leaving but ruins, wherewith to rebuild
Upon the same foundation, and renew
Dungeons and thrones, which the same hour re-fill'd,
As heretofore, because ambition was self-will'd.

83

But this will not endure, nor be endured!   280
Mankind have felt their strength, and made it felt.
They might have used it better, but, allured
By their new vigour, sternly have they dealt
On one another; pity ceased to melt
With her once natural charities. But they,
Who in oppression's darkness caved had dwelt,
They were not eagles, nourish'd with the day;
What marvel then, at times, if they mistook their prey?

84

What deep wounds ever closed without a scar?
The heart's bleed longest, and but heal to wear   290
That which disfigures it; and they who war
With their own hopes, and have been vanquish'd, bear
Silence, but not submission: in his lair
Fix'd Passion holds his breath, until the hour
Which shall atone for years; none need despair:
It came, it cometh, and will come,—the power
To punish or forgive—in *one* we shall be slower.

92

The sky is changed!—and such a change! Oh night,
And storm, and darkness, ye are wondrous strong,
Yet lovely in your strength, as is the light   300
Of a dark eye in woman! Far along,
From peak to peak, the rattling crags among
Leaps the live thunder! Not from one lone cloud,
But every mountain now hath found a tongue,
And Jura answers, through her misty shroud,
Back to the joyous Alps, who call to her aloud!

93

And this is in the night:—Most glorious night!
Thou wert not sent for slumber! let me be
A sharer in thy fierce and far delight,—
A portion of the tempest and of thee!   310
How the lit lake shines, a phosphoric sea,
And the big rain comes dancing to the earth!
And now again 'tis black,—and now, the glee
Of the loud hills shakes with its mountain-mirth,
As if they did rejoice o'er a young earthquake's birth.

94

Now, where the swift Rhone cleaves his way between
Heights which appear as lovers who have parted
In hate, whose mining depths so intervene,
That they can meet no more, though broken-hearted;
Though in their souls, which thus each other thwarted,   320
Love was the very root of the fond rage
Which blighted their life's bloom, and then departed:—
Itself expired, but leaving them an age
Of years all winters,—war within themselves to wage.

95

Now, where the quick Rhone thus hath cleft his way,
The mightiest of the storms hath ta'en his stand:
For here, not one, but many, make their play,
And fling their thunder-bolts from hand to hand,
Flashing and cast around: of all the band,
The brightest through these parted hills hath fork'd   330
His lightnings,—as if he did understand,
That in such gaps as desolation work'd,
There the hot shaft should blast whatever therein lurk'd.

96

Sky, mountains, river, winds, lake, lightnings! ye!
With night, and clouds, and thunder, and a soul
To make these felt and feeling, well may be
Things that have made me watchful; the far roll
Of your departing voices, is the knoll
Of what in me is sleepless,—if I rest.
But where of ye, oh tempests! is the goal?   340
Are ye like those within the human breast?
Or do ye find, at length, like eagles, some high nest?

97

Could I embody and unbosom now
That which is most within me,—could I wreak
My thoughts upon expression, and thus throw
Soul, heart, mind, passions, feelings, strong or weak,
All that I would have sought, and all I seek,
Bear, know, feel, and yet breathe—into *one* word,
And that one word were Lightning, I would speak;
But as it is, I live and die unheard,   350
With a most voiceless thought, sheathing it as a sword.

(Canto III)

[1817]

PERCY BYSSHE SHELLEY
1792–1822

168   *Hymn to Intellectual Beauty*

I

THE awful shadow of some unseen Power
     Floats though unseen amongst us,—visiting
     This various world with as inconstant wing
As summer winds that creep from flower to flower.—
Like moonbeams that behind some piny mountain shower,
          It visits with inconstant glance
          Each human heart and countenance;
Like hues and harmonies of evening,—
          Like clouds in starlight widely spread,—

Like memory of music fled,—   10
Like aught that for its grace may be
Dear, and yet dearer for its mystery.

2

Spirit of BEAUTY, that doth consecrate
  With thine own hues all thou dost shine upon
  Of human thought or form,—where art thou gone?
Why dost thou pass away and leave our state,
This dim vast vale of tears, vacant and desolate?
        Ask why the sunlight not forever
        Weaves rainbows o'er yon mountain river,
Why aught should fail and fade that once is shown,   20
        Why fear and dream and death and birth
        Cast on the daylight of this earth
        Such gloom,—why man has such a scope
For love and hate, despondency and hope?

3

No voice from some sublimer world hath ever
  To sage or poet these responses given—
  Therefore the name of God, and ghosts, and Heaven,
Remain the records of their vain endeavour,
Frail spells—whose uttered charm might not avail to sever,   30
        From all we hear and all we see,
        Doubt, chance, and mutability.
Thy light alone—like mist o'er mountains driven,
        Or music by the night wind sent
        Through strings of some still instrument,
        Or moonlight on a midnight stream,
Gives grace and truth to life's unquiet dream.

4

Love, Hope, and Self-esteem, like clouds depart
  And come, for some uncertain moments lent.
  Man were immortal, and omnipotent,
Didst thou, unknown and awful as thou art,   40
Keep with thy glorious train firm state within his heart.
        Thou messenger of sympathies
        That wax and wane in lovers' eyes—
Thou—that to human thought art nourishment,
        Like darkness to a dying flame!
        Depart not as thy shadow came,
        Depart not—lest the grave should be,
Like life and fear, a dark reality.

5

While yet a boy I sought for ghosts, and sped
   Through many a listening chamber, cave and ruin,
   And starlight wood, with fearful steps pursuing   50
Hopes of high talk with the departed dead.
I called on poisonous names with which our youth is fed,
      I was not heard—I saw them not—
      When musing deeply on the lot
Of life, at that sweet time when winds are wooing
      All vital things that wake to bring
      News of buds and blossoming,—
      Sudden, thy shadow fell on me;
I shrieked, and clasped my hands in ecstasy!   60

6

I vowed that I would dedicate my powers
   To thee and thine—have I not kept the vow?
   With beating heart and streaming eyes, even now
I call the phantoms of a thousand hours
Each from his voiceless grave: they have in visioned bowers
      Of studious zeal or love's delight
      Outwatched with me the envious night—
They know that never joy illumed my brow
      Unlinked with hope that thou wouldst free
      This world from its dark slavery,
      That thou—O awful LOVELINESS,   70
Wouldst give whate'er these words cannot express.

7

The day becomes more solemn and serene
   When noon is past—there is a harmony
   In autumn, and a lustre in its sky,
Which through the summer is not heard or seen,
As if it could not be, as if it had not been!
      Thus let thy power, which like the truth
      Of nature on my passive youth
Descended, to my onward life supply   80
      Its calm—to one who worships thee,
      And every form containing thee,
      Whom, SPIRIT fair, thy spells did bind
To fear himself, and love all human kind.

169   *Mont Blanc*

Lines Written in the Vale of Chamouni

I

THE everlasting universe of things
Flows through the mind, and rolls its rapid waves,
Now dark—now glittering—now reflecting gloom—
Now lending splendour, where from secret springs
The source of human thought its tribute brings
Of waters,—with a sound but half its own,
Such as a feeble brook will oft assume
In the wild woods, among the mountains lone,
Where waterfalls around it leap for ever,
Where woods and winds contend, and a vast river   10
Over its rocks ceaselessly bursts and raves.

II

Thus thou, Ravine of Arve—dark, deep Ravine—
Thou many-coloured, many-voicèd vale,
Over whose pines, and crags, and caverns sail
Fast cloud shadows and sunbeams: awful scene,
Where Power in likeness of the Arve comes down
From the ice gulfs that gird his secret throne,
Bursting through these dark mountains like the flame
Of lightning through the tempest;—thou dost lie,
Thy giant brood of pines around thee clinging,   20
Children of elder time, in whose devotion
The chainless winds still come and ever came
To drink their odours, and their mighty swinging
To hear—an old and solemn harmony;
Thine earthly rainbows stretched across the sweep
Of the etherial waterfall, whose veil
Robes some unsculptured image; the strange sleep
Which when the voices of the desert fail
Wraps all in its own deep eternity;—
Thy caverns echoing to the Arve's commotion,   30
A loud, lone sound no other sound can tame;
Thou art pervaded with that ceaseless motion,
Thou art the path of that unresting sound—
Dizzy Ravine! and when I gaze on thee
I seem as in a trance sublime and strange
To muse on my own separate fantasy,
My own, my human mind, which passively

Now renders and receives fast influencings,
Holding an unremitting interchange
With the clear universe of things around;   40
One legion of wild thoughts, whose wandering wings
Now float above thy darkness, and now rest
Where that or thou art no unbidden guest,
In the still cave of the witch Poesy,
Seeking among the shadows that pass by,
Ghosts of all things that are, some shade of thee,
Some phantom, some faint image; till the breast
From which they fled recalls them, thou art there!

III

Some say that gleams of a remoter world
Visit the soul in sleep,—that death is slumber,   50
And that its shapes the busy thoughts outnumber
Of those who wake and live.—I look on high;
Has some unknown omnipotence unfurled
The veil of life and death? or do I lie
In dream, and does the mightier world of sleep
Spread far around and inaccessibly
Its circles? For the very spirit fails,
Driven like a homeless cloud from steep to steep
That vanishes among the viewless gales!
Far, far above, piercing the infinite sky,   60
Mont Blanc appears,—still, snowy, and serene—
Its subject mountains their unearthly forms
Pile around it, ice and rock; broad vales between
Of frozen floods, unfathomable deeps,
Blue as the overhanging heaven, that spread
And wind among the accumulated steeps;
A desert peopled by the storms alone,
Save when the eagle brings some hunter's bone,
And the wolf tracks her there—how hideously
Its shapes are heaped around! rude, bare, and high,   70
Ghastly, and scarred, and riven.—Is this the scene
Where the old Earthquake-daemon taught her young
Ruin? Were these their toys? or did a sea
Of fire envelop once this silent snow?
None can reply—all seems eternal now.
The wilderness has a mysterious tongue
Which teaches awful doubt, or faith so mild,
So solemn, so serene, that man may be
But for such faith with nature reconciled;
Thou hast a voice, great Mountain, to repeal   80

Large codes of fraud and woe; not understood
By all, but which the wise, and great, and good
Interpret, or make felt, or deeply feel.

IV

The fields, the lakes, the forests, and the streams,
Ocean, and all the living things that dwell
Within the daedal earth; lightning, and rain,
Earthquake, and fiery flood, and hurricane,
The torpor of the year when feeble dreams
Visit the hidden buds, or dreamless sleep
Holds every future leaf and flower;—the bound   90
With which from that detested trance they leap;
The works and ways of man, their death and birth,
And that of him and all that his may be;
All things that move and breathe with toil and sound
Are born and die; revolve, subside and swell.
Power dwells apart in its tranquillity
Remote, serene, and inaccessible:
And *this*, the naked countenance of earth,
On which I gaze, even these primeval mountains
Teach the adverting mind. The glaciers creep   100
Like snakes that watch their prey, from their far fountains,
Slow rolling on; there, many a precipice,
Frost and the Sun in scorn of mortal power
Have piled: dome, pyramid, and pinnacle,
A city of death, distinct with many a tower
And wall impregnable of beaming ice.
Yet not a city, but a flood of ruin
Is there, that from the boundaries of the sky
Rolls its perpetual stream; vast pines are strewing
Its destined path, or in the mangled soil   110
Branchless and shattered stand; the rocks, drawn down
From yon remotest waste, have overthrown
The limits of the dead and living world,
Never to be reclaimed. The dwelling-place
Of insects, beasts, and birds, becomes its spoil;
Their food and their retreat for ever gone,
So much of life and joy is lost. The race
Of man flies far in dread; his work and dwelling
Vanish, like smoke before the tempest's stream,
And their place is not known. Below, vast caves   120
Shine in the rushing torrent's restless gleam,
Which from those secret chasms in tumult welling
Meet in the vale, and one majestic River,

The breath and blood of distant lands, for ever
Rolls its loud waters to the ocean waves,
Breathes its swift vapours to the circling air.

V

Mont Blanc yet gleams on high:—the power is there,
The still and solemn power of many sights
And many sounds, and much of life and death.
In the calm darkness of the moonless nights,   130
In the lone glare of day, the snows descend
Upon that Mountain; none beholds them there,
Nor when the flakes burn in the sinking sun,
Or the star-beams dart through them:—Winds contend
Silently there, and heap the snow with breath
Rapid and strong, but silently! Its home
The voiceless lightning in these solitudes
Keeps innocently, and like vapour broods
Over the snow. The secret strength of things
Which governs thought, and to the infinite dome   140
Of heaven is as a law, inhabits thee!
And what were thou, and earth, and stars, and sea,
If to the human mind's imaginings
Silence and solitude were vacancy?

GEORGE GORDON, LORD BYRON

170   *Manfred*

A Dramatic Poem

> *There are more things in heaven and earth, Horatio,*
> *Than are dreamt of in your philosophy.*

DRAMATIS PERSONAE

MANFRED
CHAMOIS HUNTER
ABBOT OF ST MAURICE
MANUEL
HERMAN

WITCH OF THE ALPS
ARIMANES
NEMESIS
THE DESTINIES
SPIRITS, etc.

The Scene of the Drama is amongst the Higher Alps—partly in the Castle of Manfred, and partly in the Mountains.

Act I

SCENE I

MANFRED *alone—Scene, a Gothic gallery—Time, Midnight.*

MAN. The lamp must be replenish'd, but even then
   It will not burn so long as I must watch:
   My slumbers—if I slumber—are not sleep,
   But a continuance of enduring thought,
   Which then I can resist not: in my heart
   There is a vigil, and these eyes but close
   To look within; and yet I live, and bear
   The aspect and the form of breathing men.
   But grief should be the instructor of the wise;
   Sorrow is knowledge: they who know the most   10
   Must mourn the deepest o'er the fatal truth,
   The Tree of Knowledge is not that of Life.
   Philosophy and science, and the springs
   Of wonder, and the wisdom of the world,
   I have essayed, and in my mind there is
   A power to make these subject to itself—
   But they avail not: I have done men good,
   And I have met with good even among men—
   But this avail'd not: I have had my foes,
   And none have baffled, many fallen before me—   20
   But this avail'd not:—Good, or evil, life,
   Powers, passions, all I see in other beings,
   Have been to me as rain unto the sands,
   Since that all-nameless hour. I have no dread,
   And feel the curse to have no natural fear,
   Nor fluttering throb, that beats with hopes or wishes,
   Or lurking love of something on the earth.—
   Now to my task.—
             Mysterious Agency!
   Ye spirits of the unbounded Universe!
   Whom I have sought in darkness and in light—   30
   Ye, who do compass earth about, and dwell
   In subtler essence—ye, to whom the tops
   Of mountains inaccessible are haunts,
   And earth's and ocean's caves familiar things—
   I call upon ye by the written charm
   Which gives me power upon you——Rise! appear!   [*A pause*

They come not yet.—Now by the voice of him
Who is the first among you—by this sign,
Which makes you tremble—by the claims of him
Who is undying,—Rise! appear!——Appear!   [*A pause*   40
If it be so.—Spirits of earth and air,
Ye shall not thus elude me: by a power,
Deeper than all yet urged, a tyrant-spell,
Which had its birth-place in a star condemn'd,
The burning wreck of a demolish'd world,
A wandering hell in the eternal space;
By the strong curse which is upon my soul,
The thought which is within me and around me,
I do compel ye to my will.—Appear!

[*A star is seen at the darker end of the gallery; it is stationary; and
a voice is heard singing*]

FIRST SPIRIT.
Mortal! to thy bidding bow'd,   50
From my mansion in the cloud,
Which the breath of twilight builds,
And the summer's sun-set gilds
With the azure and vermilion,
Which is mix'd for my pavilion;
Though thy quest may be forbidden,
On a star-beam I have ridden;
To thine adjuration bow'd,
Mortal—be thy wish avow'd!

Voice of the SECOND SPIRIT.
Mont Blanc is the monarch of mountains,   60
   They crowned him long ago
On a throne of rocks, in a robe of clouds,
   With a diadem of snow.
Around his waist are forests braced,
   The Avalanche in his hand;
But ere it fall, that thundering ball
   Must pause for my command.
The Glacier's cold and restless mass
   Moves onward day by day;
But I am he who bids it pass,   70
   Or with its ice delay.
I am the spirit of the place,
   Could make the mountain bow
And quiver to his cavern'd base—
   And what with me wouldst *Thou*?

Voice of the THIRD SPIRIT.

In the blue depth of the waters,
   Where the wave hath no strife,
Where the wind is a stranger,
   And the sea-snake hath life,
Where the Mermaid is decking   80
   Her green hair with shells;
Like the storm on the surface
   Came the sound of thy spells;
O'er my calm Hall of Coral
   The deep echo roll'd—
To the Spirit of Ocean
   Thy wishes unfold!

FOURTH SPIRIT.

Where the slumbering earthquake
   Lies pillow'd on fire,
And the lakes of bitumen   90
   Rise boilingly higher;
Where the roots of the Andes
   Strike deep in the earth,
As their summits to heaven
   Shoot soaringly forth;
I have quitted my birth-place,
   Thy bidding to bide—
Thy spell hath subdued me,
   Thy will be my guide!

FIFTH SPIRIT.

I am the Rider of the wind,   100
   The Stirrer of the storm;
The hurricane I left behind
   Is yet with lightning warm;
To speed to thee, o'er shore and sea
   I swept upon the blast:
The fleet I met sailed well, and yet
   'Twill sink ere night be past.

SIXTH SPIRIT.

My dwelling is the shadow of the night,
Why doth thy magic torture me with light?

SEVENTH SPIRIT.

The star which rules thy destiny,   110
Was ruled, ere earth began, by me:

It was a world as fresh and fair
As e'er revolved round sun in air;
Its course was free and regular,
Space bosom'd not a lovelier star.
The hour arrived—and it became
A wandering mass of shapeless flame,
A pathless comet, and a curse,
The menace of the universe;
Still rolling on with innate force,   120
Without a sphere, without a course,
A bright deformity on high,
The monster of the upper sky!
And thou! beneath its influence born—
Thou worm! whom I obey and scorn—
Forced by a power (which is not thine,
And lent thee but to make thee mine)
For this brief moment to descend,
Where these weak spirits round thee bend
And parley with a thing like thee—   130
What wouldst thou, Child of Clay! with me?

The SEVEN SPIRITS.

Earth, ocean, air, night, mountains, winds, thy star,
   Are at thy beck and bidding, Child of Clay!
Before thee at thy quest their spirits are—
   What wouldst thou with us, son of mortals—say?

MAN. Forgetfulness——
FIRST SPIRIT. Of what—of whom—and why?
MAN. Of that which is within me; read it there—
   Ye know it, and I cannot utter it.
SPIRIT. We can but give thee that which we possess:
   Ask of us subjects, sovereignty, the power   140
   O'er earth, the whole, or portion, or a sign
   Which shall control the elements, whereof
   We are the dominators, each and all,
   These shall be thine.
MAN.   Oblivion, self-oblivion—
   Can ye not wring from out the hidden realms
   Ye offer so profusely what I ask?
SPIRIT. It is not in our essence, in our skill;
   But—thou mayst die.
MAN.   Will death bestow it on me?
SPIRIT. We are immortal, and do not forget;
   We are eternal; and to us the past   150

Is, as the future, present. Art thou answered?

MAN. Ye mock me—but the power which brought ye here
    Hath made you mine. Slaves, scoff not at my will!
    The mind, the spirit, the Promethean spark,
    The lightning of my being, is as bright,
    Pervading, and far-darting as your own,
    And shall not yield to yours, though coop'd in clay!
    Answer, or I will teach ye what I am.

SPIRIT. We answer as we answered; our reply
    Is even in thine own words.

MAN.   Why say ye so?   160

SPIRIT. If, as thou say'st, thine essence be as ours,
    We have replied in telling thee, the thing
    Mortals call death hath nought to do with us.

MAN. I then have call'd ye from your realms in vain;
    Ye cannot, or ye will not, aid me.

SPIRIT.   Say;
    What we possess we offer; it is thine:
    Bethink ere thou dismiss us, ask again—
    Kingdom, and sway, and strength, and length of days——

MAN. Accursed! what have I to do with days?
    They are too long already.—Hence—begone!   170

SPIRIT. Yet pause: being here, our will would do thee service;
    Bethink thee, is there then no other gift
    Which we can make not worthless in thine eyes?

MAN. No, none: yet stay—one moment, ere we part—
    I would behold ye face to face. I hear
    Your voices, sweet and melancholy sounds,
    As music on the waters; and I see
    The steady aspect of a clear large star;
    But nothing more. Approach me as ye are,
    Or one, or all, in your accustom'd forms.   180

SPIRIT. We have no forms beyond the elements
    Of which we are the mind and principle:
    But choose a form—in that we will appear.

MAN. I have no choice; there is no form on earth
    Hideous or beautiful to me. Let him,
    Who is most powerful of ye, take such aspect
    As unto him may seem most fitting.—Come!

SEVENTH SPIRIT [*Appearing in the shape of a beautiful female figure*].
    Behold!

MAN.   Oh God! if it be thus, and *thou*
    Art not a madness and a mockery,
    I yet might be most happy.—I will clasp thee,   190
    And we again will be——   [*The figure vanishes*
        My heart is crush'd!

[MANFRED *falls senseless*

[*A voice is heard in the Incantation which follows*]

When the moon is on the wave,
  And the glow-worm in the grass,
And the meteor on the grave,
  And the wisp on the morass;
When the falling stars are shooting,
And the answer'd owls are hooting,
And the silent leaves are still
In the shadow of the hill,
Shall my soul be upon thine, 200
With a power and with a sign.

Though thy slumber may be deep,
Yet thy spirit shall not sleep,
There are shades which will not vanish,
There are thoughts thou canst not banish;
By a power to thee unknown,
Thou canst never be alone;
Thou art wrapt as with a shroud,
Thou art gathered in a cloud;
And for ever shalt thou dwell 210
In the spirit of this spell.

Though thou seest me not pass by,
Thou shalt feel me with thine eye
As a thing that, though unseen,
Must be near thee, and hath been;
And when in that secret dread
Thou hast turn'd around thy head,
Thou shalt marvel I am not
As thy shadow on the spot,
And the power which thou dost feel 220
Shall be what thou must conceal.

And a magic voice and verse
Hath baptized thee with a curse;
And a spirit of the air
Hath begirt thee with a snare;
In the wind there is a voice
Shall forbid thee to rejoice;
And to thee shall Night deny
All the quiet of her sky;
And the day shall have a sun, 230
Which shall make thee wish it done.

From thy false tears I did distil
An essence which hath strength to kill;
From thy own heart I then did wring
The black blood in its blackest spring;
From thy own smile I snatch'd the snake,
For there it coil'd as in a brake;
From thy own lip I drew the charm
Which gave all these their chiefest harm;
In proving every poison known,   240
I found the strongest was thine own.

By thy cold breast and serpent smile,
By thy unfathom'd gulfs of guile,
By that most seeming virtuous eye,
By thy shut soul's hypocrisy;
By the perfection of thine art
Which pass'd for human thine own heart;
By thy delight in others' pain,
And by thy brotherhood of Cain,
I call upon thee! and compel   250
Thyself to be thy proper Hell!

And on thy head I pour the vial
Which doth devote thee to this trial;
Nor to slumber, nor to die,
Shall be in thy destiny;
Though thy death shall still seem near
To thy wish, but as a fear;
Lo! the spell now works around thee,
And the clankless chain hath bound thee;
O'er thy heart and brain together   260
Hath the word been pass'd—now wither!

SCENE II

The Mountain of the Jungfrau.—*Time, Morning.*—MANFRED *alone upon the Cliffs.*

MAN. The spirits I have raised abandon me—
The spells which I have studied baffle me—
The remedy I reck'd of tortured me;
I lean no more on super-human aid,
It hath no power upon the past, and for
The future, till the past be gulf'd in darkness,
It is not of my search.—My mother Earth!
And thou fresh breaking Day, and you, ye Mountains,
Why are ye beautiful? I cannot love ye.

425

And thou, the bright eye of the universe,   10
That openest over all, and unto all
Art a delight—thou shin'st not on my heart.
And you, ye crags, upon whose extreme edge
I stand, and on the torrent's brink beneath
Behold the tall pines dwindled as to shrubs
In dizziness of distance; when a leap,
A stir, a motion, even a breath, would bring
My breast upon its rocky bosom's bed
To rest for ever—wherefore do I pause?
I feel the impulse—yet I do not plunge;   20
I see the peril—yet do not recede;
And my brain reels—and yet my foot is firm:
There is a power upon me which withholds
And makes it my fatality to live;
If it be life to wear within myself
This barrenness of spirit, and to be
My own soul's sepulchre, for I have ceased
To justify my deeds unto myself—
The last infirmity of evil. Ay,
Thou winged and cloud-cleaving minister,   *[An eagle passes*
Whose happy flight is highest into heaven,
Well mayst thou swoop so near me—I should be
Thy prey, and gorge thine eaglets; thou art gone
Where the eye cannot follow thee; but thine
Yet pierces downward, onward, or above
With a pervading vision.—Beautiful!
How beautiful is all this visible world!
How glorious in its action and itself;
But we, who name ourselves its sovereigns, we,
Half dust, half deity, alike unfit   40
To sink or soar, with our mix'd essence make
A conflict of its elements, and breathe
The breath of degradation and of pride,
Contending with low wants and lofty will
Till our mortality predominates,
And men are—what they name not to themselves,
And trust not to each other. Hark! the note,
                    [The Shepherd's pipe in the distance is heard
The natural music of the mountain reed—
For here the patriarchal days are not
A pastoral fable—pipes in the liberal air,   50
Mix'd with the sweet bells of the sauntering herd;
My soul would drink those echoes.—Oh, that I were
The viewless spirit of a lovely sound,
A living voice, a breathing harmony,

A bodiless enjoyment—born and dying
With the blest tone which made me!

Enter from below a CHAMOIS HUNTER

CHAMOIS HUNTER.   Even so
This way the chamois leapt: her nimble feet
Have baffled me; my gains to-day will scarce
Repay my break-neck travail.—What is here?
Who seems not of my trade, and yet hath reach'd   60
A height which none even of our mountaineers,
Save our best hunters, may attain: his garb
Is goodly, his mien manly, and his air
Proud as a free-born peasant's, at this distance.—
I will approach him nearer.
MAN. [*not perceiving the other*]. To be thus—
Grey-hair'd with anguish, like these blasted pines,
Wrecks of a single winter, barkless, branchless,
A blighted trunk upon a cursed root,
Which but supplies a feeling to decay—
And to be thus, eternally but thus,   70
Having been otherwise! Now furrow'd o'er
With wrinkles, plough'd by moments, not by years;
And hours—all tortured into ages—hours
Which I outlive!—Ye toppling crags of ice!
Ye avalanches, whom a breath draws down
In mountainous o'erwhelming, come and crush me—
I hear ye momently above, beneath,
Crash with a frequent conflict; but ye pass,
And only fall on things which still would live;
On the young flourishing forest, or the hut   80
And hamlet of the harmless villager.
C. HUN. The mists begin to rise from up the valley;
I'll warn him to descend, or he may chance
To lose at once his way and life together.
MAN. The mists boil up around the glaciers; clouds
Rise curling fast beneath me, white and sulphury,
Like foam from the roused ocean of deep Hell,
Whose every wave breaks on a living shore,
Heaped with the damn'd like pebbles.—I am giddy.
C. HUN. I must approach him cautiously; if near,   90
A sudden step will startle him, and he
Seems tottering already.
MAN.   Mountains have fallen
Leaving a gap in the clouds, and with the shock
Rocking their Alpine brethren; filling up
The ripe green valleys with destruction's splinters;

Damming the rivers with a sudden dash,
Which crush'd the waters into mist, and made
Their fountains find another channel—thus,
Thus, in its old age, did Mount Rosenberg—
Why stood I not beneath it?

C. HUN.   Friend! have a care,   100
Your next step may be fatal!—for the love
Of him who made you, stand not on that brink!

MAN. [*not hearing him*]. Such would have been for me a fitting tomb;
My bones had then been quiet in their depth;
They had not then been strewn upon the rocks
For the wind's pastime—as thus—thus they shall be—
In this one plunge.—Farewell, ye opening heavens!
Look not upon me thus reproachfully—
Ye were not meant for me—Earth! take these atoms!

[*As* MANFRED *is in act to spring from the cliff, the* CHAMOIS
HUNTER *seizes and retains him with a sudden grasp*]

C. HUN. Hold, madman!—though aweary of thy life,   110
Stain not our pure vales with thy guilty blood.—
Away with me——I will not quit my hold.

MAN. I am most sick at heart—nay, grasp me not—
I am all feebleness—the mountains whirl
Spinning around me—I grow blind—What art thou?

C. HUN. I'll answer that anon.—Away with me—
The clouds grow thicker—there—now lean on me—
Place your foot here—here, take this staff, and cling
A moment to that shrub—now give me your hand,
And hold fast by my girdle—softly—well—   120
The Chalet will be gained within an hour—
Come on, we'll quickly find a surer footing,
And something like a pathway, which the torrent
Hath wash'd since winter.—Come, 'tis bravely done—
You should have been a hunter.—Follow me.

[*As they descend the rocks with difficulty, the scene closes*]

END OF ACT THE FIRST

Act II

SCENE I

A Cottage amongst the Bernese Alps.

MANFRED *and the* CHAMOIS HUNTER.

C. HUN. No, no—yet pause—thou must not yet go forth:
　　Thy mind and body are alike unfit
　　To trust each other, for some hours, at least;
　　When thou art better, I will be thy guide—
　　But whither?
MAN.　　　　　　It imports not: I do know
　　My route full well, and need no further guidance.
C. HUN. Thy garb and gait bespeak thee of high lineage—
　　One of the many chiefs, whose castled crags
　　Look o'er the lower valleys—which of these
　　May call thee Lord? I only know their portals;　　　　　　10
　　My way of life leads me but rarely down
　　To bask by the huge hearths of those old halls,
　　Carousing with the vassals; but the paths,
　　Which step from out our mountains to their doors,
　　I know from childhood—which of these is thine?
MAN. No matter.
C. HUN.　　　　　Well, sir, pardon me the question,
　　And be of better cheer. Come, taste my wine;
　　'Tis of an ancient vintage; many a day
　　'T has thawed my veins among our glaciers, now
　　Let it do thus for thine—Come, pledge me fairly.　　　　　20
MAN. Away, away! there's blood upon the brim!
　　Will it then never—never sink in the earth?
C. HUN. What dost thou mean? thy senses wander from thee.
MAN. I say 'tis blood—my blood! the pure warm stream
　　Which ran in the veins of my fathers, and in ours
　　When we were in our youth, and had one heart,
　　And loved each other as we should not love,
　　And this was shed: but still it rises up,
　　Colouring the clouds, that shut me out from heaven,
　　Where thou art not—and I shall never be.　　　　　　　　30
C. HUN. Man of strange words, and some half-maddening sin,
　　Which makes thee people vacancy, whate'er
　　Thy dread and sufferance be, there's comfort yet—
　　The aid of holy men, and heavenly patience——
MAN. Patience and patience! Hence—that word was made
　　For brutes of burthen, not for birds of prey;
　　Preach it to mortals of a dust like thine,—
　　I am not of thine order.

C. HUN.   Thanks to heaven!
  I would not be of thine for the free fame
  Of William Tell; but whatsoe'er thine ill,   40
  It must be borne, and these wild starts are useless.
MAN. Do I not bear it?—Look on me—I live.
C. HUN. This is convulsion, and no healthful life.
MAN. I tell thee, man! I have lived many years,
  Many long years, but they are nothing now
  To those which I must number: ages—ages—
  Space and eternity—and consciousness,
  With the fierce thirst of death—and still unslaked!
C. HUN. Why, on thy brow the seal of middle age
  Hath scarce been set; I am thine elder far.   50
MAN. Think'st thou existence doth depend on time?
  It doth; but actions are our epochs: mine
  Have made my days and nights imperishable,
  Endless, and all alike, as sands on the shore,
  Innumerable atoms, and one desart,
  Barren and cold, on which the wild waves break,
  But nothing rests, save carcasses and wrecks,
  Rocks, and the salt-surf weeds of bitterness.
C. HUN. Alas! he's mad—but yet I must not leave him.
MAN. I would I were—for then the things I see   60
  Would be but a distempered dream.
C. HUN.   What is it
  That thou dost see, or think thou look'st upon?
MAN. Myself, and thee—a peasant of the Alps—
  Thy humble virtues, hospitable home,
  And spirit patient, pious, proud and free;
  Thy self-respect, grafted on innocent thoughts;
  Thy days of health, and nights of sleep; thy toils,
  By danger dignified, yet guiltless; hopes
  Of cheerful old age and a quiet grave,
  With cross and garland over its green turf,   70
  And thy grandchildren's love for epitaph;
  This do I see—and then I look within—
  It matters not—my soul was scorch'd already!
C. HUN. And wouldst thou then exchange thy lot for mine?
MAN. No, friend! I would not wrong thee, nor exchange
  My lot with living being: I can bear—
  However wretchedly, 'tis still to bear—
  In life what others could not brook to dream,
  But perish in their slumber.
C. HUN.   And with this—
  This cautious feeling for another's pain,   80
  Canst thou be black with evil?—say not so.

Can one of gentle thoughts have wreak'd revenge
Upon his enemies?
MAN.   Oh! no, no, no!
My injuries came down on those who loved me—
On those whom I best loved: I never quell'd
An enemy, save in my just defence—
My wrongs were all on those I should have cherished—
But my embrace was fatal.
C. HUN.   Heaven give thee rest!
And penitence restore thee to thyself;
My prayers shall be for thee.
MAN.   I need them not,   90
But can endure thy pity. I depart—
'Tis time—farewell!—Here's gold, and thanks for thee—
No words—it is thy due.—Follow me not—
I know my path—the mountain peril's past:—
And once again, I charge thee, follow not!

                                        [*Exit* MANFRED

SCENE II

A lower Valley in the Alps.—A Cataract.

Enter MANFRED

MAN. It is not noon—the sunbow's rays still arch
The torrent with the many hues of heaven,
And roll the sheeted silver's waving column
O'er the crag's headlong perpendicular,
And fling its lines of foaming light along,
And to and fro, like the pale courser's tail,
The Giant steed, to be bestrode by Death,
As told in the Apocalypse. No eyes
But mine now drink this sight of loveliness;
I should be sole in this sweet solitude,   10
And with the Spirit of the place divide
The homage of these waters.—I will call her.

    [MANFRED *takes some of the water into the palm of his hand, and
    flings it in the air, muttering the adjuration. After a pause, the* WITCH
    OF THE ALPS *rises beneath the arch of the sunbow of the torrent*]

MAN. Beautiful Spirit! with thy hair of light,
And dazzling eyes of glory, in whose form
The charms of Earth's least-mortal daughters grow
To an unearthly stature, in an essence
Of purer elements; while the hues of youth,—

Carnation'd like a sleeping infant's cheek,
Rock'd by the beating of her mother's heart,
Or the rose tints, which summer's twilight leaves   20
Upon the lofty glacier's virgin snow,
The blush of earth embracing with her heaven,—
Tinge thy celestial aspect, and make tame
The beauties of the sunbow which bends o'er thee.
Beautiful Spirit! in thy calm clear brow,
Wherein is glass'd serenity of soul,
Which of itself shows immortality,
I read that thou wilt pardon to a Son
Of Earth, whom the abstruser powers permit
At times to commune with them—if that he   30
Avail him of his spells—to call thee thus,
And gaze on thee a moment.
WITCH.   Son of Earth!
I know thee, and the powers which give thee power;
I know thee for a man of many thoughts,
And deeds of good and ill, extreme in both,
Fatal and fated in thy sufferings.
I have expected this—what wouldst thou with me?
MAN. To look upon thy beauty—nothing further.
The face of the Earth hath madden'd me, and I
Take refuge in her mysteries, and pierce   40
To the abodes of those who govern her—
But they can nothing aid me. I have sought
From them what they could not bestow, and now
I search no further.
WITCH.   What could be the quest
Which is not in the power of the most powerful,
The rulers of the invisible?
MAN.   A boon;
But why should I repeat it? 'twere in vain.
WITCH. I know not that; let thy lips utter it.
MAN. Well, though it torture me, 'tis but the same;
My pang shall find a voice. From my youth upwards   50
My spirit walk'd not with the souls of men,
Nor look'd upon the earth with human eyes;
The thirst of their ambition was not mine,
The aim of their existence was not mine;
My joys, my griefs, my passions, and my powers,
Made me a stranger; though I wore the form,
I had no sympathy with breathing flesh,
Nor midst the creatures of clay that girded me
Was there but one who——but of her anon.
I said, with men, and with the thoughts of men,   60

432

I held but slight communion; but instead,
My joy was in the Wilderness, to breathe
The difficult air of the iced mountain's top,
Where the birds dare not build, nor insect's wing
Flit o'er the herbless granite; or to plunge
Into the torrent, and to roll along
On the swift whirl of the new breaking wave
Of river-stream, or ocean, in their flow.
In these my early strength exulted; or
To follow through the night the moving moon,   70
The stars and their developement; or catch
The dazzling lightnings till my eyes grew dim;
Or to look, list'ning, on the scattered leaves,
While Autumn winds were at their evening song.
These were my pastimes, and to be alone;
For if the beings, of whom I was one,—
Hating to be so,—cross'd me in my path,
I felt myself degraded back to them,
And was all clay again. And then I dived,
In my lone wanderings, to the caves of death,   80
Searching its cause in its effect; and drew
From wither'd bones, and skulls, and heap'd up dust,
Conclusions most forbidden. Then I pass'd
The nights of years in sciences untaught,
Save in the old-time; and with time and toil,
And terrible ordeal, and such penance
As in itself hath power upon the air,
And spirits that do compass air and earth,
Space, and the peopled infinite, I made
Mine eyes familiar with Eternity,   90
Such as, before me, did the Magi, and
He who from out their fountain dwellings raised
Eros and Anteros, at Gadara,
As I do thee;—and with my knowledge grew
The thirst of knowledge, and the power and joy
Of this most bright intelligence, until——
WITCH. Proceed.
MAN.   Oh! I but thus prolonged my words,
Boasting these idle attributes, because
As I approach the core of my heart's grief—
But to my task. I have not named to thee   100
Father or mother, mistress, friend, or being,
With whom I wore the chain of human ties;
If I had such, they seem'd not such to me—
Yet there was one——
WITCH.   Spare not thyself—proceed.

433

MAN. She was like me in lineaments—her eyes,
  Her hair, her features, all, to the very tone
  Even of her voice, they said were like to mine;
  But soften'd all, and temper'd into beauty;
  She had the same lone thoughts and wanderings,
  The quest of hidden knowledge, and a mind   110
  To comprehend the universe: nor these
  Alone, but with them gentler powers than mine,
  Pity, and smiles, and tears—which I had not;
  And tenderness—but that I had for her;
  Humility—and that I never had.
  Her faults were mine—her virtues were her own—
  I loved her, and destroy'd her!
WITCH.   With thy hand?
MAN. Not with my hand, but heart—which broke her heart—
  It gazed on mine, and withered. I have shed
  Blood, but not hers—and yet her blood was shed—   120
  I saw—and could not staunch it.
WITCH.   And for this—
  A being of the race thou dost despise,
  The order which thine own would rise above,
  Mingling with us and ours, thou dost forgo
  The gifts of our great knowledge, and shrink'st back
  To recreant mortality——Away!
MAN. Daughter of Air! I tell thee, since that hour—
  But words are breath—look on me in my sleep,
  Or watch my watchings—Come and sit by me!
  My solitude is solitude no more,   130
  But peopled with the Furies;—I have gnash'd
  My teeth in darkness till returning morn,
  Then cursed myself till sunset;—I have pray'd
  For madness as a blessing—'tis denied me.
  I have affronted death—but in the war
  Of elements the waters shrunk from me,
  And fatal things pass'd harmless—the cold hand
  Of an all-pitiless demon held me back,
  Back by a single hair, which would not break.
  In phantasy, imagination, all   140
  The affluence of my soul—which one day was
  A Croesus in creation—I plunged deep,
  But, like an ebbing wave, it dash'd me back
  Into the gulf of my unfathom'd thought.
  I plunged amidst mankind—Forgetfulness
  I sought in all, save where 'tis to be found,
  And that I have to learn—my sciences,
  My long pursued and super-human art,

434

Is mortal here—I dwell in my despair—
And live—and live for ever.
WITCH.   It may be   150
That I can aid thee.
MAN.   To do this thy power
Must wake the dead, or lay me low with them.
Do so—in any shape—in any hour—
With any torture—so it be the last.
WITCH. That is not in my province; but if thou
Wilt swear obedience to my will, and do
My bidding, it may help thee to thy wishes.
MAN. I will not swear—Obey! and whom? the spirits
Whose presence I command, and be the slave
Of those who served me—Never!
WITCH.   Is this all?   160
Hast thou no gentler answer—Yet bethink thee,
And pause ere thou rejectest.
MAN.   I have said it.
WITCH. Enough!—I may retire then—say!
MAN.   Retire!
                              [*The* WITCH *disappears*
MAN. [*alone*]. We are the fools of time and terror: Days
Steal on us and steal from us; yet we live,
Loathing our life, and dreading still to die.
In all the days of this detested yoke—
This heaving burthen, this accursed breath—
This vital weight upon the struggling heart,
Which sinks with sorrow, or beats quick with pain,   170
Or joy that ends in agony or faintness—
In all the days of past and future, for
In life there is no present, we can number
How few—how less than few—wherein the soul
Forbears to pant for death, and yet draws back
As from a stream in winter, though the chill
Be but a moment's. I have one resource
Still in my science—I can call the dead,
And ask them what it is we dread to be:
The sternest answer can but be the Grave,   180
And that is nothing—if they answer not—
The buried Prophet answered to the Hag
Of Endor; and the Spartan Monarch drew
From the Byzantine maid's unsleeping spirit
An answer and his destiny—he slew
That which he loved, unknowing what he slew,
And died unpardon'd—though he call'd in aid
The Phyxian Jove, and in Phigalia roused

The Arcadian Evocators to compel
The indignant shadow to depose her wrath,   190
Or fix her term of vengeance—she replied
In words of dubious import, but fulfill'd.

If I had never lived, that which I love
Had still been living; had I never loved,
That which I love would still be beautiful—
Happy and giving happiness. What is she?
What is she now?—a sufferer for my sins—
A thing I dare not think upon—or nothing.
Within few hours I shall not call in vain—
Yet in this hour I dread the thing I dare: 200
Until this hour I never shrunk to gaze
On spirit, good or evil—now I tremble,
And feel a strange cold thaw upon my heart,
But I can act even what I most abhor,
And champion human fears.—The night approaches.   [*Exit*

SCENE III

The Summit of the Jungfrau Mountain

Enter FIRST DESTINY

The moon is rising broad, and round, and bright;
And here on snows, where never human foot
Of common mortal trod, we nightly tread,
And leave no traces; o'er the savage sea,
The glassy ocean of the mountain ice,
We skim its rugged breakers, which put on
The aspect of a tumbling tempest's foam,
Frozen in a moment—a dead whirlpool's image;
And this most steep fantastic pinnacle,
The fretwork of some earthquake—where the clouds   10
Pause to repose themselves in passing by—
Is sacred to our revels, or our vigils;
Here do I wait my sisters, on our way
To the Hall of Arimanes, for to-night
Is our great festival—'tis strange they come not.

A Voice without, singing
The Captive Usurper,
    Hurl'd down from the throne,
Lay buried in torpor,
    Forgotten and lone;

436

    I broke through his slumbers,   20
       I shivered his chain,
    I leagued him with numbers—
       He's Tyrant again!
With the blood of a million he'll answer my care,
With a nation's destruction—his flight and despair.

Second Voice, without
The ship sail'd on, the ship sail'd fast,
But I left not a sail, and I left not a mast;
There is not a plank of the hull or the deck,
And there is not a wretch to lament o'er his wreck;
Save one, whom I held, as he swam, by the hair,   30
And he was a subject well worthy my care;
A traitor on land, and a pirate at sea—
But I saved him to wreak further havoc for me!

FIRST DESTINY, *answering*
    The city lies sleeping;
      The morn, to deplore it,
    May dawn on it weeping:
      Sullenly, slowly,
    The black plague flew o'er it—
      Thousands lie lowly;
    Tens of thousands shall perish—   40
      The living shall fly from
    The sick they should cherish;
      But nothing can vanquish
    The touch that they die from.
      Sorrow and anguish,
    And evil and dread,
      Envelope a nation—
    The blest are the dead,
      Who see not the sight
    Of their own desolation.—   50
      This work of a night—
This wreck of a realm—this deed of my doing—
For ages I've done, and shall still be renewing!

Enter the SECOND *and* THIRD DESTINIES
THE THREE
Our hands contain the hearts of men,
    Our footsteps are their graves;
We only give to take again
    The spirits of our slaves!

437

FIRST DES. Welcome!—Where's Nemesis?
SECOND DES.   At some great work;
  But what I know not, for my hands were full.
THIRD DES. Behold she cometh.

Enter NEMESIS

FIRST DES.   Say, where hast thou been?—   60
  My sisters and thyself are slow to-night.
NEM. I was detain'd repairing shattered thrones,
  Marrying fools, restoring dynasties,
  Avenging men upon their enemies,
  And making them repent their own revenge;
  Goading the wise to madness; from the dull
  Shaping out oracles to rule the world
  Afresh, for they were waxing out of date,
  And mortals dared to ponder for themselves,
  To weigh kings in the balance, and to speak   70
  Of freedom, the forbidden fruit.—Away!
  We have outstaid the hour—mount we our clouds!   [*Exeunt*

SCENE IV

The Hall of Arimanes—Arimanes on his Throne, a Globe of Fire, surrounded
by the Spirits.

Hymn of the SPIRITS

Hail to our Master!—Prince of Earth and Air!—
  Who walks the clouds and waters—in his hand
The sceptre of the elements, which tear
  Themselves to chaos at his high command!
He breatheth—and a tempest shakes the sea;
  He speaketh—and the clouds reply in thunder;
He gazeth—from his glance the sunbeams flee;
  He moveth—earthquakes rend the world asunder.
Beneath his footsteps the volcanos rise;
  His shadow is the Pestilence; his path   10
The comets herald through the crackling skies;
  And planets turn to ashes at his wrath.
To him War offers daily sacrifice;
  To him Death pays his tribute; Life is his,
With all its infinite of agonies—
  And his the spirit of whatever is!

438

Enter the DESTINIES *and* NEMESIS

FIRST DES. Glory to Arimanes! on the earth
    His power increaseth—both my sisters did
    His bidding, nor did I neglect my duty!
SECOND DES. Glory to Arimanes! we who bow   20
    The necks of men, bow down before his throne!
THIRD DES. Glory to Arimanes!—we await
    His nod!
NEM.   Sovereign of Sovereigns! we are thine,
    And all that liveth, more or less, is ours,
    And most things wholly so; still to increase
    Our power increasing thine, demands our care,
    And we are vigilant—Thy late commands
    Have been fulfilled to the utmost.

Enter MANFRED

A SPIRIT.   What is here?
    A mortal!—Thou most rash and fatal wretch,
    Bow down and worship!
SECOND SPIRIT.   I do know the man—   30
    A Magian of great power, and fearful skill!
THIRD SPIRIT. Bow down and worship, slave!—What, know'st
        thou not
    Thine and our Sovereign?—Tremble, and obey!
ALL THE SPIRITS. Prostrate thyself, and thy condemned clay,
    Child of the Earth! or dread the worst.
MAN.   I know it;
    And yet ye see I kneel not.
FOURTH SPIRIT.   'Twill be taught thee.
MAN. 'Tis taught already;—many a night on the earth,
    On the bare ground, have I bow'd down my face,
    And strew'd my head with ashes; I have known
    The fulness of humiliation, for   40
    I sunk before my vain despair, and knelt
    To my own desolation.
FIFTH SPIRIT.   Dost thou dare
    Refuse to Arimanes on his throne
    What the whole earth accords, beholding not
    The terror of his Glory—Crouch! I say.
MAN. Bid *him* bow down to that which is above him,
    The overruling Infinite—the Maker
    Who made him not for worship—let him kneel,
    And we will kneel together.
THE SPIRITS.   Crush the worm!
    Tear him in pieces!—

439

FIRST DES.   Hence! Avaunt!—he's mine.   50
  Prince of the Powers invisible! This man
  Is of no common order, as his port
  And presence here denote; his sufferings
  Have been of an immortal nature, like
  Our own; his knowledge and his powers and will,
  As far as is compatible with clay,
  Which clogs the etherial essence, have been such
  As clay hath seldom borne; his aspirations
  Have been beyond the dwellers of the earth,
  And they have only taught him what we know—   60
  That knowledge is not happiness, and science
  But an exchange of ignorance for that
  Which is another kind of ignorance.
  This is not all—the passions, attributes
  Of earth and heaven, from which no power, nor being,
  Nor breath from the worm upwards is exempt,
  Have pierced his heart; and in their consequence
  Made him a thing, which I, who pity not,
  Yet pardon those who pity. He is mine,
  And thine, it may be—be it so, or not,   70
  No other Spirit in this region hath
  A soul like his—or power upon his soul.
NEM. What doth he here then?
FIRST DES.   Let *him* answer that.
MAN. Ye know what I have known; and without power
  I could not be amongst ye: but there are
  Powers deeper still beyond—I come in quest
  Of such, to answer unto what I seek.
NEM. What wouldst *thou*?
MAN.   Thou can'st not reply to me.
  Call up the dead—my question is for them.
NEM. Great Arimanes, doth thy will avouch   80
  The wishes of this mortal?
ARI.   Yea.
NEM.   Whom wouldst thou
  Uncharnel?
MAN.   One without a tomb—call up
  Astarte.

NEMESIS.
Shadow! or Spirit!
  Whatever thou art,
Which still doth inherit
  The whole or a part
Of the form of thy birth,
  Of the mould of thy clay,

440

Which returned to the earth,   90
   Re-appear to the day!
Bear what thou borest,
   The heart and the form,
And the aspect thou worest
   Redeem from the worm.
Appear!—Appear!—Appear!
Who sent thee there requires thee here!

[*The Phantom of* ASTARTE *rises and stands in the midst*]

MAN. Can this be death? there's bloom upon her cheek;
  But now I see it is no living hue,
  But a strange hectic—like the unnatural red   100
  Which Autumn plants upon the perish'd leaf.
  It is the same! Oh, God! that I should dread
  To look upon the same—Astarte!—No,
  I cannot speak to her—but bid her speak—
  Forgive me or condemn me.

NEMESIS.
By the power which hath broken
   The grave which enthrall'd thee,
Speak to him who hath spoken,
   Or those who have call'd thee!

MAN.   She is silent,   110
  And in that silence I am more than answered.
NEM. My power extends no further. Prince of air!
  It rests with thee alone—command her voice,
ARI. Spirit—obey this sceptre!
NEM.   Silent still!
  She is not of our order, but belongs
  To the other powers. Mortal! thy quest is vain,
  And we are baffled also.
MAN.   Hear me, hear me—
  Astarte! my beloved! speak to me:
  I have so much endured—so much endure—
  Look on me! the grave hath not changed thee more   120
  Than I am changed for thee. Thou lovedst me
  Too much, as I loved thee: we were not made
  To torture thus each other, though it were
  The deadliest sin to love as we have loved.
  Say that thou loath'st me not—that I do bear
  This punishment for both—that thou wilt be
  One of the blessed—and that I shall die,
  For hitherto all hateful things conspire
  To bind me in existence—in a life

Which makes me shrink from immortality—   130
A future like the past. I cannot rest.
I know not what I ask, nor what I seek:
I feel but what thou art—and what I am;
And I would hear yet once before I perish
The voice which was my music—Speak to me!
For I have call'd on thee in the still night,
Startled the slumbering birds from the hush'd boughs,
And woke the mountain wolves, and made the caves
Acquainted with thy vainly echoed name,
Which answered me—many things answered me—   140
Spirits and men—but thou wert silent all.
Yet speak to me! I have outwatch'd the stars,
And gazed o'er heaven in vain in search of thee.
Speak to me! I have wandered o'er the earth
And never found thy likeness—Speak to me!
Look on the fiends around—they feel for me:
I fear them not, and feel for thee alone—
Speak to me! though it be in wrath;—but say—
I reck not what—but let me hear thee once—
This once—once more!

PHANTOM OF ASTARTE. Manfred!
MAN.   Say on, say on—   150
I live but in the sound—it is thy voice!
PHAN. Manfred! To-morrow ends thine earthly ills.
Farewell!
MAN.   Yet one word more—am I forgiven?
PHAN. Farewell!
MAN.   Say, shall we meet again?
PHAN.   Farewell!
MAN. One word for mercy! Say, thou lovest me.
PHAN. Manfred!

                    [*The Spirit of* ASTARTE *disappears*
NEM.   She's gone, and will not be recall'd;
Her words will be fulfill'd. Return to the earth.
A SPIRIT. He is convulsed—This is to be a mortal
And seek the things beyond mortality.
ANOTHER SPIRIT. Yet, see, he mastereth himself, and makes   160
His torture tributary to his will.
Had he been one of us, he would have made
An awful spirit.
NEM.   Hast thou further question
Of our great Sovereign, or his worshippers?
MAN. None.
NEM.   Then for a time farewell.
MAN.   We meet then—

                    442

Where? On the earth?
NEM.   That will be seen hereafter.
MAN. Even as thou wilt: and for the grace accorded
  I now depart a debtor. Fare ye well!

                                        [*Exit* MANFRED

                    [*Scene closes*]

              END OF ACT SECOND

                       Act III

                       SCENE I
            A Hall in the Castle of Manfred

                 MANFRED *and* HERMAN

MAN. What is the hour?
HER.   It wants but one till sunset,
  And promises a lovely twilight.
MAN.   Say,
  Are all things so disposed of in the tower
  As I directed?
HER.   All, my lord, are ready;
  Here is the key and casket.
MAN.   It is well:
  Thou mayst retire.   [*Exit* HERMAN
MAN. [*alone*].   There is a calm upon me—
  Inexplicable stillness! which till now
  Did not belong to what I knew of life.
  If that I did not know philosophy
  To be of all our vanities the motliest,   10
  The merest word that ever fool'd the ear
  From out the schoolman's jargon, I should deem
  The golden secret, the sought 'Kalon', found,
  And seated in my soul. It will not last,
  But it is well to have known it, though but once:
  It hath enlarged my thoughts with a new sense,
  And I within my tablets would note down
  That there is such a feeling. Who is there?

                 Re-enter HERMAN

HER. My lord, the abbot of St Maurice craves
  To greet your presence.

             Enter the ABBOT OF ST MAURICE

ABBOT.   Peace be with Count Manfred!   20

                       443

MAN. Thanks, holy father! welcome to these walls;
 Thy presence honours them, and blesseth those
 Who dwell within them.
ABBOT.   Would it were so, Count!—
 But I would fain confer with thee alone.
MAN. Herman, retire. What would my reverend guest?

              [*Exit* HERMAN

ABBOT. Thus, without prelude:—Age and zeal, my office,
 And good intent, must plead my privilege;
 Our near, though not acquainted neighbourhood,
 May also be my herald. Rumours strange,
 And of unholy nature, are abroad,   30
 And busy with thy name; a noble name
 For centuries; may he who bears it now
 Transmit it unimpair'd!
MAN.   Proceed,—I listen.
ABBOT. 'Tis said thou holdest converse with the things
 Which are forbidden to the search of man;
 That with the dwellers of the dark abodes,
 The many evil and unheavenly spirits
 Which walk the valley of the shade of death,
 Thou communest. I know that with mankind,
 Thy fellows in creation, thou dost rarely   40
 Exchange thy thoughts, and that thy solitude
 Is as an anchorite's, were it but holy.
MAN. And what are they who do avouch these things?
ABBOT. My pious brethren—the scared peasantry—
 Even thy own vassals—who do look on thee
 With most unquiet eyes. Thy life's in peril.
MAN. Take it.
ABBOT.   I come to save, and not destroy—
 I would not pry into thy secret soul;
 But if these things be sooth, there still is time
 For penitence and pity: reconcile thee   50
 With the true church, and through the church to heaven.
MAN. I hear thee. This is my reply; whate'er
 I may have been, or am, doth rest between
 Heaven and myself.—I shall not choose a mortal
 To be my mediator. Have I sinn'd
 Against your ordinances? prove and punish!
ABBOT. My son! I did not speak of punishment,
 But penitence and pardon;—with thyself
 The choice of such remains—and for the last,
 Our institutions and our strong belief   60
 Have given me power to smooth the path from sin
 To higher hope and better thoughts; the first

444

I leave to heaven—'Vengeance is mine alone!'
So saith the Lord, and with all humbleness
His servant echoes back the awful word.
MAN. Old man! there is no power in holy men,
Nor charm in prayer—nor purifying form
Of penitence—nor outward look—nor fast—
Nor agony—nor, greater than all these,
The innate tortures of that deep despair,   70
Which is remorse without the fear of hell,
But all in all sufficient to itself
Would make a hell of heaven—can exorcise
From out the unbounded spirit, the quick sense
Of its own sins, wrongs, sufferance, and revenge
Upon itself; there is no future pang
Can deal that justice on the self-condemn'd
He deals on his own soul.
ABBOT.   All this is well;
For this will pass away, and be succeeded
By an auspicious hope, which shall look up   80
With calm assurance to that blessed place,
Which all who seek may win, whatever be
Their earthly errors, so they be atoned:
And the commencement of atonement is
The sense of its necessity.—Say on—
And all our church can teach thee shall be taught;
And all we can absolve thee, shall be pardon'd.
MAN. When Rome's sixth Emperor was near his last,
The victim of a self-inflicted wound,
To shun the torments of a public death   90
From senates once his slaves, a certain soldier,
With show of loyal pity, would have staunch'd
The gushing throat with his officious robe;
The dying Roman thrust him back and said—
Some empire still in his expiring glance,
'It is too late—is this fidelity?'
ABBOT. And what of this?
MAN.   I answer with the Roman—
'It is too late!'
ABBOT.   It never can be so,
To reconcile thyself with thy own soul,
And thy own soul with heaven. Hast thou no hope?   100
'Tis strange—even those who do despair above,
Yet shape themselves some phantasy on earth,
To which frail twig they cling, like drowning men.
MAN. Ay—father! I have had those earthly visions
And noble aspirations in my youth,

To make my own the mind of other men,
The enlightener of nations; and to rise
I knew not whither—it might be to fall;
But fall, even as the mountain-cataract,
Which having leapt from its more dazzling height,   110
Even in the foaming strength of its abyss,
(Which casts up misty columns that become
Clouds raining from the re-ascended skies)
Lies low but mighty still.—But this is past,
My thoughts mistook themselves.

ABBOT.   And wherefore so?

MAN. I could not tame my nature down; for he
Must serve who fain would sway—and soothe—and sue—
And watch all time—and pry into all place—
And be a living lie—who would become
A mighty thing amongst the mean, and such   120
The mass are; I disdained to mingle with
A herd, though to be leader—and of wolves.
The lion is alone, and so am I.

ABBOT. And why not live and act with other men?

MAN. Because my nature was averse from life;
And yet not cruel; for I would not make,
But find a desolation:—Like the wind,
The red-hot breath of the most lone Simoom,
Which dwells but in the desert, and sweeps o'er
The barren sands which bear no shrubs to blast,   130
And revels o'er their wild and arid waves,
And seeketh not, so that it is not sought,
But being met is deadly; such hath been
The course of my existence; but there came
Things in my path which are no more.

ABBOT.   Alas!
I 'gin to fear that thou art past all aid
From me and from my calling; yet so young,
I still would——

MAN.   Look on me! there is an order
Of mortals on the earth, who do become
Old in their youth, and die ere middle age,   140
Without the violence of warlike death;
Some perishing of pleasure—some of study—
Some worn with toil—some of mere weariness—
Some of disease—and some insanity—
And some of withered, or of broken hearts;
For this last is a malady which slays
More than are numbered in the lists of Fate,
Taking all shapes, and bearing many names.

446

Look upon me! for even of all these things
Have I partaken; and of all these things,   150
One were enough; then wonder not that I
Am what I am, but that I ever was,
Or, having been, that I am still on earth.
ABBOT. Yet, hear me still——
MAN.   Old man! I do respect
Thine order, and revere thine years; I deem
Thy purpose pious, but it is in vain:
Think me not churlish; I would spare thyself,
Far more than me, in shunning at this time
All further colloquy—and so—farewell.   [*Exit* MANFRED
ABBOT. This should have been a noble creature: he   160
Hath all the energy which would have made
A goodly frame of glorious elements,
Had they been wisely mingled; as it is,
It is an awful chaos—light and darkness—
And mind and dust—and passions and pure thoughts,
Mix'd, and contending without end or order,
All dormant or destructive: he will perish,
And yet he must not; I will try once more,
For such are worth redemption; and my duty
Is to dare all things for a righteous end.   170
I'll follow him—but cautiously, though surely.   [*Exit* ABBOT

SCENE II
Another Chamber

MANFRED *and* HERMAN.

HER. My Lord, you bade me wait on you at sunset:
He sinks behind the mountain.
MAN.   -   Doth he so?
I will look on him.
                        [MANFRED *advances to the Window of the Hall*
                        Glorious Orb! the idol
Of early nature, and the vigorous race
Of undiseased mankind, the giant sons
Of the embrace of angels, with a sex
More beautiful than they, which did draw down
The erring spirits who can ne'er return.—
Most glorious orb! that wert a worship, ere
The mystery of thy making was reveal'd!   10
Thou earliest minister of the Almighty,
Which gladden'd, on their mountain tops, the hearts
Of the Chaldean shepherds, till they pour'd
Themselves in orisons! Thou material God!

447

And representative of the Unknown—
Who chose thee for his shadow! Thou chief star!
Centre of many stars! which mak'st our earth
Endurable, and temperest the hues
And hearts of all who walk within thy rays!
Sire of the seasons! Monarch of the climes,   20
And those who dwell in them! for near or far,
Our inborn spirits have a tint of thee,
Even as our outward aspects;—thou dost rise,
And shine, and set in glory. Fare thee well!
I ne'er shall see thee more. As my first glance
Of love and wonder was for thee, then take
My latest look: thou wilt not beam on one
To whom the gifts of life and warmth have been
Of a more fatal nature. He is gone:
I follow.   30
                                             [*Exit* MANFRED

SCENE III

The Mountains.—The Castle of Manfred at some distance.—A Terrace before
a Tower.—Time, Twilight.

HERMAN, MANUEL, *and other Dependents of* MANFRED.

HER. 'Tis strange enough; night after night, for years,
     He hath pursued long vigils in this tower,
     Without a witness. I have been within it,—
     So have we all been oft-times; but from it,
     Or its contents, it were impossible
     To draw conclusions absolute, of aught
     His studies tend to. To be sure, there is
     One chamber where none enter; I would give
     The fee of what I have to come these three years,
     To pore upon its mysteries.
MANUEL.   'Twere dangerous;   10
     Content thyself with what thou knowest already.
HER. Ah! Manuel! thou art elderly and wise,
     And couldst say much; thou hast dwelt within the castle—
     How many years is't?
MANUEL.   Ere Count Manfred's birth,
     I served his father, whom he nought resembles.
HER. There be more sons in like predicament.
     But wherein do they differ?
MANUEL.   I speak not
     Of features or of form, but mind and habits:
     Count Sigismund was proud,—but gay and free,—
     A warrior and a reveller; he dwelt not   20

448

With books and solitude, nor made the night
A gloomy vigil, but a festal time,
Merrier than day; he did not walk the rocks
And forests like a wolf, nor turn aside
From men and their delights.

HER.   Beshrew the hour,
But those were jocund times! I would that such
Would visit the old walls again; they look
As if they had forgotten them.

MANUEL.   These walls
Must change their chieftain first. Oh! I have seen
Some strange things in them, Herman.

HER.   Come, be friendly;   30
Relate me some to while away our watch:
I've heard thee darkly speak of an event
Which happened hereabouts, by this same tower.

MANUEL. That was a night indeed; I do remember
'Twas twilight, as it may be now, and such
Another evening;—yon red cloud, which rests
On Eigher's pinnacle, so rested then,—
So like that it might be the same; the wind
Was faint and gusty, and the mountain snows
Began to glitter with the climbing moon;   40
Count Manfred was, as now, within his tower,—
How occupied, we knew not, but with him
The sole companion of his wanderings
And watchings—her, whom of all earthly things
That lived, the only thing he seem'd to love,—
As he, indeed, by blood was bound to do,
The lady Astarte, his——
                         Hush! who comes here?

Enter the ABBOT

ABBOT. Where is your master?

HER.   Yonder, in the tower.

ABBOT. I must speak with him.

MANUEL.   'Tis impossible;
He is most private, and must not be thus   50
Intruded on.

ABBOT.   Upon myself I take
The forfeit of my fault, if fault there be—
But I must see him.

HER.   Thou hast seen him once
This eve already.

ABBOT.   Sirrah! I command thee,
Knock, and apprize the Count of my approach.

HER. We dare not.
ABBOT.   Then it seems I must be herald
  Of my own purpose.
MANUEL.   Reverend father, stop—
  I pray you pause.
ABBOT.   Why so?
MANUEL.   But step this way,
  And I will tell you further.

                                        [*Exeunt*

SCENE IV

Interior of the Tower.

MANFRED *alone.*

MAN. The stars are forth, the moon above the tops
  Of the snow-shining mountains.—Beautiful!
  I linger yet with Nature, for the night
  Hath been to me a more familiar face
  Than that of man; and in her starry shade
  Of dim and solitary loveliness,
  I learn'd the language of another world.
  I do remember me, that in my youth,
  When I was wandering,—upon such a night
  I stood within the Colosseum's wall,   10
  'Midst the chief relics of almighty Rome;
  The trees which grew along the broken arches
  Waved dark in the blue midnight, and the stars
  Shone through the rents of ruin; from afar
  The watchdog bayed beyond the Tiber; and
  More near from out the Caesars' palace came
  The owl's long cry, and, interruptedly,
  Of distant sentinels the fitful song
  Begun and died upon the gentle wind.
  Some cypresses beyond the time-worn breach   20
  Appeared to skirt the horizon, yet they stood
  Within a bowshot—where the Caesars dwelt,
  And dwell the tuneless birds of night; amidst
  A grove which springs through levell'd battlements,
  And twines its roots with the imperial hearths,
  Ivy usurps the laurel's place of growth;—
  But the gladiators' bloody Circus stands,
  A noble wreck in ruinous perfection!
  While Caesar's chambers, and the Augustan halls,
  Grovel on earth in indistinct decay.—   30
  And thou didst shine, thou rolling moon, upon
  All this, and cast a wide and tender light,

Which soften'd down the hoar austerity
Of rugged desolation, and fill'd up,
As 'twere, anew, the gaps of centuries;
Leaving that beautiful which still was so,
And making that which was not, till the place
Became religion, and the heart ran o'er
With silent worship of the great of old!—
The dead, but sceptred sovereigns, who still rule   40
Our spirits from their urns.—
                   'Twas such a night!
'Tis strange that I recall it at this time;
But I have found our thoughts take wildest flight
Even at the moment when they should array
Themselves in pensive order.

Enter the ABBOT

ABBOT.   My good Lord!
I crave a second grace for this approach;
But yet let not my humble zeal offend
By its abruptness—all it hath of ill
Recoils on me; its good in the effect
May light upon your head—could I say *heart*—   50
Could I touch *that*, with words or prayers, I should
Recall a noble spirit which hath wandered,
But is not yet all lost.
MAN.   Thou know'st me not;
My days are numbered, and my deeds recorded:
Retire, or 'twill be dangerous—Away!
ABBOT. Thou dost not mean to menace me?
MAN.   Not I;
I simply tell thee peril is at hand,
And would preserve thee.
ABBOT.   What dost mean?
MAN.   Look there!
What dost thou see?
ABBOT.   Nothing.
MAN.   Look there, I say,   60
And steadfastly;—now tell me what thou seest?
ABBOT. That which should shake me,—but I fear it not—
I see a dusk and awful figure rise
Like an infernal god from out the earth;
His face wrapt in a mantle, and his form
Robed as with angry clouds; he stands between
Thyself and me—but I do fear him not.
MAN. Thou hast no cause—he shall not harm thee—but
His sight may shock thine old limbs into palsy.
I say to thee—Retire!

ABBOT.   And, I reply—
  Never—till I have battled with this fiend—   70
  What doth he here?
MAN.   Why—ay—what doth he here?
  I did not send for him,—he is unbidden.
ABBOT. Alas! lost mortal! what with guests like these
  Hast thou to do? I tremble for thy sake;
  Why doth he gaze on thee, and thou on him?
  Ah! he unveils his aspect; on his brow
  The thunder-scars are graven; from his eye
  Glares forth the immortality of hell—
  Avaunt!——
MAN.   Pronounce—what is thy mission?
SPIRIT.   Come!
ABBOT. What art thou, unknown being? answer!—speak!   80
SPIRIT. The genius of this mortal.—Come! 'tis time.
MAN. I am prepared for all things, but deny
  The power which summons me. Who sent thee here?
SPIRIT. Thou'lt know anon—Come! come!
MAN.   I have commanded
  Things of an essence greater far than thine,
  And striven with thy masters. Get thee hence!
SPIRIT. Mortal! thine hour is come—Away! I say.
MAN. I knew, and know my hour is come, but not
  To render up my soul to such as thee:
  Away! I'll die as I have lived—alone.   90
SPIRIT. Then I must summon up my brethren.—Rise!
                              [Other Spirits rise up
ABBOT. Avaunt! ye evil ones!—Avaunt! I say,—
  Ye have no power where piety hath power,
  And I do charge ye in the name——
SPIRIT.   Old man!
  We know ourselves, our mission, and thine order;
  Waste not thy holy words on idle uses,
  It were in vain; this man is forfeited.
  Once more I summon him—Away! away!
MAN. I do defy ye,—though I feel my soul
  Is ebbing from me, yet I do defy ye;   100
  Nor will I hence, while I have earthly breath
  To breathe my scorn upon ye—earthly strength
  To wrestle, though with spirits; what ye take
  Shall be ta'en limb by limb.
SPIRIT.   Reluctant mortal!
  Is this the Magian who would so pervade
  The world invisible, and make himself
  Almost our equal?—Can it be that thou

Art thus in love with life? the very life
Which made thee wretched!
MAN.   Thou false fiend, thou liest!
My life is in its last hour,—*that* I know,   110
Nor would redeem a moment of that hour;
I do not combat against death, but thee
And thy surrounding angels; my past power
Was purchased by no compact with thy crew,
But by superior science—penance—daring—
And length of watching—strength of mind—and skill
In knowledge of our fathers—when the earth
Saw men and spirits walking side by side,
And gave ye no supremacy: I stand
Upon my strength—I do defy—deny—   120
Spurn back, and scorn ye!—
SPIRIT.   But thy many crimes
Have made thee——
MAN.   What are they to such as thee?
Must crimes be punish'd but by other crimes,
And greater criminals?—Back to thy hell!
Thou hast no power upon me, *that* I feel;
Thou never shalt possess me, *that* I know:
What I have done is done; I bear within
A torture which could nothing gain from thine:
The mind which is immortal makes itself
Requital for its good or evil thoughts—   130
Is its own origin of ill and end—
And its own place and time—its innate sense,
When stripp'd of this mortality, derives
No colour from the fleeting things without,
But is absorb'd in sufferance or in joy,
Born from the knowledge of its own desert.
Thou didst not tempt me, and thou couldst not tempt me;
I have not been thy dupe, nor am thy prey—
But was my own destroyer, and will be
My own hereafter.—Back, ye baffled fiends!   140
The hand of death is on me—but not yours!
                              [*The Demons disappear*
ABBOT. Alas! how pale thou art—thy lips are white—
And thy breast heaves—and in thy gasping throat
The accents rattle—Give thy prayers to heaven—
Pray—albeit but in thought,—but die not thus.
MAN. 'Tis over—my dull eyes can fix thee not;
But all things swim around me, and the earth
Heaves as it were beneath me. Fare thee well—
Give me thy hand.

ABBOT.   Cold—cold—even to the heart—
  But yet one prayer—alas! how fares it with thee?—   150
MAN. Old man! 'tis not so difficult to die.

                                          [MANFRED *expires*

ABBOT. He's gone—his soul hath ta'en its earthless flight—
  Whither? I dread to think—but he is gone.

CHARLES WOLFE
1791–1823

171   *The Burial of Sir John Moore*

I

Not a drum was heard, not a funeral note,
    As his corse to the rampart we hurried;
Not a soldier discharged his farewell shot
    O'er the grave where our hero we buried.

II

We buried him darkly at dead of night,
    The sods with our bayonets turning;
By the struggling moonbeam's misty light,
    And the lantern dimly burning.

III

No useless coffin enclosed his breast,
    Not in sheet or in shroud we wound him;   10
But he lay like a warrior taking his rest,
    With his martial cloak around him.

IV

Few and short were the prayers we said,
    And we spoke not a word of sorrow;
But we steadfastly gazed on the face that was dead,
    And we bitterly thought of the morrow.

V

We thought, as we hollowed his narrow bed,
    And smoothed down his lonely pillow,
That the foe and the stranger would tread o'er his head,
    And we far away on the billow!   20

VI

Lightly they'll talk of the spirit that's gone,
    And o'er his cold ashes upbraid him,—
But little he'll reck, if they let him sleep on
    In the grave where a Briton has laid him.

VII

But half of our heavy task was done,
    When the clock struck the hour for retiring;
And we heard the distant and random gun
    That the foe was sullenly firing.

VIII

Slowly and sadly we laid him down,
    From the field of his fame fresh and gory;   30
We carved not a line, and we raised not a stone—
    But we left him alone with his glory!

JAMES HOGG
1770–1835

172   *A Witch's Chant*

THOU art weary, weary, weary,
    Thou art weary and far away,
Hear me, gentle spirit, hear me,
    Come before the dawn of day.

I hear a small voice from the hill,
The vapour is deadly, pale, and still—
A murmuring sough is on the wood,
And the witching star is red as blood.

And in the cleft of heaven I scan
The giant form of a naked man,   10
His eye is like the burning brand,
And he holds a sword in his right hand.

All is not well. By dint of spell,
Somewhere between the heaven and hell

455

There is this night a wild deray,
The spirits have wander'd from their way.

The purple drops shall tinge the moon
As she wanders through the midnight noon;
And the dawning heaven shall all be red
With blood by guilty angels shed.   20

Be as it will, I have the skill
To work by good or work by ill;
Then here's for pain, and here's for thrall,
And here's for conscience, worst of all.

Another chant, and then, and then,
Spirits shall come or Christian men—
Come from the earth, the air, or the sea,
Great Gil-Moules, I cry to thee!

Sleep'st thou, wakest thou, lord of the wind,
Mount thy steeds and gallop them blind;   30
And the long-tailed fiery dragon outfly,
The rocket of heaven, the bomb of the sky.

Over the dog-star, over the wain,
Over the cloud, and the rainbow's mane,
Over the mountain, and over the sea,
    Haste—haste—haste to me!

Then here's for trouble, and here's for smart,
And here's for the pang that seeks the heart;
Here's for madness, and here's for thrall,
And here's for conscience, the worst of all!   40

[1818]

THOMAS MOORE

173   from *The Fudge Family in Paris*
Letter 1

from Miss Biddy Fudge to Miss Dorothy ——, of Clonkilty, in Ireland

Amiens

DEAR DOLL, while the tails of our horses are plaiting,
   The trunks tying on, and Papa, at the door,
Into very bad French is, as usual, translating
   His English resolve not to give a *sou* more,
I sit down to write you a line—only think!—
A letter from France, with French pens and French ink,
How delightful! though, would you believe it, my dear?
I have seen nothing yet *very* wonderful here;
No adventure, no sentiment, far as we've come,
But the corn-fields and trees quite as dull as at home;   10
And *but* for the post-boy, his boots and his queue,
I might *just* as well be at Clonkilty with you!
In vain, at DESSEIN'S, did I take from my trunk
That divine fellow, STERNE, and fall reading 'The Monk';
In vain did I think of his charming Dead Ass,
And remember the crust and the wallet—alas!
No monks can be had now for love or for money,
(All owing, Pa says, to that infidel BONEY;)
And, though *one* little Neddy we saw in our drive
Out of classical Nampont, the beast was alive!   20

  .   .   .   .

Our party consists (in a neat Calais job)
Of Papa and myself, Mr. CONNOR and BOB.
You remember how sheepish BOB looked at Kilrandy,
But, Lord! he's quite altered—they've made him a Dandy;
A thing, you know, whiskered, great-coated, and laced,
Like an hour-glass, exceedingly small in the waist:
Quite a new sort of creatures, unknown yet to scholars,
With heads, so immovably stuck in shirt collars,
That seats, like our music-stools, soon must be found them,
To twirl, when the creatures may wish to look round them.   30

In short, dear, 'a Dandy' describes what I mean,
And BOB's far the best of the *genus* I've seen:

An improving young man, fond of learning, ambitious,
And goes now to Paris to study French dishes,
Whose names—think, how quick! he already knows pat,
À la braise, petits pâtés, and—what d'ye call that
They inflict on potatoes!—oh! *maître d'hôtel*—
I assure you, dear DOLLY, he knows them as well
As if nothing else all his life he had eat,
Though a bit of them BOBBY has never touched yet;   40
But just knows the names of French dishes and cooks,
As dear Pa knows the titles of authors and books.

As to Pa, what d'ye think! mind, it's all *entre nous*,
But you know, love, I never keep secrets from you—
Why, he's writing a book—what! a tale? a romance?
No, ye Gods, would it were! but his Travels in France;
At the special desire (he let out t'other day)
Of his great friend and patron, my Lord C[A]STL[E]R[EA]GH,
Who said, 'My dear FUDGE'—I forget th' exact words,
And, it's strange, no one ever remembers my Lord's;   50
But 'twas something to say that, as all must allow
A good orthodox work is much wanting just now,
To expound to the world the new—thingummie—science,
Found out by the—what's-its-name—Holy Alliance,
And to prove to mankind that their rights are but folly,
Their freedom a joke, (which it *is*, you know, DOLLY).
'There's none,' said his Lordship, 'if I may be judge,
Half so fit for this great undertaking as FUDGE!'

The matter's soon settled—Pa flies to *the Row*
(The *first* stage your tourists now usually go),   60
Settles all for his quarto—advertisements, praises—
Starts post from the door, with his tablets—French phrases—
'SCOTT's Visit,' of course—in short, everything *he* has
An author can want, except words, and ideas:—
And, lo! the first thing, in the spring of the year,
Is PHIL. FUDGE at the front of a Quarto, my dear!

But, bless me, my paper's near out, so I'd better
Draw fast to a close: this exceeding long letter
You owe to a *déjeuner à la fourchette*,
Which BOBBY *would* have, and is hard at it yet.—   70
What's next? oh, the tutor, the last of the party,

Young CONNOR:—they say he's so like BONAPARTE,
His nose and his chin—which Papa rather dreads,
As the Bourbons, you know, are suppressing all heads
That resemble old NAP's, and who knows but their honours
May think, in their fright, of suppressing poor CONNOR's?
Au reste (as we say), the young lad's well enough,
Only talks much of Athens, Rome, virtue, and stuff;
A third cousin of ours, by the way—poor as Job
   (Though of royal descent by the side of Mamma),   80
And for charity made private tutor to BOB;—
   Entre nous, too, a Papist—how lib'ral of Pa!

This is all, dear,—forgive me for breaking off thus,
But BOB's *déjeuner*'s done, and Papa's in a fuss.

                                        B.F.

  P.S.
How provoking of Pa! he will not let me stop
Just to run in and rummage some milliner's shop;
And my *début* in Paris, I blush to think on it,
Must now, DOLL, be made in a hideous low bonnet.
But Paris, dear Paris!—oh, *there* will be joy,
And romance, and high bonnets, and Madame Le ROI!   90

GEORGE GORDON, LORD BYRON

from *Beppo*
A Venetian Story

ROSALIND. Farewell, Monsieur Traveller: Look you lisp, and wear strange
   suits; disable all the benefits of your own country; be out of love with your
   Nativity, and almost chide God for making you that countenance you are;
   or I will scarce think that you have swam in a GONDOLA.

As You Like It, IV. i

Annotation of the Commentators

That is, been at *Venice*, which was much visited by the young English
gentlemen of those times, and was then what *Paris* is *now*—the seat of all
dissoluteness. S.A.

1

'TIS known, at least it should be, that throughout
   All countries of the Catholic persuasion,
Some weeks before Shrove Tuesday comes about,
   The people take their fill of recreation,
And buy repentance, ere they grow devout,
   However high their rank, or low their station,
With fiddling, feasting, dancing, drinking, masquing,
And other things which may be had for asking.

2

The moment night with dusky mantle covers
   The skies (and the more duskily the better),   10
The time less liked by husbands than by lovers
   Begins, and prudery flings aside her fetter;
And gaiety on restless tiptoe hovers,
   Giggling with all the gallants who beset her;
And there are songs and quavers, roaring, humming,
Guitars, and every other sort of strumming.

3

And there are dresses splendid, but fantastical,
   Masks of all times and nations, Turks and Jews,
And harlequins and clowns, with feats gymnastical,
   Greeks, Romans, Yankee-doodles, and Hindoos;   20
All kinds of dress, except the ecclesiastical,
   All people, as their fancies hit, may choose,
But no one in these parts may quiz the clergy,
Therefore take heed, ye Freethinkers! I charge ye.

4

You'd better walk about begirt with briars,
    Instead of coat and smallclothes, than put on
A single stitch reflecting upon friars,
    Although you swore it only was in fun;
They'd haul you o'er the coals, and stir the fires
    Of Phlegethon with every mother's son,   30
Nor say one mass to cool the cauldron's bubble
That boiled your bones, unless you paid them double.

5

But saving this, you may put on whate'er
    You like by way of doublet, cape, or cloak,
Such as in Monmouth-street, or in Rag Fair,
    Would rig you out in seriousness or joke;
And even in Italy such places are
    With prettier names in softer accents spoke,
For, bating Covent Garden, I can hit on
No place that's called 'Piazza' in Great Britain.   40

6

This feast is named the Carnival, which being
    Interpreted, implies 'farewell to flesh':
So call'd, because the name and thing agreeing,
    Through Lent they live on fish both salt and fresh.
But why they usher Lent with so much glee in,
    Is more than I can tell, although I guess
'Tis as we take a glass with friends at parting,
In the stage-coach or packet, just at starting.

7

And thus they bid farewell to carnal dishes,
    And solid meats, and highly spic'd ragouts,   50
To live for forty days on ill-dress'd fishes,
    Because they have no sauces to their stews,
A thing which causes many 'poohs' and 'pishes',
    And several oaths (which would not suit the Muse),
From travellers accustom'd from a boy
To eat their salmon, at the least, with soy;

8

And therefore humbly I would recommend
    'The curious in fish-sauce', before they cross
The sea, to bid their cook, or wife, or friend,
    Walk or ride to the Strand, and buy in gross   60

(Or if set out beforehand, these may send
  By any means least liable to loss),
Ketchup, Soy, Chili-vinegar, and Harvey,
Or, by the Lord! a Lent will well nigh starve ye;

9

That is to say, if your religion's Roman,
  And you at Rome would do as Romans do,
According to the proverb,—although no man,
  If foreign, is oblig'd to fast; and you,
If protestant, or sickly, or a woman,
  Would rather dine in sin on a ragout—   70
Dine, and be d—d! I don't mean to be coarse,
But that's the penalty, to say no worse.

10

Of all the places where the Carnival
  Was most facetious in the days of yore,
For dance, and song, and serenade, and ball,
  And masque, and mime, and mystery, and more
Than I have time to tell now, or at all,
  Venice the bell from every city bore,
And at the moment when I fix my story,
That sea-born city was in all her glory.   80

11

They've pretty faces yet, those same Venetians,
  Black eyes, arch'd brows, and sweet expressions still,
Such as of old were copied from the Grecians,
  In ancient arts by moderns mimick'd ill;
And like so many Venuses of Titian's
  (The best's at Florence—see it, if ye will)
They look when leaning over the balcony,
Or stepp'd from out a picture by Giorgione,

12

Whose tints are truth and beauty at their best;
  And when you to Manfrini's palace go,   90
That picture (howsoever fine the rest)
  Is loveliest to my mind of all the show;
It may perhaps be also to *your* zest,
  And that's the cause I rhyme upon it so,
'Tis but a portrait of his son, and wife,
And self; but *such* a woman! love in life!

13

Love in full life and length, not love ideal,
  No, nor ideal beauty, that fine name,
But something better still, so very real,
  That the sweet model must have been the same;   100
A thing that you would purchase, beg, or steal,
  Wer't not impossible, besides a shame:
The face recalls some face, as 'twere with pain,
You once have seen, but ne'er will see again;

14

One of those forms which flit by us, when we
  Are young, and fix our eyes on every face;
And, oh! the loveliness at times we see
  In momentary gliding, the soft grace,
The youth, the bloom, the beauty which agree,
  In many a nameless being we retrace,   110
Whose course and home we knew not, nor shall know,
Like the lost Pleiad seen no more below.

175   from *Childe Harold's Pilgrimage*

93

What from this barren being do we reap?
Our senses narrow, and our reason frail,
Life short, and truth a gem which loves the deep,
And all things weigh'd in custom's falsest scale;
Opinion an omnipotence,—whose veil
Mantles the earth with darkness, until right
And wrong are accidents, and men grow pale
Lest their own judgments should become too bright,
And their free thoughts be crimes, and earth have too
    much light.

94

And thus they plod in sluggish misery,   10
Rotting from sire to son, and age to age,
Proud of their trampled nature, and so die,
Bequeathing their hereditary rage
To the new race of inborn slaves, who wage
War for their chains, and rather than be free,
Bleed gladiator-like, and still engage
Within the same arena where they see
Their fellows fall before, like leaves of the same tree.

95

I speak not of men's creeds—they rest between
Man and his Maker—but of things allowed,   20
Averr'd, and known,—and daily, hourly seen—
The yoke that is upon us doubly bowed,
And the intent of tyranny avowed,
The edict of Earth's rulers, who are grown
The apes of him who humbled once the proud,
And shook them from their slumbers on the throne;
Too glorious, were this all his mighty arm had done.

96

Can tyrants but by tyrants conquered be,
And Freedom find no champion and no child
Such as Columbia saw arise when she   30
Sprung forth a Pallas, armed and undefiled?
Or must such minds be nourished in the wild,
Deep in the unpruned forest, 'midst the roar
Of cataracts, where nursing Nature smiled
On infant Washington? Has Earth no more
Such seeds within her breast, or Europe no such shore?

97

But France got drunk with blood to vomit crime,
And fatal have her Saturnalia been
To Freedom's cause; in every age and clime;
Because the deadly days which we have seen,   40
And vile Ambition, that built up between
Man and his hopes an adamantine wall,
And the base pageant last upon the scene,
Are grown the pretext for the eternal thrall
Which nips life's tree, and dooms man's worst—
        his second fall.

98

Yet, Freedom! yet thy banner, torn, but flying,
Streams like the thunder-storm *against* the wind;
Thy trumpet voice, though broken now and dying,
The loudest still the tempest leaves behind;
Thy tree hath lost its blossoms, and the rind,   50
Chopp'd by the axe, looks rough and little worth,
But the sap lasts,—and still the seed we find
Sown deep, even in the bosom of the North,
So shall a better spring less bitter fruit bring forth.

115

Egeria! sweet creation of some heart
Which found no mortal resting-place so fair
As thine ideal breast; whate'er thou art
Or wert,—a young Aurora of the air,
The nympholepsy of some fond despair;
Or, it might be, a beauty of the earth,   60
Who found a more than common votary there
Too much adoring; whatso'er thy birth,
Thou wert a beautiful thought, and softly bodied forth.

116

The mosses of thy fountain still are sprinkled
With thine Elysian water-drops; the face
Of thy cave-guarded spring, with years unwrinkled,
Reflects the meek-eyed genius of the place,
Whose green, wild margin now no more erase
Art's works; nor must the delicate waters sleep,
Prisoned in marble, bubbling from the base   70
Of the cleft statue, with a gentle leap
The rill runs o'er, and round, fern, flowers, and ivy, creep,

117

Fantastically tangled; the green hills
Are clothed with early blossoms, through the grass
The quick-eyed lizard rustles, and the bills
Of summer-birds sing welcome as ye pass;
Flowers fresh in hue, and many in their class,
Implore the pausing step, and with their dyes
Dance in the soft breeze in a fairy mass;
The sweetness of the violet's deep blue eyes,   80
Kiss'd by the breath of heaven, seems coloured by its skies.

118

Here didst thou dwell, in this enchanted cover,
Egeria! thy all heavenly bosom beating
For the far footsteps of thy mortal lover;
The purple Midnight veil'd that mystic meeting
With her most starry canopy, and seating
Thyself by thine adorer, what befell?
This cave was surely shaped out for the greeting
Of an enamour'd Goddess, and the cell
Haunted by holy Love—the earliest oracle!   90

465

119

And didst thou not, thy breast to his replying,
Blend a celestial with a human heart;
And Love, which dies as it was born, in sighing,
Share with immortal transports? could thine art
Make them indeed immortal, and impart
The purity of heaven to earthly joys,
Expel the venom and not blunt the dart—
The dull satiety which all destroys—
And root from out the soul the deadly weed which cloys?

120

Alas! our young affections run to waste,   100
Or water but the desart; whence arise
But weeds of dark luxuriance, tares of haste,
Rank at the core, though tempting to the eyes,
Flowers whose wild odours breathe but agonies,
And trees whose gums are poison; such the plants
Which spring beneath her steps as Passion flies
O'er the world's wilderness, and vainly pants
For some celestial fruit forbidden to our wants.

121

Oh Love! no habitant of earth thou art—
An unseen seraph, we believe in thee,   110
A faith whose martyrs are the broken heart,
But never yet hath seen, nor e'er shall see
The naked eye, thy form, as it should be;
The mind hath made thee, as it peopled heaven,
Even with its own desiring phantasy,
And to a thought such shape and image given,
As haunts the unquench'd soul—parch'd—wearied—
        wrung—and riven.

122

Of its own beauty is the mind diseased,
And fevers into false creation:—where,
Where are the forms the sculptor's soul hath seized?   120
In him alone. Can Nature show so fair?
Where are the charms and virtues which we dare
Conceive in boyhood and pursue as men,
The unreach'd Paradise of our despair,
Which o'er-informs the pencil and the pen,
And overpowers the page where it would bloom again?

123

Who loves, raves—'tis youth's frenzy—but the cure
Is bitterer still; as charm by charm unwinds
Which robed our idols, and we see too sure
Nor worth nor beauty dwells from out the mind's   130
Ideal shape of such; yet still it binds
The fatal spell, and still it draws us on,
Reaping the whirlwind from the oft-sown winds;
The stubborn heart, its alchemy begun,
Seems ever near the prize,—wealthiest when most undone.

124

We wither from our youth, we gasp away—
Sick—sick; unfound the boon—unslaked the thirst,
Though to the last, in verge of our decay,
Some phantom lures, such as we sought at first—
But all too late,—so are we doubly curst.   140
Love, fame, ambition, avarice—'tis the same,
Each idle—and all ill—and none the worst—
For all are meteors with a different name,
And Death the sable smoke where vanishes the flame.

125

Few—none—find what they love or could have loved,
Though accident, blind contact, and the strong
Necessity of loving, have removed
Antipathies—but to recur, ere long,
Envenomed with irrevocable wrong;
And Circumstance, that unspiritual god   150
And miscreator, makes and helps along
Our coming evils with a crutch-like rod,
Whose touch turns Hope to dust,—the dust we all have trod.

126

Our life is a false nature—'tis not in
The harmony of things,—this hard decree,
This uneradicable taint of sin,
This boundless upas, this all-blasting tree,
Whose root is earth, whose leaves and branches be
The skies which rain their plagues on men like dew—
Disease, death, bondage—all the woes we see—   160
And worse, the woes we see not—which throb through
The immedicable soul, with heart-aches ever new.

467

127

Yet let us ponder boldly—'tis a base
Abandonment of reason to resign
Our right of thought—our last and only place
Of refuge; this, at least, shall still be mine:
Though from our birth the faculty divine
Is chain'd and tortured—cabin'd, cribb'd, confined,
And bred in darkness, lest the truth should shine
Too brightly on the unprepared mind,   170
The beam pours in, for time and skill will couch the blind.

179

Roll on, thou deep and dark blue ocean—roll!
Ten thousand fleets sweep over thee in vain;
Man marks the earth with ruin—his control
Stops with the shore;—upon the watery plain
The wrecks are all thy deed, nor doth remain
A shadow of man's ravage, save his own,
When, for a moment, like a drop of rain,
He sinks into thy depths with bubbling groan,
Without a grave, unknell'd, uncoffin'd, and unknown.   180

180

His steps are not upon thy paths,—thy fields
Are not a spoil for him,—thou dost arise
And shake him from thee; the vile strength he wields
For earth's destruction thou dost all despise,
Spurning him from thy bosom to the skies,
And send'st him, shivering in thy playful spray
And howling, to his Gods, where haply lies
His petty hope in some near port or bay,
And dashest him again to earth:—there let him lay.

181

The armaments which thunderstrike the walls   190
Of rock-built cities, bidding nations quake,
And monarchs tremble in their capitals,
The oak leviathans, whose huge ribs make
Their clay creator the vain title take
Of lord of thee, and arbiter of war;
These are thy toys, and, as the snowy flake,
They melt into thy yeast of waves, which mar
Alike the Armada's pride, or spoils of Trafalgar.

182

Thy shores are empires, changed in all save thee—
Assyria, Greece, Rome, Carthage, what are they?   200
Thy waters washed them power while they were free,
And many a tyrant since; their shores obey
The stranger, slave, or savage, their decay
Has dried up realms to desarts:—not so thou,
Unchangeable save to thy wild waves' play—
Time writes no wrinkle on thine azure brow—
Such as creation's dawn beheld, thou rollest now.

183

Thou glorious mirror, where the Almighty's form
Glasses itself in tempests; in all time,
Calm or convuls'd—in breeze, or gale, or storm,   210
Icing the pole, or in the torrid clime
Dark-heaving;—boundless, endless, and sublime—
The image of Eternity—the throne
Of the Invisible, even from out thy slime
The monsters of the deep are made; each zone
Obeys thee; thou goest forth, dread, fathomless, alone.

184

And I have loved thee, Ocean! and my joy
Of youthful sports was on thy breast to be
Borne, like thy bubbles, onward: from a boy
I wantoned with thy breakers—they to me   220
Were a delight; and if the freshening sea
Made them a terror—'twas a pleasing fear,
For I was as it were a child of thee,
And trusted to thy billows far and near,
And laid my hand upon thy mane—as I do here.

(Canto IV)

THOMAS LOVE PEACOCK
1785–1866

176   from *Rhododaphne*

MAGIC and mystery, spells Circæan,
The Siren voice, that calmed the sea,
And steeped the soul in dews Lethæan;
The enchanted chalice, sparkling free
With wine, amid whose ruby glow
Love couched, with madness linked and woe;
Mantle and zone, whose woof beneath
Lurked wily grace, in subtle wreath
With blandishment and young desire
And soft persuasion intertwined,   10
Whose touch, with sympathetic fire,
Could melt at once the sternest mind;
Have passed away: for vestal Truth
Young Fancy's foe, and Reason chill,
Have chased the dreams that charmed the youth
Of nature and the world, which still,
Amid that vestal light severe,
Our colder spirits leap to hear
Like echoes from a fairy hill.
Yet deem not so. The Power of Spells   20
Still lingers on the earth, but dwells
In deeper folds of close disguise,
That baffle Reason's searching eyes:
Nor shall that mystic Power resign
To Truth's cold sway his webs of guile,
Till woman's eyes have ceased to shine,
And woman's lips have ceased to smile,
And woman's voice has ceased to be
The earthly soul of melody.

(Canto IV. 1–29)

JOHN KEATS

from *Endymion*

A Poetic Romance

A THING of beauty is a joy for ever:
Its loveliness increases; it will never
Pass into nothingness; but still will keep
A bower quiet for us, and a sleep
Full of sweet dreams, and health, and quiet breathing.
Therefore, on every morrow, are we wreathing
A flowery band to bind us to the earth,
Spite of despondence, of the inhuman dearth
Of noble natures, of the gloomy days,
Of all the unhealthy and o'er-darkened ways   10
Made for our searching: yes, in spite of all,
Some shape of beauty moves away the pall
From our dark spirits. Such the sun, the moon,
Trees old, and young sprouting a shady boon
For simple sheep; and such are daffodils
With the green world they live in; and clear rills
That for themselves a cooling covert make
'Gainst the hot season; the mid forest brake,
Rich with a sprinkling of fair musk-rose blooms:
And such too is the grandeur of the dooms   20
We have imagined for the mighty dead;
All lovely tales that we have heard or read:
An endless fountain of immortal drink,
Pouring unto us from the heaven's brink.

Nor do we merely feel these essences
For one short hour; no, even as the trees
That whisper round a temple become soon
Dear as the temple's self, so does the moon,
The passion poesy, glories infinite,
Haunt us till they become a cheering light   30
Unto our souls, and bound to us so fast,
That, whether there be shine, or gloom o'ercast,
They alway must be with us, or we die.

(Book I, lines 1–33)

178 *[Proud Maisie]*

PROUD Maisie is in the wood,
  Walking so early;
Sweet Robin sits on the bush,
  Singing so rarely.

'Tell me, thou bonny bird,
  When shall I marry me?'
'When six braw gentlemen
  Kirkward shall carry ye.'

'Who makes the bridal bed,
  Birdie, say truly?'   10
'The grey-headed sexton
  That delves the grave duly.

'The glow-worm o'er grave and stone
  Shall light thee steady.
The owl from the steeple sing,
  "Welcome, proud lady." '

WILLIAM HONE
1780–1842

179

The Political House that Jack Built

'A straw—thrown up to show which way the wind blows.'

WITH THIRTEEN CUTS.

The Pen and the Sword.

LONDON:
PRINTED BY AND FOR WILLIAM HONE, LUDGATE HILL.

> ——'Many, whose sequester'd lot
> Forbids their interference, looking on,
> Anticipate perforce some dire event;
> And, seeing the old castle of the state,
> That promis'd once more firmness, so assail'd,
> That all its tempest-beaten turrets shake,
> Stand motionless expectants of its fall.'
>
> *Cowper.*

NOTE.

Each Motto that follows, is from Cowper's 'Task.'

WILLIAM HONE

The Author's Dedication to his Political Godchild.

TO

DOCTOR SLOP,

in acknowledgement of many public testimonials
of his filial gratitude; and to

THE NURSERY OF CHILDREN, SIX FEET HIGH,

HIS READERS,

for the delight and instruction of their uninformed minds;

THIS JUVENILE PUBLICATION

is affectionately inscribed, by the Doctor's Political Godfather,

THE AUTHOR.

NOTE.—*The Publication wherein the Author of 'The Political House that Jack Built' conferred upon Dr. Slop the lasting distinction of his name, was a Jeu d'Esprit, entitled 'Buonaparte-phobia, or Cursing made easy to the meanest capacity,'—it is reprinted, and may be had of the Publisher, Price One Shilling.*

'A distant age asks where the fabric stood.'

THIS IS THE HOUSE THAT JACK BUILT.

——'Not to understand a treasure's worth,
Till time has stolen away the slighted good,
Is cause of half the poverty we feel,
And makes the world the wilderness it is.'

THIS IS

THE WEALTH

that lay
In the House that Jack built.

——'A race obscene,
Spawn'd in the muddy beds of Nile, came forth,
Polluting Egypt: gardens, fields, and plains,
Were cover'd with the pest;
The croaking nuisance lurk'd in every nook;

Nor palaces, nor even chambers, 'scap'd;
And the land stank—so num'rous was the fry.'

THESE ARE
THE VERMIN

That Plunder the Wealth,
That lay in the House,
That Jack built.

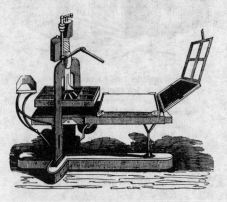

'Once enslaved, farewell!

*   *   *   *

Do I forebode impossible events,
And tremble at vain dreams? Heav'n grant I may!'

THIS IS
THE THING,

   that, in spite of new Acts,
And attempts to restrain it,
   by Soldiers or Tax,
Will *poison* the Vermin,
That plunder the Wealth,
That lay in the House,
That Jack built.

'The seals of office glitter in his eyes;
He climbs, he pants, he grasps them—
To be a pest where he was useful once.'

THIS IS

THE PUBLIC INFORMER,

who
Would put down the *Thing*,
that, in spite of new Acts,
And attempts to restrain it,
by Soldiers or Tax,
Will *poison* the Vermin, that plunder the Wealth,
That lay in the House, that Jack built.

'Ruffians are abroad——
*   *   *   *
Leviathan is not *so* tamed.'

WILLIAM HONE

THESE ARE

THE *REASONS* OF LAWLESS POWER

That back the Public Informer,
who
Would put down the *Thing*,
that, in spite of new Acts,
And attempts to restrain it,
by Soldiers or Tax,
Will *poison* the Vermin,
That plunder the Wealth,
That lay in the House,
That Jack built.

————'Great offices will have
Great talents.'

This is THE MAN—all shaven and shorn,
All cover'd with Orders—and all forlorn;
THE DANDY OF SIXTY,
   who bows with a grace,
And has *taste* in wigs, collars,
   cuirasses and lace;
Who, to tricksters, and fools,
   leaves the State and its treasure,
And, when Britain's in tears,
   sails about at his pleasure:
Who spurn'd from his presence
   the Friends of his youth,
And now has not one
   who will tell him the truth;
Who took to his counsels,
   in evil hour,
The Friends to the Reasons
   of lawless Power;
That back the Public Informer,
   who
Would put down the *Thing*,
   that, in spite of new Acts,
And attempts to restrain it,
   by Soldiers or Tax,
Will *poison* the Vermin,
That plunder the Wealth,
That lay in the House,
That Jack built.

'Portentous, unexampled, unexplain'd!
————What man seeing this,

And having human feelings, does not blush,
And hang his head, to think himself a man?
——————————I cannot rest
A silent witness of the headlong rage,
Or heedless folly, by which thousands die——
Bleed gold for Ministers to sport away.'

THESE ARE

THE PEOPLE

   all tatter'd and torn,
Who curse the day
    wherein they were born,
On account of Taxation
    too great to be borne,
And pray for relief,
    from night to morn;
Who, in vain, Petition
    in every form,
Who, peaceably Meeting,
    to ask for Reform,
Were sabred by Yeomanry Cavalry,
    who,
Were thank'd by THE MAN,
    all shaven and shorn,
All cover'd with Orders—
    and all forlorn;
THE DANDY OF SIXTY,
    who bows with a grace,
And has *taste* in wigs, collars,
    cuirasses, and lace;
Who, to tricksters, and fools,
    leaves the State and its treasure,
And when Britain's in tears,
    sails about at his pleasure;
Who spurn'd from his presence
    the Friends of his youth,
And now has not one
    who will tell him the truth;
Who took to his counsels, in evil hour,
The Friends to the Reasons of lawless Power,
That back the Public Informer, who
Would put down the *Thing*, that, in spite of new Acts,
And attempts to restrain it, by Soldiers or Tax,
Will *poison* the Vermin, that plunder the Wealth,
That lay in the House, that Jack built.

THE DOCTOR.
'At his last gasp—as if with opium drugg'd.'

DERRY-DOWN TRIANGLE.
'He that sold his country.'

THE SPOUTER OF FROTH.
'With merry descants on a nation's woes—
There is a public mischief in his mirth.'

THE GUILTY TRIO.
'Great skill have they in *palmistry*, and more
To conjure clean away the gold they touch,
Conveying worthless dross into its place;
Loud when they beg, dumb only when they steal.

         *   *   *   *

              Dream after dream ensues;
And still they dream, that they shall still succeed,
And still are disappointed.'

This is THE DOCTOR
              of *Circular* fame,
A Driv'ller, a Bigot, a Knave
              without shame:
And *that's* DERRY DOWN TRIANGLE
              by name,
From the Land of mis-rule,
              and half-hanging, and flame:
And *that* is THE SPOUTER OF FROTH
              BY THE HOUR,
The worthless colleague
              of their infamous power;
Who dubb'd *him* 'the Doctor'
              whom now he calls 'brother',
And, to get at his Place,
              took a shot at the other;

481

Who haunts their *Bad House*,
   a base living to earn,
By playing Jack-pudding, and Ruffian,
   in turn;
Who bullies, for those
   whom he bullied before;
Their *Flash*-man, their Bravo,
   a son of a ———;
The hate of the People,
   all tatter'd and torn,
Who curse the day
   wherein they were born,
On account of Taxation
   too great to be borne,
And pray for relief
   from night to morn;
Who, in vain, Petition
   in every form,
Who peaceably Meeting,
   to ask for Reform,
Were sabred by Yeomanry Cavalry,
   who,
Were thank'd by THE MAN,
   all shaven and shorn,
All cover'd with Orders—
   and all forlorn;
THE DANDY OF SIXTY,
   who bows with a grace,
And has *taste* in wigs, collars,
   cuirasses, and lace:
Who to tricksters and fools,
   leaves the State and its treasure,
And, when Britain's in tears,
   sails about at his pleasure:
Who spurn'd from his presence
   the Friends of his youth,
And now has not one
   who will tell him the truth;
Who took to his counsels, in evil hour,
The Friends to the Reasons of lawless Power;
That back the Public Informer, who
Would put down the *Thing*, that, in spite of new Acts,
And attempts to restrain it, by Soldiers or Tax,
Will *poison* the Vermin, that plunder the Wealth,
That lay in the House, that Jack built.

—————'Burghers, men immaculate perhaps
In all their private functions, once combin'd,
Become a loathsome body, only fit
For dissolution.
————————————Power usurp'd
Is weakness when oppos'd; conscious of wrong,
'Tis pusillanimous and prone to flight.
————————————I could endure
Chains nowhere patiently; and chains at home,
Where I am free by birthright, not at all.'

This WORD is the Watchword—
                the talisman word,
That the WATERLOO-MAN's to crush
                with his sword;
But, if shielded by NORFOLK
                and BEDFORD's alliance,
It will set both his sword,
                and him, at defiance;
If FITZWILLIAM, and GROSVENOR, and
                ALBEMARLE aid it,
And assist its best Champions,
                who then dare invade it?
'Tis the terrible WORD OF FEAR,
                night and morn,
To the *Guilty Trio*,
                all cover'd with scorn;

First, to the Doctor,
          of *Circular* fame,
A Driv'ller, a Bigot, a Knave
          without shame:
And next, Derry Down Triangle
          by name,
From the Land of Mis-rule,
          and Half-hanging, and Flame:
And then, to the Spouter of Froth
          by the hour,
The worthless Colleague
          of their infamous power;
Who dubb'd *him* 'the Doctor',
          whom now he calls 'brother',
And, to get at his Place,
          took a shot at the other;
Who haunts their *Bad House*,
          a base living to earn,
By playing Jack-Pudding, and Ruffian,
          in turn;
Who bullies for those,
          whom he bullied before;
Their *Flash*-man, their Bravo,
          a son of a ———;
The hate of the People,
          all tatter'd and torn,
Who curse the day
          wherein they were born,
On account of Taxation
          too great to be borne,
And pray for relief,
          from night to morn,
Who in vain Petition
          in every form,
Who peaceably Meeting
          to ask for Reform,
Were sabred by Yeomanry Cavalry,
          who
Were thank'd by THE MAN,
          all shaven and shorn,
All cover'd with Orders—
          and all forlorn;
THE DANDY OF SIXTY,
          who bows with a grace,
And has *taste* in wigs, collars,
          cuirasses, and lace;

Who, to tricksters, and fools,
           leaves the State and its treasure,
And, when Britain's in tears
           sails about at his pleasure;
Who spurn'd from his presence
           the Friends of his Youth,
And now has not one
           who will tell him the Truth;
Who took to his Counsels,
           in evil hour,
The Friends to the Reasons
           of lawless Power;
That back the Public Informer,
           who
Would put down the Thing,
           that, in spite of new Acts,
And attempts to restrain it
           by Soldiers or Tax,
Will *poison* the Vermin,
That plunder the Wealth,
That lay in the House,
That Jack built.

END OF THE HOUSE THAT JACK BUILT.

THE CLERICAL MAGISTRATE.

'*The Bishop.*   Will you be diligent in Prayers—laying aside the study of the
world and the flesh?——*The Priest.*   I will.
The Bishop.   Will you maintain and set forwards, as much as lieth in you,
quietness, peace, and love, among all Christian People?——*Priest.*   I will.
The Bishop laying his hand upon the head of him that receiveth the order of
Priesthood, shall say, RECEIVE THE HOLY GHOST.'

The Form of Ordination for a Priest.

————'The pulpit (in the sober use
Of its legitimate peculiar pow'rs)
Must stand acknowledg'd, while the world shall stand,
The most important and effectual guard,
Support, and ornament of virtue's cause.'

*   *   *   *

Behold the picture! Is it like?

THIS IS A PRIEST,

made 'according to Law',
Who, on being ordain'd,
vow'd, by rote, like a daw,
That, he felt himself call'd,
by the Holy Spirit,
To teach men the Kingdom of Heaven
to merit;
That, to think of the World and the flesh
he'd cease,

And keep men in quietness,
     love and peace;
And, making thus his profession
     and boast,
Receiv'd, from the Bishop,
     the Holy Ghost:
Then—not having the fear of God
     before him—
Is sworn in a Justice,
     and one of the *Quorum;*
'Gainst his spiritual Oath,
     puts his Oath of the Bench,
And, instead of his Bible,
     examines a wench;
Gets Chairman of Sessions—leaves his flock,
     sick, or dying,
To license Ale-houses—and assist
     in the trying
Of prostitutes, poachers, pickpockets
     and thieves;——
Having *charged* the Grand Jury,
     dines with them, and gives
'CHURCH AND KING without day-light;'
     gets *fresh*, and puts in—
To the stocks vulgar people
     who fuddle with gin:
Stage coachmen, and toll-men,
     convicts as he pleases;
And beggars and paupers
     incessantly teazes:
Commits starving vagrants,
     and orders Distress
On the Poor, for their Rates—
     signs warrants to press,
And beats up for names
     to a Loyal Address:
Would indict, for Rebellion,
     those who Petition;
And, all who look peaceable,
     try for Sedition;
If the People were legally Meeting,
     in quiet,
Would pronounce it, decidedly—*sec. Stat.*—
     a Riot,
And order the Soldiers
     'to aid and assist',

That is—kill the helpless,
          Who cannot resist.
He, though vowing 'from all worldly studies
          to cease',
Breaks the Peace of the Church,
          to be Justice of Peace;
Breaks his vows made to Heaven—
          a pander for Power;
A Perjurer—a guide to the People
          no more;
On God turns his back,
          when he turns the State's Agent;
And damns his own Soul,
          to be friends with the ———.

THE END.

' 'Tis Liberty alone, that gives the flow'r
Of fleeting life its lustre and perfume;
And we are weeds without it.'

180   from *Don Juan*, Canto 1

[*Julia and Juan in Love*]

75

POOR Julia's heart was in an awkward state;
     She felt it going, and resolved to make
The noblest efforts for herself and mate,
     For honour's, pride's, religion's, virtue's sake;
Her resolutions were most truly great,
     And almost might have made a Tarquin quake;
She pray'd the Virgin Mary for her grace,
As being the best judge of a lady's case.

76

She vow'd she never would see Juan more,
     And next day paid a visit to his mother,   10
And look'd extremely at the opening door,
     Which, by the Virgin's grace, let in another;
Grateful she was, and yet a little sore—
     Again it opens, it can be no other,
'Tis surely Juan now—No! I'm afraid
That night the Virgin was no further pray'd.

77

She now determined that a virtuous woman
     Should rather face and overcome temptation,
That flight was base and dastardly, and no man
     Should ever give her heart the least sensation;   20
That is to say, a thought beyond the common
     Preference, that we must feel upon occasion,
For people who are pleasanter than others,
But then they only seem so many brothers.

78

And even if by chance—and who can tell?
     The devil's so very sly—she should discover
That all within was not so very well,
     And, if still free, that such or such a lover
Might please perhaps, a virtuous wife can quell
     Such thoughts, and be the better when they're over;   30

And if the man should ask, 'tis but denial:
I recommend young ladies to make trial.

79

And then there are such things as love divine,
  Bright and immaculate, unmix'd and pure,
Such as the angels think so very fine,
  And matrons, who would be no less secure,
Platonic, perfect, 'just such love as mine':
  Thus Julia said—and thought so, to be sure,
And so I'd have her think, were I the man
On whom her reveries celestial ran.   40

80

Such love is innocent, and may exist
  Between young persons without any danger,
A hand may first, and then a lip be kist;
  For my part, to such doings I'm a stranger,
But *hear* these freedoms form the utmost list
  Of all o'er which such love may be a ranger:
If people go beyond, 'tis quite a crime,
But not my fault—I tell them all in time.

81

Love, then, but love within its proper limits,
  Was Julia's innocent determination   50
In young Don Juan's favour, and to him its
  Exertion might be useful on occasion;
And, lighted at too pure a shrine to dim its
  Etherial lustre, with what sweet persuasion
He might be taught, by love and her together—
I really don't know what, nor Julia either.

82

Fraught with this fine intention, and well fenced
  In mail of proof—her purity of soul,
She, for the future of her strength convinced,
  And that her honour was a rock, or mole,   60
Exceeding sagely from that hour dispensed
  With any kind of troublesome control;
But whether Julia to the task was equal
Is that which must be mentioned in the sequel.

83

Her plan she deem'd both innocent and feasible,
   And, surely, with a stripling of sixteen
Not scandal's fangs could fix on much that's seizable,
   Or if they did so, satisfied to mean
Nothing but what was good, her breast was peaceable—
   A quiet conscience makes one so serene!   70
Christians have burnt each other, quite persuaded
That all the Apostles would have done as they did.

84

And if in the mean time her husband died,
   But heaven forbid that such a thought should cross
Her brain, though in a dream! (and then she sigh'd)
   Never could she survive that common loss;
But just suppose that moment should betide,
   I only say suppose it—*inter nos*—
(This should be *entre nous*, for Julia thought
In French, but then the rhyme would go for nought).   80

85

I only say suppose this supposition:
   Juan being then grown up to man's estate
Would fully suit a widow of condition,
   Even seven years hence it would not be too late;
And in the interim (to pursue this vision)
   The mischief, after all, could not be great,
For he would learn the rudiments of love,
I mean the seraph way of those above.

86

So much for Julia. Now we'll turn to Juan,
   Poor little fellow! he had no idea   90
Of his own case, and never hit the true one;
   In feelings quick as Ovid's Miss Medea,
He puzzled over what he found a new one,
   But not as yet imagined it could be a
Thing quite in course, and not at all alarming,
Which, with a little patience, might grow charming.

87

Silent and pensive, idle, restless, slow,
   His home deserted for the lonely wood,
Tormented with a wound he could not know,
   His, like all deep grief, plunged in solitude: 100

I'm fond myself of solitude or so,
    But then, I beg it may be understood,
By solitude I mean a sultan's, not
A hermit's, with a haram for a grot.

88

'Oh Love! in such a wilderness as this,
    Where transport and security entwine,
Here is the empire of thy perfect bliss,
    And here thou art a god indeed divine.'
The bard I quote from does not sing amiss,
    With the exception of the second line,   110
For that same twining 'transport and security'
Are twisted to a phrase of some obscurity.

89

The poet meant, no doubt, and thus appeals
    To the good sense and senses of mankind,
The very thing which every body feels,
    As all have found on trial, or may find,
That no one likes to be disturb'd at meals
    Or love.—I won't say more about 'entwined'
Or 'transport', as we knew all that before,
But beg 'Security' will bolt the door.   120

90

Young Juan wander'd by the glassy brooks
    Thinking unutterable things; he threw
Himself at length within the leafy nooks
    Where the wild branch of the cork forest grew;
There poets find materials for their books,
    And every now and then we read them through,
So that their plan and prosody are eligible,
Unless, like Wordsworth, they prove unintelligible.

91

He, Juan, (and not Wordsworth) so pursued
    His self-communion with his own high soul,   130
Until his mighty heart, in its great mood,
    Had mitigated part, though not the whole
Of its disease; he did the best he could
    With things not very subject to control,
And turn'd, without perceiving his condition,
Like Coleridge, into a metaphysician.

92

He thought about himself, and the whole earth,
    Of man the wonderful, and of the stars,
And how the deuce they ever could have birth;
    And then he thought of earthquakes, and of wars,   140
How many miles the moon might have in girth,
    Of air-balloons, and of the many bars
To perfect knowledge of the boundless skies;
And then he thought of Donna Julia's eyes.

93

In thoughts like these true wisdom may discern
    Longings sublime, and aspirations high,
Which some are born with, but the most part learn
    To plague themselves withal, they know not why:
'Twas strange that one so young should thus concern
    His brain about the action of the sky;   150
If *you* think 'twas philosophy that this did,
I can't help thinking puberty assisted.

94

He pored upon the leaves, and on the flowers,
    And heard a voice in all the winds; and then
He thought of wood nymphs and immortal bowers,
    And how the goddesses came down to men:
He miss'd the pathway, he forgot the hours,
    And when he look'd upon his watch again,
He found how much old Time had been a winner—
He also found that he had lost his dinner.   160

95

Sometimes he turn'd to gaze upon his book,
    Boscan, or Garcilasso;—by the wind
Even as the page is rustled while we look,
    So by the poesy of his own mind
Over the mystic leaf his soul was shook,
    As if 'twere one whereon magicians bind
Their spells, and give them to the passing gale,
According to some good old woman's tale.

96

Thus would he while his lonely hours away
    Dissatisfied, nor knowing what he wanted;   170
Nor glowing reverie, nor poet's lay,
    Could yield his spirit that for which it panted,

A bosom whereon he his head might lay,
 And hear the heart beat with the love it granted,
With——several other things, which I forget,
Or which, at least, I need not mention yet.

97

Those lonely walks, and lengthening reveries,
 Could not escape the gentle Julia's eyes;
She saw that Juan was not at his ease;
 But that which chiefly may, and must surprise,
Is, that the Donna Inez did not tease   180
 Her only son with question or surmise;
Whether it was she did not see, or would not,
Or, like all very clever people, could not.

98

This may seem strange, but yet 'tis very common;
 For instance—gentlemen, whose ladies take
Leave to o'erstep the written rights of woman,
 And break the——Which commandment is't they break?
(I have forgot the number, and think no man
 Should rashly quote, for fear of a mistake)
I say, when these same gentlemen are jealous, 190
They make some blunder, which their ladies tell us.

99

A real husband always is suspicious,
 But still no less suspects in the wrong place,
Jealous of some one who had no such wishes,
 Or pandering blindly to his own disgrace
By harbouring some dear friend extremely vicious;
 The last indeed's infallibly the case:
And when the spouse and friend are gone off wholly,
He wonders at their vice, and not his folly.

100

Thus parents also are at times short-sighted; 200
 Though watchful as the lynx, they ne'er discover,
The while the wicked world beholds delighted,
 Young Hopeful's mistress, or Miss Fanny's lover,
Till some confounded escapade has blighted
 The plan of twenty years, and all is over;
And then the mother cries, the father swears,
And wonders why the devil he got heirs.

101

But Inez was so anxious, and so clear
  Of sight, that I must think, on this occasion,
She had some other motive much more near   210
  For leaving Juan to this new temptation;
But what that motive was, I shan't say here;
  Perhaps to finish Juan's education,
Perhaps to open Don Alfonso's eyes,
In case he thought his wife too great a prize.

102

It was upon a day, a summer's day;—
  Summer's indeed a very dangerous season,
And so is spring about the end of May;
  The sun, no doubt, is the prevailing reason;
But whatsoe'er the cause is, one may say,   220
  And stand convicted of more truth than treason,
That there are months which nature grows more merry in,
March has its hares, and May must have its heroine.

103

'Twas on a summer's day—the sixth of June:—
  I like to be particular in dates,
Not only of the age, and year, but moon;
  They are a sort of post-house, where the Fates
Change horses, making history change its tune,
  Then spur away o'er empires and o'er states,
Leaving at last not much besides chronology,   230
Excepting the post-obits of theology.

104

'Twas on the sixth of June, about the hour
  Of half-past six—perhaps still nearer seven,
When Julia sate within as pretty a bower
  As e'er held houri in that heathenish heaven
Described by Mahomet, and Anacreon Moore,
  To whom the lyre and laurels have been given,
With all the trophies of triumphant song—
He won them well, and may he wear them long!

105

She sate, but not alone; I know not well   240
  How this same interview had taken place,

495

And even if I knew, I should not tell—
  People should hold their tongues in any case;
No matter how or why the thing befell,
  But there were she and Juan, face to face—
When two such faces are so, 'twould be wise,
But very difficult, to shut their eyes.

106

How beautiful she look'd! her conscious heart
  Glow'd in her cheek, and yet she felt no wrong.
Oh Love! how perfect is thy mystic art,   250
  Strengthening the weak, and trampling on the strong,
How self-deceitful is the sagest part
  Of mortals whom thy lure hath led along—
The precipice she stood on was immense,
So was her creed in her own innocence.

107

She thought of her own strength, and Juan's youth,
  And of the folly of all prudish fears,
Victorious virtue, and domestic truth,
  And then of Don Alfonso's fifty years;
I wish these last had not occurr'd, in sooth,   260
  Because that number rarely much endears,
And through all climes, the snowy and the sunny,
Sounds ill in love, whate'er it may in money.

108

When people say, 'I've told you *fifty* times,'
  They mean to scold, and very often do;
When poets say, 'I've written *fifty* rhymes,'
  They make you dread that they'll recite them too;
In gangs of *fifty*, thieves commit their crimes;
  At *fifty* love for love is rare, 'tis true,
But then, no doubt, it equally as true is,   270
A good deal may be bought for *fifty* Louis.

109

Julia had honour, virtue, truth, and love,
  For Don Alfonso; and she inly swore,
By all the vows below to powers above,
  She never would disgrace the ring she wore,
Nor leave a wish which wisdom might reprove;

And while she ponder'd this, besides much more,
One hand on Juan's carelessly was thrown,
Quite by mistake—she thought it was her own;

110

Unconsciously she lean'd upon the other,   280
   Which play'd within the tangles of her hair;
And to contend with thoughts she could not smother,
   She seem'd by the distraction of her air.
'Twas surely very wrong in Juan's mother
   To leave together this imprudent pair,
She who for many years had watch'd her son so—
I'm very certain *mine* would not have done so.

111

The hand which still held Juan's, by degrees
   Gently, but palpably confirm'd its grasp,
As if it said 'detain me, if you please';   290
   Yet there's no doubt she only meant to clasp
His fingers with a pure Platonic squeeze;
   She would have shrunk as from a toad, or asp,
Had she imagined such a thing could rouse
A feeling dangerous to a prudent spouse.

112

I cannot know what Juan thought of this,
   But what he did, is much what you would do;
His young lip thank'd it with a grateful kiss,
   And then, abash'd at its own joy, withdrew
In deep despair, lest he had done amiss,   300
   Love is so very timid when 'tis new:
She blush'd, and frown'd not, but she strove to speak,
And held her tongue, her voice was grown so weak.

113

The sun set, and up rose the yellow moon:
   The devil's in the moon for mischief; they
Who call'd her CHASTE, methinks, began too soon
   Their nomenclature; there is not a day,
The longest, not the twenty-first of June,
   Sees half the business in a wicked way
On which three single hours of moonshine smile—   310
And then she looks so modest all the while.

114

There is a dangerous silence in that hour,
  A stillness, which leaves room for the full soul
To open all itself, without the power
  Of calling wholly back its self-control;
The silver light which, hallowing tree and tower,
  Sheds beauty and deep softness o'er the whole,
Breathes also to the heart, and o'er it throws
A loving languor, which is not repose.

115

And Julia sate with Juan, half embraced   320
  And half retiring from the glowing arm,
Which trembled like the bosom where 'twas placed;
  Yet still she must have thought there was no harm,
Or else 'twere easy to withdraw her waist;
  But then the situation had its charm,
And then——God knows what next—I can't go on;
I'm almost sorry that I e'er begun.

116

Oh Plato! Plato! you have paved the way,
  With your confounded fantasies, to more
Immoral conduct by the fancied sway   330
  Your system feigns o'er the controlless core
Of human hearts, than all the long array
  Of poets and romancers:—You're a bore,
A charlatan, a coxcomb—and have been,
At best, no better than a go-between.

117

And Julia's voice was lost, except in sighs,
  Until too late for useful conversation;
The tears were gushing from her gentle eyes,
  I wish, indeed, they had not had occasion,
But who, alas! can love, and then be wise?   340
  Not that remorse did not oppose temptation,
A little still she strove, and much repented,
And whispering 'I will ne'er consent'—consented.

118

'Tis said that Xerxes offer'd a reward
  To those who could invent him a new pleasure;

Methinks, the requisition's rather hard,
    And must have cost his majesty a treasure:
For my part, I'm a moderate-minded bard,
    Fond of a little love (which I call leisure);
I care not for new pleasures, as the old   350
Are quite enough for me, so they but hold.

119

Oh Pleasure! you're indeed a pleasant thing,
    Although one must be damn'd for you, no doubt;
I make a resolution every spring
    Of reformation, ere the year run out,
But, somehow, this my vestal vow takes wing,
    Yet still, I trust, it may be kept throughout:
I'm very sorry, very much ashamed,
And mean, next winter, to be quite reclaim'd.

[Julia's Farewell Letter]

192

'They tell me 'tis decided; you depart: 360
    'Tis wise—'tis well, but not the less a pain;
I have no further claim on your young heart,
    Mine was the victim, and would be again;
To love too much has been the only art
    I used;—I write in haste, and if a stain
Be on this sheet, 'tis not what it appears,
My eyeballs burn and throb, but have no tears.

193

'I loved, I love you, for that love have lost
    State, station, heaven, mankind's, my own esteem,
And yet can not regret what it hath cost,   370
    So dear is still the memory of that dream;
Yet, if I name my guilt, 'tis not to boast,
    None can deem harshlier of me than I deem:
I trace this scrawl because I cannot rest—
I've nothing to reproach, nor to request.

194

'Man's love is of his life a thing apart,
    'Tis woman's whole existence; man may range
The court, camp, church, the vessel, and the mart,
    Sword, gown, gain, glory, offer in exchange

Pride, fame, ambition, to fill up his heart,   380
    And few there are whom these can not estrange;
Man has all these resources, we but one,
To love again, and be again undone.

195

'My breast has been all weakness, is so yet;
    I struggle, but cannot collect my mind;
My blood still rushes where my spirit's set,
    As roll the waves before the settled wind;
My brain is feminine, nor can forget—
    To all, except your image, madly blind;
As turns the needle trembling to the pole   390
It ne'er can reach, so turns to you, my soul.

196

'You will proceed in beauty, and in pride,
    Beloved and loving many; all is o'er
For me on earth, except some years to hide
    My shame and sorrow deep in my heart's core;
These I could bear, but cannot cast aside
    The passion which still rends it as before,
And so farewell—forgive me, love me—No,
That word is idle now—but let it go.

197

'I have no more to say, but linger still,   400
    And dare not set my seal upon this sheet,
And yet I may as well the task fulfil,
    My misery can scarce be more complete:
I had not lived till now, could sorrow kill;
    Death flies the wretch who fain the blow would meet,
And I must even survive this last adieu,
And bear with life, to love and pray for you!'

198

This note was written upon gilt-edged paper
    With a neat crow-quill, rather hard, but new;
Her small white fingers scarce could reach the taper,   410
    But trembled as magnetic needles do,
And yet she did not let one tear escape her;
    The seal a sunflower; '*Elle vous suit partout*',
The motto, cut upon a white cornelian;
The wax was superfine, its hue vermilion.

JOHN KEATS

Ode to a Nightingale

1

My heart aches, and a drowsy numbness pains
   My sense, as though of hemlock I had drunk,
Or emptied some dull opiate to the drains
   One minute past, and Lethe-wards had sunk:
'Tis not through envy of thy happy lot,
   But being too happy in thine happiness,—
      That thou, light-winged Dryad of the trees,
        In some melodious plot
   Of beechen green, and shadows numberless,
      Singest of summer in full-throated ease.   10

2

O, for a draught of vintage! that hath been
   Cool'd a long age in the deep-delved earth,
Tasting of Flora and the country green,
   Dance, and Provencal song, and sunburnt mirth!
O for a beaker full of the warm South,
   Full of the true, the blushful Hippocrene,
      With beaded bubbles winking at the brim,
        And purple-stained mouth;
   That I might drink, and leave the world unseen,
      And with thee fade away into the forest dim: 20

3

Fade far away, dissolve, and quite forget
   What thou among the leaves hast never known,
The weariness, the fever, and the fret
   Here, where men sit and hear each other groan;
Where palsy shakes a few, sad, last gray hairs,
   Where youth grows pale, and spectre-thin, and dies;
      Where but to think is to be full of sorrow
        And leaden-eyed despairs,
   Where Beauty cannot keep her lustrous eyes,
      Or new Love pine at them beyond to-morrow.   30

4

Away! away! for I will fly to thee,
   Not charioted by Bacchus and his pards,

But on the viewless wings of Poesy,
　　Though the dull brain perplexes and retards:
Already with thee! tender is the night,
　　And haply the Queen-Moon is on her throne,
　　　　Cluster'd around by all her starry Fays;
　　　　　　But here there is no light,
　　Save what from heaven is with the breezes blown
　　　　Through verdurous glooms and winding mossy ways.   40

　　　　　　　　　　5

I cannot see what flowers are at my feet,
　　Nor what soft incense hangs upon the boughs,
But, in embalmed darkness, guess each sweet
　　Wherewith the seasonable month endows
The grass, the thicket, and the fruit-tree wild;
　　White hawthorn, and the pastoral eglantine;
　　　　Fast fading violets cover'd up in leaves;
　　　　　　And mid-May's eldest child,
　　The coming musk-rose, full of dewy wine,
　　　　The murmurous haunt of flies on summer eves.   50

　　　　　　　　　　6

Darkling I listen; and, for many a time
　　I have been half in love with easeful Death,
Call'd him soft names in many a mused rhyme,
　　To take into the air my quiet breath;
Now more than ever seems it rich to die,
　　To cease upon the midnight with no pain,
　　　　While thou art pouring forth thy soul abroad
　　　　　　In such an ecstasy!
　　Still wouldst thou sing, and I have ears in vain—
　　　　To thy high requiem become a sod.   60

　　　　　　　　　　7

Thou wast not born for death, immortal Bird!
　　No hungry generations tread thee down;
The voice I hear this passing night was heard
　　In ancient days by emperor and clown:
Perhaps the self-same song that found a path
　　Through the sad heart of Ruth, when, sick for home,
　　　　She stood in tears amid the alien corn;
　　　　　　The same that oft-times hath
　　Charm'd magic casements, opening on the foam
　　　　Of perilous seas, in faery lands forlorn.   70

8

Forlorn! the very word is like a bell
  To toll me back from thee to my sole self!
Adieu! the fancy cannot cheat so well
  As she is fam'd to do, deceiving elf.
Adieu! adieu! thy plaintive anthem fades
  Past the near meadows, over the still stream,
    Up the hill-side; and now 'tis buried deep
      In the next valley-glades:
  Was it a vision, or a waking dream?
  Fled is that music:—Do I wake or sleep?   80

SAMUEL BAMFORD
1788–1872

182   *Touch Him!*

TOUCH him, aye! touch him, if you dare;
Pluck from his head one single hair—
  Ye sneaking, coward crew:
Touch him—and blasted be the hand
That graspeth not a vengeful brand,
To rid our long oppressed land
  Of reptiles such as you.

Touch him—and by the eternal pow'r,
That very day, that very hour,
  Is curst oppression's last: 10
Then vengeance shall no longer stay,
The mighty flood shall break away:
Our purse-proud tyrants vanity
  Shall to the earth be cast.

You *whisker'd whelp*, of borough-breed,
Shall surely rue his dastard deed,
  And so shall *Sawney*, too:
Their chicken hearts, in that dread day,
Shall melt before their enemy;
A tougher game they'll have to play   20
  Than that of *Waterloo*.

Lift but a finger for his harm
Thou bloated ban-dog of the swarm,
    That crowd to yonder den.
Dare it, and thy black sin-clad soul
Shall, in an instant, hell-ward howl!
To join Cerberus' damned growl,
    Barr'd down from God and men.

Why did the sparks, on Monday night,
With fallen crests decline the fight,   30
    And silent sneak away?
Oh! there were country clogs, I ween,
And trusty cudgels, too, were seen;
And sturdy tykes, so gaunt and keen,
    All come to see the play.

The Dandies' shins, like rotten sticks,
Had snapp'd before the bumpkins' kicks,
    Had they but dar'd the tug:
Their ulcer'd throats had felt a grasp,
Crush'd flat, as in a giant's clasp,   40
    Or wild-bear's fatal hug.

Whiskers, and stays, and periwigs,
Had been pluck'd off by Burke's rude pigs,
    And trampled in the mire;
False teeth and noses would have flown,
Which the scabb'd rascals call their own,
Before the clog of country clown,
    Or cudgel's bruise so dire.

But true to Dandy stile and trim,
They risked neither life nor limb;   50
    Oh! it had cheered me,
To see our gallant gang so stout,
At clog and cudgel have a bout;
So fast, so firm, amid the rout,
    For *Hunt and Liberty*.

Oh! it had been well worth one's while
To travel many a weary mile,
    'Midst cold, and wind, and rain;
But come, my lads, some other day
We'll pin them, e'er they sneak away,   60
And they shall either play or pay
    When *Hunt* returns again.

GEORGE CRABBE

Delay Has Danger

Morning Excursion—Lady at Silford, who?—Reflections on Delay—Cecilia and Henry—The Lovers contracted—Visit to the Patron—Whom he finds there—Fanny described—The yielding of Vanity—Delay—Resentment—Want of Resolution—Further Entanglement—Danger—How met—Conclusion.

THREE weeks had past, and Richard rambles now
Far as the dinners of the day allow;
He rode to Farley Grange and Finley Mere,
That house so ancient, and that lake so clear:
He rode to Ripley through that river gay,
Where in the shallow stream the loaches play,
And stony fragments stay the winding stream,
And gilded pebbles at the bottom gleam,
Giving their yellow surface to the sun,
And making proud the waters as they run: 10
It is a lovely place, and at the side
Rises a mountain-rock in rugged pride;
And in that rock are shapes of shells, and forms
Of creatures in old worlds, of nameless worms,
Whose generations lived and died ere man,
A worm of other class, to crawl began.

There is a town call'd Silford, where his steed
Our traveller rested—He the while would feed
His mind by walking to and fro, to meet,
He knew not what adventure, in the street: 20
A stranger there, but yet a window-view
Gave him a face that he conceived he knew;
He saw a tall, fair, lovely lady, dress'd
As one whom taste and wealth had jointly bless'd;
He gazed, but soon a footman at the door
Thundering, alarm'd her, who was seen no more.

'This was the lady whom her lover bound
In solemn contract, and then proved unsound:
Of this affair I have a clouded view,
And should be glad to have it clear'd by you.'   30
So Richard spake, and instant George replied,
'I had the story from the injured side,

505

But when resentment and regret were gone,
And pity (shaded by contempt) came on.

'Frail was the hero of my tale, but still
Was rather drawn by accident than will;
Some without meaning into guilt advance,
From want of guard, from vanity, from chance;
Man's weakness flies his more immediate pain,
A little respite from his fears to gain;   40
And takes the part that he would gladly fly,
If he had strength and courage to deny.

'But now my tale, and let the moral say,
When hope can sleep, there's Danger in Delay.
Not that for rashness, Richard, I would plead,
For unadvised alliance: No, indeed:
Think ere the contract—but, contracted, stand
No more debating, take the ready hand:
When hearts are willing, and when fears subside,
Trust not to time, but let the knot be tied;   50
For when a lover has no more to do,
He thinks in leisure, what shall I pursue?
And then who knows what objects come in view?
For when, assured, the man has nought to keep
His wishes warm and active, then they sleep:
Hopes die with fears; and then a man must lose
All the gay visions, and delicious views,
Once his mind's wealth! He travels at his ease,
Nor horrors now nor fairy-beauty sees;
When the kind goddess gives the wish'd assent,   60
No mortal business should the deed prevent;
But the blest youth should legal sanction seek
Ere yet th'assenting blush has fled the cheek.

'And—hear me, Richard,—man has reptile-pride
That often rises when his fears subside;
When, like a trader feeling rich, he now
Neglects his former smile, his humble bow,
And, conscious of his hoarded wealth, assumes
New airs, nor thinks how odious he becomes.

'There is a wandering, wavering train of thought   70
That something seeks where nothing should be sought,
And will a self-delighted spirit move
To dare the danger of pernicious love.'

—————

First be it granted all was duly said
By the fond youth to the believing maid;
Let us suppose with many a sigh there came
The declaration of the deathless flame;—
And so her answer—'She was happy then,
Blest in herself, and did not think of men;
And with such comforts in her present state,   80
A wish to change it was to tempt her fate;
That she would not; but yet she would confess
With him she thought her hazard would be less;
Nay, more, she would esteem, she would regard express:
But to be brief—if he could wait and see
In a few years what his desires would be.'—

Henry for years read months, then weeks, nor found
The lady thought his judgment was unsound;
'For months read weeks,' she read it to his praise,
And had some thoughts of changing it to *days*.   90

And here a short excursion let me make,
A lover tried, I think, for lovers' sake;
And teach the meaning in a lady's mind
When you can none in her expressions find:
Words are design'd that meaning to convey,
But often *Yea* is hidden in a *Nay!*
And what the charmer wills, some gentle hints betray.
Then, too, when ladies mean to yield at length,
They match their reasons with the lover's strength,
And, kindly cautious, will no force employ   100
But such as he can baffle or destroy.

As when heroic lovers beauty woo'd,
And were by magic's mighty art withstood,
The kind historian, for the dame afraid,
Gave to the faithful knight the stronger aid.

A downright *No!* would make a man despair,
Or leave for kinder nymph the cruel fair;
But '*No!* because I'm very happy now,
Because I dread th' irrevocable vow,
Because I fear papa will not approve,   110
Because I love not—No, I cannot love;
Because you men of Cupid make a jest,
Because——in short, a single life is best.'
A *No!* when back'd by reasons of such force,
Invites approach, and will recede of course.

507

Ladies, like towns besieged, for honour's sake,
Will some defence or its appearance make;
On first approach there's much resistance made,
And conscious weakness hides in bold parade;
With lofty looks, and threat'nings stern and proud,   120
'Come, if you dare,' is said in language loud,
But if th'attack be made with care and skill,
'Come,' says the yielding party, 'if you will;'
Then each the other's valiant acts approve,
And twine their laurels in a wreath of love.—

We now retrace our tale, and forward go,—
Thus Henry rightly read Cecilia's No!
His prudent father, who had duly weigh'd,
And well approved the fortune of the maid,
Not much resisted, just enough to show   130
He knew his power, and would his son should know.

'Harry, I will, while I your bargain make,
That you a journey to our patron take:
I know her guardian; care will not become
A lad when courting; as you must be dumb,
You may be absent; I for you will speak,
And ask what you are not supposed to seek.'

Then came the parting hour, and what arise
When lovers part! expressive looks and eyes,
Tender and tear-full,—many a fond adieu,   140
And many a call the sorrow to renew;
Sighs such as lovers only can explain,
And words that they might undertake in vain.

Cecilia liked it not; she had, in truth,
No mind to part with her enamour'd youth;
But thought it foolish thus themselves to cheat,
And part for nothing but again to meet.

Now Henry's father was a man whose heart
Took with his interest a decided part;
He knew his Lordship, and was known for acts   150
That I omit,—they were acknowledged facts;
An interest somewhere; I the place forget,
And the good deed—no matter—'twas a debt:
Thither must Henry, and in vain the maid
Express'd dissent—the father was obey'd.

But though the maid was by her fears assail'd,
Her reason rose against them, and prevail'd;
Fear saw him hunting, leaping, falling—led,
Maim'd and disfigured, groaning to his bed;
Saw him in perils, duels,—dying,—dead.   160
But Prudence answer'd, 'Is not every maid
With equal cause for him she loves afraid?'
And from her guarded mind Cecilia threw
The groundless terrors that will love pursue.

She had no doubts, and her reliance strong
Upon the honour that she would not wrong:
Firm in herself, she doubted not the truth
Of him, the chosen, the selected youth;
Trust of herself a trust in him supplied,
And she believed him faithful, though untried: 170
On her he might depend, in him she would confide.

If some fond girl express'd a tender pain
Lest some fair rival should allure her swain,
To such she answer'd, with a look severe,
'Can one you doubt be worthy of your fear?'

My lord was kind,—a month had pass'd away,
And Henry stay'd,—he sometimes named a day;
But still my lord was kind, and Henry still must stay:
His father's words to him were words of fate—
'Wait, 'tis your duty; 'tis my pleasure, wait!'   180

In all his walks, in hilly heath or wood,
Cecilia's form the pensive youth pursued;
In the gray morning, in the silent noon,
In the soft twilight, by the sober moon,
In those forsaken rooms, in that immense saloon;
And he, now fond of that seclusion grown,
There reads her letters, and there writes his own.

'Here none approach,' said he, 'to interfere,
But I can think of my Cecilia here!'

But there did come—and how it came to pass   190
Who shall explain?—a mild and blue-eyed lass;—
It was the work of accident, no doubt—
The cause unknown—we say, 'as things fall out;'—
The damsel enter'd there, in wand'ring round about:
At first she saw not Henry; and she ran,
As from a ghost, when she beheld a man.

She was esteem'd a beauty through the hall,
And so admitted, with consent of all;
And, like a treasure, was her beauty kept
From every guest who in the mansion slept;   200
Whether as friends who join'd the noble pair,
Or those invited by the steward there.

She was the daughter of a priest, whose life
Was brief and sad: he lost a darling wife,
And Fanny then her father, who could save
But a small portion; but his all he gave,
With the fair orphan, to a sister's care,
And her good spouse: they were the ruling pair—
Steward and steward's lady—o'er a tribe,
Each under each, whom I shall not describe.   210

This grave old couple, childless and alone,
Would, by their care, for Fanny's loss atone:
She had been taught in schools of honest fame;
And to the Hall, as to a home, she came,
My lord assenting: yet, as meet and right,
Fanny was held from every hero's sight,
Who might in youthful error cast his eyes
On one so gentle as a lawful prize,
On border land, whom, as their right or prey,
A youth from either side might bear away.   220

Some handsome lover of th'inferior class
Might as a wife approve the lovely lass;
Or some invader from the class above,
Who, more presuming, would his passion prove
By asking less—love only for his love.

This much experienced aunt her fear express'd,
And dread of old and young, of host and guest.

'Go not, my Fanny, in their way,' she cried,
'It is not right that virtue should be tried;
So, to be safe, be ever at my side.'   230

She was not ever at that side; but still
Observed her precepts, and obey'd her will.

But in the morning's dawn and evening's gloom
She could not lock the damsel in her room;
And Fanny thought, 'I will ascend these stairs
To see the chapel,—there are none at prayers;

None,' she believed, 'had yet to dress return'd,
By whom a timid girl might be discern'd:'
In her slow motion, looking, as she glides,
On pictures, busts, and what she met besides,   240
And speaking softly to herself alone,
Or singing low in melancholy tone;
And thus she rambled through the still domain,
Room after room, again, and yet again.

But, to retrace our story, still we say,
To this saloon the maiden took her way;
Where she beheld our youth, and frighten'd ran,
And so their friendship in her fear began.

But dare she thither once again advance,
And still suppose the man will think it chance?   250
Nay, yet again, and what has chance to do
With this?—I know not: doubtless Fanny knew.

Now, of the meeting of a modest maid
And sober youth why need we be afraid?
And when a girl's amusements are so few
As Fanny's were, what would you have her do?
Reserved herself, a decent youth to find,
And just be civil, sociable, and kind,
And look together at the setting sun,
Then at each other—What the evil done?   260

Then Fanny took my little lord to play,
And bade him not intrude on Henry's way:
'O, he intrudes not!' said the youth, and grew
Fond of the child, and would amuse him too;
Would make such faces, and assume such looks—
He loved it better than his gayest books.

When man with man would an acquaintance seek,
He will his thoughts in chosen language speak;
And they converse on divers themes, to find
If they possess a corresponding mind;   270
But man with woman has foundation laid,
And built up friendship ere a word is said:
'Tis not with words that they their wishes tell,
But with a language answering quite as well;
And thus they find, when they begin t'explore
Their way by speech, they knew it all before.

And now it chanced again the pair, when dark,
Met in their way, when wandering in the park;
Not in the common path, for so they might,
Without a wonder, wander day or night;   280
But, when in pathless ways their chance will bring
A musing pair, we do admire the thing.

The youth in meeting read the damsel's face,
As if he meant her inmost thoughts to trace;
On which her colour changed, as if she meant
To give her aid, and help his kind intent.

Both smiled and parted, but they did not speak—
The smile implied, 'Do tell me what you seek:'
They took their different ways with erring feet,
And met again, surprised that they could meet;   290
Then must they speak—and something of the air
Is always ready—' 'Tis extremely fair!'

'It was so pleasant!' Henry said; 'the beam
Of that sweet light so brilliant on the stream;
And chiefly yonder, where that old cascade
Has for an age its simple music made;
All so delightful, soothing, and serene!
Do you not feel it? not enjoy the scene?
Something it has that words will not express,
But rather hide, and make th'enjoyment less: 300
'Tis what our souls conceive, 'tis what our hearts confess.'

Poor Fanny's heart at these same words confess'd
How well he painted, and how rightly guess'd;
And, while they stood admiring their retreat,
Henry found something like a mossy seat;
But Fanny sat not; no, she rather pray'd
That she might leave him, she was so afraid.

'Not, sir, of you; your goodness I can trust,
But folks are so censorious and unjust,
They make no difference, they pay no regard   310
To our true meaning, which is very hard
And very cruel; great the pain it cost
To lose such pleasure, but it must be lost:
Did people know how free from thought of ill
One's meaning is, their malice would be still.'

At this she wept; at least a glittering gem
Shone in each eye, and there was fire in them,

For as they fell, the sparkles, at his feet,
He felt emotions very warm and sweet.

'A lovely creature! not more fair than good,   320
By all admired, by some, it seems, pursued,
Yet self-protected by her virtue's force
And conscious truth—What evil in discourse
With one so guarded, who is pleased to trust
Herself with me, reliance strong and just?'

Our lover then believed he must not seem
Cold to the maid who gave him her esteem;
Not manly this; Cecilia had his heart,
But it was lawful with his time to part;
It would be wrong in her to take amiss   330
A virtuous friendship for a girl like this;
False or disloyal he would never prove,
But kindness here took nothing from his love:
Soldiers to serve a foreign prince are known,
When not on present duty to their own;
So, though our bosom's queen we still prefer,
We are not always on our knees to her.
'Cecilia present, witness yon fair moon,
And yon bright orbs, that fate would change as soon
As my devotion; but the absent sun   340
Cheers us no longer when his course is run;
And then those starry twinklers may obtain
A little worship till he shines again.'

The father still commanded 'Wait awhile,'
And the son answered in submissive style,
Grieved, but obedient; and obedience teased
His lady's spirit more than grieving pleased:
That he should grieve in absence was most fit,
But not that he to absence should submit;
And in her letters might be traced reproof,   350
Distant indeed, but visible enough;
This should the wandering of his heart have stay'd;
Alas! the wanderer was the vainer made.

The parties daily met, as by consent,
And yet it always seem'd by accident;
Till in the nymph the shepherd had been blind
If he had fail'd to see a manner kind,
With that expressive look, that seem'd to say,
'You do not speak, and yet you see you may.'

O! yes, he saw, and he resolved to fly,
And blamed his heart, unwilling to comply:
He sometimes wonder'd how it came to pass,
That he had all this freedom with the lass;
Reserved herself, with strict attention kept,
And care and vigilance that never slept:
'How is it thus that they a beauty trust
With me, who feel the confidence is just?
And they, too, feel it; yes, they may confide,'—
He said in folly, and he smiled in pride.
'Tis thus our secret passions work their way,   370
And the poor victims know not they obey.

Familiar now became the wandering pair,
And there was pride and joy in Fanny's air;
For though his silence did not please the maid,
She judged him only modest and afraid;
The gentle dames are ever pleased to find
Their lovers dreading they should prove unkind;
So, blind by hope, and pleased with prospects gay,
The generous beauty gave her heart away
Before he said, 'I love!'—alas! he dared not say.   380

Cecilia yet was mistress of his mind,
But oft he wish'd her, like his Fanny, kind;
Her fondness sooth'd him, for the man was vain,
And he perceived that he could give her pain:
Cecilia liked not to profess her love,
But Fanny ever was the yielding dove;
Tender and trusting, waiting for the word,
And then prepared to hail her bosom's lord.

Cecilia once her honest love avow'd,
To make him happy, not to make him proud;   390
But she would not, for every asking sigh,
Confess the flame that waked his vanity;
But this poor maiden, every day and hour,
Would, by fresh kindness, feed the growing power;
And he indulged, vain being! in the joy,
That he alone could raise it, or destroy;
A present good, from which he dared not fly,
Cecilia absent, and his Fanny by.

O! vain desire of youth, that in the hour
Of strong temptation, when he feels the power,   400
And knows how daily his desires increase,

Yet will he wait, and sacrifice his peace,
Will trust to chance to free him from the snare,
Of which, long since, his conscience said, beware!
Or look for strange deliverance from that ill,
That he might fly, could he command the will!

How can he freedom from the future seek,
Who feels already that he grows too weak?
And thus refuses to resist, till time
Removes the power, and makes the way for crime: 410
Yet thoughts he had, and he would think, 'Forego
My dear Cecilia? not for kingdoms! No!
But may I, ought I not the friend to be
Of one who feels this fond regard for me?
I wrong no creature by a kindness lent
To one so gentle, mild, and innocent;
And for that fair one, whom I still adore,
By feeling thus I think of her the more;'
And not unlikely, for our thoughts will tend
To those whom we are conscious we offend.   420

Had Reason whisper'd, 'Has Cecilia leave
Some gentle youth in friendship to receive,
And be to him the friend that you appear
To this soft girl?—would not some jealous fear
Proclaim your thoughts, that he approach'd too near?'

But Henry, blinded still, presumed to write
Of one in whom Cecilia would delight;
A mild and modest girl, a gentle friend,
If, as he hoped, her kindness would descend—
But what he fear'd to lose or hoped to gain   430
By writing thus, he had been ask'd in vain.

It was his purpose, every morn he rose,
The dangerous friendship he had made to close;
It was his torment nightly, ere he slept,
To feel his prudent purpose was not kept.

True, he has wonder'd why the timid maid
Meets him so often, and is not afraid;
And why that female dragon, fierce and keen,
Has never in their private walks been seen;
And often he has thought, 'What can their silence
        mean?   440

515

'They can have no design, or plot, or plan,—
In fact, I know not how the thing began,—
'Tis their dependence on my credit here,
And fear not, nor, in fact, have cause to fear.'

But did that pair, who seemed to think that all
Unwatch'd will wander and unguarded fall,
Did they permit a youth and maid to meet
Both unreproved? were they so indiscreet?

This sometimes enter'd Henry's mind, and then,
'Who shall account for women or for men?'   450
He said, 'or who their secret thoughts explore?
Why do I vex me? I will think no more.'

My Lord of late had said, in manner kind,
'My good friend Harry, do not think us blind!'
Letters had past, though he had nothing seen,
His careful father and my Lord between;
But to what purpose was to him unknown—
It might be borough business, or their own.

Fanny, it seem'd, was now no more in dread,
If one approach'd, she neither fear'd nor fled: 460
He mused on this,—'But wherefore her alarm?
She knows me better, and she dreads no harm.'

Something his father wrote that gave him pain:
'I know not, son, if you should yet remain;—
Be cautious, Harry, favours to procure
We strain a point, but we must first be sure:
Love is a folly,—that, indeed, is true,—
But something still is to our honour due,
So I must leave the thing to my good Lord and you.'

But from Cecilia came remonstrance strong: 470
'You write too darkly, and you stay too long;
We hear reports; and, Henry,—mark me well,—
I heed not every tale that triflers tell;—
Be you no trifler; dare not to believe
That I am one whom words and vows deceive:
You know your heart, your hazard you will learn,
And this your trial——instantly return.'

'Unjust, injurious, jealous, cruel maid!
Am I a slave, of haughty words afraid?
Can she who thus commands expect to be obey'd?   480
O! how unlike this dear assenting soul,
Whose heart a man might at his will control!'

Uneasy, anxious, fill'd with self-reproof,
He now resolved to quit his patron's roof;
And then again his vacillating mind
To stay resolved, and that her pride should find:
Debating thus, his pen the lover took,
And chose the words of anger and rebuke.

Again, yet once again, the conscious pair
Met, and 'O, speak!' was Fanny's silent prayer;   490
And, 'I must speak,' said the embarrass'd youth,
'Must save my honour, must confess the truth:
Then I must lose her; but, by slow degrees,
She will regain her peace, and I my ease.'

Ah! foolish man! to virtue true nor vice,
He buys distress, and self-esteem the price;
And what his gain?—a tender smile and sigh
From a fond girl to feed his vanity.

Thus, every day they lived, and every time
They met, increased his anguish and his crime.   500

Still in their meetings they were ofttimes nigh
The darling theme, and then past trembling by;
On those occasions Henry often tried
For the sad truth—and then his heart denied
The utterance due: thus daily he became
The prey of weakness, vanity, and shame.

But soon a day, that was their doubts to close,
On the fond maid and thoughtless youth arose.

Within the park, beside the bounding brook,
The social pair their usual ramble took;   510
And there the steward found them: they could trace
News in his look, and gladness in his face.

He was a man of riches, bluff and big,
With clean brown broad-cloth, and with white cut wig:
He bore a cane of price, with riband tied,
And a fat spaniel waddled at his side:
To every being whom he met he gave
His looks expressive; civil, gay, or grave,
But condescending all; and each declared
How much he govern'd, and how well he fared.   520

This great man bow'd, not humbly, but his bow
Appear'd familiar converse to allow:

The trembling Fanny, as he came in view,
Within the chestnut grove in fear withdrew;
While Henry wonder'd, not without a fear,
Of that which brought th'important man so near:
Doubt was dispersed by—'My esteem'd young man!'
As he with condescending grace began——

'Though you with youthful frankness nobly trust
Your Fanny's friends, and doubtless think them just;   530
Though you have not, with craving soul, applied
To us, and ask'd the fortune of your bride,
Be it our care that you shall not lament
That love has made you so improvident.

'An orphan maid——Your patience! you shall have
Your time to speak, I now attention crave;—
Fanny, dear girl! has in my spouse and me
Friends of a kind we wish our friends to be,
None of the poorest——nay, sir, no reply,
You shall not need——and we are born to die: 540
And one yet crawls on earth, of whom, I say,
That what he has he cannot take away;
Her mother's father, one who has a store
Of this world's good, and always looks for more;
But, next his money, loves the girl at heart,
And she will have it when they come to part.'

'Sir,' said the youth, his terrors all awake,
'Hear me, I pray, I beg,—for mercy's sake!
Sir, were the secrets of my soul confess'd,
Would you admit the truths that I protest   550
Are such——your pardon'——
                    'Pardon! good, my friend,
I not alone will pardon, I commend:
Think you that I have no remembrance left
Of youthful love, and Cupid's cunning theft?
How nymphs will listen when their swains persuade,
How hearts are gain'd, and how exchange is made?—
Come sir, your hand'——
                    'In mercy, hear me now!'
'I cannot hear you, time will not allow:
You know my station, what on me depends,
For ever needed—but we part as friends;   560
And here comes one who will the whole explain,
My better self—and we shall meet again.'

'Sir, I entreat'——
            'Then be entreaty made
To her, a woman, one you may persuade;
A little teasing, but she will comply,
And loves her niece too fondly to deny.'

'O! he is mad, and miserable I!'
Exclaim'd the youth; 'But let me now collect
My scatter'd thoughts, I something must effect.'

Hurrying she came—'Now, what has he confess'd,   570
Ere I could come to set your heart at rest?
What! he has grieved you! Yet he, too, approves
The thing! but man will tease you, if he loves.

'But now for business: tell me, did you think
That we should always at your meetings wink?
Think you, you walk'd unseen? There are who bring
To me all secrets—O, you wicked thing!
Poor Fanny! now I think I see her blush,
All red and rosy, when I beat the bush;
"And hide your secret," said I, "if you dare!"   580
So out it came, like an affrighten'd hare.

' "Miss", said I, gravely; and the trembling maid
Pleased me at heart to see her so afraid;
And then she wept;—now, do remember this,
Never to chide her when she does amiss;
For she is tender as the callow bird,
And cannot bear to have her temper stirr'd;—
"Fanny," I said, then whisper'd her the name,
And caused such looks—Yes, yours are just the same;
But hear my story—When your love was known   590
For this our child—she is, in fact, our own—
Then, first debating, we agreed at last
To seek my Lord, and tell him what had past.'

'To tell the Earl?'
              'Yes, truly, and why not?
And then together we contrived our plot.'

'Eternal God!'
         'Nay, be not so surprised,—
In all the matter we were well advised;
We saw my Lord, and Lady Jane was there,
And said to Johnson, "Johnson, take a chair:"

True, we are servants in a certain way,   600
But in the higher places so are they;
We are obey'd in ours, and they in theirs obey—
So Johnson bow'd, for that was right and fit,
And had no scruple with the Earl to sit—
Why look you so impatient while I tell
What they debated?—you must like it well.

' "Let them go on," our gracious Earl began;
"They will go off," said, joking, my good man:
"Well!" said the Countess,—she's a lover's friend,—
"What if they do, they make the speedier end"——   610
But be you more composed, for that dear child
Is with her joy and apprehension wild:
O! we have watch'd you on from day to day,
"There go the lovers!" we were wont to say—
But why that look?'—
                              'Dear Madam, I implore
A single moment!'
                              'I can give no more:
Here are your letters—"That's a female pen,"
Said I to Fanny—" 'Tis his sister's, then,"
Replied the maid.—No! never must you stray;
Or hide your wanderings, if you should, I pray;   620
I know, at least I fear, the best may err,
But keep the by-walks of your life from her:
That youth should stray is nothing to be told,
When they have sanction in the grave and old,
Who have no call to wander and transgress,
But very love of change and wantonness.

'I prattle idly, while your letters wait,
And then my Lord has much that he would state,
All good to you—do clear that clouded face,
And with good looks your lucky lot embrace.   630

'Now, mind that none with her divide your heart,
For she would die ere lose the smallest part;
And I rejoice that all has gone so well,
For who th'effect of Johnson's rage can tell?
He had his fears when you began to meet,
But I assured him there was no deceit:
He is a man who kindness will requite,
But injured once, revenge is his delight;
And he would spend the best of his estates
To ruin, goods and body, them he hates;   640

While he is kind enough when he approves
A deed that's done, and serves the man he loves:
Come, read your letters—I must now be gone,
And think of matters that are coming on.'

Henry was lost,—his brain confused, his soul
Dismay'd and sunk, his thoughts beyond control;
Borne on by terror, he foreboding read
Cecilia's letter! and his courage fled;
All was a gloomy, dark, and dreadful view,
He felt him guilty, but indignant too:—   650
And as he read, he felt the high disdain
Of injured men—'She may repent, in vain.'

Cecilia much had heard, and told him all
That scandal taught—'A servant at the Hall,
Or servant's daughter, in the kitchen bred,
Whose father would not with her mother wed,
Was now his choice! a blushing fool, the toy,
Or the attempted, both of man and boy;
More than suspected, but without the wit
Or the allurements for such creatures fit;   660
Not virtuous though unfeeling, cold as ice
And yet not chaste, the weeping fool of vice;
Yielding, not tender; feeble, not refined;
Her form insipid, and without a mind.

'Rival! she spurn'd the word; but let him stay,
Warn'd as he was! beyond the present day,
Whate'er his patron might object to this,
The uncle-butler, or the weeping miss—
Let him from this one single day remain,
And then return! he would to her, in vain;   670
There let him then abide, to earn, or crave
Food undeserved! and be with slaves a slave.'

Had reason guided anger, govern'd zeal,
Or chosen words to make a lover feel,
She might have saved him—anger and abuse
Will but defiance and revenge produce.

'Unjust and cruel, insolent and proud!'
He said, indignant, and he spoke aloud.
'Butler! and servant! Gentlest of thy sex,
Thou wouldst not thus a man who loved thee vex;   680
Thou wouldst not thus to vile report give ear,

Nor thus enraged for fancied crimes appear;
I know not what, dear maid!—if thy soft smiles were here.'

And then, that instant, there appear'd the maid,
By his sad looks in her approach dismay'd;
Such timid sweetness, and so wrong'd, did more
Than all her pleading tenderness before.

In that weak moment, when disdain and pride,
And fear and fondness, drew the man aside,
In this weak moment—'Wilt thou,' he began,   690
'Be mine?' and joy o'er all her features ran;
'I will!' she softly whisper'd; but the roar
Of cannon would not strike his spirit more;
Ev'n as his lips the lawless contract seal'd
He felt that conscience lost her seven-fold shield,
And honour fled, but still he spoke of love,
And all was joy in the consenting dove.

That evening all in fond discourse was spent,
When the sad lover to his chamber went,
To think on what had past, to grieve and to repent: 700
Early he rose, and look'd with many a sigh
On the red light that fill'd the eastern sky;
Oft had he stood before, alert and gay,
To hail the glories of the new-born day:
But now dejected, languid, listless, low,
He saw the wind upon the water blow,
And the cold stream curl'd onward as the gale
From the pine-hill blew harshly down the dale;
On the right side the youth a wood survey'd,
With all its dark intensity of shade;   710
Where the rough wind alone was heard to move,
In this, the pause of nature and of love,
When now the young are rear'd, and when the old,
Lost to the tie, grow negligent and cold—
Far to the left he saw the huts of men,
Half hid in mist, that hung upon the fen;
Before him swallows, gathering for the sea,
Took their short flights, and twitter'd on the lea;
And near the bean-sheaf stood, the harvest done,
And slowly blacken'd in the sickly sun;   720
All these were sad in nature, or they took
Sadness from him, the likeness of his look,
And of his mind—he ponder'd for a while,
Then met his Fanny with a borrow'd smile.

Not much remain'd; for money and my Lord
Soon made the father of the youth accord;
His prudence half resisted, half obey'd,
And scorn kept still the guardians of the maid:
Cecilia never on the subject spoke,
She seem'd as one who from a dream awoke;   730
So all was peace, and soon the married pair
Fix'd with fair fortune in a mansion fair.

Five years had past, and what was Henry then?
The most repining of repenting men;
With a fond, teasing, anxious wife, afraid
Of all attention to another paid;
Yet powerless she her husband to amuse,
Lives but t'intreat, implore, resent, accuse;
Jealous and tender, conscious of defects,
She merits little, and yet much expects;   740
She looks for love that now she cannot see,
And sighs for joy that never more can be;
On his retirements her complaints intrude,
And fond reproof endears his solitude:
While he her weakness (once her kindness) sees,
And his affections in her languor freeze;
Regret, uncheck'd by hope, devours his mind,
He feels unhappy, and he grows unkind.

'Fool! to be taken by a rosy cheek,
And eyes that cease to sparkle or to speak;   750
Fool! for this child my freedom to resign,
When one the glory of her sex was mine;
While from this burthen to my soul I hide,
To think what Fate has dealt, and what denied.

'What fiend possess'd me when I tamely gave
My forced assent to be an idiot's slave?
Her beauty vanish'd, what for me remains?
Th'eternal clicking of the galling chains:
Her person truly I may think my own,
Seen without pleasure, without triumph shown: 760
Doleful she sits, her children at her knees,
And gives up all her feeble powers to please;
Whom I, unmoved, or moved with scorn, behold,
Melting as ice, as vapid and as cold.'

Such was his fate, and he must yet endure
The self-contempt that no self-love can cure:

GEORGE CRABBE

Some business call'd him to a wealthy town
When unprepared for more than Fortune's frown;
There at a house he gave his luckless name,
The master absent, and Cecilia came;   770
Unhappy man! he could not, dared not speak,
But look'd around, as if retreat to seek:
This she allow'd not; but, with brow severe,
Ask'd him his business, sternly bent to hear;
He had no courage, but he view'd that face
As if he sought for sympathy and grace;
As if some kind returning thought to trace:
In vain; not long he waited, but with air,
That of all grace compell'd him to despair,
She rang the bell, and, when a servant came,   780
Left the repentant traitor to his shame;
But, going, spoke, 'Attend this person out,
And if he speaks, hear what he comes about!'
Then, with cool curtesy, from the room withdrew,
That seem'd to say, 'Unhappy man, adieu!'

Thus will it be when man permits a vice
First to invade his heart, and then entice;
When wishes vain and undefined arise,
And that weak heart deceive, seduce, surprise;
When evil Fortune works on Folly's side,   790
And rash Resentment adds a spur to Pride;
Then life's long troubles from those actions come,
In which a moment may decide our doom.

[1820]

JOHN KEATS

184   *Ode on a Grecian Urn*

I

THOU still unravish'd bride of quietness,
    Thou foster-child of silence and slow time,
Sylvan historian, who canst thus express
    A flowery tale more sweetly than our rhyme:

What leaf-fring'd legend haunts about thy shape
  Of deities or mortals, or of both,
    In Tempe or the dales of Arcady?
  What men or gods are these? What maidens loth?
What mad pursuit? What struggle to escape?
    What pipes and timbrels? What wild ecstasy? 10

2

Heard melodies are sweet, but those unheard
  Are sweeter; therefore, ye soft pipes, play on:
Not to the sensual ear, but, more endear'd,
  Pipe to the spirit ditties of no tone:
Fair youth, beneath the trees, thou canst not leave
  Thy song, nor ever can those trees be bare;
    Bold Lover, never, never canst thou kiss,
Though winning near the goal—yet, do not grieve;
    She cannot fade, though thou hast not thy bliss,
  For ever wilt thou love, and she be fair! 20

3

Ah, happy, happy boughs! that cannot shed
  Your leaves, nor ever bid the Spring adieu;
And, happy melodist, unwearied,
  For ever piping songs for ever new;
More happy love! more happy, happy love!
  For ever warm and still to be enjoy'd,
    For ever panting, and for ever young;
All breathing human passion far above,
  That leaves a heart high-sorrowful and cloy'd,
    A burning forehead, and a parching tongue. 30

4

Who are these coming to the sacrifice?
  To what green altar, O mysterious priest,
Lead'st thou that heifer lowing at the skies,
  And all her silken flanks with garlands drest?
What little town by river or sea shore,
  Or mountain-built with peaceful citadel,
    Is emptied of this folk, this pious morn?
And, little town, thy streets for evermore
  Will silent be; and not a soul to tell
    Why thou art desolate, can e'er return. 40

5

O Attic shape! Fair attitude! with brede
  Of marble men and maidens overwrought,
With forest branches and the trodden weed;
  Thou, silent form, dost tease us out of thought
As doth eternity: Cold Pastoral!
  When old age shall this generation waste,
    Thou shalt remain, in midst of other woe
  Than ours, a friend to man, to whom thou say'st,
'Beauty is truth, truth beauty,'—that is all
    Ye know on earth, and all ye need to know.   50

185   *La Belle Dame Sans Mercy*

AH, what can ail thee, wretched wight,
  Alone and palely loitering;
The sedge is wither'd from the lake,
  And no birds sing.

Ah, what can ail thee, wretched wight,
  So haggard and so woe-begone?
The squirrel's granary is full,
  And the harvest's done.

I see a lilly on thy brow
  With anguish moist and fever dew;   10
And on thy cheek a fading rose
  Fast withereth too.

I met a lady in the meads,
  Full beautiful, a fairy's child;
Her hair was long, her foot was light,
  And her eyes were wild.

I set her on my pacing steed,
  And nothing else saw all day long;
For sideways would she lean, and sing
  A faery's song.   20

I made a garland for her head,
  And bracelets too, and fragrant zone;
She look'd at me as she did love,
  And made sweet moan.

She found me roots of relish sweet,
  And honey wild, and manna dew,
And sure in language strange she said,
  I love thee true.

She took me to her elfin grot,
  And there she gaz'd and sighed deep,   30
And there I shut her wild sad eyes—
  So kiss'd to sleep.

And there we slumber'd on the moss,
  And there I dream'd, ah woe betide
The latest dream I ever dream'd
  On the cold hill side.

I saw pale kings and princes too,
  Pale warriors, death-pale were they all;
Who cry'd—'La belle Dame sans mercy
  Hath thee in thrall!'   40

I saw their starv'd lips in the gloom
  With horrid warning gaped wide,
And I awoke and found me here
  On the cold hill side.

And this is why I sojourn here
  Alone and palely loitering,
Though the sedge is wither'd from the lake,
  And no birds sing.

186   *A Dream, after Reading Dante's Episode*
                of Paolo and Francesca

As Hermes once took to his feathers light,
  When lulled Argus, baffled, swoon'd and slept,
So on a Delphic reed, my idle spright
  So play'd, so charm'd, so conquer'd, so bereft
The dragon-world of all its hundred eyes;
  And, seeing it asleep, so fled away—
Not unto Ida with its snow-cold skies,
  Nor unto Tempe, where Jove griev'd a day,
But to that second circle of sad hell,
  Where 'mid the gust, the world-wind, and the flaw   10

Of rain and hail-stones, lovers need not tell
   Their sorrows. Pale were the sweet lips I saw,
Pale were the lips I kiss'd, and fair the form
I floated with, about that melancholy storm.

JOHN CLARE
1793–1864

187   *My Mary*

WHO lives where beggars rarely speed,
And leads a hum-drum life indeed,
As none beside herself would lead?
              My Mary.

Who lives where noises never cease,
And what with hogs and ducks and geese
Can never have a minute's peace?
              My Mary.

Who, nearly battled to her chin,
Bangs down the yard through thick and thin,   10
Nor picks her road, nor cares a pin?
              My Mary.

Who, save in Sunday's bib and tuck,
Goes daily waddling like a duck,
O'er head and ears in grease and muck?
              My Mary.

Unus'd to pattens or to clogs,
Who takes the swill to serve the hogs,
And steals the milk for cats and dogs?
              My Mary.   20

Who, frost and snow, as hard as nails,
Stands out o' doors, and never fails
To wash up things and scour the pails?
              My Mary.

Who bustles night and day, in short,
At all catch jobs of every sort,
And gains her mistress' favour for't?
                    My Mary.

And who is oft repaid with praise,
In doing what her mistress says,   30
And yielding to her whimmy ways?
                    My Mary.

For there's none apter, I believe,
At 'creeping up a mistress' sleeve,'
Than this low kindred stump of Eve,
                    My Mary.

Who, when the baby's all unfit,
To please its mamma kisses it,
And vows no rose on earth's so sweet?
                    My Mary.   40

But when her mistress is not nigh,
Who swears, and wishes it would die,
And pinches it and makes it cry?
                    My Mary.

Oh, rank deceit! what soul could think—
But gently there, revealing ink:
At faults of thine thy friend must wink,
                    My Mary.

Who, not without a 'spark o' pride,'
Though strong as grunter's bristly hide,   50
Doth keep her hair in papers tied?
                    My Mary.

And, mimicking the gentry's way,
Who strives to speak as fine as they,
And minds but every word they say?
                    My Mary.

And who, though's well bid blind to see
As her to tell ye A from B,
Thinks herself none o' low degree?
                    My Mary.   60

Who prates and runs o'er silly stuff,
And 'mong the boys makes sport enough,
So ugly, silly, droll and rough?

                My Mary.

Ugly! Muse, for shame of thee,
What faults art thou a-going to see
In one, that's 'lotted out to be

                My Mary?

Who, low in stature, thick and fat,
Turns brown from going without a hat,   70
Though not a pin the worse for that?

                My Mary.

Who's laugh'd at too by every whelp,
For failings which she cannot help?
But silly fools will laugh and chelp,

                My Mary.

For though in stature mighty small,
And near as thick as thou art tall,
The hand made thee that made us all,

                My Mary.   80

And though thy nose hooks down too much,
And prophesies thy chin to touch,
I'm not so nice to look at such,

                My Mary.

No, no; about thy nose and chin,
Its hooking out, or bending in,
I never heed or care a pin,

                My Mary.

And though thy skin is brown and rough,
And form'd by nature hard and tough,   90
All suiteth me! so that's enough,

                My Mary.

HENRY LUTTRELL

1765–1821

188   from *Letters to Julia, in Rhyme*

Have you not seen (you must remember)
A fog in London—time, November?
That non-descript elsewhere, and grown
In our congenial soil alone?
First, at the dawn of lingering day
It rises, of an ashey grey,
Then, deepening with a sordid stain
Of yellow, like a lion's mane,
Vapour importunate and dense,
It wars at once with every sense,   10
Invades the eyes, is tasted, smelt,
And, like Egyptian darkness, felt.
The ears escape not. All around
Returns a dull unwonted sound.
Loth to stand still, afraid to stir,
The chilled and puzzled passenger,
Oft-blundering from the pavement, fails
To feel his way along the rails,
Or, at the crossings, in the roll
Of every carriage dreads its pole.   20

Scarce an eclipse with pall so dun
Blots from the face of heaven the sun,
If sun indeed he can be called,
With orb so beamless and so bald;
When not an arrow from his quiver
Alights unblunted on the river.
But soon a thicker darker cloak
Wraps all the town. Behold! The smoke
Which steam-compelling trade disgorges
From all her furnaces and forges,   30
In pitchy clouds, too dense to rise,
Descends, rejected, from the skies,
Till struggling day, extinguished quite,
At noon gives place to candle-light!

O Chemistry, *attractive* maid,
Descend in pity to our aid!
Come, with thy all-pervading gasses,

Thy crucibles, retorts, and glasses,
Thy fearful energies and wonders,
Thy dazzling lights and mimic thunders!   40
Let Carbon in thy train be seen,
Dark Azote, and fair Oxygene,
And Woolaston, and Davy guide
The car that bears thee, at thy side.
If any power can any how
Abate these nuisances, 'tis thou.
And see, to aid thee in the blow,
The bill of Michael Angelo!
O join (success a thing of course is)
Thy heav'nly to his mortal forces,   50
Make all our chimneys chew the cud
Like hungry cows, as chimneys should,
And since 'tis only smoke we draw
Within our lungs, at common law,
Into their thirsty tubes be sent
Fresh air—by act of Parliament!

  Enough.—From sights and sounds like these
Return we to the Tuilleries.

(from 'Letter II')

  London, within thy ample verge
What crowds lie sheltered, or emerge
Buoyant in every shape and form,
As smiles the calm or drives the storm;
Blest if they reach the harbour free
Of golden Mediocrity!
Here, ev'n the dwellings of the poor
And lonely are, at least, obscure,
And, in obscurity, exempt
From poverty's worst plague, contempt.   10
Unmarked the poor man seeks his den;
Unheeded issues forth again.
Wherefore appears he? None inquires,
Nor why nor whither he retires.
All that his pride would fain conceal,
All that Shame blushes to reveal,
The petty shifts, the grovelling cares
To which the sons of Want are heirs,
Those ills, which, grievous to be borne,
Call forth—not sympathy but scorn,   20

Here lost, elude the searching eye
Of callous Curiosity.

   And what though Poverty environ
Full many a wretch with chains of iron?
These in no stricter bondage hold
Their slaves than manacles of gold.
The costliest fetters are as strong
As common ones, and last as long.
Whom gall they most?—'Tis doubtful which,
The very poor, or very rich;   30
Those scourged by wants and discontents,
Or these by their establishments;
Victims, from real evils free,
To nerves, *cui bono?* and ennui.
Don't fancy now that this "cui bono"
Has some strange meaning, Julia. No, no.
Be not alarmed, nor blush, nor smile.
The words but ask—Is Life worth while?

   Still, Poverty, in every place
Still ghastly is thy spectre-face.   40
But he whose lips have never quaffed
From thy lean hands the bitter draught,
Who joins to health and competence
Good temper and a grain of sense,
Here may defy or follow Fashion;
Indulge his whim, his taste, or passion,
Pursue his pleasures or his labours,
Aloof from squires, unwatched by neighbours.

   What though to rail or laugh at money
Be over-dull, or over-funny,   50
(Since who would ridicule employment,
Or cry down power, or quiz enjoyment,)
London is, surely, to a tittle
The place for those who have but little.
Here I endure no throbs, no twitches
Of envy at another's riches,
But, smiling, from my window see
A dozen twice as rich as he;
And, if I stroll, am sure to meet
A dozen more in every street.   60
None are distinguished, none are rare
From wealth which hundreds round them share,
But, neutralized by one another

Whene'er they think to raise a pother,
Be they kind-hearted, or capricious,
Vain, prodigal, or avaricious,
Proud, popular, or what they will,
Are elbowed by their rivals still.

  Should one among them dare be dull,
Or prose, because his purse is full;   70
Should he, in breach of all decorum,
Make the least mention of the Quorum;
Drop but a hint of what transgressions
Are punished at the Quarter-sessions;
Or murmur at those vile encroachers
On rural privilege—the poachers;
Soon would a general yawn or cough
From such a trespass warn him off,
Spite of his India-bonds, and rents,
His acres, and his three-per-cents.   80
None would endure such parish-prate,
Were half the island his estate;
Though he in ready cash were sharing
The wealth, without the sense, of Baring.

(from 'Letter III')

EDWARD QUILLINAN
1791–1851

189   *The Hour Glass*

POETS loiter all their leisure,
  Culling flowers of rhyme;
Thus they twine the wreath of pleasure
  Round the glass of time:
  Twining flowers of rhyme.

Fancy's Children, ever heedless!
  Why thus bribe the hours?
Death, to prove the trouble needless,
  Withers all your flowers:
  Why then bribe the hours?   10

Like the Sand, so fast retreating,
  Thus your hopes shall fall;
Life and fame are just as fleeting;
  Poets, flowers, and all:
  Thus your fancies fall.

PERCY BYSSHE SHELLEY

190   from *Prometheus Unbound*

A Lyrical Drama

DRAMATIS PERSONAE

PROMETHEUS
DEMOGORGON
JUPITER
THE EARTH
OCEAN
APOLLO
MERCURY
ASIA
PANTHEA ⎫ Oceanides
IONE   ⎭
HERCULES
THE PHANTASM OF JUPITER
THE SPIRIT OF THE EARTH
THE SPIRIT OF THE MOON
SPIRITS OF THE HOURS
SPIRITS, ECHOES, FAUNS
FURIES

from *Act I*

SCENE.—*A Ravine of Icy Rocks in the Indian Caucasus.* PROMETHEUS
is discovered bound to the Precipice. PANTHEA *and* IONE *are seated at
his feet. Time, night. During the Scene, morning slowly breaks.*

PROMETHEUS. Monarch of Gods and Dæmons, and all Spirits
  But One, who throng those bright and rolling worlds

Which Thou and I alone of living things
Behold with sleepless eyes! regard this Earth
Made multitudinous with thy slaves, whom thou
Requitest for knee-worship, prayer, and praise,
And toil, and hecatombs of broken hearts,
With fear and self-contempt and barren hope.
Whilst me, who am thy foe, eyeless in hate,
Hast thou made reign and triumph, to thy scorn,   10
O'er mine own misery and thy vain revenge.
Three thousand years of sleep-unsheltered hours,
And moments aye divided by keen pangs
Till they seemed years, torture and solitude,
Scorn and despair,—these are mine empire:—
More glorious far than that which thou surveyest
From thine unenvied throne, O Mighty God!
Almighty, had I deigned to share the shame
Of thine ill tyranny, and hung not here
Nailed to this wall of eagle-baffling mountain,   20
Black, wintry, dead, unmeasured; without herb,
Insect, or beast, or shape or sound of life.
Ah me! alas, pain, pain ever, for ever!

No change, no pause, no hope! Yet I endure.
I ask the Earth, have not the mountains felt?
I ask yon Heaven, the all-beholding Sun,
Has it not seen? The Sea, in storm or calm,
Heaven's ever-changing Shadow, spread below,
Have its deaf waves not heard my agony?
Ah me! alas, pain, pain ever, for ever!   30

The crawling glaciers pierce me with the spears
Of their moon-freezing crystals, the bright chains
Eat with their burning cold into my bones.
Heaven's wingèd hound, polluting from thy lips
His beak in poison not his own, tears up
My heart; and shapeless sights come wandering by,
The ghastly people of the realm of dream,
Mocking me: and the Earthquake-fiends are charged
To wrench the rivets from my quivering wounds
When the rocks split and close again behind: 40
While from their loud abysses howling throng
The genii of the storm, urging the rage
Of whirlwind, and afflict me with keen hail.
And yet to me welcome is day and night,
Whether one breaks the hoar frost of the morn,
Or starry, dim, and slow, the other climbs

The leaden-coloured east; for then they lead
The wingless, crawling hours, one among whom
—As some dark Priest hales the reluctant victim—
Shall drag thee, cruel King, to kiss the blood   50
From these pale feet, which then might trample thee
If they disdained not such a prostrate slave.
Disdain! Ah no! I pity thee. What ruin
Will hunt thee undefended through the wide Heaven!
How will thy soul, cloven to its depth with terror,
Gape like a hell within! I speak in grief,
Not exultation, for I hate no more,
As then ere misery made me wise. The curse
Once breathed on thee I would recall. Ye Mountains,
Whose many-voicèd Echoes, through the mist   60
Of cataracts, flung the thunder of that spell!
Ye icy Springs, stagnant with wrinkling frost,
Which vibrated to hear me, and then crept
Shuddering through India! Thou serenest Air,
Through which the Sun walks burning without beams!
And ye swift Whirlwinds, who on poisèd wings
Hung mute and moveless o'er yon hushed abyss,
As thunder, louder than your own, made rock
The orbèd world! If then my words had power,
Though I am changed so that aught evil wish   70
Is dead within; although no memory be
Of what is hate, let them not lose it now!
What was that curse? for ye all heard me speak.

FIRST VOICE (*from the Mountains*).
Thrice three hundred thousand years
  O'er the Earthquake's couch we stood:
Oft, as men convulsed with fears,
  We trembled in our multitude.

SECOND VOICE (*from the Springs*).
Thunderbolts had parched our water,
  We had been stained with bitter blood,
And had run mute, 'mid shrieks of slaughter,   80
  Thro' a city and a solitude.

THIRD VOICE (*from the Air*).
I had clothed, since Earth uprose,
  Its wastes in colours not their own,
And oft had my serene repose
  Been cloven by many a rending groan.

537

FOURTH VOICE (*from the Whirlwinds*).
We had soared beneath these mountains
    Unresting ages; nor had thunder,
Nor yon volcano's flaming fountains,
    Nor any power above or under
    Ever made us mute with wonder.   90

FIRST VOICE.
But never bowed our snowy crest
As at the voice of thine unrest.

SECOND VOICE.
Never such a sound before
To the Indian waves we bore.
A pilot asleep on the howling sea
Leaped up from the deck in agony,
And heard, and cried, 'Ah, woe is me!'
And died as mad as the wild waves be.

THIRD VOICE.
By such dread words from Earth to Heaven
My still realm was never riven: 100
When its wound was closed, there stood
Darkness o'er the day like blood.

FOURTH VOICE.
And we shrank back: for dreams of ruin
To frozen caves our flight pursuing
Made us keep silence—thus—and thus—
Though silence is as hell to us.

THE EARTH. The tongueless Caverns of the craggy hills
    Cried, 'Misery!' then; the hollow Heaven replied,
    'Misery!' and the Ocean's purple waves,
    Climbing the land, howled to the lashing winds,   110
        And the pale nations heard it, 'Misery!'
PROMETHEUS. I heard a sound of voices: not the voice
    Which I gave forth. Mother, thy sons and thou
    Scorn him, without whose all-enduring will
    Beneath the fierce omnipotence of Jove,
    Both they and thou had vanished, like thin mist
    Unrolled on the morning wind. Know ye not me,
    The Titan? He who made his agony
    The barrier to your else all-conquering foe?
    Oh, rock-embosomed lawns, and snow-fed streams,   120
    Now seen athwart frore vapours, deep below,

538

Through whose o'ershadowing woods I wandered once
With Asia, drinking life from her loved eyes;
Why scorns the spirit which informs ye, now
To commune with me? me alone, who checked,
As one who checks a fiend-drawn charioteer,
The falsehood and the force of him who reigns
Supreme, and with the groans of pining slaves
Fills your dim glens and liquid wildernesses:
Why answer ye not, still? Brethren!

THE EARTH.   They dare not.

PROMETHEUS. Who dares? for I would hear that curse again.   130
    Ha, what an awful whisper rises up!
    'Tis scarce like sound: it tingles through the frame
    As lightning tingles, hovering ere it strike.
    Speak, Spirit! from thine inorganic voice
    I only know that thou art moving near
    And love. How cursed I him?

THE EARTH.   How canst thou hear
    Who knowest not the language of the dead?

PROMETHEUS. Thou art a living spirit; speak as they.

THE EARTH. I dare not speak like life, lest Heaven's fell King   140
    Should hear, and link me to some wheel of pain
    More torturing than the one whereon I roll.
    Subtle thou art and good, and though the Gods
    Hear not this voice, yet thou art more than God,
    Being wise and kind: earnestly hearken now.

PROMETHEUS. Obscurely through my brain, like shadows dim,
    Sweep awful thoughts, rapid and thick. I feel
    Faint, like one mingled in entwining love;
    Yet 'tis not pleasure.

THE EARTH.   No, thou canst not hear:
    Thou art immortal, and this tongue is known   150
    Only to those who die.

PROMETHEUS.   And what art thou,
    O, melancholy Voice?

THE EARTH.   I am the Earth,
    Thy mother; she within whose stony veins,
    To the last fibre of the loftiest tree
    Whose thin leaves trembled in the frozen air,
    Joy ran, as blood within a living frame,
    When thou didst from her bosom, like a cloud
    Of glory, arise, a spirit of keen joy!
    And at thy voice her pining sons uplifted
    Their prostrate brows from the polluting dust,   160
    And our almighty Tyrant with fierce dread
    Grew pale, until his thunder chained thee here.

539

Then, see those million worlds which burn and roll
Around us: their inhabitants beheld
My spherèd light wane in wide Heaven; the sea
Was lifted by strange tempest, and new fire
From earthquake-rifted mountains of bright snow
Shook its portentous hair beneath Heaven's frown;
Lightning and Inundation vexed the plains;
Blue thistles bloomed in cities; foodless toads   170
Within voluptuous chambers panting crawled:
When Plague had fallen on man, and beast, and worm,
And Famine; and black blight on herb and tree;
And in the corn, and vines, and meadow-grass,
Teemed ineradicable poisonous weeds
Draining their growth, for my wan breast was dry
With grief; and the thin air, my breath, was stained
With the contagion of a mother's hate
Breathed on her child's destroyer; ay, I heard
Thy curse, the which, if thou rememberest not,   180
Yet my innumerable seas and streams,
Mountains, and caves, and winds, and yon wide air,
And the inarticulate people of the dead,
Preserve, a treasured spell. We meditate
In secret joy and hope those dreadful words,
But dare not speak them.
PROMETHEUS.   Venerable mother!
All else who live and suffer take from thee
Some comfort; flowers, and fruits, and happy sounds,
And love, though fleeting; these may not be mine.
But mine own words, I pray, deny me not.   190
THE EARTH. They shall be told. Ere Babylon was dust,
The Magus Zoroaster, my dead child,
Met his own image walking in the garden.
That apparition, sole of men, he saw.
For know there are two worlds of life and death:
One that which thou beholdest; but the other
Is underneath the grave, where do inhabit
The shadows of all forms that think and live
Till death unite them and they part no more;
Dreams and the light imaginings of men,   200
And all that faith creates or love desires,
Terrible, strange, sublime and beauteous shapes.
There thou art, and dost hang, a writhing shade,
'Mid whirlwind-peopled mountains; all the gods
Are there, and all the powers of nameless worlds,
Vast, sceptred phantoms; heroes, men, and beasts;
And Demogorgon, a tremendous gloom;

And he, the supreme Tyrant, on his throne
Of burning gold. Son, one of these shall utter
The curse which all remember. Call at will   210
Thine own ghost, or the ghost of Jupiter,
Hades or Typhon, or what mightier Gods
From all-prolific Evil, since thy ruin
Have sprung, and trampled on my prostrate sons.
Ask, and they must reply: so the revenge
Of the Supreme may sweep through vacant shades,
As rainy wind through the abandoned gate
Of a fallen palace.
PROMETHEUS.   Mother, let not aught,
Of that which may be evil pass again
My lips, or those of aught resembling me.   220
Phantasm of Jupiter, arise, appear!

IONE.
My wings are folded o'er mine ears:
    My wings are crossèd o'er mine eyes:
Yet through their silver shade appears,
    And through their lulling plumes arise,
A Shape, a throng of sounds;
    May it be no ill to thee
O thou of many wounds!
Near whom, for our sweet sister's sake,
Ever thus we watch and wake.   230

PANTHEA.
The sound is of whirlwind underground,
    Earthquake, and fire, and mountains cloven;
The shape is awful like the sound,
    Clothed in dark purple, star-inwoven.
A sceptre of pale gold
    To stay steps proud, o'er the slow cloud
His veinèd hand doth hold.
Cruel he looks, but calm and strong,
Like one who does, not suffers wrong.

PHANTASM OF JUPITER. Why have the secret powers of this
    strange world   240
    Driven me, a frail and empty phantom, hither
    On direst storms? What unaccustomed sounds
    Are hovering on my lips, unlike the voice
    With which our pallid race hold ghastly talk

In darkness? And, proud sufferer, who art thou?

PROMETHEUS. Tremendous Image, as thou art must be
He whom thou shadowest forth. I am his foe,
The Titan. Speak the words which I would hear,
Although no thought inform thine empty voice.

THE EARTH. Listen! And though your echoes must be
    mute,   250
Gray mountains, and old woods, and haunted springs,
Prophetic caves, and isle-surrounding streams,
Rejoice to hear what yet ye cannot speak.

PHANTASM. A spirit seizes me and speaks within:
It tears me as fire tears a thunder-cloud.

PANTHEA. See, how he lifts his mighty looks, the
    Heaven
Darkens above.

IONE.   He speaks! O shelter me!

PROMETHEUS. I see the curse on gestures proud and
    cold,
And looks of firm defiance, and calm hate,
And such despair as mocks itself with smiles,   260
Written as on a scroll: yet speak: Oh, speak!

PHANTASM.

Fiend, I defy thee! with a calm, fixed mind,
    All that thou canst inflict I bid thee do;
Foul Tyrant both of Gods and Human-kind,
    One only being shalt thou not subdue.
Rain then thy plagues upon me here,
Ghastly disease, and frenzying fear;
And let alternate frost and fire
Eat into me, and be thine ire
Lightning, and cutting hail, and legioned forms   270
Of furies, driving by upon the wounding storms.

Ay, do thy worst. Thou art omnipotent.
    O'er all things but thyself I gave thee power,
And my own will. Be thy swift mischiefs sent
    To blast mankind, from yon ethereal tower.
Let thy malignant spirit move
In darkness over those I love:
On me and mine I imprecate
The utmost torture of thy hate;
And thus devote to sleepless agony,   280
This undeclining head while thou must reign on high.

But thou, who art the god and lord: o, thou,
   Who fillest with thy soul this world of woe,
To whom all things of Earth and Heaven do bow
   In fear and worship: all-prevailing foe!
I curse thee! let a sufferer's curse
Clasp thee, his torturer, like remorse;
Till thine Infinity shall be
A robe of envenomed agony;
And thine Omnipotence a crown of pain,   290
To cling like burning gold round thy dissolving brain.

Heap on thy soul, by virtue of this Curse,
   Ill deeds, then be thou damned, beholding good;
Both infinite as is the universe,
   And thou, and thy self-torturing solitude.
An awful image of calm power
Though now thou sittest, let the hour
Come, when thou must appear to be
That which thou art internally;
And after many a false and fruitless crime   300
Scorn track thy lagging fall through boundless space and
     time.

PROMETHEUS. Were these my words, O Parent?
THE EARTH.   They were thine.
PROMETHEUS. It doth repent me: words are quick and vain;
  Grief for awhile is blind, and so was mine.
  I wish no living thing to suffer pain.

THE EARTH.

Misery, Oh misery to me,
That Jove at length should vanquish thee.
Wail, howl aloud, Land and Sea,
The Earth's rent heart shall answer ye.
Howl, Spirits of the living and the dead,   310
Your refuge, your defence lies fallen and vanquishèd.

Act II

SCENE I.—*Morning. A lovely Vale in the Indian Caucasus.* ASIA *alone.*

ASIA. From all the blasts of heaven thou hast descended:
  Yes, like a spirit, like a thought, which makes
  Unwonted tears throng to the horny eyes,
  And beatings haunt the desolated heart,
  Which should have learnt repose: thou hast descended
  Cradled in tempests; thou dost wake, O Spring!
  O child of many winds! As suddenly
  Thou comest as the memory of a dream,
  Which now is sad because it hath been sweet;
  Like genius, or like joy which riseth up   10
  As from the earth, clothing with golden clouds
  The desert of our life.
  This is the season, this the day, the hour;
  At sunrise thou shouldst come, sweet sister mine,
  Too long desired, too long delaying, come!
  How like death-worms the wingless moments crawl!
  The point of one white star is quivering still
  Deep in the orange light of widening morn
  Beyond the purple mountains: through a chasm
  Of wind-divided mist the darker lake   20
  Reflects it: now it wanes: it gleams again
  As the waves fade, and as the burning threads
  Of woven cloud unravel in pale air:
  'Tis lost! and through yon peaks of cloud-like snow
  The roseate sunlight quivers: hear I not
  The Aeolian music of her sea-green plumes
  Winnowing the crimson dawn?   [PANTHEA *enters.*
                    I feel, I see
  Those eyes which burn through smiles that fade in tears,
  Like stars half quenched in mists of silver dew.
  Belovèd and most beautiful, who wearest   30
  The shadow of that soul by which I live,
  How late thou art! the spherèd sun had climbed
  The sea; my heart was sick with hope, before
  The printless air felt thy belated plumes.
PANTHEA. Pardon, great Sister! but my wings were faint
  With the delight of a remembered dream,
  As are the noontide plumes of summer winds
  Satiate with sweet flowers. I was wont to sleep
  Peacefully, and awake refreshed and calm
  Before the sacred Titan's fall, and thy   40
  Unhappy love, had made, through use and pity,
  Both love and woe familiar to my heart

As they had grown to thine: erewhile I slept
Under the glaucous caverns of old Ocean
Within dim bowers of green and purple moss,
Our young Ione's soft and milky arms
Locked then, as now, behind my dark, moist hair,
While my shut eyes and cheek were pressed within
The folded depth of her life-breathing bosom:
But not as now, since I am made the wind   50
Which fails beneath the music that I bear
Of thy most wordless converse; since dissolved
Into the sense with which love talks, my rest
Was troubled and yet sweet; my waking hours
Too full of care and pain.
ASIA.   Lift up thine eyes,
And let me read thy dream.
PANTHEA.   As I have said
With our sea-sister at his feet I slept.
The mountain mists, condensing at our voice
Under the moon, had spread their snowy flakes,
From the keen ice shielding our linkèd sleep.   60
Then two dreams came. One, I remember not.
But in the other his pale wound-worn limbs
Fell from Prometheus, and the azure night
Grew radiant with the glory of that form
Which lives unchanged within, and his voice fell
Like music which makes giddy the dim brain,
Faint with intoxication of keen joy:
'Sister of her whose footsteps pave the world
With loveliness—more fair than aught but her,
Whose shadow thou art—lift thine eyes on me.'   70
I lifted them: the overpowering light
Of that immortal shape was shadowed o'er
By love; which, from his soft and flowing limbs,
And passion-parted lips, and keen, faint eyes,
Steamed forth like vaporous fire; an atmosphere
Which wrapped me in its all-dissolving power,
As the warm aether of the morning sun
Wraps ere it drinks some cloud of wandering dew.
I saw not, heard not, moved not, only felt
His presence flow and mingle through my blood   80
Till it became his life, and his grew mine,
And I was thus absorbed, until it passed,
And like the vapours when the sun sinks down,
Gathering again in drops upon the pines,
And tremulous as they, in the deep night
My being was condensed; and as the rays

Of thought were slowly gathered, I could hear
His voice, whose accents lingered ere they died
Like footsteps of weak melody: thy name
Among the many sounds alone I heard   90
Of what might be articulate; though still
I listened through the night when sound was none.
Ione wakened then, and said to me:
'Canst thou divine what troubles me to-night?
I always knew what I desired before,
Nor ever found delight to wish in vain.
But now I cannot tell thee what I seek;
I know not; something sweet, since it is sweet
Even to desire; it is thy sport, false sister;
Thou hast discovered some enchantment old,   100
Whose spells have stolen my spirit as I slept
And mingled it with thine: for when just now
We kissed, I felt within thy parted lips
The sweet air that sustained me, and the warmth
Of the life-blood, for loss of which I faint,
Quivered between our intertwining arms.'
I answered not, for the Eastern star grew pale,
But fled to thee.
ASIA.   Thou speakest, but thy words
Are as the air: I feel them not: Oh, lift
Thine eyes, that I may read his written soul!   110
PANTHEA. I lift them though they droop beneath the load
Of that they would express: what canst thou see
But thine own fairest shadow imaged there?
ASIA. Thine eyes are like the deep, blue, boundless heaven
Contracted to two circles underneath
Their long, fine lashes; dark, far, measureless,
Orb within orb, and line through line inwoven.
PANTHEA. Why lookest thou as if a spirit passed?
ASIA. There is a change: beyond their inmost depth
I see a shade, a shape: 'tis He, arrayed   120
In the soft light of his own smiles, which spread
Like radiance from the cloud-surrounded morn.
Prometheus, it is thine! depart not yet!
Say not those smiles that we shall meet again
Within that bright pavilion which their beams
Shall build o'er the waste world? The dream is told.
What shape is that between us? Its rude hair
Roughens the wind that lifts it, its regard
Is wild and quick, yet 'tis a thing of air,
For through its gray robe gleams the golden dew   130
Whose stars the noon has quenched not.

DREAM.   Follow! Follow!
PANTHEA. It is mine other dream.
ASIA.   It disappears.
PANTHEA. It passes now into my mind. Methought
  As we sate here, the flower-infolding buds
  Burst on yon lightning-blasted almond-tree,
  When swift from the white Scythian wilderness
  A wind swept forth wrinkling the Earth with frost:
  I looked, and all the blossoms were blown down;
  But on each leaf was stamped, as the blue bells
  Of Hyacinth tell Apollo's written grief,   140
  O, FOLLOW, FOLLOW!
ASIA.   As you speak, your words
  Fill, pause by pause, my own forgotten sleep
  With shapes. Methought among these lawns together
  We wandered, underneath the young gray dawn,
  And multitudes of dense white fleecy clouds
  Were wandering in thick flocks along the mountains
  Shepherded by the slow, unwilling wind;
  And the white dew on the new-bladed grass,
  Just piercing the dark earth, hung silently;
  And there was more which I remember not: 150
  But on the shadows of the morning clouds,
  Athwart the purple mountain slope, was written
  FOLLOW, O, FOLLOW! as they vanished by;
  And on each herb, from which Heaven's dew had fallen,
  The like was stamped, as with a withering fire,
  A wind arose among the pines; it shook
  The clinging music from their boughs, and then
  Low, sweet, faint sounds, like the farewell of ghosts,
  Were heard: O, FOLLOW, FOLLOW, FOLLOW ME!
  And then I said: 'Panthea, look on me.'   160
  But in the depth of those belovèd eyes
  Still I saw, FOLLOW, FOLLOW!
ECHO.   Follow, follow!
PANTHEA. The crags, this clear spring morning, mock our voices
  As they were spirit-tongued.
ASIA.   It is some being
  Around the crags. What fine clear sounds! O, list!

ECHOES (unseen).
Echoes we: listen!
We cannot stay:
As dew-stars glisten
Then fade away—
Child of Ocean!   170

ASIA. Hark! Spirits speak. The liquid responses
  Of their aëreal tongues yet sound.
PANTHEA.   I hear.

ECHOES.
O, follow, follow,
  As our voice recedeth
Through the caverns hollow,
  Where the forest spreadeth;
    (*More distant.*)
O, follow, follow!
Through the caverns hollow,
As the song floats thou pursue,
Where the wild bee never flew,   180
Through the noontide darkness deep,
By the odour-breathing sleep
Of faint night flowers, and the waves
At the fountain-lighted caves,
While our music, wild and sweet,
Mocks thy gently falling feet,
    Child of Ocean!

ASIA. Shall we pursue the sound? It grows more faint
  And distant.
PANTHEA. List! the strain floats nearer now.

ECHOES.
In the world unknown   190
  Sleeps a voice unspoken;
By thy step alone
  Can its rest be broken;
    Child of Ocean!

ASIA. How the notes sink upon the ebbing wind!

ECHOES.
O, follow, follow!
Through the caverns hollow,
As the song floats thou pursue,
By the woodland noontide dew;
By the forest, lakes, and fountains,   200
Through the many-folded mountains;
To the rents, and gulfs, and chasms,
Where the Earth reposed from spasms,
On the day when He and thou
Parted, to commingle now;
    Child of Ocean!

ASIA. Come, sweet Panthea, link thy hand in mine,
  And follow, ere the voices fade away.

SCENE II.—*A Forest, intermingled with Rocks and Caverns.* ASIA *and*
PANTHEA *pass into it. Two young Fauns are sitting on a Rock listening.*

SEMICHORUS I OF SPIRITS.
        The path through which that lovely twain
          Have passed, by cedar, pine, and yew,
          And each dark tree that ever grew,
          Is curtained out from Heaven's wide blue;
        Nor sun, nor moon, nor wind, nor rain,
            Can pierce its interwoven bowers,
          Nor aught, save where some cloud of dew,
        Drifted along the earth-creeping breeze,
        Between the trunks of the hoar trees,
            Hangs each a pearl in the pale flowers   10
          Of the green laurel, blown anew;
        And bends, and then fades silently,
        One frail and fair anemone:
        Or when some star of many a one
        That climbs and wanders through steep night,
        Has found the cleft through which alone
        Beams fall from high those depths upon
        Ere it is borne away, away,
        By the swift Heavens that cannot stay,
        It scatters drops of golden light,   20
        Like lines of rain that ne'er unite:
        And the gloom divine is all around,
        And underneath is the mossy ground.

SEMICHORUS II.
        There the voluptuous nightingales,
          Are awake through all the broad noonday,
        When one with bliss or sadness fails,
            And through the windless ivy-boughs
            Sick with sweet love, droops dying away
        On its mate's music-panting bosom;
        Another from the swinging blossom,   30
            Watching to catch the languid close
          Of the last strain, then lifts on high
          The wings of the weak melody,
        'Till some new strain of feeling bear
          The song, and all the woods are mute;
        When there is heard through the dim air

The rush of wings, and rising there
　　Like many a lake-surrounded flute,
Sounds overflow the listener's brain
So sweet, that joy is almost pain.　　　　　　40

SEMICHORUS I.
There those enchanted eddies play
　　Of echoes, music-tongued, which draw,
　　By Demogorgon's mighty law,
　　With melting rapture, or sweet awe,
All spirits on that secret way;
　　As inland boats are driven to Ocean
Down streams made strong with mountain-thaw:
　　　　And first there comes a gentle sound
　　　　To those in talk or slumber bound,
　　And wakes the destined soft emotion,　　　　50
Attracts, impels them; those who saw
　　Say from the breathing earth behind
　　There steams a plume-uplifting wind
Which drives them on their path, while they
　　Believe their own swift wings and feet
The sweet desires within obey:
And so they float upon their way,
Until, still sweet, but loud and strong,
The storm of sound is driven along,
　　　　Sucked up and hurrying: as they fleet　　60
　　　　Behind, its gathering billows meet
And to the fatal mountain bear
Like clouds amid the yielding air.

FIRST FAUN. Canst thou imagine where those spirits live
　　Which make such delicate music in the woods?
　　We haunt within the least frequented caves
　　And closest coverts, and we know these wilds,
　　Yet never meet them, though we hear them oft:
　　Where may they hide themselves?
SECOND FAUN.　　　　　　　　'Tis hard to tell:
　　I have heard those more skilled in spirits say,　　70
　　The bubbles, which the enchantment of the sun
　　Sucks from the pale faint water-flowers that pave
　　The oozy bottom of clear lakes and pools,
　　Are the pavilions where such dwell and float
　　Under the green and golden atmosphere
　　Which noontide kindles through the woven leaves;
　　And when these burst, and the thin fiery air,
　　The which they breathed within those lucent domes,

Ascends to flow like meteors through the night,
They ride on them, and rein their headlong speed.   80
And bow their burning crests, and glide in fire
Under the waters of the earth again.

FIRST FAUN. If such live thus, have others other lives,
Under pink blossoms or within the bells
Of meadow flowers, or folded violets deep,
Or on their dying odours, when they die,
Or in the sunlight of the spherèd dew?

SECOND FAUN. Ay, many more which we may well divine.
But, should we stay to speak, noontide would come,
And thwart Silenus find his goats undrawn,   90
And grudge to sing those wise and lovely songs
Of Fate, and Chance, and God, and Chaos old,
And Love, and the chained Titan's woful doom,
And how he shall be loosed, and make the earth
One brotherhood: delightful strains which cheer
Our solitary twilights, and which charm
To silence the unenvying nightingales.

SCENE V.—*The Car pauses within a Cloud on the top of a snowy
Mountain.* ASIA, PANTHEA, *and the* SPIRIT OF THE HOUR.

SPIRIT.

On the brink of the night and the morning
  My coursers are wont to respire;
But the Earth has just whispered a warning
  That their flight must be swifter than fire:
  They shall drink the hot speed of desire!

ASIA. Thou breathest on their nostrils, but my breath
Would give them swifter speed.
SPIRIT.   Alas! it could not.
PANTHEA. Oh Spirit! pause, and tell whence is the light
Which fills the cloud? the sun is yet unrisen.
SPIRIT. The sun will rise not until noon. Apollo   10
Is held in heaven by wonder; and the light
Which fills this vapour, as the aëreal hue
Of fountain-gazing roses fills the water,
Flows from thy mighty sister.
PANTHEA.   Yes, I feel—
ASIA. What is it with thee, sister? Thou art pale.
PANTHEA. How thou art changed! I dare not look on thee;
I feel but see thee not. I scarce endure
The radiance of thy beauty. Some good change

Is working in the elements, which suffer
Thy presence thus unveiled. The Nereids tell   20
That on the day when the clear hyaline
Was cloven at thine uprise, and thou didst stand
Within a veinèd shell, which floated on
Over the calm floor of the crystal sea,
Among the Aegean isles, and by the shores
Which bear thy name; love, like the atmosphere
Of the sun's fire filling the living world,
Burst from thee, and illumined earth and heaven
And the deep ocean and the sunless caves
And all that dwells within them; till grief cast   30
Eclipse upon the soul from which it came:
Such art thou now; nor is it I alone,
Thy sister, thy companion, thine own chosen one,
But the whole world which seeks thy sympathy.
Hearest thou not sounds i' the air which speak the love
Of all articulate beings? Feelest thou not
The inanimate winds enamoured of thee? List!   [*Music.*

ASIA. Thy words are sweeter than aught else but his
  Whose echoes they are: yet all love is sweet,
  Given or returned. Common as light is love,   40
  And its familiar voice wearies not ever.
  Like the wide heaven, the all-sustaining air,
  It makes the reptile equal to the God:
  They who inspire it most are fortunate,
  As I am now; but those who feel it most
  Are happier still, after long sufferings,
  As I shall soon become.

PANTHEA.   List! Spirits speak.

            VOICE IN THE AIR, *singing.*
          Life of Life! thy lips enkindle
            With their love the breath between them;
          And thy smiles before they dwindle   50
            Make the cold air fire; then screen them
          In those looks, where whoso gazes
          Faints, entangled in their mazes.

          Child of Light! thy limbs are burning
            Through the vest which seems to hide them;
          As the radiant lines of morning
            Through the clouds ere they divide them;
          And this atmosphere divinest
          Shrouds thee wheresoe'er thou shinest.

Fair are others; none beholds thee,   60
   But thy voice sounds low and tender
Like the fairest, for it folds thee
   From the sight, that liquid splendour,
And all feel, yet see thee never,
As I feel now, lost for ever!

Lamp of Earth! where'er thou movest
   Its dim shapes are clad with brightness,
And the souls of whom thou lovest
   Walk upon the winds with lightness,
Till they fail, as I am failing,   70
Dizzy, lost, yet unbewailing!

ASIA.

My soul is an enchanted boat,
   Which, like a sleeping swan, doth float
Upon the silver waves of thy sweet singing;
   And thine doth like an angel sit
   Beside the helm conducting it,
Whilst all the winds with melody are ringing.
   It seems to float ever, for ever,
   Upon that many-winding river,
   Between mountains, woods, abysses,   80
   A paradise of wildernesses!
Till, like one in slumber bound,
Borne to the ocean, I float down, around,
Into a sea profound, of ever-spreading sound:

   Meanwhile thy spirit lifts its pinions
   In music's most serene dominions;
Catching the winds that fan that happy heaven.
   And we sail on, away, afar,
   Without a course, without a star,
But, by the instinct of sweet music driven;   90
   Till through Elysian garden islets
   By thee, most beautiful of pilots,
   Where never mortal pinnace glided,
   The boat of my desire is guided:
Realms where the air we breathe is love,
Which in the winds and on the waves doth move,
Harmonizing this earth with what we feel above.

   We have passed Age's icy caves,
   And Manhood's dark and tossing waves,
And Youth's smooth ocean, smiling to betray: 100

Beyond the glassy gulfs we flee
Of shadow-peopled Infancy,
Through Death and Birth, to a diviner day;
A paradise of vaulted bowers,
Lit by downward-gazing flowers,
And watery paths that wind between
Wildernesses calm and green,
Peopled by shapes too bright to see,
And rest, having beheld; somewhat like thee;
Which walk upon the sea, and chant melodiously!   110

Act III

SCENE I.—*Heaven.* JUPITER *on his Throne;* THETIS *and the other Deities assembled.*

JUPITER. Ye congregated powers of heaven, who share
The glory and the strength of him ye serve,
Rejoice! henceforth I am omnipotent.
All else had been subdued to me; alone
The soul of man, like unextinguished fire,
Yet burns towards heaven with fierce reproach, and doubt,
And lamentation, and reluctant prayer,
Hurling up insurrection, which might make
Our antique empire insecure, though built
On eldest faith, and hell's coeval, fear;   10
And though my curses through the pendulous air,
Like snow on herbless peaks, fall flake by flake,
And cling to it; though under my wrath's night
It climbs the crags of life, step after step,
Which wound it, as ice wounds unsandalled feet,
It yet remains supreme o'er misery,
Aspiring, unrepressed, yet soon to fall:
Even now have I begotten a strange wonder,
That fatal child, the terror of the earth,
Who waits but till the destined hour arrive,   20
Bearing from Demogorgon's vacant throne
The dreadful might of ever-living limbs
Which clothed that awful spirit unbeheld,
To redescend, and trample out the spark.
Pour forth heaven's wine, Idæan Ganymede,
And let it fill the Dædal cups like fire,
And from the flower-inwoven soil divine
Ye all-triumphant harmonies arise,

554

As dew from earth under the twilight stars:
Drink! be the nectar circling through your veins   30
The soul of joy, ye ever-living Gods,
Till exultation burst in one wide voice
Like music from Elysian winds.
                              And thou
Ascend beside me, veilèd in the light
Of the desire which makes thee one with me,
Thetis, bright image of eternity!
When thou didst cry, 'Insufferable might!
God! Spare me! I sustain not the quick flames,
The penetrating presence; all my being,
Like him whom the Numidian seps did thaw   40
Into a dew with poison, is dissolved,
Sinking through its foundations:' even then
Two mighty spirits, mingling, made a third
Mightier than either, which, unbodied now,
Between us floats, felt, although unbeheld,
Waiting the incarnation, which ascends,
(Hear ye the thunder of the fiery wheels
Griding the winds?) from Demogorgon's throne.
Victory! victory! Feel'st thou not, O world,
The earthquake of his chariot thundering up   50
Olympus?
          [*The Car of the* HOUR *arrives.* DEMOGORGON *descends, and moves*
                              towards the Throne of JUPITER.
          Awful shape, what art thou? Speak!
DEMOGORGON. Eternity. Demand no direr name.
Descend, and follow me down the abyss.
I am thy child, as thou wert Saturn's child;
Mightier than thee: and we must dwell together
Henceforth in darkness. Lift thy lightnings not.
The tyranny of heaven none may retain,
Or reassume, or hold, succeeding thee:
Yet if thou wilt, as 'tis the destiny
Of trodden worms to writhe till they are dead,   60
Put forth thy might.
JUPITER.   Detested prodigy!
Even thus beneath the deep Titanian prisons
I trample thee! thou lingerest?
                              Mercy! mercy!
No pity, no release, no respite! Oh,
That thou wouldst make mine enemy my judge,
Even where he hangs, seared by my long revenge,
On Caucasus! he would not doom me thus.
Gentle, and just, and dreadless, is he not

The monarch of the world? What then art thou?
No refuge! no appeal!
            Sink with me then,   70
We two will sink on the wide waves of ruin,
Even as a vulture and a snake outspent
Drop, twisted in inextricable fight,
Into a shoreless sea. Let hell unlock
Its mounded oceans of tempestuous fire,
And whelm on them into the bottomless void
This desolated world, and thee, and me,
The conqueror and the conquered, and the wreck
Of that for which they combated.
                Ai! Ai!
The elements obey me not. I sink   80
Dizzily down, ever, for ever, down.
And, like a cloud, mine enemy above
Darkens my fall with victory! Ai, Ai!

from SCENE IV

[*The* SPIRIT OF THE HOUR *enters.*

PROMETHEUS. We feel what thou hast heard and seen: yet speak.
SPIRIT OF THE HOUR. Soon as the sound had ceased whose
    thunder filled
The abysses of the sky and the wide earth,
There was a change: the impalpable thin air
And the all-circling sunlight were transformed,
As if the sense of love dissolved in them
Had folded itself round the spherèd world.
My vision then grew clear, and I could see
Into the mysteries of the universe:
Dizzy as with delight I floated down,   10
Winnowing the lightsome air with languid plumes,
My coursers sought their birthplace in the sun,
Where they henceforth will live exempt from toil,
Pasturing flowers of vegetable fire;
And where my moonlike car will stand within
A temple, gazed upon by Phidian forms
Of thee, and Asia, and the Earth, and me,
And you fair nymphs looking the love we feel,—
In memory of the tidings it has borne,—
Beneath a dome fretted with graven flowers,   20
Poised on twelve columns of resplendent stone,
And open to the bright and liquid sky.
Yoked to it by an amphisbaenic snake
The likeness of those wingèd steeds will mock

The flight from which they find repose. Alas,
Whither has wandered now my partial tongue
When all remains untold which ye would hear?
As I have said, I floated to the earth:
It was, as it is still, the pain of bliss
To move, to breathe, to be; I wandering went   30
Among the haunts and dwellings of mankind,
And first was disappointed not to see
Such mighty change as I had felt within
Expressed in outward things; but soon I looked,
And behold, thrones were kingless, and men walked
One with the other even as spirits do,
None fawned, none trampled; hate, disdain, or fear,
Self-love, or self-contempt, on human brows
No more inscribed, as o'er the gate of hell,
'All hope abandon ye who enter here;'   40
None frowned, none trembled, none with eager fear
Gazed on another's eye of cold command,
Until the subject of a tyrant's will
Became, worse fate, the abject of his own,
Which spurred him, like an outspent horse, to death.
None wrought his lips in truth-entangling lines
Which smiled the lie his tongue disdained to speak;
None, with firm sneer, trod out in his own heart
The sparks of love and hope till there remained
Those bitter ashes, a soul self-consumed,   50
And the wretch crept a vampire among men,
Infecting all with his own hideous ill;
None talked that common, false, cold, hollow talk
Which makes the heart deny the *yes* it breathes,
Yet question that unmeant hypocrisy
With such a self-mistrust as has no name.
And women, too, frank, beautiful, and kind
As the free heaven which rains fresh light and dew
On the wide earth, past; gentle radiant forms,
From custom's evil taint exempt and pure,   60
Speaking the wisdom once they could not think,
Looking emotions once they feared to feel,
And changed to all which once they dared not be,
Yet being now, made earth like heaven; nor pride,
Nor jealousy, nor envy, nor ill shame,
The bitterest of those drops of treasured gall,
Spoilt the sweet taste of the nepenthe, love.

Thrones, altars, judgement-seats, and prisons; wherein,
And beside which, by wretched men were borne

Sceptres, tiaras, swords, and chains, and tomes   70
Of reasoned wrong, glozed on by ignorance,
Were like those monstrous and barbaric shapes,
The ghosts of a no-more-remembered fame,
Which, from their unworn obelisks, look forth
In triumph o'er the palaces and tombs
Of those who were their conquerors, mouldering round.
Those imaged to the pride of kings and priests
A dark yet mighty faith, a power as wide
As is the world it wasted, and are now
But an astonishment; even so the tools   80
And emblems of its last captivity,
Amid the dwellings of the peopled earth,
Stand, not o'erthrown, but unregarded now.
And those foul shapes, abhorred by god and man,—
Which, under many a name and many a form
Strange, savage, ghastly, dark and execrable,
Were Jupiter, the tyrant of the world;
And which the nations, panic-stricken, served
With blood, and hearts broken by long hope, and love
Dragged to his altars soiled and garlandless,   90
And slain amid men's unreclaiming tears,
Flattering the thing they feared, which fear was hate,—
Frown, mouldering fast, o'er their abandoned shrines:
The painted veil, by those who were, called life,
Which mimicked, as with colours idly spread,
All men believed or hoped, is torn aside;
The loathsome mask has fallen, the man remains
Sceptreless, free, uncircumscribed, but man
Equal, unclassed, tribeless, and nationless,
Exempt from awe, worship, degree, the king   100
Over himself; just, gentle, wise: but man
Passionless?—no, yet free from guilt or pain,
Which were, for his will made or suffered them,
Nor yet exempt, though ruling them like slaves,
From chance, and death, and mutability,
The clogs of that which else might oversoar
The loftiest star of unascended heaven,
Pinnacled dim in the intense inane.

(lines 97–204)

from *Act IV*

DEMOGORGON.

This is the day, which down the void abysm
At the Earth-born's spell yawns for Heaven's despotism,
   And Conquest is dragged captive through the deep:
Love, from its awful throne of patient power
In the wise heart, from the last giddy hour
   Of dread endurance, from the slippery, steep,
And narrow verge of crag-like agony, springs
And folds over the world its healing wings.

Gentleness, Virtue, Wisdom, and Endurance,
These are the seals of that most firm assurance   10
   Which bars the pit over Destruction's strength;
And if, with infirm hand, Eternity,
Mother of many acts and hours, should free
   The serpent that would clasp her with his length;
These are the spells by which to reassume
An empire o'er the disentangled doom.

To suffer woes which Hope thinks infinite;
To forgive wrongs darker than death or night;
   To defy power, which seems omnipotent;
To love, and bear; to hope till Hope creates   20
From its own wreck the thing it contemplates;
   Neither to change, nor falter, nor repent;
This, like thy glory, Titan, is to be
Good, great and joyous, beautiful and free;
This is alone Life, Joy, Empire, and Victory.

(lines 494–518)

191   *Ode to the West Wind*

I

O WILD West Wind, thou breath of Autumn's being,
Thou, from whose unseen presence the leaves dead
Are driven, like ghosts from an enchanter fleeing,

Yellow, and black, and pale, and hectic red,
Pestilence-stricken multitudes: O thou,
Who chariotest to their dark wintry bed

The winged seeds, where they lie cold and low,
Each like a corpse within its grave, until
Thine azure sister of the Spring shall blow

Her clarion o'er the dreaming earth, and fill   10
(Driving sweet buds like flocks to feed in air)
With living hues and odours plain and hill:

Wild Spirit, which art moving everywhere;
Destroyer and Preserver; hear, oh, hear!

II

Thou on whose stream, 'mid the steep sky's commotion,
Loose clouds like earth's decaying leaves are shed,
Shook from the tangled boughs of Heaven and Ocean,

Angels of rain and lightning: there are spread
On the blue surface of thine aëry surge,
Like the bright hair uplifted from the head   20

Of some fierce Mænad, even from the dim verge
Of the horizon to the zenith's height,
The locks of the approaching storm. Thou dirge

Of the dying year, to which this closing night
Will be the dome of a vast sepulchre,
Vaulted with all thy congregated might

Of vapours, from whose solid atmosphere
Black rain, and fire, and hail will burst: oh, hear!

III

Thou who didst waken from his summer dreams
The blue Mediterranean, where he lay,   30
Lulled by the coil of his chrystàlline streams,

Beside a pumice isle in Baiae's bay,
And saw in sleep old palaces and towers
Quivering within the wave's intenser day,

All overgrown with azure moss and flowers
So sweet, the sense faints picturing them! Thou
For whose path the Atlantic's level powers

Cleave themselves into chasms, while far below

The sea-blooms and the oozy woods which wear
The sapless foliage of the ocean, know   40

Thy voice, and suddenly grow gray with fear,
And tremble and despoil themselves: oh, hear!

IV

If I were a dead leaf thou mightest bear;
If I were a swift cloud to fly with thee;
A wave to pant beneath thy power, and share

The impulse of thy strength, only less free
Than thou, O uncontrollable! If even
I were as in my boyhood, and could be

The comrade of thy wanderings over Heaven,
As then, when to outstrip thy skiey speed   50
Scarce seemed a vision; I would ne'er have striven

As thus with thee in prayer in my sore need.
Oh! lift me as a wave, a leaf, a cloud!
I fall upon the thorns of life! I bleed!

A heavy weight of hours has chained and bowed
One too like thee: tameless, and swift, and proud.

V

Make me thy lyre, even as the forest is:
What if my leaves are falling like its own!
The tumult of thy mighty harmonies

Will take from both a deep, autumnal tone,   60
Sweet though in sadness. Be thou, Spirit fierce,
My spirit! Be thou me, impetuous one!

Drive my dead thoughts over the universe
Like withered leaves to quicken a new birth!
And, by the incantation of this verse,

Scatter, as from an unextinguished hearth
Ashes and sparks, my words among mankind!
Be through my lips to unawakened Earth

The trumpet of a prophecy! O, Wind,
If Winter comes, can Spring be far behind?   70

192   *To a Skylark*

HAIL to thee, blithe Spirit!
   Bird thou never wert,
That from Heaven, or near it,
   Pourest thy full heart
In profuse strains of unpremeditated art.

Higher still and higher
   From the earth thou springest
Like a cloud of fire;
   The blue deep thou wingest,
And singing still dost soar, and soaring ever singest.   10

In the golden lightning
   Of the sunken sun,
O'er which clouds are bright'ning,
   Thou dost float and run;
Like an unbodied joy whose race is just begun.

The pale purple even
   Melts around thy flight;
Like a star of Heaven,
   In the broad daylight
Thou art unseen, but yet I hear thy shrill delight,   20

Keen as are the arrows
   Of that silver sphere,
Whose intense lamp narrows
   In the white dawn clear
Until we hardly see—we feel that it is there.

All the earth and air
   With thy voice is loud,
As, when night is bare,
   From one lonely cloud
The moon rains out her beams, and Heaven is overflowed.   30

What thou art we know not;
   What is most like thee?
From rainbow clouds there flow not
   Drops so bright to see
As from thy presence showers a rain of melody.

Like a Poet hidden
   In the light of thought,

Singing hymns unbidden,
   Till the world is wrought
To sympathy with hopes and fears it heeded not: 40

Like a high-born maiden
   In a palace-tower,
Soothing her love-laden
   Soul in secret hour
With music sweet as love, which overflows her bower:

Like a glow-worm golden
   In a dell of dew,
Scattering unbeholden
   Its aëreal hue
Among the flowers and grass, which screen it from the view!   50

Like a rose embowered
   In its own green leaves,
By warm winds deflowered,
   Till the scent it gives
Makes faint with too much sweet these heavy-wingèd thieves:

Sound of vernal showers
   On the twinkling grass,
Rain-awakened flowers,
   All that ever was
Joyous, and clear, and fresh, thy music doth surpass: 60

Teach us, Sprite or Bird,
   What sweet thoughts are thine:
I have never heard
   Praise of love or wine
That panted forth a flood of rapture so divine.

Chorus Hymeneal,
   Or triumphal chant,
Matched with thine would be all
   But an empty vaunt,
A thing wherein we feel there is some hidden want.   70

What objects are the fountains
   Of thy happy strain?
What fields, or waves, or mountains?
   What shapes of sky or plain?
What love of thine own kind? what ignorance of pain?

With thy clear keen joyance
   Languor cannot be:

Shadow of annoyance
 Never came near thee:
Thou lovest—but ne'er knew love's sad satiety.   80

Waking or asleep,
 Thou of death must deem
Things more true and deep
 Than we mortals dream,
Or how could thy notes flow in such a crystal stream?

We look before and after,
 And pine for what is not:
Our sincerest laughter
 With some pain is fraught;
Our sweetest songs are those that tell of saddest thought. 90

Yet if we could scorn
 Hate, and pride, and fear;
If we were things born
 Not to shed a tear,
I know not how thy joy we ever should come near.

Better than all measures
 Of delightful sound,
Better than all treasures
 That in books are found,
Thy skill to poet were, thou scorner of the ground! 100

Teach me half the gladness
 That thy brain must know,
Such harmonious madness
 From my lips would flow
The world should listen then—as I am listening now.

JOHN KEATS

193   from *Lamia*

PART I

UPON a time, before the faery broods
Drove Nymph and Satyr from the prosperous woods,
Before King Oberon's bright diadem,
Sceptre, and mantle, clasp'd with dewy gem,
Frighted away the Dryads and the Fauns
From rushes green, and brakes, and cowslip'd lawns,
The ever-smitten Hermes empty left

His golden throne, bent warm on amorous theft:
From high Olympus had he stolen light,
On this side of Jove's clouds, to escape the sight   10
Of his great summoner, and made retreat
Into a forest on the shores of Crete.
For somewhere in that sacred island dwelt
A nymph, to whom all hoofed Satyrs knelt;
And at whose feet the languid Tritons poured
Pearls, while on land they wither'd and adored.
Fast by the springs where she to bathe was wont,
And in those meads where sometime she might haunt,
Were strewn rich gifts, unknown to any Muse,
Though Fancy's casket were unlock'd to choose.   20
Ah, what a world of love was at her feet!
So Hermes thought, and a celestial heat
Burnt from his winged heels to either ear,
That from a whiteness, as the lily clear,
Blush'd into roses 'mid his golden hair,
Fallen in jealous curls about his shoulders bare.

From vale to vale, from wood to wood, he flew,
Breathing upon the flowers his passion new,
And wound with many a river to its head,
To find where this sweet nymph prepar'd her secret bed: 30
In vain; the sweet nymph might nowhere be found,
And so he rested, on the lonely ground,
Pensive, and full of painful jealousies
Of the Wood-Gods, and even the very trees.
There as he stood, he heard a mournful voice,
Such as once heard, in gentle heart, destroys
All pain but pity: thus the lone voice spake:
'When from this wreathed tomb shall I awake!
When move in a sweet body fit for life,
And love, and pleasure, and the ruddy strife   40
Of hearts and lips! Ah, miserable me!'
The God, dove-footed, glided silently
Round bush and tree, soft-brushing, in his speed,
The taller grasses and full-flowering weed,
Until he found a palpitating snake,
Bright, and cirque-couchant in a dusky brake.

She was a gordian shape of dazzling hue,
Vermilion-spotted, golden, green, and blue;
Striped like a zebra, freckled like a pard,
Eyed like a peacock, and all crimson barr'd;   50
And full of silver moons, that, as she breathed,

Dissolv'd, or brighter shone, or interwreathed
Their lustres with the gloomier tapestries—
So rainbow-sided, touch'd with miseries,
She seem'd, at once, some penanced lady elf,
Some demon's mistress, or the demon's self.
Upon her crest she wore a wannish fire
Sprinkled with stars, like Ariadne's tiar:
Her head was serpent, but ah, bitter-sweet!
She had a woman's mouth with all its pearls complete: 60
And for her eyes: what could such eyes do there
But weep, and weep, that they were born so fair?
As Proserpine still weeps for her Sicilian air.
Her throat was serpent, but the words she spake
Came, as through bubbling honey, for Love's sake,
And thus; while Hermes on his pinions lay,
Like a stoop'd falcon ere he takes his prey.

'Fair Hermes, crown'd with feathers, fluttering light,
I had a splendid dream of thee last night:
I saw thee sitting, on a throne of gold,   70
Among the Gods, upon Olympus old,
The only sad one; for thou didst not hear
The soft, lute-finger'd Muses chaunting clear,
Nor even Apollo when he sang alone,
Deaf to his throbbing throat's long, long melodious moan.
I dreamt I saw thee, robed in purple flakes,
Break amorous through the clouds, as morning breaks,
And, swiftly as a bright Phœbean dart,
Strike for the Cretan isle; and here thou art!
Too gentle Hermes, hast thou found the maid?'   80
Whereat the star of Lethe not delay'd
His rosy eloquence, and thus inquired:
'Thou smooth-lipp'd serpent, surely high inspired!
Thou beauteous wreath, with melancholy eyes,
Possess whatever bliss thou canst devise,
Telling me only where my nymph is fled,—
Where she doth breathe!' 'Bright planet, thou hast said,'
Return'd the snake, 'but seal with oaths, fair God!'
'I swear,' said Hermes, 'by my serpent rod,
And by thine eyes, and by thy starry crown!'   90
Light flew his earnest words, among the blossoms blown.
Then thus again the brilliance feminine:
'Too frail of heart! for this lost nymph of thine,
Free as the air, invisibly, she strays
About these thornless wilds; her pleasant days
She tastes unseen; unseen her nimble feet

Leave traces in the grass and flowers sweet;
From weary tendrils, and bow'd branches green,
She plucks the fruit unseen, she bathes unseen:
And by my power is her beauty veil'd   100
To keep it unaffronted, unassail'd
By the love-glances of unlovely eyes,
Of Satyrs, Fauns, and blear'd Silenus' sighs.
Pale grew her immortality, for woe
Of all these lovers, and she grieved so
I took compassion on her, bade her steep
Her hair in weïrd syrops, that would keep
Her loveliness invisible, yet free
To wander as she loves, in liberty.
Thou shalt behold her, Hermes, thou alone,   110
If thou wilt, as thou swearest, grant my boon!'
Then, once again, the charmed God began
An oath, and through the serpent's ears it ran
Warm, tremulous, devout, psalterian.
Ravish'd, she lifted her Circean head,
Blush'd a live damask, and swift-lisping said,
'I was a woman, let me have once more
A woman's shape, and charming as before.
I love a youth of Corinth—O the bliss!
Give me my woman's form, and place me where he is.   120
Stoop, Hermes, let me breathe upon thy brow,
And thou shalt see thy sweet nymph even now.'
The God on half-shut feathers sank serene,
She breath'd upon his eyes, and swift was seen
Of both the guarded nymph near-smiling on the green.
It was no dream; or say a dream it was,
Real are the dreams of Gods, and smoothly pass
Their pleasures in a long immortal dream.
One warm, flush'd moment, hovering, it might seem
Dash'd by the wood-nymph's beauty, so he burn'd;   130
Then, lighting on the printless verdure, turn'd
To the swoon'd serpent, and with languid arm,
Delicate, put to proof the lythe Caducean charm.
So done, upon the nymph his eyes he bent
Full of adoring tears and blandishment,
And towards her stept: she, like a moon in wane,
Faded before him, cower'd, nor could restrain
Her fearful sobs, self-folding like a flower
That faints into itself at evening hour:
But the God fostering her chilled hand,   140
She felt the warmth, her eyelids open'd bland,
And she, like flowers at morning song of bees,

Bloom'd, and gave up her honey to the lees.
Into the green-recessed woods they flew;
Nor grew they pale, as mortal lovers do.

   Left to herself, the serpent now began
To change; her elfin blood in madness ran,
Her mouth foam'd, and the grass, therewith besprent,
Wither'd at dew so sweet and virulent;
Her eyes in torture fix'd, and anguish drear,   150
Hot, glaz'd, and wide, with lid-lashes all sear,
Flash'd phosphor and sharp sparks, without one cooling
tear.
The colours all inflam'd throughout her train,
She writh'd about, convuls'd with scarlet pain:
A deep volcanian yellow took the place
Of all her milder-mooned body's grace;
And, as the lava ravishes the mead,
Spoilt all her silver mail, and golden brede;
Made gloom of all her frecklings, streaks and bars,
Eclips'd her crescents, and lick'd up her stars: 160
So that, in moments few, she was undrest
Of all her sapphires, greens, and amethyst,
And rubious-argent: of all these bereft,
Nothing but pain and ugliness were left.
Still shone her crown; that vanish'd, also she
Melted and disappear'd as suddenly;
And in the air, her new voice luting soft,
Cried, 'Lycius! gentle Lycius!'—Borne aloft
With the bright mists about the mountains hoar
These words dissolv'd: Crete's forests heard no more.   170

194   *The Eve of St Agnes*

                            I

      ST Agnes' Eve—Ah, bitter chill it was!
      The owl, for all his feathers, was a-cold;
      The hare limp'd trembling through the frozen grass,
      And silent was the flock in woolly fold:
      Numb were the Beadsman's fingers, while he told
      His rosary, and while his frosted breath,
      Like pious incense from a censer old,
         Seem'd taking flight for heaven, without a death,
   Past the sweet Virgin's picture, while his prayer he saith.

2

His prayer he saith, this patient, holy man;   10
Then takes his lamp, and riseth from his knees,
And back returneth, meagre, barefoot, wan,
Along the chapel aisle by slow degrees:
The sculptur'd dead, on each side, seem to freeze,
Emprison'd in black, purgatorial rails:
Knights, ladies, praying in dumb orat'ries,
He passeth by; and his weak spirit fails
To think how they may ache in icy hoods and mails.

3

Northward he turneth through a little door,
And scarce three steps, ere Music's golden tongue   20
Flatter'd to tears this aged man and poor;
But no—already had his deathbell rung;
The joys of all his life were said and sung:
His was harsh penance on St Agnes' Eve:
Another way he went, and soon among
Rough ashes sat he for his soul's reprieve,
And all night kept awake, for sinners' sake to grieve.

4

That ancient Beadsman heard the prelude soft;
And so it chanc'd, for many a door was wide,
From hurry to and fro. Soon, up aloft,   30
The silver, snarling trumpets 'gan to chide:
The level chambers, ready with their pride,
Were glowing to receive a thousand guests:
The carved angels, ever eager-eyed,
Star'd, where upon their heads the cornice rests,
With hair blown back, and wings put cross-wise on their
    breasts.

5

At length burst in the argent revelry,
With plume, tiara, and all rich array,
Numerous as shadows haunting fairily
The brain, new stuff'd, in youth, with triumphs gay   40
Of old romance. These let us wish away,
And turn, sole-thoughted, to one Lady there,
Whose heart had brooded, all that wintry day,
On love, and wing'd St Agnes' saintly care,
As she had heard old dames full many times declare.

6

They told her how, upon St Agnes' Eve,
Young virgins might have visions of delight,
And soft adorings from their loves receive
Upon the honey'd middle of the night,
If ceremonies due they did aright;   50
As, supperless to bed they must retire,
And couch supine their beauties, lily white;
Nor look behind, nor sideways, but require
Of Heaven with upward eyes for all that they desire.

7

Full of this whim was thoughtful Madeline:
The music, yearning like a God in pain,
She scarcely heard: her maiden eyes divine,
Fix'd on the floor, saw many a sweeping train
Pass by—she heeded not at all: in vain
Came many a tiptoe, amorous cavalier,   60
And back retir'd, not cool'd by high disdain;
But she saw not: her heart was otherwhere:
She sigh'd for Agnes' dreams, the sweetest of the year.

8

She danc'd along with vague, regardless eyes,
Anxious her lips, her breathing quick and short:
The hallow'd hour was near at hand: she sighs
Amid the timbrels, and the throng'd resort
Of whisperers in anger, or in sport;
'Mid looks of love, defiance, hate, and scorn,
Hoodwink'd with faery fancy; all amort,   70
Save to St Agnes and her lambs unshorn,
And all the bliss to be before to-morrow morn.

9

So, purposing each moment to retire,
She linger'd still. Meantime, across the moors,
Had come young Porphyro, with heart on fire
For Madeline. Beside the portal doors,
Buttress'd from moonlight, stands he, and implores
All saints to give him sight of Madeline,
But for one moment in the tedious hours,
That he might gaze and worship all unseen;   80
Perchance speak, kneel, touch, kiss—in sooth such things
      have been.

10

He ventures in: let no buzz'd whisper tell:
All eyes be muffled, or a hundred swords
Will storm his heart, Love's fev'rous citadel:
For him, those chambers held barbarian hordes,
Hyena foemen, and hot-blooded lords,
Whose very dogs would execrations howl
Against his lineage: not one breast affords
Him any mercy, in that mansion foul,
Save one old beldame, weak in body and in soul. 90

11

Ah, happy chance! the aged creature came,
Shuffling along with ivory-headed wand,
To where he stood, hid from the torch's flame,
Behind a broad hall-pillar, far beyond
The sound of merriment and chorus bland:
He startled her; but soon she knew his face,
And grasp'd his fingers in her palsied hand,
Saying, 'Mercy, Porphyro! hie thee from this place;
They are all here to-night, the whole blood-thirsty race!

12

'Get hence! get hence! there's dwarfish Hildebrand; 100
He had a fever late, and in the fit
He cursed thee and thine, both house and land:
Then there's that old Lord Maurice, not a whit
More tame for his gray hairs—Alas me! flit!
Flit like a ghost away.'—'Ah, Gossip dear,
We're safe enough; here in this arm-chair sit,
And tell me how'—'Good Saints! not here, not here;
Follow me, child, or else these stones will be thy bier.'

13

He follow'd through a lowly arched way,
Brushing the cobwebs with his lofty plume, 110
And as she mutter'd 'Well-a—well-a-day!'
He found him in a little moonlight room,
Pale, lattic'd, chill, and silent as a tomb.
'Now tell me where is Madeline,' said he,
'O tell me, Angela, by the holy loom
Which none but secret sisterhood may see,
When they St Agnes' wool are weaving piously.'

14

'St Agnes! Ah! it is St Agnes' Eve—
Yet men will murder upon holy days:
Thou must hold water in a witch's sieve,   120
And be liege-lord of all the Elves and Fays,
To venture so: it fills me with amaze
To see thee, Porphyro!—St Agnes' Eve!
God's help! my lady fair the conjuror plays
This very night: good angels her deceive!
But let me laugh awhile, I've mickle time to grieve.'

15

Feebly she laugheth in the languid moon,
While Porphyro upon her face doth look,
Like puzzled urchin on an aged crone
Who keepeth clos'd a wond'rous riddle-book,   130
As spectacled she sits in chimney nook.
But soon his eyes grew brilliant, when she told
His lady's purpose; and he scarce could brook
Tears, at the thought of those enchantments cold,
And Madeline asleep in lap of legends old.

16

Sudden a thought came like a full-blown rose,
Flushing his brow, and in his pained heart
Made purple riot: then doth he propose
A stratagem, that makes the beldame start:
'A cruel man and impious thou art: 140
Sweet lady, let her pray, and sleep, and dream
Alone with her good angels, far apart
From wicked men like thee. Go, go!—I deem
Thou canst not surely be the same that thou didst seem.'

17

'I will not harm her, by all saints I swear,'
Quoth Porphyro: 'O may I ne'er find grace
When my weak voice shall whisper its last prayer,
If one of her soft ringlets I displace,
Or look with ruffian passion in her face:
Good Angela, believe me by these tears;   150
Or I will, even in a moment's space,
Awake, with horrid shout, my foemen's ears,
And beard them, though they be more fang'd than wolves and
        bears.'

18

'Ah! why wilt thou affright a feeble soul?
A poor, weak, palsy-stricken, churchyard thing,
Whose passing-bell may ere the midnight toll;
Whose prayers for thee, each morn and evening,
Were never miss'd.'—Thus plaining, doth she bring
A gentler speech from burning Porphyro;
So woful, and of such deep sorrowing,   160
That Angela gives promise she will do
Whatever he shall wish, betide her weal or woe.

19

Which was, to lead him, in close secrecy,
Even to Madeline's chamber, and there hide
Him in a closet, of such privacy
That he might see her beauty unespied,
And win perhaps that night a peerless bride,
While legion'd fairies pac'd the coverlet,
And pale enchantment held her sleepy-eyed.
Never on such a night have lovers met,   170
Since Merlin paid his Demon all the monstrous debt.

20

'It shall be as thou wishest,' said the Dame:
'All cates and dainties shall be stored there
Quickly on this feast-night: by the tambour frame
Her own lute thou wilt see: no time to spare,
For I am slow and feeble, and scarce dare
On such a catering trust my dizzy head.
Wait here, my child, with patience; kneel in prayer
The while: Ah! thou must needs the lady wed,
Or may I never leave my grave among the dead.'   180

21

So saying, she hobbled off with busy fear.
The lover's endless minutes slowly pass'd;
The dame return'd, and whisper'd in his ear
To follow her; with aged eyes aghast
From fright of dim espial. Safe at last,
Through many a dusky gallery, they gain
The maiden's chamber, silken, hush'd, and chaste;
Where Porphyro took covert, pleas'd amain.
His poor guide hurried back with agues in her brain.

22

Her falt'ring hand upon the balustrade,   190
Old Angela was feeling for the stair,
When Madeline, St Agnes' charmed maid,
Rose, like a mission'd spirit, unaware:
With silver taper's light, and pious care,
She turn'd, and down the aged gossip led
To a safe level matting. Now prepare,
  Young Porphyro, for gazing on that bed;
She comes, she comes again, like ring-dove fray'd and fled.

23

Out went the taper as she hurried in;
Its little smoke, in pallid moonshine, died: 200
She clos'd the door, she panted, all akin
To spirits of the air, and visions wide:
No uttered syllable, or, woe betide!
But to her heart, her heart was voluble,
Paining with eloquence her balmy side;
  As though a tongueless nightingale should swell
Her throat in vain, and die, heart-stifled, in her dell.

24

A casement high and triple-arch'd there was,
All garlanded with carven imag'ries
Of fruits, and flowers, and bunches of knot-grass,   210
And diamonded with panes of quaint device,
Innumerable of stains and splendid dyes,
As are the tiger-moth's deep-damask'd wings;
And in the midst, 'mong thousand heraldries,
  And twilight saints, and dim emblazonings,
A shielded scutcheon blush'd with blood of queens and kings.

25

Full on this casement shone the wintry moon,
And threw warm gules on Madeline's fair breast,
As down she knelt for heaven's grace and boon;
Rose-bloom fell on her hands, together prest,   220
And on her silver cross soft amethyst,
And on her hair a glory, like a saint:
She seem'd a splendid angel, newly drest,
  Save wings, for heaven:—Porphyro grew faint:
She knelt, so pure a thing, so free from mortal taint.

26

Anon his heart revives: her vespers done,
Of all its wreathed pearls her hair she frees;
Unclasps her warmed jewels one by one;
Loosens her fragrant boddice; by degrees
Her rich attire creeps rustling to her knees: 230
Half-hidden, like a mermaid in sea-weed,
Pensive awhile she dreams awake, and sees,
In fancy, fair St Agnes in her bed,
But dares not look behind, or all the charm is fled.

27

Soon, trembling in her soft and chilly nest,
In sort of wakeful swoon, perplex'd she lay,
Until the poppied warmth of sleep oppress'd
Her soothed limbs, and soul fatigued away;
Flown, like a thought, until the morrow-day;
Blissfully haven'd both from joy and pain;   240
Clasp'd like a missal where swart Paynims pray;
Blinded alike from sunshine and from rain,
As though a rose should shut, and be a bud again.

28

Stol'n to this paradise, and so entranced,
Porphyro gazed upon her empty dress,
And listen'd to her breathing, if it chanced
To wake into a slumberous tenderness;
Which when he heard, that minute did he bless,
And breath'd himself: then from the closet crept,
Noiseless as fear in a wide wilderness,   250
And over the hush'd carpet, silent, stept,
And 'tween the curtains peep'd, where, lo!—how fast she slept.

29

Then by the bed-side, where the faded moon
Made a dim, silver twilight, soft he set
A table, and, half anguish'd, threw thereon
A cloth of woven crimson, gold, and jet:—
O for some drowsy Morphean amulet!
The boisterous, midnight, festive clarion,
The kettle-drum, and far-heard clarionet,
Affray his ears, though but in dying tone:—   260
The hall door shuts again, and all the noise is gone.

30

And still she slept an azure-lidded sleep,
In blanched linen, smooth, and lavender'd,
While he from forth the closet brought a heap
Of candied apple, quince, and plum, and gourd;
With jellies soother than the creamy curd,
And lucent syrops, tinct with cinnamon;
Manna and dates, in argosy transferr'd
From Fez; and spiced dainties, every one,
From silken Samarcand to cedar'd Lebanon.   270

31

These delicates he heap'd with glowing hand
On golden dishes and in baskets bright
Of wreathed silver: sumptuous they stand
In the retired quiet of the night,
Filling the chilly room with perfume light.—
'And now, my love, my seraph fair, awake!
Thou art my heaven, and I thine eremite:
Open thine eyes, for meek St Agnes' sake,
Or I shall drowse beside thee, so my soul doth ache.'

32

Thus whispering, his warm, unnerved arm   280
Sank in her pillow. Shaded was her dream
By the dusk curtains:—'twas a midnight charm
Impossible to melt as iced stream:
The lustrous salvers in the moonlight gleam;
Broad golden fringe upon the carpet lies:
It seem'd he never, never could redeem
From such a stedfast spell his lady's eyes;
So mus'd awhile, entoil'd in woofed phantasies.

33

Awakening up, he took her hollow lute,—
Tumultuous,—and, in chords that tenderest be,   290
He play'd an ancient ditty, long since mute,
In Provence call'd, 'La belle dame sans mercy':
Close to her ear touching the melody;—
Wherewith disturb'd, she utter'd a soft moan:
He ceased—she panted quick—and suddenly
Her blue affrayed eyes wide open shone:
Upon his knees he sank, pale as smooth-sculptured stone.

34

Her eyes were open, but she still beheld,
Now wide awake, the vision of her sleep:
There was a painful change, that nigh expell'd   300
The blisses of her dream so pure and deep:
At which fair Madeline began to weep,
And moan forth witless words with many a sigh;
While still her gaze on Porphyro would keep;
Who knelt, with joined hands and piteous eye,
Fearing to move or speak, she look'd so dreamingly.

35

'Ah, Porphyro!' said she, 'but even now
Thy voice was at sweet tremble in mine ear,
Made tuneable with every sweetest vow;
And those sad eyes were spiritual and clear: 310
How chang'd thou art! how pallid, chill, and drear!
Give me that voice again, my Porphyro,
Those looks immortal, those complainings dear!
Oh leavé me not in this eternal woe,
For if thou diest, my Love, I know not where to go.'

36

Beyond a mortal man impassion'd far
At these voluptuous accents, he arose,
Ethereal, flush'd, and like a throbbing star
Seen mid the sapphire heaven's deep repose;
Into her dream he melted, as the rose   320
Blendeth its odour with the violet,—
Solution sweet: meantime the frost-wind blows
Like Love's alarum pattering the sharp sleet
Against the window-panes; St Agnes' moon hath set.

37

'Tis dark: quick pattereth the flaw-blown sleet:
'This is no dream, my bride, my Madeline!'
'Tis dark: the iced gusts still rave and beat:
'No dream, alas! alas! and woe is mine!
Porphyro will leave me here to fade and pine.—
Cruel! what traitor could thee hither bring?   330
I curse not, for my heart is lost in thine,
Though thou forsakest a deceived thing;—
A dove forlorn and lost with sick unpruned wing.'

38

'My Madeline! sweet dreamer! lovely bride!
Say, may I be for aye thy vassal blest?
Thy beauty's shield, heart-shap'd and vermeil dyed?
Ah, silver shrine, here will I take my rest
After so many hours of toil and quest,
A famish'd pilgrim,—saved by miracle.
Though I have found, I will not rob thy nest   340
Saving of thy sweet self; if thou think'st well
To trust, fair Madeline, to no rude infidel.

39

'Hark! 'tis an elfin-storm from faery land,
Of haggard seeming, but a boon indeed:
Arise—arise! the morning is at hand:—
The bloated wassaillers will never heed:—
Let us away, my love, with happy speed;
There are no ears to hear, or eyes to see,—
Drown'd all in Rhenish and the sleepy mead:
Awake! arise! my love, and fearless be,   350
For o'er the southern moors I have a home for thee.'

40

She hurried at his words, beset with fears,
For there were sleeping dragons all around,
At glaring watch, perhaps, with ready spears—
Down the wide stairs a darkling way they found.—
In all the house was heard no human sound.
A chain-droop'd lamp was flickering by each door;
The arras, rich with horseman, hawk, and hound,
Flutter'd in the besieging wind's uproar;
And the long carpets rose along the gusty floor.   360

41

They glide, like phantoms, into the wide hall;
Like phantoms, to the iron porch, they glide;
Where lay the Porter, in uneasy sprawl,
With a huge empty flaggon by his side:
The wakeful bloodhound rose, and shook his hide,
But his sagacious eye an inmate owns:
By one, and one, the bolts full easy slide:—
The chains lie silent on the footworn stones;—
The key turns, and the door upon its hinges groans.

42

And they are gone: ay, ages long ago   370
These lovers fled away into the storm.
That night the Baron dreamt of many a woe,
And all his warrior-guests, with shade and form
Of witch, and demon, and large coffin-worm,
Were long be-nightmar'd. Angela the old
Died palsy-twitch'd, with meagre face deform;
The Beadsman, after thousand aves told,
For aye unsought for slept among his ashes cold.

195   from *Hyperion*

A Fragment

BOOK I

DEEP in the shady sadness of a vale
Far sunken from the healthy breath of morn,
Far from the fiery noon, and eve's one star,
Sat gray-hair'd Saturn, quiet as a stone,
Still as the silence round about his lair;
Forest on forest hung above his head
Like cloud on cloud. No stir of air was there,
Not so much life as on a summer's day
Robs not one light seed from the feather'd grass,
But where the dead leaf fell, there did it rest.   10
A stream went voiceless by, still deadened more
By reason of his fallen divinity
Spreading a shade: the Naiad 'mid her reeds
Press'd her cold finger closer to her lips.

Along the margin-sand large foot-marks went,
No further than to where his feet had stray'd,
And slept there since. Upon the sodden ground
His old right hand lay nerveless, listless, dead,
Unsceptred; and his realmless eyes were closed;
While his bow'd head seem'd list'ning to the Earth,   20
His ancient mother, for some comfort yet.

It seem'd no force could wake him from his place;
But there came one, who with a kindred hand
Touch'd his wide shoulders, after bending low
With reverence, though to one who knew it not.
She was a Goddess of the infant world;

By her in stature the tall Amazon
Had stood a pigmy's height: she would have ta'en
Achilles by the hair and bent his neck;
Or with a finger stay'd Ixion's wheel.   30
Her face was large as that of Memphian sphinx,
Pedestal'd haply in a palace court,
When sages look'd to Egypt for their lore.
But oh! how unlike marble was that face:
How beautiful, if sorrow had not made
Sorrow more beautiful than Beauty's self.
There was a listening fear in her regard,
As if calamity had but begun;
As if the vanward clouds of evil days
Had spent their malice, and the sullen rear   40
Was with its stored thunder labouring up.
One hand she press'd upon that aching spot
Where beats the human heart, as if just there,
Though an immortal, she felt cruel pain:
The other upon Saturn's bended neck
She laid, and to the level of his ear
Leaning with parted lips, some words she spake
In solemn tenour and deep organ tone:
Some mourning words, which in our feeble tongue
Would come in these like accents; O how frail   50
To that large utterance of the early Gods!
'Saturn, look up!—though wherefore, poor old King?
I have no comfort for thee, no not one:
I cannot say, "O wherefore sleepest thou?"
For heaven is parted from thee, and the earth
Knows thee not, thus afflicted, for a God;
And ocean too, with all its solemn noise,
Has from thy sceptre pass'd; and all the air
Is emptied of thine hoary majesty.
Thy thunder, conscious of the new command,   60
Rumbles reluctant o'er our fallen house;
And thy sharp lightning in unpractised hands
Scorches and burns our once serene domain.
O aching time! O moments big as years!
All as ye pass swell out the monstrous truth,
And press it so upon our weary griefs
That unbelief has not a space to breathe.
Saturn, sleep on:—O thoughtless, why did I
Thus violate thy slumbrous solitude?
Why should I ope thy melancholy eyes?   70
Saturn, sleep on! while at thy feet I weep.'

As when, upon a tranced summer-night,
Those green-rob'd senators of mighty woods,
Tall oaks, branch-charmed by the earnest stars,
Dream, and so dream all night without a stir,
Save from one gradual solitary gust
Which comes upon the silence, and dies off,
As if the ebbing air had but one wave;
So came these words and went; the while in tears
She touch'd her fair large forehead to the ground,   80
Just where her falling hair might be outspread,
A soft and silken mat for Saturn's feet.

One moon, with alteration slow, had shed
Her silver seasons four upon the night,
And still these two were postured motionless,
Like natural sculpture in cathedral cavern;
The frozen God still couchant on the earth,
And the sad Goddess weeping at his feet:
Until at length old Saturn lifted up
His faded eyes, and saw his kingdom gone,   90
And all the gloom and sorrow of the place,
And that fair kneeling Goddess; and then spake,
As with a palsied tongue, and while his beard
Shook horrid with such aspen-malady:
'O tender spouse of gold Hyperion,
Thea, I feel thee ere I see thy face;
Look up, and let me see our doom in it;
Look up, and tell me if this feeble shape
Is Saturn's; tell me, if thou hear'st the voice
Of Saturn; tell me, if this wrinkling brow,   100
Naked and bare of its great diadem,
Peers like the front of Saturn. Who had power
To make me desolate? whence came the strength?
How was it nurtur'd to such bursting forth,
While Fate seem'd strangled in my nervous grasp?
But it is so; and I am smother'd up,
And buried from all godlike exercise
Of influence benign on planets pale,
Of admonitions to the winds and seas,
Of peaceful sway above man's harvesting,   110
And all those acts which Deity supreme
Doth ease its heart of love in.—I am gone
Away from my own bosom: I have left
My strong identity, my real self,
Somewhere between the throne, and where I sit
Here on this spot of earth. Search, Thea, search!
Open thine eyes eterne, and sphere them round

Upon all space: space starr'd, and lorn of light;
Space region'd with life-air; and barren void;
Spaces of fire, and all the yawn of hell.—   120
Search, Thea, search! and tell me, if thou seest
A certain shape or shadow, making way
With wings or chariot fierce to repossess
A heaven he lost erewhile: it must—it must
Be of ripe progress—Saturn must be King.
Yes, there must be a golden victory;
There must be Gods thrown down, and trumpets blown
Of triumph calm, and hymns of festival
Upon the gold clouds metropolitan,
Voices of soft proclaim, and silver stir   130
Of strings in hollow shells; and there shall be
Beautiful things made new, for the surprise
Of the sky-children; I will give command:
Thea! Thea! Thea! where is Saturn?'

    This passion lifted him upon his feet,
And made his hands to struggle in the air,
His Druid locks to shake and ooze with sweat,
His eyes to fever out, his voice to cease.
He stood, and heard not Thea's sobbing deep;   140
A little time, and then again he snatch'd
Utterance thus.—'But cannot I create?
Cannot I form? Cannot I fashion forth
Another world, another universe,
To overbear and crumble this to nought?
Where is another chaos? Where?'—That word
Found way unto Olympus, and made quake
The rebel three.—Thea was startled up,
And in her bearing was a sort of hope,
As thus she quick-voic'd spake, yet full of awe.

    'This cheers our fallen house: come to our friends,   150
O Saturn! come away, and give them heart;
I know the covert, for thence came I hither.'
Thus brief; then with beseeching eyes she went
With backward footing through the shade a space:
He follow'd, and she turn'd to lead the way
Through aged boughs, that yielded like the mist
Which eagles cleave upmounting from their nest.

    Meanwhile in other realms big tears were shed,
More sorrow like to this, and such like woe,
Too huge for mortal tongue or pen of scribe: 160

The Titans fierce, self-hid, or prison-bound,
Groan'd for the old allegiance once more,
And listen'd in sharp pain for Saturn's voice.
But one of the whole mammoth-brood still kept
His sov'reignty, and rule, and majesty;—
Blazing Hyperion on his orbed fire
Still sat, still snuff'd the incense, teeming up
From man to the sun's God; yet unsecure:
For as among us mortals omens drear
Fright and perplex, so also shuddered he—   170
Not at dog's howl, or gloom-bird's hated screech,
Or the familiar visiting of one
Upon the first toll of his passing-bell,
Or prophesyings of the midnight lamp;
But horrors, portion'd to a giant nerve,
Oft made Hyperion ache. His palace bright,
Bastion'd with pyramids of glowing gold,
And touch'd with shade of bronzed obelisks,
Glar'd a blood-red through all its thousand courts,
Arches, and domes, and fiery galleries;   180
And all its curtains of Aurorian clouds
Flush'd angerly: while sometimes eagle's wings,
Unseen before by Gods or wondering men,
Darken'd the place; and neighing steeds were heard,
Not heard before by Gods or wondering men.
Also, when he would taste the spicy wreaths
Of incense, breath'd aloft from sacred hills,
Instead of sweets, his ample palate took
Savour of poisonous brass and metal sick:
And so, when harbour'd in the sleepy west,   190
After the full completion of fair day,—
For rest divine upon exalted couch
And slumber in the arms of melody,
He pac'd away the pleasant hours of ease
With stride colossal, on from hall to hall;
While far within each aisle and deep recess,
His winged minions in close clusters stood,
Amaz'd and full of fear; like anxious men
Who on wide plains gather in panting troops,
When earthquakes jar their battlements and towers.   200
Even now, while Saturn, rous'd from icy trance,
Went step for step with Thea through the woods,
Hyperion, leaving twilight in the rear,
Came slope upon the threshold of the west;
Then, as was wont, his palace-door flew ope
In smoothest silence, save what solemn tubes,

Blown by the serious Zephyrs, gave of sweet
And wandering sounds, slow-breathed melodies;
And like a rose in vermeil tint and shape,
In fragrance soft, and coolness to the eye,   210
That inlet to severe magnificence
Stood full blown, for the God to enter in.

He enter'd, but he enter'd full of wrath;
His flaming robes stream'd out beyond his heels,
And gave a roar, as if of earthly fire,
That scar'd away the meek ethereal Hours
And made their dove-wings tremble. On he flared,
From stately nave to nave, from vault to vault,
Through bowers of fragrant and enwreathed light,
And diamond-paved lustrous long arcades,   220
Until he reach'd the great main cupola;
There standing fierce beneath, he stampt his foot,
And from the basements deep to the high towers
Jarr'd his own golden region; and before
The quavering thunder thereupon had ceas'd,
His voice leapt out, despite of godlike curb,
To this result: 'O dreams of day and night!
O monstrous forms! O effigies of pain!
O spectres busy in a cold, cold gloom!
O lank-eared Phantoms of black-weeded pools!   230
Why do I know ye? why have I seen ye? why
Is my eternal essence thus distraught
To see and to behold these horrors new?
Saturn is fallen, am I too to fall?
Am I to leave this haven of my rest,
This cradle of my glory, this soft clime,
This calm luxuriance of blissful light,
These crystalline pavilions, and pure fanes,
Of all my lucent empire? It is left
Deserted, void, nor any haunt of mine.   240
The blaze, the splendor, and the symmetry,
I cannot see—but darkness, death and darkness.
Even here, into my centre of repose,
The shady visions come to domineer,
Insult, and blind, and stifle up my pomp.—
Fall!—No, by Tellus and her briny robes!
Over the fiery frontier of my realms
I will advance a terrible right arm
Shall scare that infant thunderer, rebel Jove,
And bid old Saturn take his throne again.'—   250
He spake, and ceas'd, the while a heavier threat

Held struggle with his throat but came not forth;
For as in theatres of crowded men
Hubbub increases more they call out 'Hush!'
So at Hyperion's words the Phantoms pale
Bestirr'd themselves, thrice horrible and cold;
And from the mirror'd level where he stood
A mist arose, as from a scummy marsh.
At this, through all his bulk an agony
Crept gradual, from the feet unto the crown,   260
Like a lithe serpent vast and muscular
Making slow way, with head and neck convuls'd
From over-strained might. Releas'd, he fled
To the eastern gates, and full six dewy hours
Before the dawn in season due should blush,
He breath'd fierce breath against the sleepy portals,
Clear'd them of heavy vapours, burst them wide
Suddenly on the ocean's chilly streams.
The planet orb of fire, whereon he rode
Each day from east to west the heavens through,   270
Spun round in sable curtaining of clouds;
Not therefore veiled quite, blindfold, and hid,
But ever and anon the glancing spheres,
Circles, and arcs, and broad-belting colure,
Glow'd through, and wrought upon the muffling dark
Sweet-shaped lightnings from the nadir deep
Up to the zenith,—hieroglyphics old,
Which sages and keen-eyed astrologers
Then living on the earth, with labouring thought
Won from the gaze of many centuries: 280
Now lost, save what we find on remnants huge
Of stone, or marble swart; their import gone,
Their wisdom long since fled.—Two wings this orb
Possess'd for glory, two fair argent wings,
Ever exalted at the God's approach:
And now, from forth the gloom their plumes immense
Rose, one by one, till all outspreaded were;
While still the dazzling globe maintain'd eclipse,
Awaiting for Hyperion's command.
Fain would he have commanded, fain took throne   290
And bid the day begin, if but for change.
He might not:—No, though a primeval God:
The sacred seasons might not be disturb'd.
Therefore the operations of the dawn
Stay'd in their birth, even as here 'tis told.
Those silver wings expanded sisterly,
Eager to sail their orb; the porches wide

Open'd upon the dusk demesnes of night;
And the bright Titan, phrenzied with new woes,
Unus'd to bend, by hard compulsion bent   300
His spirit to the sorrow of the time;
And all along a dismal rack of clouds,
Upon the boundaries of day and night,
He stretch'd himself in grief and radiance faint.
There as he lay, the Heaven with its stars
Look'd down on him with pity, and the voice
Of Cœlus, from the universal space,
Thus whisper'd low and solemn in his ear.
'O brightest of my children dear, earth-born
And sky-engendered, Son of Mysteries   310
All unrevealed even to the powers
Which met at thy creating; at whose joys
And palpitations sweet, and pleasures soft,
I, Cœlus, wonder, how they came and whence;
And at the fruits thereof what shapes they be,
Distinct, and visible; symbols divine,
Manifestations of that beauteous life
Diffus'd unseen throughout eternal space:
Of these new-form'd art thou, oh brightest child!
Of these, thy brethren and the Goddesses!   320
There is sad feud among ye, and rebellion
Of son against his sire. I saw him fall,
I saw my first-born tumbled from his throne!
To me his arms were spread, to me his voice
Found way from forth the thunders round his head!
Pale wox I, and in vapours hid my face.
Art thou, too, near such doom? vague fear there is:
For I have seen my sons most unlike Gods.
Divine ye were created, and divine
In sad demeanour, solemn, undisturb'd,   330
Unruffled, like high Gods, ye liv'd and ruled:
Now I behold in you fear, hope, and wrath;
Actions of rage and passion; even as
I see them, on the mortal world beneath,
In men who die.—This is the grief, O Son!
Sad sign of ruin, sudden dismay, and fall!
Yet do thou strive; as thou art capable,
As thou canst move about, an evident God;
And canst oppose to each malignant hour
Ethereal presence:—I am but a voice;   340
My life is but the life of winds and tides,
No more than winds and tides can I avail:—
But thou canst.—Be thou therefore in the van

Of circumstance; yea, seize the arrow's barb
Before the tense string murmur.—To the earth!
For there thou wilt find Saturn, and his woes.
Meantime I will keep watch on thy bright sun,
And of thy seasons be a careful nurse.'—
Ere half this region-whisper had come down,
Hyperion arose, and on the stars   350
Lifted his curved lids, and kept them wide
Until it ceas'd; and still he kept them wide:
And still they were the same bright, patient stars.
Then with a slow incline of his broad breast,
Like to a diver in the pearly seas,
Forward he stoop'd over the airy shore,
And plung'd all noiseless into the deep night.

196   *Ode to Psyche*

O GODDESS! hear these tuneless numbers, wrung
    By sweet enforcement and remembrance dear,
And pardon that thy secrets should be sung
    Even into thine own soft-conched ear:
Surely I dreamt to-day, or did I see
    The winged Psyche with awaken'd eyes?
I wander'd in a forest thoughtlessly,
    And, on the sudden, fainting with surprise,
Saw two fair creatures, couched side by side
    In deepest grass, beneath the whisp'ring roof   10
    Of leaves and trembled blossoms, where there ran
        A brooklet, scarce espied:
'Mid hush'd, cool-rooted flowers, fragrant-eyed,
    Blue, silver-white, and budded Tyrian,
They lay calm-breathing on the bedded grass;
    Their arms embraced, and their pinions too;
    Their lips touch'd not, but had not bade adieu,
As if disjoined by soft-handed slumber,
And ready still past kisses to outnumber   20
    At tender eye-dawn of aurorean love:
        The winged boy I knew;
    But who wast thou, O happy, happy dove?
        His Psyche true!

O latest born and loveliest vision far
    Of all Olympus' faded hierarchy!

Fairer than Phœbe's sapphire-region'd star,
    Or Vesper, amorous glow-worm of the sky;
Fairer than these, though temple thou hast none,
      Nor altar heap'd with flowers;
Nor virgin-choir to make delicious moan   30
    Upon the midnight hours;
No voice, no lute, no pipe, no incense sweet
    From chain-swung censer teeming;
No shrine, no grove, no oracle, no heat
    Of pale-mouth'd prophet dreaming.

O brightest! though too late for antique vows,
    Too, too late for the fond believing lyre,
When holy were the haunted forest boughs,
    Holy the air, the water, and the fire;
Yet even in these days so far retir'd   40
    From happy pieties, thy lucent fans,
    Fluttering among the faint Olympians,
I see, and sing, by my own eyes inspired.
So let me be thy choir, and make a moan
    Upon the midnight hours;
Thy voice, thy lute, thy pipe, thy incense sweet
    From swinged censer teeming;
Thy shrine, thy grove, thy oracle, thy heat
    Of pale-mouth'd prophet dreaming.

Yes, I will be thy priest, and build a fane   50
    In some untrodden region of my mind,
Where branched thoughts, new grown with pleasant pain,
    Instead of pines shall murmur in the wind:
Far, far around shall those dark-cluster'd trees
    Fledge the wild-ridged mountains steep by steep;
And there by zephyrs, streams, and birds, and bees,
    The moss-lain Dryads shall be lull'd to sleep;
And in the midst of this wide quietness
A rosy sanctuary will I dress
With the wreath'd trellis of a working brain,   60
    With buds, and bells, and stars without a name,
With all the gardener Fancy e'er could feign,
    Who breeding flowers, will never breed the same:
And there shall be for thee all soft delight
    That shadowy thought can win,
A bright torch, and a casement ope at night,
    To let the warm Love in!

197   *To Autumn*

1

SEASON of mists and mellow fruitfulness,
　　Close bosom-friend of the maturing sun;
Conspiring with him how to load and bless
　　With fruit the vines that round the thatch-eves run;
To bend with apples the moss'd cottage-trees,
　　And fill all fruit with ripeness to the core;
　　　　To swell the gourd, and plump the hazel shells
With a sweet kernel; to set budding more,
And still more, later flowers for the bees,
Until they think warm days will never cease,   10
　　　　For Summer has o'er-brimm'd their clammy cells.

2

Who hath not seen thee oft amid thy store?
　　Sometimes whoever seeks abroad may find
Thee sitting careless on a granary floor,
　　Thy hair soft-lifted by the winnowing wind;
Or on a half-reap'd furrow sound asleep,
　　Drows'd with the fume of poppies, while thy hook
　　　　Spares the next swath and all its twined flowers:
And sometimes like a gleaner thou dost keep
　　Steady thy laden head across a brook;   20
　　Or by a cyder-press, with patient look,
　　　　Thou watchest the last oozings hours by hours.

3

Where are the songs of Spring? Ay, where are they?
　　Think not of them, thou hast thy music too,—
While barred clouds bloom the soft-dying day,
　　And touch the stubble-plains with rosy hue;
Then in a wailful choir the small gnats mourn
　　Among the river sallows, borne aloft
　　　　Or sinking as the light wind lives or dies;
And full-grown lambs loud bleat from hilly bourn;   30
　　Hedge-crickets sing; and now with treble soft
　　The red-breast whistles from a garden-croft;
　　　　And gathering swallows twitter in the skies.

GEORGE DARLEY
1795–1846

198   *To Helene*

On a gifte-ringe carelesslie loste
AD 1672

I SENTE a ringe, a little bande
   Of Emeraud and rubie stone;
Ande bade it, sparklinge onne thy hande,
   Telle thee sweete tales of one,
      Whose constante memorie,
      Was fulle of lovelinesse ande thee.

A spelle was gravenne in its golde,
   'Twas Cupide fixede, without his winges.
To HELENE once it would have tolde
   More thanne was everre tolde bie ringes,   10
      But now alle's past ande gone,
      Her love is buriede with thatte stone.

Thou shalte not see the teares thatte starte
   Fromme eyes bie thoughtes like those beguilde,
Thou shalte not knowe the beatinge hearte,
   Ever a victime ande a childe.
      Yette HELENE love, believe
      The hearte thatt never coulde deceive.

I'll heare thy voice of melodie
   In the sweete whisperres of the aire;   20
I'll see the brightnesse of thine eye
   In the blue Eveninge's dewie starre;
      In crystalle streames thy puritie,
      And looke on Heavenne, to look on thee.

                          Guilliame

CHARLES LLOYD

1775–1839

199   from *Desultory Thoughts in London*

110

WHERE have I wander'd, London, from thy haunts?
  Yet still, at times, in this erratic strain
My heart has turn'd to thee, and still it pants
  To pay its debt of gratitude for pain,
By thee abated: nor let him who vaunts
  Of joys imaginary, where the reign
Of nature's most complete, presume to swear
Imagination's joys are only there.

111

'Tis not the form that is th' essential thing,
  It is the soul, the spirit, that is there;   10
It is a mystery whence th' elastic spring
  Of inspiration comes, but it is clear
That, where it is, mere trifles,—any thing,—
  The passing bell, some scrannel notes we hear
From vagrant ballad-singer, may invoke
Thoughts that disclaim reality's dull yoke.

112

Yes, I have caught from seeing—as I went
  To childhood's bed—through ice-glaz'd lattice shine
The moon's cold gleam; or when the day was spent,
  From Christmas-carol, not, in notes like thine,   20
Oh, Mara, sung; perhaps when the flame, sent
  Towards mirror, shone in it, whence it would shine
Back bickering through the room;—if at this hour
So apt to yield us to thy witching power;—

113

From distant fife, upon my ears, there fell
  Some notes;—from these—have caught such impulses:
The ice-glaz'd lattice so to me would tell
  Of winter's pleasures; of such *jocos dulces*
The carol speak to me;—with such a spell,
  At close of day, would Fancy *still* my pulses;   30

In parlour twilight such sweet melancholy
Steal over me, so passionate, so holy,

114

That there has seem'd from all these little sources,
   Bliss to arise, which could not be exceeded!
Thus, when the mind is rich in all its forces,
   A flower, a scent, which, in some place, I'd heeded,
Still dear to me,—impell'd by these resources,
   That feeling strange has risen, as if indeed it
Were true that we elsewhere had had existence:—
And this of past identity were instance.   40

115

I wist not whether those, who may, by chance,
   Cast on these lines their eyes, have ever known it,
But 'tis a strange sensation—this swift glance
   At past existence, which, as soon as shewn, it
Vanishes; but the mind feels, while the trance
   Doth last, (a sense of past life so doth own it)
As if the self-same forms it saw again,
Which, though it knew not where, it erst had seen.

JOANNA BAILLIE
1762–1851

200   *The Ghost of Fadon*

On Gask's deserted ancient hall
   Was twilight closing fast,
And, in its dismal shadows, all
   Seem'd lofty, void, and vast.

All sounds of life, now reft and bare,
   From its walls had pass'd away,
But the stir of small birds shelter'd there,
   Dull owl, or clatt'ring jay.

Loop-hole and window, dimly seen,
   With faint light passing through,   10
Grew dimmer still, and the dreary scene
   Was fading from the view:

When the trampling sound of banded men
    Came from the court without;
Words of debate and call, and then
    A loud and angry shout.

But mingled echoes from within
    A mimick mock'ry made,
And the bursting door, with furious din,
    On jarring hinges bray'd.   20

An eager band, press'd rear on van,
    Rush'd in with clam'rous sound,
And their chief, the goodliest, bravest man,
    That e'er trode Scottish ground.

Then spoke forthwith that leader bold,
    'We war with wayward fate:
These walls are bare, the hearth is cold,
    And all is desolate.

'With fast unbroke and thirst unslaked,
    Must we on the hard ground sleep?   30
Or, like ghosts from vaulted charnel waked
    Our cheerless vigil keep?

'Hard hap this day in bloody field,
    Ye bravely have sustain'd,
And for your pains this dismal bield,
    And empty board have gain'd.

'Hie, Malcom, to that varlet's steed,
    And search if yet remain
Some homely store, but good at need,
    Spent nature to sustain.   40

'Cheer up, my friends! still, heart in hand,
    Tho' few and spent we be,
We are the pith of our native land,
    And she shall still be free.

'Cheer up! tho' scant and coarse our meal,
    In this our sad retreat,
We'll fill our horn to Scotland's weal,
    And that will make it sweet.'

Then all, full cheerly, as they could,
    Their willing service lent,   50

Some broke the boughs, some heap'd the wood,
  Some struck the sparkling flint.

And a fire they kindled speedily,
  Where the hall's last fire had been,
And pavement, walls, and rafters high,
  In the rising blaze were seen.

Red gleam on each tall buttress pour'd,
  The lengthen'd hall along,
And tall and black behind them lower'd
  Their shadows deep and strong.   60

The ceiling, ribb'd with massy oak,
  From bick'ring flames below,
As light and shadow o'er it broke,
  Seem'd wav'ring to and fro.

Their scanty meal was on the ground,
  Spread by the friendly light,
And they made the brown-horn circle round,
  As cheerly as they might.

Some talk of horses, weapons, mail,
  Some of their late defeat,   70
By treach'ry caused, and many a tale
  Of Southron spy's retreat.

'Aye, well,' says one, 'my sinking heart
  Did some disaster bode,
When faithless Fadon's wily art
  Beguiled us from the road.'

'But well repaid by Providence
  Are such false deeds we see;
He's had his rightful recompence,
  And cursed let him be.'   80

'Oh! curse him not! I needs must rue
  That stroke so rashly given:
If he to us were false or true,
  Is known to righteous Heaven.'

So spoke their chief, then silent all
  Remain'd in sombre mood,

Till they heard a bugle's larum call
   Sound distant thro' the wood.

'Rouse ye, my friends!' the chieftain said,
   That blast, from friend or foe,   90
Comes from the west; thro' forest shade
   With wary caution go.

'And bring me tidings. Speed ye well!'
   Forth three bold warriors past.
Then from the east with fuller swell
   Was heard the bugle blast.

Out past three warriors more; then shrill,
   The horn blew from the north,
And other eager warriors still,
   As banded scouts, went forth.   100

Till from their chief each war-mate good
   Had to the forest gone,
And he, who fear'd not flesh and blood,
   Stood by the fire alone.

He stood, wrapp'd in a musing dream,
   Nor rais'd his drooping head,
Till a sudden, alter'd, paly gleam
   On all around was spread.

Such dull, diminish'd, sombre sheen
   From moon eclips'd, by swain   110
Belated, or lone herd is seen
   O'er-mantling hill and plain.

Then to the fitful fire he turn'd,
   Which higher and brighter grew,
Till the flame like a baleful meteor burn'd
   Of clear sulphureous blue.

Then wist the chief, some soul unblest,
   Or spirit of power was near;
And his eyes adown the hall he cast,
   Yet naught did there appear.   120

But he felt a strange unearthly breath
   Upon the chill air borne,

And he heard at the gate, like a blast of wrath,
  The sound of Fadon's horn.

Owls, bats, and swallows, flutt'ring, out
  From hole and crevice flew,
Circling the lofty roof about,
  As loud and long it blew.

His noble hound sprang from his lair,
  The midnight rouse to greet,   130
Then, like a timid trembling hare,
  Couch'd at his master's feet.

Between his legs his drooping tail,
  Like dog of vulgar race,
He hid, and with strange piteous wail,
  Look'd in his master's face.

The porch seem'd void, but vapour dim
  Soon fill'd the lowering room,
Then was he aware of a figure grim,
  Approaching thro' the gloom.   140

And striding as it onward came,
  The vapour wore away,
Till it stood distinctly by the flame,
  Like a form in the noon of day.

Well Wallace knew that form, that head,
  That throat unbraced and bare,
Mark'd deep with streaming circlet red,
  And he utter'd a rapid prayer.

But when the spectre rais'd its arm,
  And brandish'd its glitt'ring blade,   150
That moment broke fear's chilly charm
  On noble Wallace laid.

The threaten'd combat was to him
  Relief; with weapon bare,
He rush'd upon the warrior grim,
  But his sword shore empty air.

Then the spectre smiled with a ghastly grin,
  And its warrior-semblance fled,
And its features grew stony, fix'd, and thin,
  Like the face of the stiffen'd dead.   160

The head a further moment crown'd
  The body's stately wreck,
Shook hideously, and to the ground
  Dropt from the bolter'd neck.

Back shrunk the noble chief aghast,
  And longer tarried not,
But quickly to the portal past,
  To shun the horrid spot.

But in the portal, stiff and tall,
  The apparition stood,   170
And Wallace turn'd and cross'd the hall,
  Where entrance to the wood

By other door he hoped to snatch,
  Whose pent arch darkly lower'd,
But there, like sentry on his watch,
  The dreadful phantom tower'd.

Then up the ruin'd stairs so steep,
  He ran with panting breath,
And from a window—desp'rate leap!
  Sprang to the court beneath.   180

O'er wall and ditch he quickly got,
  Thro' brake and bushy stream,
When suddenly thro' darkness shot
  A red and lurid gleam.

He look'd behind, and that lurid light
  Forth from the castle came;
Within its circuit thro' the night
  Appear'd an elrich flame.

Red glow'd each window, slit, and door,
  Like mouths of furnace hot,   190
And tint of deepest blackness wore
  The walls and steepy moat.

But soon it rose with bright'ning power,
  Till bush and ivy green,
And wall-flower, fringing breach and tower,
  Distinctly might be seen.

Then a spreading blaze with eddying sweep,
  Its spiral surges rear'd,
And then aloft on the stately keep,
  Fadon's Ghost appear'd.   200

A burning rafter, blazing bright,
  It wielded in its hand;
And its warrior-form, of human height,
  Dilated grew, and grand.

Coped by a curling tawny cloud,
  With tints sulphureous blent,
It rose with burst of thunder loud,
  And up the welkin went.

High, high it rose with wid'ning glare,
  Sent far o'er land and main,   210
And shot into the lofty air,
  And all was dark again.

A spell of horror lapt him round,
  Chill'd, motionless, amazed,
His very pulse of life was bound
  As on black night he gazed.

Till harness'd warriors' heavy tread,
  From echoing dell arose;
'Thank God!' with utter'd voice, he said,
  'For here come living foes.'   220

With kindling soul that brand he drew
  Which boldest Southron fears,
But soon the friendly call he knew,
  Of his gallant brave compeers.

With haste each wond'rous tale was told,
  How still, in vain pursuit,
They follow'd the horn thro' wood and wold,
  And Wallace alone was mute.

Day rose; but silent, sad, and pale,
  Stood the bravest of Scottish race;   230
And each warrior's heart began to quail,
  When he look'd in his leader's face.

GEORGE GORDON, LORD BYRON

from *Don Juan*, Canto III

[*Haidée's and Juan's Feast*]

67

Haidée and Juan carpeted their feet
  On crimson satin, border'd with pale blue;
Their sofa occupied three parts complete
  Of the apartment—and appear'd quite new;
The velvet cushions—(for a throne more meet)—
  Were scarlet, from whose glowing centre grew
A sun emboss'd in gold, whose rays of tissue,
Meridian-like, were seen all light to issue.

68

Crystal and marble, plate and porcelain,
  Had done their work of splendour; Indian mats   10
And Persian carpets, which the heart bled to stain,
  Over the floors were spread; gazelles and cats,
And dwarfs and blacks, and such like things, that gain
  Their bread as ministers and favourites—(that's
To say, by degradation)—mingled there
As plentiful as in a court or fair.

69

There was no want of lofty mirrors, and
  The tables, most of ebony inlaid
With mother of pearl or ivory, stood at hand,
  Or were of tortoise-shell or rare woods made,   20
Fretted with gold or silver:—by command
  The greater part of these were ready spread
With viands and sherbets in ice—and wine—
Kept for all comers, at all hours to dine.

70

Of all the dresses I select Haidée's:
  She wore two jelicks—one was of pale yellow;
Of azure, pink, and white was her chemise—
  'Neath which her breast heaved like a little billow;
With buttons form'd of pearls as large as peas,
  All gold and crimson shone her jelick's fellow,   30

599

And the striped white gauze baracan that bound her,
Like fleecy clouds about the moon, flow'd round her.

71

One large gold bracelet clasp'd each lovely arm,
    Lockless—so pliable from the pure gold
That the hand stretch'd and shut it without harm,
    The limb which it adorn'd its only mould;
So beautiful—its very shape would charm,
    And clinging as if loth to lose its hold,
The purest ore enclosed the whitest skin
That e'er by precious metal was held in.   40

72

Around, as princess of her father's land,
    A like gold bar above her instep roll'd
Announced her rank; twelve rings were on her hand;
    Her hair was starr'd with gems; her veil's fine fold
Below her breast was fasten'd with a band
    Of lavish pearls, whose worth could scarce be told;
Her orange silk full Turkish trousers furl'd
About the prettiest ankle in the world.

73

Her hair's long auburn waves down to her heel
    Flow'd like an Alpine torrent which the sun   50
Dyes with his morning light,—and would conceal
    Her person if allow'd at large to run,
And still they seem resentfully to feel
    The silken fillet's curb, and sought to shun
Their bonds whene'er some Zephyr caught began
To offer his young pinion as her fan.

74

Round her she made an atmosphere of life,
    The very air seem'd lighter from her eyes,
They were so soft and beautiful, and rife
    With all we can imagine of the skies,   60
And pure as Psyche ere she grew a wife—
    Too pure even for the purest human ties;
Her overpowering presence made you feel
It would not be idolatry to kneel.

75

Her eyelashes, though dark as night, were tinged
    (It is the country's custom), but in vain;
For those large black eyes were so blackly fringed,
    The glossy rebels mock'd the jetty stain,
And in their native beauty stood avenged:
    Her nails were touch'd with henna; but again   70
The power of art was turn'd to nothing, for
They could not look more rosy than before.

76

The henna should be deeply dyed to make
    The skin relieved appear more fairly fair;
She had no need of this, day ne'er will break
    On mountain tops more heavenly white than her:
The eye might doubt if it were well awake,
    She was so like a vision; I might err,
But Shakespeare also says 'tis very silly,
'To gild refined gold, or paint the lily'.   80

77

Juan had on a shawl of black and gold,
    But a white baracan, and so transparent
The sparkling gems beneath you might behold,
    Like small stars through the milky way apparent;
His turban, furl'd in many a graceful fold,
    An emerald aigrette with Haidée's hair in't
Surmounted as its clasp—a glowing crescent,
Whose rays shone ever trembling, but incessant.

78

And now they were diverted by their suite,
    Dwarfs, dancing girls, black eunuchs, and a poet,   90
Which made their new establishment complete;
    The last was of great fame, and liked to show it:
His verses rarely wanted their due feet—
    And for his theme—he seldom sung below it,
He being paid to satirize or flatter,
As the psalm says, 'inditing a good matter.'

79

He praised the present, and abused the past,
    Reversing the good custom of old days,

An eastern antijacobin at last
   He turn'd, preferring pudding to *no* praise—   100
For some few years his lot had been o'ercast
   By his seeming independent in his lays,
But now he sung the Sultan and the Pacha
With truth like Southey and with verse like Crashaw.

80

He was a man who had seen many changes,
   And always changed as true as any needle;
His polar star being one which rather ranges,
   And not the fix'd—he knew the way to wheedle:
So vile, he 'scaped the doom which oft avenges;
   And being fluent (save indeed when fee'd ill),   110
He lied with such a fervour of intention—
There was no doubt he earn'd his laureate pension.

81

But he had genius,—when a turncoat has it
   The 'Vates irritabilis' takes care
That without notice few full moons shall pass it;
   Even good men like to make the public stare:—
But to my subject—let me see—what was it?—
   Oh!—the third canto—and the pretty pair—
Their loves, and feasts, and house, and dress, and mode
Of living in their insular abode.   120

82

Their poet, a sad trimmer, but no less
   In company a very pleasant fellow,
Had been the favourite of full many a mess
   Of men, and made them speeches when half mellow;
And though his meaning they could rarely guess,
   Yet still they deign'd to hiccup or to bellow
The glorious meed of popular applause,
Of which the first ne'er knows the second cause.

83

But now being lifted into high society,
   And having pick'd up several odds and ends   130
Of free thoughts in his travels, for variety,
   He deem'd, being in a lone isle, among friends,
That without any danger of a riot, he
   Might for long lying make himself amends;

And singing as he sung in his warm youth,
Agree to a short armistice with truth.

84

He had travell'd 'mongst the Arabs, Turks, and Franks,
    And knew the self-loves of the different nations;
And having lived with people of all ranks,
    Had something ready upon most occasions—   140
Which got him a few presents and some thanks.
    He varied with some skill his adulations;
To 'do at Rome as Romans do', a piece
Of conduct was which he observed in Greece.

85

Thus, usually, when he was ask'd to sing,
    He gave the different nations something national;
'Twas all the same to him—'God save the king,'
    Or '*Ça ira*', according to the fashion all;
His muse made increment of any thing,
    From the high lyric down to the low rational: 150
If Pindar sang horse-races, what should hinder
Himself from being as pliable as Pindar?

86

In France, for instance, he would write a chanson;
    In England, a six canto quarto tale;
In Spain, he'd make a ballad or romance on
    The last war—much the same in Portugal;
In Germany, the Pegasus he'd prance on
    Would be old Goethe's—(see what says de Staël)
In Italy, he'd ape the 'Trecentisti';
In Greece, he'd sing some sort of hymn like this t'ye: 160

1

The isles of Greece, the isles of Greece!
    Where burning Sappho loved and sung,
Where grew the arts of war and peace,—
    Where Delos rose, and Phoebus sprung!
Eternal summer gilds them yet,
But all, except their sun, is set.

2

The Scian and the Teian muse,
    The hero's harp, the lover's lute,

Have found the fame your shores refuse;
 Their place of birth alone is mute   170
To sounds which echo further west
Than your sires' 'Islands of the Blest'.

3

The mountains look on Marathon—
 And Marathon looks on the sea;
And musing there an hour alone,
 I dream'd that Greece might still be free;
For standing on the Persian's grave,
I could not deem myself a slave.

4

A king sate on the rocky brow
 Which looks o'er sea-born Salamis;   180
And ships, by thousands, lay below,
 And men in nations;—all were his!
He counted them at break of day—
And when the sun set where were they?

5

And where are they? and where art thou,
 My country? On thy voiceless shore
The heroic lay is tuneless now—
 The heroic bosom beats no more!
And must thy lyre, so long divine,
Degenerate into hands like mine?   190

6

'Tis something, in the dearth of fame,
 Though link'd among a fetter'd race,
To feel at least a patriot's shame,
 Even as I sing, suffuse my face;
For what is left the poet here?
For Greeks a blush—for Greece a tear.

7

Must *we* but weep o'er days more blest?
 Must *we* but blush?—Our fathers bled.
Earth! render back from out thy breast
 A remnant of our Spartan dead!   200
Of the three hundred grant but three,
To make a new Thermopylae!

8

What, silent still? and silent all?
    Ah! no;—the voices of the dead
Sound like a distant torrent's fall,
    And answer, 'Let one living head,
But one arise,—we come, we come!'
'Tis but the living who are dumb.

9

In vain—in vain: strike other chords:
    Fill high the cup with Samian wine!   210
Leave battles to the Turkish hordes,
    And shed the blood of Scio's vine!
Hark! rising to the ignoble call—
How answers each bold bacchanal!

10

You have the Pyrrhic dance as yet,
    Where is the Pyrrhic phalanx gone?
Of two such lessons, why forget
    The nobler and the manlier one?
You have the letters Cadmus gave—
Think ye he meant them for a slave?   220

11

Fill high the bowl with Samian wine!
    We will not think of themes like these!
It made Anacreon's song divine:
    He served—but served Polycrates—
A tyrant; but our masters then
Were still, at least, our countrymen.

12

The tyrant of the Chersonese
    Was freedom's best and bravest friend;
That tyrant was Miltiades!
    Oh! that the present hour would lend   230
Another despot of the kind!
Such chains as his were sure to bind.

13

Fill high the bowl with Samian wine!
    On Suli's rock, and Parga's shore,

Exists the remnant of a line
  Such as the Doric mothers bore;
And there, perhaps, some seed is sown,
The Heracleidan blood might own.

14

Trust not for freedom to the Franks—
  They have a king who buys and sells: 240
In native swords, and native ranks,
  The only hope of courage dwells;
But Turkish force, and Latin fraud,
Would break your shield, however broad.

15

Fill high the bowl with Samian wine!
  Our virgins dance beneath the shade—
I see their glorious black eyes shine;
  But gazing on each glowing maid,
My own the burning tear-drop laves,
To think such breasts must suckle slaves.   250

16

Place me on Sunium's marbled steep,
  Where nothing, save the waves and I,
May hear our mutual murmurs sweep;
  There, swan-like, let me sing and die:
A land of slaves shall ne'er be mine—
Dash down yon cup of Samian wine!

87

Thus sung, or would, or could, or should have sung,
  The modern Greek, in tolerable verse;
If not like Orpheus quite, when Greece was young,
  Yet in these times he might have done much worse: 260
His strain display'd some feeling—right or wrong;
  And feeling, in a poet, is the source
Of others' feeling; but they are such liars,
And take all colours—like the hands of dyers.

88

But words are things, and a small drop of ink,
  Falling like dew, upon a thought, produces
That which makes thousands, perhaps millions, think;
  'Tis strange, the shortest letter which man uses

Instead of speech, may form a lasting link
   Of ages; to what straits old Time reduces   270
Frail man, when paper—even a rag like this,
Survives himself, his tomb, and all that's his.

89

And when his bones are dust, his grave a blank,
   His station, generation, even his nation,
Become a thing, or nothing, save to rank
   In chronological commemoration,
Some dull MS oblivion long has sank,
   Or graven stone found in a barrack's station
In digging the foundation of a closet,
May turn his name up, as a rare deposit.   280

90

And glory long has made the sages smile;
   'Tis something, nothing, words, illusion, wind—
Depending more upon the historian's style
   Than on the name a person leaves behind:
Troy owes to Homer what whist owes to Hoyle;
   The present century was growing blind
To the great Marlborough's skill in giving knocks,
Until his late Life by Archdeacon Coxe.

91

Milton's the prince of poets—so we say;
   A little heavy, but no less divine: 290
An independent being in his day—
   Learn'd, pious, temperate in love and wine;
But his life falling into Johnson's way,
   We're told this great high priest of all the Nine
Was whipt at college—a harsh sire—odd spouse,
For the first Mrs Milton left his house.

92

All these are, *certes*, entertaining facts,
   Like Shakespeare's stealing deer, Lord Bacon's bribes;
Like Titus' youth, and Caesar's earliest acts;
   Like Burns (whom Doctor Currie well describes);   300
Like Cromwell's pranks;—but although truth exacts
   These amiable descriptions from the scribes,
As most essential to their hero's story,
They do not much contribute to his glory.

93

All are not moralists, like Southey, when
   He prated to the world of 'Pantisocrasy';
Or Wordsworth unexcised, unhired, who then
   Season'd his pedlar poems with democracy;
Or Coleridge, long before his flighty pen
   Lent to the Morning Post its aristocracy;   310
When he and Southey, following the same path,
Espoused two partners (milliners of Bath.)

94

Such names at present cut a convict figure,
   The very Botany Bay in moral geography;
Their loyal treason, renegado rigour,
   Are good manure for their more bare biography.
Wordsworth's last quarto, by the way, is bigger
   Than any since the birthday of typography;
A drowsy frowzy poem, call'd the 'Excursion',
Writ in a manner which is my aversion.   320

95

He there builds up a formidable dyke
   Between his own and others' intellect;
But Wordsworth's poem, and his followers, like
   Joanna Southcote's Shiloh, and her sect,
Are things which in this century don't strike
   The public mind, so few are the elect;
And the new births of both their stale virginities
Have proved but dropsies, taken for divinities.

96

But let me to my story: I must own,
   If I have any fault, it is digression;   330
Leaving my people to proceed alone,
   While I soliloquize beyond expression;
But these are my addresses from the throne,
   Which put off business to the ensuing session:
Forgetting each omission is a loss to
The world, not quite so great as Ariosto.

from *Don Juan*, Canto IV

[*The Death of Haidée*]

54

I leave Don Juan for the present, safe—
 Not sound, poor fellow, but severely wounded;
Yet could his corporal pangs amount to half
 Of those with which his Haidée's bosom bounded!
She was not one to weep, and rave, and chafe,
 And then give way, subdued because surrounded;
Her mother was a Moorish maid, from Fez,
Where all is Eden, or a wilderness.

55

There the large olive rains its amber store
 In marble fonts; there grain, and flower, and fruit,   10
Gush from the earth until the land runs o'er;
 But there too many a poison-tree has root,
And midnight listens to the lion's roar,
 And long, long deserts scorch the camel's foot,
Or heaving whelm the helpless caravan,
And as the soil is, so the heart of man.

56

Afric is all the sun's, and as her earth
 Her human clay is kindled; full of power
For good or evil, burning from its birth,
 The Moorish blood partakes the planet's hour,   20
And like the soil beneath it will bring forth:
 Beauty and love were Haidée's mother's dower;
But her large dark eye show'd deep Passion's force,
Though sleeping like a lion near a source.

57

Her daughter, temper'd with a milder ray,
 Like summer clouds all silvery, smooth, and fair,
Till slowly charged with thunder they display
 Terror to earth, and tempest to the air,
Had held till now her soft and milky way;
 But overwrought with passion and despair,   30
The fire burst forth from her Numidian veins,
Even as the Simoom sweeps the blasted plains.

58

The last sight which she saw was Juan's gore,
 And he himself o'ermaster'd and cut down;
His blood was running on the very floor
 Where late he trod, her beautiful, her own;
Thus much she view'd an instant and no more,—
 Her struggles ceased with one convulsive groan;
On her sire's arm, which until now scarce held
Her writhing, fell she like a cedar fell'd.   40

59

A vein had burst, and her sweet lips' pure dyes
 Were dabbled with the deep blood which ran o'er;
And her head droop'd as when the lily lies
 O'ercharged with rain: her summon'd handmaids bore
Their lady to her couch with gushing eyes;
 Of herbs and cordials they produced their store,
But she defied all means they could employ,
Like one life could not hold, nor death destroy.

60

Days lay she in that state unchanged, though chill
 With nothing livid, still her lips were red;   50
She had no pulse, but death seem'd absent still;
 No hideous sign proclaim'd her surely dead;
Corruption came not in each mind to kill
 All hope; to look upon her sweet face bred
New thoughts of life, for it seem'd full of soul,
She had so much, earth could not claim the whole.

61

The ruling passion, such as marble shows
 When exquisitely chisell'd, still lay there,
But fix'd as marble's unchanged aspect throws
 O'er the fair Venus, but for ever fair;   60
O'er the Laocoon's all eternal throes,
 And ever-dying Gladiator's air,
Their energy like life forms all their fame,
Yet looks not life, for they are still the same.

62

She woke at length, but not as sleepers wake,
 Rather the dead, for life seem'd something new,

A strange sensation which she must partake
  Perforce, since whatsoever met her view
Struck not on memory, though a heavy ache
  Lay at her heart, whose earliest beat still true   70
Brought back the sense of pain without the cause,
For, for a while, the furies made a pause.

63

She look'd on many a face with vacant eye,
  On many a token without knowing what;
She saw them watch her without asking why,
  And reck'd not who around her pillow sat;
Not speechless though she spoke not; not a sigh
  Relieved her thoughts; dull silence and quick chat
Were tried in vain by those who served; she gave
No sign, save breath, of having left the grave.   80

64

Her handmaids tended, but she heeded not;
  Her father watch'd, she turn'd her eyes away;
She recognized no being, and no spot
  However dear or cherish'd in their day;
They changed from room to room, but all forgot,
  Gentle, but without memory she lay;
At length those eyes, which they would fain be weaning
Back to old thoughts, wax'd full of fearful meaning.

65

And then a slave bethought her of a harp;
  The harper came, and tuned his instrument;   90
At the first notes, irregular and sharp,
  On him her flashing eyes a moment bent,
Then to the wall she turn'd as if to warp
  Her thoughts from sorrow through her heart re-sent,
And he begun a long low island song
Of ancient days, ere tyranny grew strong.

66

Anon her thin wan fingers beat the wall
  In time to his old tune; he changed the theme,
And sung of love; the fierce name struck through all
  Her recollection; on her flash'd the dream   100
Of what she was, and is, if ye could call
  To be so being; in a gushing stream

611

The tears rush'd forth from her o'erclouded brain,
Like mountain mists at length dissolved in rain.

67

Short solace, vain relief!—thought came too quick,
    And whirl'd her brain to madness; she arose
As one who ne'er had dwelt among the sick,
    And flew at all she met, as on her foes;
But no one ever heard her speak or shriek,
    Although her paroxysm drew towards its close: 110
Hers was a phrensy which disdain'd to rave,
Even when they smote her, in the hope to save.

68

Yet she betray'd at times a gleam of sense;
    Nothing could make her meet her father's face,
Though on all other things with looks intense
    She gazed, but none she ever could retrace;
Food she refused, and raiment; no pretence
    Avail'd for either; neither change of place,
Nor time, nor skill, nor remedy, could give her
Senses to sleep—the power seem'd gone for ever.   120

69

Twelve days and nights she wither'd thus; at last,
    Without a groan, or sigh, or glance, to show
A parting pang, the spirit from her past:
    And they who watch'd her nearest could not know
The very instant, till the change that cast
    Her sweet face into shadow, dull and slow,
Glazed o'er her eyes—the beautiful, the black—
Oh! to possess such lustre—and then lack!

70

She died, but not alone; she held within
    A second principle of life, which might   130
Have dawn'd a fair and sinless child of sin;
    But closed its little being without light,
And went down to the grave unborn, wherein
    Blossom and bough lie wither'd with one blight;
In vain the dews of Heaven descend above
The bleeding flower and blasted fruit of love.

71

Thus lived—thus died she; never more on her
    Shall sorrow light, or shame. She was not made
Through years or moons the inner weight to bear,
    Which colder hearts endure till they are laid   140
By age in earth; her days and pleasures were
    Brief, but delightful—such as had not staid
Long with her destiny; but she sleeps well
By the sea shore, whereon she loved to dwell.

72

That isle is now all desolate and bare,
    Its dwellings down, its tenants past away;
None but her own and father's grave is there,
    And nothing outward tells of human clay;
Ye could not know where lies a thing so fair,
    No stone is there to show, no tongue to say   150
What was; no dirge, except the hollow sea's,
Mourns o'er the beauty of the Cyclades.

73

But many a Greek maid in a loving song
    Sighs o'er her name; and many an islander
With her sire's story makes the night less long;
    Valour was his, and beauty dwelt with her;
If she loved rashly, her life paid for wrong—
    A heavy price must all pay who thus err,
In some shape, let none think to fly the danger;
For soon or late Love is his own avenger.   160

74

But let me change this theme, which grows too sad,
    And lay this sheet of sorrows on the shelf;
I don't much like describing people mad,
    For fear of seeming rather touch'd myself—
Besides I've no more on this head to add;
    And as my Muse is a capricious elf,
We'll put about, and try another tack
With Juan, left half-kill'd some stanzas back.

JOHN MOULTRIE
1799–1874

202   *The Fairy Maimounè*

SHE came on Earth soon after the creation,
   And was akin to Oberon, 'tis said:
In Faeryland received her education,
   But never yet had been induced to wed,
Though she was woo'd by half the Elfin nation—
   But still a free and roving life she led;
And sought diversion for her gentle mind
Chiefly among the haunts of humankind.

There was a deep and solitary well in
   The palace where the Prince was now confined,   10
Which served this lovely Fairy for a dwelling,
   A spot just suited to a Fairy's mind;
Much like the fountain where Narcissus fell in
   Love with her own fair face, and pined, and pined
To death (the passion 's not at all uncommon
In Man, and very prevalent in woman).

Beneath this fountain's fresh and bubbling water,
   Unfathomably deep, the livelong day,
This wondrous Fairy, Time's most radiant daughter,
   In unimaginable visions lay;   20
Where never earthly care or sorrow sought her,
   But o'er her head did the wild waters play,
And flitting spirits of the Earth and Air
Scattered sweet dreams and lulling music there.

For she was well beloved by all th' immortal
   Beings that roam through Ocean, Earth, or Sky;
And oft would blessed spirits pass the portal
   Of the vast Eden of Eternity
To be her slaves, and to her did resort all
   Angelic thoughts, each heavenly phantasy,   30
That mortals may not know—all came to bless
This gentle Being's dreams of happiness.

And all around that fountain, the pure air
   Breathed of her presence; every leaf was hung

614

With music, and each flower that blossom'd there
   A fine and supernatural fragrance flung
On the glad sense; and thither did repair
   Garlanded maids, and lovers fond and young;
And by the side of the low-murmuring stream
Would youthful poets lay them down to dream.   40

And ever on that spot the rays of Morning
   Fell thickest, and the Sun's meridian light
Sparkled and danced amid the waves, adorning
   The crystal chamber of the sleeping Sprite.
But when proud Dian walk'd, with maiden scorn, in
   The Eastern skies, and the sweet dews of Night
Lay heavy on the Earth, that Sprite arose
Fresh from the visions of the day's repose.

And then, she gaily wander'd through the world,
   Where'er her fancy led her, and would stray   50
(The sails of her bright meteor-wings unfurl'd)
   Through many a populous city, and survey
The chambers of the sleeping; oft she curl'd
   The locks of young chaste maidens, as they lay,
And lit new lustre in their sleeping eyes,
And breathed upon their cheeks the bloom of Paradise.

And she would scatter o'er the Poet's brain
   (As he lay smiling through swift-springing tears)
A strange and unintelligible train
   Of fancies, and ring loud into his ears   60
A long, mysterious, and perplexing strain
   Of music, or combine the joy of years
In half an hour of slumber; till he started
From such sweet visions, weeping and wild-hearted.

And, in her mirthful moments, would she seek
   The bachelor's room, and spoil his lonely rest;
Or with old maids play many a wicked freak;
   Or rattle loudly at the miser's chest,
Till he woke trembling; she would often wreak
   Her vengeance on stern fathers who repress'd   70
Their children's young and innocent loves, and sold
(Like our two Kings) their happiness for gold.

PERCY BYSSHE SHELLEY

203   *Adonais*

An Elegy on the Death of John Keats

Αστήρ πρὶν μὲν ἐλαμπες ενι ζῶοισιν εῶος.
Νυν δε θανῶν, λαμπεις ἔοπερος εν φθίμενοις.

PLATO

I

I WEEP for Adonais—he is dead!
O, weep for Adonais! though our tears
Thaw not the frost which binds so dear a head!
And thou, sad Hour, selected from all years
To mourn our loss, rouse thy obscure compeers,
And teach them thine own sorrow, say: with me
Died Adonais; till the Future dares
Forget the Past, his fate and fame shall be
An echo and a light unto eternity!

II

Where wert thou mighty Mother, when he lay,   10
When thy Son lay, pierced by the shaft which flies
In darkness? where was lorn Urania
When Adonais died? With veiled eyes,
'Mid listening Echoes, in her Paradise
She sate, while one, with soft enamoured breath,
Rekindled all the fading melodies,
With which, like flowers that mock the corse beneath,
He had adorned and hid the coming bulk of death.

III

O, weep for Adonais—he is dead!
Wake, melancholy Mother, wake and weep!   20
Yet wherefore? Quench within their burning bed
Thy fiery tears, and let thy loud heart keep
Like his, a mute and uncomplaining sleep;
For he is gone, where all things wise and fair
Descend;—oh, dream not that the amorous Deep
Will yet restore him to the vital air;
Death feeds on his mute voice, and laughs at our despair.

IV

Most musical of mourners, weep again!
Lament anew, Urania!—He died,
Who was the Sire of an immortal strain,   30
Blind, old, and lonely, when his country's pride,
The priest, the slave, and the liberticide,
Trampled and mocked with many a loathed rite
Of lust and blood; he went, unterrified,
Into the gulf of death; but his clear Sprite
Yet reigns o'er earth; the third among the sons of light.

V

Most musical of mourners, weep anew!
Not all to that bright station dared to climb;
And happier they their happiness who knew,
Whose tapers yet burn through that night of time   40
In which suns perished; others more sublime,
Struck by the envious wrath of man or God,
Have sunk, extinct in their refulgent prime;
And some yet live, treading the thorny road,
Which leads, through toil and hate, to Fame's serene abode.

VI

But now, thy youngest, dearest one, has perished
The nursling of thy widowhood, who grew,
Like a pale flower by some sad maiden cherished,
And fed with true love tears, instead of dew;
Most musical of mourners, weep anew!   50
Thy extreme hope, the loveliest and the last,
The bloom, whose petals nipt before they blew
Died on the promise of the fruit, is waste;
The broken lily lies—the storm is overpast.

VII

To that high Capital, where kingly Death
Keeps his pale court in beauty and decay,
He came; and bought, with price of purest breath,
A grave among the eternal.—Come away!
Haste, while the vault of blue Italian day
Is yet his fitting charnel-roof! while still   60
He lies, as if in dewy sleep he lay;
Awake him not! surely he takes his fill
Of deep and liquid rest, forgetful of all ill.

VIII

He will awake no more, oh, never more!—
Within the twilight chamber spreads apace,
The shadow of white Death, and at the door
Invisible Corruption waits to trace
His extreme way to her dim dwelling-place;
The eternal Hunger sits, but pity and awe
Soothe her pale rage, nor dares she to deface   70
So fair a prey, till darkness, and the law
Of mortal change, shall fill the grave which is her maw.

IX

O, weep for Adonais!—The quick Dreams,
The passion-winged Ministers of thought,
Who were his flocks, whom near the living streams
Of his young spirit he fed, and whom he taught
The love which was its music, wander not,—
Wander no more, from kindling brain to brain,
But droop there, whence they sprung; and mourn their lot
Round the cold heart, where, after their sweet pain,   80
They ne'er will gather strength, or find a home again.

X

And one with trembling hands clasps his cold head,
And fans him with her moonlight wings, and cries;
'Our love, our hope, our sorrow, is not dead;
See, on the silken fringe of his faint eyes,
Like dew upon a sleeping flower, there lies
A tear some Dream has loosened from his brain.'
Lost Angel of a ruined Paradise!
She knew not 'twas her own; as with no stain
She faded, like a cloud which had outwept its rain.   90

XI

One from a lucid urn of starry dew
Washed his light limbs as if embalming them;
Another clipt her profuse locks, and threw
The wreath upon him, like an anadem,
Which frozen tears instead of pearls begem;
Another in her wilful grief would break
Her bow and winged reeds, as if to stem
A greater loss with one which was more weak;
And dull the barbed fire against his frozen cheek.

XII

Another Splendour on his mouth alit,   100
That mouth, whence it was wont to draw the breath
Which gave it strength to pierce the guarded wit,
And pass into the panting heart beneath
With lightning and with music: the damp death
Quenched its caress upon his icy lips;
And, as a dying meteor stains a wreath
Of moonlight vapour, which the cold night clips,
It flushed through his pale limbs, and past to its eclipse.

XIII

And others came . . . Desires and Adorations,
Winged Persuasions and veiled Destinies,   110
Splendours, and Glooms, and glimmering Incarnations
Of hopes and fears, and twilight Phantasies;
And Sorrow, with her family of Sighs,
And Pleasure, blind with tears, led by the gleam
Of her own dying smile instead of eyes,
Came in slow pomp;—the moving pomp might seem
Like pageantry of mist on an autumnal stream.

XIV

All he had loved, and moulded into thought,
From shape, and hue, and odour, and sweet sound,
Lamented Adonais. Morning sought   120
Her eastern watchtower, and her hair unbound,
Wet with the tears which should adorn the ground,
Dimmed the aerial eyes that kindle day;
Afar the melancholy thunder moaned,
Pale Ocean in unquiet slumber lay,
And the wild winds flew round, sobbing in their dismay.

XV

Lost Echo sits amid the voiceless mountains,
And feeds her grief with his remembered lay,
And will no more reply to winds or fountains,
Or amorous birds perched on the young green spray,   130
Or herdsman's horn, or bell at closing day;
Since she can mimic not his lips, more dear
Than those for whose disdain she pined away
Into a shadow of all sounds:—a drear
Murmur, between their songs, is all the woodmen hear.

XVI

Grief made the young Spring wild, and she threw down
Her kindling buds, as if she Autumn were,
Or they dead leaves; since her delight is flown
For whom should she have waked the sullen year?
To Phœbus was not Hyacinth so dear   140
Nor to himself Narcissus, as to both
Thou Adonais: wan they stand and sere
Amid the drooping comrades of their youth,
With dew all turned to tears; odour, to sighing ruth.

XVII

Thy spirit's sister, the lorn nightingale
Mourns not her mate with such melodious pain;
Not so the eagle, who like thee could scale
Heaven, and could nourish in the sun's domain
Her mighty youth with morning, doth complain,
Soaring and screaming round her empty nest,   150
As Albion wails for thee: the curse of Cain
Light on his head who pierced thy innocent breast,
And scared the angel soul that was its earthly guest!

XVIII

Ah woe is me! Winter is come and gone,
But grief returns with the revolving year;
The airs and streams renew their joyous tone;
The ants, the bees, the swallows reappear;
Fresh leaves and flowers deck the dead Seasons' bier;
The amorous birds now pair in every brake,
And build their mossy homes in field and brere;   160
And the green lizard, and the golden snake,
Like unimprisoned flames, out of their trance awake.

XIX

Through wood and stream and field and hill and Ocean
A quickening life from the Earth's heart has burst
As it has ever done, with change and motion,
From the great morning of the world when first
God dawned on Chaos; in its steam immersed
The lamps of Heaven flash with a softer light;
All baser things pant with life's sacred thirst;
Diffuse themselves; and spend in love's delight,   170
The beauty and the joy of their renewed might.

XX

The leprous corpse touched by this spirit tender
Exhales itself in flowers of gentle breath;
Like incarnations of the stars, when splendour
Is changed to fragrance, they illumine death
And mock the merry worm that wakes beneath;
Nought we know, dies. Shall that alone which knows
Be as a sword consumed before the sheath
By sightless lightning?—th' intense atom glows
A moment, then is quenched in a most cold repose.   180

XXI

Alas! that all we loved of him should be,
But for our grief, as if it had not been,
And grief itself be mortal! Woe is me!
Whence are we, and why are we? of what scene
The actors or spectators? Great and mean
Meet massed in death, who lends what life must borrow.
As long as skies are blue, and fields are green,
Evening must usher night, night urge the morrow,
Month follow month with woe, and year wake year to sorrow.

XXII

He will awake no more, oh, never more!   190
'Wake thou,' cried Misery, 'childless Mother, rise
Out of thy sleep, and slake, in thy heart's core,
A wound more fierce than his with tears and sighs.'
And all the Dreams that watched Urania's eyes,
And all the Echoes whom their sister's song
Had held in holy silence, cried: 'Arise!'
Swift as a Thought by the snake Memory stung,
From her ambrosial rest the fading Splendour sprung.

XXIII

She rose like an autumnal Night, that springs
Out of the East, and follows wild and drear   200
The golden Day, which, on eternal wings,
Even as a ghost abandoning a bier,
Had left the Earth a corpse. Sorrow and fear
So struck, so roused, so rapt Urania;
So saddened round her like an atmosphere
Of stormy mist; so swept her on her way
Even to the mournful place where Adonais lay.

XXIV

Out of her secret Paradise she sped,
Through camps and cities rough with stone, and steel,
And human hearts, which to her aery tread   210
Yielding not, wounded the invisible
Palms of her tender feet where'er they fell:
And barbed tongues, and thoughts more sharp than they
Rent the soft Form they never could repel,
Whose sacred blood, like the young tears of May,
Paved with eternal flowers that undeserving way.

XXV

In the death chamber for a moment Death
Shamed by the presence of that living Might
Blushed to annihilation, and the breath
Revisited those lips, and life's pale light   220
Flashed through those limbs, so late her dear delight.
'Leave me not wild and drear and comfortless,
As silent lightning leaves the starless night!
Leave me not!' cried Urania: her distress
Roused Death: Death rose and smiled, and met her vain caress.

XXVI

'Stay yet awhile! speak to me once again;
Kiss me, so long but as a kiss may live;
And in my heartless breast and burning brain
That word, that kiss shall all thoughts else survive,
With food of saddest memory kept alive,   230
Now thou art dead, as if it were a part
Of thee, my Adonais! I would give
All that I am to be as thou now art!
But I am chained to Time, and cannot thence depart!

XXVII

'Oh gentle child, beautiful as thou wert,
Why didst thou leave the trodden paths of men
Too soon, and with weak hands though mighty heart
Dare the unpastured dragon in his den?
Defenceless as thou wert, oh where was then
Wisdom the mirrored shield, or scorn the spear?   240
Or hadst thou waited the full cycle, when
Thy spirit should have filled its crescent sphere,
The monsters of life's waste had fled from thee like deer.

XXVIII

'The herded wolves, bold only to pursue;
The obscene ravens, clamorous oer the dead;
The vultures to the conqueror's banner true
Who feed where Desolation first has fed,
And whose wings rain contagion;—how they fled,
When like Apollo, from his golden bow,
The Pythian of the age one arrow sped   250
And smiled!—The spoilers tempt no second blow,
They fawn on the proud feet that spurn them as they go.

XXIX

'The sun comes forth, and many reptiles spawn;
He sets, and each ephemeral insect then
Is gathered into death without a dawn,
And the immortal stars awake again;
So is it in the world of living men:
A godlike mind soars forth, in its delight
Making earth bare and veiling heaven, and when
It sinks, the swarms that dimmed or shared its light   260
Leave to its kindred lamps the spirit's awful night.'

XXX

Thus ceased she: and the mountain shepherds came
Their garlands sere, their magic mantles rent;
The Pilgrim of Eternity, whose fame
Over his living head like Heaven is bent,
An early but enduring monument,
Came, veiling all the lightnings of his song
In sorrow; from her wilds Ierne sent
The sweetest lyrist of her saddest wrong,
And love taught grief to fall like music from his tongue.   270

XXXI

Midst others of less note, came one frail Form,
A phantom among men; companionless
As the last cloud of an expiring storm
Whose thunder is its knell; he, as I guess,
Had gazed on Nature's naked loveliness,
Actæon-like, and now he fled astray
With feeble steps o'er the world's wilderness,
And his own thoughts, along that rugged way,
Pursued, like raging hounds, their father and their prey.

XXXII

A pardlike Spirit beautiful and swift—   280
A Love in desolation masked;—a Power
Girt round with weakness;—it can scarce uplift
The weight of the superincumbent hour;
It is a dying lamp, a falling shower,
A breaking billow;—even whilst we speak
Is it not broken? On the withering flower
The killing sun smiles brightly: on a cheek
The life can burn in blood, even while the heart may break.

XXXIII

His head was bound with pansies overblown,
And faded violets, white, and pied, and blue;   290
And a light spear topped with a cypress cone,
Round whose rude shaft dark ivy tresses grew
Yet dripping with the forest's noonday dew,
Vibrated, as the ever-beating heart
Shook the weak hand that grasped it; of that crew
He came the last, neglected and apart;
A herd-abandoned deer struck by the hunter's dart.

XXXIV

All stood aloof, and at his partial moan
Smiled through their tears; well knew that gentle band
Who in another's fate now wept his own;   300
As in the accents of an unknown land,
He sung new sorrow; sad Urania scanned
The Stranger's mien, and murmured: 'who art thou?'
He answered not, but with a sudden hand
Made bare his branded and ensanguined brow,
Which was like Cain's or Christ's—Oh! that it should be so!

XXXV

What softer voice is hushed over the dead?
Athwart what brow is that dark mantle thrown?
What form leans sadly o'er the white death-bed,
In mockery of monumental stone,   310
The heavy heart heaving without a moan?
If it be He, who, gentlest of the wise,
Taught, soothed, loved, honoured the departed one;
Let me not vex, with inharmonious sighs
The silence of that heart's accepted sacrifice.

XXXVI

Our Adonais has drunk poison—oh!
What deaf and, viperous murderer could crown
Life's early cup with such a draught of woe?
The nameless worm would now itself disown:
It felt, yet could escape the magic tone   320
Whose prelude held all envy, hate, and wrong,
But what was howling in one breast alone,
Silent with expectation of the song,
Whose master's hand is cold, whose silver lyre unstrung.

XXXVII

Live thou, whose infamy is not thy fame!
Live! fear no heavier chastisement from me,
Thou noteless blot on a remembered name!
But be thyself, and know thyself to be!
And ever at thy season be thou free
To spill the venom when thy fangs o'er flow: 330
Remorse and Self-contempt shall cling to thee;
Hot Shame shall burn upon thy secret brow,
And like a beaten hound tremble thou shalt—as now.

XXXVIII

Nor let us weep that our delight is fled
Far from these carrion kites that scream below;
He wakes or sleeps with the enduring dead;
Thou canst not soar where he is sitting now.—
Dust to the dust! but the pure spirit shall flow
Back to the burning fountain whence it came,
A portion of the Eternal, which must glow   340
Through time and change, unquenchably the same,
Whilst thy cold embers choke the sordid hearth of shame.

XXXIX

Peace, peace! he is not dead, he doth not sleep—
He hath awakened from the dream of life—
'Tis we, who lost in stormy visions, keep
With phantoms an unprofitable strife,
And in mad trance, strike with our spirit's knife
Invulnerable nothings.—*We* decay
Like corpses in a charnel; fear and grief
Convulse us and consume us day by day,   350
And cold hopes swarm like worms within our living clay.

XL

He has outsoared the shadow of our night;
Envy and calumny and hate and pain,
And that unrest which men miscall delight,
Can touch him not and torture not again;
From the contagion of the world's slow stain
He is secure, and now can never mourn
A heart grown cold, a head grown grey in vain;
Nor, when the spirit's self has ceased to burn,
With sparkless ashes load an unlamented urn.   360

XLI

He lives, he wakes—'tis Death is dead, not he;
Mourn not for Adonais.—Thou young Dawn
Turn all thy dew to splendour, for from thee
The spirit thou lamentest is not gone;
Ye caverns and ye forests, cease to moan!
Cease ye faint flowers and fountains, and thou Air
Which like a mourning veil thy scarf hadst thrown
O'er the abandoned Earth, now leave it bare
Even to the joyous stars which smile on its despair!

XLII

He is made one with Nature: there is heard   370
His voice in all her music, from the moan
Of thunder, to the song of night's sweet bird;
He is a presence to be felt and known
In darkness and in light, from herb and stone,
Spreading itself where'er that Power may move
Which has withdrawn his being to its own;
Which wields the world with never wearied love,
Sustains it from beneath, and kindles it above.

XLIII

He is a portion of the loveliness
Which once he made more lovely: he doth bear   380
His part, while the one Spirit's plastic stress
Sweeps through the dull dense world, compelling there,
All new successions to the forms they wear;
Torturing th'unwilling dross that checks its flight
To its own likeness, as each mass may bear;
And bursting in its beauty and its might
From trees and beasts and men into the Heaven's light.

626

XLIV

The splendours of the firmament of time
May be eclipsed, but are extinguished not;
Like stars to their appointed height they climb   390
And death is a low mist which cannot blot
The brightness it may veil. When lofty thought
Lifts a young heart above its mortal lair,
And love and life contend in it, for what
Shall be its earthly doom, the dead live there
And move like winds of light on dark and stormy air.

XLV

The inheritors of unfulfilled renown
Rose from their thrones, built beyond mortal thought,
Far in the Unapparent. Chatterton
Rose pale, his solemn agony had not   400
Yet faded from him; Sidney, as he fought
And as he fell and as he lived and loved
Sublimely mild, a Spirit without spot,
Arose; and Lucan, by his death approved:
Oblivion as they rose shrank like a thing reproved.

XLVI

And many more, whose names on Earth are dark
But whose transmitted effluence cannot die
So long as fire outlives the parent spark,
Rose, robed in dazzling immortality.
'Thou art become as one of us', they cry,   410
'It was for thee yon kingless sphere has long
Swung blind in unascended majesty,
Silent alone amid an Heaven of song.
Assume thy winged throne, thou Vesper of our throng!'

XLVII

Who mourns for Adonais? oh come forth
Fond wretch! and know thyself and him aright.
Clasp with thy panting soul the pendulous Earth;
As from a centre, dart thy spirit's light
Beyond all worlds, until its spacious might
Satiate the void circumference: then shrink   420
Even to a point within our day and night;
And keep thy heart light lest it make thee sink
When hope has kindled hope, and lured thee to the brink.

XLVIII

Or go to Rome, which is the sepulchre
O, not of him, but of our joy: 'tis nought
That ages, empires, and religions there
Lie buried in the ravage they have wrought;
For such as he can lend,—they borrow not
Glory from those who made the world their prey;
And he is gathered to the kings of thought   430
Who waged contention with their time's decay,
And of the past are all that cannot pass away.

XLIX

Go thou to Rome,—at once the Paradise,
The grave, the city, and the wilderness;
And where its wrecks like shattered mountains rise,
And flowering weeds, and fragrant copses dress
The bones of Desolation's nakedness
Pass, till the Spirit of the spot shall lead
Thy footsteps to a slope of green access
Where, like an infant's smile, over the dead,   440
A light of laughing flowers along the grass is spread.

L

And gray walls moulder round, on which dull Time
Feeds, like slow fire upon a hoary brand;
And one keen pyramid with wedge sublime,
Pavilioning the dust of him who planned
This refuge for his memory, doth stand
Like flame transformed to marble; and beneath,
A field is spread, on which a newer band
Have pitched in Heaven's smile their camp of death
Welcoming him we lose with scarce extinguished breath.   450

LI

Here pause: these graves are all too young as yet
To have out grown the sorrow which consigned
Its charge to each; and if the seal is set,
Here, on one fountain of a mourning mind,
Break it not thou! too surely shalt thou find
Thine own well full, if thou returnest home,
Of tears and gall. From the world's bitter wind
Seek shelter in the shadow of the tomb.
What Adonais is, why fear we to become?

LII

The One remains, the many change and pass;   460
Heaven's light forever shines, Earth's shadows fly;
Life, like a dome of many-coloured glass,
Stains the white radiance of Eternity,
Until Death tramples it to fragments.—Die,
If thou wouldst be with that which thou dost seek!
Follow where all is fled!—Rome's azure sky,
Flowers, ruins, statues, music, words, are weak
The glory they transfuse with fitting truth to speak.

LIII

Why linger, why turn back, why shrink, my Heart?
Thy hopes are gone before: from all things here   470
They have departed; thou shouldst now depart!
A light is past from the revolving year,
And man, and woman; and what still is dear
Attracts to crush, repels to make thee wither.
The soft sky smiles,—the low wind whispers near:
'Tis Adonais calls! oh, hasten thither,
No more let Life divide what Death can join together.

LIV

That Light whose smile kindles the Universe,
That Beauty in which all things work and move,
That Benediction which the eclipsing Curse   480
Of birth can quench not, that sustaining Love
Which through the web of being blindly wove
By man and beast and earth and air and sea,
Burns bright or dim, as each are mirrors of
The fire for which all thirst; now beams on me,
Consuming the last clouds of cold mortality.

LV

The breath whose might I have invoked in song
Descends on me; my spirit's bark is driven,
Far from the shore, far from the trembling throng
Whose sails were never to the tempest given;   490
The massy earth and sphered skies are riven!
I am borne darkly, fearfully, afar;
Whilst burning through the inmost veil of Heaven,
The soul of Adonais, like a star,
Beacons from the abode where the Eternal are.

204   from *Cain, A Mystery*

[*Lucifer and Intellectual Freedom*]

LUCIFER. And now I will convey thee to thy world,
  Where thou shalt multiply the race of Adam,
  Eat, drink, toil, tremble, laugh, weep, sleep, and die.
CAIN. And to what end have I beheld these things
  Which thou hast shown me?
LUCIFER.   Didst thou not require
  Knowledge? And have I not, in what I show'd,
  Taught thee to know thyself?
CAIN.   Alas! I seem
  Nothing.
LUCIFER.   And this should be the human sum
  Of knowledge, to know mortal nature's nothingness;
  Bequeath that science to thy children, and   10
  'Twill spare them many tortures.
CAIN.   Haughty spirit!
  Thou speak'st it proudly; but thyself, though proud,
  Hast a superior.
LUCIFER.   No! By heaven, which He
  Holds, and the abyss, and the immensity
  Of worlds and life, which I hold with him—No!
  I have a victor—true; but no superior.
  Homage he has from all—but none from me:
  I battle it against him, as I battled
  In highest heaven. Through all eternity,
  And the unfathomable gulfs of Hades,   20
  And the interminable realms of space,
  And the infinity of endless ages,
  All, all, will I dispute! And world by world,
  And star by star, and universe by universe
  Shall tremble in the balance, till the great
  Conflict shall cease, if ever it shall cease,
  Which it ne'er shall, till he or I be quench'd!
  And what can quench our immortality,
  Or mutual and irrevocable hate?
  He as a conqueror will call the conquer'd   30
  Evil; but what will be the *good* he gives?
  Were I the victor, *his* works would be deem'd
  The only evil ones. And you, ye new
  And scarce-born mortals, what have been his gifts

To you already in your little world?
CAIN. But few; and some of those but bitter.
LUCIFER.   Back
  With me, then, to thine earth, and try the rest
  Of his celestial boons to ye and yours.
  Evil and good are things in their own essence,
  And not made good or evil by the giver;   40
  But if he gives you good—so call him; if
  Evil springs from *him*, do not name it *mine*,
  Till ye know better its true fount; and judge
  Not by words, though of spirits, but the fruits
  Of your existence, such as it must be.
  One good gift has the fatal apple given—
  Your *reason*:—let it not be over-sway'd
  By tyrannous threats to force you into faith
  'Gainst all external sense and inward feeling:
  Think and endure,—and form an inner world   50
  In your own bosom—where the outward fails;
  So shall you nearer be the spiritual
  Nature, and war triumphant with your own.

                                                           [*They disappear*

                          (II. ii. 414–66)

                     [*Eve's Curse on Cain*]

EVE.   Hear, Jehovah!
  May the eternal serpent's curse be on him!
  For he was fitter for his seed than ours.
  May all his days be desolate! May——
ADAM.   Hold!
  Curse him not, mother, for he is thy son—
  Curse him not, mother, for he is my brother,
  And my betroth'd.
EVE.   He hath left thee no brother—   60
  Zillah no husband—me *no son*!—for thus
  I curse him from my sight for evermore!
  All bonds I break between us, as he broke
  That of his nature, in yon——Oh death! death!
  Why didst thou not take *me*, who first incurr'd thee?
  Why dost thou not so now?
ADAM.   Eve! let not this,
  Thy natural grief, lead to impiety!
  A heavy doom was long forespoken to us;
  And now that it begins, let it be borne
  In such sort as may show our God, that we   70
  Are faithful servants to his holy will.

                              631

EVE [*pointing to Cain*]. *His will!!* the will of yon incarnate spirit
    Of death, whom I have brought upon the earth
    To strew it with the dead. May all the curses
    Of life be on him! and his agonies
    Drive him forth o'er the wilderness, like us
    From Eden, till his children do by him
    As he did by his brother! May the swords
    And wings of fiery cherubim pursue him
    By day and night—snakes spring up in his path—   80
    Earth's fruits be ashes in his mouth—the leaves
    On which he lays his head to sleep be strew'd
    With scorpions! May his dreams be of his victim!
    His waking a continual dread of death!
    May the clear rivers turn to blood as he
    Stoops down to stain them with his raging lip!
    May every element shun or change to him!
    May he live in the pangs which others die with!
    And death itself wax something worse than death
    To him who first acquainted him with man!   90
    Hence, fratricide! henceforth that word is *Cain*,
    Through all the coming myriads of mankind,
    Who shall abhor thee, though thou wert their sire!
    May the grass wither from thy feet! the woods
    Deny thee shelter! earth a home! the dust
    A grave! the sun his light! and heaven her God!   [*Exit* EVE

(III. i. 401–43)

THOMAS MOORE

205   *Echo*

HOW sweet the answer Echo makes
      To music at night,
When, roused by lute or horn, she wakes,
And far away, o'er lawns and lakes,
      Goes answering light!

Yet Love hath echoes truer far,
      And far more sweet,
Than e'er beneath the moonlight's star,
Of horn or lute, or soft guitar,
      The songs repeat.   10

'Tis when the sigh, in youth sincere,
 And only then,—
The sigh that's breath'd for one to hear,
Is by that one, that only dear,
 Breath'd back again!

[1822]

LAETITIA ELIZABETH LANDON
1802–1838

206   *Lines Written Under a Picture of a Girl
        Burning a Love-Letter*

*The lines were filled with many a tender thing,
All the impassioned heart's fond communing.*

I TOOK the scroll: I could not brook
  An eye to gaze on it, save mine;
I could not bear another's look
  Should dwell upon one thought of thine.
My lamp was burning by my side,
  I held thy letter to the flame,
I marked the blaze swift o'er it glide,
  It did not even spare thy name.
Soon the light from the embers past,
  I felt so sad to see it die,   10
So bright at first, so dark at last,
  I feared it was love's history.

GEORGE CROLY
1780–1860

207   *An Aestuary*

A Calm Evening

LOOK on these waters, with how soft a kiss
They woo the pebbled shore! then steal away,
Like wanton lovers,—but to come again,
And die in music!—There, the bending skies
See all their stars,—and the beach-loving trees,
Osiers and willows, and the wat'ry flowers,
That wreathe their pale roots round the ancient stones,
Make pictures of themselves!

GEORGE DARLEY

208   *The Rebellion of the Waters*

*The Sea, in tremendous commotion, calls on its tributary streams for succour,
whilst Triton blows his threatening conch in vain. Simois and Scamander
awake from their dream of ages, into pristine glory, and the floods subside
not even at the rebuke of Neptune.*

'ARISE!—the Sea-god's groaning shell
    Cries madly from his breathless caves,
And staring rocks its echoes tell
    Along the wild and shouting waves.
Arise! awake! ye other streams
    That wear the plains of ruined Troy,
Ida's dark sons, have burst their dreams,
    And shake the very hills for joy.'

Press'd by the King of Tides, from far
    With nostril split, and bloodshot eye,   10
The web-foot minions of his car
    Shriek at the wave, they lighten by.
The noise of total hell was there,
    As fled the rebel deeps along;
A reckless, joyous prank they dare,
    Though thunder fall from Neptune's tongue.

[1823]

WILLIAM PROBERT
1790–1870

209   from *The Triads of Britain*

1. THERE were three names given to the Isle of Britain from the first: before it was inhabited, it was called the Sea-girt Green Space; after it was inhabited, it was called the Honey Island; and after the people were formed into a common-wealth, by Prydain the son of Aedd the Great, it was denominated the Isle of Britain. And no one has any right to it but the tribe of the Cambrians, for they first took possession; and before that time were no persons living in it, but it was full of bears, wolves, crocodiles, and bisons.

9. There were three treacherous invasions of the Isle of Britain: the first were the red Irishmen from Ireland, who came to Alban; the second were the Scandinavians; and the third were the Saxons. These last came to this Island in peace and by the permission of the tribe of the Cambrians, and in the protection of God and his truth, as well as in the protection of the country and of the tribe; and by treachery and mischief they opposed the tribe of the Cambrians, and were able to wrest from them the sovereign power of the Isle of Britain, and they mutually confederated themselves in Lloegria and Alban, where they still reside. This happened in the age of Vortigern.

10. There were three disappearances by loss in the Isle of Britain. The first were Gavran and his men, who went in search of the Green Islands of the floods, and were never heard of after. The second were Merddin the bard of Emrys, and his nine attendant bards, who went to sea in a house of glass, and the place where they went is unknown. The third was Madog the son of Owain king of North Wales, who went to sea with three hundred persons in ten ships, but the place to which they went is unknown.

13. There were three awful events in the Isle of Britain. The first was the bursting of the Lake of Floods, and the rushing of an inundation over all the lands, until all persons were destroyed, except Dwyvan and Dwyvach who escaped in an open vessel; and from them the Isle of Britain was repeopled. The second was the trembling of the fiery torrent, until the earth was rent to the abyss, and the greatest part of all life was destroyed. The third was the Hot Summer, when the trees and plants

635

took fire by the burning heat of the sun, and many people and animals, various kinds of birds, vermin, trees and plants, were entirely lost.

52.   The three tremendous slaughters of the Isle of Britain. The first, when Medrawd went to Galliwig, he did not leave in the court meat and drink to support a fly, but consumed and wasted it all; and he pulled Gwenhwyvar from her throne, and committed adultery with her. The second was, when Arthur went to the court of Medrawd, he left neither meat nor drink that he did not destroy; and killed every living thing in the hundred, both man and beast. The third was, when the traitorous Aeddan went to the court of Rhydderch the Generous, he destroyed all the meat and drink in the court, without leaving as much as would feed a fly; and he did not leave either a man or beast alive, but destroyed the whole. These were called the three dreadful slaughters because the Cambrians were compelled, according to law and custom, to answer and grant redress for what was done in that irregular, unusual, and lawless manner.

53.   The three concealments and disclosures of the Isle of Britain. The first was the head of Bran the Blessed, the son of Llyr, that Owain the son of Ambrosius had concealed in the white hill in London; and whilst it remained in that state, no injury could happen to this Island. The second were the bones of Gwrthevyr the Blessed, which were buried in the principal ports of the Island, and while they remained there no molestation could happen to this Island. The third were the dragons which were concealed by Lludd the son of Beli in the fortress of Pharaon among the rocks of Snowdon. And these three concealments were placed under the protection of God and his attributes, so that misery should fall upon the hour and the person who should disclose them. Vortigern revealed the dragons out of revenge for the opposition of the Cambrians towards him, and he invited the Saxons under the semblance of auxiliaries to fight with the Irish Picts; and after that, he revealed the bones of Gwrthevyr the Blessed out of love to Rowena the daughter of Hengist the Saxon. And Arthur revealed the head of Bran the Blessed, the son of Llyr, because he scorned to keep the Island but by his own might; and after these three disclosures, the invaders obtained the superiority over the Cambrian nation.

THOMAS CAMPBELL

The Last Man

ALL worldly shapes shall melt in gloom,
　The Sun himself must die,
Before this mortal shall assume
　Its Immortality!
I saw a vision in my sleep
That gave my spirit strength to sweep
　Adown the gulf of Time!
I saw the last of human mould
That shall Creation's death behold.
　As Adam saw her prime!　　　　　　　　　　10

The Sun's eye had a sickly glare,
　The Earth with age was wan,
The skeletons of nations were
　Around that lonely man!
Some had expired in fight,—the brands
Still rusted in their bony hands;
　In plague and famine some!
Earth's cities had no sound nor tread;
And ships were drifting with the dead
　To shores where all was dumb!　　　　　　　20

Yet, prophet-like, that lone one stood
　With dauntless words and high,
That shook the sere leaves from the wood
　As if a storm passed by,
Saying, 'We are twins in death, proud Sun!
Thy face is cold, thy race is run,
　'Tis Mercy bids thee go;
For thou ten thousand thousand years
Hast seen the tide of human tears,
　That shall no longer flow.　　　　　　　　　30

'What though beneath thee man put forth
　His pomp, his pride, his skill,
And arts that made fire, flood, and earth
　The vassals of his will?
Yet mourn I not thy parted sway,
Thou dim discrownèd king of day:
　For all those trophied arts
And triumphs that beneath thee sprang

637

Healed not a passion or a pang
  Entailed on human hearts.   40

'Go, let oblivion's curtain fall
  Upon the stage of men,
Nor with thy rising beams recall
  Life's tragedy again.
Its piteous pageants bring not back,
Nor waken flesh upon the rack
  Of pain anew to writhe—
Stretched in disease's shapes abhorred,
Or mown in battle by the sword
  Like grass beneath the scythe.   50

'Even I am weary in yon skies
  To watch thy fading fire;
Test of all sumless agonies,
  Behold not me expire!
My lips that speak thy dirge of death—
Their rounded gasp and gargling breath
  To see thou shalt not boast;
The eclipse of Nature spreads my pall,—
The majesty of Darkness shall
  Receive my parting ghost!   60

'This spirit shall return to Him
  That gave its heavenly spark;
Yet think not, Sun, it shall be dim
  When thou thyself are dark!
No! it shall live again, and shine
In bliss unknown to beams of thine,
  By Him recalled to breath
Who captive led captivity,
Who robbed the grave of Victory,
  And took the sting from Death!   70

'Go, Sun, while Mercy holds me up
  On Nature's awful waste
To drink this last and bitter cup
  Of grief that man shall taste—
Go, tell the night that hides thy face
Thou saw'st the last of Adam's race
  On Earth's sepulchral clod
The darkening universe defy
To quench his immortality
  Or shake his trust in God!'   80

WINTHROP MACKWORTH PRAED
1802–1839

211   *Chancery Morals*

> Around, around, around, about,
> All ill come running in, all good keep out.
>   MACBETH

BOLD BENBOW rubs his jovial eyes,
    And lauds the law's refinement;
Dense DUGDALE is in ecstacies,
    Though CARLILE's in confinement:
And Guilt has wed Legality,
    And useful, through the nation,
Is prurience to publicity,
    And sin to circulation.
'*Don Juan* was a horrid beast,
    And that was why we sell'd 'un;   10
So say the statutes—or at least
    So says the Earl of ELDON.'

Pert POLL has come from Kentish Town,
    With sixpence in her pocket;
Red ROSE has sold her yellow gown,
    Meek MEG her little locket;
And MOLLY, who with Mrs FRY
    Has learnt a load of cant, goes
To pawn her prayers for poetry,
    Her Canticles for Cantos.   20
'*Don Juan* is a very feast,
    So wicked, and so well-done;
We thank God for it—or at least
    We thank the Earl of ELDON!'

The City hath its myriads sent
    To learn what BYRON's pen does;
And bakers study sentiment,
    And butchers innuendoes;
And big Bow-bells unheeded chime,
    For Beaux and Belles grow tender;   30
And Taste applauds a double rhyme,
    And Ton—'*a double 'tendre.*'

639

And frail ones, whose illicit trade
  Could never else have held on,
Cry 'Bless my soul! our fortune's made—
  Long live the Earl of ELDON!'

The girls of the Academy,
  With empty heads and purses,
Bless Charity and Chancery
  For cheapening naughty verses;   40
And MAUDES and MARYS peep and pay,
  With sigh and shilling ready;
And ANNA envies '*Julia*,'
  And ARAMINTA '*Haidee*.'
And Governantes are furious quite—
  'Lord! what have BET and BELL done!
They've read *Don Juan* through to-night!—
  And bless'd the Earl of ELDON.'

Bad BYRON loathes the legal fence,
  The guardian of good order,   50
The conqueror of common sense,
  From Cornwall to the border:
And damns the doubts and the delays,
  The quibblings and quotations,
The knowing nods and solemn says,
  The robes and revelations:
'This piracy will never do;
  I'll send you down to hell, *Don*,
The Devils have a right to you!
  So says the Earl of ELDON.'   60

GEORGE GORDON, LORD BYRON

212   *Don Juan*, Canto XI

I

WHEN Bishop Berkeley said 'there was no matter',
  And proved it—'twas no matter what he said:
They say his system 'tis in vain to batter,
  Too subtle for the airiest human head;
And yet who can believe it! I would shatter
  Gladly all matters, down to stone or lead,
Or adamant, to find the World a spirit,
And wear my head, denying that I wear it.

2

What a sublime discovery 'twas to make the
    Universe universal Egotism!   10
That all's ideal—*all ourselves*: I'll stake the
    World (be it what you will) that *that's* no Schism.
Oh, Doubt!—if thou be'st Doubt, for which some take thee,
    But which I doubt extremely—thou sole prism
Of the Truth's rays, spoil not my draught of spirit!
Heaven's brandy,—though our brain can hardly bear it.

3

For ever and anon comes Indigestion,
    (Not the most 'dainty Ariel') and perplexes
Our soarings with another sort of question:
    And that which after all my spirit vexes,   20
Is, that I find no spot where man can rest eye on,
    Without confusion of the sorts and sexes,
Of being, stars, and this unriddled wonder,
The World, which at the worst's a glorious blunder—

4

If it be Chance; or if it be according
    To the Old Text, still better:—lest it should
Turn out so, we'll say nothing 'gainst the wording,
    As several people think such hazards rude:
They're right; our days are too brief for affording
    Space to dispute what *no one* ever could   30
Decide, and *every body one day* will
Know very clearly—or at least lie still.

5

And therefore will I leave off metaphysical
    Discussion, which is neither here nor there:
If I agree that what is, is; then this I call
    Being quite perspicuous and extremely fair.
The truth is, I've grown lately rather phthisical:
    I don't know what the reason is—the air
Perhaps; but as I suffer from the shocks
Of illness, I grow much more orthodox.   40

6

The first attack at once proved the Divinity;
    (But *that* I never doubted, nor the Devil);
The next, the Virgin's mystical virginity;
    The third, the usual Origin of Evil;

641

The fourth at once established the whole Trinity
 On so uncontrovertible a level,
That I devoutly wished the three were four,
On purpose to believe so much the more.

7

To our theme:—The man who has stood on the Acropolis,
 And looked down over Attica; or he   50
Who has sailed where picturesque Constantinople is,
 Or seen Timbuctoo, or hath taken tea
In small-eyed China's crockery-ware metropolis,
 Or sat amidst the bricks of Nineveh,
May not think much of London's first appearance—
But ask him what he thinks of it a year hence?

8

Don Juan had got out on Shooter's Hill;
 Sunset the time, the place the same declivity
Which looks along that vale of good and ill
 Where London streets ferment in full activity; 60
While every thing around was calm and still,
 Except the creak of wheels, which on their pivot he
Heard,—and that bee-like, bubbling, busy hum
Of cities, that boil over with their scum:—

9

I say, Don Juan, wrapt in contemplation,
 Walked on behind his carriage, o'er the summit,
And lost in wonder of so great a nation,
 Gave way to't, since he could not overcome it.
'And here,' he cried, 'is Freedom's chosen station;
 Here peals the people's voice, nor can entomb it 70
Racks, prisons, inquisitions; resurrection
Awaits it, each new meeting or election.

10

'Here are chaste wives, pure lives; here people pay
 But what they please; and if that things be dear,
'Tis only that they love to throw away
 Their cash, to show how much they have a-year.
Here laws are all inviolate; none lay
 Traps for the traveller; every highway's clear:
Here'——he was interrupted by a knife,
With, 'Damn your eyes! your money or your life!' 80

11

These freeborn sounds proceeded from four pads,
    In ambush laid, who had perceived him loiter
Behind his carriage; and, like handy lads,
    Had seized the lucky hour to reconnoitre,
In which the heedless gentleman who gads
    Upon the road, unless he prove a fighter,
May find himself within that Isle of riches
Exposed to lose his life as well as breeches.

12

Juan, who did not understand a word
    Of English, save their shibboleth, 'God damn!'   90
And even that he had so rarely heard,
    He sometimes thought 'twas only their 'Salām,'
Or 'God be with you!'—and 'tis not absurd
    To think so; for half English as I am
(To my misfortune) never can I say
I heard them wish 'God with you,' save that way;—

13

Juan yet quickly understood their gesture,
    And being somewhat choleric and sudden,
Drew forth a pocket-pistol from his vesture,
    And fired it into one assailant's pudding—   100
Who fell, as rolls an ox o'er in his pasture,
    And roared out, as he writhed his native mud in,
Unto his nearest follower or henchman,
'Oh Jack! I'm floored by that 'ere bloody Frenchman!'

14

On which Jack and his train set off at speed,
    And Juan's suite, late scattered at a distance,
Came up, all marvelling at such a deed,
    And offering, as usual, late assistance.
Juan, who saw the Moon's late minion bleed
    As if his veins would pour out his existence,   110
Stood calling out for bandages and lint,
And wished he had been less hasty with his flint.

15

'Perhaps,' thought he, 'it is the country's Wont
    To welcome foreigners in this way: now

I recollect some innkeepers who don't
   Differ, except in robbing with a bow,
In lieu of a bare blade and brazen front.
   But what is to be done? I can't allow
The fellow to lie groaning on the road:
So take him up; I'll help you with the load.'   120

16

But ere they could perform this pious duty,
   The dying man cried, 'Hold! I've got my gruel!
Oh! for a glass of *max*! We've miss'd our booty—
   Let me die where I am!' And as the fuel
Of life shrunk in his heart, and thick and sooty
   The drops fell from his death-wound, and he drew ill
His breath,—he from his swelling throat untied
A kerchief, crying 'Give Sal that!'—and died.

17

The cravat stained with bloody drops fell down
   Before Don Juan's feet: he could not tell   130
Exactly why it was before him thrown,
   Nor what the meaning of the man's farewell.
Poor Tom was once a kiddy upon town,
   A thorough varmint, and a *real* swell,
Full flash, all fancy, until fairly diddled,
His pockets first, and then his body riddled.

18

Don Juan, having done the best he could
   In all the circumstances of the case,
As soon as 'Crowner's 'quest' allowed, pursued
   His travels to the capital apace;—   140
Esteeming it a little hard he should
   In twelve hours' time, and very little space,
Have been obliged to slay a freeborn native
In self-defence:—this made him meditative.

19

He from the world had cut off a great man,
   Who in his time had made heroic bustle.
Who in a row like Tom could lead the van,
   Booze in the ken, or at the spellken hustle?
Who queer a flat? Who (spite of Bow-street's ban)
   On the high toby-spice so flash the muzzle?   150

Who on a lark, with black-eyed Sal (his blowing)
So prime, so swell, so nutty, and so knowing?

20

But Tom's no more—and so no more of Tom.
   Heroes must die; and by God's blessing 'tis
Not long before the most of them go home.—
   Hail! Thamis, hail! Upon thy verge it is
That Juan's chariot, rolling like a drum
   In thunder, holds the way it can't well miss,
Through Kennington and all the other 'tons,'
Which make us wish ourselves in town at once;—   160

21

Through Groves, so called as being void of trees,
   (Like *lucus* from *no* light); through prospects named
Mounts Pleasant, as containing nought to please,
   Nor much to climb; through little boxes framed
Of bricks, to let the dust in at your ease,
   With 'To be let,' upon their doors proclaimed;
Through 'Rows' most modestly called 'Paradise,'
Which Eve might quit without much sacrifice;—

22

Through coaches, drays, choked turnpikes, and a whirl
   Of wheels, and roar of voices and confusion;   170
Here taverns wooing to a pint of 'purl',
   There mails fast flying off like a delusion;
There barber's blocks with periwigs in curl
   In windows; here the lamplighter's infusion
Slowly distilled into the glimmering glass,
(For in those days we had not got to gas:)—

23

Through this, and much, and more, is the approach
   Of travellers to mighty Babylon:
Whether they come by horse, or chaise, or coach,
   With slight exceptions, all the ways seem one.   180
I could say more, but do not choose to encroach
   Upon the guide-book's privilege. The Sun
Had set some time, and night was on the ridge
Of twilight, as the party crossed the bridge.

645

24

That's rather fine, the gentle sound of Thamis—
    Who vindicates a moment too his stream—
Though hardly heard through multifarious 'damme's.'
    The lamps of Westminster's more regular gleam,
The breadth of pavement, and yon shrine where Fame is
    A spectral resident—whose pallid beam   190
In shape of moonshine hovers o'er the pile—
Make this a sacred part of Albion's Isle.

25

The Druid's groves are gone—so much the better:
    Stone-Henge is not—but what the devil is it?—
But Bedlam still exists with its sage fetter,
    That madmen may not bite you on a visit;
The Bench too seats or suits full many a debtor;
    The Mansion House too (though some people quiz it)
To me appears a stiff yet grand erection;
But then the Abbey's worth the whole collection.   200

26

The line of lights too up to Charing Cross,
    Pall Mall, and so forth, have a coruscation
Like gold as in comparison to dross,
    Matched with the Continent's illumination,
Whose cities Night by no means deigns to gloss:
    The French were not yet a lamp-lighting nation,
And when they grew so—on their new-found lanthorn,
Instead of wicks, they made a wicked man turn.

27

A row of gentlemen along the streets
    Suspended, may illuminate mankind,   210
As also bonfires made of country seats;
    But the old way is best for the purblind:
The other looks like phosphorus on sheets,
    A sort of Ignis-fatuus to the mind,
Which, though 'tis certain to perplex and frighten,
Must burn more mildly ere it can enlighten.

28

But London's so well lit, that if Diogenes
    Could recommence to hunt his *honest man*,

And found him not amidst the various progenies
   Of this enormous city's spreading spawn,   220
'Twere not for want of lamps to aid his dodging his
   Yet undiscovered treasure. What *I* can,
I've done to find the same throughout life's journey,
But see the world is only one attorney.

29

Over the stones still rattling up Pall Mall,
   Through crowds and carriages, but waxing thinner
As thundered knockers broke the long-sealed spell
   Of doors 'gainst duns, and to an early dinner
Admitted a small party as night fell,—
   Don Juan, our young diplomatic sinner,   230
Pursued his path, and drove past some Hotels,
St James's Palace, and St James's 'Hells'.

30

They reached the hotel: forth streamed from the front door
   A tide of well-clad waiters, and around
The mob stood, and as usual, several score
   Of those pedestrian Paphians, who abound
In decent London when the daylight's o'er;
   Commodious but immoral, they are found
Useful, like Malthus, in promoting marriage:—
But Juan now is stepping from his carriage   240

31

Into one of the sweetest of hotels,
   Especially for foreigners—and mostly
For those whom favour or whom fortune swells,
   And cannot find a bill's small items costly.
There many an envoy either dwelt or dwells,
   (The den of many a diplomatic lost lie)
Until to some conspicuous square they pass,
And blazon o'er the door their names in brass.

32

Juan, whose was a delicate commission,
   Private, though publicly important, bore   250
No title to point out with due precision
   The exact affair on which he was sent o'er.

'Twas merely known that on a secret mission
   A foreigner of rank had graced our shore,
Young, handsome, and accomplished, who was said
(In whispers) to have turned his Sovereign's head.

33

Some rumour also of some strange adventures
   Had gone before him, and his wars and loves;
And as romantic heads are pretty painters,
   And, above all, an Englishwoman's roves   260
Into the excursive, breaking the indentures
   Of sober reason, wheresoe'er it moves,
He found himself extremely in the fashion,
Which serves our thinking people for a passion.

34

I don't mean that they are passionless, but quite
   The contrary; but then 'tis in the head;
Yet as the consequences are as bright
   As if they acted with the heart instead,
What after all can signify the site
   Of ladies' lucubrations? So they lead   270
In safety to the place for which you start,
What matters if the road be head or heart?

35

Juan presented in the proper place,
   To proper placemen, every Russ credential;
And was received with all the due grimace,
   By those who govern in the mood potential;
Who, seeing a handsome stripling with smooth face,
   Thought (what in state affairs is most essential)
That they as easily might *do* the youngster,
As hawks may pounce upon a woodland songster.   280

36

They erred, as aged men will do; but by
   And by we'll talk of that; and if we don't,
'Twill be because our notion is not high
   Of politicians and their double front,
Who live by lies, yet dare not boldly lie:
   Now what I love in women is, they won't
Or can't do otherwise than lie, but do it
So well, the very truth seems falsehood to it.

37

And, after all, what is a lie? 'Tis but
   The truth in masquerade; and I defy   290
Historians, heroes, lawyers, priests to put
   A fact without some leaven of a lie.
The very shadow of true Truth would shut
   Up annals, revelations, poesy,
And prophecy—except it should be dated
Some years before the incidents related.

38

Praised be all liars and all lies! Who now
   Can tax my mild Muse with misanthropy?
She rings the world's 'Te Deum,' and her brow
   Blushes for those who will not:—but to sigh   300
Is idle; let us like most others bow,
   Kiss hands, feet, any part of Majesty,
After the good example of 'Green Erin,'
Whose Shamrock now seems rather worse for wearing.

39

Don Juan was presented, and his dress
   And mien excited general admiration—
I don't know which was most admired or less:
   One monstrous diamond drew much observation,
Which Catherine in a moment of 'ivresse'
   (In love or brandy's fervent fermentation)   310
Bestowed upon him, as the public learned;
And, to say truth, it had been fairly earned.

40

Besides the Ministers and underlings,
   Who must be courteous to the accredited
Diplomatists of rather wavering kings,
   Until their royal riddle's fully read,
The very clerks—those somewhat dirty springs
   Of office, or the House of Office, fed
By foul corruption into streams,—even they
Were hardly rude enough to earn their pay.   320

41

And insolence no doubt is what they are
   Employed for, since it is their daily labour,

In the dear offices of peace and war;
   And should you doubt, pray ask of your next neighbour,
When for a passport, or some other bar
   To freedom, he applied (a grief and a bore)
If he found not this spawn of tax-born riches,
Like lap-dogs, the least civil sons of b——s.

42

But Juan was received with much 'empressement:'—
   These phrases of refinement I must borrow   330
From our next neighbour's land, where, like a chessman,
   There is a move set down for joy or sorrow
Not only in mere talking, but the press. Man
   In islands is, it seems, downright and thorough,
More than on continents—as if the sea
(See Billingsgate) made even the tongue more free.

43

And yet the British 'Damme's' rather Attic:
   Your Continental oaths are but incontinent,
And turn on things which no Aristocratic
   Spirit would name, and therefore even I won't anent   340
This subject quote; as it would be schismatic
   In politesse, and have a sound affronting in't:—
But 'Damme's' quite ethereal, though too daring—
Platonic blasphemy, the soul of swearing.

44

For downright rudeness, ye may stay at home;
   For true or false politeness (and scarce *that*
Now) you may cross the blue deep and white foam—
   The first the emblem (rarely though) of what
You leave behind— the next of much you come
   To meet. However, 'tis no time to chat   350
On general topics: poems must confine
Themselves to Unity, like this of mine.

45

In the Great World,—which being interpreted
   Meaneth the West or worst end of a city,
And about twice two thousand people bred
   By no means to be very wise or witty,
But to sit up while others lie in bed,
   And look down on the universe with pity,—

Juan, as an inveterate Patrician,
Was well received by persons of condition.   360

46

He was a bachelor, which is a matter
    Of import both to Virgin and to Bride,
The former's hymeneal hopes to flatter;
    And (should she not hold fast by love or pride)
'Tis also of some moment to the latter:
    A rib's a thorn in a wed Gallant's side,
Requires decorum, and is apt to double
The horrid sin—and what's still worse, the trouble.

47

But Juan was a bachelor—of arts,
    And parts, and hearts: he danced and sung, and had   370
An air as sentimental as Mozart's
    Softest of melodies; and could be sad
Or cheerful, without any 'flaws or starts',
    Just at the proper time; and though a lad,
Had seen the world—which is a curious sight,
And very much unlike what people write.

48

Fair virgins blushed upon him; wedded dames
    Bloomed also in less transitory hues;
For both commodities dwell by the Thames,
    The painting and the painted; youth, ceruse,   380
Against his heart preferred their usual claims,
    Such as no gentleman can quite refuse;
Daughters admired his dress, and pious mothers
Enquired his income, and if he had brothers.

49

The milliners who furnish 'drapery Misses'
    Throughout the season, upon speculation
Of payment ere the honeymoon's last kisses
    Have waned into a crescent's coruscation,
Thought such an opportunity as this is,
    Of a rich foreigner's initiation,   390
Not to be overlooked,—and gave such credit,
That future bridegrooms swore, and sighed, and paid it.

50

The Blues, that tender tribe, who sigh o'er sonnets,
  And with the pages of the last Review
Line the interior of their heads or bonnets,
  Advanced in all their azure's highest hue:
They talked bad French of Spanish, and upon its
  Late authors asked him for a hint or two;
And which was softest, Russian or Castilian?
And whether in his travels he saw Ilion?   400

51

Juan, who was a little superficial,
  And not in literature a great Drawcansir,
Examined by this learned and especial
  Jury of matrons, scarce knew what to answer:
His duties warlike, loving, or official,
  His steady application as a dancer,
Had kept him from the brink of Hippocrene,
Which now he found was blue instead of green.

52

However, he replied at hazard, with
  A modest confidence and calm assurance,   410
Which lent his learned lucubrations pith,
  And passed for arguments of good endurance.
That prodigy, Miss Araminta Smith,
  (Who at sixteen translated 'Hercules Furens'
Into as furious English) with her best look,
Set down his sayings in her common-place book.

53

Juan knew several languages—as well
  He might—and brought them up with skill, in time
To save his fame with each accomplished belle,
  Who still regretted that he did not rhyme.   420
There wanted but this requisite to swell
  His qualities (with them) into sublime:
Lady Fitz-Frisky, and Miss Maevia Mannish,
Both longed extremely to be sung in Spanish.

54

However, he did pretty well, and was
   Admitted as an aspirant to all
The Coteries; and, as in Banquo's glass,
   At great assemblies or in parties small,
He saw ten thousand living authors pass,
   That being about their average numeral;   430
Also the eighty 'greatest living poets,'
As every paltry magazine can show *its*.

55

In twice five years the 'greatest living poet,'
   Like to the champion in the fisty ring,
Is called on to support his claim, or show it,
   Although 'tis an imaginary thing.
Even I—albeit I'm sure I did not know it,
   Nor sought of foolscap subjects to be king,—
Was reckoned, a considerable time,
The grand Napoleon of the realms of rhyme.   440

56

But Juan was my Moscow, and Faliero
   My Leipsic, and my Mont Saint Jean seems Cain:
'La Belle Alliance' of dunces down at zero,
   Now that the Lion's fall'n, may rise again:
But I will fall at least as fell my hero;
   Nor reign at all, or as a *monarch* reign;
Or to some lonely isle of Jailors go,
With turncoat Southey for my turnkey Lowe.

57

Sir Walter reigned before me; Moore and Campbell
   Before and after; but now grown more holy,   450
The Muses upon Sion's hill must ramble,
   With poets almost clergymen, or wholly;
And Pegasus hath a psalmodic amble
   Beneath the reverend Cambyses Croly,
Who shoes the glorious animal with stilts,
A modern Ancient Pistol—'by these Hilts!'

58

Still he excels that artificial hard
   Labourer in the same vineyard, though the vine
Yields him but vinegar for his reward,—
   That neutralized dull Dorus of the Nine;   460

That swarthy Sporus, neither man nor bard;
  That ox of verse, who *ploughs* for every line:—
Cambyses' roaring Romans beat at least
The howling Hebrews of Cybele's priest.—

59

Then there's my gentle Euphues; who, they say,
  Sets up for being a sort of *moral me*;
He'll find it rather difficult some day
  To turn out both, or either, it may be.
Some persons think that Coleridge hath the sway;
  And Wordsworth has supporters, two or three;   470
And that deep-mouthed Boeotian, 'Savage Landor,'
Has taken for a swan rogue Southey's gander.

60

John Keats, who was killed off by one critique,
  Just as he really promised something great,
If not intelligible,—without Greek
  Contrived to talk about the Gods of late,
Much as they might have been supposed to speak.
  Poor fellow! His was an untoward fate:—
'Tis strange the mind, that very fiery particle,
Should let itself be snuffed out by an Article.   480

61

The list grows long of live and dead pretenders
  To that which none will gain—or none will know
The Conqueror at least; who, ere time renders
  His last award, will have the long grass grow
Above his burnt-out brain, and sapless cinders.
  If I might augur, I should rate but low
Their chances;—they're too numerous, like the thirty
Mock tyrants, when Rome's annals waxed but dirty.

62

This is the literary *lower* Empire,
  Where the Praetorian bands take up the matter;—   490
A 'dreadful trade,' like his who 'gathers samphire',
  The insolent soldiery to soothe and flatter,
With the same feelings as you'd coax a vampire.
  Now, were I once at home, and in good satire,
I'd try conclusions with those Janizaries,
And show them *what* an intellectual war is.

63

I think I know a trick or two, would turn
  Their flanks;—but it is hardly worth my while
With such small gear to give myself concern:
  Indeed I've not the necessary bile;   500
My natural temper's really aught but stern,
  And even my Muse's worst reproof's a smile;
And then she drops a brief and modern curtsey,
And glides away, assured she never hurts ye.

64

My Juan, whom I left in deadly peril
  Amongst live poets and blue ladies, past
With some small profit through that field so sterile.
  Being tired in time, and neither least nor last
Left it before he had been treated very ill;
  And henceforth found himself more gaily classed   510
Amongst the higher spirits of the day,
The sun's true son, no vapour, but a ray.

65

His morns he passed in business—which dissected,
  Was like all business, a laborious nothing,
That leads to lassitude, the most infected
  And Centaur–Nessus garb of mortal clothing,
And on our sophas makes us lie dejected,
  And talk in tender horrors of our loathing
All kinds of toil, save for our country's good—
Which grows no better, though 'tis time it should.   520

66

His afternoons he passed in visits, luncheons,
  Lounging, and boxing; and the twilight hour
In riding round those vegetable puncheons
  Called 'Parks,' where there is neither fruit nor flower
Enough to gratify a bee's slight munchings;
  But after all it is the only 'bower,'
(In Moore's phrase) where the fashionable fair
Can form a slight acquaintance with fresh air.

67

Then dress, then dinner, then awakes the world!
  Then glare the lamps, then whirl the wheels, then roar   530
Through street and square fast flashing chariots, hurled
  Like harnessed meteors; then along the floor

Chalk mimics painting; then festoons are twirled;
  Then roll the brazen thunders of the door,
Which opens to the thousand happy few
An earthly Paradise of 'Or Molu'.

68

There stands the noble Hostess, nor shall sink
  With the three-thousandth curtsey; there the Waltz,
The only dance which teaches girls to think,
  Makes one in love even with its very faults.   540
Saloon, room, hall o'erflow beyond their brink,
  And long the latest of arrivals halts,
'Midst royal dukes and dames condemned to climb,
And gain an inch of staircase at a time.

69

Thrice happy he, who, after a survey
  Of the good company, can win a corner,
A door that's *in*, or boudoir *out* of the way,
  Where he may fix himself, like small 'Jack Horner,'
And let the Babel round run as it may,
  And look on as a mourner, or a scorner,   550
Or an approver, or a mere spectator,
Yawning a little as the night grows later.

70

But this won't do, save by and by; and he
  Who, like Don Juan, takes an active share,
Must steer with care through all that glittering sea
  Of gems and plumes, and pearls and silks, to where
He deems it is his proper place to be;
  Dissolving in the waltz to some soft air,
Or proudlier prancing with mercurial skill
Where Science marshals forth her own quadrille.   560

71

Or, if he dance not, but hath higher views
  Upon an heiress or his neighbour's bride,
Let him take care that that which he pursues
  Is not at once too palpably descried.
Full many an eager gentleman oft rues
  His haste: impatience is a blundering guide
Amongst a people famous for reflection,
Who like to play the fool with circumspection.

72

But, if you can contrive, get next at supper;
   Or, if forestalled, get opposite and ogle:—   570
Oh, ye ambrosial moments! always upper
   In mind, a sort of sentimental bogle,
Which sits for ever upon Memory's crupper,
   The ghost of vanished pleasures once in vogue! Ill
Can tender souls relate the rise and fall
Of hopes and fears which shake a single ball.

73

But these precautionary hints can touch
   Only the common run, who must pursue,
And watch, and ward; whose plans a word too much
   Or little overturns; and not the few   580
Or many (for the number's sometimes such)
   Whom a good mien, especially if new,
Or fame, or name, for wit, war, sense, or nonsense,
Permits whate'er they please, or *did* not long since.

74

Our hero, as a hero, young and handsome,
   Noble, rich, celebrated, and a stranger,
Like other slaves of course must pay his ransom
   Before he can escape from so much danger
As will environ a conspicuous man. Some
   Talk about poetry, and 'rack and manger',   590
And ugliness, disease, as toil and trouble,—
I wish they knew the life of a young noble.

75

They are young, but know not youth—it is anticipated;
   Handsome but wasted, rich without a sou;
Their vigour in a thousand arms is dissipated;
   Their cash comes *from*, their wealth goes *to* a Jew;
Both senates see their nightly votes participated
   Between the tyrant's and the tribunes' crew;
And having voted, dined, drank, gamed, and whored,
The family vault receives another lord.   600

76

'Where is the world,' cries Young, 'at *eighty*? Where
   The world in which a man was born?' Alas!

Where is the world of *eight* years past? 'Twas there—
  I look for it—'tis gone, a Globe of Glass!
Cracked, shivered, vanished, scarcely gazed on, ere
  A silent change dissolves the glittering mass.
Statesmen, chiefs, orators, queens, patriots, kings,
And dandies, all are gone on the wind's wings.

77

Where is Napoleon the Grand? God knows:
  Where little Castlereagh? The devil can tell: 610
Where Grattan, Curran, Sheridan, all those
  Who bound the bar or senate in their spell?
Where is the unhappy Queen, with all her woes?
  And where the Daughter, whom the Isles loved well?
Where are those martyred Saints the Five per Cents?
And where—oh where the devil are the Rents!

78

Where's Brummell? Dished. Where's Long Pole Wellesley?
  Diddled.
  Where's Whitbread? Romilly? Where's George the Third?
Where is his will? (That's not so soon unriddled.)
  And where is 'Fum' the Fourth, our 'royal bird'?   620
Gone down it seems to Scotland, to be fiddled
  Unto by Sawney's violin, we have heard:
'Caw me, caw thee'—for six months hath been hatching
This scene of royal itch and loyal scratching.

79

Where is Lord This? And where my Lady That?
  The Honourable Mistresses and Misses?
Some laid aside like an old opera hat,
  Married, unmarried, and remarried: (this is
An evolution oft performed of late).
  Where are the Dublin shouts—and London hisses?   630
Where are the Grenvilles? Turned as usual. Where
My friends the Whigs? Exactly where they were.

80

Where are the Lady Carolines and Franceses?
  Divorced or doing thereanent. Ye annals
So brilliant, where the list of routs and dances is,—
  Thou Morning Post, sole record of the panels

Broken in carriages, and all the phantasies
   Of fashion,—say what streams now fill those channels?
Some die, some fly, some languish on the Continent,
Because the times have hardly left them *one* tenant.   640

81

Some who once set their caps at cautious Dukes,
   Have taken up at length with younger brothers:
Some heiresses have bit at sharpers' hooks;
   Some maids have been made wives, some merely mothers;
Others have lost their fresh and fairy looks:
   In short, the list of alterations bothers:
There's little strange in this, but something strange is
The unusual quickness of these common changes.

82

Talk not of seventy years as age! in seven
   I have seen more changes, down from monarchs to   650
The humblest individual under heaven,
   Than might suffice a moderate century through.
I knew that nought was lasting, but now even
   Change grows too changeable, without being new:
Nought's permanent among the human race,
Except the Whigs *not* getting into place.

83

I have seen Napoleon, who seemed quite a Jupiter,
   Shrink to a Saturn. I have seen a Duke
(No matter which) turn politician stupider,
   If that can well be, than his wooden look.   660
But it is time that I should hoist my 'blue Peter',
   And sail for a new theme:—I have seen—and shook
To see it—the King hissed, and then carest;
And don't pretend to settle which was best.

84

I have seen the landholders without a rap—
   I have seen Johanna Southcote—I have seen
The House of Commons turned to a tax-trap—
   I have seen that sad affair of the late Queen—
I have seen crowns worn instead of a fool's-cap—
   I have seen a Congress doing all that's mean—   670
I have seen some nations like o'erloaded asses
Kick off their burthens—meaning the high classes.

85

I have seen small poets, and great prosers, and
    Interminable—*not eternal*—speakers—
I have seen the Funds at war with house and land—
    I've seen the Country Gentlemen turn squeakers—
I've seen the people ridden o'er like sand
    By slaves on horseback—I have seen malt liquors
Exchanged for 'thin potations' by John Bull—
I have seen John half detect himself a fool.—   680

86

But 'Carpe diem,' Juan, 'Carpe, carpe!'
    To-morrow sees another race as gay
And transient, and devoured by the same harpy.
    'Life's a poor player,'—then 'play out the play,
Ye villains!' and above all keep a sharp eye
    Much less on what you do than what you say:
Be hypocritical, be cautious, be
Not what you *seem*, but always what you *see*.

87

But how shall I relate in other Cantos
    Of what befell our hero in the land,   690
Which 'tis the common cry and lie to vaunt as
    A moral country? But I hold my hand—
For I disdain to write an Atalantis;
    But 'tis as well at once to understand,
You are *not* a moral people, and you know it
Without the aid of too sincere a poet.

88

What Juan saw and underwent, shall be
    My topic, with of course the due restriction
Which is required by proper courtesy;
    And recollect the work is only fiction,   700
And that I sing of neither mine nor me,   .
    Though every scribe, in some slight turn of diction,
Will hint allusions never *meant*. Ne'er doubt
This—when I speak, I *don't hint*, but *speak out*.

89

Whether he married with the third or fourth
    Offspring of some sage, husband-hunting Countess,
Or whether with some virgin of more worth
    (I mean in Fortune's matrimonial bounties)

He took to regularly peopling Earth,
   Of which your lawful awful wedlock fount is,— 710
Or whether he was taken in for damages,
For being too excursive in his homages,—

90

Is yet within the unread events of time.
   Thus far, go forth, thou Lay! which I will back
Against the same given quantity of rhyme,
   For being as much the subject of attack
As ever yet was any work sublime,
   By those who love to say that white is black.
So much the better!—I may stand alone,
And would not change my free thoughts for a throne. 720

BRIAN WALLER PROCTER
1787–1874

213   *Sonnet*
A Still Place

UNDER what beechen shade, or silent oak,
Lies the mute sylvan now,—mysterious Pan?
Once (while rich Peneus and Ilissus ran
Clear from their fountains)—as the morning broke,
Tis said, the Satyr with Apollo spoke,
And to harmonious strife, with his wild reed,
Challenged the God, whose music was indeed
Divine, and fit for Heaven.—Each play'd, and woke
Beautiful sounds to life, deep melodies:
One blew his pastoral pipe with such nice care,   10
That flocks and birds all answer'd him; and one
Shook his immortal showers upon the air.
—*That* music hath ascended to the sun;
But where the other?—Speak! ye dells and trees!

CATHERINE MARIA FANSHAWE
1765–1834

A Riddle

'TWAS in heaven pronounced, and 'twas muttered in hell
And echo caught faintly the sound as it fell:
On the confines of earth 'twas permitted to rest,
And the depths of the ocean its presence confest;
'Twill be found in the sphere when 'tis riven asunder,
Be seen in the lightning, and heard in the thunder.
'Twas allotted to man with his earliest breath,
Attends at his birth, and awaits him in death,
Presides o'er his happiness, honour, and health,
Is the prop of his house, and the end of his wealth.   10
In the heaps of the miser 'tis hoarded with care,
But is sure to be lost on his prodigal heir.
It begins every hope, every wish it must bound,
With the husbandman toils, and with monarchs is crown'd.
Without it the soldier, the seaman may roam,
But wo to the wretch who expels it from home!
In the whispers of conscience its voice will be found,
Nor e'en in the whirlwind of passion be drown'd.
'Twill not soften the heart; but though deaf be the ear,
It will make it acutely and instantly hear.   20
Yet in shade let it rest like a delicate flower,
Ah breathe on it softly—it dies in an hour.

CAROLINE OLIPHANT, later
BARONESS NAIRNE
1766–1845

215   *The Laird o' Cockpen*

Air: 'When she cam' ben, she bobbit'

THE laird o' Cockpen, he's proud an' he's great,
His mind is ta'en up wi' things o' the State;
He wanted a wife, his braw house to keep,
But favour wi' wooin' was fashous to seek.

Down by the dyke-side a lady did dwell,
At his table head he thought she'd look well,
McClish's ae daughter o' Clavers-ha' Lee,
A penniless lass wi' a lang pedigree.

His wig was weel pouther'd and as gude as new,
His waistcoat was white, his coat it was blue;   10
He put on a ring, a sword, and cock't hat,
And wha could refuse the laird wi' a' that?

He took the grey mear, an' rade cannily,
An' rapp'd at the yett o' Clavers-ha' Lee;
'Gae tell Mistress Jean to come speedily ben,—
She's wanted to speak to the Laird o' Cockpen.'

Mistress Jean was makin' the elder-flower wine;
'An' what brings the laird at sic a like time?'
She pat aff her aprin, and on her silk gown,
Her mutch wi' red ribbons, and gaed awa' down.   20

An' when she cam' ben he boued fu' low,
An' what was his errand he soon let her know;
Amazed was the laird when the Ladye said 'Na,'
And wi' a laigh curtsie, she turned awa'.

215:   3 braw] fine   4 fashous] troublesome   14 yett] gate

Dumfounder'd was he, nae sigh did he gie,
He mounted his mear—he rade cannily;
An' aften he thought, as he gaed thro' the glen,
She's daft to refuse the laird o' Cockpen.

216   *The Land o' the Leal*

Air: 'Hey tutti taiti'

I'M wearin' awa', John,
Like snaw-wreaths in thaw, John,
I'm wearin' awa'
    To the land o' the leal.
There's nae sorrow there, John,
There's neither cauld nor care, John,
The day's aye fair
    In the land o' the leal.

Our bonnie bairn's there, John,
She was baith gude and fair, John,   10
And oh! we grudged her sair
    To the land o' the leal.
But sorrow's sel' wears past, John,
And joy's a-comin' fast, John,
The joy that's aye to last,
    In the land o' the leal.

Sae dear's that joy was bought, John,
Sae free the battle fought, John,
That sinfu' man e'er brought
    To the land o' the leal.   20
Oh! dry your glist'ning e'e, John,
My saul langs to be free, John,
And angels beckon me
    To the land o' the leal.

Oh! haud ye leal and true, John,
Your day it's wearin' through, John,
And I'll welcome you
    To the land o' the leal.
Now fare-ye-weel, my ain John,
This warld's cares are vain, John,   30
We'll meet, and we'll be fain,
    In the land o' the leal.

PERCY BYSSHE SHELLEY

217

Julian and Maddalo

A Conversation

I RODE one evening with Count Maddalo
Upon the bank of land which breaks the flow
Of Adria towards Venice: a bare strand
Of hillocks, heaped from ever-shifting sand,
Matted with thistles and amphibious weeds,
Such as from earth's embrace the salt ooze breeds,
Is this; an uninhabited sea-side,
Which the lone fisher, when his nets are dried,
Abandons; and no other object breaks
The waste, but one dwarf tree and some few stakes   10
Broken and unrepaired, and the tide makes
A narrow space of level sand thereon,
Where 'twas our wont to ride while day went down.
This ride was my delight. I love all waste
And solitary places; where we taste
The pleasure of believing what we see
Is boundless, as we wish our souls to be:
And such was this wide ocean, and this shore
More barren than its billows; and yet more
Than all, with a remembered friend I love   20
To ride as then I rode;—for the winds drove
The living spray along the sunny air
Into our faces; the blue heavens were bare,
Stripped to their depths by the awakening north;
And, from the waves, sound like delight broke forth
Harmonising with solitude, and sent
Into our hearts aëreal merriment.
So, as we rode, we talked; and the swift thought,
Winging itself with laughter, lingered not,
But flew from brain to brain,—such glee was ours,   30
Charged with light memories of remembered hours,
None slow enough for sadness: till we came
Homeward, which always makes the spirit tame.
This day had been cheerful but cold, and now
The sun was sinking, and the wind also.
Our talk grew somewhat serious, as may be
Talk interrupted with such raillery
As mocks itself, because it cannot scorn

The thoughts it would extinguish:—'twas forlorn,
Yet pleasing, such as once, so poets tell,   40
The devils held within the dales of Hell
Concerning God, freewill and destiny:
Of all that earth has been or yet may be,
All that vain men imagine or believe,
Or hope can paint or suffering may achieve,
We descanted, and I (for ever still
Is it not wise to make the best of ill?)
Argued against despondency, but pride
Made my companion take the darker side.
The sense that he was greater than his kind   50
Had struck, methinks, his eagle spirit blind
By gazing on its own exceeding light.
Meanwhile the sun paused ere it should alight,
Over the horizon of the mountains;—Oh,
How beautiful is sunset, when the glow
Of Heaven descends upon a land like thee,
Thou Paradise of exiles, Italy!
Thy mountains, seas, and vineyards, and the towers
Of cities they encircle!—it was ours
To stand on thee, beholding it: and then,   60
Just where we had dismounted, the Count's men
Were waiting for us with the gondola.—
As those who pause on some delightful way
Though bent on pleasant pilgrimage, we stood
Looking upon the evening, and the flood
Which lay between the city and the shore,
Paved with the image of the sky . . . the hoar
And aëry Alps towards the North appeared
Through mist, an heaven-sustaining bulwark reared
Between the East and West; and half the sky   70
Was roofed with clouds of rich emblazonry
Dark purple at the zenith, which still grew
Down the steep West into a wondrous hue
Brighter than burning gold, even to the rent
Where the swift sun yet paused in his descent
Among the many-folded hills: they were
Those famous Euganean hills, which bear,
As seen from Lido thro' the harbour piles,
The likeness of a clump of peakèd isles—
And then—as if the Earth and Sea had been   80
Dissolved into one lake of fire, were seen
Those mountains towering as from waves of flame
Around the vaporous sun, from which there came
The inmost purple spirit of light, and made

Their very peaks transparent. 'Ere it fade,'
Said my companion, 'I will show you soon
A better station'—so, o'er the lagune
We glided; and from that funereal bark
I leaned, and saw the city, and could mark
How from their many isles, in evening's gleam,   90
Its temples and its palaces did seem
Like fabrics of enchantment piled to Heaven.
I was about to speak, when—'We are even
Now at the point I meant,' said Maddalo,
And bade the gondolieri cease to row.
'Look, Julian, on the west, and listen well
If you hear not a deep and heavy bell.'
I looked, and saw between us and the sun
A building on an island; such a one
As age to age might add, for uses vile,   100
A windowless, deformed and dreary pile;
And on the top an open tower, where hung
A bell, which in the radiance swayed and swung;
We could just hear its hoarse and iron tongue:
The broad sun sunk behind it, and it tolled
In strong and black relief.—'What we behold
Shall be the madhouse and its belfry tower,'
Said Maddalo, 'and ever at this hour
Those who may cross the water, hear that bell
Which calls the maniacs, each one from his cell,   110
To vespers.'—'As much skill as need to pray
In thanks or hope for their dark lot have they
To their stern maker,' I replied. 'O ho!
You talk as in years past,' said Maddalo.
' 'Tis strange men change not. You were ever still
Among Christ's flock a perilous infidel,
A wolf for the meek lambs—if you can't swim
Beware of Providence.' I looked on him,
But the gay smile had faded in his eye.
'And such,'—he cried, 'is our mortality,   120
And this must be the emblem and the sign
Of what should be eternal and divine!—
And like that black and dreary bell, the soul,
Hung in a heaven-illumined tower, must toll
Our thoughts and our desires to meet below
Round the rent heart and pray—as madmen do
For what? they know not,—till the night of death
As sunset that strange vision, severeth
Our memory from itself, and us from all
We sought and yet were baffled.' I recall   130

The sense of what he said, although I mar
The force of his expressions. The broad star
Of day meanwhile had sunk behind the hill,
And the black bell became invisible,
And the red tower looked gray, and all between
The churches, ships and palaces were seen
Huddled in gloom;—into the purple sea
The orange hues of heaven sunk silently.
We hardly spoke, and soon the gondola
Conveyed me to my lodgings by the way.   140
    The following morn was rainy, cold and dim:
Ere Maddalo arose, I called on him,
And whilst I waited with his child I played;
A lovelier toy sweet Nature never made,
A serious, subtle, wild, yet gentle being,
Graceful without design and unforeseeing,
With eyes—Oh speak not of her eyes!—which seem
Twin mirrors of Italian Heaven, yet gleam
With such deep meaning, as we never see
But in the human countenance: with me   150
She was a special favourite: I had nursed
Her fine and feeble limbs when she came first
To this bleak world; and she yet seemed to know
On second sight her ancient playfellow,
Less changed than she was by six months or so;
For after her first shyness was worn out
We sate there, rolling billiard balls about,
When the Count entered. Salutations past—
'The word you spoke last night might well have cast
A darkness on my spirit—if man be   160
The passive thing you say, I should not see
Much harm in the religions and old saws
(Tho' I may never own such leaden laws)
Which break a teachless nature to the yoke:
Mine is another faith'—thus much I spoke
And noting he replied not, added: 'See
This lovely child, blithe, innocent and free;
She spends a happy time with little care,
While we to such sick thoughts subjected are
As came on you last night—it is our will   170
That thus enchains us to permitted ill—
We might be otherwise—we might be all
We dream of happy, high, majestical.
Where is the love, beauty, and truth we seek
But in our mind? and if we were not weak
Should we be less in deed than in desire?'

'Ay, if we were not weak—and we aspire
How vainly to be strong!' said Maddalo:
'You talk Utopia.' 'It remains to know,'
I then rejoined, 'and those who try may find   180
How strong the chains are which our spirit bind;
Brittle perchance as straw ... We are assured
Much may be conquered, much may be endured,
Of what degrades and crushes us. We know
That we have power over ourselves to do
And suffer—what, we know not till we try;
But something nobler than to live and die—
So taught those kings of old philosophy
Who reigned, before Religion made men blind;
And those who suffer with their suffering kind   190
Yet feel their faith, religion.' 'My dear friend,'
Said Maddalo, 'my judgement will not bend
To your opinion, though I think you might
Make such a system refutation-tight
As far as words go. I knew one like you
Who to this city came some months ago,
With whom I argued in this sort, and he
Is now gone mad,—and so he answered me,—
Poor fellow! but if you would like to go
We'll visit him, and his wild talk will show   200
How vain are such aspiring theories.'
'I hope to prove the induction otherwise,
And that a want of that true theory, still,
Which seeks a "soul of goodness" in things ill
Or in himself or others, has thus bowed
His being—there are some by nature proud,
Who patient in all else demand but this—
To love and be beloved with gentleness;
And being scorned, what wonder if they die
Some living death? this is not destiny   210
But man's own wilful ill.'
                    As thus I spoke
Servants announced the gondola, and we
Through the fast-falling rain and high-wrought sea
Sailed to the island where the madhouse stands.
We disembarked. The clap of tortured hands,
Fierce yells and howlings and lamentings keen,
And laughter where complaint had merrier been,
Moans, shrieks, and curses, and blaspheming prayers
Accosted us. We climbed the oozy stairs
Into an old courtyard. I heard on high,   220
Then, fragments of most touching melody,

But looking up saw not the singer there—
Through the black bars in the tempestuous air
I saw, like weeds on a wrecked palace growing,
Long tangled locks flung wildly forth, and flowing,
Of those who on a sudden were beguiled
Into strange silence, and looked forth and smiled
Hearing sweet sounds.—Then I: 'Methinks there were
A cure of these with patience and kind care,
If music can thus move ... but what is he   230
Whom we seek here?' 'Of his sad history
I know but this,' said Maddalo: 'he came
To Venice a dejected man, and fame
Said he was wealthy, or he had been so;
Some thought the loss of fortune wrought him woe;
But he was ever talking in such sort
As you do—far more sadly—he seemed hurt,
Even as a man with his peculiar wrong,
To hear but of the oppression of the strong,
Or those absurd deceits (I think with you   240
In some respects, you know) which carry through
The excellent impostors of this earth
When they outface detection—he had worth,
Poor fellow! but a humourist in his way'—
'Alas, what drove him mad?' 'I cannot say:
A lady came with him from France, and when
She left him and returned, he wandered then
About yon lonely isles of desert sand
Till he grew wild—he had no cash or land
Remaining,—the police had brought him here—   250
Some fancy took him and he would not bear
Removal; so I fitted up for him
Those rooms beside the sea, to please his whim,
And sent him busts and books and urns for flowers,
Which had adorned his life in happier hours,
And instruments of music—you may guess
A stranger could do little more or less
For one so gentle and unfortunate:
And those are his sweet strains which charm the weight
From madmen's chains, and make this Hell appear   260
A heaven of sacred silence, hushed to hear.'—
'Nay, this was kind of you—he had no claim,
As the world says'—'None—but the very same
Which I on all mankind were I as he
Fallen to such deep reverse;—his melody
Is interrupted—now we hear the din
Of madmen, shriek on shriek, again begin;

Let us now visit him; after this strain
He ever communes with himself again,
And sees nor hears not any.' Having said   270
These words we called the keeper, and he led
To an apartment opening on the sea—
There the poor wretch was sitting mournfully
Near a piano, his pale fingers twined
One with the other, and the ooze and wind
Rushed through an open casement, and did sway
His hair, and starred it with the brackish spray;
His head was leaning on a music book,
And he was muttering, and his lean limbs shook;
His lips were pressed against a folded leaf   280
In hue too beautiful for health, and grief
Smiled in their motions as they lay apart—
As one who wrought from his own fervid heart
The eloquence of passion, soon he raised
His sad meek face and eyes lustrous and glazed
And spoke—sometimes as one who wrote, and thought
His words might move some heart that heeded not,
If sent to distant lands: and then as one
Reproaching deeds never to be undone
With wondering self-compassion; then his speech   290
Was lost in grief, and then his words came each
Unmodulated, cold, expressionless,—
But that from one jarred accent you might guess
It was despair made them so uniform:
And all the while the loud and gusty storm
Hissed through the window, and we stood behind
Stealing his accents from the envious wind
Unseen. I yet remember what he said
Distinctly: such impression his words made.

'Month after month,' he cried, 'to bear this load   300
And as a jade urged by the whip and goad
To drag life on, which like a heavy chain
Lengthens behind with many a link of pain!—
And not to speak my grief—O, not to dare
To give a human voice to my despair,
But live and move, and, wretched thing! smile on
As if I never went aside to groan,
And wear this mask of falsehood even to those
Who are most dear—not for my own repose—
Alas! no scorn or pain or hate could be   310
So heavy as that falsehood is to me—
But that I cannot bear more altered faces

Than needs must be, more changed and cold embraces,
More misery, disappointment, and mistrust
To own me for their father . . . Would the dust
Were covered in upon my body now!
That the life ceased to toil within my brow!
And then these thoughts would at the least be fled;
Let us not fear such pain can vex the dead.

'What Power delights to torture us? I know   320
That to myself I do not wholly owe
What now I suffer, though in part I may.
Alas! none strewed sweet flowers upon the way
Where wandering heedlessly, I met pale Pain
My shadow, which will leave me not again—
If I have erred, there was no joy in error,
But pain and insult and unrest and terror;
I have not as some do, bought penitence
With pleasure, and a dark yet sweet offence,
For then,—if love and tenderness and truth   330
Had overlived hope's momentary youth,
My creed should have redeemed me from repenting;
But loathèd scorn and outrage unrelenting
Met love excited by far other seeming
Until the end was gained . . . as one from dreaming
Of sweetest peace, I woke, and found my state
Such as it is.——
                          'O Thou, my spirit's mate
Who, for thou art compassionate and wise,
Wouldst pity me from thy most gentle eyes
If this sad writing thou shouldst ever see—   340
My secret groans must be unheard by thee,
Thou wouldst weep tears bitter as blood to know
Thy lost friend's incommunicable woe.

'Ye few by whom my nature has been weighed
In friendship, let me not that name degrade
By placing on your hearts the secret load
Which crushes mine to dust. There is one road
To peace and that is truth, which follow ye!
Love sometimes leads astray to misery.
Yet think not though subdued—and I may well   350
Say that I am subdued—that the full Hell
Within me would infect the untainted breast
Of sacred nature with its own unrest;
As some perverted beings think to find
In scorn or hate a medicine for the mind
Which scorn or hate have wounded—O how vain!

The dagger heals not but may rend again . . .
Believe that I am ever still the same
In creed as in resolve, and what may tame
My heart, must leave the understanding free,   360
Or all would sink in this keen agony—
Nor dream that I will join the vulgar cry;
Or with my silence sanction tyranny;
Or seek a moment's shelter from my pain
In any madness which the world calls gain,
Ambition or revenge or thoughts as stern
As those which make me what I am; or turn
To avarice or misanthropy or lust . . .
Heap on me soon, O grave, thy welcome dust!
Till then the dungeon may demand its prey,   370
And Poverty and Shame may meet and say—
Halting beside me on the public way—
"That love-devoted youth is ours—let's sit
Beside him—he may live some six months yet."
Or the red scaffold, as our country bends,
May ask some willing victim, or ye friends
May fall under some sorrow which this heart
Or hand may share or vanquish or avert;
I am prepared—in truth with no proud joy—
To do or suffer aught, as when a boy   380
I did devote to justice and to love
My nature, worthless now! . . .
                                   'I must remove
A veil from my pent mind. 'Tis torn aside!
O, pallid as Death's dedicated bride,
Thou mockery which art sitting by my side,
Am I not wan like thee? at the grave's call
I haste, invited to thy wedding-ball
To greet the ghastly paramour, for whom
Thou hast deserted me . . . and made the tomb
Thy bridal bed . . . But I beside your feet   390
Will lie and watch ye from my winding sheet—
Thus . . . wide awake tho' dead . . . yet stay, O stay!
Go not so soon—I know not what I say—
Hear but my reasons . . I am mad, I fear,
My fancy is o'erwrought . . thou art not here . . .
Pale art thou, 'tis most true . . but thou art gone,
Thy work is finished . . . I am left alone!—
         .   .   .   .   .

'Nay, was it I who wooed thee to this breast
Which, like a serpent, thou envenomest
As in repayment of the warmth it lent?   400

673

Didst thou not seek me for thine own content?
Did not thy love awaken mine? I thought
That thou wert she who said, "You kiss me not
Ever, I fear you do not love me now"—
In truth I loved even to my overthrow
Her, who would fain forget these words: but they
Cling to her mind, and cannot pass away.

   .   .   .   .   .   .

  'You say that I am proud—that when I speak
My lip is tortured with the wrongs which break
The spirit it expresses . . . Never one   410
Humbled himself before, as I have done!
Even the instinctive worm on which we tread
Turns, though it wound not—then with prostrate head
Sinks in the dusk and writhes like me—and dies?
No: wears a living death of agonies!
As the slow shadows of the pointed grass
Mark the eternal periods, his pangs pass
Slow, ever-moving,—making moments be
As mine seem—each an immortality!

   .   .   .   .   .   .

  'That you had never seen me—never heard   420
My voice, and more than all had ne'er endured
The deep pollution of my loathed embrace—
That your eyes ne'er had lied love in my face—
That, like some maniac monk, I had torn out
The nerves of manhood by their bleeding root
With mine own quivering fingers, so that ne'er
Our hearts had for a moment mingled there
To disunite in horror—these were not
With thee, like some suppressed and hideous thought
Which flits athwart our musings, but can find   430
No rest within a pure and gentle mind . . .
Thou sealedst them with many a bare broad word,
And searedst my memory o'er them,—for I heard
And can forget not . . . they were ministered
One after one, those curses. Mix them up
Like self-destroying poisons in one cup,
And they will make one blessing which thou ne'er
Didst imprecate for, on me,—death.

   .   .   .   .   .   .

                       'It were
A cruel punishment for one most cruel,
If such can love, to make that love the fuel   440
Of the mind's hell; hate, scorn, remorse, despair:
But *me*—whose heart a stranger's tear might wear

674

As water-drops the sandy fountain-stone,
Who loved and pitied all things, and could moan
For woes which others hear not, and could see
The absent with the glance of phantasy,
And with the poor and trampled sit and weep,
Following the captive to his dungeon deep;
Me—who am as a nerve o'er which do creep
The else unfelt oppressions of this earth,   450
And was to thee the flame upon thy hearth,
When all beside was cold—that thou on me
Shouldst rain these plagues of blistering agony—
Such curses are from lips once eloquent
With love's too partial praise—let none relent
Who intend deeds too dreadful for a name
Henceforth, if an example for the same
They seek . . . for thou on me lookedst so, and so—
And didst speak thus . . and thus . . . I live to show
How much men bear and die not!

      . . . .

               'Thou wilt tell,   460
With the grimace of hate, how horrible
It was to meet my love when thine grew less;
Thou wilt admire how I could e'er address
Such features to love's work . . . this taunt, though true,
(For indeed Nature nor in form nor hue
Bestowed on me her choicest workmanship)
Shall not be thy defence . . . for since thy lip
Met mine first, years long past, since thine eye kindled
With soft fire under mine, I have not dwindled
Nor changed in mind or body, or in aught   470
But as love changes what it loveth not
After long years and many trials.
                 'How vain
Are words! I thought never to speak again,
Not even in secret,—not to my own heart—
But from my lips the unwilling accents start,
And from my pen the words flow as I write,
Dazzling my eyes with scalding tears . . . my sight
Is dim to see that charactered in vain
On this unfeeling leaf which burns the brain
And eats into it . . . blotting all things fair   480
And wise and good which time had written there.

  'Those who inflict must suffer, for they see
The work of their own hearts, and this must be
Our chastisement or recompense—O child!

I would that thine were like to be more mild
For both our wretched sakes . . . for thine the most
Who feelest already all that thou hast lost
Without the power to wish it thine again;
And as slow years pass, a funereal train
Each with the ghost of some lost hope or friend   490
Following it like its shadow, wilt thou bend
No thought on my dead memory?

  .   .   .   .

                              'Alas, love!
Fear me not . . . against thee I would not move
A finger in despite. Do I not live
That thou mayst have less bitter cause to grieve?
I give thee tears for scorn and love for hate;
And that thy lot may be less desolate
Than his on whom thou tramplest, I refrain
From that sweet sleep which medicines all pain.
Then, when thou speakest of me, never say   500
"He could forgive not." Here I cast away
All human passions, all revenge, all pride;
I think, speak, act no ill; I do but hide
Under these words, like embers, every spark
Of that which has consumed me—quick and dark
The grave is yawning . . . as its roof shall cover
My limbs with dust and worms under and over
So let Oblivion hide this grief . . . the air
Closes upon my accents, as despair
Upon my heart—let death upon despair!'   510

  He ceased, and overcome leant back awhile,
Then rising, with a melancholy smile
Went to a sofa, and lay down, and slept
A heavy sleep, and in his dreams he wept
And muttered some familiar name, and we
Wept without shame in his society.
I think I never was impressed so much;
The man who were not, must have lacked a touch
Of human nature . . . then we lingered not,
Although our argument was quite forgot,   520
But calling the attendants, went to dine
At Maddalo's; yet neither cheer nor wine
Could give us spirits, for we talked of him
And nothing else, till daylight made stars dim;
And we agreed his was some dreadful ill
Wrought on him boldly, yet unspeakable,
By a dear friend; some deadly change in love

Of one vowed deeply which he dreamed not of;
For whose sake he, it seemed, had fixed a blot
Of falsehood on his mind which flourished not   530
But in the light of all-beholding truth;
And having stamped this canker on his youth
She had abandoned him—and how much more
Might be his woe, we guessed not—he had store
Of friends and fortune once, as we could guess
From his nice habits and his gentleness;
These were now lost . . . it were a grief indeed
If he had changed one unsustaining reed
For all that such a man might else adorn.
The colours of his mind seemed yet unworn;   540
For the wild language of his grief was high,
Such as in measure were called poetry;
And I remember one remark which then
Maddalo made. He said: 'Most wretched men
Are cradled into poetry by wrong,
They learn in suffering what they teach in song.'

   If I had been an unconnected man
I, from this moment, should have formed some plan
Never to leave sweet Venice,—for to me
It was delight to ride by the lone sea;   550
And then, the town is silent—one may write
Or read in gondolas by day or night,
Having the little brazen lamp alight,
Unseen, uninterrupted; books are there,
Pictures, and casts from all those statues fair
Which were twin-born with poetry, and all
We seek in towns, with little to recall
Regrets for the green country. I might sit
In Maddalo's great palace, and his wit
And subtle talk would cheer the winter night   560
And make me know myself, and the firelight
Would flash upon our faces, till the day
Might dawn and make me wonder at my stay:
But I had friends in London too: the chief
Attraction here, was that I sought relief
From the deep tenderness that maniac wrought
Within me—'twas perhaps an idle thought—
But I imagined that if day by day
I watched him, and but seldom went away,
And studied all the beatings of his heart   570
With zeal, as men study some stubborn art
For their own good, and could by patience find

An entrance to the caverns of his mind,
I might reclaim him from his dark estate:
In friendships I had been most fortunate—
Yet never saw I one whom I would call
More willingly my friend; and this was all
Accomplished not; such dreams of baseless good
Oft come and go in crowds or solitude
And leave no trace—but what I now designed   580
Made for long years impression on my mind.
The following morning, urged by my affairs,
I left bright Venice.
                        After many years
And many changes I returned; the name
Of Venice, and its aspect, was the same;
But Maddalo was travelling far away
Among the mountains of Armenia.
His dog was dead. His child had now become
A woman; such as it has been my doom
To meet with few,—a wonder of this earth,   590
Where there is little of transcendent worth,—
Like one of Shakespeare's women: kindly she,
And, with a manner beyond courtesy,
Received her father's friend; and when I asked
Of the lorn maniac, she her memory tasked,
And told as she had heard the mournful tale:
'That the poor sufferer's health began to fail
Two years from my departure, but that then
The lady who had left him, came again.
Her mien had been imperious, but she now   600
Looked meek—perhaps remorse had brought her low.
Her coming made him better, and they stayed
Together at my father's—for I played,
As I remember, with the lady's shawl—
I might be six years old—but after all
She left him' . . . 'Why, her heart must have been tough:
How did it end?' 'And was not this enough?
They met—they parted'—'Child, is there no more?'
'Something within that interval which bore
The stamp of *why* they parted, *how* they met: 610
Yet if thine agèd eyes disdain to wet
Those wrinkled cheeks with youth's remembered tears,
Ask me no more, but let the silent years
Be closed and cered over their memory
As yon mute marble where their corpses lie.'
I urged and questioned still, she told me how
All happened—but the cold world shall not know.

218

The Triumph of Life

SWIFT as a spirit hastening to his task
Of glory and of good, the Sun sprang forth
Rejoicing in his splendour, and the mask

Of darkness fell from the awakened Earth—
The smokeless altars of the mountain snows
Flamed above crimson clouds, and at the birth

Of light, the Ocean's orison arose,
To which the birds tempered their matin lay.
All flowers in field or forest which unclose

Their trembling eyelids to the kiss of day,   10
Swinging their censers in the element,
With orient incense lit by the new ray

Burned slow and inconsumably, and sent
Their odorous sighs up to the smiling air;
And, in succession due, did continent,

Isle, ocean, and all things that in them wear
The form and character of mortal mould,
Rise as the Sun their father rose, to bear

Their portion of the toil, which he of old
Took as his own, and then imposed on them: 20
But I, whom thoughts which must remain untold

Had kept as wakeful as the stars that gem
The cone of night, now they were laid asleep
Stretched my faint limbs beneath the hoary stem

Which an old chestnut flung athwart the steep
Of a green Apennine: before me fled
The night; behind me rose the day; the deep

Was at my feet, and Heaven above my head,—
When a strange trance over my fancy grew
Which was not slumber, for the shade it spread   30

Was so transparent, that the scene came through
As clear as when a veil of light is drawn
O'er evening hills they glimmer; and I knew

That I had felt the freshness of that dawn
Bathed in the same cold dew my brow and hair,
And sate as thus upon that slope of lawn

Under the self-same bough, and heard as there
The birds, the fountains and the ocean hold
Sweet talk in music through the enamoured air,
And then a vision on my brain was rolled.   40

As in that trance of wondrous thought I lay,
This was the tenour of my waking dream:—
Methought I sate beside a public way

Thick strewn with summer dust, and a great stream
Of people there was hurrying to and fro,
Numerous as gnats upon the evening gleam,

All hastening onward, yet none seemed to know
Whither he went, or whence he came, or why
He made one of the multitude, and so

Was borne amid the crowd, as through the sky   50
One of the million leaves of summer's bier;
Old age and youth, manhood and infancy,

Mixed in one mighty torrent did appear,
Some flying from the thing they feared, and some
Seeking the object of another's fear;

And others, as with steps towards the tomb,
Pored on the trodden worms that crawled beneath,
And others mournfully within the gloom

Of their own shadow walked, and called it death;
And some fled from it as it were a ghost,   60
Half fainting in the affliction of vain breath:

But more, with motions which each other crossed,
Pursued or shunned the shadows the clouds threw,
Or birds within the noonday aether lost,

Upon that path where flowers never grew,—
And, weary with vain toil and faint for thirst,
Heard not the fountains, whose melodious dew

Out of their mossy cells forever burst;
Nor felt the breeze which from the forest told
Of grassy paths and wood-lawns interspersed   70

With overarching elms and caverns cold,
And violet banks where sweet dreams brood, but they
Pursued their serious folly as of old.

And as I gazed, methought that in the way
The throng grew wilder, as the woods of June
When the south wind shakes the extinguished day,

And a cold glare, intenser than the noon,
But icy cold, obscured with blinding light
The sun, as he the stars. Like the young moon—

When on the sunlit limits of the night   80
Her white shell trembles amid crimson air,
And whilst the sleeping tempest gathers might—

Doth, as a herald of its coming, bear
The ghost of her dead mother, whose dim form
Bends in dark aether from her infant's chair,—

So came a chariot on the silent storm
Of its own rushing splendour, and a Shape
So sate within, as one whom years deform,

Beneath a dusky hood and double cape,
Crouching within the shadow of a tomb;   90
And o'er what seemed the head a cloud-like crape

Was bent, a dun and faint aethereal gloom
Tempering the light. Upon the chariot's beam
A Janus-visaged Shadow did assume

The guidance of that wonder-wingèd team;
The shapes which drew it in thick lightnings
Were lost:—I heard alone on the air's soft stream

The music of their ever-moving wings.
All the four faces of that Charioteer
Had their eyes banded; little profit brings   100

Speed in the van and blindness in the rear,
Nor then avail the beams that quench the sun,—
Or that these banded eyes could pierce the sphere

681

Of all that is, has been or will be done;
So ill was the car guided—but it passed
With solemn speed majestically on.

The crowd gave way, and I arose aghast,
Or seemed to rise, so mighty was the trance,
And saw, like clouds upon the thunder-blast,

The million with fierce song and maniac dance   110
Raging around—such seemed the jubilee
As when to greet some conqueror's advance

Imperial Rome poured forth her living sea
From senate-house, and prison, and theatre,
When Freedom left those who upon the free

Had bound a yoke, which soon they stooped to bear.
Nor wanted here the just similitude
Of a triumphal pageant, for where'er

The chariot rolled, a captive multitude
Was driven;—all those who had grown old in power   120
Or misery,—all who have their age subdued

By action or by suffering, and whose hour
Was drained to its last sand in weal or woe,
So that the trunk survived both fruit and flower;—

All those whose fame or infamy must grow
Till the great winter lay the form and name
Of their own earth with them for ever low;—

All but the sacred few who could not tame
Their spirits to the conqueror—but as soon
As they had touched the world with living flame,   130

Fled back like eagles to their native noon,
Or those who put aside the diadem
Of earthly thrones or gems, till the last one

Were there, for they of Athens and Jerusalem,
Were neither mid the mighty captives seen,
Nor mid the ribald crowd that followed them,

Or fled before ... Swift, fierce and obscene.
The wild dance maddens in the van, and those
Who lead it—fleet as shadows on the green,

Outspeed the chariot, and without repose   140
Mix with each other in tempestuous measure
To savage music, wilder as it grows,

They, tortured by their agonizing pleasure,
Convulsed and on the rapid whirlwinds spun
Of that fierce Spirit, whose unholy leisure

Was soothed by mischief since the world begun,
Throw back their heads and loose their streaming hair;
And in their dance round her who dims the sun,

Maidens and youths fling their wild arms in air
As their feet twinkle; now recede, and now   150
Bending within each other's atmosphere,

Kindle invisibly—and as they glow,
Like moths by light attracted and repelled,
Oft to new bright destruction come and go,

Till like two clouds into one vale impelled,
That shake the mountains when their lightnings mingle
And die in rain—the fiery band which held

Their natures, snaps—ere the shock cease to tingle;
One falls and then another in the path
Senseless—nor is the desolation single,   160

Yet ere I can say *where*—the chariot hath
Passed over them—nor other trace I find
But as of foam after the ocean's wrath

Is spent upon the desert shore;—behind,
Old men and women foully disarrayed,
Shake their gray hairs in the insulting wind,

Limp in the dance and strain with limbs decayed,
To reach the car of light which leaves them still
Farther behind and deeper in the shade.

But not the less with impotence of will   170
They wheel, though ghastly shadows interpose
Round them and round each other, and fulfil

Their work, and in the dust whence they arose
Sink, and corruption veils them as they lie,
And frost in these performs what fire in those.

Struck to the heart by this sad pageantry,
Half to myself I said—'And what is this?
Whose shape is that within the car? And why—'

I would have added—'is all here amiss?—'
But a voice answered—'Life!'—I turned, and knew   180
(O Heaven, have mercy on such wretchedness!)

That what I thought was an old root which grew
To strange distortion out of the hill side,
Was indeed one of that deluded crew,

And that the grass, which methought hung so wide
And white, was but his thin discoloured hair,
And that the holes it vainly sought to hide,

Were or had been eyes:—'If thou canst, forbear
To join the dance, which I had well forborne!'
Said the grim Feature, of my thought aware.   190

'I will tell all that which to this deep scorn
Led me and my companions, and relate
The progress of the pageant since the morn;

'If thirst of knowledge doth not thus abate,
Follow it even to the night, but I
Am weary.'—Then like one who with the weight

Of his own words is staggered, wearily
He paused; and ere he could resume, I cried:
'First, who art thou?'—'Before thy memory,

'I feared, loved, hated, suffered, did and died,   200
And if the spark with which Heaven lit my spirit
Earth had with purer nutriment supplied,

'Corruption would not now thus much inherit
Of what was once Rousseau,—nor this disguise
Stained that within which still disdains to wear it;

'If I have been extinguished, yet there rise
A thousand beacons from the spark I bore'—
'And who are those chained to the car?'—'The wise,

'The great, the unforgotten,—they who wore
Mitres and helms and crowns, or wreaths of light,   210
Signs of thought's empire over thought—their lore

'Taught them not this, to know themselves; their might
Could not repress the mutiny within,
And for the morn of truth they feigned, deep night

'Caught them ere evening.'—'Who is he with chin
Upon his breast, and hands crossed on his chain?'—
'The child of a fierce hour; he sought to win

'The world, and lost all that it did contain
Of greatness, in its hope destroyed; and more
Of fame and peace than virtue's self can gain   220

'Without the opportunity which bore
Him on its eagle pinions to the peak
From which a thousand climbers have before

'Fallen, as Napoleon fell.'—I felt my cheek
Alter, to see the great form pass away,
Whose grasp had left the giant world so weak

That every pigmy kicked it as it lay;
And much I grieved to think how power and will
In opposition rule our mortal day,

And why God made irreconcilable   230
Good and the means of good; and for despair
I half disdained mine eyes' desire to fill

With the spent vision of the times that were
And scarce have ceased to be.—'Dost thou behold,'
Said my guide, 'those spoilers spoiled, Voltaire,

'Frederick, and Kant, Catherine, and Leopold,
And hoary anarchs, demagogue, and sage—
Whose name the fresh world thinks already old—

'For in the battle Life and they did wage,
She remained conqueror. I was overcome   240
By my own heart alone, which neither age,

'Nor tears, nor infamy, nor now the tomb
Could temper to its object.'—'Let them pass,'
I cried, 'the world and its mysterious doom

'Is not so much more glorious than it was,
That I desire to worship those who drew
New figures on its false and fragile glass

'As the old faded.'—'Figures ever new
Rise on the bubble, paint them how you may;
We have but thrown, as those before us threw,   250

'Our shadows on it as it passed away.
But mark how chained to the triumphal chair
The mighty phantoms of an elder day;

'All that is mortal of great Plato there
Expiates the joy and woe his master knew not;
The star that ruled his doom was far too fair,

'And life, where long that flower of Heaven grew not,
Conquered the heart by love, which gold, or pain,
Or age, or sloth, or slavery could subdue not.

'And near him walk the   twain,   260
The tutor and his pupil, whom Dominion
Followed as tame as vulture in a chain.

'The world was darkened beneath either pinion
Of him whom from the flock of conquerors
Fame singled as her thunder-bearing minion;

'The other long outlived both woes and wars,
Throned in new thoughts of men, and still had kept
The jealous keys of Truth's eternal doors,

'If Bacon's eagle spirit had not lept
Like lightning out of darkness—he compelled   270
The Proteus shape of Nature, as it slept

'To wake, and to unbar the caves that held
The treasure of the secrets of its reign.
See the great bards of old who inly quelled

'The passions which they sung, as by their strain
May well be known: their living melody
Tempers its own contagion to the vein

'Of those who are infected with it—I
Have suffered what I wrote, or viler pain!
And so my words have seeds of misery—   280

'Even as the deeds of others.' 'Not as theirs,'
I said—he pointed to a company,

In which I recognized amid the heirs
Of Caesar's crime, from him to Constantine;
The anarch old, whose force and murderous snares

Had founded many a sceptre-bearing line,
And spread the plague of gold and blood abroad:
And Gregory and John, and men divine,

Who rose like shadows between man and God;
Till that eclipse, still hanging over heaven,   290
Was worshipped by the world o'er which they strode,

For the true sun it quenched—'Their power was given
But to destroy,' replied the leader:—'I
Am one of those who have created, even

'If it be but a world of agony.'—
'Whence camest thou? and whither goest thou?
How did thy course begin?' I said, 'and why?

'Mine eyes are sick of this perpetual flow
Of people, and my heart of one sad thought—
Speak!'—'Whence I came, I partly seem to know,   300

'And how and by what paths I have been brought
To this dread pass, methinks even thou mayst guess;—
Why this should be, my mind can compass not;

'Whither the conqueror hurries me, still less;—
But follow thou, and from spectator turn
Actor or victim in this wretchedness,

'And what thou wouldst be taught I then may learn
From thee. Now listen:—In the April prime,
When all the forest-tops began to burn

'With kindling green, touched by the azure clime   310
Of the young year, I found myself asleep
Under a mountain, which from unknown time

'Had yawned into a cavern, high and deep;
And from it came a gentle rivulet,
Whose water, like clear air, in its calm sweep

'Bent the soft grass, and kept for ever wet
The stems of the sweet flowers, and filled the grove
With sound, which all who hear must needs forget

'All pleasure and all pain, all hate and love,
Which they had known before that hour of rest;   320
A sleeping mother then would dream not of

'Her only child who died upon the breast
At eventide—a king would mourn no more
The crown of which his brow was dispossessed

'When the sun lingered o'er the ocean floor
To gild his rival's new prosperity.
Thou wouldst forget thus vainly to deplore

'Ills, which if ills can find no cure from thee,
The thought of which no other sleep will quell,
Nor other music blot from memory,   330

'So sweet and deep is the oblivious spell;
Whether my life had been before that sleep
The Heaven which I imagine, or a Hell

'Like this harsh world in which I wake to weep,
I know not. I arose, and for a space
The scene of woods and waters seemed to keep,

'Though it was now broad day, a gentle trace
Of light diviner than the common sun
Sheds on the common earth, but all the place

'Was filled with many sounds woven into one   340
Oblivious melody, confusing sense
Amid the gliding waves and shadows dun;

'And, as I looked, the bright omnipresence
Of morning through the orient cavern flowed,
And the sun's image radiantly intense

'Burned on the waters of the well that glowed
Like gold, and threaded all the forest's maze
With winding paths of emerald fire; there stood

'Amid the sun, as he amid the blaze
Of his own glory, on the vibrating   350
Floor of the fountain, paved with flashing rays,

'A Shape all light, which with one hand did fling
Dew on the earth, as if she were the dawn,
Whose invisible rain for ever seemed to sing

'A silver music on the mossy lawn;
And still before her on the dusky grass,
Iris her many-coloured scarf had drawn:

'In her right hand she bore a crystal glass,
Mantling with bright Nepenthe; the fierce splendour
Fell from her as she moved under the mass   360

'Of the deep cavern, and with palms so tender,
Their tread broke not the mirror of its billow,
Glided along the river, and did bend her

'Head under the dark boughs, till like a willow
Her fair hair swept the bosom of the stream
That whispered with delight to be their pillow.

'As one enamoured is upborne in dream
O'er lily-paven lakes, mid silver mist,
To wondrous music, so this shape might seem

'Partly to tread the waves with feet which kissed   370
The dancing foam; partly to glide along
The airs that roughened the moist amethyst,

'Or the slant morning beams that fell among
The trees, or the soft shadows of the trees;
And her feet, ever to the ceaseless song

'Of leaves, and winds, and waves, and birds, and bees,
And falling drops, moved in a measure new
Yet sweet, as on the summer evening breeze,

'Up from the lake a shape of golden dew
Between two rocks, athwart the rising moon,   380
Dances i' the wind, where eagle never flew;

'And still her feet, no less than the sweet tune
To which they moved, seemed as they moved to blot
The thoughts of him who gazed on them; and soon

'All that was, seemed as if it had been not;
As if the gazer's mind was strewn beneath
Her feet like embers; and she, thought by thought,

'Trampled its fires into the dust of death;
As day upon the threshold of the east
Treads out the lamps of night, until the breath   390

'Of darkness re-illumines even the least
Of heaven's living eyes—like day she came,
Making the night a dream; and ere she ceased

'To move, as one between desire and shame
Suspended, I said—If, as it doth seem,
Thou comest from the realm without a name

'Into this valley of perpetual dream,
Show whence I came, and where I am, and why—
Pass not away upon the passing stream.

'Arise and quench thy thirst, was her reply.   400
And as a shut lily stricken by the wand
Of dewy morning's vital alchemy,

'I rose; and, bending at her sweet command,
Touched with faint lips the cup she raised,
And suddenly my brain became as sand

'Where the first wave had more than half erased
The track of deer on desert Labrador;
Whilst the fierce wolf, from which they fled amazed,

'Leaves his stamp visibly upon the shore,
Until the second bursts;—so on my sight   410
Burst a new vision, never seen before,

'And the fair shape waned in the coming light,
As veil by veil the silent splendour drops
From Lucifer, amid the chrysolite

'Of sunrise, ere it strike the mountain-tops;
And as the presence of that fairest planet,
Although unseen, is felt by one who hopes

'That his day's path may end as he began it,
In that star's smile, whose light is like the scent
Of a jonquil when evening breezes fan it,   420

'Or the soft notes in which his dear lament
The Brescian shepherd breathes, or the caress
That turned his weary slumber to content;

'So knew I in that light's severe excess
The presence of that Shape which on the stream
Moved, as I moved along the wilderness,

'More dimly than a day-appearing dream,
The ghost of a forgotten form of sleep;
A light from heaven, whose half-extinguished beam

'Through the sick day in which we wake to weep   430
Glimmers, for ever sought, for ever lost;
So did that shape its obscure tenour keep

'Beside my path, as silent as a ghost;
But the new Vision, and its cold bright car,
With savage music, stunning music, crossed

'The forest, and as if from some dread war
Triumphantly returning, the loud million
Fiercely extolled the fortune of her star.

'A moving arch of victory, the vermilion
And green and azure plumes of Iris had   440
Built high over her wind-wingèd pavilion,

'And underneath aethereal glory clad
The wilderness, and far before her flew
The tempest of the splendour, which forbade

'Shadow to fall from leaf or stone; the crew
Seemed in that light, like atomies that dance
Within a sunbeam;—some upon the new

'Embroidery of flowers, that did enhance
The grassy vesture of the desert, played,
Forgetful of the chariot's swift advance;   450

'Others stood gazing, till within the shade
Of the great mountain its light left them dim;
Others outspeeded it; and others made

'Circles around it, like the clouds that swim
Round the high moon in a bright sea of air;
And more did follow, with exulting hymn,

'The chariot and the captives fettered there:—
But all like bubbles on an eddying flood
Fell into the same track at last, and were

'Borne onward.—I among the multitude   460
Was swept—me, sweetest flowers delayed not long;
Me, not the shadow nor the solitude;

'Me, not the falling stream's Lethean song;
Me, not the phantom of that early Form
Which moved upon its motion—but among

'The thickest billows of the living storm
I plunged, and bared my bosom to the clime
Of that cold light, whose airs too soon deform.

'Before the chariot had begun to climb
The opposing steep of that mysterious dell,   470
Behold a wonder worthy of the rhyme

'Of him who from the lowest depths of hell,
Through every paradise and through all glory,
Love led serene, and who returned to tell

'In words of hate and awe the wondrous story
How all things are transfigured except Love;
For deaf as is a sea, which wrath makes hoary,

'The world can hear not the sweet notes that move
The sphere whose light is melody to lovers—
A wonder worthy of his rhyme.—The grove   480

'Grew dense with shadows to its inmost covers,
The earth was gray with phantoms, and the air
Was peopled with dim forms, as when there hovers

'A flock of vampire-bats before the glare
Of the tropic sun, bringing, ere evening,
Strange night upon some Indian isle;—thus were

'Phantoms diffused around; and some did fling
Shadows of shadows, yet unlike themselves,
Behind them; some like eaglets on the wing

'Were lost in the white day; others like elves   490
Danced in a thousand unimagined shapes
Upon the sunny streams and grassy shelves;

'And others sate chattering like restless apes
On vulgar paws and voluble like fire.
Some made a cradle of the ermined capes

'Of kingly mantles; some across the tiar
Of pontiffs sate like vultures; others played
Within the crown which girt with empire

'A baby's or an idiot's brow, and made
Their nests in it. The old anatomies   500
Sate hatching their bare brood under the shade

'Of daemon wings, and laughed from their dead eyes
To reassume the delegated power,
Arrayed in which those worms did monarchize,

'Who make this earth their charnel. Others more
Humble, like falcons, sate upon the fist
Of common men, and round their heads did soar;

'Or like small gnats and flies, as thick as mist
On evening marshes, thronged about the brow
Of lawyer, statesman, priest and theorist;—   510

'And others, like discoloured flakes of snow
On fairest bosoms and the sunniest hair,
Fell, and were melted by the youthful glow

'Which they extinguished; for like tears, they were
A veil to those from whose faint lids they rained
In drops of sorrow. I became aware

'Of whence those forms proceeded which thus stained
The track in which we moved. After brief space,
From every form the beauty slowly waned;

'From every firmest limb and fairest face   520
The strength and freshness fell like dust, and left
The action and the shape without the grace

'Of life. The marble brow of youth was cleft
With care; and in the eyes where once hope shone,
Desire, like a lioness bereft

'Of its last cub, glared ere it died; each one
Of that great crowd sent forth incessantly
These shadows, numerous as the dead leaves blown

'In autumn evening from a poplar tree.
Each like himself and like each other were   530
At first; but soon distorted seemed to be

'Obscure clouds, moulded by the casual air;
And of this stuff the car's creative ray
Wrought all the busy phantoms that were there,

'As the sun shapes the clouds; thus on the way
Mask after mask fell from the countenance
And form of all; and long before the day

'Was old, the joy which waked like heaven's glance
The sleepers in the oblivious valley, died;
And some grew weary of the ghastly dance,   540

'And fell, as I have fallen, by the wayside;—
Those soonest from whose forms most shadows passed,
And least of strength and beauty did abide.'

'Then, what is life?' I said—the cripple cast
His eye upon the car which now had rolled
Onward, as if that look must be the last,

And answered—'Happy those for whom the fold
Of

219   *Sonnet*

> Lift not the painted veil which those who live
> Call Life: though unreal shapes be pictured there,
> And it but mimic all we would believe
> With colours idly spread,—behind, lurk Fear
> And Hope, twin Destinies; who ever weave
> Their shadows, o'er the chasm, sightless and drear.
> I knew one who had lifted it—he sought,
> For his lost heart was tender, things to love,
> But found them not, alas! nor was there aught
> The world contains, the which he could approve.   10
> Through the unheeding many he did move,
> A splendour among shadows, a bright blot
> Upon this gloomy scene, a Spirit that strove
> For truth, and like the Preacher found it not.

GEORGE GORDON, LORD BYRON

220   *Messalonghi. January 22, 1824.*
On this day I Complete my Thirty-Sixth Year

> 'Tis time this heart should be unmoved,
>   Since others it hath ceased to move:
> Yet though I cannot be beloved,
>   Still let me love!
>
> My days are in the yellow leaf;
>   The flowers and fruits of Love are gone;
> The worm—the canker, and the grief
>   Are mine alone!
>
> The fire that on my bosom preys
>   Is lone as some Volcanic Isle;   10
> No torch is kindled at its blaze
>   A funeral pile!
>
> The hope, the fear, the jealous care,
>   The exalted portion of the pain
> And power of Love I cannot share,
>   But wear the chain.

But 'tis not *thus*—and 'tis not *here*
  Such thoughts should shake my Soul, nor *now*
Where Glory decks the hero's bier
        Or binds his brow.   20

The Sword, the Banner, and the Field,
  Glory and Greece around us see!
The Spartan borne upon his shield
        Was not more free!

Awake (not Greece—she *is* awake!)
  Awake, my Spirit! think through *whom*
Thy life-blood tracks its parent lake
        And then strike home!

Tread those reviving passions down
  Unworthy Manhood—unto thee   30
Indifferent should the smile or frown
        Of Beauty be.

If thou regret'st thy Youth, *why live?*
  The land of honourable Death
Is here:—up to the Field, and give
        Away thy Breath!

Seek out—less often sought than found—
  A Soldier's Grave, for thee the best;
Then look around, and choose thy Ground,
        And take thy Rest!   40

[1825]

FELICIA DOROTHEA HEMANS
1793–1835

221   *The Lost Pleiad*

Like the lost Pleiad seen no more below.
BYRON

AND is there glory from the heavens departed?
  —Oh! void unmark'd!—thy sisters of the sky
    Still hold their place on high,

Though from its rank thine orb so long hath started,
Thou, that no more art seen of mortal eye.

Hath the night lost a gem, the regal night?
    She wears her crown of old magnificence,
        Though thou art exil'd thence—
No desert seems to part those urns of light,
'Midst the far depths of purple gloom intense.   10

They rise in joy, the starry myriads burning—
    The shepherd greets them on his mountains free;
        And from the silvery sea
To them the sailor's wakeful eye is turning—
Unchang'd they rise, they have not mourn'd for thee.

Couldst thou be shaken from thy radiant place
    Ev'n as a dew-drop from the myrtle spray,
        Swept by the wind away?
Wert thou not peopled by some glorious race,
And was there power to smite them with decay?   20

Why, who shall talk of thrones, of sceptres riven?
    —Bow'd be our hearts to think of what *we* are,
        When from its height afar
A world sinks thus—and yon majestic heaven
Shines not the less for that one vanish'd star!

222   *The Hour of Death*

    LEAVES have their time to fall,
And flowers to wither at the north-wind's breath,
    And stars to set—but all,
Thou hast all seasons for thine own, oh! Death.

    Day is for mortal care,
Eve for glad meetings round the joyous hearth,
   Night for the dreams of sleep, the voice of prayer—
But all for thee, thou Mightiest of the earth.

    The banquet hath its hour,
Its feverish hour of mirth, and song, and wine;   10
   There comes a day for grief's o'erwhelming power,
A time for softer tears—but all are thine.

Youth and the opening rose
May look like things too glorious for decay,
    And smile at thee—but thou art not of those
That wait the ripen'd bloom to seize their prey.

Leaves have their time to fall,
And flowers to wither at the north-wind's breath,
    And stars to set—but all,
Thou hast all seasons for thine own, oh! Death.   20

We know when moons shall wane,
When summer-birds from far shall cross the sea,
    When autumn's hue shall tinge the golden grain—
But who shall teach us when to look for thee?—

Is it when Spring's first gale
Comes forth to whisper where the violets lie?
    Is it when roses in our paths grow pale?—
They have *one* season—*all* are ours to die!

Thou art where billows foam,
Thou art where music melts upon the air;   30
    Thou art around us in our peaceful home,
And the world calls us forth—and thou art there.

Thou art where friend meets friend,
Beneath the shadow of the elm to rest—
    Thou art where foe meets foe, and trumpets rend
The skies, and swords beat down the princely crest.

Leaves have their time to fall,
And flowers to wither at the north-wind's breath,
    And stars to set—but all,
Thou hast all seasons for thine own, oh! Death.   40

223   *A Child Screening a Dove from a Hawk*

By Stewardson

AY, screen thy favourite dove, fair child,
    Ay, screen it if you may,—
Yet I misdoubt thy trembling hand
    Will scare the hawk away.

That dove will die, that child will weep,—
    Is this their destinie?
Ever amid the sweets of life
    Some evil thing must be.

Ay, moralize,—is it not thus
    We've mourn'd our hope and love?   10
Alas! there's tears for every eye,
    A hawk for every dove.

224   *The Enchanted Island*

By Danby

AND there the island lay, the waves around
Had never known a storm; for the north wind
Was charm'd from coming, and the only airs
That blew brought sunshine on their azure wings,
Or tones of music from the sparry caves,
Where the sea-maids make lutes of the pink conch.
These were sea breezes,—those that swept the land
Brought other gifts,—sighs from blue violets,
Or from June's sweet Sultana, the bright rose,
Stole odours. On the silver mirror's face   10
Was but a single ripple that was made
By a flamingo's beak, whose scarlet wings
Shone like a meteor on the stream: around,
Upon the golden sands, were coral plants,
And shells of many colours, and sea weeds,
Whose foliage caught and chain'd the Nautilus,

Where lay they as at anchor. On each side
Were grottoes, like fair porticoes with steps
Of the green marble; and a lovely light,
Like the far radiance of a thousand lamps,   20
Half-shine, half-shadow, or the glorious track
Of a departing star but faintly seen
In the dim distance, through those caverns shone,
And play'd o'er the tall trees which seem'd to hide
Gardens, where hyacinths rang their soft bells
To call the bees from the anemone,
Jealous of their bright rivals' golden wealth.
—Amid those arches floated starry shapes,
Just indistinct enough to make the eye
Dream of surpassing beauty; but in front,   30
Borne on a car of pearl, and drawn by swans,
There lay a lovely figure,—she was queen
Of the Enchanted Island, which was raised
From ocean's bosom but to pleasure her:
And spirits, from the stars, and from the sea,
The beautiful mortal had them for her slaves.

She was the daughter of a king, and loved
By a young Ocean Spirit from her birth,—
He hover'd o'er her in her infancy,
And bade the rose grow near her, that her cheek   40
Might catch its colour,—lighted up her dreams
With fairy wonders, and made harmony
The element in which she moved; at last,
When that she turn'd away from earthly love,
Enamour'd of her visions, he became
Visible with his radiant wings, and bore
His bride to the fair island.

THOMAS HOOD
1799–1845

225 *Faithless Nelly Gray*

A Pathetic Ballad

BEN Battle was a soldier bold,
　　And used to war's alarms;
But a cannon-ball took off his legs,
　　So he laid down his arms!

Now as they bore him off the field,
　　Said he, 'Let others shoot,
For here I leave my second leg,
　　And the Forty-second Foot!'

The army-surgeons made him limbs:
　　Said he,—'They're only pegs:　　　　10
But there's as wooden members quite,
　　As represent my legs!'

Now Ben he loved a pretty maid,
　　Her name was Nelly Gray;
So he went to pay her his devours,
　　When he'd devour'd his pay!

But when he called on Nelly Gray,
　　She made him quite a scoff;
And when she saw his wooden legs,
　　Began to take them off!　　　　20

'O, Nelly Gray! O, Nelly Gray!
　　Is this your love so warm?
The love that loves a scarlet coat,
　　Should be more uniform!'

Said she, 'I loved a soldier once,
　　For he was blythe and brave;
But I will never have a man
　　With both legs in the grave!

'Before you had those timber toes,
   Your love I did allow,
But then, you know, you stand upon
   Another footing now!'   30

'O, Nelly Gray! O, Nelly Gray!
   For all your jeering speeches,
At duty's call, I left my legs
   In Badajos's *breaches!*'

'Why, then,' said she, 'you've lost the feet
   Of legs in war's alarms,
And now you cannot wear your shoes
   Upon your feats of arms!'   40

'O, false and fickle Nelly Gray!
   I know why you refuse:—
Though I've no feet—some other man
   Is standing in my shoes!

'I wish I ne'er had seen your face;
   But, now, a long farewell!
For you will be my death:—alas!
   You will not be my *Nell!*'

Now when he went from Nelly Gray,
   His heart so heavy got—   50
And life was such a burthen grown,
   It made him take a knot!

So round his melancholy neck,
   A rope he did entwine,
And, for his second time in life,
   Enlisted in the Line!

One end he tied around a beam,
   And then removed his pegs,
And, as his legs were off,—of course,
   He soon was off his legs!   60

And there he hung, till he was dead
   As any nail in town,—
For though distress had cut him up,
   It could not cut him down!

A dozen men sat on his corpse,
    To find out why he died—
And they buried Ben in four cross-roads,
    With a *stake* in his inside!

226   *Jack Hall*

'TIS very hard when men forsake
This melancholy world, and make
A bed of turf, they cannot take
                    A quiet doze,
But certain rogues will come and break
                    Their 'bone repose.'

'Tis hard we can't give up our breath,
And to the earth our earth bequeath,
Without Death Fetches after death,
                    Who thus exhume us;   10
And snatch us from our homes beneath,
                    And hearths posthumous.

The tender lover comes to rear
The mournful urn, and shed his tear—
Her glorious dust, he cries, is here!
                    Alack! alack!
The while his Sacharissa dear
                    Is in a sack!

'Tis hard one cannot lie amid
The mould, beneath a coffin-lid,   20
But thus the Faculty will bid
                    Their rogues break thro' it!
If they don't want us there, why did
                    They send us to it?

One of these sacrilegious knaves,
Who crave as hungry vulture craves,
Behaving as the ghoul behaves,
                    'Neath church-yard wall—
Mayhap because he fed on graves,
                    Was nam'd Jack Hall.   30

By day it was his trade to go
Tending the black coach to and fro;

And sometimes at the door of woe,
    With emblems suitable,
He stood with brother Mute, to show
    That life is mutable.

But long before they pass'd the ferry,
The dead that he had help'd to bury,
He sack'd—(he had a sack to carry
    The bodies off in.)   40
In fact, he let them have a very
    Short fit of coffin.

Night after night, with crow and spade,
He drove this dead but thriving trade,
Meanwhile his conscience never weigh'd
    A single horsehair;
On corses of all kinds he prey'd,
    A perfect corsair!

At last—it may be, Death took spite,
Or jesting only meant to fright—   50
He sought for Jack night after night
    The churchyards round;
And soon they met, the man and sprite,
    In Pancras' ground.

Jack, by the glimpses of the moon,
Perceiv'd the bony knacker soon,
An awful shape to meet at noon
    Of night and lonely;
But Jack's tough courage did but swoon
    A minute only.   60

Anon he gave his spade a swing
Aloft, and kept it brandishing,
Ready for what mishaps might spring
    From this conjunction;
Funking indeed was quite a thing
    Beside his function.

'Hollo!' cried Death, 'd'ye wish your sands
Run out? the stoutest never stands
A chance with me,—to my commands
    The strongest truckles;   70
But I'm your friend—so let's shake hands,
    I should say—knuckles.'

Jack, glad to see th' old sprite so sprightly,
And meaning nothing but uprightly,
Shook hands at once, and, bowing slightly,
            His mull did proffer:
But Death, who had no nose, politely
            Declin'd the offer.

Then sitting down upon a bank,
Leg over leg, shank over shank,   80
Like friends for conversation frank,
            That had no check on:
Quoth Jack unto the Lean and Lank,
            'You're Death, I reckon.'

The Jaw-bone grinn'd:—'I am that same,
You've hit exactly on my name;
In truth it has some little fame
            Where burial sod is.'
Quoth Jack, (and wink'd,) 'of course ye came
            Here after bodies.'   90

Death grinn'd again and shook his head:—
'I've little business with the dead;
When they are fairly sent to bed
            I've done my turn;
Whether or not the worms are fed
            Is your concern.

'My errand here, in meeting you,
Is nothing but a "how-d'ye do;"
I've done what jobs I had—a few
            Along this way;   100
If I can serve a crony too,
            I beg you'll say.'

Quoth Jack, 'Your Honour's very kind:
And now I call the thing to mind,
This parish very strict I find;
            But in the next 'un
There lives a very well-inclin'd
            Old sort of sexton.'

Death took the hint, and gave a wink
As well as eyelet holes can blink;   110
Then stretching out his arm to link
            The other's arm,—

'Suppose,' says he, 'we have a drink
              Of something warm.'

Jack nothing loth, with friendly ease
Spoke up at once:—'Why, what ye please;
Hard by there is the Cheshire Cheese,
              A famous tap.'
But this suggestion seem'd to teaze
              The bony chap.   120

'No, no—your mortal drinks are heady,
And only make my hand unsteady;
I do not even care for Deady,
              And loathe your rum;
But I've some glorious brewage ready,
              My drink is—mum!'

And off they set, each right content—
Who knows the dreary way they went?
But Jack felt rather faint and spent,
              And out of breath;   130
At last he saw, quite evident,
              The door of Death.

All other men had been unmann'd
To see a coffin on each hand,
That served a skeleton to stand
              By way of sentry;
In fact, Death has a very grand
              And awful entry.

Throughout his dismal sign prevails,
His name is writ in coffin nails,
The mortal darts make area rails;   140
              A scull that mocketh,
Grins on the gloomy gate, and quails
              Whoever knocketh.

And lo! on either side, arise
Two monstrous pillars—bones of thighs;
A monumental slab supplies
              The step of stone,
Where waiting for his master lies
              A dog of bone.   150

The dog leapt up, but gave no yell,
The wire was pull'd, but woke no bell,
The ghastly knocker rose and fell,
              But caused no riot;
The ways of Death, we all know well
              Are very quiet.

Old Bones stept in; Jack stepp'd behind.
Quoth Death, 'I really hope you'll find
The entertainment to your mind,
              As I shall treat ye—   160
A friend or two of goblin kind,
              I've asked to meet ye.'

And lo! a crowd of spectres tall,
Like jack-a-lanterns on a wall,
Were standing—every ghastly ball
              An eager watcher.
'My friends,' says Death—'friends, Mr. Hall,
              The body-snatcher.'

Lord, what a tumult it produc'd,
When Mr. Hall was introduced!   170
Jack even, who had long been used
              To frightful things,
Felt just as if his back was sluic'd
              With freezing springs!

Each goblin face began to make
Some horrid mouth—ape—gorgon—snake;
And then a spectre-hag would shake
              An airy thigh-bone;
And cried, (or seem'd to cry,) I'll break
              Your bone, with *my* bone!   180

Some ground their teeth—some seem'd to spit—
(Nothing, but nothing came of it,)
A hundred awful brows were knit
              In dreadful spite.
Thought Jack—I'm sure I'd better quit,
              Without good night.

One skip and hop and he was clear,
And running like a hunted deer,
As fleet as people run by fear
              Well spurr'd and whipp'd,   190

Death, ghosts, and all in that career
            Were quite outstripp'd.

But those who live by death must die;
Jack's soul at last prepar'd to fly;
And when his latter end drew nigh,
            Oh! what a swarm
Of doctors came,—but not to try
            To keep him warm.

No ravens ever scented prey
So early where a dead horse lay,   200
Nor vultures sniff'd so far away
            A last convulse;
A dozen 'guests' day after day
            Were 'at his pulse.'

'Twas strange, altho' they got no fees,
How still they watch'd by twos and threes:
But Jack a very little ease
            Obtain'd from them;
In fact he did not find M. D.s
            Worth one D—M.   210

The passing bell with hollow toll
Was in his thought—the dreary hole!
Jack gave his eyes a horrid roll,
            And then a cough:—
'There's something weighing on my soul
            I wish was off;

'All night it roves about my brains,
All day it adds to all my pains,
It is concerning my remains
            When I am dead;'   220
Twelve wigs and twelve gold-headed canes
            Drew near his bed.

'Alas!' he sighed, 'I'm sore afraid,
A dozen pangs my heart invade;
But when I drove a certain trade
            In flesh and bone,
There was a little bargain made
            About my own.'

Twelve suits of black began to close,
Twelve pair of sleek and sable hose,   230
Twelve flowing cambric frills in rows,
   At once drew round;
Twelve noses turn'd against his nose,
   Twelve snubs profound.

'Ten guineas did not quite suffice,
And so I sold my body twice;
Twice did not do—I sold it thrice,
   Forgive my crimes!
In short I have received its price
   A dozen times!'   240

Twelve brows got very grim and black,
Twelve wishes stretch'd him on the rack,
Twelve pair of hands for fierce attack
   Took up position,
Ready to share the dying Jack
   By long division.

Twelve angry doctors wrangled so,
That twelve had struck an hour ago,
Before they had an eye to throw
   On the departed;   250
Twelve heads turn'd round at once, and lo!
   Twelve doctors started.

Whether some comrade of the dead,
Or Satan took it in his head
To steal the corpse—the corpse had fled!
   'Tis only written,
That *'there was nothing in the bed,*
   But twelve were bitten!'

WINTHROP MACKWORTH PRAED

227 *The Chaunts of the Brazen Head*

II

As for me, I am growing sick of all things: every day there is the
same routine of pleasure or of weariness; the same loungers at the
Club, the same fashionables in the Park; the same criticisms on
the last Opera, the same anticipations of the next; the same speeches
in Parliament, the same advertisements in the Newspaper. There is
nothing new beneath the sun.

The Head

THE world pursues the very track
   Which it pursued at its creation;
And mortals shrink in horror back
   From any hint of innovation:
From year to year the children do
   Exactly what their sires have done;
Time is! time was!—there's nothing new,—
   There's nothing new beneath the sun!

Still lovers hope to be believed,
   Still clients hope to win their causes;   10
Still plays and farces are received
   With most encouraging applauses;
Still dancers have fantastic toes;
   Still dandies shudder at a dun;
Still dinners have their fricandeaus,—
   There's nothing new beneath the sun!

Still cooks torment the hapless eels,
   Still boys torment the dumb cockchafers;
Lord Eldon still adores the seals,
   Lord Clifford still adores the wafers;   20
Still asses have enormous ears,
   Still gambling bets are lost and won;
Still opera-dancers marry peers,—
   There's nothing new beneath the sun!

Still women are absurdly weak,
   Still infants dote upon a rattle;
Still Mr. Martin cannot speak
   Of any thing but beaten cattle;

Still brokers swear the shares will rise,
  Still cockneys boast of Manton's gun;   30
Still listeners swallow monstrous lies,—
  There's nothing new beneath the sun!

Still genius is a jest to earls,
  Still honesty is down to zero;
Still heroines have spontaneous curls,
  Still novels have a handsome hero;
Still Madame Vestris plays a man,
  Still fools adore her, I for one;
Still youths write sonnets to a fan,—
  There's nothing new beneath the sun!   40

Still people make a plaguy fuss,
  About all things that don't concern them,
As if it matters aught to us,
  What happens to our grandsons, burn them!
Still life is nothing to the dead,
  Still Folly's toil is Wisdom's fun;
And still, except the Brazen Head,—
  There's nothing new beneath the sun!

[1827]

SAMUEL BAMFORD

228   *The Pass of Death*

*Written Shortly after the Decease of the Right Honourable
George Canning, and with reference to that Event*

ANOTHER'S gone, and who comes next,
  Of all the sons of pride?
And is humanity perplex'd
  Because this man hath died?
The sons of men did raise their voice
  And criéd in despair,
'We will not come, we will not come,
  Whilst Death is waiting there!'

But Time went forth and dragg'd them on,
  By one, by two, by three;   10

Nay, sometimes thousands came as one,
    So merciless was he!
And still they go, and still they go,
    The slave, the lord, the king;
And disappear, like flakes of snow,
    Before the sun of spring!

For Death stood in the path of Time,
    And slew them as they came,
And not a soul escap'd his hand,
    So certain was his aim.
The beggar fell across his staff,
    The soldier on his sword,
The king sank down beneath his crown,
    The priest beside the Word.

And Youth came in his blush of health,
    And in a moment fell;
And Avarice, grasping still at wealth,
    Was rolléd into hell;
And Age stood trembling at the pass,
    And would have turned again;
But Time said, 'No, 'tis never so,
    Thou canst not here remain.'

The bride came in her wedding robe—
    But that did nought avail;
Her ruby lips went cold and blue,
    Her rosy cheek turn'd pale!
And some were hurried from the ball,
    And some came from the play;
And some were eating to the last,
    And some with wine were gay.

And some were ravenous for food,
    And rais'd seditious cries;
But, being a 'legitimate,'
    Death quickly stopp'd their noise!
The father left his infant brood
    Amid the world to weep;
The mother died whilst her babe
    Lay smiling in its sleep!

And some did offer bribes of gold,
    If they might but survive;
But he drew his arrow to the head,
    And left them not alive!

And some were plighting vows of love,
  When their very hearts were torn;
And eyes that shone so bright at eve
  Were closéd ere the morn!

And one had just attained to pow'r,
  He wist not he should die;
Till the arrow smote his stream of life,
  And left the cistern dry!—   60
Another's gone, and who comes next,
  Of all the sons of pride?
And is humanity perplexed
  Because this man hath died?

And still they come, and still they go,
  And still there is no end,—
The hungry grave is yawning yet,
  And who shall next descend?
Oh! shall it be a crownéd head,
  Or one of noble line?   70
Or doth the slayer turn to smite
  A life so frail as mine?

GEORGE DARLEY

229   from *Sylvia; or, The May Queen*

A VIEW like one of Fairy-land,
As gay, as gorgeous, and as grand;
Millions of bright star-lustres hung
The glittering leaves and boughs among;
High-battled, domy palaces,
Seen crystal through the glimmering trees,
With spires and glancing minarets,
Just darting from their icy seats:
Pavilions, diamond-storied towers,
Dull'd by the aromatic bowers;   10
Transparent peaks and pinnacles,
Like streams shot upward from their wells,
Or cave-dropt, Parian icicles.
  Green haunts, and deep enquiring lanes,
Wind through the trunks their grassy trains;
Millions of chaplets curl unweft
From boughs, beseeching to be reft,

To prune the clustering of their groves,
And wreathe the brows that Beauty loves.
Millions of blossoms, fruits, and gems,   20
Bend with rich weight the massy stems;
Millions of restless dizzy things,
With ruby tufts, and rainbow wings,
Speckle the eye-refreshing shades,
Burn through the air, or swim the glades:
As if the tremulous leaves were tongues,
Millions of voices, sounds, and songs,
Breathe from the aching trees that sigh,
Near sick of their own melody.
   Raised by a magic breath whene'er   30
The pow'rs of Fairyland are here,
And by a word as potent blown
To sightless air, when they are gone,
This scene of beauty now displays
Both flank and front in sheets of blaze:
Spirits in an ascending quire
Touch with soft palm the golden wire:
While some on wing, some on the ground,
In mazy circles whirl around;
Kissing and smiling, as they pass,   40
Like sweet winds o'er the summer grass.

(from I. ii)

FELICIA DOROTHEA HEMANS

230   *Night-Blowing Flowers*

CALL back your odours, lonely flowers,
   From the night-wind call them back,
And fold your leaves till the laughing hours
   Come forth on the sunbeam's track!

The lark lies couch'd in his grassy nest,
   And the honey-bee is gone,
And all bright things are away to rest—
   Why watch ye thus alone?

Is not your world a mournful one,
   When your sisters close their eyes,   10
And your soft breath meets not a lingering tone
   Of song in the starry skies?

Take ye no joy in the dayspring's birth,
   When it kindles the sparks of dew?
And the thousand strains of the forest's mirth,
   Shall they gladden all but you?

Shut your sweet bells till the fawn comes out
   On the sunny turf to play,
And the woodland child, with a fairy shout,
   Goes dancing on his way.   20

Nay, let our shadowy beauty bloom
   When the stars give quiet light;
And let us offer our faint perfume
   On the silent shrine of night.

Call it not wasted, the scent we lend
   To the breeze when no step is nigh;
Oh! thus for ever the earth should send
   Her grateful breath on high!

And love us as emblems, night's dewy flowers,
   Of hopes unto sorrow given,   30
That spring through the gloom of the darkest hours,
   Looking alone to Heaven!

LAETITIA ELIZABETH LANDON

from *The Golden Violet*

231   *Song*

My heart is like the failing hearth
      Now by my side,
One by one its bursts of flame
      Have burnt and died
There are none to watch the sinking blaze,
      And none to care,
Or if it kindle into strength,
      Or waste in air.
My fate is as yon faded wreath
      Of summer flowers;   10
They've spent their store of fragrant health
      On sunny hours,

Which reck'd them not, which heeded not
    When they were dead;
Other flowers, unwarn'd by them
    Will spring instead.
And my own heart is as the lute
    I am now waking;
Wound to too fine and high a pitch
    They both are breaking.   20
And of their song what memory
    Will stay behind?
An echo, like a passing thought,
    Upon the wind.
Silence, forgetfulness, and rust,
    Lute, are for thee:
And such my lot; neglect, the grave,
    These are for me.

232   *Song*

    WHERE, O! where's the chain to fling,
    One that will bind CUPID's wing,
    One that will have longer power
    Than the April sun or shower?
    Form it not of Eastern gold,
    All too weighty it to hold;
    Form it neither all of bloom,
    Never does love find a tomb
    Sudden, soon, as when he meets
    Death amid unchanging sweets: 10
    But if you would fling a chain,
    And not fling it all in vain,
    Like a fairy form a spell
    Of all that is changeable,
    Take the purple tints that deck,
    Meteorlike, the peacock's neck;
    Take the many hues that play
    On the rainbow's colour'd way;
    Never let a hope appear
    Without its companion fear;   20
    Only smile to sigh, and then
    Change into a smile again;
    Be to-day as sad, as pale,
    As minstrel with his lovelorn tale;
    But to-morrow gay as all

Life had been one festival.
If a woman would secure
All that makes her reign endure,
And, alas! her reign must be
Ever most in fantasy,   30
Never let an envious eye
Gaze upon the heart too nigh;
Never let the veil be thrown
Quite aside, as all were known
Of delight and tenderness,
In the spirit's last recess;
And, one spell all spells above,
Never let her own her love.

[1828]

JOHN HERMAN MERIVALE
1779–1844

233   from [*Meleager*]

HAIL, universal mother! lightly rest
      On that dead form,
Which, when with life invested, ne'er oppress'd
      Its fellow worm.

FELICIA DOROTHEA HEMANS

234   *The Effigies*

Der rasche Kampf verewigt einen Mann:
Er falle gleich, so preiset ihn das Lied.
Allein die Thränen, die unendlichen
Der überbleibnen, der verlass'nen Frau,
Zählt keine Nachwelt.

                                        GOETHE

WARRIOR! whose image on thy tomb,
      With shield and crested head,
Sleeps proudly in the purple gloom
      By the stain'd window shed;

The records of thy name and race
　　Have faded from the stone,
Yet, through a cloud of years I trace
　　What thou hast been and done.

A banner, from its flashing spear
　　Flung out o'er many a fight,　　　　　　　　10
A war-cry ringing far and clear,
　　And strong to turn the flight;
An arm that bravely bore the lance
　　On for the holy shrine;
A haughty heart and a kingly glance—
　　Chief! were not these things thine?

A lofty place where leaders sate
　　Around the council-board;
In festive halls a chair of state
　　When the blood-red wine was pour'd;　　　20
A name that drew a prouder tone
　　From herald, harp, and bard;—
Surely these things were all thine own,
　　So hadst thou thy reward.

Woman! whose sculptur'd form at rest
　　By the arm'd knight is laid,
With meek hands folded o'er a breast
　　In matron robes array'd;
What was *thy* tale?—Oh! gentle mate
　　Of him, the bold and free,　　　　　　　　30
Bound unto his victorious fate,
　　What bard hath sung of *thee?*

He wooed a bright and burning star—
　　Thine was the void, the gloom,
The straining eye that follow'd far
　　His fast receding plume;
The heart-sick listening while his steed
　　Sent echoes on the breeze;
The pang—but when did *Fame* take heed
　　Of griefs obscure as these?　　　　　　　　40

Thy silent and secluded hours
　　Through many a lonely day,
While bending o'er thy broider'd flowers,
　　With spirit far away;
Thy weeping midnight prayers for him
　　Who fought on Syrian plains,

Thy watchings till the torch grew dim—
  These fill no minstrel strains.

A still, sad life was thine!—long years
  With tasks unguerdon'd fraught,   50
Deep, quiet love, submissive tears,
  Vigils of anxious thought;
Prayer at the cross in fervor pour'd,
  Alms to the pilgrim given—
Oh! happy, happier than thy lord,
  In that lone path to heaven!

235   *The Graves of a Household*

THEY grew in beauty, side by side,
  They fill'd one home with glee;—
Their graves are sever'd, far and wide,
  By mount, and stream, and sea.

The same fond mother bent at night
  O'er each fair sleeping brow;
She had each folded flower in sight,—
  Where are those dreamers now?

One, midst the forests of the west,
  By a dark stream is laid—   10
The Indian knows his place of rest,
  Far in the cedar shade.

The sea, the blue lone sea, hath one,
  He lies where pearls lie deep;
He was the lov'd of all, yet none
  O'er his low bed may weep.

One sleeps where southern vines are drest
  Above the noble slain:
He wrapt his colours round his breast,
  On a blood-red field of Spain.   20

And one—o'er *her* the myrtle showers
  Its leaves, by soft winds fann'd;
She faded midst Italian flowers,—
  The last of that bright band.

And parted thus they rest, who play'd
    Beneath the same green tree;
Whose voices mingled as they pray'd
    Around one parent knee!

They that with smiles lit up the hall,
    And cheer'd with song the hearth,—   30
Alas! for love, if *thou* wert all,
    And nought beyond, oh, earth!

236   *The Image in Lava*

THOU thing of years departed!
    What ages have gone by,
Since here the mournful seal was set
    By love and agony!

Temple and tower have moulder'd,
    Empires from earth have pass'd,—
And woman's heart hath left a trace
    Those glories to outlast!

And childhood's fragile image,
    Thus fearfully enshrin'd,   10
Survives the proud memorials rear'd
    By conquerors of mankind.

Babe! wert thou brightly slumbering
    Upon thy mother's breast,
When suddenly the fiery tomb
    Shut round each gentle guest?

A strange, dark fate o'ertook you,
    Fair babe and loving heart!
One moment of a thousand pangs—
    Yet better than to part!   20

Haply of that fond bosom,
    On ashes here impress'd,
Thou wert the only treasure, child!
    Whereon a hope might rest.

Perchance all vainly lavish'd
    Its other love had been,

And where it trusted, nought remain'd
  But thorns on which to lean.

Far better then to perish,
  Thy form within its clasp,   30
Than live and lose thee, precious one!
  From that impassion'd grasp.

Oh! I could pass all relics
  Left by the pomps of old,
To gaze on this rude monument,
  Cast in affection's mould.

Love, human love! what art thou?
  Thy print upon the dust
Outlives the cities of renown
  Wherein the mighty trust!   40

237   *The Homes of England*

> Where's the coward that would not dare
> To fight for such a land?
>
>   *Marmion*

THE stately Homes of England,
  How beautiful they stand!
Amidst their tall ancestral trees,
  O'er all the pleasant land.
The deer across their greensward bound
  Thro' shade and sunny gleam,
And the swan glides past them with the sound
  Of some rejoicing stream.

The merry Homes of England!
  Around their hearths by night,   10
What gladsome looks of household love
  Meet, in the ruddy light!
There woman's voice flows forth in song,
  Or childhood's tale is told,
Or lips move tunefully along
  Some glorious page of old.

The blessed Homes of England!
  How softly on their bowers

Is laid the holy quietness
 That breathes from Sabbath-hours!   20
Solemn, yet sweet, the church-bell's chime
 Floats thro' their woods at morn;
All other sounds, in that still time,
 Of breeze and leaf are born.

The Cottage Homes of England!
 By thousands on her plains,
They are smiling o'er the silvery brooks,
 And round the hamlet-fanes.
Thro' glowing orchards forth they peep,
 Each from its nook of leaves,   30
And fearless there the lowly sleep,
 As the bird beneath their eaves.

The free, fair Homes of England!
 Long, long, in hut and hall,
May hearts of native proof be rear'd
 To guard each hallow'd wall!
And green for ever be the groves,
 And bright the flowery sod,
Where first the child's glad spirit loves
 Its country and its God!   40

GEORGE DARLEY

238   *A Song*

IT is not beautie I demande,
 A christalle browe, the moone's despaire,
Nor the snowe's daughter, a whyte hand,
 Nor mermaide's yellowe pryde of haire.

Tell mee not of youre starrie eies,
 Your lips that seeme on roses fedde, .
Your breastes where Cupide tombling lyes,
 Nor sleepes for kissing of his bedde.

A bloomie paire of vermeil cheekes
 Like Hebe's in her roddiest houres,   10
A breath that softer musicke speakes
 Than summer windes a-wooing floures.

These are but gawdes: nay, what are lips?
  Corall beneathe the ocean-streame,
Whose brinke when youre adventurer slips,
  Full oft hee perisheth on themme.

And what are cheekes but ensignes ofte
  That wave hot youthe to fieldes of bloode?
Did Helene's breaste, though ere so softe,
  Do Greece or Ilium anie goode?   20

Eies can with balefulle ardoure burne,
  Poison can breath that erste perfumede,
There's manie a whyte hande holdes an urne
  With lovers' hearts to dust consumede.

For christalle browes, there's nought within,
  They are but emptie cells for pryde;
Hee who the syrenne's haire woulde winne
  Is mostlie stranglede in the tyde.

Give mee, insteade of beautie's buste,
  A tender heart, a loyale minde,   30
Which with temptation I coulde truste,
  Yet never linkde with erroure finde.

One in whose gentle bosome, I
  Coulde poure mie secrete heart of woes,
Like the care-burthenede honie flie
  That hides his murmurrs in the rose.

Mie earthlie comfortoure! whose love
  So indefeisible might bee,
That when mie spirite wonne above,
  Hers could not staye for sympathie.   40

CHARLES LAMB

Verses for an Album

FRESH clad from heaven in robes of white,
A young probationer of light,
Thou wert, my soul, an Album bright,

A spotless leaf; but thought, and care,
And friends, and foes, in foul or fair,
Have 'written strange defeature' there;

And Time, with heaviest hand of all,
Like that fierce writing on the wall,
Hath stamp'd sad dates—he can't recal;

And error, gilding worst designs—   10
Like speckled snake that strays and shines—
Betrays his path by crooked lines;

And vice hath left his ugly blot;
And good resolves, a moment hot,
Fairly began—but finish'd not;

And fruitless, late remorse doth trace—
Like Hebrew lore, a backward pace—
Her irrecoverable race.

Disjointed numbers; sense unknit;
Huge reams of folly; shreds of wit;   20
Compose the mingled mass of it.

My scalded eyes no longer brook
Upon this ink-blurr'd thing to look—
Go, shut the leaves, and clasp the book.

240   *Constancy to an Ideal Object*

SINCE all that beat about in Nature's range,
Or veer or vanish; why should'st thou remain
The only constant in a world of change,
O yearning Thought! that liv'st but in the brain?
Call to the Hours, that in the distance play,
The faery people of the future day——

Fond Thought! not one of all that shining swarm
Will breathe on thee with life-enkindling breath,
Till when, like strangers shelt'ring from a storm,
Hope and Despair meet in the porch of Death!   10
Yet still thou haunt'st me; and though well I see,
She is not thou, and only thou art she,
Still, still as though some dear embodied Good,
Some living Love before my eyes there stood
With answering look a ready ear to lend,
I mourn to thee and say—'Ah! loveliest friend!
That this the meed of all my toils might be,
To have a home, an English home, and thee!'
Vain repetition! Home and Thou are one.
The peacefull'st cot, the moon shall shine upon,   20
Lulled by the thrush and wakened by the lark,
Without thee were but a becalméd bark,
Whose Helmsman on an ocean waste and wide
Sits mute and pale his mouldering helm beside.

And art thou nothing? Such thou art, as when
The woodman winding westward up the glen
At wintry dawn, where o'er the sheep-track's maze
The viewless snow-mist weaves a glist'ning haze,
Sees full before him, gliding without tread,
An image with a glory round its head;   30
The enamoured rustic worships its fair hues,
Nor knows he makes the shadow, he pursues!

WINTHROP MACKWORTH PRAED

241   *Arrivals at a Watering-Place*

SCENE—*A Conversazione at Lady Crumpton's.—Whist and weariness, Cari-
catures and Chinese Puzzle.—Young Ladies making tea, and Young Gentlemen
making the agreeable.—The Stable-Boy handing rout-cakes.—Music expressive
of there being nothing to do.*

I PLAY a spade:—Such strange new faces
    Are flocking in from near and far:
Such frights—Miss Dobbs holds all the aces,—
    One can't imagine who they are!
The Lodgings at enormous prices,
    New Donkeys, and another fly;
And Madame Bonbon out of ices,
    Although we're scarcely in July:
We're quite as sociable as any,
    But our old horse can scarcely crawl;   10
And really where there are so many,
    We can't tell where we ought to call.

Pray who has seen the odd old fellow
    Who took the Doctor's house last week?—
A pretty chariot,—livery yellow,
    Almost as yellow as his cheek:
A widower, sixty-five, and surly,
    And stiffer than a poplar-tree;
Drinks rum and water, gets up early
    To dip his carcass in the sea: 20
He's always in a monstrous hurry,
    And always talking of Bengal;
They say his cook makes noble curry;—
    I think, Louisa, we should call.

And so Miss Jones, the mantua-maker,
    Has let her cottage on the hill?—
The drollest man, a sugar-baker,—
    Last year imported from the till:
Prates of his 'orses and his 'oney,
    Is quite in love with fields and farms;   30

726

A horrid Vandal,—but his money
   Will buy a glorious coat of arms;
Old Clyster makes him take the waters;
   Some say he means to give a ball;
And after all, with thirteen daughters,
   I think, Sir Thomas, you might call.

That poor young man!—I'm sure and certain
   Despair is making up his shroud:
He walks all night beneath the curtain
   Of the dim sky and murky cloud: 40
Draws landscapes,—throws such mournful glances!—
   Writes verses,—has such splendid eyes;
An ugly name,—but Laura fancies
   He's some great person in disguise!—
And since his dress is all the fashion,
   And since he's very dark and tall,
I think that, out of pure compassion,
   I'll get Papa to go and call.

So Lord St Ives is occupying
   The whole of Mr Ford's Hotel;   50
Last Saturday his man was trying
   A little nag I want to sell.
He brought a lady in the carriage;
   Blue eyes,—eighteen, or thereabouts;—
Of course, you know, we *hope* it's marriage!
   But yet the *femme de chambre* doubts.
She look'd so pensive when we met her;
   Poor thing! and such a charming shawl!—
Well! till we understand it better,
   It's quite impossible to call!   60

Old Mr Fund, the London banker,
   Arrived to-day at Premium Court;
I would not, for the world, cast anchor
   In such a horrid dangerous port;
Such dust and rubbish, lath and plaster,—
   (Contractors play the meanest tricks)—
The roof's as crazy as its master,
   And he was born in fifty-six:
Stairs creaking—cracks in every landing,—
   The colonnade is sure to fall;—   70
We shan't find post or pillar standing,
   Unless we make great haste to call.

Who was that sweetest of sweet creatures,
    Last Sunday, in the Rector's seat?
The finest shape,—the loveliest features,—
    I never saw such tiny feet.
My brother,—(this is quite between us)
    Poor Arthur,—'twas a sad affair!
Love at first sight,—she's quite a Venus,—
    But then she's poorer far than fair: 80
And so my father and my mother
    Agreed it would not do at all;
And so,—I'm sorry for my brother!—
    It's settled that we're not to call.

And there's an Author, full of knowledge;
    And there's a Captain on half-pay;
And there's a Baronet from college,
    Who keeps a boy, and rides a bay;
And sweet Sir Marcus from the Shannon,
    Fine specimen of brogue and bone;   90
And Doctor Calipee, the canon,
    Who weighs, I fancy, twenty stone:
A maiden Lady is adorning
    The faded front of Lily Hall:—
Upon my word, the first fine morning,
    We'll make a round, my dear, and call.

Alas! disturb not, maid and matron,
    The swallow in my humble thatch;
Your son may find a better patron,
    Your niece may meet a richer match: 100
I can't afford to give a dinner,
    I never was on Almack's list;
And since I seldom rise a winner,
    I never like to play at whist;
Unknown to me the stocks are falling;
    Unwatched by me the glass may fall;
Let all the world pursue its calling,—
    I'm not at home if people call.

242

Beauty and her Visitors

I

I LOOKED for Beauty:—on a throne,
   A dazzling throne of light, I found her;
And music poured its softest tone,
   And flowers their sweetest breath, around her.
A score or two of idle gods,
   Some dressed as Peers, and some as Peasants
Were watching all her smiles and nods,
   And making compliments, and presents.

II

And first young Love, the rosy boy,
   Exhibited his bow and arrows,   10
And gave her many a pretty toy,
   Torches, and bleeding hearts, and sparrows:
She told him, as he passed, she knew
   Her court would scarcely do without him;
But yet—she hoped they were not true—
   There *were* some awkward tales about him.

III

Wealth deemed that magic had no charm
   More mighty than the gifts he brought her,
And linked around her radiant arm
   Bright diamonds of the purest water: 20
The Goddess, with a scornful touch,
   Unclasped the gaudy, galling fetter;
And said,—she thanked him very much,—
   She liked a wreath of roses better.

IV

Then Genius snatched his golden lute,
   And told a tale of love and glory;
The crowd around were hushed and mute
   To hear so sad and sweet a story;
And Beauty marked the minstrel's cheek,
   So very pale—no bust was paler;—   30
Vowed she could listen for a week;
   But really—he *should* change his tailor!

V

As died the echo of the strings,
   A shadowy Phantom kneeled before her,
Looked all unutterable things,
   And swore to see was to adore her;
He called her veil a cruel cloud,
   Her cheek a rose, her smile a battery;
She fancied it was Wit that bowed,—
   I'm almost certain it was Flattery.   40

VI

There was a Beldame finding fault
   With every person's every feature,
And by the sneer, and by the halt,
   I knew at once the odious creature;
'You see,' quoth Envy, 'I am come
   To bow—as is my bounden duty;—
They tell me Beauty is at home;—
   Impossible! that *can't* be Beauty!'

VII

I heard a murmur far and wide
   Of 'Lord! how quick the dotard passes!'   50
As Time threw down at Beauty's side
   The prettiest of his clocks and glasses:
But it was noticed in the throng,
   How Beauty marred the maker's cunning;
For, when she talked, the hands went wrong,
   And, when she smiled, the sands stopped running.

VIII

Death, in a Doctor's wig and gown,
   Came, arm in arm with Lethe, thither,
And crowned her with a withered crown,
   And hinted, Beauty too must wither!   60
'Avaunt!' she cried; 'how came he here?
   The frightful fiend—he's my abhorrence!'
I went and whispered in her ear,
   'He shall not hurt you;—sit to Lawrence!'

243

Casabianca

Young Casabianca, a boy about thirteen years old, son to the admiral of the Orient, remained at his post (in the battle of the Nile), after the ship had taken fire, and all the guns had been abandoned; and perished in the explosion of the vessel, when the flames had reached the powder.

THE boy stood on the burning deck,
    Whence all but him had fled;
The flame that lit the battle's wreck,
    Shone round him o'er the dead.

Yet beautiful and bright he stood,
    As born to rule the storm;
A creature of heroic blood,
    A proud, though child-like form.

The flames roll'd on—he would not go,
    Without his father's word;   10
That father, faint in death below,
    His voice no longer heard.

He call'd aloud—'Say, father, say
    If yet my task is done?'
He knew not that the chieftain lay
    Unconscious of his son.

'Speak, Father!' once again he cried,
    'If I may yet be gone!'
—And but the booming shots replied,
    And fast the flames roll'd on.   20

Upon his brow he felt their breath
    And in his waving hair;
And look'd from that lone post of death,
    In still, yet brave despair.

And shouted but once more aloud,
    'My father! must I stay?'
While o'er him fast, through sail and shroud,
    The wreathing fires made way.

They wrapt the ship in splendor wild,
   They caught the flag on high,   30
And stream'd above the gallant child,
   Like banners in the sky.

There came a burst of thunder sound—
   The boy—oh! where was he?
—Ask of the winds that far around
   With fragments strew'd the sea!

With mast, and helm, and pennon fair,
   That well had borne their part—
But the noblest thing that perish'd there,
   Was that young faithful heart.   40

LAETITIA ELIZABETH LANDON

244   *Revenge*

Ay, gaze upon her rose-wreath'd hair,
   And gaze upon her smile:
Seem as you drank the very air
   Her breath perfumed the while:

And wake for her the gifted line,
   That wild and witching lay,
And swear your heart is as a shrine,
   That only owns her sway.

'Tis well: I am revenged at last,—
   Mark you that scornful cheek,—   10
The eye averted as you pass'd,
   Spoke more than words could speak.

Ay, now by all the bitter tears,
   That I have shed for thee,—
The racking doubts, the burning fears,—
   Avenged they well may be—

By the nights pass'd in sleepless care,
   The days of endless wo;
All that you taught my heart to bear,
   All that yourself will know.   20

I would not wish to see you laid
    Within an early tomb;
I should forget how you betray'd,
    And only weep your doom:

But this is fitting punishment
    To live and love in vain,—
O my wrung heart, be thou content,
    And feed upon his pain.

Go thou and watch her lightest sigh,—
    Thine own it will not be;
And back beneath her sunny eye,—   30
    It will not turn on thee.

'Tis well: the rack, the chain, the wheel,
    Far better hadst thou proved;
Ev'n I could almost pity feel,
    For thou art not beloved.

245   *Lines of Life*

Orphan in my first years, I early learnt
To make my heart suffice itself, and seek
Support and sympathy in its own depths.

    WELL, read my cheek, and watch my eye,—
        Too strictly school'd are they,
    One secret of my soul to show,
        One hidden thought betray.

    I never knew the time my heart
        Look'd freely from my brow;
    It once was check'd by timidness,
        'T is taught by caution now.

    I live among the cold, the false,
        And I must seem like them;   10
    And such I am, for I am false
        As those I most condemn.

    I teach my lip its sweetest smile,
        My tongue its softest tone;
    I borrow others' likeness, till
        Almost I lose my own.

733

I pass through flattery's gilded sieve,
    Whatever I would say;
In social life, all, like the blind,
    Must learn to feel their way.   20

I check my thoughts like curbed steeds
    That struggle with the rein;
I bid my feelings sleep, like wrecks
    In the unfathom'd main.

I hear them speak of love, the deep,
    The true, and mock the name;
Mock at all high and early truth,
    And I too do the same.

I hear them tell some touching tale,
    I swallow down the tear;   30
I hear them name some generous deed,
    And I have learnt to sneer.

I hear the spiritual, the kind,
    The pure, but named in mirth;
Till all of good, ay, even hope,
    Seems exiled from our earth.

And one fear, withering ridicule,
    Is all that I can dread;
A sword hung by a single hair
    For ever o'er the head.   40

We bow to a most servile faith,
    In a most servile fear;
While none among us dares to say
    What none will choose to hear.

And if we dream of loftier thoughts,
    In weakness they are gone;
And indolence and vanity
    Rivet our fetters on.

Surely I was not born for this!
    I feel a loftier mood   50
Of generous impulse, high resolve,
    Steal o'er my solitude!

I gaze upon the thousand stars
    That fill the midnight sky;

And wish, so passionately wish,
    A light like theirs on high.

I have such eagerness of hope
    To benefit my kind;
And feel as if immortal power
    Were given to my mind.   60

I think on that eternal fame,
    The sun of earthly gloom,
Which makes the gloriousness of death,
    The future of the tomb—

That earthly future, the faint sign
    Of a more heavenly one;
—A step, a word, a voice, a look,—
    Alas! my dream is done.

And earth, and earth's debasing stain,
    Again is on my soul;   70
And I am but a nameless part
    Of a most worthless whole.

Why write I this? because my heart
    Towards the future springs,
That future where it loves to soar
    On more than eagle wings.

The present, it is but a speck
    In that eternal time,
In which my lost hopes find a home,
    My spirit knows its clime.   80

Oh! not myself,—for what am I?—
    The worthless and the weak,
Whose every thought of self should raise
    A blush to burn my cheek.

But song has touch'd my lips with fire,
    And made my heart a shrine;
For what, although alloy'd, debased,
    Is in itself divine.

I am myself but a vile link
    Amid life's weary chain;   90
But I have spoken hallow'd words,
    Oh do not say in vain!

My first, my last, my only wish,
   Say will my charmed chords
Wake to the morning light of fame,
   And breathe again my words?

Will the young maiden, when her tears
   Alone in moonlight shine—
Tears for the absent and the loved—
   Murmur some song of mine?   100

Will the pale youth by his dim lamp,
   Himself a dying flame,
From many an antique scroll beside,
   Choose that which bears my name?

Let music make less terrible
   The silence of the dead;
I care not, so my spirit last
   Long after life has fled.

246   ['Lady, thy face is very beautiful']

LADY, thy face is very beautiful,
A calm and stately beauty: thy dark hair
Hangs as the passing winds paid homage there;
And gems, such gems as only princes cull
From earth's rich veins, are round thy neck and arm;
Ivory, with just one touch of colour warm;
And thy white robe floats queen-like, suiting well
A shape such as in ancient pictures dwell!
  If thou hadst lived in that old haunted time,
When sovereign Beauty was a thing sublime,   10
For which knights went to battle, and her glove
Had even more of glory than of love;—
Hadst thou lived in those days, how chivalrie,
With brand and banner, would have honour'd thee!
Then had this picture been a chronicle,
Of whose contents might only poets tell
What king had worn thy chains, what heroes sigh'd,
What thousands nameless, hopeless, for thee died.
But thou art of the Present—there is nought
About thee for the dreaming minstrel's thought,   20
Save vague imagination, which still lives

Upon the charmed light all beauty gives.
What hath romancing lute, or fancied line,
Or colour'd words to do with thee or thine?
No, the chords sleep in silence at thy feet,
They have no measures for thy music meet;
The poet hath no part in it, his dream
Would too much idleness of flattery seem;
And to that lovely picture only pays
The wordless homage of a lingering gaze.   30

EBENEZER ELLIOTT
1781–1849

247   from *The Village Patriarch*

FIVE rivers, like the fingers of a hand,
Flung from black mountains, mingle, and are one
Where sweetest valleys quit the wild and grand,
And eldest forests, o'er the silvan Don,
Bid their immortal brother journey on,
A stately pilgrim, watch'd by all the hills.
Say, shall we wander, where, through warriors' graves,
The infant Yewden, mountain-cradled, trills
Her doric notes? Or, where the Locksley raves
Of broil and battle, and the rocks and caves   10
Dream yet of ancient days? Or, where the sky
Darkens o'er Rivilin, the clear and cold,
That throws his blue length, like a snake, from high?
Or, where deep azure brightens into gold
O'er Sheaf, that mourns in Eden? Or, where roll'd
On tawny sands, through regions passion-wild,
And groves of love, in jealous beauty dark,
Complains the Porter, Nature's thwarted child,
Born in the waste, like headlong Wiming? Hark!
The pois'd hawk calls thee, Village Patriarch!   20
He calls thee to his mountains! Up, away!
Up, up, to Stanedge! higher still ascend,
Till kindred rivers, from the summit grey,
To distant seas their course in beauty bend,
And, like the lives of human millions, blend
Disparted waves in one immensity!

                                                (Book V. iii)

THOMAS LOVE PEACOCK

The War-Song of Dinas Vawr

I

THE mountain sheep are sweeter,
But the valley sheep are fatter;
We therefore deem'd it meeter
To carry off the latter.
We made an expedition;
We met a host and quell'd it;
We forced a strong position,
And kill'd the men who held it.

II

On Dyfed's richest valley,
Where herds of kine were browsing,   10
We made a mighty sally,
To furnish our carousing.
Fierce warriors rushed to meet us;
We met them, and o'erthrew them:
They struggled hard to beat us;
But we conquer'd them, and slew them.

III

As we drove our prize at leisure,
The king march'd forth to catch us:
His rage surpass'd all measure,
But his people could not match us.   20
He fled to his hall-pillars;
And, ere our force we led off,
Some sack'd his house and cellars,
While others cut his head off.

IV

We there, in strife bewild'ring,
Spilt blood enough to swim in:
We orphan'd many children,
And widow'd many women.
The eagles and the ravens
We glutted with our foemen: 30
The heroes and the cravens,
The spearmen and the bowmen.

V

We brought away from battle,
And much their land bemoan'd them,
Two thousand head of cattle,
And the head of him who owned them:
Ednyfed, King of Dyfed,
His head was borne before us;
His wine and beasts supplied our feasts,
And his overthrow, our chorus.   40

[1830]

FELICIA DOROTHEA HEMANS

249   *The Magic Glass*

How lived, how loved, how died they?
                                                      BYRON

'THE Dead! the glorious Dead!—And shall they rise?
Shall they look on thee with their proud bright eyes?
                  Thou ask'st a fearful spell!
Yet say, from shrine or dim sepulchral hall,
What kingly vision shall obey my call?
                  The deep grave knows it well!

'Wouldst thou behold earth's conquerors? shall they pass
Before thee, flushing all the Magic Glass
                  With triumph's long array?
Speak! and those dwellers of the marble urn,   10
Robed for the feast of victory, shall return,
                  As on their proudest day.

'Or wouldst thou look upon the lords of song?—
O'er the dark mirror that immortal throng
                  Shall waft a solemn gleam!
Passing, with lighted eyes and radiant brows,
Under the foliage of green laurel-boughs,
                  But silent as a dream.'

'Not these, O mighty master!—Though their lays
Be unto man's free heart, and tears, and praise,   20
                  Hallow'd for evermore!

And not the buried conquerors! Let them sleep,
And let the flowery earth her Sabbaths keep
   In joy, from shore to shore!

'But, if the narrow house may so be moved,
Call the bright shadows of the most beloved,
   Back from their couch of rest!
That I may learn if *their* meek eyes be fill'd
With peace, if human love hath ever still'd
   The yearning human breast.'   30

'Away, fond youth!—An idle quest is thine;
These have no trophy, no memorial shrine;
   I know not of their place!
'Midst the dim valleys, with a secret flow,
Their lives, like shepherd reed-notes, faint and low,
   Have pass'd, and left no trace.

'Haply, begirt with shadowy woods and hills,
And the wild sounds of melancholy rills,
   Their covering turf may bloom;
But ne'er hath Fame made relics of its flowers,— 40
Never hath pilgrim sought their household bowers,
   Or poet hail'd their tomb.'

'Adieu, then, master of the midnight spell!
Some voice, perchance, by those lone graves may tell
   That which I pine to know!
I haste to seek, from woods and valleys deep,
Where the beloved are laid in lowly sleep,
   Records of joy and woe.'

250   *The Dreaming Child*

  Alas! what kind of grief should thy years know?
  Thy brow and cheek are smooth as waters be
  When no breath troubles them.

      BEAUMONT AND FLETCHER

AND is there sadness in *thy* dreams, my boy?
What should the cloud be made of?—blessed child!
Thy spirit, borne upon a breeze of joy,
All day hath ranged through sunshine, clear, yet mild:

And now thou tremblest!—wherefore?—in *thy* soul
There lies no past, no future.—Thou hast heard
No sound of presage from the distance roll,
Thy heart bears traces of no arrowy word.

From thee no love hath gone; thy mind's young eye
Hath look'd not into Death's, and thence become   10
A questioner of mute Eternity,
A weary searcher for a viewless home:

Nor hath thy sense been quicken'd unto pain,
By feverish watching for some step beloved;
Free are thy thoughts, an ever-changeful train,
Glancing like dewdrops, and as lightly moved.

Yet now, on billows of strange passion toss'd,
How art thou wilder'd in the cave of sleep!
My gentle child! 'midst what dim phantoms lost,
Thus in mysterious anguish dost thou weep?   20

Awake! they sadden me—those early tears,
First gushings of the strong dark river's flow,
That *must* o'ersweep thy soul with coming years
Th' unfathomable flood of human woe!

Awful to watch, ev'n rolling through a dream,
Forcing wild spray-drops but from childhood's eyes!
Wake, wake! as yet *thy* life's transparent stream
Should wear the tinge of none but summer skies.

Come from the shadow of those realms unknown,
Where now thy thoughts dismay'd and darkling rove;   30
Come to the kindly region all thine own,
The home, still bright for thee with guardian love.

Happy, fair child! that yet a mother's voice
Can win thee back from visionary strife!—
Oh! shall *my* soul, thus waken'd to rejoice,
Start from the dreamlike wilderness of life?

251   *The Mirror in the Deserted Hall*

O, DIM, forsaken mirror!
How many a stately throng
Hath o'er thee gleam'd, in vanish'd hours
Of the wine-cup and the song!

The song hath left no echo;
The bright wine hath been quaff'd;
And hush'd is every silvery voice
That lightly here hath laugh'd.

Oh! mirror, lonely mirror,
Thou of the silent hall!   10
Thou hast been flush'd with beauty's bloom—
Is this, too, vanish'd all?

It is, with the scatter'd garlands
Of triumphs long ago;
With the melodies of buried lyres;
With the faded rainbow's glow.

And for all the gorgeous pageants,
For the glance of gem and plume,
For lamp, and harp, and rosy wreath,
And vase of rich perfume.   20

Now, dim, forsaken mirror,
Thou givest but faintly back
The quiet stars, and the sailing moon,
On her solitary track.

And thus with man's proud spirit
Thou tellest me 'twill be,
When the forms and hues of this world fade
From his memory, as from thee:

And his heart's long-troubled waters
At last in stillness lie,   30
Reflecting but the images
Of the solemn world on high.

252   'In the days of old'

In the days of old,
Lovers felt true passion,
Deeming years of sorrow
By a smile repaid.
Now the charms of gold,
Spells of pride and fashion,
Bid them say good morrow
To the best-loved maid.

Through the forests wild,
O'er the mountains lonely,   10
They were never weary
Honour to pursue:
If the damsel smiled
Once in seven years only,
All their wanderings dreary
Ample guerdon knew.

Now one day's caprice
Weighs down years of smiling,
Youthful hearts are rovers,
Love is bought and sold: 20
Fortune's gifts may cease,
Love is less beguiling;
Wiser were the lovers,
In the days of old.

ALFRED TENNYSON
1809–1892

Mariana

Mariana in the moated grange.
Measure for Measure

[I]

WITH blackest moss the flowerplots
    Were thickly crusted, one and all,
The rusted nails fell from the knots
    That held the peach to the gardenwall.
The broken sheds looked sad and strange,
    Unlifted was the clinking latch,
    Weeded and worn the ancient thatch
Upon the lonely moated grange.
      She only said 'My life is dreary,
        He cometh not,' she said;
      She said 'I am aweary, aweary;
        I would that I were dead!'

II

Her tears fell with the dews at even,
    Her tears fell ere the dews were dried,
She could not look on the sweet heaven,
    Either at morn or eventide.
After the flitting of the bats,
    When thickest dark did trance the sky,
    She drew her casementcurtain by,
And glanced athwart the glooming flats.
      She only said 'The night is dreary,
        He cometh not,' she said:
      She said 'I am aweary, aweary,
        I would that I were dead!'

III

Upon the middle of the night,
    Waking she heard the nightfowl crow:
The cock sung out an hour ere light:
    From the dark fen the oxen's low
Came to her: without hope of change,
    In sleep she seemed to walk forlorn,
    Till cold winds woke the grey-eyed morn

About the lonely moated grange.
    She only said, 'The day is dreary,
     He cometh not,' she said;
    She said, 'I am aweary, aweary,
     I would that I were dead!'

IV

About a stonecast from the wall,
  A sluice with blackened waters slept,
And o'er it many, round and small,
  The clustered marishmosses crept.   40
Hard by a poplar shook alway,
  All silvergreen with gnarled bark,
  For leagues no other tree did dark
The level waste, the rounding grey.
    She only said, 'My life is dreary,
     He cometh not,' she said;
    She said, 'I am aweary, aweary,
     I would that I were dead!'

V

And ever when the moon was low,
  And the shrill winds were up an' away,   50
In the white curtain, to and fro,
  She saw the gusty shadow sway.
But when the moon was very low,
  And wild winds bound within their cell,
  The shadow of the poplar fell
Upon her bed, across her brow.
    She only said, 'The night is dreary,
     He cometh not,' she said;
    She said, 'I am aweary, aweary,
     I would that I were dead!'   60

VI

All day within the dreamy house,
  The doors upon their hinges creaked,
The blue fly sung i' the pane; the mouse
  Behind the mouldering wainscot shrieked,
Or from the crevice peered about.
    Old faces glimmered through the doors,
    Old footsteps trod the upper floors,
Old voices called her from without.
    She only said, 'My life is dreary,
     He cometh not,' she said;   70

ALFRED TENNYSON

She said, 'I am aweary, aweary,
I would that I were dead!'

VII

The sparrow's chirrup on the roof,
    The slow clock ticking, and the sound
Which to the wooing wind aloof
    The poplar made, did all confound
Her sense; but most she loathed the hour
    When the thickmoted sunbeam lay
    Athwart the chambers, and the day
Downsloped was westering in his bower.   80
        Then, said she, 'I am very dreary,
            He will not come,' she said;
        She wept, 'I am aweary, aweary,
            Oh God, that I were dead!'

[1831]

EBENEZER ELLIOTT

254   *'Child, is thy father dead?'*

Tune: 'Robin Adair'

CHILD, is thy father dead?
    Father is gone!
Why did they tax his bread?
    God's will be done!
Mother has sold her bed;
Better to die than wed!
Where shall she lay her head?
    Home we have none!

Father clamm'd thrice a week,
    God's will be done!   10
Long for work did he seek,
    Work he found none.
Tears on his hollow cheek
Told what no tongue could speak:
Why did his master break?
    God's will be done!

    Doctor said air was best,
       Food we had none;
    Father, with panting breast,
       Groan'd to be gone: 20
    Now he is with the blest—
    Mother says death is best!
    We have no place of rest—
       Yes, ye have one!

THOMAS TOD STODDART
1810–1880

255   from *The Death-Wake; or, Lunacy*

Song

'Tis light to love thee living, girl, when hope is full and fair,
In the springtide of thy beauty, when there is no sorrow there—
No sorrow on thy brow, and no shadow on thy heart!
When, like a floating sea-bird, bright and beautiful thou art!

'Tis light to love thee living, girl—to see thee ever so,
With health, that, like a crimson flower, lies blushing in the snow;
And thy tresses falling over, like the amber on the pearl—
Oh! true it is a lightsome thing, to love thee living, girl!

But when the brow is blighted, like a star of morning tide,
And faded is the crimson blush upon the cheek beside;   10
It is to love, as seldom love, the brightest and the best,
When our love lies like a dew upon the one that is at rest.

Because of hopes, that, fallen, are changing to despair,
And the heart is always dreaming on the ruin that is there,
Oh, true! 'tis weary, weary, to be gazing over thee,
And the light of thy pure vision breaketh never upon me!

                       (from 'Chimera II')

[*'He sate like winter o'er the wasted year'*]

He sate like winter o'er the wasted year—
Like melancholy winter, drawing near
To its own death.—'Oh me! the worm, at last,
Will gorge upon me, and the autumn blast
Howl by!—Where?—where?—there is no worm to creep

Amid the waters of the lonely deep;
But I will take me Agathè upon
This sorrowful, sore bosom, and anon,
Down, down, through azure silence, we shall go,
Unepitaph'd, to cities far below;   10
Where the sea triton, with his winding shell,
Shall sound our blessed welcome. We shall dwell
With many a mariner in his pearly home,
In bowers of amber weed and silver foam,
Amid the crimson corals; we shall be
Together, Agathè! fair Agathè!—
But thou art sickly, ladye—thou art sad;
And I am weary, ladye—I am mad!
They bring no food to feed us, and I feel
A frost upon my vitals, very chill,   20
Like winter breaking on the golden year
Of life. This bark shall be our floating bier,
And the dark waves our mourners; and the white,
Pure swarm of sunny sea birds, basking bright
On some far isle, shall sorrowfully pour
Their wail of melancholy o'er and o'er,
At evening, on the waters of the sea,—
While, with its solemn burden, silently,
Floats forward our lone bark.—Oh, Agathè!
Methinks that I shall meet thee far away,   30
Within the awful centre of the earth,
Where, earliest, we had our holy birth—
In some huge cavern, arching wide below,
Upon whose airy pivot, years ago,
The world went round: 'tis infinitely deep,
But never dismal; for above it sleep,
And under it, blue waters, hung aloof,
And held below,—an amethystine roof,
A sapphire pavement; and the golden sun,
Afar, looks through alternately, like one   40
That watches round some treasure: often, too,
Through many a mile of ocean, sparkling through,
Are seen the stars and moon, all gloriously,
Bathing their angel brilliance in the sea!

'And there are shafted pillars, that beyond,
Are ranged before a rock of diamond,
Awfully heaving its eternal heights,
From base of silver strewn with chrysolites;
And over it are chasms of glory seen,
With crimson rubies clustering between,   50

On sward of emerald, with leaves of pearl,
And topazes hung brilliantly on beryl.
So Agathè!—but thou art sickly sad,
And tellest me, poor Julio is mad—
Ay, mad!—was he not madder when he sware
A vow to Heaven? was there no madness there,
That he should do—for why?—a holy string
Of penances? No penances will bring
The stricken conscience to the blessed light
Of peace,—Oh! I am lost, and there is night,   60
Despair and darkness, darkness and despair,
And want, that hunts me to the lion-lair
Of wild perdition: and I hear them all—
All cursing me! The very sun-rays fall
In curses, and the shadow of the moon,
And the pale star light, and the winds that tune
Their voices to the music of the sea,—
And thou,—yes, thou! my gentle Agathè!—
All curse me!—Oh! that I were never, never!—
Or but a breathless fancy, that was ever   70
Adrift upon the wilderness of Time,
That knew no impulse, but was left sublime
To play at its own will!—that I were hush'd
At night by silver cataracts, that gush'd
Through flowers of fairy hue, and then to die
Away, with all before me passing by,
Like a fair vision I had lived to see,
And died to see no more!—It cannot be!
By this right hand! I feel it is not so,
And by the beating of a heart below,   80
That strangely feareth for eternity!'

                                        (from 'Chimera II')

['Beautiful Lunacy!']

Beautiful Lunacy! that shapest flight
For love to blessed bowers of delight,
And buildest holy monarchies within
The fancy, till the very heart is queen
Of all her golden wishes. Lunacy!
Thou empress of the passions! though they be
A sister group of wild, unearthly forms,
Like lightnings playing in their home of storms!
I see thee, striking at the silver strings
Of the pure heart, and holy music springs   10

Before thy touch, in many a solemn strain,
Like that of sea-waves rolling from the main!

But say, is Melancholy by thy side,
With tresses in a raven shower, that hide
Her pale and weeping features? Is she never
Flowing before thee, like a gloomy river,
The sister of thyself? but cold and chill,
And winter-born, and sorrowfully still,
And not like thee, that art in merry mood,
And frolicksome amid thy solitude!   20

Fair Lunacy! I see thee, with a crown
Of hawthorn and sweet daisies, bending down
To mirror thy young image in a spring;
And thou wilt kiss that shadow of a thing
As soul-less as thyself. 'Tis tender, too,
The smile that meeteth thine! the holy hue
Of health! the pearly radiance of the brow!
All, all as tender—beautiful as thou!

And wilt thou say, my sister, there is none
Will answer thee? Thou art—thou art alone,   30
A pure, pure being! but the God on high
Is with thee ever, as thou goest by.

Thou poetess! that harpest to the moon,
And, in soft concert to the silver tune
Of waters, play'd on by the magic wind,
As he comes streaming, with his hair untwined,
Dost sing light strains of melody and mirth,—
I hear thee, hymning on thy holy birth,
How thou wert moulded of thy mother Love,
That came, like seraph, from the stars above,   40
And was so sadly wedded unto Sin,
That thou wert born, and Sorrow was thy twin.
Sorrow and mirthful Lunacy! that be
Together link'd for time, I deem of ye
That ye are worshipp'd as none others are,—
One as a lonely shadow, one a star!

                                    (from 'Chimera III')

WINTHROP MACKWORTH PRAED

The Belle of the Ball-Room

An Every-Day Character

Il faut juger des femmes depuis la chaussure jusqu'à la coiffure
exclusivement, à peu près comme on mesure le poisson entre
queue et tête.

LA BRUYÈRE

YEARS, years ago,—ere yet my dreams
    Had been of being wise or witty;—
Ere I had done with writing themes,
    Or yawned o'er this infernal Chitty;
Years, years ago,—while all my joy
    Was in my fowling-piece and filly;—
In short, while I was yet a boy,
    I fell in love with Laura Lily.

I saw her at the Country-Ball:
    There, when the sounds of flute and fiddle   10
Gave signal sweet in that old hall,
    Of hands across and down the middle,
Hers was the subtlest spell by far
    Of all that set young hearts romancing;
She was our queen, our rose, our star;
    And then she danced,—Oh heaven, her dancing!

Dark was her hair; her hand was white;
    Her voice was exquisitely tender;
Her eyes were full of liquid light;
    I never saw a waist so slender;   20
Her every look, her every smile,
    Shot right and left a score of arrows;
I thought 'twas Venus from her isle,
    And wondered where she'd left her sparrows.

She talked—of politics, or prayers;
    Of Southey's prose, or Wordsworth's sonnets;
Of danglers, or of dancing bears,
    Of battles, or the last new bonnets:
By candlelight, at twelve o'clock,
    To me it mattered not a tittle;   30

If those bright lips had quoted Locke,
  I might have thought they murmured Little.

Through sunny May, through sultry June,
  I loved her with a love eternal;
I spoke her praises to the moon,
  I wrote them to the Sunday Journal:
My mother laughed;—I soon found out
  That ancient ladies have no feeling:
My father frowned;—but how should gout
  See any happiness in kneeling?   40

She was the daughter of a Dean,
  Rich, fat, and rather apoplectic;
She had one brother, just thirteen,
  Whose colour was extremely hectic:
Her grandmother for many a year
  Had fed the parish with her bounty;
Her second cousin was a peer,
  And Lord Lieutenant of the county.

But titles, and the three per cents.,
  And mortgages, and great relations,   50
And India bonds, and tithes, and rents,
  Oh, what are they to love's sensations!
Black eyes, fair forehead, clustering locks,
  Such wealth, such honours, Cupid chuses;
He cares as little for the Stocks,
  As Baron Rothschild for the Muses.

She sketched;—the vale, the wood, the beach
  Grew lovelier from her pencil's shading:
She botanized;—I envied each
  Young blossom in her boudoir fading;   60
She warbled Handel; it was grand;
  She made the Catalani jealous;
She touched the organ;—I could stand
  For hours and hours to blow the bellows.

She kept an Album too at home,
  Well filled with all an Album's glories;
Paintings of butterflies, and Rome,
  Patterns for trimmings, Persian stories;
Soft songs to Julia's cockatoo,
  Fierce odes to Famine and to Slaughter;   70
And autographs of Prince Leboo,
  And recipes for elder-water.

And she was flattered, worshipped, bored;
   Her steps were watched, her dress was noted;
Her poodle dog was quite adored,
   Her sayings were extremely quoted.
She laughed, and every heart was glad,
   As if the taxes were abolished;
She frowned, and every look was sad,
   As if the Opera were demolished.   80

She smiled on many just for fun,—
   I knew that there was nothing in it;
I was the first,—the only one,
   Her heart had thought of for a minute.
I knew it; for she told me so,
   In phrase which was divinely moulded;
She wrote a charming hand,—and oh!
   How sweetly all her notes were folded!

Our love was like most other loves;—
   A little glow, a little shiver,   90
A rose-bud, and a pair of gloves,
   And 'Fly not yet' upon the river;
Some jealousy of some one's heir,
   Some hopes of dying broken-hearted;
A miniature, a lock of hair,
   The usual vows, and then we parted.

We parted—months and years rolled by;
   We met again four summers after;
Our parting was all sob and sigh;
   Our meeting was all mirth and laughter: 100
For in my heart's most secret cell
   There had been many other lodgers;
And she was not the Ball-Room's Belle,
   But only Mrs Something Rogers.

257 ['Past ruin'd Ilion']

PAST ruin'd Ilion Helen lives,
    Alcestis rises from the shades;
Verse calls them forth; 'tis verse that gives
    Immortal youth to mortal maids.

Soon shall Oblivion's deepening veil
    Hide all the peopled hills you see,
The gay, the proud, while lovers hail
    These many summers you and me.

The tear for fading beauty check,
    For passing glory cease to sigh;   10
One form shall rise above the wreck,
    One name, Ianthe, shall not die.

[1832]

ALFRED TENNYSON

258   *The Lady of Shalott*

PART THE FIRST

ON either side the river lie
Long fields of barley and of rye,
That clothe the wold, and meet the sky.
And thro' the field the road runs by
            To manytowered Camelot.
The yellowleavèd waterlily,
The greensheathèd daffodilly,
Tremble in the water chilly,
            Round about Shalott.

Willows whiten, aspens shiver,   10
The sunbeam-showers break and quiver
In the stream that runneth ever
By the island in the river,
            Flowing down to Camelot.

Four gray walls and four gray towers
Overlook a space of flowers,
And the silent isle imbowers
      The Lady of Shalott.

Underneath the bearded barley,
The reaper, reaping late and early,   20
Hears her ever chanting cheerly,
Like an angel, singing clearly,
      O'er the stream of Camelot.
Piling the sheaves in furrows airy,
Beneath the moon, the reaper weary
Listening whispers, ''tis the fairy
      Lady of Shalott.'

The little isle is all inrailed
With a rose-fence, and overtrailed
With roses: by the marge unhailed   30
The shallop flitteth silkensailed,
      Skimming down to Camelot.
A pearlgarland winds her head:
She leaneth on a velvet bed,
Full royally apparellèd,
      The Lady of Shalott.

PART THE SECOND

No time hath she to sport and play:
A charmèd web she weaves alway.
A curse is on her, if she stay
Her weaving, either night or day,   40
      To look down to Camelot.
She knows not what the curse may be;
Therefore she weaveth steadily,
Therefore no other care hath she,
      The Lady of Shalott.

She lives with little joy or fear.
Over the water, running near,
The sheepbell tinkles in her ear.
Before her hangs a mirror clear,
      Reflecting towered Camelot.   50
And, as the mazy web she whirls,
She sees the surly village-churls,
And the red cloaks of market-girls,
      Pass onward from Shalott.

Sometimes a troop of damsels glad,
An abbot on an ambling pad,
Sometimes a curly shepherd lad,
Or longhaired page, in crimson clad,
　　　　Goes by to towered Camelot.
And sometimes thro' the mirror blue,　　　　　　　　60
The knights come riding, two and two.
She hath no loyal knight and true,
　　　　The Lady of Shalott.

But in her web she still delights
To weave the mirror's magic sights:
For often thro' the silent nights
A funeral, with plumes and lights
　　　　And music, came from Camelot.
Or, when the moon was overhead,
Came two young lovers, lately wed:　　　　　　　　70
'I am half-sick of shadows,' said
　　　　The Lady of Shalott.

PART THE THIRD

A bowshot from her bower-eaves.
He rode between the barleysheaves:
The sun came dazzling thro' the leaves,
And flamed upon the brazen greaves
　　　　Of bold Sir Launcelot.
A redcross knight for ever kneeled
To a lady in his shield,
That sparkled on the yellow field,　　　　　　　　80
　　　　Beside remote Shalott.

The gemmy bridle glittered free,
Like to some branch of stars we see
Hung in the golden galaxy.
The bridle-bells rang merrily,
　　　　As he rode down from Camelot.
And, from his blazoned baldric slung,
A mighty silver bugle hung,
And, as he rode, his armour rung,
　　　　Beside remote Shalott.　　　　　　　　　　90

All in the blue unclouded weather,
Thickjewelled shone the saddle-leather.
The helmet, and the helmet-feather
Burned like one burning flame together,
　　　　As he rode down from Camelot.

As often thro' the purple night,
Below the starry clusters bright,
Some bearded meteor, trailing light,
     Moves over green Shalott.

His broad clear brow in sunlight glowed.   100
On burnished hooves his warhorse trode.
From underneath his helmet flowed
His coalblack curls, as on he rode,
     As he rode down from Camelot.
From the bank, and from the river,
He flashed into the crystal mirror,
'Tirra lirra, tirra lirra,'
     Sang Sir Launcelot.

She left the web: she left the loom:
She made three paces thro' the room: 110
She saw the waterflower bloom:
She saw the helmet and the plume:
     She looked down to Camelot.
Out flew the web, and floated wide,
The mirror cracked from side to side,
'The curse is come upon me,' cried
     The Lady of Shalott.

PART THE FOURTH

In the stormy eastwind straining
The pale-yellow woods were waning,
The broad stream in his banks complaining,   120
Heavily the low sky raining
     Over towered Camelot:
Outside the isle a shallow boat
Beneath a willow lay afloat,
Below the carven stern she wrote,
     THE LADY OF SHALOTT.

A cloudwhite crown of pearl she dight.
All raimented in snowy white
That loosely flew, (her zone in sight,
Clasped with one blinding diamond bright,)   130
     Her wide eyes fixed on Camelot,
Though the squally eastwind keenly
Blew, with folded arms serenely
By the water stood the queenly
     Lady of Shalott.

With a steady, stony glance—
Like some bold seer in a trance,
Beholding all his own mischance,
Mute, with a glassy countenance—
            She looked down to Camelot.   140
It was the closing of the day,
She loosed the chain, and down she lay,
The broad stream bore her far away,
            The Lady of Shalott.

As when to sailors while they roam,
By creeks and outfalls far from home,
Rising and dropping with the foam,
From dying swans wild warblings come,
            Blown shoreward; so to Camelot
Still as the boathead wound along   150
The willowy hills and fields among,
They heard her chanting her deathsong,
            The Lady of Shalott.

A longdrawn carol, mournful, holy,
She chanted loudly, chanted lowly,
Till her eyes were darkened wholly,
And her smooth face sharpened slowly
            Turned to towered Camelot:
For ere she reached upon the tide
The first house by the waterside,   160
Singing in her song she died,
            The Lady of Shalott.

Under tower and balcony,
By gardenwall and gallery,
A pale, pale corpse she floated by,
Deadcold, between the houses high,
            Dead into towered Camelot.
Knight and burgher, lord and dame,
To the plankèd wharfage came:
Below the stern they read her name,   170
            'The Lady of Shalott.'

They crossed themselves, their stars they blest,
Knight, minstrel, abbot, squire and guest.
There lay a parchment on her breast,
That puzzled more than all the rest,
            The wellfed wits at Camelot.

'*The web was woven curiously*
The charm is broken utterly,
Draw near and fear not—this is I,
The Lady of Shalott.'   180

259   *To ——. With the Following Poem*

I SEND you, Friend, a sort of allegory,
(You are an artist and will understand
Its many lesser meanings) of a soul,
A sinful soul possessed of many gifts,
A spacious garden full of flowering weeds,
A glorious Devil, large in heart and brain,
That did love Beauty only, (Beauty seen
In all varieties of mould and mind)
And Knowledge for its beauty; or if Good,
Good only for its beauty, seeing not   10
That Beauty, Good, and Knowledge, are three sisters
That doat upon each other, friends to man,
Living together under the same roof,
And never can be sundered without tears.
And he that shuts Love out, in turn shall be
Shut out from Love, and on her threshold lie
Howling in outer darkness. Not for this
Was common clay ta'en from the common earth,
Moulded by God, and tempered with the tears
Of angels to the perfect shape of man.   20

260   *The Palace of Art*

I

I BUILT my soul a lordly pleasurehouse,
    Wherein at ease for aye to dwell.
I said, 'Oh Soul, make merry and carouse,
    Dear Soul, for all is well.'

II

A huge crag-platform, smooth as burnished brass,
    I chose, whose rangèd ramparts bright
From great broad meadowbases of deep grass
    Suddenly scaled the light.

III

Thereon I built it firm. Of ledge or shelf
    The rock rose clear, or winding stair.   10
My soul would live alone unto herself
    In her high palace there.

IV

'While the great world runs round and round,' I said,
    'Reign thou apart, a quiet king;
Still, as, while Saturn whirls, his steadfast shade
    Sleeps on his luminous ring.

V

'And richly feast within thy palacehall,
    Like to the dainty bird that sups,
Lodged in the lustrous crown-imperial,
    Draining the honeycups.'   20

VI

To which my soul made answer readily.
    'Trust me, in bliss I shall abide
In this great mansion that is built for me
    So royalrich and wide.'

VII

Full of long sounding corridors it was
    That overvaulted grateful glooms,
Roofed with thick plates of green and orange glass
    Ending in stately rooms.

VIII

Full of great rooms and small the palace stood,
    All various, all beautiful,   30
Looking all ways, fitted to every mood
    And change of my still soul.

IX

For some were hung with arras green and blue
    Showing a gaudy summer morn,
Where with puffed cheek the belted hunter blew
    His wreathèd buglehorn.

X

One showed an English home—gray twilight poured
    On dewy pastures, dewy trees,
Softer than sleep—all things in order stored—
    A haunt of ancient Peace.   40

XI

Some were all dark and red, a glimmering land
    Lit with a low round moon,
Among brown rocks a man upon the sand
    Went weeping all alone.

XII

One seemed a foreground black with stones and slags.
    Below sunsmitten icy spires
Rose striped with long white cloud the scornful crags,
    Deeptrenched with thunderfires.

XIII

Some showed far-off thick woods mounted with towers,
    Nearer, a flood of mild sunshine   50
Poured on long walks and lawns and beds and bowers
    Trellised with bunchy vine.

XIV

Or the maidmother by a crucifix,
    In yellow pastures sunnywarm,
Beneath branchwork of costly sardonyx,
    Sat smiling, babe in arm.

XV

Or Venus in a snowy shell alone,
    Deepshadowed in the glassy brine,
Moonlike glowed double on the blue, and shone
    A naked shape divine.   60

XVI

Or in a clearwalled city on the sea,
    Near gilded organpipes (her hair
Wound with white roses) slept Saint Cecily;
    An angel looked at her.

XVII

Or that deepwounded child of Pendragon
      Mid misty woods on sloping greens
Dozed in the valley of Avilion,
      Tended by crownèd queens.

XVIII

Or blue-eyed Kriemhilt from a craggy hold,
      Athwart the lightgreen rows of vine,   70
Poured blazing hoards of Nibelungen gold,
      Down to the gulfy Rhine.

XIX

Europa's scarf blew in an arch, unclasped,
      From her bare shoulder backward borne;
From one hand drooped a crocus: one hand grasped
      The mild bull's golden horn.

XX

He thro' the streaming crystal swam, and rolled
      Ambrosial breaths that seemed to float
In lightwreathed curls. She from the ripple cold
      Updrew her sandalled foot.   80

XXI

Or else flushed Ganymede, his rosy thigh
      Half-buried in the eagle's down,
Sole, as a flying star, shot thro' the sky
      Over the pillared town.

XXII

Not these alone: but many a legend fair,
      Which the supreme Caucasian mind
Carved out of nature for itself, was there
      Broidered in screen and blind.

XXIII

So that my soul beholding in her pride
      All these, from room to room did pass;   90
And all things that she saw, she multiplied,
      A manyfacèd glass;

XXIV

And, being both the sower and the seed,
    Remaining in herself became
All that she saw, Madonna, Ganymede,
    Or the Asiatic dame—

XXV

Still changing, as a lighthouse in the night
    Changeth athwart the gleaming main,
From red to yellow, yellow to pale white,
    Then back to red again.   100

XXVI

'From change to change four times within the womb
    The brain is moulded,' she began,
'So thro' all phases of all thought I come
    Into the perfect man.

XXVII

'All nature widens upward: evermore
    The simpler essence lower lies.
More complex is more perfect, owning more
    Discourse, more widely wise.

XXVIII

'I take possession of men's minds and deeds.
    I live in all things great and small.   110
I dwell apart, holding no forms of creeds,
    But contemplating all.'

XXIX

Four ample courts there were, East, West, South, North,
    In each a squarèd lawn wherefrom
A golden-gorgèd dragon spouted forth
    The fountain's diamond foam.

XXX

All round the cool green courts there ran a row
    Of cloisters, branched like mighty woods,
Echoing all night to that sonorous flow
    Of spouted fountain floods.   120

XXXI

From those four jets four currents in one swell
    Over the black rock streamed below
In steamy folds, that, floating as they fell,
    Lit up a torrentbow;

XXXII

And round the roofs ran gilded galleries
    That gave large view to distant lands,
Tall towns and mounds, and close beneath the skies
    Long lines of amber sands.

XXXIII

Huge incense-urns along the balustrade,
    Hollowed of solid amethyst,   130
Each with a different odour fuming, made
    The air a silver mist.

XXXIV

Far-off 'twas wonderful to look upon
    Those sumptuous towers between the gleam
Of that great foambow trembling in the sun,
    And the argent incense-steam;

XXXV

And round the terraces and round the walls,
    While day sank lower or rose higher,
To see those rails with all their knobs and balls,
    Burn like a fringe of fire.   140

XXXVI

Likewise the deepset windows, stained and traced,
    Burned, like slowflaming crimson fires,
From shadowed grots of arches interlaced,
    And topped with frostlike spires.

XXXVII

Up in the towers I placed great bells that swung
    Moved of themselves with silver sound:
And with choice paintings of wise men I hung
    The royal daïs round.

XXXVIII

There deephaired Milton like an angel tall
    Stood limnèd, Shakspeare bland and mild,   150
Grim Dante pressed his lips, and from the wall
    The bald blind Homer smiled.

XXXIX

And underneath freshcarved in cedarwood,
    Somewhat alike in form and face,
The Genii of every climate stood,
    All brothers of one race:

XL

Angels who sway the seasons by their art,
    And mould all shapes in earth and sea;
And with great effort build the human heart
    From earliest infancy.   160

XLI

And in the sunpierced Oriel's coloured flame
    Immortal Michael Angelo
Looked down, bold Luther, largebrowed Verulam,
    The king of those who know.

XLII

Cervantes, the bright face of Calderon,
    Robed David touching holy strings,
The Halicarnasseän, and alone,
    Alfred the flower of kings,

XLIII

Isaïah with fierce Ezekiel,
    Swarth Moses by the Coptic sea,   170
Plato, Petrarca, Livy, and Raphaël,
    And eastern Confutzee:

XLIV

And many more, that in their lifetime were
    Fullwelling fountainheads of Change,
Between the stone shafts glimmered, blazoned fair
    In divers raiment strange.

XLV

Thro' which the lights, rose, amber, emerald, blue,
    Flushed in her temples and her eyes,
And from her lips, as morn from Memnon, drew
    Rivers of melodies.   180

XLVI

No nightingale delighteth to prolong
    Her low preamble all alone,
More than my soul to hear her echoed song
    Throb thro' the ribbèd stone.

XLVII

Singing and murmuring in her feastful mirth
    Joying to feel herself alive,
Lord over nature, lord o' the visible earth,
    Lord of the senses five—

XLVIII

As some rich tropic mountain, that infolds
    All change, from flats of scattered palms   190
Sloping thro' five great zones of climate, holds
    His head in snows and calms—

XLIX

Full of her own delight and nothing else,
    My vainglorious, gorgeous soul
Sat throned between the shining oriels,
    In pomp beyond control;

L

With piles of flavorous fruits in basket-twine
    Of gold, upheapèd, crushing down
Muskscented blooms—all taste—grape, gourd or pine—
    In bunch, or singlegrown—   200

LI

Our growths, and such as brooding Indian heats
    Make out of crimson blossoms deep,
Ambrosial pulps and juices, sweets from sweets
    Sunchanged, when seawinds sleep.

LII

With graceful chalices of curious wine,
    Wonders of art—and costly jars,
And bossèd salvers. Ere young night divine
    Crowned dying day with stars,

LIII

Making sweet close of his delicious toils,
    She lit white streams of dazzling gas,   210
And soft and fragrant flames of precious oils
    In moons of purple glass

LIV

Ranged on the fretted woodwork to the ground.
    Thus her intense untold delight,
In deep or vivid colour, smell and sound,
    Was flattered day and night.

LV

Sometimes the riddle of the painful earth
    Flashed thro' her as she sat alone,
Yet not the less held she her solemn mirth,
    And intellectual throne   220

LVI

Of fullsphered contemplation. So three years
    She throve, but on the fourth she fell,
Like Herod, when the shout was in his ears,
    Struck thro' with pangs of hell.

LVII

Lest she should fail and perish utterly,
    God, before whom ever lie bare
The abysmal deeps of Personality,
    Plagued her with sore despair.

LVIII

When she would think, where'er she turned her sight
    The airy hand confusion wrought,   230
Wrote 'Mene, mene,' and divided quite
    The kingdom of her thought.

LIX

Deep dread and loathing of her solitude
    Fell on her, from which mood was born
Scorn of herself; again, from out that mood
    Laughter at her selfscorn.

LX

'Who hath drawn dry the fountains of delight,
    That from my deep heart everywhere
Moved in my blood and dwelt, as power and might
    Abode in Sampson's hair?   240

LXI

'What, is not this my place of strength,' she said,
    'My spacious mansion built for me,
Whereof the strong foundationstones were laid
    Since my first memory?'

LXII

But in dark corners of her palace stood
    Uncertain shapes, and unawares
On white-eyed phantasms weeping tears of blood
    And horrible nightmares,

LXIII

And hollow shades enclosing hearts of flame,
    And, with dim fretted foreheads all,   250
On corpses three-months-old at noon she came
    That stood against the wall.

LXIV

A spot of dull stagnation, without light
    Or power of movement, seemed my soul,
Mid downward-sloping motions infinite
    Making for one sure goal.

LXV

A still salt pool, locked in with bars of sand,
    Left on the shore, that hears all night
The plunging seas draw backward from the land
    Their moonled waters white.   260

LXVI

A star that with the choral starry dance
    Joined not, but stood, and standing saw
The hollow orb of moving Circumstance
    Rolled round by one fixed law.

LXVII

Back on herself her serpent pride had curled.
    'No voice,' she shrieked in that lone hall,
'No voice breaks through the stillness of this world—
    One deep, deep silence all.'

LXVIII

She, mouldering with the dull earth's mouldering sod,
    Inwrapt tenfold in slothful shame,   270
Lay there exilèd from eternal God,
    Lost to her place and name;

LXIX

And death and life she hated equally,
    And nothing saw, for her despair,
But dreadful time, dreadful eternity,
    No comfort anywhere;

LXX

Remaining utterly confused with fears,
    And ever worse with growing time,
And ever unrelieved by dismal tears,
    And all alone in crime;   280

LXXI

Shut up as in a crumbling tomb, girt round
    With blackness as a solid wall,
Far off she seemed to hear the dully sound
    Of human footsteps fall.

LXXII

As in strange lands a traveller walking slow,
    In doubt and great perplexity,
A little before moonrise hears the low
    Moan of an unknown sea,

LXXIII

And knows not if it be thunder or the sound
    Of stones thrown down, or one deep cry   290
Of great wild beasts; then thinketh, 'I have found
    A new land, but I die.'

LXXIV

She howled aloud 'I am on fire within.
    There comes no murmur of reply.
What is it that will take away my sin
    Dying the death I die?'

LXXV

So when four years were wholly finishèd,
    She threw her royal robes away.
'Make me a cottage in the vale,' she said,
    'Where I may mourn and pray.   300

LXXVI

'Yet pull not down my palace towers, that are
    So lightly, beautifully built:
Perchance I may return with others there
    When I have purged my guilt.'

APPENDIX
NOTES AND REFERENCES
INDEXES

APPENDIX

WILLIAM WORDSWORTH

from the Preface to the *Lyrical Ballads* (1805 version)

THE first volume of these poems has already been submitted to general perusal. It was published as an experiment, which I hoped might be of some use to ascertain how far, by fitting to metrical arrangement a selection of the real language of men in a state of vivid sensation, that sort of pleasure and that quantity of pleasure may be imparted which a poet may rationally endeavour to impart. . . .

It is supposed that by the act of writing in verse an author makes a formal engagement that he will gratify certain known habits of association; that he not only thus apprises the reader that certain classes of ideas and expressions will be found in his book, but that others will be carefully excluded. This exponent or symbol held forth by metrical language must in different eras of literature have excited very different expectations: for example, in the age of Catullus, Terence and Lucretius, and that of Statius or Claudian; and in our own country, in the age of Shakespeare and Beaumont and Fletcher, and that of Donne and Cowley, or Dryden, or Pope. I will not take upon me to determine the exact import of the promise which, by the act of writing in verse, an author in the present day makes to his reader; but I am certain it will appear to many persons that I have not fulfilled the terms of an engagement thus voluntarily contracted. They who have been accustomed to the gaudiness and inane phraseology of many modern writers, if they persist in reading this book to its conclusion, will no doubt frequently have to struggle with feelings of strangeness and awkwardness; they will look round for poetry, and will be induced to enquire by what species of courtesy these attempts can be permitted to assume that title. I hope therefore the reader will not censure me if I attempt to state what I have proposed to myself to perform, and also (as far as the limits of a preface will permit) to explain some of the chief reasons which have determined me in the choice of my purpose; that at least he may be spared any unpleasant feeling of disappointment, and that I myself may be protected from the most dishonourable accusation which can be brought against an author— namely, that of an indolence which prevents him from endeavouring to ascertain what is his duty, or, when his duty is ascertained, prevents him from performing it.

The principal object, then, which I proposed to myself in these poems was to choose incidents and situations from common life, and to relate or describe them throughout, as far as was possible, in a selection of language really used by men; and at the same time to throw over them a certain colouring of imagination, whereby ordinary things should be presented to the mind in an unusual way; and further, and above all, to make these incidents and situations interesting by tracing in them, truly though not ostentatiously, the primary laws of our nature: chiefly as far as regards the manner in which we associate ideas in a state of excitement. Low and rustic life was generally chosen, because in that condition the essential passions of the heart find a better soil in which they can attain their maturity, are less under restraint, and speak a plainer and more emphatic language; because in that condition of life our elementary feelings co-exist in a state of greater simplicity, and consequently may be more accurately contemplated and more forcibly communicated; because the manners of rural life germinate from those elementary feelings, and from the necessary character of rural occupations are more easily comprehended, and are more durable; and lastly, because in that condition the passions of men are incorporated with the beautiful and permanent forms of nature. The language, too, of these men is adopted (purified indeed from what appear to be its real defects, from all lasting and rational causes of dislike or disgust) because such men hourly communicate with the best objects from which the best part of language is originally derived; and because, from their rank in society and the sameness and narrow circle of their intercourse being less under the influence of social vanity, they convey their feelings and notions in simple and unelaborated expressions. Accordingly such a language, arising out of repeated experience and regular feelings, is a more permanent and a far more philosophical language than that which is frequently substituted for it by poets, who think that they are conferring honour upon themselves and their art in proportion as they separate themselves from the sympathies of men, and indulge in arbitrary and capricious habits of expression in order to furnish food for fickle tastes and fickle appetites of their own creation.*

I cannot, however, be insensible of the present outcry against the triviality and meanness both of thought and language which some of my contemporaries have occasionally introduced into their metrical compositions; and I acknowledge that this defect, where it exists, is more dishonourable to the writer's own character than false refinement or arbitrary innovation, though I should contend at the same time that it is far less pernicious in the sum of its consequences. From such verses the poems in these volumes will be found distinguished at least by one mark of difference, that each of them has a worthy *purpose*. Not that I mean to say that I always began to write with a distinct purpose formally conceived; but I believe that my habits of meditation have so formed my feelings, as that my descriptions of such objects as strongly excite those feelings will be found to carry along with them a *purpose*. If in this opinion I am mistaken, I can have little right to the name of a poet. For all good poetry is the spontaneous overflow of powerful feelings; but though this be true, poems to which any value can be attached were never produced on any variety of subjects but by a man who, being possessed of more than usual organic sensibility, had also thought long and deeply. For our continued influxes of feeling are modified and directed by our thoughts, which are indeed the representatives of all our past feelings; and as by contemplating the relation of these general representatives to each other we discover what is really important to men, so by the repetition and continuance of this act our feelings will be connected with important subjects, till at length, if we be originally possessed of much sensibility, such habits of mind will be produced that, by obeying blindly and mechanically the impulses of those habits, we shall describe objects and utter sentiments of such a nature and in such connection with each other that the understanding of the being to whom we address ourselves, if he be in a healthful state of association, must necessarily be in some degree enlightened and his affections ameliorated.

I have said that each of these poems has a purpose. I have also informed my reader what this purpose will be found principally to be: namely, to illustrate the

---

* It is worth while here to observe that the affecting parts of Chaucer are almost always expressed in language pure and universally intelligible to this day.

manner in which our feelings and ideas are associated in a state of excitement. But speaking in language somewhat more appropriate, it is to follow the fluxes and refluxes of the mind when agitated by the great and simple affections of our nature. This object I have endeavoured in these short essays to attain by various means: by tracing the maternal passion through many of its more subtle windings, as in the poems of *The Idiot Boy* and *The Mad Mother*; by accompanying the last struggles of a human being at the approach of death, cleaving in solitude to life and society, as in the poem of *The Forsaken Indian*; by showing, as in the stanzas entitled *We are Seven*, the perplexity and obscurity which in childhood attend our notion of death, or rather our utter inability to admit that notion; or by displaying the strength of fraternal or, to speak more philosophically, of moral attachment when early associated with the great and beautiful objects of nature, as in *The Brothers*; or, as in the incident of *Simon Lee*, by placing my reader in the way of receiving from ordinary moral sensations another and more salutary impression than we are accustomed to receive from them. It has also been part of my general purpose to attempt to sketch characters under the influence of less impassioned feelings, as in *The Two April Mornings*, *The Fountain*, *The Old Man Travelling*, *The Two Thieves*, etc., characters of which the elements are simple, belonging rather to nature than to manners, such as exist now and will probably always exist, and which from their constitution may be distinctly and profitably contemplated. I will not abuse the indulgence of my reader by dwelling longer upon this subject, but it is proper that I should mention one other circumstance which distinguishes these poems from the popular poetry of the day: it is this, that the feeling therein developed gives importance to the action and situation, and not the action and situation to the feeling. My meaning will be rendered perfectly intelligible by referring my reader to the poems entitled *Poor Susan* and *The Childless Father*, particularly to the last stanza of the latter poem.

I will not suffer a sense of false modesty to prevent me from asserting that I point my reader's attention to this mark of distinction far less for the sake of these particular poems than from the general importance of the subject. The subject is indeed important! For the human mind is capable of being excited without the application of gross and violent stimulants; and he must have a very faint perception of its beauty and dignity who does not know this, and who does not further know that one being is elevated above another in proportion as he possesses this capability. It has therefore appeared to me that to endeavour to produce or enlarge this capability is one of the best services in which, at any period, a writer can be engaged; but this service, excellent at all times, is especially so at the present day. For a multitude of causes unknown to former times are now acting with a combined force to blunt the discriminating powers of the mind and, unfitting it for all voluntary exertion, to reduce it to a state of almost savage torpor. The most effective of these causes are the great national events which are daily taking place and the increasing accumulation of men in cities, where the uniformity of their occupations produces a craving for extraordinary incident, which the rapid communication of intelligence hourly gratifies. To this tendency of life and manners the literature and theatrical exhibitions of the country have conformed themselves. The invaluable works of our elder writers, I had almost said the works of Shakespeare and Milton, are driven into neglect by frantic novels, sickly and stupid German tragedies, and deluges of idle and extravagant stories in verse. . . .

Having dwelt thus long on the subjects and aim of these poems, I shall request the reader's permission to apprise him of a few circumstances relating to their *style*, in order, among other reasons, that I may not be censured for not having performed what I never attempted.... There will also be found in these volumes little of what is usually called poetic diction; I have taken as much pains to avoid it as others ordinarily take to produce it; this I have done for the reason already alleged, to bring my language near to the language of men, and further, because the pleasure which I have proposed to myself to impart is of a kind very different from that which is supposed by many persons to be the proper object of poetry....

I have previously asserted that a large portion of the language of every good poem can in no respect differ from that of good prose. I will go further. I do not doubt that it may be safely affirmed, that there neither is, nor can be, any essential difference between the language of prose and metrical composition. We are fond of tracing the resemblance between poetry and painting, and accordingly we call them sisters: but where shall we find bonds of connection sufficiently strict to typify the affinity betwixt metrical and prose composition? They both speak by and to the same organs; the bodies in which both of them are clothed may be said to be of the same substance, their affections are kindred and almost identical, not necessarily differing even in degree. Poetry* sheds no tears 'such as angels weep,' but natural and human tears; she can boast of no celestial ichor that distinguishes her vital juices from those of prose; the same human blood circulates through the veins of them both.

If it be affirmed that rhyme and metrical arrangement of themselves constitute a distinction which overturns what I have been saying on the strict affinity of metrical language with that of prose, and paves the way for other artificial distinctions which the mind voluntarily admits, I answer that the language of such poetry as I am recommending is, as far as is possible, a selection of the language really spoken by men; that this selection, wherever it is made with true taste and feeling, will of itself form a distinction far greater than would at first be imagined, and will entirely separate the composition from the vulgarity and meanness of ordinary life; and if metre be superadded thereto I believe that a dissimilitude will be produced altogether sufficient for the gratification of a rational mind....

Taking up the subject, then, upon general grounds, I ask what is meant by the word *poet*? What is a poet? To whom does he address himself? And what language is to be expected from him? He is a man speaking to men: a man, it is true, endued with more lively sensibility, more enthusiasm and tenderness, who has a greater knowledge of human nature, and a more comprehensive soul, than are supposed to be common among mankind; a man pleased with his own passions and volitions, and who rejoices more than other men in the spirit of life that is in him; delighting to contemplate similar volitions and passions as manifested in the goings-on of the universe, and habitually impelled to create them where he does not find them. To these qualities he has added a disposition to be affected more than other men by absent things as if they were present: an ability of conjuring up in himself passions which are indeed far from being the same as those produced by real events, yet (especially in those parts of the general sympathy which are pleasing and delightful) do more nearly resemble the passions produced by real events than anything which, from the motions of their own minds merely, other men are accustomed to feel in

---

* I here use the word *poetry* (though against my own judgment) as opposed to the word *prose*, and synonymous with metrical composition. But much confusion has been introduced into criticism by this contradistinction of poetry and prose, instead of the more philosophical one of poetry and matter of fact, or science. The only strict antithesis to prose is metre; nor is this in truth a *strict* antithesis, because lines and passages of metre so naturally occur in writing prose that it would be scarcely possible to avoid them, even were it desirable.

themselves; whence, and from practice, he has acquired a greater readiness and power in expressing what he thinks and feels, and especially those thoughts and feelings which by his own choice, or from the structure of his own mind, arise in him without immediate external excitement.

But whatever portion of this faculty we may suppose even the greatest poet to possess, there cannot be a doubt but that the language which it will suggest to him must in liveliness and truth fall far short of that which is uttered by men in real life under the actual pressure of those passions, certain shadows of which the poet thus produces or feels to be produced in himself. However exalted a notion we would wish to cherish of the character of a poet, it is obvious that while he describes and imitates passions his situation is altogether slavish and mechanical compared with the freedom and power of real and substantial action and suffering. So that it will be the wish of the poet to bring his feelings near to those of the persons whose feelings he describes—nay, for short spaces of time perhaps to let himself slip into an entire delusion, and even confound and identify his own feelings with theirs; modifying only the language which is thus suggested to him by a consideration that he describes for a particular purpose, that of giving pleasure. Here, then, he will apply the principle on which I have so much insisted, namely that of selection: on this he will depend for removing what would otherwise be painful or disgusting in the passion; he will feel that there is no necessity to trick out or to elevate nature; and the more industriously he applies this principle, the deeper will be his faith that no words which his fancy or imagination can suggest will be to be compared with those which are the emanations of reality and truth.

But it may be said by those who do not object to the general spirit of these remarks that, as it is impossible for the poet to produce upon all occasions language as exquisitely fitted for the passion as that which the real passion itself suggests, it is proper that he should consider himself as in the situation of a translator, who deems himself justified when he substitutes excellences of another kind for those which are unattainable by him; and endeavours occasionally to surpass his original in order to make some amends for the general inferiority to which he feels that he must submit. But this would be to encourage idleness and unmanly despair. Further, it is the language of men who speak of what they do not understand; who talk of poetry as of a matter of amusement and idle pleasure; who will converse with us as gravely about a *taste* for poetry, as they express it, as if it were a thing as indifferent as a taste for rope-dancing, or Frontiniac, or sherry. Aristotle, I have been told, hath said that poetry is the most philosophic of all writing: it is so: its object is truth, not individual and local, but general and operative; not standing upon external testimony, but carried alive into the heart by passion; truth which is its own testimony, which gives strength and divinity to the tribunal to which it appeals, and receives them from the same tribunal. Poetry is the image of man and nature. The obstacles which stand in the way of the fidelity of the biographer and historian, and of their consequent utility, are incalculably greater than those which are to be encountered by the poet who has an adequate notion of the dignity of his art. The poet writes under one restriction only, namely, that of the necessity of giving immediate pleasure to a human being possessed of that information which may be expected from him, not as a lawyer, a physician, a mariner, an astronomer or a natural philosopher, but as a man. Except this one restriction, there is no object standing between the poet and the image of things: between this and the biographer and historian there are a thousand.

Nor let this necessity of producing immediate pleasure be considered as a degradation of the poet's art. It is far otherwise. It is an acknowledgment of the beauty of the universe, an acknowledgment the more sincere because it is not formal, but indirect; it is a task light and easy to him who looks at the world in the spirit of love; further, it is a homage paid to the native and naked dignity of man, to the grand elementary principle of pleasure, by which he knows, and feels, and lives, and moves. We have no sympathy but what is propagated by pleasure: I would not be misunderstood; but wherever we sympathise with pain it will be found that the sympathy is produced and carried on by subtle combinations with pleasure. We have no knowledge, that is no general principles drawn from the contemplation of particular facts, but what has been built up by pleasure, and exists in us by pleasure alone. The man of science, the chemist and mathematician, whatever difficulties and disgusts they may have had to struggle with, know and feel this. However painful may be the objects with which the anatomist's knowledge is connected, he feels that his knowledge is pleasure; and where he has no pleasure he has no knowledge. What then does the poet? He considers man and the objects that surround him as acting and reacting upon each other so as to produce an infinite complexity of pain and pleasure; he considers man in his own nature and in his ordinary life as contemplating this with a certain quantity of immediate knowledge, with certain convictions, intuitions, and deductions which by habit become of the nature of intuitions; he considers him as looking upon this complex scene of ideas and sensations, and finding everywhere objects that immediately excite in him sympathies which, from the necessities of his nature, are accompanied by an over-balance of enjoyment.

To this knowledge which all men carry about with them, and to these sympathies in which without any other discipline than that of our daily life we are fitted to take delight, the poet principally directs his attention. He considers man and nature as essentially adapted to each other, and the mind of man as naturally the mirror of the fairest and most interesting qualities of nature. And thus the poet, prompted by this feeling of pleasure which accompanies him through the whole course of his studies, converses with general nature with affections akin to those which, through labour and length of time, the man of science has raised up in himself by conversing with those particular parts of nature which are the objects of his studies. The knowledge both of the poet and the man of science is pleasure: but the knowledge of the one cleaves to us as a necessary part of our existence, our natural and unalienable inheritance; the other is a personal and individual acquisition, slow to come to us, and by no habitual and direct sympathy connecting us with our fellow-beings. The man of science seeks truth as a remote and unknown bene-factor; he cherishes and loves it in his solitude: the poet, singing a song in which all human beings join with him, rejoices in the presence of truth as our visible friend and hourly companion. Poetry is the breath and finer spirit of all knowledge; it is the impassioned expression which is in the countenance of all science. Emphatically may it be said of the poet, as Shakespeare hath said of man, 'that he looks before and after.' He is the rock of defence of human nature, an upholder and preserver, carrying everywhere with him relationship and love. In spite of difference of soil and climate, of language and manners, of laws and customs, in spite of things silently gone out of mind and things violently destroyed, the poet binds together by passion and knowledge the vast empire of human society, as it is spread over the whole earth, and over all time. The objects of the poet's thoughts are everywhere: though the eyes and senses of men are, it is true, his favourite guides, yet he will follow wheresoever he can find an atmosphere of sensation in which to move his wings. Poetry is the first and last of all knowledge: it is as immortal as the heart of man. If the labours of men of science should ever create any material revolution, direct or indirect, in our condition and in the impressions which we habitually receive, the poet will sleep then no more than at present, but he will be ready to follow the steps of the man of science, not only in those general indirect effects, but he will be at his side, carrying sensation into the midst of the objects of the science itself. The remotest discoveries of the chemist, the botanist or mineralogist will be as proper objects of the poet's art as any upon which it can be employed, if the time should ever come when these things shall be familiar to us, and the relations under which they are contemplated by the followers of these respective sciences shall be manifestly and palpably material to us as enjoying and suffering beings. If the time should ever come when what is now called science, thus familiarised to men, shall be ready to put on, as it were, a form of flesh and blood, the poet will lend his divine spirit to aid the transfiguration, and will welcome the being thus produced as a dear and genuine inmate of the household of man. It is not, then, to be supposed that any one who holds that sublime notion of poetry which I have attempted to convey will break in upon the sanctity and truth of his pictures by transitory and accidental ornaments, and endeavour to excite admiration of himself by arts the necessity of which must manifestly depend upon the assumed meanness of his subject.

What I have thus far said applies to poetry in general, but especially to those parts of composition where the poet speaks through the mouths of his characters; and upon this point it appears to have such weight that I will conclude: there are few persons of good sense who would not allow that the dramatic parts of composition are defective in proportion as they deviate from the real language of nature and are coloured by a diction of the poet's own, either peculiar to him as an individual poet or belonging simply to poets in general—to a body of men who, from the circumstance of their compositions being in metre, it is expected will employ a particular language.

It is not, then, in the dramatic parts of composition that we look for this distinction of language; but still it may be proper and necessary where the poet speaks to us in his own person and character. To this I answer by referring my reader to the description which I have before given of a poet. Among the qualities which I have enumerated as principally conducing to form a poet is implied nothing differing in kind from other men, but only in degree. The sum of what I have there said is that the poet is chiefly distinguished from other men by a greater promptness to think and feel without immediate external excitement, and a greater power in expressing such thoughts and feelings as are produced in him in that manner. But these passions and thoughts and feelings are the general passions and thoughts and feelings of men. And with what are they connected? Undoubtedly with our moral sentiments and animal sensations, and with the causes which excite these: with the operations of the elements and the appearances of the visible universe; with storm and sunshine, with the revolutions of the seasons, with cold and heat, with loss of friends and kindred, with injuries and resentments, gratitude and hope, with fear and sorrow. These and the like are the sensations and objects which the poet describes, as they are the sensations of other men and the objects which interest them. The poet thinks and feels in the spirit of the passions of men. How then can his language differ in any material degree from that of all other men who feel vividly and see clearly? It might be *proved* that it is impossible. . . .

I have said that poetry is the spontaneous overflow of powerful feelings; it takes its origin from emotion recollected in tranquillity; the emotion is contemplated till by a species of reaction the tranquillity gradually disappears, and an emotion, kindred to that which was before the subject of contemplation, is gradually produced and does itself actually exist in the mind. In this mood successful composition generally begins, and in a mood similar to this it is carried on; but the emotion, of whatever kind and in whatever degree, from various causes is qualified by various pleasures, so that in describing any passions whatsoever which are voluntarily described the mind will upon the whole be in a state of enjoyment. Now, if Nature be thus cautious in preserving in a state of enjoyment a being thus employed, the poet ought to profit by the lesson thus held forth to him, and ought especially to take care that whatever passions he communicates to his reader, those passions, if his reader's mind be sound and vigorous, should always be accompanied with an overbalance of pleasure. Now the music of harmonious metrical language, the sense of difficulty overcome, and the blind association of pleasure which has been previously received from works of rhyme or metre of the same or similar construction, an indistinct perception perpetually renewed of language closely resembling that of real life, and yet in the circumstance of metre differing from it so widely—all these imperceptibly make up a complex feeling of delight, which is of the most important use in tempering the painful feeling which will always be found intermingled with powerful descriptions of the deeper passions. This effect is always produced in pathetic and impassioned poetry; while in lighter compositions the ease and gracefulness with which the poet manages his numbers are themselves confessedly a principal source of the gratification of the reader. I might perhaps include all which it is *necessary* to say upon this subject by affirming, what few persons will deny, that of two descriptions either of passions, manners or characters, each of them equally well executed, the one in prose and the other in verse, the verse will be read a hundred times where the prose is read once. We see that Pope, by the power of verse alone, has contrived to render the plainest common sense interesting, and even frequently to invest it with the appearance of passion. In consequence of these convictions I related in metre the tale of *Goody Blake and Harry Gill*, which is one of the rudest of this collection. I wished to draw attention to the truth, that the power of the human imagination is sufficient to produce such changes even in our physical nature as might almost appear miraculous. The truth is an important one: the fact (for it is a *fact*) is a valuable illustration of it. And I have the satisfaction of knowing that it has been communicated to many hundreds of people who would never have heard of it had it not been narrated as a ballad, and in a more impressive metre than is usual in ballads. . . .

I am sensible that my associations must have sometimes been particular instead of general, and that consequently, giving to things a false importance, sometimes from diseased impulses I may have written upon unworthy subjects; but I am less apprehensive on this account, than that my language may frequently have suffered from those arbitrary connections of feelings and ideas with particular words and phrases, from which no man can altogether protect himself. Hence I have no doubt that in some instances feelings even of the ludicrous may be given to my readers by expressions which appeared to me tender and pathetic. Such faulty expressions, were I convinced they were faulty at present and that they must necessarily continue to be so, I would willingly take all reasonable pains to correct. But it is dangerous to make these alterations on the simple authority of a few individuals, or even of certain classes of men; for where the understanding of an author is not convinced or his feelings altered, this cannot be done without great injury to himself: for his own feelings are his stay and support, and if he sets them aside in one instance he may be induced to repeat this act till his mind loses all confidence in itself and becomes utterly debilitated. To this it may be added that the reader ought never to forget that he is himself exposed to the same errors as the poet, and perhaps in a much greater degree: for there can be no presumption in saying that it is not probable he will be so well acquainted with the various stages of meaning through which words have passed, or with the fickleness or stability of the relations of particular ideas to each other; and above all, since he is so much less interested in the subject, he may decide lightly and carelessly. . . .

NOTES AND REFERENCES

In the references to sources that follow, the place of publication is London unless stated otherwise.

1785

1. This is the first of Sir William Jones's celebrated translations from the Sanskrit (see below, nos. 10, 21, 81–2). Published in Francis Gladwin (ed.), *The Asiatick Miscellany* (Calcutta, 1785). In his Argument to the poem Jones refers to the orientalist Nathaniel Brassey Halhed (1751–1830) and his translation of Vasishtha, *A Code of Gentoo Laws etc.* (1776). For the quotation ('We know this only . . .') see Pope's *Essay on Man* 4. 260; the thought was attributed to Socrates by Diogenes Laertius. The 'author of Cyrus' was John Hoole (1727–1803); his tragedy appeared in 1768. He is not known to have written a commentary on Plato.

2–3. These two poems are from *The Florence Miscellany* (privately printed in Florence, 1785), the work which launched the Della Cruscan movement. Though now fallen into considerable obscurity, the Della Cruscans had a powerful influence on the course of romanticism in England. Behind the movement stand the German *Sturm und Drang*, Rousseau, and (most plainly) the legacy of Richardson and Sterne's sentimentalism. Initially the group formed a coterie of Italians and English expatriates around Mrs Hester Piozzi. The poems in *The Florence Miscellany*, with a Preface by Mrs Piozzi, found their way to London, where they were printed in several periodicals, including *The Oracle* and *The World*, and quickly gained great celebrity. Robert Merry, the chief figure of the group, returned to England and increased his fame with many further publications, including several plays. His intense commitment to ideas associated with personal liberty and the French Revolution would eventually make him the focus of attack by reactionary circles (see the selection below by William Gifford, poem no. **37**). The women associated with the Della Cruscan movement were particularly satirized in Richard Polwhele's *The Unsex'd Females* (below, no. **69**). Parsons was a minor Della Cruscan writer. His translation is of course from the *Orlando Furioso*.

4. Published in Yearsley's first book *Poems on Several Occasions* (1785). Celebrated and condescended to as 'Lactilla, the milkmaid poet', Yearsley was in fact a fiercely independent spirit—as her first patron, Hannah More, would painfully discover (Anna Seward would speak of Yearsley's 'gloomy and jealous dignity of spirit'). Yearsley came from humble Bristol origins and married a labourer, John Yearsley, in 1774. Between then and 1784, when More discovered her and her work, Yearsley read and wrote poetry in the evenings after her day's work. More sponsored her first book, which was supported by over a thousand subscribers. Yearsley and More had a bitter falling out afterwards, but Yearsley went on to have a distinguished career.

Yearsley's 1785 volume was prefaced by More's letter to Elizabeth Montagu in which More recounted her view of Yearsley's life and character. This should be compared with Yearsley's own account which she printed in her next book, *Poems on Various Subjects* (1787).

1786

5–9. These poems are from the first edition of Burns's celebrated and influential

NOTES AND REFERENCES

Poems, Chiefly in the Scottish Dialect, published by subscription in Kilmarnock, 1786.

5. Epigraph: *Paradise Lost*, I. 128–9.
    111.   *Sin' that day MICHAEL*: *vide* Milton, Book 6th [line 320]. [RB]

6. The notes below are Robert Burns's:
[Prefatory note:] The following POEM will, by many readers, be well enough understood; but, for the sake of those who are unacquainted with the manners and traditions of the country where the scene is cast, Notes are added, to give some account of the principal Charms and Spells of the Night, so big with Prophecy to the Peasantry in the West of Scotland. The passion of prying into Futurity makes a striking part of the history of Human-nature, in its rude state, in all ages and nations; and it may be some entertainment to a philosophic mind, if any such should honor the Author with a perusal, to see the remains of it, among the more unenlightened in our own.
[Title:] is thought to be a night when Witches, Devils, and other mischief-making beings, are all abroad on their baneful, midnight errands: particularly, those aerial people, the Fairies, are said, on that night, to hold a grand Anniversary.
Epigraph: *The Deserted Village*, lines 251–4.
    2. *Cassilis Downans*: certain little, romantic, rocky, green hills in the neighbourhood of the ancient seat of the Earls of Cassilis.
    7. *Cove*: a noted cavern near Colean-house, called the Cove of Colean; which, as well as Cassilis Downans, is famed, in country story, for being a favourite haunt of Fairies.
    12. *BRUCE*: the famous family of that name, the ancestors of ROBERT the great Deliverer of his country, were Earls of Carrick.
    29. *stocks*: the first ceremony of Halloween, is pulling each a *Stock*, or plant of kail. They must go out, hand in hand, with eyes shut, and pull the first they meet with; its being big or little, straight or crooked, is prophetic of the size and shape of the grand object of all their Spells—the husband or wife. If any *yird*, or earth, stick to the root, that is the *tocher*, or fortune; and the taste of the *custoc*, that is, the heart of the stem, is indicative of the natural temper and disposition. Lastly, the stems, or to give them their ordinary appellation, the *runts*, are placed somewhere above the head of the door; and the christian names of people whom chance brings into the house, are, according to the priority of placing the *runts*, the names in question.
    47. *stalks o' corn*: they go to the barn-yard, and pull each, at three several times, a stalk of Oats. If the third stalk wants the *top-pickle*, that is, the grain at the top of the stalk, the party in question will want the Maidenhead.
    53. *Fause-house*: when the corn is in a doubtful state, by being too green, or wet, the Stack-builder, by means of old timber, &c. makes a large apartment in his stack, with an opening in the side which is fairest exposed to the wind: this he calls a *Fause-house*.
    55. *nits*: burning the nuts is a favourite charm. They name the lad and lass to each particular nut, as they lay them in the fire; and according as they burn quietly together, or start from beside one another, the course and issue of Courtship will be.
    98. *blue-clue*: whoever would, with success, try this spell, must strictly observe these directions. Steal out, all alone, to the *kiln*, and, darkling, throw into the *pot*, a clew of blue yarn: wind it in a new clew off the old one; and towards the latter end, something will hold the thread: demand, *wha hands?* i.e. who holds? and

answer will be returned from the kiln-pot, by naming the christian and sirname of your future Spouse.

111. *eat the apple*: take a candle, and go, alone, to a looking glass: eat an apple before it, and some traditions say you should comb your hair all the time: the face of your conjugal companion, *to be*, will be seen in the glass, as if peeping over your shoulder.

140. *hemp-seed*: steal out, unperceived, and sow a handful of hemp-seed; harrowing it with anything you can conveniently draw after you. Repeat, now and then, 'Hemp seed I saw thee, Hemp seed I saw thee; and him (or her) that is to be my true-love, come after me and pou thee.' Look over your left shoulder, and you will see the appearance of the person invoked, in the attitude of pulling hemp. Some traditions say, 'come after me and shaw thee,' that is, show thyself; in which case it simply appears. Others omit the harrowing, and say, 'come after me and harrow thee.'

182. *To winn three wechts o' naething*: this charm must likewise be performed, unperceived and alone. You go to the *barn*, and open both doors; taking them off the hinges, if possible; for there is danger, that the Being, about to appear, may shut the doors, and do you some mischief. Then take that instrument used in winnowing the corn, which, in our country-dialect, we call a *wecht*; and go thro' all the attitudes of letting down corn against the wind. Repeat it three times; and the third time, an apparition will pass thro' the barn, in at the windy door, and out at the other, having both the figure in question, and the appearance or retinue, marking the employment or station in life.

201. *It chanc'd the Stack he faddom't thrice*: take the opportunity of going, unnoticed, to a *Bear-stack*, and fathom it three times round. The last fathom of the last time, you will catch in your arms, the appearance of your future conjugal yoke-fellow.

214–15. *three Lairds' lan's met at a burn*: you go out, one or more, for this is a social spell, to a south-running spring or rivulet, where 'three Lairds' lands meet,' and dip your left shirt-sleeve. Go to bed in sight of a fire, and hang your wet sleeve before it to dry. Ly awake; and sometime near midnight, an apparition, having the exact figure of the grand object in question, will come and turn the sleeve, as if to dry the other side of it.

236. *The Luggies*: take three dishes; put clean water in one, foul water in another, and leave the third empty: blindfold a person, and lead him to the hearth where the dishes are ranged; he (or she) dips the left hand; if by chance in the clean water, the future husband or wife will come to the bar of Matrimony, a Maid; if in the foul, a widow; if in the empty dish, it foretells, with equal certainty, no marriage at all. It is repeated three times; and every time the arrangement of the dishes is altered.

248. *butter'd So'ns*: Sowens, with butter instead of milk to them, is always the *Halloween Supper*.

7. Dedication: Robert Aiken (1739–1807) was chiefly responsible for getting most of the subscribers for the 1786 Kilmarnock edition.

Epigraph: Thomas Gray, 'Elegy Written in a Country Church Yard', lines 29–32.

138. 'Hope "springs exhulting on triumphant wing," ' Pope's Windsor Forest [lines 111–12]. [RB]

10. Published in *The Asiatick Miscellany* (1786). In the Argument Jones refers to Sir Charles Wilkins (1749?–1836) and his translation of the *Bhagavad-gita* (1785),

from the *Mahabharata*. The line from Quintus Ennius (239–170 BC) may be rendered 'Behold this wondrous light, whom all invoke as Jove.'

1787

11–14. Published in the *World*, 29 June and 10 July 1787 and 3 Jan., 22 Feb., 17 May 1788. Nos. 11 and 13 inaugurated the amazing poetical correspondence in the pages of the *World* between Merry and Mrs Cowley, who would meet each other only much later (in April 1788, shortly before they brought their interchanges to a conclusion). The principal topics taken up in these highly personal and mannered exchanges were erotic sentiment, poetry, and social alienation. The poetical interplay between Della Crusca and Anna Matilda concluded in the *World* on 26 May 1788 with the latter's final poem 'To Della Crusca'. The sentimental love dialogue, carried out in public, became a feature of Della Cruscan poetry.

12. It is helpful to recall, in reading this poem, that it is playing with the contemporary ambiguity in the term 'horror', which can signify either a painful or a reverent feeling of fear (see *OED*, 'horror', 3*a* and 4).

1788

15. The epigraph may be rendered 'Go, now is the end of my loves.'

   47. *Lion Virgin Sphinx*: The overflowing of the Nile always happens while the sun is in Leo and Virgo. [RM]

16. Andrews was a minor Della Cruscan. Text from *The Poetry of the World*, ii (1788).

17. Published in the *World*, 8 May 1788. Sarah Hussey, Lady Tyrconnell (1763–1800): she was married to Lord Tyrconnell as a minor in 1780, but left her husband in 1791 to live (openly) with Lord Strathmore.

   Headnote: 'There is a gentleman about town, not a little remarkable for his talent at extempore verse. Not many weeks ago, he was requested by *Lady T‑rc——l* to give her a proof of it. The subject she chose, was the *Ring on her finger*: after a moment's pause, he repeated the following Stanza, the neatness of which has not an equal.'

1789

18. First published 1789.

19–20. Published posthumously in William Howley (ed.), *Sonnets and Miscellaneous Poems* ... (1789).

19. Title: Valclusa was the place where Petrarch spent a number of years living a hermit's life and devoting himself to study and writing. He wrote the sonnets to Laura during this period.

20. 3. *Great Pæan's Son*: Hephaestus, the son of Zeus and Hera ('Pæan' was a surname applied to various gods), and the god of fire. He was thrown from Olympus by his mother when a child because of his frailty, and lived for nine years in a grotto by the sea (see lines 2, 6). Later, he was thrown from Olympus a second time by Zeus in a quarrel, and landed upon the island of Lemnos in the Aegean. Russell appears to have combined these two incidents.

21. Published in Francis Gladwin (ed.), *The New Asiatic Miscellany* (Calcutta, 1789).
   102. *and pours insufferable light*: see Gray's Letters, p. 382, 4to. and the note. [SWJ]

22. From *Fourteen Sonnets . . .* (1789). Bowles's first edition was reissued in 1789 in a revised edition of twenty-one sonnets, and in a series of further augmented editions through 1800. The text here is from the ninth edition (1805).

23–30. From *Songs of Innocence*, which carries the imprint 'The Author & Printer W Blake 1789'. Nos. **29–30** were later transferred to some copies of the *Songs of Experience* (see below, nos. **43–54**). When the latter were completed, the two groups of Songs were gathered together as *The Songs of Innocence and of Experience*, an arrangement which highlighted the dialogic character of the works (e.g. 'The Lamb'/'The Tyger'; the two 'Holy Thursday' poems; 'A Divine Image'/'The Human Abstract').

1790

31. Published in the *Scots Musical Museum*, iii (1790). Text from James Kinsley's *Poems and Songs* (Oxford, 1968).

32. Published in *Julia; a Novel* (1790).

9. The song of the bards or minstrels of Otaheite was unpremeditated, and accompanied with music. They were continually going about from place to place; and they were rewarded by the master of the house with such things as the one wanted, and the other could spare. *Cook's Voyage*. [HMW]

33. Published in a quarto pamphlet in 1790.

47. See above, nos. **11–14**.

1791

34. Published in Francis Grose, *The Antiquities of Scotland* (1791), ii. 199–201 as a note to Grose's discussion of Alloway Church, Ayrshire. Grose's headnote to the poem reads: 'This church is also famous for being the place wherein the witches and warlocks used to hold their infernal meetings, or sabbaths, and prepare their magical unctions: here too they used to amuse themselves with dancing to the pipes of the muckle-horned Deel. Diverse stories of these horrid rites are still current; one of which my worthy friend Mr Burns has here favoured me with in verse.'

143–6. *Three lawyers tongues . . . in every neuk*: These four lines, printed by Grose and present in the MS, were later removed as being too strong, and most texts do not restore them.

210. *key-stane*: it is a well known fact that witches, or any evil spirits, have no power to follow a poor wight any farther than the middle of the next running stream.—It may be proper likewise to mention to the benighted traveller, that when he falls in with *bogles*, whatever danger may be his in going forward, there is much more hazard in turning back. [RB, MS n. printed in later edns.]

35. Published in vol. i of her *Poems* (1791). Her Della Cruscan pseudonym was Laura Maria.

36. Published in vol. i of *The Romance of the Forest* (1791).

37. *The Baviad* was the most famous of the many conservative attacks on the Della Cruscan movement. For Gifford's references see above nos. **2–3**, **11–14**, **31**, **33**, and nn. Gifford appended a series of ponderous notes to his text; the notes for this brief passage are exemplary:

1. *Lo, DELLA CRUSCA!*:

> 'O thou, to whom superior worth's allied,
> Thy country's honour, and the Muses pride—'

So says Laura Maria—

et solem quis dicere falsum
Audeat?

Indeed, she says a great deal more; but as I do not understand it, I forebear to lengthen my quotation.

Innumerable Odes, Sonnets, &c. published from time to time to time in the papers, have justly procured this gentleman the reputation of the first poet of the age: but the performance which called forth the high-sounding panegyric above mentioned, is a philosophical rhapsody on the French Revolution, called the 'Wreath of Liberty.'

Of this poem no reader (provided he can read) is at this time ignorant: but as there are various opinions concerning it, and as I do not choose perhaps to dispute with a lady of Mrs Robinson's critical abilities, I shall select a few passages from it, and leave the world to judge how truly its author can be said to be

> —'gifted with the sacred lyre,
> Whose sounds can more than mortal thoughts inspire.'

This supernatural effort of genius, then, is chiefly distinguished by three very prominent features.—1. Downright nonsense. 2. Downright frigidity. 3. Downright doggerel.—Of each of these in its turn: and first of the first.

> 'Hang o'er his eye the gossamery tear.
> Wreath round her airy harp the tim'rous joy.
> Recumbent eve rock the reposing tide.
> A web-work of despair, a mass of woes.
> And o'er my lids the scalding tumor roll.'

'TUMOUR, a morbid swelling.' JOHNSON. An excellent thing to roll over an eye, especially if it happen to be hot and hot, as in the present case.

> —'summer-tints begemm'd the scene,
> And silky ocean slept in glossy green.

> While air's nocturnal ghost, in paly shroud,
> Glances with grisly glare from cloud to cloud.

> And gauzy zephyrs, flutt'ring o'er the plain,
> On twilight's boom drop their filmy rain.'

Unus instar omnium! This couplet staggered me. I should be loth to be found correcting a madman and yet more folly seems unequal to the production of such exquisite nonsense.

2do.

> —'the explosion came
> And burst the o'ercharg'd culverin of shame.'

> —'days of old
> Their perish'd, proudest, pageantry unfold.'

> —'nothing I descry,
> But the bare boast of barren heraldry.'

> —'The huntress queen,
> Showers her shafts of silver o'er the scene.'

To these add, 'moody monarchs,' 'turgid tyrants,' 'pampered popes,' 'radiant rivers,' 'cooling cataracts,' 'lazy Loires,' (of which, by the bye, there are none) 'gay

Garrones,' 'gloomy glass,' 'mingling murder,' 'dauntless day,' 'lettered lightnings,' 'delicious dilatings,' 'sinking sorrows,' 'blissful blessings,' 'rich reasoning,' 'meliorating mercies,' 'vicious venalities,' 'sublunary suns,' 'dewy vapours damp, that sweep the silent swamp;' and a world of others, to be found in the compass of half a dozen pages.

3tio.

> 'In phosphor blaze of genealogic line.'

N.B. Written to 'the turning of a brazen candlestick.'

> 'O better were it ever to be lost
> In black negation's sea, than reach the coast.'

This couplet may be placed to advantage under the first head.

> 'Should the zeal of parliament be empty words.
> turn to France, and see
> Four million men in arms for liberty.'

> —'doom for a breath
> A hundred reasoning hecatomb to death.'

A hecatomb is a sacrifice of a hundred head of oxen. Where did this gentleman hear of their *reasoning*?

> 'Awhile I'll ruminate on time and fate;
> And the most probable event of things'—

EUGE, MAGNE POETA! Well may Laura Maria say,

> 'That GENIUS glows in every classic line,
> And NATURE dictates—every thing that's thine.'

7. Scilicet haec populo, pexusque togaque recenti
    Et natalitia tandem cum sardonyche albus
    Sede leges celsa, liquido cum plasmate guttur
    Mobile collueris, patranti fractus ocello.

19. 'GENIUS or MUSE, whoe'er thou art, whose thrill
    Exhalts the fancy, and inflames the will,
    Bids o'er the heart sublime sensation roll,
    And wakes ecstatic fervour in the soul.'

See the commencement of the Wreath of Liberty, where our great poet, with a dexterity peculiar to himself, has contrived to fill several quarto pages without a single idea.

> Hic neque more probo videas, neque voca serena,
> Ingentes trepidare Titos, cum carmina lumbum
> Intrant, et tremulo scalpuntur ubi intima versu.

25–6. I learn from Della Crusca's lamentations that he is declined into the vale of years; that the women say to him, as they formerly said to Anacreon, —— and that Love, about two years since,

> —'tore his name from his bright page,
> And gave it to approaching age.'

> Tun' vetule, auriculis alienis colligas escas
> Auriculis, quibus et dicas cute perditus, ohe!
> Quo didicisse, nisi hoc fermentum, et quae semel intus
> Innata est, rupto jecore exierit caprificus?

38. Printed anonymously in the *Norfolk Chronicle*, 16 July 1791. Text here is from the *Cambridge Intelligencer*, 29 Nov. 1794, where it appeared under the title 'The Triumph of Freedom'.

1792

39. Published in the *Scots Musical Museum*, iv (1792). Text from James Kinsley's *Poems and Songs*, 3 vols. (Oxford, 1968).

1793

40. The publication date of Blake's *Marriage* is approximate. The poem's political context is the early years of the French Revolution as that event was perceived by an antinomian liberal mind. The text here is organized by (numbered) plates plus lines of verse. Plate numbers for this and the other Blake texts are those of Gerald E. Bentley, Jr. (ed.), *William Blake's Writings* (Oxford, 1978).

pl. 2, line 1. *Rintrah*: spirit of revolutionary prophecy; the new day is appropriately announced by a word (and name) only just 'now perceived by the minds of men' [pl. 7].

pl. 3. *thirty-three years*: i.e. 1790, the year the *Marriage* was begun, which is thirty-three years after the birth of Blake. See also below, n. for pl. 21.

pl. 6. *a mighty Devil*: another ironic self-reference; the text projects an image of Blake the revolutionary engraver.

pl. 21. The philosopher and mystic Emanuel Swedenborg (1688–1772) was a powerful influence on Blake; the *Marriage* is at once an imitation, parody, and critique of Swedenborg's *Heaven and Hell* (1758), which Blake may also be recalling in pl. 3.

pl. 24. *The Bible of Hell*: see below, no. 55.

41–42. Published in the *Gentleman's Magazine* (July and Oct. 1793).

1794

43–54. The title-page of *Songs of Experience* carries the imprint 'The Author & Printer W Blake 1794'. Though a separate title-page for the sequence was printed, none of the extant copies of *Experience* appear by themselves, separated from the *Songs of Innocence*.

43–4. Though engraved on separate plates, the poems are in dialogue with each other.

47. The engraved text arranges the stanzas in the spatial relation represented here. The arrangement establishes an ambiguity in the stanza sequencing.

49–51. The three poems are engraved together on a single plate.

55. The imprint on *The Book of Urizen* is 'Lambeth. Printed by Will Blake 1794'. On the title-page, the word 'First' is erased in some copies; the word signals Blake's original intention to have written several other 'books' for this bible of hell. *Urizen* is a parody of Genesis, the 'first book' of Moses. The duplicate chapter iv in *Urizen* probably represents Blake's effort to parody similar duplications in the early books of the orthodox bible. The title is a homophonic word play meant to recall both 'your reason' and 'horizon'. There are gaps in the plate sequence because some of the text's plates contain only pictorial material.

pl. 5, line 38. *Los*: Blake's eternal form of imagination as it operates in time and space; the name is 'Sol' backwards, and it also signifies 'Los[s]'. Los's female emanation is Enitharmon.

pl. 19, line 45. This is *Orc*, the demonic child meant to recall (in the biblical context) Cain.

pl. 23, lines 13, 15. *Utha, Grodna*: names meant to signal primitive (pagan) deities.

pl. 28. *Fuzon* is Blake's imagination of Moses, and this final chapter glances at the biblical Exodus.

56–7. Published in the *Cambridge Intelligencer* (15 Mar., 13 Sept. 1794). National fast days were called during the war; Coleridge in 1796 would write his 'Essay on Fasts' in protest against them.

58. Published in the *Champion*. The text here is from *The Poetical Recreations of the Champion* . . . (1822).

59. Published in the *Scots Magazine* (Dec. 1794).

1795

60. The *Watchman* text of the poem has the following headnote: We are happy in being able to present our readers with the following admirable lines, written by MR CROWE, the public Orator of the University of Oxford: they were intended to have been spoken by an Under-Graduate at the Installation of the Duke of Portland; but were rejected by the Vice-Chancellor, on account of the *too free* sentiments which they conveyed. MR CROWE is the Author of LEWESDON-HILL, a Poem.

—Quod qui non legit, legat, qui legit, relegat.

[Text from the *Watchman*, 5 (2 Apr. 1796), 144–5.]

The poem first appeared in the *European Magazine* (June 1795), 418–19, but the version from the *Watchman* is given here because of the interesting headnote. The Latin motto 'Those who have not read it, read it; those who have read it, read it again' may have been by Coleridge.

1796

61. Published in the *Scots Musical Museum*, v (1796).

62. Published in Coleridge's first collection, *Poems on Various Occasions* (1796). The title here was fixed in 1817, but this is the 1796 text. (Original title: 'Effusion XXXV. Composed August 20th, 1795, at Clevedon, Somersetshire'.) Sara is Sara Fricker, whom Coleridge married in Oct. 1795. Clevedon is where the couple took their honeymoon.

51. L'athée n'est point à mes yeux un faux esprit; je puis vivre avec lui aussi bien et mieux qu'avec le dévot, car il raisonne davantage, mais il lui manque un sens, et mon ame ne se fond point entièrement avec le sienne: il est froid au spectacle le plus ravissant, et il cherche un syllogisme lorsque je rends une action de grace. 'Appel a l'impartiale postérité', par la Citoyenne Roland, troisième partie, p. 67. [STC, 1796]

63. Taylor translates the original ballad by Gottfried August Burger (1747–94), the German *Sturm und Drang* poet. Taylor moves the scene of the action from the seven years' war to the time of the crusades. The translation had been circulating in MS since 1790, when Taylor wrote it. Scott wrote and published his translation —which is deeply in debt to Taylor's—in 1796 under the title 'William and Helen'. Taylor's translation appeared in the *Monthly Magazine* (Mar. 1796) and in a separately printed pamphlet; the latter is the text printed here.

64–5. 'The Erl-King' was first published in the *Monthly Mirror* (Oct. 1796); it was reprinted in Lewis's two-volume collection *Tales of Wonder* (1801), i, no. 9, with the following headnote: 'Though founded on a Danish tradition, this Ballad was originally written in German, and is the production of the celebrated Goethe, author of Werter etc.' The second ballad was one of the poems published in *The Monk* (1796), vol. iii.

1797

66–7. Southey's poem appeared in his *Poems* (1797); it was soon parodied by Canning and Frere in the *Anti-Jacobin* (27 Nov. 1797).

1798

68. Published in the *Anti-Jacobin*, 19 Feb. 1798. The work parodies Richard Payne Knight's (1750–1824) *The Progress of Civil Society, a Didactic Poem in Six Books* (1796).

69. Published in 1798 and 'addressed to the author of *The Pursuits of Literature*' (1794–7), i.e. T. J. Matthias (1754–1835), another conservative critic of the period. The epigraph of Polwhele's work is from a note in Matthias's poem: 'Our unsex'd female writers now instruct, or confuse, us and themselves, in the labyrinth of politics, or turn us wild with Gallic frenzy' (7th edn., p. 238). Mary Wollstonecraft is the chief object of attack, but Polwhele also singles out Mrs Barbauld, Mary Robinson, Charlotte Smith, Helen Maria Williams, Ann Yearsley, Mary Hays (1760–1843), the painter Angelica Kauffmann (1741–1807), and Emma Crewe.

The notes below are Polwhele's:

1. *all the poet's*: in my opinion, the Author of 'the Pursuits of Literature' has discovered, in his animated Satire, a true poetical genius. And (as a writer, who had very little pretensions to the character himself, observes) 'a true poet is a public good.' The satire in question, seems to have produced effects, resembling those which distinguished the poetry of Greece and Rome. For I can assert, on the best authorities, that many in this country, whose politics and even religion have been long wavering, are now fixed in their principles by 'the Pursuits of Literature.'

4. by the muse I mean literature in general.

5. *from her beam*: I agree with the Author of 'the Pursuits,' both in his praises and his censures of the writers of this country, with a few exceptions only. To his eulogia, indeed, I heartily assent: but, I think, his animadversions on [Erasmus] Darwin and [William] Hayley [1745–1820] in particular, are unmerited. In composing his Botanic Garden, Dr Darwin was aware, that though imagination refuse to enlist under the banner of science, yet science may sometimes be brought forward, not unhappily, under the conduct of imagination: and of the latter, if I am any way a judge, we are presented with a complete specimen in that admirable poem. With respect to the structure of the poem, we have been told, that it wants connexion—that there is a reciprocal repulsion between the scientific and imaginative particles, and so little affinity even between the latter, that they cannot possibly cohere. But on this topic, let us hear the Author himself; who invites us to contemplate, in his poem, 'a great variety of little pictures, connected only by a slight festoon of ribbons.' And they are pictures glowing in the richest colors—the most beautiful, in short, that were ever delineated by the poetic pencil. I defy any one of Dr Darwin's censurers, to point out a single picture, which is not finished with touches the most exquisite—'with all the magic charms of light and shade.'

NOTES AND REFERENCES

I had intended to examine the style, the versification, the poetry; but rather let me desire my Reader to open either of the volumes, at a venture, and take the first description that presents itself: and he will find painting sublime as [Henry] Fuseli's, or as beautiful as Emma Crewe's. It is easy to run over the changes of 'artificial glitter'—'glaring varnish'—'deliciousness that cloys.' Thus was Gibbon treated. Gibbon forsooth, was required to bring down the haughtiness of his style to a level with that of vulgar 'prosers.' And Darwin must lower his eagle wing, to silence the clamour of the poetic sparrow-hawks, that, whilst they arraign his flights, are pining at their own imbecility.—Of the other poet, Mr Hayley, whose merit has been much depreciated by the author of 'the Pursuits,' I have always entertained the highest opinion. In graceful negligence, and in harmony of numbers, he surely stands unrivalled. He has all that lucid imagery, and that chaste elegance which characterise the poet of Eloisa: and his imagery is his own. Pope's was borrowed. In copiousness of expression, he is vastly superior to Pope. But from his command of language, he is sometimes tempted to riot in redundancies, or to expand a sentiment where he ought to compress it. I need not enumerate his various productions, both in verse and prose; all of which will probably descend to posterity, with honor to his name. But his 'Triumphs of Temper' [1781] is a poem, in which the invention of Spenser is blended with the perspicuity and melody of Pope.—I might mention other names which the Author of 'the Pursuits' seems to have slighted—but I shall hint only, that he has entirely omitted several names of literary respectability—particularly in the west of England. What does he think of [John] Whitaker [1735–1808]? Doubtless a gentleman of such high eminence as the historian of Manchester [1771], the memorialist of Mary Queen of Scots [1787], &c. &c. must have his share 'in affecting public order, regulated government and polished society.'

9. 'Greatly think, or nobly die.' Pope [slightly misquoted from 'Elegy to the Memory of an Unfortunate Lady', line 10].

12. NATURE'S law: Nature is the grand basis of all laws human and divine: and the woman, who has no regard to nature, either in the decoration of her person, or the culture of her mind, will soon 'walk after the flesh, in the lust of uncleanness, and despise government' [2 Peter 2: 10].

13.   A troop came next, who crowns and armour wore,
             And proud defiance in their looks they bore. Pope.

The Amazonian band—the female Quixotes of the new philosophy, are, here, too justly characterised. Nor could they read, I suspect, some passages in the sixth satire of Juvenal without an uneasy sensation:

           Quam praestare potest mulier galeata pudorem?

I have seen in MS Mr Gifford's masterly translation of this satire. Our expectations, I hope, will soon be gratified by his entire version of Juvenal. [It was finally published in 1802.]

35.   However gross, indeed, the food might be,
             .   .   .   .   .   . to taste
             Think not, she would be nice .   .
                        .   for what redounds, transpires
             Thro' spirits with ease!

                              Paradise Lost [v. 432 ff.]

38. Miss Wollstonecraft used often to meet Mr Fuseli at the house of a common friend, where she was so charmed with his talents, and the tout ensemble, that she

suffered herself to fall in love with him, though a married man. See [William] Godwin's *Memoirs* [1798].

43. The vegetable passion of love is agreeably seen in the flower of the Parnassia, in which the males alternately approach and recede from the female, and in the flower of Nigella, or Devil in the Bush, in which the tall females bend down to their dwarf husbands. But I was, this morning, surprised to observe, among Sir Brooke Boothby's valuable collection of plants at Asbourn, the manifest adultery of several females of the plant Collinsonia, who had bent themselves into contact with the males of other flowers of the same plant, in their vicinity, neglectful of their own. Botanic Garden, Part the First, p. 197—3rd Edit.

52. To smother in dissipation her passion for Fuseli, Miss W. had fled to France. There she met with a paramour responsive to her sighs, a Mr [Gilbert] Imlay [1754–1828]: with him she formed a connexion, though not a matrimonial one; being always of opinion, with Eloisa, that

> Love, free as air, at sight of human ties,
> Spreads his light wings, and in a moment flies!

> [*Eloisa to Abelard*, lines 75–6]

56. Imlay soon left his lady to her own imaginations. Thus abandoned, she returned to London; and driven to desperation, attempted to put an end to her life, but was recovered. She soon, however, made a second effort to plunge into eternity. In a dark and tempestuous night, she repaired to Putney-bridge; where, determined to throw herself into the river, she walked up and down, for half an hour, through the rain, that her clothes, being thoroughly drenched and heavy, might facilitate her descent into the water. She then leaped from the top of the bridge; but finding a difficulty in sinking, tried to press her clothes closely around her, and at last became insensible; but at this moment she was discovered, and brought back to life. See Godwin's *Memoirs*.

70. Published in the *Courier*, 8 Nov. 1798.

71. Published 1798.

Book 7. 17. *tho' they saw*: If this were not taken parenthetically, and read so, it would convey a double sense. Charoba told the attendants that she was rising, 'tho' they saw'—tho' they were in the apartment, and could perceive that there were no preparations for that purpose. [WSL, n. in 1803.]

72. Composed Jan. 1798. Printed in *Blank Verse* (1798).

73–9. The poems appeared in this order in the one-volume 1798 edition of *Lyrical Ballads*. A second volume was added for the second edition (1800), when Wordsworth added his famous Preface. The Preface was expanded in the 1805 edition; the latter text is printed here as an appendix, pp. 771–9. For the poems from vol. ii of 1800 see below, nos. 87–94. 73. This is the 1798 text. The poem was the first in the 1798 *Lyrical Ballads*; in the 1800 (second) edition it was placed at the end of vol. i under the title 'The Ancient Mariner: A Poet's Reverie'. ('Expostulation and Reply' was placed first.) When Coleridge printed it again in *Sibylline Leaves* (1817) the text was much revised, and the well-known glosses were added in the margin. (The glosses are an antiquarian touch, intended to be read as if written by a seventeenth-century commentator.) The 1816 text is in effect a new poem.

348. *Lavrock*: Sky-lark (1800 text).

79. 4. The river is not affected by the tides a few miles above Tintern. [WW]

107. This line has a close resemblance to an admirable line of Young, the exact expression of which I cannot recollect. [WW, *Night Thoughts*, VI. 424.]

80. Published in a quarto pamphlet, 1798. The 'cradled infant' is Coleridge's eldest son Hartley (1796–1849).

15. In all parts of the animal kingdom these films are called *strangers*, and supposed to portend the arrival of some absent friend. [STC]

1799

81–2. Both translations published posthumously in *The Works of Sir William Jones . . .* (1799).

83. Written in 1785–6, the poem was first printed (partially) in 1799 as a chapbook; first published complete in 1802 by Thomas Stewart in Glasgow under the title *The Jolly Beggars; or, Tatterdemallions. A Cantata.* The text here is from Kinsley's *Poems and Songs*.

2. *Buackie-bird*: the old Scotch name for the bat. [RB]

9. *Poosie-Nancie's*: the Hostess of a noted Caravansary in M[auchline], well known to and much frequented by the lowest orders of Travellers and Pilgrims. [RB]

33–4. *where my LEADER . . . ABRAM*: Referring to the battle of Quebec (1759), when General James Wolfe died after taking the Heights of Abraham from the French (under General Montcalm).

35–6. *when the gallant* game . . . *drum*: The British attacked the Moro (a fortress guarding the harbour of Santiago) in 1762.

37–40. *with Curtis . . . drum*: Refers to the defence of Gibraltar against Spanish attack in 1782; Admiral Roger Curtis commanded the English, and General George Eliott destroyed the enemy's floating batteries.

178. *Kilbaigie*: a peculiar sort of Whiskie so called is a great favourite with Poosie Nansie's Clubs. [RB]

188. *clunk*: sound made when a narrow-necked bottle is being emptied.

194. Homer is allowed to be the eldest Ballad singer on record. [RB]

84. Published in the *Monthly Magazine* (July 1799).

85–6. Published in the *Morning Post*, 28 Dec. 1799 and 3 Jan. 1800, under her frequent pseudonym Tabitha Bramble. Except for the original titles, the texts here are from the corrected and slightly revised *Poetical Works* (1806).

1800

87–94. From vol. ii of *Lyrical Ballads*. 92. 4. The house at which I was boarded during the time I was at school. [WW]

93. The poem is better known by the title Wordsworth later gave it, 'The Danish Boy'. Lines 45–55 were dropped in the 1802 edition of *Lyrical Ballads* and thereafter.

94. 179. Clipping is the word used in the North of England for shearing. [WW]

1801

95. Written in 1785. The 'Sessional process' against Hamilton had begun in 1784, but the charges were dismissed early in the next year. The original of Holy Willie was the Mauchline farmer William Fisher (1737–1809). First printed in *Poems ascribed to Robert Burns . . .*, ed. Thomas Stewart (1801). Epigraph from *The Rape*

of the Lock, IV. 64. Text here from Kinsley's *Poems and Songs*.

96. Published in M. G. Lewis's collection *Tales of Wonder* (1801), ii, no. 52, with the following headnote: 'I am not at liberty to publish the name of the author of this Ballad: it is founded on the fourth chapter of the Romance of "Ambrosio, or the Monk".' The ballad's climax varies from the story as told in Lewis's famous novel.

97. This is from Williams's sequence 'Sonnets from Paul and Virginia'. Published in *Poems Moral, Elegant, and Pathetic . . . and Original Sonnets by Helen Maria Williams* (1801). Bernardin de Saint-Pierre's (1737–1814) sentimental novel *Paul et Virginie* (1783) had a great influence on writers of the romantic period.

98. Published 1801.

99. Published in *The Poetical Works of the Late Thomas Little, Esq.* (1801).

1802

100. Composed probably summer 1800. Printed in *John Woodvil: A Tragedy*. By C. Lamb &c. (1802).

101. Published in the *Morning Post* under Robinson's pseudonym Oberon; text here from the *Spirit of the Public Journals*, 5 (1802), 234.

102. At least three integral versions of the poem exist; an MS version sent in a letter to William Sotheby dated 19 July 1802; the version printed in *Sibylline Leaves* (1816); and the first printed version (given here), which appeared in the *Morning Post*, 4 Oct. 1802.

   25. *EDMUND*: 'William' (i.e. Wordsworth) in the MS; 'Lady' (presumably Sara Hutchinson, with whom Coleridge was in love) in the 1816 text.

   87–8. Coleridge's hiatus is a highly expressive feature in this version of the poem.

   94. Tairn, a small lake, generally, if not always, applied to the lakes up in the mountains, and which are the feeders of those in the vallies. This address to the wind will not appear extravagant to those who have heard it at night, in a mountainous country. [STC]

1803

103. This was the last poem Cowper wrote in English (in 1799). It was first published by William Hayley in his *Life, and Posthumous Writings, of William Cowper* (1803), vol. ii. The story is drawn from an incident related in Richard Walter's *A Voyage Round the World . . . by George Anson* (1748).

104. Published in the seventh edition of *The Pleasures of Hope* (1803).

1804

105. Published in the *European Magazine*, Feb. 1804.

106–7. The dating for both signals when Blake began work on his two epic poems. Both were finished some time later—in the case of *Jerusalem*, probably much later (perhaps 1818–20). The *Milton* excerpts are from pls. 2, 24, 30–1; from *Jerusalem*, pls. 15–16. *Milton* pls. 30–1 introduce the descent of Ololon, who is Milton's female emanation in the poem.

1805

108. Composed around 1803–4 when England was threatened by invasion from France. The poem is the font of much Lancashire dialect poetry. The weaver and teacher Joseph Lees of Glodwick was probably the sole author, though the issue has been hotly disputed. Text here is taken from John Harland's *Ballads and Songs of Lancashire* (1865).

109–13. Published in *Hours of Solitude* (1805).

114. *Psyche* was privately printed in 1805, but the edition of 1811 (*Psyche, with other poems*) established her reputation. The latter supplies the text here.

1806

115. Published in *Simonidea* (1806) without title, but under the general heading 'On the Dead'. Rose Aylmer (1779–1800) was the only daughter of the fourth Baron Aylmer.

116. Published in *Rhymes for the Nursery* (1806). The poem rewrites Blake's 'The Tyger' (no. **48**).

117. First published in the *Gentleman's Magazine* (Nov. 1806); printed as a small book (4 × 5 inches), the first in the famous series known as *Harris's Cabinet*, in Jan. 1807, with coloured illustrations by the painter William Mulready (1786–1863). Text here is from the edition of 1808.

1807

118. This is the opening passage of the poem; published in *Beachy Head and Other Poems* (1807). The notes below are Charlotte Smith's:
  3. In crossing the Channel from the coast of France, Beachy-Head is the first land made.
  6–7. Alluding to an idea that this island was once joined to the continent of Europe, and torn from it by some convulsion of Nature. I confess I never could trace the resemblances between the two countries. Yet the cliffs around Dieppe resemble the chalk cliffs on the Southern coast. But Normandy has no likeness whatever to the part of England opposite to it.
  23. *Terns.*—Sterna hirundo, or sea swallow. *Gulls.*—Larus canus. *Tarrocks.*—Larus tridactylus.
  25. *Gray Choughs.*—Corvus Graculens, Cornish Choughs, or, as these birds are called by the Sussex people, Saddle-backed Crows, build in great numbers on this coast.

119. Published in *The Lay of an Irish Harp . . .* (1807).
  Epigraph: Edward Young, *Night Thoughts*, VIII. 967.

120–31. All published in *Poems, in Two Volumes* (1807). Nos. **120–5** are from vol. i; nos. **126–31** from vol. ii. Nos. **122–4** are part of the section headed 'Miscellaneous Sonnets' (of which twenty were printed); no. **125** is from the section headed 'Sonnets Dedicated to Liberty' (where Wordsworth's reactions to the war with France are most direct; twenty-six were printed); nos. **127–9** are from the section 'Moods of My Own Mind'. The poems were written between 1802 and 1807.

120. Written 1804–7.
  46. Echoes Milton's *The Doctrine and the Discipline of Divorce* (1644).

121. Written 1802. Leeches were used by physicians for bleeding patients.
  43. *Chatterton*: Thomas Chatterton (1752–70).
  45–6. *Him . . . mountain-side*: Robert Burns.

122. Probably drafted in Sept. 1802 and completed a year later.

126. Written Nov. 1805. Wordsworth's note to the poem credits a sentence from Thomas Wilkinson's MS text *Tour in Scotland* as the inspiration of the poem: 'Passed by a Female who was reaping alone: she sung in Erse [Gaelic] as she bended over her sickle; the sweetest human Voice I ever heard: her strains were tenderly melancholy and felt delicious, long after they were heard no more.'

128. Written 1802–7. Probably in debt to the *Journal* of his sister Dorothy; the entry for 15 Apr. 1802 records the pair's experience along the shore of Ullswater in prose very close to Wordsworth's verse.

130. Written May–June 1806; Wordsworth's brother John had died in 1805. Wordsworth stayed at Peele Castle, on the south coast of the Lake District, in 1794. Sir George Beaumont's painting 'A Storm: Peele Castle' was exhibited in 1806.

131. Wordsworth said lines 1–57 were written in 1802 and the rest in 1804. In 1815 the title was changed to the familiar 'Ode. Intimations of Immortality from Recollections of Early Childhood', and Wordsworth substituted the epigraph from Virgil (*Eclogues*, 4. 1) with the last three lines of '[My heart leaps up]'.

58 ff. Wordsworth commented: 'I took . . . the notion of pre-existence . . . to make . . . the best use of it I could as a Poet.'

103. *'humorous stage'*: Quoting Samuel Daniel's sonnet to Fulke Greville (line 1) in his *Musophilus*.

1808

132. Published in *The Warrior's Return and Other Poems* (1808).

133. Published in *Marmion* (1808).

1809

134. Published in *Poetic Amusement . . .* (1809).

135. Published in *Gertrude of Wyoming* (1809).

1810

136. Published 1810. The passage is the curse pronounced on Ladurlad by Kehama. The curse is demanded by the spirit of Prince Arvalan, whom Ladurlad had killed.

137–8. Published in her *Poetical Works* (Edinburgh, 1810), 3 vols., edited by Scott. The sonnet to the 'ladies of Llangollen' was written after her first visit (1795), which Seward described in her 1796 volume *Llangollen Vale, with Other Poems*. The ladies were Lady Eleanor Butler (1745–1829) and Sarah Ponsonby (1755–1831); their reclusive life together in Wales was much celebrated.

139. Published in *The Associate Minstrels* (1810), and dated July 1808.

140. Published in *The Lady of the Lake* (1810).

141. Published in *The Borough* (1810) as 'Letter XXII' in the section 'The Poor of the Borough': a tale of the evils of parish apprenticeship.

195. *Golden-eye*: a species of sea duck.

1811

142. Published in *Poems*, 2nd edn. (1811).

1812

143. Published 1812; text here is 1812 corrected against the 1814 edition. In the poem's imaginary setting, James V of Scotland (1512–42) leads the local beauty Maggie Lauder to the festival, where she will be affianced to Rob the Ranter.

51. *the flimsy Chian vest*: The island of Cos was noted for its light transparent garments.

66. *Semiramis*: Queen of Nineveh and Babylon.

144. When the first two cantos of this poem were published in 1812, Byron 'awoke and found myself famous'.

3–4. Part of the Acropolis was destroyed during a siege in 1687.

19. *Son of the morning*: a Levantine.

55. *Athena's wisest son*: Socrates.

66. *doctrine*: that there would be no resurrection.

72. *The Bactrian, Samian sage*: Zoroaster and Pythagoras.

73. *thou!—whose love and life together fled*: John Edleston, a Cambridge choirboy who died in 1811.

145–6. Both poems were published in *Poems* (1812).

Line 12 of 'The Boy of Egremond' carried the following note: In the twelfth century, William Fitz-Duncan laid waste the valleys of Craven with fire and sword; and was afterwards established by his uncle, David King of Scotland.

He was the last of his race; his son, commonly called the Boy of Egremond, dying before him in the manner here related; when a Priory was removed from Embsay to Bolton, that it might be as near as possible to the place where the accident happened. That place is still known by the name of the 'Strid;' and the mother's answer, as given in the first stanza, is to this day often repeated in Wharfedale.—See Whitaker's History of Craven. [SR]

147. Published in *Rejected Addresses; or, The New Theatrum Poetarum* (1812), in which various contemporary poets were parodied. The occasion was the opening of the new Drury Lane Theatre ('Holland's edifice', line 38), which had burned down in 1809. A poetical competition for an opening 'address' was held, and Lord Holland specifically urged Byron to write one; it was in fact chosen. 'Cui Bono?' imitates Byron's *Childe Harold*, of course.

148. Published as *Eighteen Hundred and Eleven. A Poem* (1812), in a quarto pamphlet. The satire, her last poem in print before her death, was generally attacked. Her closest friends rushed to apologize for it, giving personal unhappiness as the reason for the poem's tone. Her husband had died a few years earlier.

95. *Tadmor*: the biblical Palmyra.

96. *Stern Marius*: Gaius Marius (157–86 BC), Roman consul and general.

106–17. *Tempe* is in Greece; *Ausonia* is Italy, where the fields of Enna are located; *Hercynian* means German.

124. *'build the lofty verse'*: Misquoting Milton's *Lycidas*, line 10.

134. *Tully . . . and Maro*: Cicero and Virgil.

135. *Bonduca*: the early British queen Boadicea.

171–6. South American references: *Chimborazo*, a volcano; *La Plata*, a river; *Potosi*, a mining centre. Barbauld imagines their freedom from Spain.

149. Published in *Tales* (1812).

86. Allusion is here made . . . to the *Upas*, or poison-tree of Java . . . (GC)

183. Matthew 7: 13.

184. *tilted boats*: boats with awnings.

275. *trepann'd*: cheated.

310. *Badge-man*: a licensed beggar.

1813

150. Published 1813. In his prose Advertisement to the poem Byron placed the action at the end of the eighteenth century; the Giaour is a young Venetian. In a series of famous additions, the poem doubled its length through the first seven editions; the text here is the seventh (corrected). The prose notes are an integral feature of the work and were originally printed at the foot of the text page (first proofs).

9. *Colonna*: Cape Sunium.

566. *Liakura*: Parnassus.

151. Published in the *Monthly Magazine*, 35 (May 1813).

152. This is the entirety of the fragment published in *The World before the Flood . . . with Other Occasional Pieces* (1813).

1814

153. Published in *The Minor's Pocket Book* (1814).

154–5. Both *The Corsair* and *Lara* were published in 1814. The excerpts printed here develop a portrait of the famous Byronic Hero.

156. Published in *The Excursion, Being a Portion of The Recluse, A Poem* (1814). The composition of this long work began as early as 1797 as part of the project that included *The Prelude* and *The Recluse*; only *The Excursion* and *The Prelude* were completed. Wordsworth's Preface to *The Excursion* supplies a narrative explanation of the *Recluse* project. The extract printed here was written much earlier as an independent story titled 'The Ruined Cottage'. It culminates the section headed 'The Wanderer', which is Book 1 of the poem.

1815

157–8. 'She walks in beauty' was published in *Hebrew Melodies* (1815); 'Stanzas for Music' was first published as a separate piece of sheet music, to a setting by Sir John Stevenson, in 1815. It was revised and reprinted in Byron's *Poems* (1816), and the latter is the text printed here.

158. Epigraph: Thomas Gray, 'Alcaic Fragment'.

159. Published in *Irish Melodies*, 6 (1815).

1816

160. Published in Byron's *Poems* (1816). The poem is addressed to Lady Byron, who left the poet early in 1816 with their infant daughter Ada. The bitter separation raised scandalous rumours about Byron.

161. Begun in 1797 and originally intended for the *Lyrical Ballads*. First published by John Murray (at Byron's urging) in the 1816 volume containing as well 'Kubla Khan' and 'The Pains of Sleep'. The 'celebrated poets' of the Preface are Scott and Byron.

128–33. *The lady sank . . . not in pain*: Evil spirits, it is said, cannot cross a blessed threshold by themselves.

162. Written in 1798, not (as Coleridge states here) in 1797. Published with

'Christabel' 'at the request' of Byron. Coleridge cites *Purchas his Pilgrimage* (1626), and quotes loosely from Book IV, ch. 13. The verse quoted in the prose introduction (headed in 1816 'Of the Fragment of Kubla Khan') is from Coleridge's poem 'The Picture; or, The Lover's Resolution', lines 91–100. The Greek quotation (corrected in 1834) is from Theocritus, I. 45.

163. Published in Campbell Albyn's *Anthology* (1816). Scott's note to the poem ('The first stanza is ancient') explains the constructed character of the ballad.

164. Published as a separate pamphlet in 1816. The poem is best known for the influence it had on Byron's *Don Juan*.

165. *The Story of Rimini* (1818) elaborates Dante's Paolo and Francesca episode (*Inferno*, V. 97–142).

166. First published in the *Examiner*, 1 Dec. 1816. Balboa, not Cortez, discovered the Pacific.

167. Canto III of *Childe Harold* was published late in 1816; it is the first poem Byron wrote after leaving England following the scandalous breakup of his marriage.

1. Alluding to the poem's first instalment, *Childe Harold's Pilgrimage. A Romaunt* (1812).

42. *the apples on the Dead Sea's shore*: fabled to be fair without, but ashes within.

55. *the greatest, nor the worst of men*: Napoleon.

145. *Lake Leman*: Lake Geneva.

244. *Julie*: the heroine of Rousseau's novel of the same name (1761).

246. *the memorable kiss*: this refers to the account in his 'Confessions' of his passion for the Comptesse d'Houdetot ... and his long walk every morning for the sake of the single kiss which was the common salutation of French acquaintance ... [B]

264. *Those oracles*: Rousseau's writings had a great influence on the French revolutionists.

298. The thunder-storms to which these lines refer occurred on the 13th of June, 1816, at midnight ... [B]

1817

168. First published in the *Examiner*, 19 Jan. 1817.

169. First published in *History of a Six Weeks' Tour ...* (1817), by Mary and Percy. This is the text here, though it has been fraught with problems. A recently discovered fair-copy MS text gives a number of interesting new readings.

170. Published in June 1817, but originally written in late 1816, shortly after Byron left England following the breakup of his marriage. The poem reconsiders the Faust legend (as it were) *after* the death of Gretchen (whose equivalent is Byron's Astarte).

Epigraph: *Hamlet*, I. v. 166–7.

I. i. 192–261. *When the moon ... now wither*: Originally published separately (in 1816) under the title 'The Incantation', which Byron meant as a barely concealed curse upon his wife.

II. ii. 92. *He who from out their fountain dwellings raised*: The philosopher Iamblicus.

II. ii. 182–3. *The buried Prophet ... the Hag of Endor*: The story is in 1 Samuel 28: 7 ff.

II. ii. 183–92. *the Spartan Monarch ... fulfill'd*: The story of Pausanias, King of Sparta, who accidentally killed Cleonice, whom he loved. He tried to remove his guilt by invoking the aid of Jupiter, as well as counsel from the Arcadian evocators of souls at Phigalea.

II. iii. 16. *The Captive Usurper*: Napoleon.

II. iv. *stage direction*: Arimanes (Ahriman), the Zoroastrian principle of darkness.

III. i. 13. *Kalon*: the *summum bonum*.

III. i. 88. *Rome's sixth Emperor*: Otho.

III. ii. 5. *the giant sons*: the offspring of the intercourse between angels and mortal women, according to Genesis 6: 1 ff.

III. iv. 129–32. *The mind . . . place and time*: Echoes *Paradise Lost*, I. 254–5.

171. First published in the *Newry Telegraph*, 19 Apr. 1817. Text here from *The Burial of Sir John Moore . . .* (1909). Sir John Moore (1761–1809) was killed in Spain in the Peninsular War.

172. Published in *Dramatic Tales* (1817). Text here from *Songs, by the Ettrick Shepherd* (1831), where Hogg put a note to the poem: 'This is a most unearthly song, copied from an unearthly tragedy of my own, published anonymously with others, in two volumes, in 1817 . . . The title of the play is All-Hallow Eve. It was suggested to me by old Henry Mackenzie. . . .'

1818

173. The satire was published in 1818, comprising twelve Letters, as edited by Moore's fictitious Thomas Brown, the Younger. The scene is set after the return of Louis XVIII to France.

13–15. *In vain . . . Dead Ass*: Alluding to early sections of Laurence Sterne's *A Sentimental Journey*; the encounter with the dead ass occurs on the road to Amiens.

24. To commemorate the landing of Louis le Désiré from England, the impression of his foot is marked out on the pier at Calais, and a pillar with an inscription raised opposite to the spot. [TM]

36. Ci-git la jambe de etc etc. [TM]

114. A celebrated mantua-maker in Paris. [TM]

174. Published early in 1818, *Beppo*'s ottava rima forecasts Byron's masterwork *Don Juan*.

35. *Monmouth-street, Rag Fair*: centres for second-hand clothes.

63. *Harvey*: a popular fish sauce.

91. *That picture*: 'Triple Portrait', attributed to Giorgione but actually by Titian.

112. *the lost Pleiad*: Merope, one of the seven Pleiades; her star was dim because she married a mortal (Sisyphus).

175. The last Canto of *Childe Harold* appeared in 1818. It is a meditation in, and on, Italy.

37. *But France got drunk with blood to vomit crime*: The French Revolution.

43. *the base pageant last upon the scene*: The Congress of Vienna (1815).

53. *the bosom of the North*: England.

55. *Egeria*: the nymph who instructed Numa, the legendary lawgiver of Rome.

157. *this all-blasting tree*: the upas was supposed to poison the surrounding earth.

189. *lay*: a solecism.

176. Published in 1818 as *Rhododaphne; or, The Thessalian Spell*.

177. From *Endymion. A Poetic Romance* (1818).

178. Published in *The Heart of Midlothian* (1818), as sung by the deranged Madge Wildfire.

179. Published in 1819, with the splendid designs by George Cruickshank; it quickly went through more than fifty editions.

180. The first instalment of *Don Juan* was published in 1819. Canto I narrates the story of Juan's first love affair, with Donna Julia; the discovery of the affair; and Juan's departure from England. Canto II narrates his shipwreck and, after being washed ashore on one of the Cyclades, his meeting with Haidée, his second love.

162. *Boscan, Garcilasso*: sixteenth-century Spanish imitators of Petrarch.

236. *Anacreon Moore*: Thomas Moore translated Anacreon's Odes.

413. *'Elle vous suit partout'*: 'She follows you everywhere' (the motto on one of Byron's seals).

181. Composed May 1819; published in *Annals of the Fine Arts* (July 1819) as 'Ode to the Nightingale', first collected in Keats's 1820 volume (see below, nos. **184**, **193–7**), which is the text here.

32. *Not charioted . . . pards*: Bacchus was sometimes represented in a leopard-drawn chariot.

76. *Past the near meadows . . . stream*: Ruth 2.

182. Text here is from *Miscellaneous Poetry by Samuel Bamford . . .* (1821). The poem was written shortly after the Peterloo Massacre in August 1819 and was publicly recited and circulated at the time, though it was not printed until 1821. Bamford strangely misdates the event in the subheading he gave to his poem: 'Verses occasioned by the Outrage committed upon Mr Hunt, and His Friends, at the Theatre, Manchester, on the evening of Friday, January 22nd, by Lord Uxbridge, Captain Fraser, George Torr, and twenty or thirty other "Gemmen" of the same stamp'. Bamford's poem refers to the radical orator Henry Hunt as well as various leaders of the cavalry which attacked the crowd at Peterloo. The *'whisker'd whelp'* (line 15) is Lord Uxbridge, *'Sawney'* (line 17) was a Captain of the Scots Guards, and the 'ban-dog' (line 23) is George Torr (according to Bamford's textual notes).

183. Published in *Tales of the Hall* (1820), Book XIII. It works off the proverb 'Delays are dangerous'.

184. Written 1819, probably in May; published in *Annals of the Fine Arts* (Jan. 1820), first collected in Keats's 1820 volume (see nos. **181**, **193–7**), which is the text printed here.

7. *Tempe . . . Arcady*: Fabled spots in Greece and Greek poetry.

49. *'Beauty is truth . . .'*: Not all the texts have these quotation marks.

185. Published in the *Indicator*, 10 May 1820, and signed 'Caviar'; written Apr. 1819. The text most often reproduced in later editions is the MS text Keats sent in his letter of 14 Feb.–3 May 1819 to George and Georgiana Keats; it differs markedly from the first published text. The poem's title is from a poem once attributed to Chaucer, written by the 15th-century writer Alain Chartier.

186. Written Apr. 1819, published in the *Indicator*, 28 June 1820, signed 'Caviar'.

187. Published in *Poems Descriptive of Rural Life and Scenery* (1820). The poem was removed from the collection after the 2nd edition because it offended some of Clare's readers. It is an imitation of Cowper's famous poem of the same title.

188. Published in *Letters to Julia, in Rhyme* (1820). Text here from the 3rd edition (1822).

189. Published in *Woodcuts and Verses* (Kent, 1820).

190–2. Published in *Prometheus Unbound. A Lyrical Drama in Four Acts, with Other Poems* (1820); where necessary, these texts have been corrected against manuscripts and later printings.

190. As Shelley remarks in his Preface to the drama, his work is a rewriting of the lost *Prometheus Unbound* of Aeschylus. The latter 'supposed the reconciliation of Jupiter with his victim', but Shelley declares himself 'averse from a catastrophe so feeble as that of reconciling the Champion with the Oppressor of mankind'. Shelley's drama also continually enforces a consciousness of the contemporary relevance of the ancient and mythic struggle.

   I. 34. *Heaven's winged hound*: Jupiter's vultures (or eagles).

   I. 192. *Zoroaster*: (*fl.* 500 BC), founder of the dualistic religion that depicted the universe as struggling between forces of light and darkness.

   I. 207. *Demogorgon*: here, Fate.

   I. 212. *Typhon*: was imprisoned in Mt Aetna by Jupiter.

   II. i. 17. *one white star*: Venus.

   II. i. 26. *her*: Panthea.

   II. i. 140. *Of Hyacinth … grief*: When Apollo's beloved Hyacinthus died, the god wrote 'Ai' (i.e. 'woe') on the flowerbells.

   II. v, stage direction. *The Car*: of the Spirit of the Hour.

   II. v. 20. *The Nereids*: water nymphs.

191. Shelley appended a note to the Ode: This poem was conceived and chiefly written in a wood that skirts the Arno, near Florence, and on a day when that tempestuous wind, whose temperature is at once mild and animating, was collecting the vapours which pour down the autumnal rains. They began, as I foresaw, at sunset with a violent tempest of hail and rain, attended by that magnificent thunder and lightning peculiar to the Cisalpine regions.

   The phenomenon alluded to at the conclusion of the third stanza is well known to naturalists. The vegetation at the bottom of the sea, of rivers, and of lakes, sympathizes with that of the land in the change of seasons, and is consequently influenced by the winds which announce it.

   32–4. *Beside a pumice isle … the wave's intenser day*: Shelley recalls the reflections he had seen (in 1818) in the Bay of Baiae of the ruins of ancient villas from the days of imperial Rome.

192. 18, 22. *a star of Heaven, that silver sphere*: Venus as evening and morning star, respectively.

193–7. This group of poems was first published in Keats's third volume, *Lamia, Isabella, The Eve of St Agnes, and Other Poems* (1820).

193. 58. *Ariadne's tiar*: Bacchus gave Ariadne a crown of stars that became the constellation.

   78. *a bright Phœbean dart*: sun ray.

   81. *Too gentle Hermes*: Hermes ushered the dead to Hades.

194. The superstition on which the poem is based is sketched in st. 6. The feast of St Agnes is 21 Jan.

   133. *brook*: here, to hold back.

   171. *Merlin … his Demon*: this allusion—to Merlin and (probably) Vivien—has no clear point of reference in Arthurian materials.

NOTES AND REFERENCES

195. Written Oct. 1818–Apr. 1819. Keats later tried to recast the fragment in a Dantean form as 'The Fall of Hyperion', which was also left incomplete. The poem deals with the overthrow of the Saturnian gods by the gods of Olympus. Hyperion is the Saturnian Apollo. The poem is an act of homage to Milton and the epic tradition.

23. *one, who with a kindred hand*: Thea, wife of Hyperion.

147. *The rebel three*: Jupiter, Neptune, Pluto.

246. *Tellus*: the Earth.

307. *Cælus* is Uranus.

323. *my first-born*: Saturn.

196. Written late April, 1819. Keats's comment on the poem is useful: 'Psyche was not embodied as a goddess before the time of Apuleius the Platonist who lived after the Augustan age, and consequently the Goddess was never worshipped or sacrificed to with any of the ancient fervour' (letter to George and Georgiana Keats, 30 Apr. 1819).

197. Written 19 Sept. 1819.

1821

198. Published in the *London Magazine*, Mar. 1821.

199. Published in *Desultory Thoughts in London . . . with Other Poems* (1821).

200. Published in *Metrical Legends of Exalted Characters* (1821). The poem treats a semi-legendary event in the history of the Scottish patriot Sir William Wallace (1278?–1305) at Gask Castle in 1298. The event is based on the metrical history of Wallace written by Henry the Minstrel ('Blind Harry'). Wallace killed one of his followers, an Irishman named Fawdoun, as an English spy, and after retreating to Gask Castle is said to have experienced the visitation detailed in the poem.

201. Cantos III–V were published in 1821; they deal largely with Juan's and Haidée's brief idyllic love and its disastrous end.

III. 90. *a poet*: this figure recalls Demodocus, the court poet of the *Odyssey*; but the contemporary references are to the reactionary Southey and (Southey's opposite) Byron himself.

III. 114. *The 'Vates irritabilis'*: Horace's inspired poet.

III. 121. *trimmer*: one who plays both sides in politics.

III. 158. *what says de Staël*: in her study *De l'Allemagne* (1810).

III. 159. *the 'Trecentisti'*: Italian writers of the fourteenth century.

III. 167. *The Scian and the Teian muse*: Homer and Anacreon, respectively; the poetry of war and the poetry of love.

III. 179. *A king sate*: Xerxes watching the battle of Salamis.

III. 219. *the letters Cadmus gave*: the legendary Cadmus gave writing to the Greeks.

III. 224. Anacreon served the tyrant of Samos, Polycrates.

III. 238. *The Heracleidan blood*: descendants of Hercules.

III. 239. *the Franks*: Europeans.

III. 306. *He prated . . . 'Pantisocrasy'*: Southey planned to establish a utopian communist community in America.

III. 307. *Wordsworth unexcised, unhired*: Wordsworth had a tax-collecting sinecure from the government.

III. 312. *Espoused . . . (milliners of Bath)*: Coleridge and Southey married the Fricker sisters (who were not milliners).

III. 324. *Joanna Southcote's Shiloh, and her sect*: Joanna Southcott (1750–1814), religious millenarian.

202. Published in the *Etonian*, Aug. 1821.

203. Written in the spring of 1821, shortly after Keats's death; printed (with a prose preface) in Pisa in the summer. Shelley's models are Bion's 'Lament for Adonis' and the 'Elegy for Bion' by Moscus. The poem recurs to the savage attack on Keats's *Endymion* by an anonymous reviewer for the *Quarterly Review* (Apr. 1818).

Epigraph: not from Plato; Shelley's translation is famous: 'Thou wert the morning star among the living / Ere thy fair light had fled:— / Now, having died, thou art as Hesperus, giving / New Splendour to the dead.'

10. *mighty mother*: Urania, epic muse.

29. *He*: Milton.

36. *the sons of light*: Homer, Dante, Milton.

55. *that high Capital*: Rome.

127. *Lost Echo*: The nymph Echo vainly loved Narcissus.

141. *Narcissus*: A youth beloved and accidentally killed by Apollo.

145. *the lorn nightingale*: perhaps referring to Keats's 'Ode to a Nightingale'.

264. *The Pilgrim of Eternity*: Byron.

269. *The sweetest lyrist*: Thomas Moore.

271. Shelley.

291. *a light spear . . .* : the Dionysian thyrsus.

312. *He, who, gentlest of the wise*: Leigh Hunt.

319. *The nameless worm*: the anonymous reviewer.

399–400. *Chatterton Rose pale*: The poet Thomas Chatterton (1752–1770) killed himself.

401. *Sidney*: Sir Philip Sidney.

404. *Lucan*: the Roman poet Marcus Annaeus Lucan.

444. *one keen pyramid*: the tomb of Gaius Cestus in the Protestant cemetery in Rome, where Keats and Shelley's infant son William (line 454) were buried.

204. Published in Dec. 1821.

205. Published in *Irish Melodies*, 8 (1821).

1822

206. First published in the *Literary Gazette* (Nov. 1822); repr. in *The Improvisatrice; and Other Poems* (1824), which is the text here.

207. Published in *Cataline . . . with Other Poems* (1822).

208. Published in *The Errors of Ecstasie . . . with Other Poems* (1822).

1823

209. These translations were published in Probert's *Ancient Laws of Cambria* (1823). The Triads were first compiled by Iolo Morganwg as the 'Third Series of Triads' in the *Myvyrian Archaeology of Wales* (1801). There are fifty-three sections; the excerpts here are nos. 1, 9, 10, 13, 52, and 53, each entire.

210. First published in the *New Monthly Magazine*, Mar. 1823. The poem was written much earlier, and was read in manuscript by Byron before he composed his own 'Darkness' (1816).

211. First published in the *Morning Chronicle*, 12 Aug. 1823. The satire takes off from Lord Chancellor Eldon's refusals (in 1822) to grant injunctions against piratical publications of Byron's *Cain* and *Don Juan*. William Benbow and William Dugdale were booksellers and publishers who pirated Byron's work. Richard Carlile was a radical imprisoned from 1819 to 1825 for seditious publishing.

17. *MRS FRY*: The Quaker Elizabeth Fry (1780–1845) was a prison reformer.

43, 44. *Julia, Haidée*: characters in the early cantos of *Don Juan*.

59. Subaudi 'Printer's?' as far as the Chancellor's opinion is concerned. [WMP]

212. Cantos VI–XIV were published in three separate instalments in 1823; Cantos IX–XI appeared in August. Canto XI inaugurates the sequence of 'English Cantos'.

122. *got my gruel*: killed.

123. *max*: gin.

133. *kiddy*: street thief.

135. *Full flash*: knowing.

139. *Crowner's 'quest*: Coroner's inquest.

162. *Like lucus from no light*: example of an absurd derivation—'lucus' (grove) from 'non lucendo' (not admitting light).

176. Gas lighting came to London in 1812.

208. *they made a wicked man turn*: men were hanged from lamp-posts during the French Revolution.

232. *Hells*: gaming houses.

373. *flaws or starts*: *Macbeth*, III. iv. 63.

385. *drapery Misses*: it means a pretty, a highborn, a fashionable young woman. (LB)

402. *Drawcansir*: Braggart hero.

427. *Banquo's glass*: in *Macbeth*.

St. 56. Byron equates his works *Don Juan* (1819), *Marino Faliero*, and *Cain* (both 1821) with Napoleon's great defeats in 1812–14. Sir Hudson Lowe was governor of St Helena during Napoleon's imprisonment.

454. *the reverend Cambyses Croly*: George Croly, minor writer of the period.

456. *by these Hilts*: *I Henry IV*, II. iv. 97.

St. 58. *that artificial hard Labourer* . . . : the minor writer Henry Hart Milman.

465. *my gentle Euphues*: Bryan Waller Procter.

491. *dreadful trade . . . gathers samphire*: *King Lear*, IV. vi. 15.

516. *Centaur-Nessus garb*: Hercules was killed by the poisoned 'shirt of Nessus'.

590. *rack and manger*: waste and destruction.

601. *cries Young*: Edward Young, in his poem *Resignation* (1762).

621. *Gone down it seems to Scotland*: George IV's trip to Scotland (1822).

623. *Caw me, caw thee*: you scratch me, I'll scratch you.

633. *the Lady Carolines and Franceses*: Byron recalls his affairs with Lady Caroline Lamb and Lady Frances Wedderburn Webster.

661. *blue Peter*: naval flag signalling departure.

693. *Atalantis*: a scandalous novel.

213. Published in *The Flood of Thessaly . . . and Other Poems* (1823).

214. Published in the *Annual Register* (1823).

1824

215–16. Published anonymously in Robert Archibald Smith's *The Scottish Minstrel* (Edinburgh, 1821–4), iii. 'The Land o' the Leal' was written in 1798 and is titled

'I'm wearin' awa', John' in Smith's collection. 'The Laird o' Cockpen' has two additional (concluding) stanzas in texts of the poem published after Oliphant's death.

217–19. Published in the *Posthumous Poems* (1824), edited by Mary Shelley. The texts here incorporate substantive revisions from the 1839 *Poetical Works*, as well as from the relevant manuscripts.

217. Shelley's prose Preface identifies Maddalo as a brilliant, proud, and gloomy Venetian nobleman of 'concentered and impatient feelings'. He is widely travelled, charming, and a superb conversationalist. Julian 'is an Englishman of good family, passionately attached to those philosophical notions which assert the power of man over his own mind'; he is speculative and a free-thinker. The maniac is left unidentified except as a man 'disappointed in love'; he is described as 'very culti-vated and amiable'. In real time, Julian and Maddalo represent Shelley and Byron respectively, and the poem recollects conversations they had with each other in 1818.

143. *his child*: Allegra, Byron's natural daughter by Claire Clairmont.
204. *soul of goodness*: *Henry V*, iv. i. 4.

218. The MS readings were first restored by Donald H. Reiman.
78. *blinding*: Mary Shelley's addition to a blank in the MS.
236. *Frederick . . . Catherine . . . Leopold*: Frederick II of Prussia (1712–86); Catherine the Great of Russia (1729–96); Leopold II, Grand Duke of Tuscany (1747–92), who became Holy Roman Emperor.
255. *his master*: Socrates.
258. *Conquered the heart by love*: Plato loved a youth named Aster.
260. *him*: Mary Shelley's addition to a blank in the MS; *twain*: Aristotle and Alexander the Great.
269. *eagle*: Mary Shelley's addition.
288. *Gregory and John*: papal names.
419. *that star*: Venus, both morning and evening star.
421. *his dear lament*: the favourite song, 'Stanco di pascolar le peccorelle', is a Brescian national air. [Mary Shelley]
472. Dante.

219. 14. *the Preacher*: the speaker of Ecclesiastes.

220. First published in the *Morning Chronicle*, 29 Oct. 1824, from an imperfect copy. Text here is from *Lord Byron: The Complete Poetical Works*, ed. J. J. McGann (Oxford, 1991), vii. Byron had gone to Greece to fight for Greek independence; he died there shortly after he wrote this poem.

1825

221–2. Published in *The Forest Sanctuary and Other Poems* (1825).

221. Epigraph: *Beppo*, line 112. The lost Pleiad is Merope, one of the seven Pleiades, whose star is dim because she married a mortal (Sisyphus).

Hemans's poem is an elegy for Byron, who had just died, and whose reputation had been on the wane since 1816, when scandals surrounding his personal life erupted.

14. The Pleiades is an ancient and important constellation for navigating sailors.

223–4. Published in *The Troubadour, Catalogue of Pictures, and Historical Sketches* (1825). Thomas Stewardson (1781–1859) was best known as a portrait painter, but in his genre pictures he liked to represent children. Francis Danby (1793–1861) exhibited his painting 'An Enchanted Island' in 1825.

1826

225–6. Published in *Whims and Oddities* (1826).

225.
    8. *the Forty-second Foot*: the Black Watch (now the Royal Highlanders).
    15. *devours*: respects.
    36. In 1812 Wellington defeated the French at Badajos in the Peninsular War.
    62. *nail*: Hood is punning; in slang the word means a clever crook.
    67–8. Hood describes the traditional burial rites for a suicide.

226.
    21. *the Faculty*: the medical profession.
    37. *the ferry*: Charon's.
    54. *Pancras' ground*: the cemetery of St Pancras-in-the-Fields.
    56. *the bony knacker*: the devil.
    76. *mull*: snuff-box.
    123. *Deady*: gin.
    126. *mum*: silence; also a kind of beer.
    258. *bitten*: swindled.

227. Published in *The Brazen Head*, 10 May 1826. The poem pursues the theme of Ecclesiastes 1: 9. 'Time is! time was!', though virtually proverbial, is from Robert Greene's *History of Friar Bacon* (1589). Lord Clifford (line 20) was Roman Catholic; Richard Martin (1745–1834) was an MP with a special interest in protecting animals (lines 27–8). Madame Vestris (line 37) had recently played Apollo in a production of *Midas*.

1827

228. Published in the *Morning Herald*, 10 Aug. 1827.

229. Published 1827.

230. Published in *The Forget-Me-Not* (1827).

231–2. Published in *The Golden Violet . . . and Other Poems* (1827). Both are songs from 'The Golden Violet', a troubadour medley sequence.

1828

233. Published in *Poems Original and Translated*, i (1828).

234–7. Published in *Records of Woman, with Other Poems* (1828).

234. Epigraph: *Iphigenie*, v. 6.

236. Title: the impression of a woman's form, with an infant clasped to the bosom, found at the uncovering of Herculaneum. [FH]

237. Epigraph: *Marmion*, Canto IV, st. xxx.

238. Published in the *Literary Gazette*, 12 Apr. 1828.

239. First published in *The Bijou* (1828), which is the text here; repr. under the received title 'In my own Album', in *Album Verses* (1830).
    6. *written strange defeature*: see *Comedy of Errors*, v. i. 299.

240. Published in Coleridge's 1828 edition of his collected poems, though written (probably) much earlier.

30. This phenomenon, which the author has himself experienced, [...] is applied figuratively to the following passage in the *Aids to Reflection*:—'Pindar's fine remark respecting the different effects of Music, on different characters, holds equally true of Genius—as many as are not delighted by it are disturbed, perplexed, irritated. The beholder either recognises it as a projected form of his own Being, that moves before him with a Glory round its head, or recoils from it as a Spectre.' *Aids to Reflection* [1825], p. 220. [STC]

1829

241. Published in the *London Magazine* (Jan. 1829).

102. *Almack's*: The exclusive assembly rooms (King Street, St James's) opened in 1765.

242. Published in *The Casket* (1829).

64. *Lawrence*: Sir Thomas Lawrence (1769–1830).

243. Published in the 2nd edition of *The Forest Sanctuary and Other Poems* (1829).

244–5. Published in *The Venetian Bracelet . . . and Other Poems* (1829).

246. Published in *The Keepsake* (1829).

247. Published in *The Village Patriarch* (1829).

248. Published in *The Misfortunes of Elphin*, ch. 11 (1829).

1830

249–51. All published in *Songs of the Affections, with Other Poems* (1830); 'The Magic Glass' was first printed in *The Literary Souvenir* (1830).

250. Epigraph: see *Childe Harold's Pilgrimage*, Canto IV, st. 100.

251. Epigraph: *Philaster*, II. 3.

252. Published in *Crochet Castle* (1830), ch. 18.

253. Published in *Poems, Chiefly Lyrical* (1830).
Epigraph: *Measure for Measure*, III. i. 264.

1831

254. Published in *Corn Law Rhymes*, 3rd edn. (1831).

255. Written in 1830 and published early in 1831 (with the marvellous subtitle 'A Necromaunt in Three Chimeras'). The poem's speaker is its hero, Julio, who is keeping a vigil over the body of his dead beloved, Agathè.

256. Published in *The Literary Souvenir* (1831).
Epigraph: La Bruyère, *Charactères* (1687), ch. 3 ('Des Femmes').
32. *Little*: Thomas Moore (see above, no. 99).
62. *the Catalani*: Angelica Catalani (1780–1849), opera singer.
70. *Fierce odes . . . Slaughter*: Glancing at Coleridge's 'Fire, Famine, and Slaughter'.
71. *Prince Leboo*, of the Pelew Islands, died on a visit to England in 1784.
92. *'Fly not yet'*: Thomas Moore, 'Fly not yet, 'tis just the hour' (*Irish Melodies*).

257. Published in Landor's 1831 edition of his collected poems, in the section of poems headed 'Ianthe'.

1832

258–60. All published in *Poems* (1832), which appeared in December though the title-page is dated 1833. Like many of the poems in the 1832 volume, they were revised ('The Lady of Shalott' and 'The Palace of Art' radically so) when they were reprinted in 1842. The texts here are from 1832.

259–60. Both composed Oct. 1831–Apr. 1832; the dedicatee is R. C. Trench, whose remark ('Tennyson, we cannot live in art') occasioned 'The Palace of Art'.

260. 53. When I first conceived the plan of the Palace of Art, I intended to have introduced both sculptures and paintings into it; but it is the most difficult of all things to *devise* a statue in verse. Judge whether I have succeeded in the statues of Elijah and Olympias.

> One was the Tishbite whom the raven fed,
>   As when he stood on Carmel-steeps,
> With one arm stretched out bare, and mocked and said,
>   'Come cry aloud—he sleeps.'
>
> Tall, eager, lean and strong, his cloak windborne
>   Behind, his forehead heavenly-bright
> With the clear marble pouring glorious scorn,
>   Lit as with inner light.
>
> One was Olympias: the floating snake
>   Rolled round her ancles, round her waist
> Knotted, and folded once about her neck,
>   Her perfect lips to taste
>
> Round by the shoulder moved: she seeming blithe
>   Declined her head; on every side
> The dragon's curves melted and mingled with
>   The woman's youthful pride
>
> Of rounded limbs.   [AT]

63. *Saint Cecily*: Patroness of music.

65. *child of Pendragon*: King Arthur.

163. *Verulam*: Francis Bacon.

164. *The king of those who know*: Il maestro di color chi sanno.—Dante, *Inf[erno]* III. [AT]

179. *Memnon*: Theban statue fabled to produce music at dawn.

216. If the poem were not already too long, I should have inserted in the text the following stanzas, expressive of the joy wherewith the soul contemplated the results of astronomical experiment. In the centre of the four quadrangles rose an immense tower.

> Hither, when all the deep unsounded skies
>   Shuddered with silent stars, she clomb,
> And as with optic glasses her keen eyes
>   Pierced thro' the mystic dome,
>
> Regions of lucid matter taking forms,
>   Brushes of fire, hazy gleams,
> Clusters and beds of worlds, and bee-like swarms
>   Of suns, and starry streams.

She saw the snowy poles of moonless Mars,
  That marvellous round of milky light
Below Orion, and those double stars
  Whereof the one more bright

Is circled by the other, &c.   [AT]

223–4. Acts 12: 21–3.
230–1. Daniel 5: 17–31.

INDEX OF TITLES AND FIRST LINES

The references are to the numbers of the poems

INDEX OF TITLES AND FIRST LINES

INDEX OF TITLES AND FIRST LINES

INDEX OF TITLES AND FIRST LINES

INDEX OF TITLES AND FIRST LINES

INDEX OF TITLES AND FIRST LINES

INDEX OF TITLES AND FIRST LINES

INDEX OF TITLES AND FIRST LINES

INDEX OF AUTHORS AND WORKS

The references are to the numbers of the poems